District Gazetteers of India Series 136

MADRAS DISTRICT GAZETTEERS

COIMBATORE

District Gazetteers of India Series 136

MADRAS DISTRICT GAZETTEERS

COIMBATORE

BY

K. N. KRISHNASWAMI AYYAR

23 VOLUMES (IN 25 BINDINGS)

(VOL. 5th)

GYAN

Published by

Gyan Publishing House
5, Ansari Road
Daryaganj, New Delhi-110002
Phone: 011-47034999, 9811692060
E-mail: books@gyanbooks.com

Distribution Network
gyanbooks.com
India, USA, Canada, UK, Australia, France

ISBN: 978-93-6208-562-7 (Set) 23 Volumes (In 25 Bindings)
978-81-212-5875-3 (PB)

First Published, 1933

2nd Impression 2024

Printed at: Gyan Press, Delhi.

MADRAS DISTRICT GAZETTEERS (Vol. 5th)

K. N. KRISHNASWAMI AYYAR

LIST OF VOLUMES

S. NO.	ISBN NO.	VOLUME	TITLE	AUTHOR	PRICE	PAGES
			ASSAM DISTRICT GAZETTEERS			
1	9788121285926	1st	Cachar	B. C. Allen	600	300
2	9788121285919	2nd	Sylhet	B. C. Allen	750	378
3	9788121285902	3rd	Goalpara	B. C. Allen	400	203
4	9788121285896	4th	Kamrup	B. C. Allen	675	344
5	9788121285889	5th	Darrang	B. C. Allen	725	364
6	9788121285872	6th	Nowgong	B. C. Allen	560	280
7	9788121285865	7th	Sibsagar	B. C. Allen	675	343
8	9788121285858	8th	Lakhimpur	B. C. Allen	690	347
9	9788121285841	9th	Naga Hills and Manipur	B. C. Allen	580	294
10	9788121285834	10th	The Khasi And Jaintia Hills, The Garo Hills And The Lushai Hills	B. C. Allen	675	363
11	9788121285827	11th	The Sadiya and Balipara Frontier Tract	B. C. Allen	375	190
			BENGAL DISTRICT GAZETTEERS			
12	9788121218672	1st	Angul	L. S. S. O'Malley	340	168
13	9788121259637	2nd	Bakarganj	J. C. JACK	970	194
14	9788121218696	3rd	Balasore	L. S. S. O'Malley	450	228
15	9788121259590	4th	Bankura	L. S. S. O'Malley	1000	199
16	9788121218375	5th	Bhagalpur	J. Byrne	390	194
17	9788121218290	6th	Birbhum	L. S. S. O'Malley	300	150
18	9788121259651	7th	Eastern Bengal and Assam - Bogra	J. N. Gupta	940	188
19	9788121218351	8th	Burdwan	J. C. K. Peterson	450	227
20	9788121259538	9th	Calcutta District Gazetteer - Statistics, 1901 - 02		340	68
21	9788121218313	10th	Champaran	L. S. S. O'Malley	410	205
22	9788121259613	11th	Eastern Bengal District Gazetters - Chittagong	L. S. S. O'Malley	1080	216
23	9788121259552	12th	Chota Nagpur Tributary		130	26
24	9788121259415	13th	The Cooch Behar Gazette: Statistics		1460	292
25	9788121218412	14th	Cuttack	L. S. S. O'Malley	490	248
26	9788121261357	15th	Eastern Bengal District Gazetteers Dacca	B. C. Allen	400	207
27	9788121218436	16th	Darbhanga	L. S. S. O'Malley	360	180
28	9789362089335	17th	Darjeeling	L. S. S. O'Malley	500	248
29	9788121259453	18th	Eastern Bengal District Gazetteers - Dinajpur	F. W. Strong	890	178
30	9788121259392	19th	Faridpur	L. S. S. O'Malley	700	140
31	9788121218474	20th	Gaya	L. S. S. O'Malley	540	270
32	9788121214032	21st	Bihar and Orissa District Gazetteer: Hazaribagh	E. Lister	715	234
33	9788121218337	22nd	Hooghly	L. S. S. O'Malley	680	340
34	9788121218191	23rd	Bengal District Gazetteer Howrah	L. S. S. O'Malley	390	199
35	9788121259293	24th	Eastern Bengal and Assam - Jalpaiguri	John F. Gruning	890	178
36	9788121259279	25th	Jessore	L. S. S. O'Malley	960	192
37	9788121259231	26th	Khulna	L. S. S. O'Malley	1100	220
38	9788121259217	27th	Malda	G. E. Lambourn	670	134
39	9788121267854	28th	Manbhum	H. Coupland	600	313
40	9788121218498	29th	Midnapore	L. S. S. O'Malley	500	252
41	9788121218597	30th	Monghyr	L. S. S. O'Malley	560	280
42	9788121259156	31st	Murshidabad	L. S. S. O'Malley	1250	250
43	9788121259576	32nd	Bengal District Gazetteers - Muzaffarpur	L. S. S. O'Malley	940	188
44	9788121259132	33rd	Mymensingh	F. A. Sachse	960	192
45	9788121259118	34th	Nadia	J. H. E. Garrett	1070	214
46	9788121259095	35th	Eastern Bengal and Assam - Noakhali	J. E. Webster	580	115
47	9788121218450	36th	Feudatory States of Orissa	L. E. B. Cobdenramsay	790	395
48	9788121259071	37th	Pabna	L. S. S. O'Malley	710	142
49	9788121218511	38th	Palamau	L. S. S. O'Malley	380	190
50	9788121218634	39th	Patna	L. S. S. O'Malley	500	250
51	9788121218535	40th	Puri	L. S. S. O'Malley	650	328
52	9788121218757	41st	Purnea	L. S. S. O'Malley	440	220
53	9788121258937	42nd	Rajshahi	L. S. S. O'Malley	1080	216
54	9788121256681	43rd	Bihar and Orissa District Gazetteers: Ranchi	M. G. Hallett	1350	278
55	9788121258913	44th	Eastern Bengal and assam - Rangpur	J. A. Vas	890	178
56	9788121218559	45th	Sambalpur	L. S. S. O'Malley	480	242
57	9788121214056	46th	Santal Parganas	L. S. S. O'Malley	940	308
58	9788121218610	47th	Saran	L. S. S. O'Malley	380	190
59	9788121218658	48th	Shahabad	L. S. S. O'Malley	380	190
60	9788121256704	49th	The Gazetteer of Sikhim	H. H. Risley	960	481
61	9788121218573	50th	Singhbhum, Saraikela And Kharsawan	L. S. S. O'Malley	560	280
62	9788121259439	51st	Eastern Bengal District Gazetteers - Tippera	J. E. Webster	730	146
63	9788121259033	52nd	24 Parganas	L. S. S. O'Malley	1420	284

S. NO.	ISBN NO.	VOLUME	TITLE	AUTHOR	PRICE	PAGES
			CENTRAL PROVINCES DISTRICT GAZETTEERS			
64	9789362081728	1st, Vol. A	Akola (Descriptive)	A. E. Nelson, C. Brown	870	436
65	9789362085481	2nd, Vol. A	Amraoti (Descriptive)	S. V. Fitzgerald, A. E. Nelson	1050	524
66	9789362089267	3rd,Vol. A	Balaghat (Descriptive)	R. V. RUSSELL	430	216
67	9789362083494	4th, Vol. A	Betul (Descriptive)	R. V. RUSSELL	610	306
68	9789362085146	5th, Vol. A	Bhandara (Descriptive)	R. V. RUSSELL	580	292
69	9789362088390	6th, Vol. A	Bilaspur (Descriptive)	R. V. RUSSELL	870	434
70	9789362086044	7th, Vol. A	Buldana (Descriptive)	A. E. Nelson	1090	543
71	9789362089014	8th, Vol. B	Chanda (Descriptive)	R. V. RUSSELL	470	234
72	9789362086938	9th	Chhattisgarch Feudatory State	E. A. De Brett	880	440
73	9789362082961	10th	Chhindwara (Descriptive)	R. V. RUSSELL	550	274
74	9789362089342	11th, Vol. A & B	Damoh (Descriptive and Statistical Tables 1891-1901)	R. V. RUSSELL	830	414
75	9789362081230	12th, Vol. A	Durg (Descriptive)	A. E. Nelson	460	232
76	9789362086037	13th, Vol. A	Hoshangabad (Descriptive)	R. V. RUSSELL	860	430
77	9789362086792	14th, Vol. A	Jubbulpore (Descriptive)	A. E. Nelson	950	474
78	9789362089663	15th, Vol. A & B	Mandla (Descriptive and Statistical Tables 1891-1901)	R. V. RUSSELL	370	186
79	9789362086419	16th, Vol. A	Nagpur (Descriptive)	R. V. RUSSELL	790	394
80	9789362080646	17th, Vol. A	Narsinghpur (Descriptive)	R. V. RUSSELL	510	257
81	9789362084835	18th, Vol. A	Nimar (Descriptive)	R. V. RUSSELL	600	299
82	9789362087737	19th, Vol. A	Raipur (Descriptive)	A. E. Nelson	790	396
83	9789362080264	20th, Vol. A	Saugor (Descriptive)	R. V. RUSSELL	570	285
84	9789362081117	21st, Vol. A	Seoni (Descriptive)	R. V. RUSSELL	460	232
85	9789362084965	22nd, Vol. A	Wardha (Descriptive)	R. V. RUSSELL	600	302
86	9789362083401	23rd, Vol. A	Yeotmal (Descriptive)	R. V. RUSSELL	550	277
87	9789362080325	24th, Vol. I, Pt. I	Gwalior (Text and Tables)	R. V. RUSSELL	980	489
88	9789362087133	24th, Vol. I, Pt. II	Gwalior (Maps)	R. V. RUSSELL	400	198
89	9789362086341	24th, Vol. I, Pt. III	Gwalior (Village List)	R. V. RUSSELL	810	406
90	9789362085467	24th, Vol. I, Pt. IV	Gwalior (Photos)	R. V. RUSSELL	1400	698
91	9789362087393	25th, Vol. II	Indore (Text and Tables)	C. E. Luard	1050	524
92	9789362084422	26th, Vol. III	Bhopal (Text and Tables)	C. E. Luard	540	272
93	9789362086815	27th, Vol. IV	Rewah (Text and Tables)	C. E. Luard	500	250
94	9789362087584	28th, Vol. V, Pt. A	Western States - Malwa (Text)	C. E. Luard	1520	762
95	9789362087300	29th, Vol. VI, Pt. A	Eastern States - Bundelkhand (Text)	C. E. Luard	930	463
96	9789362082169	30th, Vol. VI, Pt. B	Eastern States - Bundelkhand (Tables)	C. E. Luard	830	417
			GAZETTEER OF THE BOMBAY PRESIDENCY:			
97	9788121283441	1st, Part I	History of Gujarat	Ed.: James M. Campbell	3220	644
98	9788121285582	1st, Part II	History of the Konkan Dakhan and Southern Maratha Country	Ed.: James M. Campbell	4200	840
99	9788121285568	2nd	Gujarat, Surat and Broach	Ed.: James M. Campbell	2990	598
100	9788121285544	3rd	Kaira and Panch Mahals	Ed.: James M. Campbell	1690	339
101	9788121285520	4th	Ahmedabad	Ed.: James M. Campbell	1860	372
102	9788121285506	5th	Cutch, Palanpur, and Mahi Kantha	Ed.: James M. Campbell	2390	478
103	9788121285483	6th	Rewa Kantha, Narukot, Cambay, and Surat States	Ed.: James M. Campbell	1450	290
104	9788121285469	7th	Baroda	Ed.: James M. Campbell	3260	652
105	9788121285445	8th	Kathiawar	Ed.: James M. Campbell	3790	758
106	9788121285421	9th, Part I	Gujarat Population - Hindus	Ed.: James M. Campbell	3170	636
107	9788121285407	9th, Part II	Gujarat Population - Musalmans and Parsis	Ed.: James M. Campbell	1520	304
108	9788121285384	10th	Ratnagiri and Savantvadi	Ed.: James M. Campbell	2500	501
109	9788121285360	11th	Kolaba and Janjira	Ed.: James M. Campbell	2550	513
110	9788121285346	12th	Khandesh	Ed.: James M. Campbell	3190	638
111	9788121285322	13th Part I	Thana	Ed.: James M. Campbell	2050	413
112	9788121285308	13th Part II	Thana	Ed.: James M. Campbell	1770	357
113	9788121285285	14th	Thana - Places of Interest	Ed.: James M. Campbell	3290	659
114	9788121285261	15th Part I	Kanara	Ed.: James M. Campbell	2340	348
115	9788121285247	15th Part II	Kanara	Ed.: James M. Campbell	1740	348
116	9788121285223	16th	Nasik	Ed.: James M. Campbell	3490	698
117	9788121285209	17th	Ahmadnagar	Ed.: James M. Campbell	3860	772
118	9788121285186	18th Part I	Poona	Ed.: James M. Campbell	2930	586
119	9788121285162	18th Part II	Poona	Ed.: James M. Campbell	2680	537
120	9788121285148	18th Part III	Poona	Ed.: James M. Campbell	2500	503
121	9788121285124	19th	Satara	Ed.: James M. Campbell	3450	692
122	9788121285100	20th	Sholapur	Ed.: James M. Campbell	2730	547
123	9788121285087	21st	Gazetteer of the Bomaby Presidency: Belgaum	Ed.: James M. Campbell	2570	514
124	9788121285063	22nd	Dharwar	Ed.: James M. Campbell	4200	841
125	9788121285049	23rd	Gazetteer of the Bombay Presidency:Bijapur	Ed.: James M. Campbell	3550	712
126	9788121285025	24th	Kolhapur	Ed.: James M. Campbell	2250	450

S. NO.	ISBN NO.	VOLUME	TITLE	AUTHOR	PRICE	PAGES
127	9788121285001	25th	Botany	Ed.: James M. Campbell	2040	408
128	9788121284981	26th, Part I	Materials Towards a Statistical Account of the Town and Island of Bombay - History	Ed.: James M. Campbell	2500	504
129	9788121284967	26th, Part II	Materials Towards a Statistical Account of the Town and Island of Bombay - Trade and Fortifications	Ed.: James M. Campbell	2690	538
130	9788121284943	26th, Part III	Materials Towards a Statistical Account of the Town And Island of Bombay - Administration	Ed.: James M. Campbell	2450	702
131	9788121284929	27th	General Index	Ed.:R. E. Enthoven	2190	428
			MADRAS DISTRICT GAZETTEERS			
132	9788121258814	1st	Anantapur	W. Francis	1140	227
133	9788121258555	2nd	Malabar	C. A Innes & F. B Evans	3010	602
134	9788121258791	3rd	Bellary	W. Francis	1890	377
135	9788121258777	4th	Statistical Appendix For Chingleput		280	56
136	9788121258753	5th	Coimbatore	K. N. Krishnaswami Ayyar	3420	628
137	9788121232814	6th	Madras District Gazetteers District Gazetteer Cuddapah	C. F. Brackenbury	1120	285
138	9788121258715	7th	Statistical Appendix For Ganjam		370	73
139	9788121256766	8th, Vol. 1st	Godavari District Gazetteer	F. R. Hemingway	650	320
140	9788121256803	8th, Vol. 2nd	Godavari District Gazetteer	F. R. Hemingway	160	83
141	9788121258678	9th	Statistical Appendix For Kistna		640	127
142	9788121258654	10th	Statistical Appendix For Kurnool		270	54
143	9788121258616	11th	Madura	W. Francis	1900	379
144	9788121258579	12th	Statistical Appendix For Madura		740	148
145	9788121258630	13th	The Nilgiris	W. Francis	2190	437
146	9788121234276	14th	Madras District Gazetteers Gazetteer Of The Nellore District Brought Upto 1938		1150	386
147	9788121258517	15th	North Arcot		590	118
148	9788121258494	16th, Vol. 1, Part I	Salem	F. J. Richards	1710	343
149	9788121258593	16th, Vol. 1, Part II	Salem	F. J. Richards	1800	360
150	9788121258456	17th	South Arcot	W. Francis	2400	480
151	9788121258470	18th	Statistical Appendix For South Canara		400	80
152	9788121258432	19th, Vol. 1st & 2nd	Tanjore: Main Volume and Statistical Appendix		2070	401
153	9788121258395	20th	Tinnevelly	H. R. Pate	2740	547
154	9788121258418	21st	Statistical Appendix For Tinnevelly		320	64
155	9788121258371	22nd, 1st & 2nd	Trichinopoly: Main Volume and Statistical Appendix	F. R. Hemingway	2440	487
156	9788121241953	23rd	Vizagapatam District Gazetteer	W. Francis	760	385
			PUNJAB DISTRICT GAZETTEERS			
157	9788121255943	1st	Ambala District 1883-84		620	124
158	9788121255967	2nd	Amritsar		1180	236
159	9788121255981	3rd	Delhi		1300	260
160	9788121256001	4th	Ferozepore		950	188
161	9788121256025	5th	Faridkot		350	70
162	9788121256049	6th	Gujranwala 1893-94		1270	254
163	9788121256063	7th	Gujrat	C. E. Luard	1140	228
164	9788121256087	8th	Gurdaspur 1891-92		1260	252
165	9788121256100	9th	Gurgaon 1883-4		1020	203
166	9788121256124	10th	Hazara	H. D. Watson	2290	458
167	9788121256148	11th	Hissar district and Lohar State		1840	367
168	9788121256162	12th	Hoshiarpur		1420	283
169	9788121256186	13th	Jhang		1070	213
170	9788121256209	14th	Jhelam		1010	202
171	9788121256223	15th	Jalandhar District 1883-84		540	108
172	9788121256247	16th, Vol. XIV-A	Jullundur District, with maps and Kapurthala		1990	398
173	9788121256261	17th, Pt. I	Kangra (Proper)		1450	290
174	9788121256285	17th, Pt. II	Kangra (Kulu, Lahual, Spiti)		1800	357
175	9788121256308	18th	Karnal		1930	386
176	9788121256322	19th	Kohat		1540	307
177	9788121256346	20th	The Lahore District 1883-84		1220	244
178	9788121256384	21st	Ludhiana and Maler Kotla		1680	335
179	9788121256407	22nd	Lyallpur		735	147
180	9788121256421	23rd	Mianwali		1170	234
181	9788121256445	24th	Montgomery	P. J. Fagan	1590	318
182	9788121258364	25th	Multan (1901-02)	E. D. Maclagan	2400	480
183	9788121258708	26th	The Rohtak District 1883-84		980	196
184	9788121258746	27th, Vol. III A	Dujana State 1904		500	16
185	9788121256483	28th	Shahpur District		1780	356
186	9788121256506	29th	Simla District		800	159

S. NO.	ISBN NO.	VOLUME	TITLE	AUTHOR	PRICE	PAGES
187	9788121256520	30th	The Chamba State		2040	408
188	9788121256544	31st	The Chenab Colony 1904		1550	310
189	9788121256568	32nd	Kalsia State		270	53
190	9788121256582	33rd	Suket and Mandi		770	154
191	9788121256605	34th	Phulkian States, Patiala Jind And Nabha 1904		2070	414
192	9788121256643	35th	Simla Hill States		2220	443
193	9788121256667	36th	Sirmur		920	183
			RAJPUTANA DISTRICT GAZETTEERS			
194	9789362088994	1st, Vol. I-A & B	Ajmer-merwara (Text and Statistics Tables)	C. C. Watson	1230	246
195	9789362080882	2nd. Vol. II-A & B	Mewar Residency (Text and Statistics Tables)	K.D. Erskine	1700	339
196	9789362088444	3rd, Vol. III-A & B	The Western Rajputana States Residency And The Bikaner Agency	K.D. Erskine	3590	718
			UNITED PROVINCES OF AGRA AND OUDH DISTRICT GAZETTEERS			
197	9789362087560	Vol. I	Agra	H. R. Nevill	2260	452
198	9789362082466	Vol. II	Aligarh	H. R. Nevill	1300	260
199	9789362089779	Vol. III	Allahabad	H. R. Nevill	2050	409
200	9789362081346	Vol. IV	Almora	H. G. Walton	1670	333
201	9789362085658	Vol. V	Azamgarh	D. L. Drake Brockman	1750	349
202	9789362080547	Vol. VI	Bahraich	H. R. Nevill	1410	281
203	9789362085214	Vol. VII	Ballia	H. R. Nevill	1750	350
204	9789362084668	Vol. VIII	Banda	D. L. Drake Brockman	1750	349
205	9789362086518	Vol. IX	Bara Banki	H. R. Nevill	1720	344
206	9789362084101	Vol. X	Bareilly	H. R. Nevill	1640	327
207	9789362086631	Vol. XI	Basti	H. R. Nevill	1610	321
208	9789362083814	Vol. XII	Benares	H. R. Nevill	2290	458
209	9789362086105	Vol. XIII	Bijnor	H. R. Nevill	1820	363
210	9789362081674	Vol. XIV	Budaun	H. R. Nevill	1890	378
211	9789362086891	Vol. XV	Bulandshahr	H. R. Nevill	2100	419
212	9789362081520	Vol. XVI	Cawnpore	H. R. Nevill	2210	442
213	9789362088031	Vol. XVII	Dehra Dun	H. G. Walton	1710	342
214	9789362088710	Vol. XVIII	Etah	E. R. Neave	1600	320
215	9789362082992	Vol. XIX	Etawah	D. L. Drake Brockman	1390	277
216	9789362082220	Vol. XX	Farrukhabad	E. R. Neave	1620	324
217	9789362083869	Vol. XXI	Fatehpur	H. R. Nevill	1890	377
218	9789362085962	Vol. XXII	Fyzabad	H. R. Nevill	1700	339
219	9789362087997	Vol. XXIII	Garhwal	H. G. Walton	1270	254
220	9789362089892	Vol. XXIV	Ghazipur	H. R. Nevill	1600	320
221	9789362085436	Vol. XXV	Gonda	H. R. Nevill	1650	330
222	9789362080271	Vol. XXVI	Gorakhpur	H. R. Nevill	1890	378
223	9789362086129	Vol. XXVII	Hamirpur	D. L. Drake Brockman	1390	277
224	9789362087638	Vol. XXVIII	Hardoi	H. R. Nevill	1680	336
225	9789362081636	Vol. XXIX	Jalaun	D. L. Drake Brockman	1180	236
226	9789362084309	Vol. XXX	Jaunpur	H. R. Nevill	1750	350
227	9789362084187	Vol. XXXI	Jhansi	D. L. Drake Brockman	1960	391
228	9789362089168	Vol. XXXII	Kheri	H. R. Nevill	1650	330
229	9789362086778	Vol. XXXIII	Lucknow	H. R. Nevill	1760	352
230	9789362088635	Vol. XXXIV	Mainpuri	H. R. Nevill	1740	348
231	9789362080424	Vol. XXXV	Meerut	H. R. Nevill	2170	434
232	9789362081087	Vol. XXXVI	Mirzapur	D. L. Drake Brockman	2430	486
233	9789362085443	Vol. XXXVII	Moradabad	H. R. Nevill	1900	380
234	9789362082763	Vol. XXXVIII	Muttra	D. L. Drake Brockman	2140	428
235	9789362089915	Vol. XXXIX	Muzaffarnagar	H. R. Nevill	2260	451
236	9789362086143	Vol. XL	Naini Tal	H. R. Nevill	1890	377
237	9789362086761	Vol. XLI	Partabgarh	H. R. Nevill	1560	312
238	9789362081124	Vol. XLII	Pilibhit	H. R. Nevill	1570	314
239	9789362084453	Vol. XLIII	Rai Bareli	H. R. Nevill	1610	322
240	9789362088284	Vol. XLIV	Rampur	H. R. Nevill	1170	234
241	9789362083654	Vol. XLV	Saharanpur	H. R. Nevill	2190	438
242	9789362083142	Vol. XLVI	Shahjahanpur	H. R. Nevill	1510	302
243	9789362083623	Vol. XLVII	Sitapur	H. R. Nevill	1590	317
244	9789362089939	Vol. XLVIII	Sultanpur	H. R. Nevill	1330	266
245	9789362080851	Vol. XLIX	Unnao	H. R. Nevill	1530	305

GAZETTEER OF INDIA
MADRAS
COIMBATORE

MADRAS DISTRICT GAZETTEERS

COIMBATORE

By

Dr. B. S. BALIGA, B.A. (Hons.), Ph.D. (Lond.),
Late Curator, Madras Record Office

GOVERNMENT OF MADRAS
1966

PRINTED BY THE DIRECTOR OF STATIONERY AND PRINTING, MADRAS, ON BEHALF OF THE GOVERNMENT OF MADRAS
1966

PREFACE

The old District Manuals and District Gazetteers prepared in the latter half of the 19th and the early years of the 20th century were valuable sources of information about the districts. In course of time the materials collected and featured in these Gazetteers became out of date. A revision of these District Gazetteers became necessary in the new situation of epoch-making changes in the country, *viz.*, independence and rapid economic and social changes.

The work of revising and rewriting the District Gazetteers was begun in the Madras State in 1954. The late Dr. B. S. Baliga, the then Curator of the Madras Record Office, was entrusted with the work of revision of the Gazetteers. Before his death in 1958 he prepared the draft chapters for four District Gazetteers, *viz.*, Thanjavur, Madurai, South Arcot and Coimbatore. The District Gazetteers of Thanjavur, Madurai and South Arcot were published in 1957, 1960 and 1962 respectively.

The old District Gazetteers were written mostly with the help of materials that could be readily collected from the sources available in the districts. In revising the District Gazetteers, Dr. B. S. Baliga pursued a pattern of his own by which he incorporated much of the materials available in the old Gazetteers and also the materials available from the records of the Madras Record Office. A special feature of the Gazetteers prepared by him was the chapter on

'Nationalism and Independence', a feature which could hardly find a place in the works prepared by the earlier civilians.

In 1958, the Government of India also sponsored a scheme for the revision of the District Gazetteers in all the States. Under the Scheme, the Government of India have supplied a new pattern for the revision of the Gazetteers so that all the District Gazetteers rewritten in the country may have a broad degree of uniformity. According to the scheme, the office of the State Editor was created in 1961 and the work of rewriting the remaining Gazetteers in accordance to the new pattern is in progress.

The revision of the District Gazetteers has been included under the Centrally Sponsored Schemes of the Third Five-Year Plan. The Ministry of Education gives a grant-in-aid towards the expenses incurred for the compilation and publication of the Gazetteers.

A number of the draft chapters of the Gazetteer were sent to the District Collector and to the Departmental Heads for their scrutiny. The chapters were later on improved by incorporating their suggestions for improvement. Our thanks are due to them in a large measure for the care and the kindness with which they scrutinised the chapters. Our thanks are due to Dr. M. Arokiaswami, Reader in History, University of Madras, for revising the chapter on "History" in the light of the suggestions from the Central Gazetteer Unit, Ministry of Education, Government of India. The Superintendent, Archaeological Survey of India, Southern Circle, Madras-9 and The Director of Information and Publicity, Madras, are also thanked for the supply of photographs, the selected copies of which have been reproduced in this Volume.

Sri M.C. Subramanian, M.A., Assistant Curator (Retired), Sri M. Natesan, B.A., Assistant Curator (Retired), and Sri N. S. Natarajan, Assistant Curator, have actively associated themselves in the compilation of the volume. The staff of the Gazetteer Unit have also borne various responsibilities connected with the printing and the publication of the volume. Our thanks are due to all of them for their unstinted labours.

The manuscripts for the Coimbatore District Gazetteer were finalised for being sent to the Press as early as 1958. The passing away of Dr. B. S. Baliga and the scheme for setting up a separate Gazetteer Unit, which was then under consideration, delayed the eventual despatch of the manuscripts to the Press. The typescripts were sent to the Press after I took over charge as State Editor and it has been my proud privilege to see it through in print in almost the manner in which the late Dr. B. S. Baliga conceived it.

GAZETTEER UNIT,
MADRAS RECORD OFFICE,
EGMORE, MADRAS-8.

14th April 1965.

A. RAMASWAMI,
State Editor, District Gazetteers

CONTENTS

99–1—B

LIST OF PLATES.

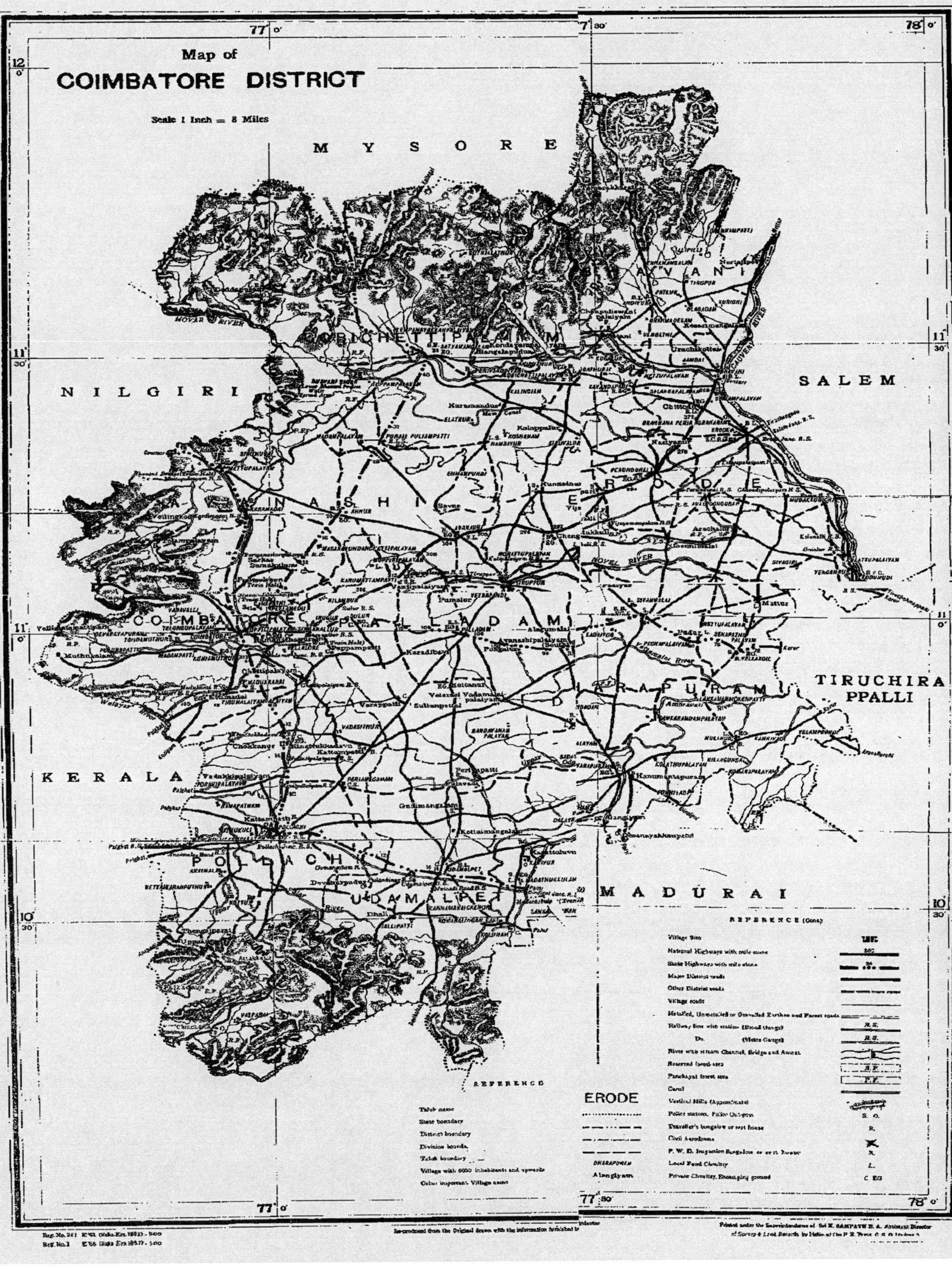

Map of
COIMBATORE DISTRICT
Scale 1 Inch = 8 Miles
MYSORE
NILGIRI
SALEM
KERALA
TIRUCHIRAPPALLI
MADURAI
ERODE
COIMBATORE
PALLADAM
POLLACHI
UDAMALPET
REFERENCE
REFERENCE (Contd)
77° 0'
78° 0'
12° 0'
11° 30'
11° 0'
10° 30'

Coimbatore District Gazetteer

CHAPTER I

PHYSICAL AND GENERAL DESCRIPTION.

Coimbatore is an inland district in the southern part of the Peninsula. It is rather elongated from north to south lying, as it is, between 76°·39' and 77° 56' of east longitude and 10° 12' and 11° 57' of the north latitude. It is bounded on the north by the Mysore State and the Salem district, on the east by the Salem and Tiruchirappalli districts, on the south by the Madurai district and the Kerala State and on the west by the Kerala State, the Nilgiri district and the Mysore State. Until recently it consisted of ten taluks but, since the reorganization of the States (November 1956), its Kollegal taluk having been ceded to the Mysore State, it now consists of nine taluks, namely, the Coimbatore, Pollachi, Udumalpet, Palladam, Dharapuram, Erode, Gobichettipalayam, Avanashi and Bhavani taluks. It has a total area of 6,024 square miles.

On the north, the district is traversed by the hill ranges of Gobichettipalayam and Bhavani; on the north-west, west and south, it is shut in by the mountain chains of the Western Ghats of which the Nilgiris on the north-west and the Anaimalais on the south are the chief ranges. In between these ranges, a few miles south-west of Coimbatore town, there is a pass to the West Coast known as the Palghat Gap, the importance of which from a climatic and commercial point of view can hardly be overestimated. The Cauvery forms the eastern boundary of the district for a considerable distance. Save for the hilly portions mentioned above, the rest of the district forms an undulating plain sloping gradually from the west to the Cauvery in the east. This sloping plain is gently undulating throughout, except in the black cotton soil tracts of the Udumalpet, Palladam and Coimbatore taluks. It is also broken by a few scattered hills of slight elevation such as the Chennimalai of the Erode and the Sivamalai of the Dharapuram taluks. The undulations consist of the great watersheds dividing river from river, as for instance, the Kangayam ridge from which the country slopes north to the Noyyal river and south to the Amaravathi river or the numerous petty ridges and bottoms which diversify a large area and afford opportunities for the hundreds of wells and rich gardens of the district[1].

The most conspicuous mountains of the district are the lofty Anaimalais which constitute its southern boundary. They are connected with the Palni hills of Madurai and are divided into the Higher or Upper and Lower ranges. The Lower ranges lying to the westward comprise the Anaimalai teak forests. Their average elevation is not more than 2,000 feet above sea level with peaks and ridges rising to 4,000 and 5,000 feet and they are almost wholly, with the exception of a few bare and rocky peaks, covered with forest. Kuchmalai, near their north-western extremity, is a noticeable landmark. The Higher ranges lying to the eastward consist of extensive open grassy hills and valleys with shola forests similar to those of the Nilgiris and the Palnis varying in elevation from 6,000 to 8,000 feet above sea level. These ranges are separated from the Palnis which lie to the east by the valley of Anjanad situated mostly in the Kerala State. This valley is not more than 12 or 15 miles across in a straight line and its western end is shut in by two blocks of well-wooded mountains with plateaux on their summits forming a connecting link between the Anaimalais and the Palnis. Viewed from Coimbatore, the Anaimalais and the Palnis appear as one continuous range of mountains; and viewed from Pollachi and Udumalpet, the Anaimalais appear most picturesque and noble.

The Higher ranges of the Anaimalais were first visited about a century ago (1851) by Major Michael, who was then in charge of the teak forests. He discovered on them a beautiful valley which now goes by his name as Michael Valley. This valley, which is 6,000 feet above sea level, is quite shut in by mountains and is well watered and well wooded. It is between 3 and 4 miles long and has a swamp at its southern end. Taking this valley as the centre of our survey, some 2,000 feet above it, on the north is the Tunukka plateau running east to west, which is narrow atthe eastern end, about half to three quarters of a mile across. It increases westward to about 2 miles in breadth and it gradually slopes to the vast forest lands of the Kerala State. To the east of this valley, and divided from it by deep wooded ravines of considerable extent, is the eastern plateau, some 4 to 5 miles long and 2 to 3 miles broad, the interior of which is broken into many abrupt ridges. To the south of this valley, at a distance of about

---

1 *Manual of the Coimbatore District* by F. A. Nicholson, 1887, pages 1–2.

5 to 7 miles, is the small but beautiful plateau of the Kumarikal Malai and to the eastwards of this spot and divided from it by the valley down which the Anjanad pass winds its way, there is a block of mountain about 7,000 feet high called the Pudukal Malai. And proceeding over the Kumarikal Malai for about 5 or 6 miles along the ridges overhanging the Anjanad Valley, the Kuratu Malai is reached. The views from this mountain are the grandest and most extensive; one can see from here a charming variety of scenery comprising undulating grassy hills, wooded valleys, rocky crags, huge overhanging precipices, the green fields of the Anjanad Valley, the grand mass of the Palnis beyond and the blue ranges in the far distance. In fine, the scenery in the Anaimalais is, in the words of Mr. Hamilton, one of its early explorers, " surprisingly grand and incomparably beautiful".[1]

The other hill ranges of the district consist of the Vellangiris, the Sholakarai and Bolampatty hills, the Lambton Peak range and the Hassanur, Bargur and Palamalai hills. The Vellangiris are the spurs of the Nilgiri mountains lying on the west and north-west of the district. The Sholakarai and Bolampatty hills lie partly in this district and partly in the Malabar district of the Kerala State. The Lambton Peak range is an offshoot of the Bolampatty range. It immediately overlooks Coimbatore town and ends on the south-east close to Tudiyalur railway station. Its highest peaks are about 4,000 feet above sea level. The Hassanur and the Bargur hills are situated in the Mysore plateau on the north-west and north-east of the district respectively[2]. The main body of the plateau here has an elevation of 2,500 to 3,000 feet; and on its south there is a chain of lofty hills rising steeply from the level of the plains to heights which are over 3,600 feet. This belt of high hills falls off eastwards and westwards and, in the middle, widens out to form the narrow plateaux of Onnaithittu, Dimbam and Kotadai. These hills contain a number of elevated peaks of which the highest is the Kambatrayan Boli which is 5,564 feet above sea level. At right angles to this southern range of hills several hill ranges run northwards intersecting the tableland into a number of large valleys and plateaux. The Palamalai hills form a long narrow plateau, 12 miles long and 4 miles broad, running roughly north to south. They are a detached block lying between the Bargur plateau on the west and the Salem hills on the east. They consist of a mass of high hills on the south, rising nearly to 5,000 feet, another fringe of hills on the east between 3,000 and 3,700 feet high, and a third lower range of hills on the west. The

[1] *Report on the High Ranges of the Anaimalai Mountains* by Lieutenant-Colonel Douglas Hamilton, 1866, pages 1, 4–7.

[2] *Manual of the Coimbatore District* by F. A. Nicholson, 1887, pages 5–7.

plateau between the eastern and western ranges is terraced, as it were, into tablelands[1].

The chief rivers of the district are the Cauvery and its tributaries, the Bhavani, the Noyyal and the Amaravathi. The Cauvery, as has already been stated, forms the eastern boundary of the district for a considerable distance. It rises, as is well known, near Mercara in Coorg and passing through the Western Ghats, which are subject to the heavy rainfall of the south-west monsoon, enters the Mysore State. Here it is joined by two tributaries, the Hemavati and the Lakshmanathirtha, and is spanned by the Krishnarajasagara Dam, near Mysore town, which impounds water for irrigation and ensures a steady supply for generating electricity, a little lower down at Sivasamudram. Before reaching Sivasamudram it is joined by another tributary, the Kabbini, as well as a number of lesser streams which contribute their quota during the north-east monsoon rains. It then takes a sharp turn from east to south at the Hogena-kal Falls. Three minor tributaries, the Palar on the west and the Chinnar and the Toppiar on the east, enter it on its course above Mettur, the site of the famous dam. It then flows south-eastwards and forms the boundary of the Bhavani taluk and the Tiruchengode taluk of the Salem district. At this part of its course it is joined by the Bhavani near the town of that name. It then turns to the south-east and forms the boundary of the Erode taluk and the Tiruchengode taluk. Near Erode it is joined by the Koranganpallam, a drainage channel which crosses the Kalingarayan and Pugalur channels near Unjalur. It then leaves the district and flows eastwards forming the boundary of the Salem and Tiruchirappalli districts. From June to August it is in full floods, thence subsiding gradually but with frequent freshes during October and November. Until it passes Erode its bed is rocky and its flow is rapid and therefore there is hardly any irrigation under it. But, after it passes Erode, its flow is slower and its bed is sandy and therefore there is a great deal of irrigation under it.

The Bhavani rises in the Silent Valley forests of the Walluvanad taluk of the Malabar district (now in the Kerala State). Before it enters the district, it receives the Siruvani, a perennial stream rising in the Attapadi Valley of the Malabar district. As it enters the district, it receives on the right the Koranganpallam which runs along the boundary of the Walluvanad taluk and the Avanashi taluk. It then enters the Avanashi taluk, and receives on the left the Kundah which rises from the Kundah range in the Ootacamund taluk of the Nilgiris, on the south the Peringapallam

---

1 *Working Plan for the North Coimbatore Forest Division*, 1934, pages 1–2.

and, a little further on the north, the Coonoor which flows from the Coonoor taluk of the Nilgiris. It next forms the boundary of the Avanashi and Gobichettipalayam taluks for some distance and then enters the latter taluk. Here it receives the Moyar (which rises in the Nilgiris and is known as the Pykara in the early part of its course) at Dhanayakankottai and, after flowing past the towns of Satyamangalam and Gobichettipalayam, goes eastwards and joins the Cauvery near the town of Bhavani, receiving on its way a few small streams from the south. It is a perennial stream and affords the best means of irrigation in the district. Being fed principally by the south-west monsoon it receives its first freshes towards the end of May and is at its highest from June to August. Thereafter it gradually subsides, though with occasional floods in the north-east monsoon. The supply of water in it has been seriously affected by the denudation of the large forest tracts at its source and on the Nilgiris.

The Noyyal, or the Noyyil, takes its rise in the Bolampatty Valley of the Velliangiri hills, and comes to be called the Swami Mudiyar, until further south, it is joined by the Periyar and the Chinnar. It runs past Perur assuming another name as the Kanchi Mahanadi, then flows within 15 miles of Coimbatore town and next forms, for a short distance, the boundary of the Coimbatore and Avanashi taluks. Here it receives on the left the Vannathankaraipallam, a drainage course which has its source in the north of Coimbatore town and, after flowing past Tirupur in the Palladam taluk, forms the boundary of the Palladam and Erode taluks where it receives the Nallar on the left. In the remaining part of its course, it forms the boundary of the Dharapuram and Erode taluks and after entering the Tiruchirappalli district, it joins the Cauvery. It is little more than a jungle stream being altogether dry for months in the year. At its source it does not receive much supply from the south-west monsoon and is largely fed by petty affluents from the plains during the north-east monsoon. It is in high and rapid floods for a short period during the north-east monsoon, its freshes then being noted for their brief duration, violence and caprice. It, however, fills up several irrigation tanks on its course, and its capriciousness is attributable to the denudation of the Bolampatty forests which supply the fuel and timber needs of Coimbatore town.

The Amaravati rises in the Anjanad Valley in the Kerala State between the Anaimalai hills and the Palnis. It descends in a northerly direction and debouches into the plains near Kallapuram at the mouth of the Anjanad Valley in the Udumalpet taluk. It then runs north-east and receives the Kudiriyar from the Madurai district on the right at Kumaralingam. Thereafter it flows into the Madurai district to emerge again into the Dharapuram taluk. Here, after passing the town of Dharapuram and receiving the Uppar on its left, it goes along a winding course, fed by a few small streams, and finally leaves the district and enters the Tiruchirappalli district and falls into the Cauvery at Kattalai in the Kulitalai taluk. Fed by the south-west monsoon, it flows with some regularity from June to the end of August; then it falls to some extent in September, but rises again with the north-east monsoon till November, when it begins to fall once more until March at the end of which it is practically dry. Its banks are low and its water is fully utilised for irrigation of good quality along its entire course.

Besides these chief rivers, there is one other river of some importance in the district and that is the Aliyar. It rises in the Peak Grass Hills of the Anaimalais in the Pollachi taluk, and is known as the Torakadavu Ar at its source. After running through reserved forests for about 14 miles and receiving several jungle streams, it enters the plains near Vannathorai bridge on the Pollachi-Vannathorai road. It is joined by the Uppar on the left near Anaimalai town and the Palar on the right a little further down. It then enters the Kerala State and joins the Ponnani which falls in the Arabian Sea. Its supplies are good except for two or three months in the year[1].

The geology of the district is simple. All the rocks, the alluvia and a few subaerial formations excepted, belong to the great gneissic series, the bottom rocks in the Indian rock series on which all other younger rock series are deposited. As a rule, the schistose, micacious and hornblendic varieties of gneiss predominate greatly, but bands of massive granitoid varieties also sometimes occur as, for instance, in the mountains north of the Palghat Gap. The formation conforms to a general strike in the direction east-north-east and west-south-west in the neighbourhood of Coimbatore town; in other parts of the district, however, it varies considerably and towards Bhavani it has a north-west strike[2].

The mineral wealth of the district is not insignificant. Limestone is found in abundance in the hills near Madukarai, about 7 miles south of Coimbatore, in extensive beds of grey and pink colours interbanded with gneissic rocks. Its beds varying from 50 yards to 450 yards in width strike in a north-east and south-west direction and have a total length of nearly 7 miles. It was formerly used for building the English Church at Coimbatore; it is now used by the Cement Works at Madukarai as raw

---

1 All this is based upon a study of the maps and a *Note on Irrigation of Coimbatore District* by V. N. Kudva, 1953.

2 *Manual of the Coimbatore District* by F. A. Nicholson, 1887, pages 20–21.

material for cement manufacture[1]. Building stones, charnockites and gneisses, are found on the Nilgiri mountains and plains and are quarried for local use[2]. Feldspar of the finest quality is abundant, especially in the Erode taluk; both the translucent pink and opaque white varieties of it occur, the former entirely free from iron and the latter slightly ferruginous on the surface from the red soil in which it is found[3]. Corundum occurs in several places. At Salangipalayam in the Bhavani taluk and at Gobichettipalayam it is found in the soil as scattered crystals, in the latter place sometimes, as big as walnuts. It is also found at Kangayam, Kandayankovil, Karatupalayam and Padiyur. Between Karatupalayam and east-south-east to Sivamalai, and especially up to Tirupur-Kangayam Road, it is found as a constituent of syenitic rock along the northern foot of a series of hillocks. In Sivamalai it is associated with elaeclite-syenite which used to be worked regularly some years ago. Here it forms crystals of good size up to 3 or 4 inches long and is of greenish grey colour[4]. Mica occurs in the northern parts of the district. There is an open cast of it measuring 120 feet×40 feet×25 feet at Vairamangalam, 4 miles west of Bhavani which has yielded pale green mica upto 12 inches across. There are two large pits of it some two furlongs west of Errappanayakanpalayam of which one measures 20 feet×20 feet. These are said to have yielded good quality green mica 3 to 4 inches across. There are also two small prospecting pits of it about 8 miles north of Bhavani near the junction of the Bhavani-Mettur Road with the cart track leading to Kuruchchi. And, in recent years, good muscovite is said to have been found at Punjai Puliyampatti about 12 miles from Satyamangalam on the Satyamangalam-Coimbatore Road[5]. Barite occurs in hillocks about half a mile west of Kuruchchi which is some 10 miles north of Bhavani. Its veins are up to 15 feet long and 8 inches thick mixed with quartz and feldspar. It is collected by women of the nearby villages as ' Kolakkal '[6]. Asbestos occurs near Perundurai and in a locality 6 furlongs from the Coimbatore-Mettupalayam railway track. It is also said to occur at Muthampalayam south of Karambadi railway station and near Bargur in the Bhavani taluk[7].

---

1 *Manual of the Coimbatore District* by F. A. Nicholson, 1887, page 22. *Mineral Resources of Madras* by M. S. Krishnan, 1951, page 189.

2 Idem, page 39.

3 *Manual of the Coimbatore District* by F. A. Nicholson, 1887, page 23.

4 *Mineral Resources of Madras* by M. S. Krishnan, 1951, page 96.

5 Idem, pages 236–237.

6 Idem, page 33.

7 Idem, page 26.

Nor is this all. Iron is said to occur in several places. It is said to occur in a rich bed in the Doddancombai forest in the Gobichettipalayam taluk near Hallagomalai and Chinnamalai[1], and in a torrent near Minkarai at the foot of the Anaimalais. The Salem Committee of the Madras Exhibition of 1851 reported on two kinds of iron produced from Coimbatore ores and the Catalogue of the 1857 Exhibition mentions both the iron stone and iron sand of rich quality collected from several localities in the district. And it was then stated that these iron ores, 'are of very fine quality, being particularly rich in metal and the most highly magnetic in the Exhibition' [2]. Manganese has been detected in the black sand from Virapaneli in the Coimbatore taluk[3]. Quartz of very fine quality is found in many places, especially in the village of Padiyur (Pattalai) near Kangayam; its crystals are sometimes deep amethyst and, when cut thick, are of rich purple or violet [4]. Zircon (gem stone) is found in the nepheline syenites of Sivamalai near Kangayam[5]. Beryl or aquamarine was formerly found in the cavities of the rocks near Padiyur. From June 1819 to June 1820, Mr. Heath, a retired Civilian, worked this beryl mine on contract with the Government and obtained, 2,196 stones weighing 22 lb. It has been surmised that this was the place from which beryl was supplied to the ancient world[6]. Finally, gold has been found in some auriferous veins in the Gobichettipalayam taluk. Several extensive old workings are found to the east, north-east and south-west of Bensibetta where a reef can be traced for 3 miles in a north-north-east direction across this hill and on a small hill one mile east-north-east of the village of Inbekombi. The southern most workings are a little to the south of the Bensibetta Trignometric station. The reef consists of stained quartz containing pyrite, limonite, hematite, chlorite, jasper etc., and strikes north-south and dips westwards. A few hundred yards east of the main out crop which was dotted with numerous old workings, Sir Henry Hayden saw some old shafts and found gold in them. He calculated that this reef was probably 5 inches thick and that it might yield 7 cwt. to the ton[7].

---

1 *Mineral Resources of Madras* by M. S. Krishnan 1951, page 96.

2 *Manual of the Coimbatore District* by F. A. Nicholson, 1887, pages, 22–23.

3 Idem, page 23.

4 Idem, page 23.

5 *Mineral Resources of Madras* by M. S. Krishnan, 1951, page 119.

6 *Manual of the Coimbatore District* by F. A. Nicholson, 1887, page 23.

7 *Mineral Resources of Madras* by M. S. Krishnan, 1951, page 122.
Memoirs of the Geological Survey of India, Vol. XXXIII—*See* the *Memoir* by H. H. Hayden, pages 55–60 and 65–66.

The soils of the district are chiefly red sand and gravel with a moderate area of red loam and black loam or sometimes black clay. Red sand occurs in 67·6 per cent of the occupied area. In the vast areas in the uplands and slopes, the soils are stony and gravelly, extremely thin with a sub-soil of raw decomposed rock, except at the bottom of the valleys where the soil is of moderate depth and somewhat rich by the wash from the uplands. In other areas the red soils are generally of fair composition chemically, owing to the presence of potash, lime and magnesia.

Black cotton soil lies in a tract consisting of portions of the Udumalpet, Palladam, Avanashi and Coimbatore taluks. Black loam and black clay are found in the south and west of the Udumalpet taluk. They are also found in the Palladam taluk, especially in the area south and south-west and in portions of the area near the railway line from Mangalam to Salur as well as in considerable tracts in the Coimbatore taluk, for example, around Coimbatore. Black loam also occurs in Avanashi, Cheyur and Anur firkas in the Avanashi taluk. Besides, there is a little black loam in the Gobichettipalayam taluk and some superior black clay and black loam in the extreme east of the Pollachi taluk.

There is a considerable amount of red loam in the Gobichettipalayam and Avanashi taluks, and a greater amount of it in the Coimbatore taluk. Soils in the latter taluk are impregnated with lime and in parts enriched by organic matter from the hills. There are some rich tracts of red loam in parts of Palladam taluk and many tracts of it in the Pollachi taluk. The soil in the Pollachi taluk is mainly sandy loam, intermixed occasionally with gravel in the Anaimalais and the red soils around the Anaimalais are extremely fertile. There is some red loam chiefly in the north, south and east of the Udumalpet taluk, a little good variety of it chiefly in the lands under the Kalingarayan channel and in beds of tanks in the Erode taluk and very little of it in the valleys of the Dharapuram taluk and in the hilly Bhavani taluk.

The soils of the Bhavani, Erode and Dharapuram taluks are mostly gravelly, stony and sandy; they are all red soils. A major portion of the soil of the Gobichettipalayam, Udumalpet and Pollachi taluks is red sand. The soil is chiefly reddish gravel at Palladam and northwards towards Avanashi [1].

---

[1] *Note on Irrigation of the Coimbatore District* by V. N. Kudva, 1953.

The talukwise distribution of soils on percentage basis is as follows[1]:—

Taluk.	Black.			Red.	
	Clay.	Loam.	Sand.	Loam.	Sand.
(1)	(2)	(3)	(4)	(5)	(6)
Gobichettipalayam ..	..	8·0	..	32·5	59·5
Bhavani	..	3·6	0·3	11·7	84·3
Erode	..	1·2	..	18·8	80·0
Dharapuram	0·2	4·0	..	10·6	85·2
Udumalpet	12·4	11·0	0·4	17·7	57·7
Palladam	6·0	7·9	8·2	14·1	63·8
Coimbatore	11·2	13·8	0·7	35·6	38·7
Avanashi	0·4	5·4	0·6	22·7	71·1
Pollachi	3·2	2·7	..	39·3	54·4

The forests of the district will be described in detail in the chapter on Forests. Here it is enough to make a few general observations. A large portion of the district is covered with forests, which lie chiefly in two sections, in the north in the Bhavani and Gobichettipalayam taluks in the hills forming the Mysore plateau and, in the south in the Pollachi and Udumalpet taluks on the Anaimalais. There is also some forest in the Coimbatore taluk in the west, at the foot of the Nilgiris and in the Bolampatty Valley. The northern forest tract is more or less interspersed with villages and is grazed over. Sandalwood and other valuable timbers are found in the neighbourhood of all the hill villages. The forests on the hills in the eastern foot of the Nilgiris do not produce very good timber, but the southern slopes of these hills produce fair timber. The preservation of the forest situated at the headwaters of the Noyyal is a matter of great local interest, the whole of the Bolampatty Valley having been disafforested within the last 130 years. The Higher ranges of the Anaimalais, which are virtually uninhabited; contain much valuable timber; but this timber is so difficult to exploit that the evergreen forest which contains it is looked upon chiefly as a protective belt of the headwaters of the various streams. The lower ranges of the Anaimalais are of much greater importance, in as much as they contain a well known belt of teak which formerly used to attain a most extraordinary growth. At the present moment they have suffered much from reckless fellings, and the open, sandy and treeless wastes, south-east of Udumalpet, present a sad spectacle to the eye. Besides teak, these forests contain most of the trees found in deciduous forests of similar elevation and produce considerable quantities of minor forest produce [2].

[1] 1951 *Census Handbook, Coimbatore District*, page 3.

[2] *Statistical Atlas of the Madras Province, Coimbatore District*, 1949, page 645.

Coming to the flora, the various kinds of trees found in the forests of the district will be described fully in the chapter on Forests. The trees found in the low country, however, are of very ordinary character and there is here a great dearth of fruit trees. Several varieties of *Acacia, Albizzia amara* and *wrightia, Ailanthus exelsa* and *Melia azadirachta* are the chief varieties of ordinary trees. The palmyra abounds in the Erode, Dharapuram and Palladam taluks and is less frequent in the other taluks. The tamarind is poorly represented, considering the opportunities for its growth. The bamboo is practically non-represented in the plains, though there are hundreds of river, channel and tank beds where it can be grown with advantage. Avenue trees are chiefly tamarind, neem, odiya-maram (*Odina wodier*) and kalathi (*Ficus tsiela*) and are usually poor in character. Among shrubs of industrial importance occurring abundantly may be named *Cassia auriculata* (avaram) found almost everywhere in profusion; *Tephrosia purpurea* (kavali) almost equally abundant ; *Balsamodendron berryi* (mullu-kiluvai) used as a hedge especially in the taluks of Erode, Bhavani and Dharapuram; several species of *Euphorbia* also used for hedge purposes; and *Zizyphus jujuba* (elandai).

The chief fibres found in the district are *Calotropis gigantea* (yerukku), *Sansevieria zeylanica* (bow-string hemp or ' marul '), *Abelmoschus esculentus* (bendikay), *Agave americana* (American aloe or anaikkaralai), *Cocos nucifera* (coconut), *Crotolaria juncea* (sunn-hemp), *gossypium arborium* (cotton), *Hardwikia binata* (acha), *Hibiscus cannabinus* (pulichi) and *Musa paradisiaca* (plantain). Less important and less abundant fibres are *Acacia arabica* (karuvelam), *Acacia leucophloea* (velvelam), *Bambusa aurundinacea* (bamboo), *Bauhinia diphylla* (akkikodi), *Grewia tilioefolia* (thadachi), *Azadirachta indica* (neem or veppam), *Guilandina bonduc* (kalachi), *Helicteres isora* (valambiri), *Isora corylifolia, Pandanus odororatissimus* (thazhai, screwpine), *Sterculia villosa* (vakkainar), etc. Of these the *acacias* are universal and abundant and bamboo abundant in the forests [1].

The chief resins and gum trees of the district are *Ailanthus malabarica* (mattipal), *Canarium strictum* (karunkungiliam or black dammar), *Boswellia glabra* (kungiliam or white dammar), *Shorea talura* (lac or kungiliam), *Aloe vulgaris* (Barbadoes aloes), *Isonadra acuminata* (Indian gutta), *Acacia arabica* (babul or karuvelam), *Acacia leucophloea* (velvelam), *Moringa oleifera* (murungai or horse radish tree), *Feronea elephantum* (wood apple or velam), *Azadirachta indica* (veppam), *Odina wodier* (Odiyamaram) and *Zizyphus jujuba* (elandai). And the chief dyes and

[1] *Manual of the Coimbatore District* by F. A. Nicholson, 1887, pages 39–40.

colours of the district are palai indigo obtained from palai (*Wrightia tinctoria*), turmeric (*curcuma longa*) and myrabolams (*Terminalia chebula et bellerica*). The other dyes of the district are safflower (*Carthamus tinctorius*), Sappan (*Coesalpinia sappan*), marking nut (*Semecarpus anacardium*), and avaram (*Cassia auriculata*). The chief tanning materials found here are the bark of avaram (*Cassia auriculata*), myrabolams, both kadukai and thanikai (*Terminalia chebula et bellerica*), abundantly in the forests ; divi-divi (*Coesalpinia coriaria*) near Coimbatore; and velvelam (*Acacia leucophloea*) which is particularly abundant in the district [1]. Among fruits, pomegranates (*Punica granatum*) are largely grown in several places and citrus fruits, especially limes, are grown in some places [2].

The fauna of the district is rich and varied. The hills here abound in almost every South Indian species of wild animals. The elephant is found on the Anaimalais and on the hills in the northern, north-eastern and north-western parts of the district, especially in the dense forests bordering on the Mysore State. The tiger is an inhabitant of all the jungly parts of the district, more particularly of the northern hills. The panther lives in scrub jungles and among the rocky hills in many places. The cheetah is sparsely distributed over a small portion of the district on either side of the Bhavani river. The hyaena is not uncommon on the low hills near Madukarai. The wolf is occasionally seen in the Palladam taluk. The jackal is met with, both on the hills and on the plains. The fox is common everywhere. The black bear is found throughout the district on the rocky sides of the wooded hills at no great distance from the jungles. The sambur, the finest of the deer tribe in the south, dwells on the slopes of the wooded hills in many parts of the district. The spotted deer is plentiful alike in the woods and plains but not usually on elevations beyond 2,500 feet. The muntjac deer, or the rib-faced deer, or the barking deer, or the jungle sheep, as it is variously called, is found in jungles. The mouse deer is met with on the northern hills. One kind of antilope, the nilgai, is sometimes seen in the low scrub jungles on the banks of the Bhavani and the Moyar; another kind, the mountain antelope, is found in several mountainous parts of the district; and a third kind, the ordinary antelope is met with in several parts of the plain open country. The ibex is found on the Anaimalais and the Nilgiris. The gaur or the bison, the grandest and the largest of the bovine family, dwells in the large forests, especially those bordering on the Mysore State.

The monkeys are fairly represented in the district. Besides the common monkeys, are to be found here the lion monkey, the Malabar langur,

---

1 Idem, pages 41–42.

2 Idem, page 241.

and the slender loris, that most curious creature with slender limbs and body, sharp features, enormous eyes and no tail. Here are also to be found the large fox bat, called the flying fox, the badger, the otter, the porcupine, the mongoose, as well as the common musk shrew or musk rat, the ordinary rat and the bandicoot. Here are likewise to be found the squirrels in plenty in the forests, the common striped squirrel, the jungle striped squirrel, and the brown flying squirrel.

Of the domestic animals, the Kangayam cattle are well known for their excellent qualities whether for labour or milk. The district also has the equally well-known Alambadi cattle imported from Mysore, the Kollegal cattle well fitted for draught, and the Bergur cattle, the swiftest and strongest of the breeds. The sheep here are of two kinds, semmari-adu and kurumbadu; the latter are usually reared by the kurumbars and yield excellent wool. The Kangayam ponies were once well-known; they were formerly bred in large numbers and even exported. But nowadays, their breeding has declined very much with the advent of faster means of traffic. The ass is common and so also is common the pariah dog.

Of birds and fishes, birds in the low country are not numerous or peculiar. The partridge, the quail, the snipe, the duck and the teal are, however, fairly abundant. But a variety of fishes are to be found in the great rivers. The masheer is found in the Cauvery and the Bhavani; the fresh water shark, the carp of several kinds as well as the murrel and the eel are found in all rivers. The spawning season is March to July but the general fishing season is all the year round [1].

The climate of some parts of the district is very pleasant. It is extremely pleasant in the Coimbatore taluk, except in its hot corners under the hills, owing partly to the elevation of the place and partly to the cooling effect produced by the south-west monsoon which begins to pour through the Palghat Gap in May, June and July. It is pleasant in the Pollachi taluk during the south-west monsoon, save in the villages situated at the foot of the hills. It is fairly good in the Udumalpet taluk where the winds of the south-west monsoon, especially in its western portion, though strong, are cool. It is tolerably good in the Dharapuram taluk, lying as this taluk is, immediately opposite the Palghat Gap. But it is comparatively hot in the Palladam taluk and very hot in the Gobichettipalayam,

---

1 *Manual of the Coimbatore District* by F. A. Nicholson, 1887, pages 27–38.

Manual of the Coimbatore District by H. A. Stuart, Vol. II, 1898, pages 336, 344, 356, 365–366, 401, 419 and 420.

Bhavani and in parts of Erode and Avanashi taluks, all which form the Bhavani and the Cauvery Valleys.

Taking the district as a whole, January and February are pleasant months everywhere. But the mornings of January are frequently misty and chilly when north-east and east winds come with occasional breezes from the south-east, at which time cold and fevers prevail. Towards the end of February the climate becomes close and sultry and March is usually very oppressive, especially along the Cauvery. During these months the rain is rare and slight, the sky is almost cloudless, the humidity is at its minimum and the wind veers to the south-east and south with oppressive calms. In April the weather gets hotter, the sun being vertical in the middle of the month, and the few thunder showers that come, instead of mitigating oppressiveness, increase it. In May, the thermometer continues to rise and thunder-showers become more frequent. Towards the close of the month, however, the wind which has for sometime been in the south and south-west gathers momentum and develops into the south-west monsoon which brings instant relief in the matter of temperature to the greater part of the district. At this time and through June, July and August, the Palghat Gap through its tunnel-shaped opening of some 16 miles broad sends forth the violent winds of the south-west which cool large parts of the country but, at the same time, overturn everything that comes in their way, even laden carts, and cause sudden and dangerous chills. Their violence and cooling effect are largely spent by the time they reach the eastern portion of the district, where they are fitful, hot and dusty. The rainfall of the south-west monsoon is irregular in the extreme as the masses of clouds are intercepted by the hills which border the district on south-west, west and north-west. No dependence can be placed upon it in June, while in July and August, droughts, most distressing to the ryots, are of frequent occurrence. A portion of the Coimbatore taluk and a great portion of the Pollachi taluk which are opposite to the Palghat Gap are exceptions where during June, July and August, the weather is cool, damp and showery. By the end of August the south-west monsoon has moderated and September, which is between the south-west and the north-east monsoons, is usually oppressive with slight and variable winds and scanty rainfall. In October the north-east monsoon sets in frequently in the early part of the month itself, but the heaviest rains are usually in the end of October and throughout November. This is practically the only cloudy month of the year for parts of the district other than those near the Palghat Gap. Rain is slight in December when the weather is chilly and raw and this brings in fevers and cold again.

The district is exceptionally dry and its rainfall is scanty, uncertain and ill-distributed. Particulars of the average annual rainfall and the average number of rainy days in a year in the various taluks are furnished below :—

Name of the taluk.	*Average annual rainfall in inches.*	*Average number of rainy days in a year.*
(1)	(2)	(3)
Gobichettipalayam	30·32	50·0
Bhavani	30·89	43·9
Avanashi	30·03	45·2
Erode	27·05	42·9
Coimbatore	28·17	45·5
Palladam	22·78	39·9
Dharapuram	23·11	35·5
Pollachi	33·04	59·8
Udumalpet	23·99	37·4

Particulars of the monthly mean of daily maximum and minimum temperature, the highest and the lowest recorded temperature and the monthly mean rainfall for the years 1881—1940 and similar particulars and actual rainfall for 1951 as recorded at Coimbatore are given below[1] :—

Month.	1881—1940. Temperature. Mean of: Daily maximum.	1881—1940. Temperature. Mean of: Daily minimum.	1881—1940. Temperature. Highest recorded.	1881—1940. Temperature. Lowest recorded.	1881—1940. Mean rainfall (inches).	1951. Temperature. Mean of: Daily maximum.	1951. Temperature. Mean of: Daily minimum.	1951. Temperature. Highest recorded.	1951. Temperature. Lowest recorded.	1951. Actual rainfall (inches).
(1)	(2)	(3)	(4)	(5)	(6)	(7)	(8)	(9)	(10)	(11)
January	86·0	64·9	95	53	0·63	87·2	67·6	90	61	0·03
February	90·9	66·5	98	55	0·36	91·0	67·0	95	63	0·01
March	95·4	70·2	102	60	0·50	94·8	72·7	98	67	0·41
April	96·5	73·6	104	64	1·58	93·1	74·2	98	71	4·64
May	94·4	73·6	103	65	2·47	93·9	74·9	97	70	1·90
June	88·8	71·9	101	65	1·52	86·6	71·7	91	69	1·17
July	86·7	71·0	96	62	1·65	86·3	71·6	91	69	1·93
August	87·4	71·0	96	63	1·23	88·1	72·5	90	71	0·19
September	88·7	70·9	96	65	1·59	89·2	72·1	95	70	3·65
October	87·7	70·7	97	59	6·31	88·5	73·1	92	71	3·11
November	85·4	69·0	94	57	4·03	85·4	72·3	90	69	7·05
December	84·3	66·0	95	54	1·36	85·8	66·5	88	63	0·13
For the year ..	89·3	69·9	104	53	23·23	89·2	71·3	98	61	24·22

1 1951 *Census Handbook, Coimbatore District*, page 2.

It will be seen from these tables that the average maximum temperature of the district over a series of years from 1881 to 1940 is 89·3° ; that the average highest and lowest recorded temperatures during the same years are 104° and 53° and that the average rainfall during the same years is 23·23 inches.

With such a scanty rainfall, the lowest in all districts in the State, it is not to be wondered that scarcities have very often, and famines have now and again, visited the district. It has been said that a full crop in the district is an exception and that a half or quarter crop is the average. Information available shows that not less than two-thirds of the seasons in the last century were unpropitious and many almost calamitous.[1] In some years the south-west monsoon which never altogether fails is scanty and partial, but in most years, it is the north-east monsoon that fails. In many cases the droughts and scarcities are exacerbated by the consecutive occurrence of bad seasons for a series of years. Sometimes the famines themselves come such as the ones that came in 1804-1805, 1806, 1808, 1812, 1813, 1823, 1831, 1832, 1834, 1836, 1861 and 1866, previous to the Great Famine of 1876-78. In 1804-05, there was a distressing failure of rain. In 1806 there was an equally bad season, the north-east monsoon failed and led to the grant of remissions. In 1808 the failure of both the monsoons caused a famine which carried off half the population. In 1812, the failure of the south-west monsoon led to a great mortality among cattle. In 1813 the failure of the north-east monsoon led to similar mortality among cattle and dried up everything, even grass. In 1823 the north-east monsoon completely failed, dried up all crops and necessitated large remissions. In 1831 the want of rains caused a famine and ' affected cultivation ', it said, 'beyond precedent' [1]. In 1832 a partial failure of the south-west monsoon was followed by a total failure of the north-east monsoon which caused immense distress. In 1834, the north-east monsoon totally failed, the rivers dried up, a large portion of the crops under the Amaravati and the Noyyal were lost and large areas of ploughed lands were left unsown. In 1836, both the monsoons failed and ushered in famine conditions. In 1861 the south-west monsoon having more or less failed, and the north-east monsoon having totally failed, a famine came and ravaged the district; even the wells went dry and the Government had to incur an expenditure amounting to Rs. 21,052 on famine works. In 1866 the north-east monsoon brought in very little rain while the south-west utterly failed. Crops suffered badly, the prices of foodgrains went up very high, even drinking water

---

1 *Manual of the Coimbatore District* by F. A. Nicholson, 1887, pages 576–581.
Manual of the Coimbatore District by H. A. Stuart, Vol. II, 1898, pages 64–71.

became scarce and thousands of people found it difficult to get any food. Arrangements had to be made for feeding the poor and for giving employment to able-bodied labourers. The Government had to spend on relief works Rs. 19,145 and on gratuitous relief Rs. 11,798[1].

Then came the great famine of 1876-78 more disastrous in effect than any of its predecessors. The year 1875 proved to be a year of scanty rainfall and it was followed in 1876 by a failure of both monsoons and the total loss of all crops, except those irrigated from wells or river channels. In 1877 the kar rains of hot season and the south-west monsoon until September failed and converted most of the country into a desert. Although the north-east monsoon followed with violence, it ruined a good deal of cumbu by its profuseness and caused great sickness and death among persons already enfeebled by want and starvation.

Early in 1877 the famine developed with alarming rapidity. The Collector (Mr. Wedderburn) had from December 1876 made preparations to face the famine, and relief works and gratuitous relief were now started at once. Until October 1877 all relief was under the Revenue Department, but from that month the relief works were handed over to the Public Works Department. The works undertaken were famine roads, improvement of village lanes, deepening of tanks, removal of prickly pear, clearance of irrigation channels and so forth. Weavers were aided by the Government by purchasing their goods. Gratuitous relief took the form of money doles and of cooked food and from September 1877, the plan of closed camps was strictly enforced. From that date, however, the improvement of the season led to the gradual decrease of relief, and though the first half of 1878 was a very trying time, by far the worst pinch of the famine was over with September 1877. The sequels of the famine had, however, to be faced even afterwards; the camps became hospitals, cholera killed thousands, dysentery, fevers and anaemia tens of thousands, and it was not till the end of 1878 that the famine was fairly over. It was estimated that 1,97,188 people and 2,06,859 cattle died during the famine. It was also asserted that but for the large number of wells of the district, the calamity would have been greater. The total State relief on works came to Rs. 23,68,768 and on gratuitous supply of food to Rs. 18,12,316. Besides the direct relief afforded to the distressed poor, 10,700 persons were helped with advances of money amounting to 1½ lakhs of rupees for cultivation and a large number of weavers were given advances amounting to Rs. 1,20,700, and very large remissions were

---

1 *Manual of the Coimbatore District* by F. A. Nicholson, 1878, pages 576–581.
Manual of the Coimbatore District by H. A. Stuart, Vol. II, 1898, page 72.

granted. The whole cost of famine of this district to the State came to upwards of 50 lakhs of rupees [1].

The next considerable famine occurred in 1891-1892. The distress which prevailed in the district during this period began as early as December 1890 and was due, at first, to the failure of the north-east monsoon of 1890-1891. This failure seriously affected cultivation and large extents of land were left untilled. It was thought that much difficulty would be experienced by agricultural labourers who were deprived of their usual work by the failure of the crops and they were, therefore, employed on public works on a small-scale to begin with. The conditions, however, became critical with the failure of the South-west monsoon. Prices shot up and cultivation became impossible. The number of persons relieved on works rose rapidly; so also rose rapidly the number of persons who were given gratuitous relief. The distress indeed became so severe that relief kitchens had to be opened for helping those who could not work. The rainfall of October at length brought relief to the district, and by November the relief works were much circumscribed, and by January, the relief kitchens were closed. The total expenditure on famine relief was Rs. 75,695, while a sum of Rs. 5,236 was spent on gratuitous relief. Besides these items of direct expenditure, the Government granted remissions of assessment amounting to Rs. 55,902. During this famine the Government also granted advances amounting to Rs. 74,000 to landowners for the improvement of their lands, especially for the construction of wells; and Rs. 80,000 for the purchase of cattle fodder and seed grain. This famine carried away about 17,000 people and 1,27,000 cattle [2].

There were scarcities in the district in 1892-1893, 1894-1895, 1904-1905, and 1905-1906 and there was also a great scarcity accompanied by a serious shortage of fodder in 1924 [3]. But there was actual famine in recent years only in 1939. This famine seriously affected the south-eastern part of the district, namely, the Dharapuram taluk and parts of the Palladam and Udumalpet taluks. Its immediate cause was the failure of the north-east monsoon of 1938. This, coupled with the failure of the south-west monsoon, rendered cultivation impossible, impoverished landowners and left the landowning as well as the landless classes in a state of despair. Relief works were started by the District Board by the end of December 1938 but very soon the situation became worse, people began to migrate along with their cattle, the prices of fodder increased three-fold,

[1] *Manual of the Coimbatore District* by H. A. Stuart, Vol. II, 1898, pages 73–79.

[2] Idem, pages 79–81.

[3] *Gazetteer of the Coimbatore District,* Vol. II, 1933, pages 126–127.

cattle were sold at half the normal price and even drinking water became scarce. The Government now started relief works and by September 1939 ten famine charges came into existence. However, good rains came in October and November, so that by the middle of November all famine works were closed. The total number of persons, including dependants, relieved at the several works were 1,73,14,033; the total number of persons who were given gratuitous relief were 16,37,708; and the total number of persons who were fed at the relief kitchens were 13,34,373. The total cost of the relief operations came to Rs. 17,49,422. Besides this, land revenue assessment amounting to Rs. 2,00,452 was postponed to next fasli and remissions of assessment amounting to Rs. 5,22,180 were given. Loans over 7 lakhs of rupees were granted under the Land Improvement Loans Act and the Agricultural Loans Act. Fodder concessions amounting to over Rs. 30,000 were also given, besides grants for sinking and deepening wells [1].

It appears that in this district (1) two successive bad years or one entire and absolute failure of crop will produce partial famine; (2) such famine will not be intense unless one or other, and especially the second year has failed to yield more than one-fourth average crop; (3) a failure of not more than one-third crop once in two years will not produce famine calling for special measures of relief; (4) a favourable season following the second bad one will extinguish famine. The wells of the district alone render these favourable inferences possible, but the protection afforded by them is aided in parts by the irrigation afforded by the river channels [2].

As may be expected the district is not subject to serious floods. There is no evidence to show that any serious floods occurred in the district in the last century. In our own century a few floods have visited the district but none of them has caused any large scale destruction. Of these the following may be mentioned: On 16th August 1923, owing to heavy and continuous rains, the Cauvery breached in two places in the Erode taluk near Kasipalayam and Kodumudi and submerged several dwelling houses and wet lands. On 19th August, however, the flood subsided having caused no loss of life or cattle [3]. The floods of 1924 proved more disastrous. Heavy rains in the Nilgiris in July caused such a volume of water to flow into the Bhavani between the 15th and 18th that, it ran 23 feet high in Satyamangalam, topped the bridge, breached the abutment, flooded the streets and destroyed several houses. At the

---

1 G.O. No. 1157, Revenue, dated 21st May 1941.

2 *Statistical Atlas of the Madras Province, Coimbatore District,* 1949, page 661.

3 G.O. No. 1349, Revenue, dated 5th September 1923.

Koduveri anicut it overflowed the head sluices of the channels at either end and breached the Thadapalli channel in several places. It also affected some 25 villages on the banks of the river, chiefly in the Gobichettipalayam taluk, resulting in many damaged huts and houses. But it did its worst in the Bhavani town. On the 18th August, the Bhavani overflowed into the town breaching its banks, tearing up roads and bringing down houses. A week later, the Cauvery too came in floods and caused much more havoc. The Madras trunk road was breached at the abutment of the Cauvery bridge whose first span was also cracked. In the Erode taluk the railway bridge spanning the river was in danger for a few days and many villages on the banks of the river suffered serious damage. There was, however, no loss of life.[1] In 1925, the floods came again. On 11th November a heavy downpour of rain in Satyamangalam breached an abandoned tank, flooded the streets and damaged several houses. This flood also washed away the road to Coimbatore near Nallur, badly tore up the road to Puliyampatti, overflowed the Kavilipalayam tank and silted up several acres of land in Puliyampatti and its neighbourhood [2]. On 10th December, the Amaravati rose in floods owing to the heavy rainfall in the Western Ghats and damaged a number of important river channels in the Udumalpet taluk[3]. In 1930 heavy rains fell from 23rd to 26th October and caused a flood in the Bhavani. In the Avanashi taluk it affected 9 villages on the bank of the river; in the Gobichettipalayam taluk, some 39 villages, and in the Bhavani taluk a few irrigation channels [4]. In 1935 unusually heavy rains fell on the Anaimalais on 15th and 16th November and brought heavy floods in the Palar and the Aliyar rivers of the Pollachi taluk. These caused damage to a number of anicuts and channels in the Pollachi, Udumalpet and Dharapuram taluks [5]. In 1936 heavy rains again fell on the Anaimalais as a result of which the Amaravati and the Aliyar rose on 2nd November and damaged many irrigation works in the same taluks, including those damaged in the previous year [6].

---

[1] *Gazetteer of the Coimbatore District*, Vol. II, 1933, pages 124–125.

[2] G.O. No. 27, Revenue, dated 5th January 1926.

[3] G.O. No. 29, Revenue, dated 6th January 1926.

[4] G.O. No. 2219, Revenue, dated 17th November 1930.
G.O. No. 2406, Revenue, dated 17th December 1930.

[5] G.O. No. 54, Revenue, dated 8th January 1936.
G.O. No 419, Revenue, dated 25th February 1936.

[6] G.O. No. 2631, Revenue, dated 8th December 1936.

CHAPTER II

EARLY HISTORY.

Long before the dawn of history, in the dim mists of antiquity, the region at present comprising the Coimbatore district was inhabited by primitive people who belonged to the Neolithic Age [1]. This is evidenced by a large number of cairns, kistvaens, dolmens or chromlechs, besides what are called Pandavakulis and Veerakals, found in the various parts of the district. All these are the graves of the dead and most of these contain traces of a bygone civilization of which we can get only a glimpse and nothing more. Cairns abound in Nallampatti, 6 miles north-north-east of Perundurai, in Kandyankoil 13 miles east of Palladam, in Kanjapalli near Annur and in Nattukkapalayam near Pollachi. The large number of them found in Nallampatti seems to show that a whole tribe with its chieftain had been buried there. Kistvaens exist in Muttukonampatti and in Pundi, 14 miles south-west of Udumalpet. Dolmens are found in several places in the Dharapuram taluk and especially (about 100) in the region around Mettupalayam. Pandavakulis or Pandukulis (which mean pits of old men) in which distinguished elders were perhaps buried are met with near Perur, Vellalur and Ellapalayam near Annur, while Veerakals (hero stones) are seen in many places, usually at the entrances of the villages [2].

The sepulchral urns found in cairns, kistvaens and dolmens have revealed burnt or unburnt bones, sometimes whole skeletons, as well as pottery and utensils of various kinds such as cups, jugs, vases, vessels with side spouts, plates and saucers, all finely glazed and exhibiting, in some cases, no mean skill in workmanship. They have also revealed metallic articles such as iron swords and daggers with wooden handles, javelins, arrows, lances, spears, spades, chisels, bronze ornamental bowl stands

---

1 *Pre-Historic South India* by V. R. Ramachandra Dikshitar, 1951, page 91.

2 *Gazetteer of the Coimbatore District*, Vol. II, 1933, pages 258–260.
The Kongu country by M. Arokiaswami, 1956, pages 30–34.

with miniature tigers for support, bronze bowls, jars, cups, sieves, strainers, bangles, beads and necklaces and, sometimes, even gold diadems [1].

Some of these relics are said to belong to the last of the pre-historic races, the Kurumbars and the Eiynars or the Vedars, the ancient pastoral and hunting tribes that were fast receding into the gloom just before the dawn of history. The Sangam literature which heralds the historic times refers to them as ancient races which once occupied almost the whole of the region now comprising the districts of Coimbatore and Salem. It refers to them as warriors skilled in archery and as builders of forts both large and small. It also refers to them as meat eaters, who were fond of toddy and of all kinds of crude games and sports. It refers especially to the Vedars as the worshippers of Korravai, a fierce goddess represented as riding on a stag, clad in tiger's skin with long teeth and horns. To this goddess they used to offer blood, meat, rice, incense and flowers and before this goddess they used to dance various kinds of dances amidst the beatings of drums and the sounding of horns [2].

On the disappearance of these people, the dawn of history comes with the first three centuries of the Christian Era. This period is lighted up by the great literature of the Sangam Age, which shows that the Coimbatore district of to-day, then formed part of what was called the Kongu country, a country which comprised also the taluk of Kollegal now belonging to Mysore, almost the whole of the Salem district as well as a part of the Kulittalai taluk of the Tiruchirappalli district and portions of the Dindigul and Palni taluks of the Madurai district [3]. That literature also shows that the Kongu country was then inhabited by the great tribes, known as the Malavar, the Kosar and the Kongar. All these tribes were in friendly relations with the Cheras of Kerala, and were well-known in the Chera, Chola and the Pandyan kingdoms for their war-like qualities. The Malavars especially were excellent soldiers. The Kosars seem to have originally come from the north under the pressure of Mauryan invasion and settled down first in the Tulu country and then in the Kongu country. They were noted for their organizing capacity, administrative ability as well as truthfulness, a circumstance which makes some historians think that they were the Satyaputras of the Asokan inscriptions. It was from the name of their capital 'Kosanputtur' that Coimbatore has probably

1 *Gazetteer of the Coimbatore District*, Vol. II, 1933, page 259,

G.O. No. 716, Public, dated 26th June 1874.

Archaeological Survey of India, Annual Report for 1902–1903, pages 111–140.

2 *The Kongu Country* by M. Arokiaswamy, 1956, pages 34–40.

3 *Gazetteer of the Coimbatore District*, Vol. II, 1933, page 257.

received its name [1]. The Kongars, from whom the name Kongu itself came to be applied to the whole country, seem to have originally come there in search of pasture from Kodagu (Coorg).

These tribes had their own kings who had their armies consisting of the corps of horses, elephants and chariots. The kings, it is said, often took the field in person and rejoiced with the common soldiers in their successes. There can be no doubt that they fought with one another and allied themselves with the Cheras and the Pandyas. They had their forts scattered in all parts of the country. They knew the use of the sword, the lance, the bow, the breast-plate, the war drum and the war banners. But they also knew and cultivated the arts of peace. The Kongars, in particular, were a great pastoral people fond of cattle breeding and agriculture. And they, as well as the Kosars and the Malavars, carried on trade not only with their neighbours but also with distant foreigners like the Romans, as is clear from the large number of Roman coins of the time found in their country. This will be explained shortly when we speak of Roman trade in the Kongu country [2].

In course of time, the Malavars, the Kosars and the Kongars, fell under the sway of their powerful neighbours, the Cheras. It would, however, appear that it was not the main line, but the collateral branch, of the Cheras, the family of the Irumporai that made inroads into the Kongu country. No less than eight rulers of this family beginning from Mantharam Peraiyan Kadungo and ending with Kanaikal Irumporai are said to have excercised supremacy in the Kongu country. Mantharam Peraiyan Kadungo's power was established by the victories of Senguttuvan at Sengalam, Viylur and Narivayal. He was succeeded by Oval-Perumcheral-Irumporai, a remarkable ruler who is said to have captured Karuvur (Karur) and defeated the Adigaman and two other chieftains at Tagadur (Dharmapuri). This Adigaman, a Malavar chieftain whom he defeated, seems to have been no other than Adigaman Neduman Anji, the patron of Avvaiyar and the ruler of the whole of East Kongu. It was possibly the growing power of this chieftain that Perumcheral wished to destroy. It is said that the Adigaman was an ally of the Tondaiman of Kanji and Ori of the Kollimalais and that he had inflicted a severe defeat on Kari of Tirukkoyilur. Perumcheral could not afford to have such a powerful

---

1 It is also held that the place was originally named 'Kovanputtur' or 'Koyenmuttur' after the Irula chieftain, Kovan or Koyen who founded it and that this name later on came to be pronounced as Coimbatore—*See Coimbatore Manual*, 1865, page 1, and *Kongu Nattu Varalaru* (Tamil) by M. Ramachandran Chettiar, pages 229–235.

2 *The Kongu Country* by M. Arokiaswami, 1956, pages 40–59 and 72–74.

chieftain in his kingdom and the victory that he won over this chieftain immediately made him feared and respected in the Kongu country.

His successor Ilamcheral is said to have defeated Perum Chola, Ilam Palayan Maran and Vicci and destroyed five forts. He was succeeded by Yanaikan-Sey-Manthram-Cheral, the Chera of the Elephant-look, in whose time Karur became the capital of the Kongu Cheras. He is praised for his just and beneficent administration and extensive foreign contacts. But it was during his time that the first check to the Chera rule over the Kongu country came. He often fought with the Pandyan king Nedunjelian and the Chola king Perunarkilli, and won several victories over them. But, in the end, he was himself defeated and taken captive at the famous battle of Talayalanganam, by the Pandyan and the Chola kings[1]. His successors had no easy time amidst the growing power of the Pandyas and the Cholas on the one side and the Velir chieftains on the other. For, it was during this period, sometime in the third century, that all the power in the Kongu country passed into the hands of the Velir chieftains. From what little evidence there is, we find that there were six of these chieftains who had established their power in the Kongu country. There was first, Vel Avi and his successors Titiyan and others who had carved out a principality in Pothini (Palni). There was, secondly, Atiyan who had conquered the southern part of the present Coimbatore district. There was thirdly, Aye Andiran who had established his power in the whole region from the Palghat Gap to Cape Comorin. And there were also three other Velir chieftains, Vel Pegan, Vel Pari and Vel Evvi who had entrenched themselves in the other parts of the Kongu country. It was these chieftains that kept the Pandyas and the Cholas away from Kongu[2].

This brings us to the middle of the third century. And here we may pause a little to give an account of the trade that had by then been firmly established between the Kongu country and Rome, Egypt and Greece. That a brisk trade was carried on in the first three centuries of the Christian Era between the Kongu country and Rome is evident by the large number of Roman coins found in the Coimbatore and Salem districts. Thus, for instance, at Vellalur, 4½ miles south-east of Coimbatore, over 600 Roman silver dinari, chiefly of Augustus (44 B.C.—14 A.D.) and Tiberius (14—37 A.D.), with a few of Caligula (37—41 A.D.), Claudius (41—51 A.D.) and Constantine (323—337 A.D.), were found in the middle of the last century. A potful of coins of Augustus and Tiberius was dug up at Pollachi in

---

1 *The Kongu Country* by M. Arokiaswami, 1956, pages 62–70.
Chera kings of the Sangam period by K. G. Sesha Aiyar, 1937, pages 44–66.

2 *The Kongu Country* by M. Arokiaswami, 1956, pages 70–72.

1800. Some Roman coins of the Caesar were also brought to light at Karur in 1806; and at Kalayamuttur, very near Palni, a number of coins ranging from Drusi (8 B.C.) to Commodius (180—193 A.D.) were unearthed in 1856. The Romans seem to have been attracted chiefly by the beryl (aqua marine) found in Padiyur. That some trade was carried on between Egypt and Greece on the one hand and Kongu on the other, possibly even before the time of the Roman Emperors, is said to be evident from a bronze jug unearthed in Avanashi, bearing Greek and Egyptian influences. The Egyptians and the Greeks seem to have been attracted chiefly by steel for which the Salem part of the Kongu country was then famous. It has also been asserted with some plausibility that the Kongu country offered these distant nations not only beryl and iron but also gold and fine hand-spun and hand-woven fabrics. It is believed that the trade route in those days lay from the Malabar Coast, through the Palghat Gap to Coimbatore, Salem and Madurai[1].

When the Roman trade was still at its height, a branch of the Rashtrakutas known as the Rattas came and occupied the whole of the Kongu country. They seem to have come from the Karnataka owing to the pressure exerted on them on all sides by the Banas, the Gangas and the Kadambas. The chronology of the Ratta kings is by no means clear; but recent[2] research has tentatively fixed it as follows :—

	A.D.
Vira Raya Chakravarti	250—270
Govinda Raya I	270—290
Krishna Raya	290—310
Govinda Raya II	330—355
Kannaradeva	355—380
Tiruvikramadeva	380—405

We know very little about the individual achievements of these kings. We are told that the last of the three kings were great warriors and conquerors. The last among them was the greatest of them all, and he conquered 'the Chola, Pandya, Kerala and Malayala countries' and wielded supremacy over the Karnataka. We are also told that all the kings, except the last, were Jains and that the last king Tiruvikramadeva gave up Jainism and embraced Saivism under the influence of Narasimha Bhatta of the Bharadwaja gotra.[3] But we know something about their

[1] *Gazetteer of the Coimbatore District,* Vol. II, 1933, pages 260–261.
Manual of the Salem District by H. Le Fanu, Vol. I, 1883, pages 21–23.
The Kongu Country by M. Arokiaswami, 1956, pages 72–79.

[2] *The Kongu Country* by M. Arokiaswami, 1956, pages 84–91.

[3] Idem, pages 91–99.

general administration. Their capital was Skandapuram, and their kingdom was divided into districts, each district consisting of groups of villages; two such districts, for instance, were Kulasta and Vijaya Skandapura. They were anointed in their capital at their installation by a solemn ceremony of consecration. They wore a crown, sat on a throne, and ruled the kingdom in accordance with the precepts of Nithisastra. They struck gold coins in their names following the way of the Romans. They showed not a little interest in architecture as is instanced by the temples built by them in their capital and other towns. They were skilled in the arts of dancing and music; they knew the Veena and the various musical drums. They encouraged agriculture and conducted a land survey; and during their time both grain measures and land measures were employed. They stimulated trade, especially trade with Rome in beryl, gold and fine cloths. They professed either Jainism or Saivism and created landed endowments for religious purposes. These endowments they made either to the Jain bastis or to the Hindu temples, sometimes as propitiary offerings on going forth to war and sometimes as thanks-offerings on their return from their campaigns. Their grants were recorded in copper plates or stones, and they dated these grants from the era of Shalivahana and added the year of the sixty years' cycles. They used the Tamil names of the months and divided each month into the waxing and waning halves. They regarded the time of the full moon and of the middle of the eclipse as auspicious moments. Nor is this all. They knew the science of warfare. They marched to war to the sound of their war drums, with their banners flying and used enchantments against their enemies. They displayed their banners which they took in battles and returned home laden with spoils and tribute [1].

From the last of the Ratta kings, Tiruvikramadeva, the Kongu country passed into the hands of the Gangas. It would appear that his attempt to subjugate Karnataka terminated in his death at the hands of Konganivarman I, the first of the long line of Ganga rulers. Available evidence shows that Konganivarman was greatly assisted in his conquest of the Kongu country by the Jains. The celebrated Jain Achariya, Simhanandi, because of the apostasy of Tiruvikramadeva, seems to have rallied all the Jains under the banner of Konganivarman and led him on to victory and finally installed him with all pomp and ceremony on the throne of the Kongu country [2].

---

1 *Manual of the Salem District* by H. Le Fanu, Vol. I, 1883, pages 19–20.
The Kongu Country by M. Arokiaswami, 1956, pages 99–101.

2 Idem 1956, pages 103–109,

The rule of the Gangas which thus began and continued for nearly five centuries is not easy to depict. Both the genealogy and the chronology of the Gangas are still vexed questions in history[1]. The Kongudesarajakkal, the chief chronicle of the Kongu kings and the inscriptions do not throw any clear light upon them. Recent research, however, has tentatively fixed the chronology of the Gangas who ruled over Kongu country as follows [2]:

	A.D.
Gangas of Skandapuram—	
Konganivarman	405—450
Madhava I	450—460
Gangas of Talakad—	
Harivarma	460—480
Vishnugopa	480—525
Madhava II (adopted son of Vishnugopa and a paruvi)—	525—535
Krishnavarma (son of Vishnugopa)	535—555
Dindikara—Regent to the unnamed daughter of Vishnugopa and Konganivarman II.)	555—610
Gangas of the Imperial period—	
Durvinita	610—655
Muskara	655—660
Tiruvikrama	660—665
Bhuvikrama	665—680
Konganivarman III	680—725
Kongu Gangas—	
Govinda	725—750
Sivakama	750—775
Prithvi Kongani	775—830
Malladeva I	830—840
Gandadeva	840—850
Satyavalkya	850—860
Gunaluttama	860—870
Malladeva II	870.

Some information is available on a few of these kings. Konganivarman I belonged to the Jahnaveya kula and the Kanavayana gotra. He distinguished himself in many battles and won a considerable victory over the Banas. His successor Madhava I was not, by any means, a warrior king ;

1 *See* for instance, *The Kongu Country* by M. Arokiaswami, 1956, pages 109–124. *List of Antiquities, Madras*, by R. Sewell, Vol. II, 1884, pages 189–191. *Ancient History of the Deccan* by G. Jouveau-Dubreuil, 1920, pages 104–110.

2 *The Kongu Country* by M. Arokiaswami, 1956, pages 124–125.

his reign was marked by peace and prosperity and great literary activity. Himself, a scholar of no mean repute, he attracted many learned poets to his court. He was also charitable to all, from his feudatories down to his servants. Both he and his father received Pallava support and cultivated Pallava alliance. But from the time of his successor, Harivarman, a change came over. It may be mentioned here that the Gangas of this period were divided into two rival houses, namely, the Paruvis who ruled from Kolar and the Gangas who ruled from Skandapuram (identified with modern Kangayam). The Pallavas having now supported the Paruvis, Harivarman allied himself with the Kadambas and shifted his capital from Skandapuram to Talakad from where he could keep an eye on the Paruvis. In the reign of his son and successor Vishnugopa, the picture changed again. The Paruvis had now no one to succeed to the Ganga throne and the whole of the Gangavadi, therefore, reverted to the Talakad Gangas. Vishnugopa, however, having no child, for a long time adopted a Paruvi, Madhava, as his son and successor. About this Madhava II, we know nothing except that he was succeeded by Krishnavarma, the son born to Vishnugopa after he adopted Madhava. The Talakad branch thus again came to occupy the Ganga throne. On Krishnavarma's death, one Dindikara is said to have acted as a regent, first to an unnamed daughter of Vishnugopa and then to her son Konganivarman II. But during the rule of Konganivarman II, the clouds began to gather. He had to permit Avanita, a scion of the Paruvi house, to rule with him conjointly. And, though, it is said, Avanita, intended the throne to be occupied by Konganivarman's son, his own son, Durvinita wrested it from him.[1]

With the accession of Durvinita the throne passed back into the Paruvi house. Durvinita seems to have fought hard to secure it; he is said to have fought several battles, at places like Andari, Alattur, Porulare and Pennagardy, identifiable in the modern districts of Salem, Coimbatore and South Arcot. He is said to have established his sway over the whole of Kongu and even extended it as far south as Tondaimandalam, the home of the Pallavas. He threw up the alliance of the Pallavas, because they had sided with the Talakad house and cemented an alliance with the Western Chalukyas, then fast coming into prominence. He gave his daughter in marriage to Pulikesin II and secured the position of Pulikesin's grandson, Vikramaditya I, after winning a victory over the Pallavas. Nor did he stop with this. He conquered the Punnata kingdom, comprising parts of south Mysore and north Coimbatore, which was then under Ravidatta, a feudary of the Cheras. He also fought against the Cheras,

[1] *The Kongu Country* by M. Arokiaswami, 1956, pages 126–138.

the Cholas and the Pandyas who were then trying to establish a foothold in the Kongu country. He, at the same time, evinced great solicitude for the welfare of his subjects. He strictly followed the Dharma Sastras and the Nithi Sastras and earned for himself the title of Manu; and, being a distinguished scholar himself, he encouraged in every way learning and literature. From all this, it would appear, that the Ganga rule reached its high water mark during his reign[1]. The Gangavadi at this time consisted of a large portion of territory extending from Madarkale on the north to the Kongu on the south, from Tondanad on the east to the Arabian Sea on the west.

Durvinita was followed by his son Muskara of whose brief reign we know next to nothing, save that he ruled over the whole of the Gangavadi region and the Kongu country, which he inherited. Nor do we know anything about his son and successor Tiruvikrama, save that he married the daughter of a Chola king. Of the reign of his son and successor Bhuvikrama, however, we know a little more. He is credited with having fought several battles against the Pandyas, the Cholas and the Pallavas side by side with his allies, the Chalukyas. He is also credited with having brought home many elephants as spoils of war and, in particular, with having snatched away the Ugrodaya, a jewelled necklace of the Pallava king Parameswaravarman, in one of his wars. Next to Durvinita he was the most powerful king of the Gangas. He was succeeded by his son Konganivarman III whose rule was characterised by peace and prosperity, but shorn somewhat of its glory by his having had to share his kingdom with his brother Vallabhagya. Konganivarman III is said to have built a bridge over the Kiline river and set up a new village called Pallava-thadakam at the request of the two Pallava princes who had been taken as hostages in the reign of Bhuvikrama. He ruled his kingdom through the members of his family appointed as Viceroys in charge of suitable divisions. One such member of his family was Ereganga, possibly his son and another Sri Purusha, his grandson[2].

On his death, the Ganga kingdom disintegrated and fell on its decline. The Kongu region now came to be governed by the sons and successors of Vallabhagya who are called Kongu Gangas. These Kongu Gangas from Govinda to Malladeva II, owed only a nominal fealty to the main branch of the Ganga Kings. Nor is this all. The Pandyas, the Pallavas, the Banas and others now began to make inroads into the Kongu country. The Pandyan king Sadayan Ranadhira (680–710) seems to have conquered

---

[1] *The Kongu Country* by M. Arokiaswami, 1956, pages 139–148.
Idem, 148–153.

parts of Kongu; his son Arikesari Maravarman (710–740) is said to have crossed the Cauvery and subdued certain hilly parts of the Kongu country; and Maravarman's son Nedunjelian (740–770) is reported to have defeated the Adigaman of Tagadur (identified with Dharmapuri in the Salem district) and erected a temple for Vishnu at Perur near Coimbatore. About the same time, the Pallavas also began to occupy parts of Kongu. During the reign of Nandivarman II called Pallavamalla (731–793), Udayachandra, his celebrated general, extended his arms into the present Salem district. The Banas too came and occupied at this time a portion of the Kongu country. Added to this, a collateral line of the Ganga kings began to rule in another portion of the Kongu country [1].

It was under these circumstances that the Kongu Ganga kings ruled over what was left of the Kongu country from 725 to 870. We can catch only a glimpse of some of these Kings. Thus, Prithvi Kongani is stated to have kept the Pallavas at bay by stationing one of his generals at Skandapuram; Gandadeva is said to have won victories over the Pallavas; and Malladeva is supposed to have taken part in the famous battle of Sri Purambiam (880), near Kumbakonam, in which the Pallava king Aparajita supported by the Chola king Aditya I and the Ganga king Prithivipati I signally defeated the Pandyan king Varagunavarman. Prithivipati is said to have lost his life in this battle. And this battle is all the more memorable because, soon after it was fought, Aditya turned his arms not only aginst the Pallavas but also against the Gangas and with remarkable swiftness conquered and occupied both Tondaimandalam and the Ganga kingdom, including Kongu [2].

Before we pass on to Chola rule, we may attempt to give a sketch of the Ganga rule in the Kongu country. From what little information we possess, the Ganga kings seem to have been no ordinary rulers. They sometimes ruled directly and sometimes through the viceroys (especially in the later period), whose duty it was, first and foremost, to protect the frontiers. Each viceroyalty was split up into several nadus and each nadu into a number of groups of villages. The village, though the last rung in the ladder of administration, was regarded as the most important. It had an assembly with a headman called the gramani or the gavunda and this assembly dealt with all village affairs and imposed even local cesses for various purposes. There is nothing to show that the Kings' Officers interfered in the local affairs conducted by these assemblies, while there is something to show that these officers made use of these assemblies for the

---

[1] *The Kongu Country* by M. Arokiaswami, 1956, pages 154–166.

[2] *Idem*, pages 166–173.

collection of land revenue. Since ' nadu ' is mentioned as a unit of administration, it must have had an assembly consisting possibly of the representatives chosen by the groups of villages. The functions of this assembly must have been similar to those of the village assembly. The Viceroy must have exercised jurisdiction over all the nadus through the King's Officers. We have no clear evidence about this, but we have clear evidence that the king was the fountain head of the whole administration. He was autocratic in theory but, in practice, he was always bound by the Dharma Sastras and the Nithi Sastras; kings like Avanita and Durvinita are specially mentioned as having been well versed in these sastras. He was also surrounded by ministers (mantris) and gurus (religious heads) who expounded these sastras to him or gave him whatever advice they deemed necessary. He had a number of important officers, both civil and military, like the senapatis, mahasandhivigrahakas, sandhivigrahakas, kayyalokanams, dandanayakas and mahaprabhus. What exactly were their duties, it is not clear, but there can be no doubt that they controlled the army and carried on the civil administration.

As may be imagined, war was the greatest pre-occupation of the king. This was inevitable, surrounded as he was by the rising power of the Cholas, the Pandyas, the Pallavas and the Chalukyas, not to mention others. He not only fought wars but practised the science of war and diplomacy. He had always ready at his command the four kinds of military corps, the elephantry, the cavalry, the chariotry and the infantry, all well equipped with bows and arrows, swords, breast-plates and other offensive and defensive weapons. He had also a perfect knowledge of the four kinds of diplomacy, ' sama, bedha, dhana and danda ' as well as a knowledge of the mantra sastras, all which he employed, it is said, successfully on many an occasion. Next to war, his most important pre-occupation was the collection of revenue. He levied chiefly assessment on land and customs duties. He collected, it would appear, one fifth or one sixth of the gross produce, depending upon the quality of the land and its facilities for irrigation. He collected also land customs, having his chowkies at the frontiers of towns and villages.

But the king was known to his subjects not merely as a protector and a tax gatherer, but as a patron of religion, learning and literature. Sometimes he professed himself a Jain, sometimes a Vaishnavite, and sometimes a Saivite; thus Konganivarman I accepted Jainism, Vishnugopa became a Vaishnavite and Sivakama a Saivite. But, whether he was a Jain, a Vaishnavite or a Saivite, he showed toleration to all religions and showered his benefactions, his land endowments and other gifts, equally on Jain bastis and Hindu temples. He was also well known for the granting of devadana and brahmadeya lands and for exempting the Brahmins from all taxes. This he did, because the Ganga King was at heart a Brahmin and a Hindu. He, however, supported Jainism, because that religion was responsible for establishing the Ganga Kingship and had made Kongu its special home ever since the dawn of the Christian era. The Brihatkathakosa of Harisena mentions without doubt the migration of the disciples of Bhadrabahu from Sravana Belgola to Punnatta in Kongu even in the centuries preceding the Christian era. When once they were settled in the Kongu country, the Jains exerted great influence in the region for a long time. We know from inscriptions and copper plates and literary records that the Jain Acharya Simhanandi is mentioned as the " promoter of the Ganga family " and he resided in Perur near Coimbatore[1]. In the later period, however, Hinduism made rapid conquest under the banners of its inspiring saints Appar, Sundarar and Sambandar and others. The king was equally well known for the encouragement he gave to all kinds of learning and literature. It was under his patronage that some celebrated works like Akalanka's Astasakti, Gunabhadra's Uttarapurana and Ugraditya's Kalyanakaraka were written. It was under his patronage again that some well known prose writers like Vimala, Udaya, Nagarjuna and Jayabandu, and poets like Bharavi, Pampa, Ponna, Asaga and Gunabhadra flourished. Nor is this all. Sometimes he himself took delight in learning; thus Madhava I specialised in law, Tiruvikrama became the master of the fourteen branches of learning, and Durvinita wrote a commentary on the XV Sarga of Kiratarjunaiya and Sanskritised the Brihatkata.

Under such a king, the subjects must have doubtless enjoyed considerable freedom of thought and freedom to profess whichever religion or philosophy they liked. Their lives in those days naturally centered round the numerous bastis and temples which the king had endowed and enriched for their sake. They also received what education they needed in the Jain monasteries and Hindu maths and agraharams. They usually followed hereditary occupations such as agriculture and trade. There were also among them numerous professional guilds, such as the guilds of goldsmiths, coiners, blacksmiths, oilmen, potters and tailors. In their social life they greatly enjoyed festivals, dancing and singing and held the women in high respect, especially those that were accomplished. There is evidence to show that some of their women were highly accomplished not only in scholarship, but also in fine arts, music, dancing, painting, etc. It would appear that even in those days, the women in general loved to wear bright coloured saris and bodice and to adorn themselves with all

[1] *The Kongu Country* by M. Arokiaswami, pages 103–109 and 185.

kinds of jewellery such as girdles, necklaces, ear-rings and bracelets. It would also appear that they showed a partiality for perfumes, preferred curly locks, applied collyrium to their eyes and wore wreaths of flowers on their hair. But the same women who did all this did also something which is revolting to our feelings today, for they sometimes committed sati to show their devotion to their husbands.[1]

So much about the Ganga regime under which the Kongu country and, therefore, the Coimbatore district, remained for about four and a half centuries. With the conquest of the Kongu country by Aditya I, the history of the district gets merged in the history of the Cholas. It is not possible to give a separate account of the Kongu country under the Cholas, for it then formed a part of the Great Chola Empire and loses all its identity.

Aditya I (871–907), the son and successor of Vijayalaya, the founder of the new dynasty of the Cholas at Thanjavur, was a remarkable ruler. As has already been stated, he not only conquered the Pallava kingdom but also subjugated the Western Gangas and conquered Kongu. And immediately after the conquest of the Kongu country, which he effected in 894, he set about to clear the country of all intruders. He drove away the Pandyas, formed friendly relations with the Chera king, Sthanu Ravi, and married a Pallava princess, and thus by using force of arms as well as diplomacy, became the unquestioned master of Kongu. He was an ardent Saivite and he built temples, it is said, all along the banks of the Cauvery from Sahyadri to the sea. He died at Tondaimanad near Kalahasti, where a temple was erected over his remains by his son Parantaka.[2]

Parantaka I (907–955) was even a more remarkable ruler, and under his leadership, the Cholas acquired a dominion which foreshadowed the greater empire of Rajaraja and Kulottunga. When he ascended the throne his kingdom embraced the country lying between Madras and Kalahasti in the north and the Cauvery in the south including, of course, Kongu but excluding the Mysore tableland and the west coast. He put an end to the Pandyan independence by conquering Madurai and chasing away the Pandyan king first to Ceylon and then to Kerala. He even invaded Ceylon but without success. He then turned his attention to the north. Here he had to face an invaṣion by Rashtrakuta Krishna II who espoused the cause of his daughter's son Kannaradeva, who was excluded

---

[1] This picture is based on the material found in the following books: *The Kongu Country* by M. Arokiaswami, 1956, pages 173–186.

The Gangas of Talkad by K. Krishna Rao, 1936, pages 120–304.

[2] *The Colas* by K. A. Nilakanta Sastri, Vol. I, 1935, pages 130–141.

from the Chola throne by Parantaka's accession. Krishna II was aided by the Banas and Vaidumbas and Parantaka by Ganga Prithivipati II. Krishna suffered a severe defeat in the battle of Vallala (modern Tiruvallam in North Arcot district) which took place round about 915 A.D.[1] As a result of this battle, he got from the Banas, the country situated to the north of the Palar between Punganur in the west and Kalahasti in the east and over this territory he appointed Prithivipati II as governor with the title of Banaditya. From the Vaidumbas he got the country near Kurnool. The defeated rulers naturally sought refuge with the Rashtrakutas, while he carried on his conquests up to Nellore which was then being ruled by the Eastern Chalukyas. But great conquests always produce great repercussions and the repercussions produced by his conquests eventually lost him all his prestige and most of his conquests. All his enemies rallied round the powerful Rashtrakuta king, Krishna III, and this king marched with a formidable force from the north-west, inflicted a great defeat upon his forces at Takkolam near Arkonam (949) and occupied large portions of his territories, including parts of the Kongu country. His eldest son Rajaditya lost his life in this battle and he himself did not survive this battle long, although, before his death, he perhaps succeeded in recovering a portion of the territories lost by him. Then followed a period of obscurity for about four decades until the accession of Rajaraja I in 985. During this period the Chola kings, Gandharaditya Arinjaya, Parantaka II, Sundara Chola, Aditya II and Uttama Chola Madhurantaka seem to have put up a stiff fight against the Rashrtakutas and the Pandyas and finally recovered much of their lost possessions, including the Kongu country.[2]

With the rise of Rajaraja I (985–1014), the son of Parantaka II, the sky begins to clear and the day dawns on a new and brilliant chapter in the history of the Cholas. Alike in war and peace, Rajaraja and his son Rajendra showed themselves as the most outstanding personalities of their time. Starting from small beginnings, for when he ascended the throne the country had hardly recovered from the effects of the Rashtrakuta invasion, Rajaraja rapidly pushed himself to the forefront by a succession of splendid victories. He conquered Kerala (the Chera country) and made it a part of his dominion. He conquered Madurai and the whole of the Pandyan country and added that too to his dominion. He conquered Malainadu (Coorg) and placed all the western countries that

[1] *History of South India* by K. A. Nilakanta Sastri, 1955, page 168.
History of India by K. A. Nilakanta Sastri, page 238.

[2] *The Colas* by K. A. Nilakanta Sastri, Vol. I, 1935, pages 142–198.
The Kongu Country by M. Arokiaswami, 1956, page 201.

he had subdued under the overlordship of his son Rajendra. He conquered the northern part of Ceylon with the aid of his powerful navy, destroyed Anuradhapura, its ancient capital, drove its king to the mountains, founded a new capital at Polonnaruwa and left there as a beautiful and lasting memorial, the little temple of Siva. He conquered almost the whole of the present Mysore State and the Bellary district from the Gangas and Nolambas and annexed them to his dominion. Nor was this all. He launched a successful war against the Western Chalukyas (then ruled by Satyasraya) in which his son Rajendra is said to have carried fire and sword into Donur (Bijapur district). He interfered in a civil war that had broken out among the Eastern Chalukyas, took up the cause of Saktivarman and Vimaladitya, the sons of Danarnava, the king of Vengi, restored the former to his ancestral throne and gave the latter his daughter, Kundavai[1] in marriage and by these masterful strokes virtually converted Vengi into a protectorate. And he closed his rule by winning a signal victory over the Cheras by conquering the Maldives.

This great conqueror was also a great statesman and administrator. He endeavoured his best to establish his empire on a firm footing. He created a standing army headed by able commanders and feudatories capable of extending his dominions from the Tungabhadra in the north to Ceylon in the south and of withstanding all external aggression and internal rebellion. He built a navy capable of carrying his victories to Ceylon and to the Maldives. He organized a civil service capable of consolidating all his conquests and restoring peace and order in all his dominions. He appointed Viceroys in charge of distant regions and it is from one of these Viceroys that the rule of Kongu-Cholas began[2] in the Kongu country as will be described shortly. He set up a centralised bureaucratic machinery both at the headquarters and in the districts, a system of survey and assessment of lands and a system of audit and control of village assemblies and quasi-public corporations. But it was in the religious sphere that he left a lasting monument of his greatness to posterity. With a colossal effort, he built the most magnificent temple of Rajarajeswara at Thanjavur, the finest specimen of Tamil architecture. Remarkable alike for its stupendous proportions and for its bold simplicity in design, it is to this day a thing of beauty and a joy for ever. He covered the temple of Siva at Chidambaram with pure gold brought from all the regions subdued by the power of his own arm. Though himself an ardent follower of Siva, he, like all great men of India, showed a broad tolerance to all religions; he encouraged his subjects to build temples not

[1] *Eastern Chalukyas* by N. Venkataramanayya, 1951, pages 206–211.

[2] *The Kongu Country* by M. Arokiaswami, 1956, page 206.

only to Siva but also to Vishnu and Buddha and liberally endowed them with grants of land and money. It is a sad circumstance that, while we have so much information about his achievements, we have no description of his personality; we have not even a statue or a painting of his. But we learn that he bore a great affection for his sister, that he married several wives and that he showed kindness to his relations and respect to his elders. And we may very well judge from all that he did that he was as brave as he was able, as masterful as he was skilful, and as broad-minded as he was pious and religious[1].

Rajaraja was succeeded by his son Rajendra I (1011–1044) who, it is clear, had jointly ruled with his father for some years before his accession. He had the advantage of possessing an empire which had already been organized on sound lines. He set about at once to improve its organisation and increase its glory. Within a few years of his accession, he appointed his son Rajadhiraja as a joint ruler and augmented the number of his Viceroys. These Viceroys were to attend to both civil and military matters, maintain public peace and repel invasions. But the maintenance of public peace was no easy matter. It was not to be expected that the several crowned heads whom Rajaraja dethroned or defeated would quietly submit to the rule of his son. Rajendra seems to have felt the smouldering discontent in the Western Chalukya country, in Ceylon, and in the Chera and Pandyan countries.

Early in his reign he crossed the sea to Ceylon, reduced the whole island to subjection, ransacked it, captured its king and returned with the captive king and a great quantity of gems and royal ornaments. He set up a Chola rule in that island during which many Hindu temples of Siva and Vishnu were constructed there. Soon after this he turned his attention nearer home and after crushing all opposition in the Chera and Pandya countries, appointed over them one of his sons as his Viceroy. He then led another successful campaign against the Western Chalukyas, this time in the Ratta country (Bellary district). But greater than all these campaigns was the expedition which he sent under one of his generals to the north in search of the Ganges. After crossing many streams by making the elephants serve as bridges across them, this intrepid general seems to have taken Sakkarakottam in the Bustar region, defeated Indraratha, the king of Orissa, and pushed through Kosala and Eastern Bengal and reached the Ganges. On his return journey with the sacred water he was met by Rajendra on the banks of the Godavari. In honour of this great expedition he assumed the title of Gangai Konda Chola and set up a new

---

1 *The Colas* by K. A. Nilakanta Sastri, Vol. I, 1935, pages 198–230.

capital called 'Gangaikondacholapuram' or 'Gangapuri' (Tiruchirappalli district) and built in it a magnificent palace and an equally magnificent Siva temple. But his most glorious expedition was that to Kedaram. Recent research has revealed that it was an expedition not to Burma, as was previously supposed, but to Kedah in the Malay Peninsula and that during its course he subjugated several cities and islands in the Malay Peninsula and the Eastern Archipelago. This expedition, more than anything else, shows the great naval strength of the Cholas. Its cause is not known; it might have been launched simply to add lustre to the Chola Crown or to remove obstacles to Chola commerce with the East, a commerce which was then at its meridian. Whatever that may be, its object was not to make the conquered countries a part of the Chola empire, for nothing was done to retain them permanently[1].

Rajendra I was succeeded by four rulers, Rajadhiraja, Rajendra II, Virarajendra and Adhirajendra, all of whom amidst much storm and stress tried their utmost to preserve in tact their vast empire. The truth is, the Chola empire had become too vast to be governed effectually from Thanjavur, while its enemies had become too stubborn to be effectually kept under subjection. Even when he had jointly ruled with his father, Rajadhiraja had enjoyed hardly any peace. He had supressed a conspiracy of the Cheras and the Pandyas and in the fighting that had resulted the Chera king had been trampled to death under an elephant and the Pandyan king (Sundara Pandya) who had organised the conspiracy had been driven out bareheaded with dishevelled hair in panic. He had attacked the Western Chalukyas led by their king Someswara Ahavamalla (Somesvara I) and burnt and ransacked their palace at Kampili (Bellary district). And, what is more, he had led an expedition to Ceylon, taken stern measures to put down a rebellion and beheaded its king. But now too, when he became the sole ruler, he found no prospects of peace. The rebellion in Ceylon raised its head again and despite his strenuous efforts, he lost the south-east portion of the island (Rohana) to king Vikkambahu. Matters became worse, when the Western Chalukyas began to interfere in the affairs of the Eastern Chalukyas who were under Chola protection. Rajadhiraja found it necessary to take the field again against Someswara. In the fierce battle of Kuppam that ensued, Rajadhiraja was killed but just at this juncture, when everything looked dark, his younger brother Rajendra who was also fighting from behind, suddenly rushed forward, rallied his forces, and launched a spirited attack against the Chalukyas which sent them flying in all directions. Rajendra II is said to have thence pressed on to Kollapuram on the banks of the Tungabhadra and planted there a

---

[1] *The Colas* by K. A. Nilakanta Sastri, Vol. I, 1935, pages 231–282.

Jayasthamba before he returned to his capital at Gangapuri. All this, however, secured only a brief respite; for, Someswara I, anxious to wipe out the disgrace that had be fallen him at Kuppam, soon gathered a powerful force and advanced to the south. Rajendra II, ably assisted by Virarajendra and an equally powerful force, met him at Kudal Sangam (at the junction of the Tungabhadra and the Krishna), defeated him in a decisive action and drove him again in disgrace. Soon afterwards when Rajendra II died and was succeeded by Virarajendra, Someswara I once more invited the Chola king to meet him at Kudal Sangam. Virarajendra greatly pleased set out for the fight and anxiously awaited him at Kudal Sangam for one full month beyond the date fixed for the meeting. But Someswara I failed to turn up, while Virarajendra carried his campaign into the Chalukyan country and set up a pillar of victory on the banks of the Tungabhadra. From there Virarajendra proceeded to Vengi, the Eastern Chalukyan country, and finding that the whole of Vengi had fallen into the hands of the Western Chalukyas, reconquered it by fighting the battle of Vijayavada. During the closing years of his reign he suppressed a rising in Ceylon and compelled the new Chalukyan king Someswara II to part with half of his dominion to his younger brother Vikramaditya VI. He also, it is stated, gave his daughter in marriage to Vikramaditya VI. There is evidence to show that this Vikramaditya patronised Bilhana and founded the Chalukya-Vikrama Era. On the death of Virarajendra, the succession was disputed and the heir Adhirajendra succeeded to the throne only by the help of his brother-in-law, Vikramaditya VI. Adhirajendra's reign was however brief and with his murder which took place in a rebellion, supposed to have been brought about by the persecution of the famous Vaishnava teacher, Sri Ramanuja, the direct Chola line became extinct.[1]

The Chola throne now passed to a new line, the Eastern Chalukyan line, which put new life into the whole old frame of the distracted empire. Rajendra Kulottunga (1070–1120), or Kulottunga I, who now ascended the throne was an extraordinary personality. A son of an Eastern Chalukyan king, Rajaraja (1022-1062) and of Ammangadevi, daughter of the Chola king, Rajendra (1012-1044), he had in early life become a favourite of his grandfather. But fate had willed that he should suffer for a time. On his father's death he had been supplanted by his uncle Vijayaditya VII at Vengi and had been forced to take refuge in the Chola country. But even in adversity he proved himself valiant. He had accompanied Virarajendra on his expedition to Sakkarakottam (Bustar) and, through his aid, regained his ancestral throne of Vengi. But now the same fate that had made him suffer made him suddenly great. The rebellion in Thanjavur gave him an

---

[1] *The Colas* by K. A. Nilakanta Sastri, Vol. I, 1935, pages 290–337.

opportunity, he made peace with his uncle Vijayaditya, marched speedily to the south and was instantly acclaimed as a deliverer by the Cholas.

Kulottunga I was more of a statesman than a warrior. During his long reign he shunned all needless wars and showed no ambition to extend his empire, he even lost some of its outposts. But by consummate diplomacy, dashed with not a little military ability, he consolidated what remained and gave it, on the whole, the blessings of peace. As soon as he ascended the throne, the Chalukyan king, Vikramaditya VI, who saw with much alarm the union of the Vengi with the Chola country, invaded Kolar with a large army. But Kulottunga induced Someswara II to attack him from behind, while he himself attacked him from the front, and in the fighting that took place routed him and conquered considerable parts of the Mysore country (Gangamandalam) and overran Konkan and the Kannada countries on the West Coast. Yet, subsequently towards the close of his rule, when the Hoysalas of Mysore rose in revolt he considered it prudent to withdraw from that country which it was becoming impossible to retain without much expenditure of blood and money. He thus lost much of the Kongu country to the Hoysalas[1]. He soon saw Ceylon slipping away from his hands under the persistent rebellions of Vijayabahu, its dispossessed ruler. He tried diplomacy to retain it, if possible, by winning over several of the ex-king's commanders and inciting a civil war. But when this civil war proved unsuccessful, he left the island to its fate and refused to send any costly expeditions for its reconquest. So far as the Chola empire proper in South India was concerned, however, he parted not a jot of its territory. With persistent efforts he reconquered the Chera and the Pandyan countries, which had become hotbeds of intrigue and declared their independence, and reduced them to complete subjection. That they might not again prove troublesome, he established a series of military out-posts in them all along important military routes and appointed as their commanders, his most trusted feudatories. When his uncle who ruled over the Vengi country died, he appointed his own sons as Viceroys in that country and when parts of that country were invaded by the king of Kalinga, he sent out two expeditions against Kalinga and not only recovered the lost parts of Vengi but also conquered the southern parts of Kalinga. All this time he did everything in his power to increase the prestige of his empire. He sent a trade embassy to China, received a trade embassy from Kedara (Malay Peninsula) and established friendly relations with the northern Indian States like Kanauj and Kamboja. Bereft of Ceylon and Gangavadi and parts of the Kongu Country, the Chola empire, when he left it to his successor, covered one compact area

[1] *The Kongu Country* by M. Arokiaswami, 1956, pages 207–212.

of Tamil land. And over his empire he must have had the satisfaction of having more or less ruled in peace for nearly half a century[1].

The wisdom of Kulottunga's policy of lopping off all turbulent non-Tamilian parts of his empire ensured peace for another half a century. From 1120 to 1163 three Chola kings succeeded him, Vikrama Chola (1120-1135), Kulottunga II (1136-1150) and Rajaraja II (1151-1163); and under all these rulers no wars or invasions distracted the country. All the same, some parts of the old empire, in Vengi, Mysore and the Kongu country, were recovered, mostly by skilful negotiations with local chieftains. These kings appointed a large number of feudatories to administer their outlying districts and frequently went on royal tours from their capital at Gangapuram to the various parts of their dominions. They also took a great delight in renovating and beautifying the great temple of Nataraja at Chidambaram. Vikrama Chola made large gifts of revenue to that temple to meet the cost of its extensive repairs. Kulottunga II made even larger gifts to the same temple, constructed its gopurams, and covered many parts of it with gold. Nor is this all. During the reign of Kulottunga II and Rajaraja II, Tamil literature was fostered and the kings as well as their vassals patronised literary men like Ottakkuttan, Sekkiliar and Kamban. Peace reigned everywhere and the country enjoyed prosperity, except during the famine of 1125 which rather severely affected some parts of North Arcot, South Arcot and Thanjavur districts. But peace has its own dangers no less than war; for the numerous feudatories upon whom the kings relied for governing the empire in the Kongu country and other countries gradually became more and more independent, though they nominally recognized the suzerainty of the king. The monarchy in fact lost much of its prestige, the Central Government, much of its authority, but the local Government—the village system of administration with its autonomous local assemblies—seems to have gone on unaffected by the change[2].

The centrifugal tendencies appeared more pronounced during the reigns of Rajadhiraja II (1163-1178) and Kulottunga III (1179–1216). Rajadhiraja saw a virulent civil war breaking out in the Pandyan country and this war, after a tortuous course, suddenly swamped the whole Chola country and ended in making his successors the vassals of the Pandyas. The outbreak of the civil war is by itself a strong indication of the growing power of the Chola vassals. In this war, the Singhalese strongly supported

1 *The Colas* by K. A. Nilakanta Sastri, Vol. I, 1935, pages 338–358, Vol. II, 1937, pages 1–60.

Eastern Chalukyas of Vengi by N. Venkataramanayya (1951), pages 249-278.

2 *The Colas* by K. A. Nilakanta Sastri, Vol. II, 1937, pages 61–88.

one claimant, Parakrama, and when he was murdered by his rival, placed his son, Vira Pandya, on the throne. The Chola king, Rajadhiraja, then intervened on behalf of the other pretender Kulasekhara, drove out the Singhalese and installed Kulasekhara on the throne. Then occurred a swift diplomatic revolution. Kulasekhara made peace with the Singhalese, while Vira Pandya sought the aid of the Cholas. Rajadhiraja again intervened and succeeded this time in installing Vira Pandya on the throne. Soon afterwards Kulottunga III succeeded Rajadhiraja. The new king too found himself faced with the increasing independence of his vassals. The Pandyan civil war flared up again after another diplomatic revolution. Vira Pandya, like Kulasekhara before him, made peace with the Singhalese, while Vikrama Pandya, perhaps a relation of Kulasekhara, sought the aid of the Cholas. By two brilliant campaigns Kulottunga drove away the Singhalese protege and for the third time installed a Chola protege. But, very soon, Vikrama Pandya's son, Jatavarman Kulasekhara proved truculent, and in order to teach him a lesson Kulottunga led a third campaign in the Pandyan country. Meanwhile the Telugu Chodas who were occupying the Nellore, Cuddapah and South Arcot districts and who were till then Chola vassals, declared independence and made it necessary for Kulottunga to conquer Kanchi. He is also said to have conquered Karur and parts of Mysore. But all these campaigns and conquests appear only as lightning streaks in a gathering gloom of storm clouds. In the twenty-third and twenty-fourth year of his reign a great famine swept over North Arcot and Thanjavur. And towards the close of his reign a greater calamity befell him. The Pandyan throne at this time passed to Maravarman Sundara Pandya and this ruler with a powerful army suddenly struck a sharp blow at Chidambaram and brought Kulottunga to his knees. However, at the strong intercession of Vira Narasimha, the rising Hoysala King, Sundara Pandya allowed Kulottunga to continue to occupy the Chola throne. But Kulottunga soon died in disgrace. Amidst all this gloom stand out in bold relief a few pious monuments of his rule, namely, the magnificent temple of Kampahareswara at Tribhuvanam, rich in sculptured panels and decorative designs and the gopura of goddess Girindraja (Sivakami) in the Chidambaram temple.[1]

These were the last great legacies of a vanishing empire. During the reigns of Rajaraja III (1216—1246) and Rajendra III (1247—1279), the Pandyas in the south and the Hoysalas in the north monopolised all power, whilst almost all the Chola feudatories, including those in the Kongu country virtually declared independence. Civil disturbances became the

---

1 *The Colas* by K. A. Nilakanta Sastri, Vol. II, 1937, pages 96–172.
The Cambridge Shorter History of India, 1934, page 192.

order of the day. And at a time when utmost tact was needed to guide the ship of State in these stormy waters, Rajaraja showed the utmost foolishness. He cast off Pandyan supremacy and began at once a campaign against them. The Pandyas sent him reeling after a pitched battle and while he was in no condition to look after himself, he fell into the hands of a daring adventurer, one of his own disaffected feudatories, Kopperunjinga, a Kadava chieftain of Sendamangalam (Tirukkoyilur taluk), who instantly captured him and kept him prisoner. The Hoysala King Narasimha again came to the rescue; he sent an expedition to the south, punished Kopperunjinga as well as the Pandyas and placed once more Rajaraja on the Chola throne. But the times were out of joint, the Chola throne had become precarious. Rajendra III who succeeded Rajaraja III showed some spurts of energy ; he plundered the Pandyan country and, for a time, claimed a sort of suzerainty over it. But the Hoysalas whose sole object was throughout to acquire an ascendancy in the south, swiftly changed sides and allied themselves with the Pandyas. And, when again after the rise of the great warrior king Jatavarman Sundara Pandya I (1251) they as quickly changed sides and allied themselves with the Cholas, they found that the times had changed completely. For, now in a succession of brilliant victories Sundara Pandya pulverised the Cholas (1258) and routed the Hoysalas (1264). This marks the end of the Chola rule and the beginning of the Pandyan supremacy in the south. From 1279 we hear nothing about Rajendra or his successors. Thanjavur and the whole Chola kingdom were now absorbed by the Pandyan empire; and the Kongu country came to be occupied partly by the Pandyas and partly by the Hoysalas.[1]

During all this period, ever since the time of Rajaraja I, a portion of the Kongu country which now forms the Coimbatore district, was ruled by the Chola Viceroys, who may be called the Kongu Cholas. As long as the Chola Emperors were strong and powerful, these Kongu Chola Viceroys remained subordinate; but the moment the Chola Emperors lost their importance, especially, since the time of Kulottunga I, they began to assert their independence. It must, however, be stated that neither the genealogy nor the chronology, of these Kongu Chola rulers is clear. Recent research, however, has tentatively fixed them as follows :—

	A.D.
Vikrama I	1004—1045
Unknown	1045—1069
Rajadhiraja	1069—1100

[1] *The Colas* by K. A. Nilakanta Sastri, Vol. II, 1937, pages 172–209.
The Kongu Country by M. Arokiaswami, 1956, pages 212–213.

	A.D.
Uttama	1100—1119
Vira Chola I	1119—1134
Vira Narayana	1134—1149
Unknown	1149—1164
Unknown	1164—1179
Vira Chola II	1179—1196
Kulottunga	1196—1230
Vira Rajendra	1207—1249
Unknown	1249—1255
Vikrama II	1255—1262
Unknown	1262—1273
Vikrama III	1273—1275

We know little about their achievements; but all that we know shows that they gave peace to the country, struck coins, built or renovated many temples and made extensive endowments to them, and followed the Chola system of administration.[1]

This Chola system of administration, which the Kongu country covering Coimbatore district enjoyed for nearly four centuries, was unique in various ways. The king was the supreme head of the executive, of the judiciary, of the army, of the navy and of the entire civil administration. He was not bound by any acts of any type of legislature—for legislature there was none in those days. Nor was he assisted or guided by any council of ministers; recent research seems to show that he had no ministers to advise him. His word was an order, a judgement or a law which none could disregard or disobey with impunity. But he was on all occasions, whether in the capital or in the camp, assisted by an able bureaucracy of top ranking civil and military officers upon whom he could rely for feeling the pulse of the people and carrying on efficienctly the central as well as the district administration. The officers who were associated with him in the central government were called ' Udankuttan ' and they were possibly the heads of various departments. Whenever the king gave audience (and he gave audience often in royal halls and temples), they explained to him orally all petitions and all matters of policy demanding his attention and he gave them, then and there, his verbal orders which were instantly recorded in writing by an officer called Tirumandira Olai. Copies of these orders were then made out and despatched to the departments concerned for taking action, and the departments in turn sent out copies of these orders to the distant local officers for inscribing them on

[1] *The Kongu Country* by M. Arokiaswami, 1956, pages 229–248.

the temple walls and carrying them into effect. This highly organized bureaucracy consisted of a hierarchy of officials bearing titles such as 'enadi', and 'marayan' (those who had distinguished themselves in civil and military affairs), 'araiyan' and 'perariyan' (those who occupied very high civil positions) and 'adigarigal' (those who held positions of trust in the army as well as in general administration).[1]

But this bureaucracy, it would appear, was by no means a menace to the people. For, normally, the king and his bureaucracy took cognizance of only high matters such as those relating to war, diplomacy, the army, the navy, and the revenue collection, and left all other matters of civil administration, including the administration of justice and police, entirely to the local assemblies. From the famous Uttaramerur and other inscriptions, it is clear that those local assemblies enjoyed complete political autonomy in local affairs. These assemblies were generally of four types, the 'ur', the 'sabha', (Kuri), the 'nagaram' and the 'nadu'. The 'ur' was the ancient Dravidian simple type of assembly which often acted by itself or sometimes acted alongside of the sabha. It was attended by all the male residents of the ur, young and old, though the leading part in its deliberations seems to have been taken by the elders alone. It had sometimes an executive body called 'alunganam' (the ruling group). The 'sabha' was an Aryan institution met with mostly in Brahmin villages. Like the 'ur' it consisted of all the male residents of the village, but, unlike the 'ur', it had a more complex machinery. It functioned largely through its committees called 'variyams', consisting of the chosen few. These few were chosen by lots for each committee by the members of the sabha from among themselves. The qualifications for membership of the committees were invariably property, learning, skill and ability. The 'sabha', it would seem, dealt with all general matters, while its committees dealt with all special matters. The 'sabha' in this manner disposed of multifarious matters such as the administration of civil and criminal justice, the provision of Kavalgars (police), the management of temples, the sales of property, the settlement of land and irrigation disputes, the raising of loans, the levying of local cesses like irrigation cesses, the collection of land revenue on behalf of the State, the repairing of tanks, the making of roads, the provision of facilities for education, the assaying of gold, in fact, all matters affecting the welfare of the people. Sometimes the king's officers attended the meetings of the 'sabha' and its committees

---

[1] *The Colas* by K. A. Nilakanta Sastri, Vol. II, 1937, pages 213–215, 224, 235–247, 254–256.

Hindu Administrative Institutions in South India by S. K. Aiyangar, 1931, pages 252–254.

to see that the royal interests were not affected. They also periodically audited the accounts of the 'sabha'. But in the whole range of hundreds of inscriptions that have come down to us we find only very few cases in which they interfered in the local affairs dealt with by the 'sabha'. Nor did they interfere in the business of the other assemblies like the 'nagaram' and the 'nadu'. The 'nagaram' was in all probability a primary assembly of merchants confined to the important towns. The 'nadu' was, as its name implies, a territorial assembly of the division consisting possibly of the representatives of the 'sabhas' and 'urs' within the division. It normally discharged all important duties connected with land transactions and charitable endowments.[1] It is thus evident that the local bodies were for all practical purposes completely autonomous in local affairs, while the king was completely autocratic in central and imperial affairs. Both served for the common good and both were restrained from exceeding or misusing their powers in those days not by any public opinion but by something more compelling than public opinion, by custom and religious sanction. Political philosophers may wonder whether this system of government of the Cholas might not have achieved as much public good as the modern systems. Whether it suits the modern age or not is a different matter; but there can be little doubt that it suited admirably the mediaeval age, infusing, as it did, an uncommon vitality into the whole system of the body politic of the Chola empire for about four centuries. Historians are not a little struck by this vitality revealed in the inscriptions of even the closing period of the Chola rule.

Of the army and the navy that built up the grand edifice of the Chola empire and spread its fame far and wide, even beyond the seas, we have very little information. The three corps upon which the Cholas depended were the elephant corps (anaiyalkal), the cavalry (kudirai-sevakar) and the infantry. They hardly made use of the chariots (ratha). The three corps were divided into a number of regiments, such as the regiments of bowmen (villigal), of swordmen (valperra kaikkolar), of King's horse body-guards (udanil-kudirai-sevakar), of fort garrisons (andalagattalar), etc. They were all stationed in the towns and cantonments (kadagams), and kept always ready in a state of emergency. One remarkable feature of the army is that it took a great deal of interest in civil and religious affairs. There are many instances of its commanders building and

---

1 *The Colas* by K. A. Nilakanta Sastri, Vol. II, 1937, pages 267–313.

Studies in Cola History and Administration by K. A. Nilakanta Sastri, 1932, pages 73–117.

Hindu Administrative Institutions in South India by S. K. Aiyangar, 1931, pages 130–211.

The Kongu Country by M. Arokiaswami, 1956, pages 225–229.

endowing temples and maths. The navy consisted of ships, great and small, which could command the respect of all the powers in the Arabian Sea and the Bay of Bengal. But we do not know how it was organized. It is, however, more or less evident that the ships which in war time assailed Ceylon, captured the Maldives and the Nicobar islands and launched an expedition to Kedaram (Malaya) were also the ships which in peace time carried on commerce with the various ports from Arabia to Indo-China.[1]

Nor have we any information as to how the whole of the empire was organized, except that its outlying parts like the Kongu Country were ruled through the Viceroys. Each of these provinces (of which there were eight or nine) was called a 'mandalam' and each 'mandalam' was divided into a number of 'nadus', and each 'nadu', was sub-divided into a number of 'kurrams' (big size villages) and 'taniyurs' (towns). There is, however, every reason to think that the administration of these parts was similar to the administration of the territory directly ruled by the King.[2]

Judicial administration was mostly left to the 'sabhas'. But in all cases, civil as well as criminal, the aggrieved parties had the right of appeal to the king and the king seems to have decided such appeals in his 'dharmasana' (court of justice) assisted by the opinions of the learned Brahmins ('dharmasana bhattas') versed in the law. Among crimes, murder, homicide, thefts, adultery and forgery were considered most heinous but even these crimes, if we are to trust the inscriptions, were visited with light punishments alike by the king and the 'sabhas'. The culprits were generally asked either to endow sufficient sums for burning lamps in the nearest temples or to pay specific fines. Even offences against the person of the king or his relations were visited only with the confiscation of property and fines. It is, however, doubtful whether this picture revealed by the inscriptions is complete and accurate. A Chinese writer of the thirteenth century, Chau-Ju-Kua, has given an altogether different picture of the Chola system of justice. He says : 'If the offence is light, the culprit is tied to a wooden frame and given fifty, seventy, or up to an hundred blows with a stick. Heinous crimes are punished with decapitation or by being trampled to death by an elephant.[3]

---

[1] *The Colas* by K. A. Nilakanta Sastri, Vol. II, 1937, pages 224–234.
Hindu Administrative Institutions by S. K. Aiyangar, 1931, pages 306–323.

[2] *The Kongu Country* by M. Arokiaswami, 1956, pages 221–223, 242–243.

[3] *The Colas* by K. A. Nilakanta Sastri, Vol. II, 1937, pages 242–266.
Hindu Administrative Institutions by S. K. Aiyangar, 1931, pages 247–252.

Land was the principal source of king's revenue. Besides land revenue, the king collected a number of taxes, duties, etc., such as customs, octroi, profession tax, fines imposed on offenders and dues from mines, forests and salt pans. Kulottunga I is said to have remitted all customs and octroi duties, but there is nothing to show that his successors did not collect them. All these taxes, duties, etc., except land revenue, were collected directly by the king's officers ; the land revenue was collected by them through the 'sabhas'. On extraordinary occasions, extraordinary contributions were also levied by the king such as the war levy during the Pandyan war in the reign of Parantaka I. These taxes and levies went by various names, but the names were indiscriminately used. The names in use were irai, vari, manrupadu, ayam and dandam. Among specific names were 'Kadamai' and 'Kudimai' meaning literally 'duty' and 'tenancy dues' respectively, and 'padikaval' meaning kavalgar's fees. Land revenue was collected both in kind and in money and non-payment of it was visited with distraint and sale of the defaulters' lands. Remissions were, however, granted for sufficient reasons like floods and famines. Temples were often allowed to commute the land revenue for reduced sums and officers were sometimes rewarded by grants of land on a permanent settlement tenure. It may also be of interest to note that whenever the local 'sabhas' found difficulty in collecting the land revenue or local cesses they obtained the aid of the Government for collecting them and that, towards the close of the Chola rule, the local chieftains imposed fresh taxes which often led to oppression and called for the intervention of the king.[1]

The State seems to have collected something well over 40 per cent of the gross produce as land revenue, a percentage which is moderate in comparison with the land revenue demand under the Vijayanagar, the Mughal and the early British rule. The only exception was temple lands, the taxes on which were limited to a third of the gross produce. Communal ownership of land, as is indicated by the terms Sabha-manjikkam, ur-manjikkam and ur-padu, existed side by side with individual ownership. All land which was not held under communal ownership by the village was either unassessed land belonging to the king or land belonging to peasant proprietors (vellan-vagai), service tenure holders, i.e., inamdars (jivita, bhoga, vritti, etc.) or eleemosynary tenure holders (bhramadeya and devadana). The peasant proprietors held their lands on ryotwari tenure ; service tenure holders held their lands either as tax-free inams or as quit-rent inams or again as feudal tenures as the case may be. In

---

1 *The Oolas* by K. A. Nilakanta Sastri, Vol. II, 1937, pages 313–349.

those days, officers were in lieu of regular salaries given either assignment of land or lands on service tenure and the important chieftains who were given land on feudal tenure were expected to contribute a stated number of soldiers ready for service whenever required by the king. Of the eleemosynary tenures, brahmadeya lands were those given to Brahmins and devadanam lands were those given to temple. Both these types of lands were liable to pay the usual taxes unless expressly exempted. There is evidence to show that a good portion of the various types of lands mentioned above was cultivated by tenants. The system of tenancy was well known and the tenants paid the landlord a fixed melvaram determined in advance and retained as their share what remained after paying the expenses of cultivation and any minor dues assessed on the land.[1]

All lands whether communal, ryotwari or inam, were periodically surveyed and carefully assessed and an accurate up-to-date record of rights—which is a great feat indeed—was maintained in every village. The assessment which was periodically revised was based on a minute classification of land; as many as twelve different tarams (grades) are mentioned in the inscriptions and the rate fixed on each taram naturally depended on its fertility. But the State was not interested in collecting land revenue alone. It undertook irrigation works, it raised the bunds of the Cauvery, removed silt from irrigation tanks and repaired them and took not a little interest in reclaiming forest and waste lands for cultivation. The landholders on the whole seem to have been prosperous as is evidenced by their endowments to temples, schools, etc., but the agricultural labourers (pulaiyars) seem to have been in a condition of serfdom bordering on slavery.[2]

Internal commerce was, it would appear, partly monopolised by the king. He used to send shiploads of merchandise and articles of luxury to distant ports in Arabia, Persia, Ceylon, Malaya and Indo-China. But a good portion of international commerce as well as all internal and coastal trade was in the hands of merchants who used to form themselves into guilds, and sometimes powerful guilds, and to enjoy exceptional privileges. The king and the 'sabhas' offered them facilities by granting lands and houses for residences and warehouses. The guilds in turn showed their gratitude by making endowments to temples and other charitable institutions. One such celebrated guild called 'Nanadesis' engaged in extensive

1 *The Colas* by K. A. Nilakanta Sastri, Vol. II, 1937, pages 325, 337–346, 379–412.

2 *Iedm*, pages 325–328, 363, 380–382.
The Kongu Country by M. Arokiaswami, 1956, pages 281–284.

foreign and internal trade is said to have been in the habit of sending its representatives for selling horses, elephants, precious stones, spices and drugs, wholesale as well as retail to 'the Chera, Chola, Pandya, Malaya, Maghada, Kausala, Sourashtra, Dhanustra, Nepala, Ekapada, Lambakarna, Stri-Rajya, Chola Mukha and many other countries.' These representatives came to the Kongu Country also and carried on trade. They often, it is stated, carried their merchandise on the backs of donkeys and buffaloes 'adorned with red trappings' under the protection of their own military guards of foot soldiers and swordsmen. Several instances can be adduced to show that the Cholas carried on a brisk trade in all parts of the country as well as in foreign countries. Among the articles exported to foreign countries, to Arabia, Persia and Indo-China, may be mentioned amber, camphor, elephants' tusks, precious stones, pearls, ivory, ebony, sandalwood, cotton and linen fabrics and spices. Internal commerce in those days depended mainly on roads and the roads were, on the whole, well maintained by the Government and the local 'sabhas'.[1]

In the field of industries, handloom industry, metal work and jewellery occupied a prominent place under the Cholas. The best of handloom fabrics, silk as well as cotton, went always to the royal palaces, temples, and foreign countries, while the rest were sold all over the country by hawkers. We are told that 'excellent napkins' and 'linen voils' were exported to Siraf and Kish in the Persian Gulf and cotton fabrics of all sorts and coloured silk threads were exported to Indo-China. Next to handlooms must have figured the manufacture of beautiful images, vessels and other utensils of copper, bronze, brass, silver and gold and all sorts of exquisite ornaments of gold and precious stones and pearls. Here too the best went to the royal palaces and temples and the rest went to the houses of the rich and the well-to-do. Some of these articles, especially jewels and ornaments, were exported to foreign countries. Besides these the manufacture of all sorts of perfumes for internal and foreign consumption must have provided a tolerable living to many people; and in that age of temple building and sculpture many people also must have lived comfortably as masons, stone cutters and sculptors.[2]

Of society in general in Chola times, it must be said that caste was the basis of social organization and that all the four castes lived, on the

---

1 *The Colas* by K. A. Nilakanta Sastri, Vol. II, 1937, pages 313-442.
The Kongu Country by M. Arokiaswami, 1956, pages 284--290.

2 *The Colas* by K. A. Nilakanta Sastri, Vol. II, 1937, pages 414-415.

whole, in peace, without manifesting any serious symptoms of jealousies and clash of interests. Conflicts between the Right Hand and the Left Hand castes were very rare, and conflicts between the Brahmins and Non-Brahmins were non-existent. The Brahmins were respected for their learning, regarded as torch bearers of civilization and encouraged to settle in all newly conquered territories. Thus the Chola kings are said to have encouraged many Brahmins to settle in the Kongu Country by granting lands to them generously.[1] The Brahmins lived usually under the patronage of kings and nobles, and although they preferred to live in strong self-regulating groups, they never forgot their duties and obligations to others. Mixed castes, such as the Rathakars which included blacksmiths, goldsmiths and stone masons, were not uncommon. Nor was heredity a bar to change of occupation. The Brahmins, for instance, sometimes took to trade, though these were exceptions. Women were not subjected to any restraint in their social life and activities, but modesty was considered chief among their graces. Such of them as belonged to the upper classes owned property in their own right and disposed of it as they chose. But the most distinguishing characteristics of the women of the higher classes in those days seem to have been piety, devotion and an ardour for social work, all which manifested themselves in their making liberal endowments to the temples, maths, schools, etc. It is indeed remarkable that even courtesans showered their largesses on temples and that the poor and the down-trodden women, instead of taking to streets, sought refuge in the temples and became dancing girls, flower girls and temple menials. Monogamy was the rule among the bulk of the people but polygamy was not infrequent among kings and nobles. Sati was rare and slavery was confined largely to women dedicated to the temples and working as domestic slaves in the houses of the rich and the powerful. The condition of temple slaves and domestic slaves does not seem to have been pitiable. The most pitiable was perhaps, as has already been stated, the condition of the agricultural labourers who were treated like slaves.[2]

Higher education was received mostly by the Brahmins and the upper classes. It was imparted in numerous temples, maths, pallis and viharas scattered throughout the country. These institutions sometimes owned big collections of manuscript literature on a variety of topics and imparted religious as well as secular education. There were also some colleges endowed by kings and nobles for teaching the Vedas, the Mimamsa, the

1 *The Kongu Country* by M. Arokiaswami, 1956, pages 196, 204, 272–278.

2 *The Colas* by K. A. Nilakanta Sastri, Vol. II, 1937, pages 350–367.
The Kongu Country by M. Arokiaswami, 1956, pages 265–267.

Vyakarana, the Sastras, the Sutras and Medicine. Some of them had a large staff of professors and a very large number of students. The professors, it would appear, were paid in kind as well as in coin and the students were given stipends. But of much more value than all these sanskrit schools and colleges must have been the Tamil schools, and the pial schools of which we have no evidence, but which, all the same, must have existed. It is these schools that must have turned out the hundreds of singers of Tiruppadigam hymns in the numerous temples and the thousands of clerks, accountants, etc., employed in the offices of the Government and the local bodies [1].

Nothing, however, occupied in society a more endearing and more important place than the temple. It was the place where the local 'sabha' commonly held its meetings to discuss and decide village affairs. It was the place where all people, young and old, came to worship God, whether Siva, Vishnu or other deities and to hear the recitation of the Ramayana, the Mahabharatha and the Puranas. It was the place where all religious and philosophical discussions were held. It was the place where all entertainments and festival, religious as well as secular and dancing as well as music, were also held. It was the place where all those who sought knowledge came and sat at the feet of the learned. It was the place where Kings, Queens and Nobles loved to display their munificence. It was the place where under their patronage all that is best in art and architecture found eloquent expression. It was the place where people sought food and shelter in times of scarcity and famine. It was the place where all disappointed girls and women sought refuge and devoted their lives to God by becoming dancing girls, flower girls, etc. It was indeed the most magnificent place where riches, beauty, sanctity, worship, learning philosophy, fine arts and even mundane things combined to attract all people. No wonder the civilization in mediaeval days grew under the protecting shade of the temple. No wonder also that in so growing it imbibed much of religion.

It is something refreshing to note that religion in those days never produced any bitter sectarian feuds. There is ample evidence to show that, although the King and the bulk of the people were Saivites, they showed a broad tolerance to all Vaishnavites, Jains and Buddhists. They made even liberal endowments to the Vaishnavite temples, Jain Pallis or Busties, and the Buddhist Viharas. As striking instances of their tolerance and broad outlook, may be mentioned the worship of

---

1 *The Colas* by K. A. Nilakanta Sastri, Vol. II, 1937, pages 463–471.
The Kongu Country by M. Arokiaswami, 1956, pages 308-310.

Nataraja as well as Govindaraja in the Chidambaram temple, and the existence side by side of the Saivite, Vaishnavite, Jain and Buddhist temples and colonies in Kancheepuram. There is nothing to show that the followers of these different faiths created any serious troubles. And when at the time of Adhirajendra, sectarianism is stated to have raised its head and led to the persecution of Sri Ramanuja, the people are said to have even risen in revolt and assassinated the King, thereby putting an end to all persecutions [1].

An age of tolerance, of broad outlook on life, is undoubtedly most favourable to literature, and the Chola age which was characterized by these noble qualities is the most creative epoch of South Indian history. The very inscriptions of that age are notable for the highly ornate and poetical prasastis written in Tamil and Sanskrit. It has been said that almost all the prasastis of the Chola Kings from the time of Rajaraja I may be classed among the best specimens of Tamil literature, exhibiting, as they do, stately diction, easy flow of verse, and animated narrative of historical events. Several of the poems of this age have been lost, but of what remains, the Perungadai by Kongu-Velir is known for its ahaval metre (blank verse) and its chaste, direct and narrative style of poetry; the Jivakasindamani by Tiruttakkadeva dealing with the story of Jivaka, an ideal hero, is counted as the greatest among the Mahakavyas of Tamil literature; the Kalingattupparani by the poet laureate Jayamkondar of Kulottunga I is considered to be the best of the paranis available to us, while the various works of Ottakkuttan who was patronised by the Chola rulers, the Ittivelupadu, the Eluppelupadu, the Takkayagapparani, etc., stand as a class by themselves. The Nalavenba (the story of Nala) by Pugalendi is well known for its simple and flexible diction and easy flow of language; and the Tiruvilaiyadal Puranam by Perumbarrappuliyur Nambi is equally well known for its rich store of legends centering round Madurai and its sixty-four miraculous sports of Siva. Above all these authors towered two literary giants, Kambar, the great author of the Ramayana, who in his treatment of the epic shows an originality and depth of experience hardly equalled in Tamil literature, and Sekkilar, the equally great author of the Peria Puranam, who in this masterpiece of Tamil literature conveys a graphic picture of the heroic age of Tamil Saivism, suffused with didactic and religious sentiments of the highest order.[2]

---

[1] *The Colas* by K. A. Nilakanta Sastri, Vol. II, pages 485–491.
The Kongu Country by M. Arokiaswami, 1956, pages 244–245, 259–261, 294–307.

[2] *The Colas* by K. A. Nilakanta Sastri, Vol. II, 1937, pages 510–536.

The age is not less famous in the field of religious literature. It was in that age that the two celebrated men, Nambi Andar Nambi and Nathamuni, arranged the Saivite and the Vaishnavite hymns and cannons respectively, substantially in the form in which we now find them. It was also in that age that several works on Saivism and Vaishnavism were written. Thus Meykandar then wrote the doctrinal work Siva-Gnana-Bodam, Arunandi wrote a similar work Siva-Gnana-Sittiyar, Manavasagan Gadandar wrote the simplest of all manuals of Saivism, Unmai-Vilakkam, and Umapati Sivacharya wrote some eight works on Saiva doctrine like Sivapprakasam, Sankarpa-Nirakaranam, etc. Among Vaishnava writers Periya Vaccan Pillai and Nambillai wrote several commentaries on the Nalairam, in whole or part, and there was also the great devotional work Ramanuja Nurrandadi by Ramanuja's disciple Tiruvarangattu Amudanar. Among works on grammar, rhetoric and lexicography the age produced the Yapparungalam and Yapparungalakkarigai of Amrita-sagara, the Virasoliyam of Buddhamitra, Neminadam of Gunavirapandita, Nannul of Bavanandi (the sage of the Kongu Country) and the Nambiyahapporul of Narkavirajanambi. Among Sanskrit works it produced the Rig-Veda Bhasha of Venkata Madhava [1].

From the last quarter of the thirteenth to the first half of the fourteenth century, the Kongu Country was ruled in parts by these distinct powers, the Pandyas (who had conquered the Cholas), the Hoysalas and the Cheras. Epigraphical evidence shows that the Pandyas employed at least two Kongu-Pandya Viceroys, that the Hoysalas appointed some chieftains subordinate to them in parts of the Kongu Country, and that the Cheras also invaded and occupied some parts of the Kongu Country opposite the Palghat Gap. The Cheras may be left out as they did not count very much at that time in the larger spheres of politics in the south. But the Hoysalas and the Pandyas required to be dealt with in some detail, as it was during their rule that the Muslim invasions took place and prepared the ground for the rise of Vijayanagar, the rulers of which had much to do with the Kongu country from the second half of the fourteenth century[2].

In the beginning years of the thirteenth century, the Hoysalas under Narasimha II established their way in the Kongu country. The *Kongudesarajakkal* referring to this period mentions names of many Hoysala officers like Sangrada Nayaka, his son Boganna Nayaka, Martanda Dandanayaka and Codanda Nayaka holding sway in Kongu. These

1 *The Colas* by K. A. Nilakanta Sastri, Vol. II, 1937, pages 475–480, 536–552. *The Kongu Country* by M. Arokiaswami, 1956, pages 310–314.

2 *Idem*, pages 248–255.

must have been the officers through whom the Hoysalas must have ruled the Kongu from their seat in Mysore. We learn from inscriptional evidence that at least three invasions were carried by Narasimha II into Magara (Magadai, a territory that is variously identified with regions of Salem and Coimbatore). It is, however, certain that this territory lay on the way to the kingdom of Kopperunjinga whom he later conquered. An inscription from Channarayapattana clearly tells us that Narasimha conquered Magara and entitled himself as *Magarajya Nirmulana.* Vira Somesvara, son of Narasimha II advanced through Kongu as far south as Tiruchirappalli. The *Kongudesarajakkal* refers to this graphically : " With many kinds of weapons setting forth, he (Vira Somesvara) went to Kongudesam and took tribute from its chieftains ". After Vira Somesvara there was a decline in the Hoysala hold of the Kongu country. Somesvara's empire became divided between his two sons Narasimha III and Vira Ramanatha. The latter took the Kongu country for his share and he had his capital at Kundani (identified in the Hosur division of the Salem district). But the partitioned empire was weak and the Pandyas took away Ramanatha's share quickly from his hands.

The great Hoysala ruler, Ballala III, however, reconquered the Kongu country and extended his sway over the whole of the Coimbatore region and went up as far as Nilgiris on the one side and the Palani Hills on the other. The powerful Pandya ruler of the time, Jatavarman Vira Pandya, was defeated by the Hoysala General, Madhava Dandanayaka, the founder of the Dandanayakan Kottai (the modern Danayakankottai of Coimbatore district). From 1291 to 1342, the Hoysalas exerted again supreme influence over the Kongu country. It is a fact worth mentioning that it was to Satyamangalam under the Hoysala ruler that the great Vedanta Desika took his learned commentary of Sri Ramanuja's Sri Bashya for safe protection from the Muslim raid of 1327.

Now turning to the Pandyas, Jatavarman Sundara Pandya (1251–1270), who brought under his feet the whole of the Chola Kingdom, including large parts of the Kongu country, was the most famous of the Pandyan Kings who ruled from Madurai. A bold, invincible, conquering monarch, he extended the bounds of the Pandyan Empire to their utmost limits and became the supreme unquestioned ruler of Southern India. He ravaged the Malainadu and destroyed the Chera King Vira Ravi Udaya Markandavarman and all his forces. He compelled Rajendra Chola to acknowledge his suzerainty and to pay him tribute. He attacked the Hoysalas in the region of the Cauvery and captured their strong fortress of Kannanur Koppam. He fought and killed several Hoysala Generals, including the brave Singanna, captured numerous elephants and horses, a large amount of treasure and a large number of women, and eventually attacked and killed Someswara, the Hoysala King himself (1262). Nor was this all. He assailed the fortress of Sendamangalam, ' struck terror into the heart ' of Kopperunjinga, conquered Magadai and the Kongu countries and pushing his arms to the north, killed Gandagopala, the ruler of Kanchi, occupied Kanchi, defeated Ganapati, the Kakatiya King, at Mudugur, drove a Bana Chief into exile and performed a Virabhisheka at Nellore. He also, between 1262 and 1264, invaded Ceylon, defeated and killed one Ceylonese prince, received the submission of two other princes, and after exacting a great booty of pearls and elephants from the ruler of Ceylon, returned victorious to Madurai. A devout Hindu, tolerant to both Saivism and Vaishnavism alike, he did much to beautify the Chidambaram temple. After his victory over the Kadava Chieftain Kopperunjinga, he is said to have repaired to Chidambaram, worshipped God Nataraja, performed many tulabharas and roofed the temple with gold. From there he is said to have proceeded to Srirangam, worshipped God Ranganatha, built a shrine to Narasimha and another to Vishvaksena, covered both of them with gold and covered also the main shrine of the temple with gold and installed in it a golden image of Vishnu. He is stated to have given away to these temples immense quantity of jewels and precious stones and pearls.[1]

He was ably assisted in his conquests by two of his co-regents, Jatavarma Vira Pandya (1253–1274) and Maravarman Kulasekara (1253–1308–9). The latter who became the supreme ruler after the death of the former had also at first two co-regents, Jatavarman Sundara Pandya, his son born to his wife, and Jatavarman Vira Pandya, his son born to his mistress.

Kulasekhara consolidated and even extended the Pandyan empire. He declared war against Hoysala Ramanatha (son of Someswara) and Chola Rajaraja III who had allied themselves and defeated them both in 1279. This was a crushing blow to the Cholas from which they never recovered. He also put down a rising in Travancore and rivetted his hold upon that country. He likewise sent an expedition under his able minister Aryachakravarti to Ceylon who ' laid waste the country on every side ', entered the fortress of Subhagiri and carried away to Madurai ' the venerable Tooth Relic (of the Budha) and all the solid wealth that was there '. This was at the time when Ceylon was ruled by Bhuvanaikabahu I. For some twenty years thereafter, the island formed part of the Pandyan Empire. Parakramabahu III (1303), who succeeded Bhuvanaikabahu as a tributary ruler of Ceylon, had to personally come to the Pandyan

---

1 *The Pandyan Kingdom* by K. A. Nilakanta Sastri, 1929, pages 158–173.
A History of South India by K. A. Nilakanta Sastri, 1955, pages 205–207.

court before he could persuade Kulasekhara to surrender the relic. Ceylon regained independence only during the civil war and the Muslim invasion that followed Kulasekhara's death.[1]

Kulasekhara's last years were embittered by quarrels between his two sons. He wanted Vira Pandya to succeed him but Sundara Pandya who had a better claim, feeling greatly incensed at the injustice done to him, murdered his father and promptly ascended the throne. Vira Pandya instantly attacked him but was defeated at Talachi and taken prisoner. He, however, soon managed to escape and with the help of his cousin Mannar Perumal, the ruler of Karamhatti, near Kalul, seized the crown and forced Sundara Pandya to take safety in flight.[2]

When Sundara was casting about his eyes in all directions to seek the aid of some strong power to regain his throne, Ala-Ud-Din Khilji, the Sultan of Delhi, was turning his attention to the south. The Sultan was as strong as he was ambitious. He had already crushed the power of Ramadeva, the Yadava ruler of Devagiri, and Prataparudra, the Kakatiya ruler of Warangal, and made them his vassals. He had no love for Sundara but he longed to possess the riches of the south associated with its temples, its palaces, its trade and commerce. He longed also to spread the light of Islam into the heathen lands and to convert them to the true faith. He, therefore, ordered the Malik Naib (Malik Kafur), one of his trusted generals to march with an army to the south. The Malik marched to Devagiri and from there, learning that Ballala III, the Hoysala ruler, was busy angling in the troubled waters of Tamilnad, immediately rushed to Devarasamudra and, in spite of the hurried arrival of Ballala to defend his capital, compelled him to surrender it with all its treasures and to become a zimmi (vassal). He then lost no time in despatching the booty to Delhi and in descending on the Pandyan empire. He put to flight Vira Pandya in a fight on the banks of the Cauvery, harried the country, sacked the rich temples and shrines of Kanchi, and, after razing them to the ground, dug up even their foundations to discover hidden treasuries, if any. From there he returned to Madurai where Sundara Pandya had taken refuge. Sundara now lost his nerve and took to flight, while the Malik forthwith ransacked the city and set fire to its temple. At this threat of dire destruction, the Pandyan brothers recovered their sanity, patched up their quarrels and, under the leadership of Vikrama Pandya, Sundara's uncle, a veteran general, gave battle to the Malik, defeated him

1 *The Pandyan Kingdom* by K. A. Nilakanta Sastri, 1929, pages 174–187.
History of South India by K. A. Nilakanta Sastri, 1955, pages 207–208.

2 *The Pandyan Kingdom* by K. A. Nilakanta Sastri, 1929, pages 201–205.

and thus rolled back the Muslim tide for a time from the south. For, the Malik is stated to have left for Delhi soon after this battle (1311), not without, however, the vast booty that he had collected in the Pandyan empire.[1]

The disappearance of the Common danger led at once to the reappearance of the common enmity. The Pandyan brothers started the civil wars again and again invited fresh dangers. Vira Pandya worsted Sundara Pandya and Sundara Pandya, who ought to have known better what to seek and what to shun, fled to Delhi and sought once more the aid of the Sultan. There is nothing to show that an expedition was actually sent from Delhi to assist him, but he seems to have, with the consent of the Sultan, collected some Muslim forces from Devagiri and returned to recapture his throne. But when he came back, he found to his dismay that during his absence, the Chera king Ravivarma Kulasekhara had made a lightening attack on Madurai and conquered it after driving away Vira Pandya. Sundara and his Muslim forces found it impossible to overthrow Kulasekhara. Sundara then sought and obtained the help of the Kakatiya ruler, Prataparudra, while Vira patched up his quarrels with Kulasekhara and joined forces with him to oppose Sundara. In the battle that was fought, the Kakatiya forces defeated Vira and Kulasekhara and installed Sundara on the Pandyan throne. But this throne had by now been shorn of all its glory. The ruler of Ceylon and the Chera king had already become independent. It was perhaps at this time that the Chera king came and occupied parts of the Kongu country. The Chola chieftain, Sambuvaraya, now became independent; and the Muslim Sultans of Delhi once again began to cast their longing eyes on the inexhaustible wealth of the distracted Pandyan empire.[2]

Sultan Qutb-ud-Din wanted no invitation to send an expedition to the south. He despatched thither a large army under his veteran general Khusrau Khan. This general came like a scourge plundering and devastating the country everywhere. On his approach, it is said, all citizens fled in terror. Sundara evaded battle, evacuated Madurai and left it to be sacked by Khusrau Khan. But the very profusion of wealth and the ease with which it could be collected turned Khusrau's head. He plotted to become independent. His generals, however, detected his

---

1 *The Early Muslim Expansion in South India* by N. Venkataramanayya, 1942, pages 13–71.

The Pandyan Kingdom by K. A. Nilakanta Sastri, 1929, pages 205-211.

A History of South India by K. A. Nilakanta Sastri, 1955, pages 219–220.

2 *The Pandyan Kingdom* by K. A. Nilakanta Sastri, 1929, page 213.

treachery and compelled him to march back to Delhi.[1] A brief respite then followed only to bring another storm, and this time a storm which swept away the Pandyan empire altogether. In the reign of Ghaiyas-ud-Din Tughluk, his son Ulugh Khan, after having conquered Warangal, marched to the South. The Pandyan Kingdom was at this time ruled by Parakrama Pandya who had succeeded Sundara Pandya. Ulugh Khan conquered the whole country, took him captive and established a Muslim rule in Madurai.[2] This Muslim rule seems to have extended over parts of the Kongu country also, previously held by the Pandyas, and thus came into a direct contact with the Hoysalas, who ruled over the other parts of the Kongu country.

Ulugh Khan who ascended the throne of Delhi under the title of Muhammad-bin-Tughlaq, was a great conquerer. He not only appointed a governor at Madurai to rule over his southern possessions but also made the weight of his arm felt by the Deccan powers. He subjugated the kingdoms of Kampili and Dwarasamudra and made both Kampila, the ruler of the former and Ballala III, the Hoysala ruler of the latter, his vassals.[3] In 1327, he fixed his capital at Devagiri so as to have a firm hold on all parts of his extensive empire. But soon afterwards, when in 1329 he retransferred his capital back to Delhi, he seems to have lost his hold on Madurai and its dependent territories. At any rate, in 1334–1335, one Syyid Jalal, one of the imperial officers, treacherously slew the governor and declared himself an independent Sultan under the title of Jalal-Ud-Din Ahsan Shah.

Thus was founded the Sultanate of Madurai. When Muhammad-bin-Tughlaq heard of this rebellion, he ordered Syyid Jalal's son, who was one of his attendants, to be instantly sawn into two and marched without delay an army to the south. But, at Warangal, a severe outbreak of cholera decimated his army and forced him to retrace his steps, having accomplished nothing. Jalal-ud-Din Ahsan Shah, however, did not enjoy the fruits of his treachery for long. He was succeeded by one of his officers, Ala-ud-Din Udauji, who was harassed by the dispossessed Pandyan princes and by the Hoysala Ballala III; and in one of his fights with the latter, he was, though victorious, killed by an arrow from an unknown hand (1341). His son-in-law succeeded him under the title of Qutb-ud-Din; but he was killed within forty days and succeeded by Ghiyas-ud-Din Damghani who was originally a trooper in the service of

[1] *Early Muslim Expansion in South India* by N. Venkataramanayya, 1942, pages 91–96.

[2] Idem, pages 122–125.

[3] Idem, pages 128–148.

the Delhi Sultan. It was during his reign that Iben Batuta saw with his own eyes the innocent slaughter of 'idolatrous Hindus' men, women and children, and recorded with horror that 'it was for this reason that God hastened the death of Ghiyas-ud-Din.'[1]

Meanwhile Ballala III stationed at Tiruvannamalai was gradually trying to consolidate his power, at the expense of the Muslims. His sway extended over portions of the Kongu country, South Arcot and North Arcot. At the time of Ghiyas-ud-Din Damghani's accession he was investing the fortress of Kannanur-Koppam after a decisive victory against the Muslim forces. The siege lasted for six months and just when the Muslim garrison was about to surrender, he, with unaccountable folly, allowed the garrison to get into touch with Ghiyas-ud-Din for settling, as he thought, the terms of surrender. Ghiyas-ud-Din, however, instead of settling the terms of surrender, at once marched with a large army, took Ballala and his troops completely by surprise and inflicted a signal defeat upon them. He took Ballala prisoner, stripped him of all his wealth, horses and elephants and then had him killed and flayed. His skin was stuffed with straw and hung upon the wall of Madurai where says Ibn Batuta, 'I saw it in the same position' (1342). This wanton cruelty had its nemisis. Soon after his return to Madurai, Ghiyas-ud-Din lost his only son, his wife and his mother, by an attack of cholera and he himself died a few days later, it is said, 'from the effects of an aphrodisiac prepared by a yogin.'[2]

Ghiyas-ud-Din was succeeded by his nephew Nasir-ud-Din (1342) who was originally a domestic servant of the Sultan of Delhi. He obtained the consent of the nobles and the army for his accession by a lavish distribution of gold. And the moment he became the Sultan he killed a son of his own paternal aunt who had married Ghiyas-ud-Din's daughter and who, therefore, was a possible candidate for the Sultanate. The last extant coin of Nasir-ud-Din belongs to the year 1344. Then follows a break in the coins till we come to 1356–1357 when we find Adil Shah ruling over the Madurai kingdom. He was succeeded by Fakr-ud-Din Mubarak Shah in 1359. Fakr-ud-Din was followed by the last of the Sultans of Madurai, Ala-ud-Din Sikander Shah (1372) during whose rule the Sultanate collapsed under the hammer of the Vijayanagar Kings (1377–1378).[3] So far as

---

[1] *South India and her Muhammadan Invaders* by S. Krishnaswami Aiyangar, 1921, pages 164–166.

[2] Idem, pages 166–168.

History of South India by K. A. Nilakanta Sastri, 1955, pages 229–230.

[3] *South India and her Muhammadan Invaders* by S. Krishnaswami Aiyangar 1921, pages 168–170.

the Kongu country is concerned, the Muslim rule in it seems to have been extinguished in 1368.[1] Throughout this Muslim rule, the Hindus were persecuted; they were slaughtered, their temples were invariably pillaged and desecrated and their idols were continually deprived of worship.[2] What happened as a result of this persecution will be described in the next chapter.

---

1 *The Kongu Country* by M. Arokiaswami, 1956, page 316.

2 *The Pandyan Kingdom* by K. A. Nilakanta Sastri, 1929, pages 241–243.

CHAPTER III.

LATER HISTORY.

Out of the holocaust of Muslim persecution was born the Hindu Kingdom of Vijayanagar which soon became a terrible menace to the Muslims. For, the rulers of this Kingdom under the blessings and inspiration of Vidyaranya, rapidly grew from strength to strength and standing forth as the champions of Hinduism and rallying round them all the Hindus of all denominations, began everywhere to attack the Muslim possessions. They sent an expedition to the south under their great general, Kumara Kampana (the son of Bukka and the brother of Harihara I) who, between 1343 and 1356, crushed the power of the Muslim Sultan of Madurai and between 1377 and 1378 put an end to the Sultanate itself.[1] There is evidence to show that Kampana conquered the Kongu country (Coimbatore and Salem) from the Muslims by 1368.[1] There is also evidence to show that the first act he did in the Kongu country after its conquest was that of rebuilding the Kuraiyur temples which had suffered destruction at the hands of the Muslims.[2]

There is, however, nothing to show what things either he or the early Vijayanagar Viceroys or kings did in the Kongu country. Inscriptions of Harihara II (1377—1404), Devaraya I (1406—1422) and Devaraya II (1422–1446) found in the Kongu country simply testify to the existence of the rule of the Vijayanagar kings in that region and nothing more.[3] It would, however, appear that during the time of Devaraya II, two Vijayanagar Viceroys, Lakkana and Madana, were ruling over the whole of the Tamil country with their headquarters at Madurai and Thanjavur, respectively and that Lakkana's sway extended over the Kongu country.[4] On the death of Devaraya II, the empire fell into disorder on account of the recurring hostilities of the Muslim Sultans of the Deccan and his hold on the southern Viceroyalties became weak. It was at this time that the Ummattur Chieftains seem to have become independent

1 *South India and her Muhammadan Invaders* by S. S. Krishnaswami Aiyangar, 1921, pages 182–188.

2 *The Kongu Country* by M. Arokiaswami, 1956, page 316.

3 *Idem*, pages 317–318.

4 *The History of the Nayaks of Madura* by R. Sathyanatha Aiyar, 1924, pages 5–8. *The Kongu Country* by M. Arokiaswami, 1956, pages 318–319.

of Vijayanagar and extended their rule over the Kongu country. In fact, what evidence there is shows that the Vijayanagar kings from Saluva Narasimha (1486—1491) to Vira Narasimha (1505–1509) exercised but little control over the Kongu country and that when Vira Narasimha demanded tribute, the Ummattur Chieftain flatly refused to pay it. It was not until the reign of Krishnadeva Raya (1509–1529) that the Kongu country was again brought under the Vijayanagar Empire.[1]

The Ummattur Chieftains seem to have ruled over the Kongu country from 1446–1520 more or less peacefully, rebuilding ruined temples and repopulating ruined towns. They seem to have also evinced considerable interest in agriculture, irrigation and trade and, by all this, did much to repair the damage done by the Muslim rule.[2]

Their rule, however, proved to be of brief duration. It was extinguished by Krishnadeva Raya (1509—1529) who is said to have come and conquered not only the Kongu country but also the Madurai and the Thanjavur countries which had shown symptoms of independence. The Kongu country now became a part of the Madurai country and came to be ruled by the Nayakas of Madurai, the rulers appointed by the Vijayanagar emperors.[3] It remained under the Nayakas from about 1530 to about 1700 and during this whole period it had no separate history, its history being bound up with the history of the Nayakas.

Tradition ascribes the foundation of the Nayaka Kingdom of Madurai to Krishnadeva Raya. It is said that he came to the south about 1520 and appointed Vira Narasimha as the Governor of the Chola country and Nagama as the Governor of the Madurai country. Nagama, a tried officer of the empire, is stated to have subdued two recalcitrant princes, one a Chola and the other a Pandya, with a stern hand and refused to reinstate the latter in his territories even when the emperor ordered it to be done. Thereupon the emperor is said to have exclaimed in a rage in open court whether there was no one who would bring the rebel captive, when Visvanatha, his betel bearer and Nagama's own son, is said to have volunteered to do so. Viswanatha, having fulfilled his task, is then said to have been rewarded by the emperor with the Nayakship of Madurai. This event is said to have occurred in 1529.[4]

This traditional account of the foundation of the Nayaka Kingdom of Madurai, embodied in chronicles like the Tanjavuru Andhra Rajulu

---

1 *The Kongu Country* by M. Arokiaswami, 1956, pages 319–324.

2 *Idem*, pages 326–327.

3 *Idem*, pages 327–334.

4 *History of the Nayaks of Madurai* by R. Satyanatha Aiyar, 1924, pages 48–52.

Charitram,has been held to be incorrect by some historians in the light of recent historical research. It has been held that Viswanatha could not have been appointed as a ruler of Madurai by Krishnadeva Raya, that even during the reign of Achyutadeva Raya he was only a Governor of Madurai, and that too for some years only, and that it was Viswanatha's son, Krishnappa, who is to be regarded as the founder of the Nayaka dynasty. It is stated that Krishnappa took advantage of the confusion caused by the battle of Rakshasi-Tangadi to declare himself as the King or Nayaka of Madurai and that the Vijayanagar emperors had to recognize him as such on account of their weakness.[1]

Whatever it is, Viswanatha (1529—1564), whether as a Governor or as a Nayaka, showed outstanding abilities both as a warrior and as a statesman. Soon after he came to Madurai he reconstructed its fort with 72 bastions with the aid of Ariyanatha, his Dalavay and Pradhani, a man born of Vellala parents, who by sheer ability had won a high position in the Vijayanagar empire. He then gave Vallam in exchange for Tiruchirappalli to the Nayaka of Thanjavur, cleared the jungles of thieves and robbers on both sides of the Cauvery to make the pilgrim route to Rameswaram as safe as possible, fortified Tiruchirappalli and subdued with the help of Ariyanatha, the Pandiya princes of Tirunelveli. He also subdued the Kambam—Gudalur country with the aid of his General Ramabhadra Nayaka. His territories seem to have comprised the modern districts of Madurai, Ramanathapuram, Tirunelveli, Tiruchirappalli, Coimbatore and Salem and parts of the Kerala State. He devised for the administration of all these territories, with the help of Ariyanatha, a system called the Palayam System, which with all its defects had a number of good points to recommend it. He divided his territories into 72 palayams and placed each of them in charge of a local chieftain called a Palayakar or Poligar. Two such palayakars seem to have been appointed over the Kongu country, one representing the Getty Mudaliars of Omalur and Taramangalam and the other representing the chieftains of Sendamangalam. All palayakars were to maintain troops for the defence of the territories, to run the civil administration of the country and to pay one-third of the land revenue collections as tribute. They were to restore peace and order, to improve agriculture, to clear the forests and to bring the waste lands under cultivation. In times of storm and stress they were to rally round the ruler and obey his orders. This system no doubt had in it the

---

1 *Studies in the History of the Third Dynasty of Vijayanagar* by N. Venkataramanayya, 1935, pages 453-461.

Further Sources of Vijayanagar History by K. A. Nilakanta Sastri and N .Venkataramanayya, 1946, pages 239-241.

seeds of misrule; the Palayakars might oppress and tyrannise the people. But it had these good points; it made use of all petty chieftains, who would otherwise have fought with one another, and sought to create unity and loyalty. So long as the ruler was strong and able he could hold the palayakars in check and get the best out of them. And Viswanatha got the best out of them; his palayakars are stated to have done much for the country by founding villages, building dams, constructing tanks and erecting temples. Viswanatha himself showed real concern for the well-being of his subjects by renovating the temples of Tiruchirappalli and Srirangam, by rebuilding the temple of God Sundara and Goddess Minakshi, by spending lavishly on works of public utility such as the enlargement of the town of Tirunelveli. He remained throughout loyal to the Vijayanagar emperor and Achyuta Raya treated him with kindness. During the presence of Rama Raja Vitthala in the south he occupied a subordinate position.[1]

Viswanatha Nayaka, as has already been stated, was succeeded by his son Krishnappa Nayaka (1564–1572). He suppressed a rebellion of one of his powerful palayakars, the palayakar of Paramakudi, and what is more, led a strong expedition to Ceylon when the King of Ceylon refused to pay tribute. Chinna Kesava, his capable General, defeated and killed the King of Ceylon and Krishnappa Nayaka is then said to have appointed his own brother-in-law as the ruler of Ceylon and returned in triumph to Madurai. He continued to remain loyal to the Vijayanagar emperor. He is said to have sent his Pradhani and Dalavay Ariyanatha to Vijayanagar to do his best to ward off the Muslim peril and it was not till about two years after the tragic battle of Rakshasi-Tangadi (Talikota 1565) that Ariyanatha is said to have come back to Madurai. His solicitude for his subjects is shown by his building two towns one called Krishnapuram and the other Kadaiyam; by his construction of some temples and by his granting endowments of land to several temples.[2]

He was followed on the throne by his son Virappa Nayaka (1572–1592) who, during his long rule, gave peace and prosperity to his kingdom. He suppressed a Pandyan rebellion, established a firm hold over all the palayakars and remained loyal to the Vijayanagar emperors. He improved the fort of Tiruchirappalli, constructed a fort at Aruppukottai, built walls round the Chidambaram temple, and granted many agraharams in charity. He is also said to have carried out several improvements to the

[1] *History of the Nayaks of Madura* by R. Sathyanatha Aiyar, 1924, pages 48–67.
Madura District Manual by J. H. Nelson, 1868, part III, pages 87–101.
The Kongu Country by M. Arokiaswami, 1956, pages 336–338.

[2] *History of the Nayaks of Madura* by R. Sathyanatha Aiyar, 1924, pages 68–76.

temple of Sundareswarar and Minakshi at Madurai. Towards the close of his rule (about 1592) he permitted the Jesuit missionaries, till then working on the coast among the Paravars, to establish a mission and to build a church and presbytery at Madurai.[1]

Krishnappa Nayaka II, son of Virappa Nayaka, ruled for a few years (1595–1601). His was a peaceful reign during which he remained loyal to the Vijayanagar emperor, Venkata II. He had, however, to keep watch over the growing power of the Pandyan Princes and the Tiruvaiyar ruler. It was during his reign that Ariyanatha, the famous Dalavay died, leaving behind him a splendid record of services to the State.[2]

Upon the death of Krishnappa Nayaka II, the throne was usurped by his youngest brother Kasturi Ranga, his other brother, Visvappa, having predeceased him. But, within a week, Kasturi Ranga was murdered and was followed by Muttu Krishnappa Nayaka (1601—1609), the son of Visvappa. He reorganized the Marava country and curbed the political influence of the Portuguese. He appointed Sadaika Teva (or the Dalavay Setupati as he is sometimes called) as the Ruler of the Marava country, on condition of his paying a fixed tribute, clearing the pilgrim route to Rameswaram of robbers and bringing the Parava coast, which was actually then ruled by the Portuguese, effectually under Madurai. These laudable objects were completely fulfilled by the Dalavay Setupati and his son Kuttan Setupati. But, while he thus put down the political power of the Portuguese, he allowed them to preach their religion unmolested. It was during his time that Robert de Nobili came to the Madurai Mission, and launched his missionary activities not only in the Madurai country but also in the Kongu country. Nobili was a remarkable personality. He saw that the reason why Christianity had failed to make headway among the higher classes was that it had failed to take into account the manners, the customs, the ideas and the language of the people. He, therefore, adopted the outer garb of the Brahmin, called himself a " Roman Brahmin ", studied the language and literature of the people, began to preach in their own language and allowed the converts to continue their harmless ceremonies and customs. He encountered the opposition of his own colleague Fernandez, but succeeded, it would seem, by his zeal and tactics, in securing several converts from among the higher classes, both in Madurai and in the Kongu country. He is said to have established friendly relations with Ramachandra Nayaka of Sendamangalam and Selapati Nayaka of Salem, the two tributaries of the Nayaka of Madurai and converted the four sons of Ramachandra Nayaka to Christianity.

---

1 *History of the Nayaks of Madura* by Sathyanatha Aiyar, 1924, pages 77–83.

2 Idem, pages 84–88.

Muttu Krishnappa, though he showed tolerance to Christianity, never failed in his duty to uphold Hinduism. He endowed the Bhagavati temple at Cape Comorin, constructed a Siva temple at Kayattar, built a number of pagodas in several places, and granted many 'agraharams'. He is also said to have built a town called Krishnapuram between Madurai and Skandamalai and constructed many tanks. He remained, like his predecessors, loyal to the Vijayanagar emperor.[1]

All these years, from the time of Viswanatha Nayaka to the time of Muttu Krishnappa Nayaka, Kongu enjoyed peace, undisturbed by any foreign invasion. But now came the time when under the successors of Muttu Krishnappa Nayaka, foreign invasions began to make their appearance. This was because Mysore now became stronger and stronger while Madurai became entangled in Vijayanagar politics and numerous wars with its neighbours.

This is what happened. When Muttu Virappa Nayaka (1609–1623), the son and successor of Muttu Krishnappa Nayaka, ascended the throne, the Vijayanagar empire was passing through a shattering experience. Venkata II died leaving behind him a succession feud which suddenly flared up into a civil war. Upon his death bed he nominated his nephew, Sriranga II Chikkaraya, as his successor, but the rights of this nephew were bitterly opposed and contested by Venkata's putative son. Very soon two parties formed themselves. The loyal chieftains under the banner of Yachama Nayaka, a veteran leader, supported the cause of the nephew, while the disloyal chieftains under the banner of Gobburi Jaggaraya, the emperor's brother-in-law, supported the cause of the putative son. Jaggaraya, having contrived to murder Sriranga II, marched to the Tamil districts for mustering strength for his cause, followed closely by Yachama Nayaka, who, having rescued Ramadeva, Sriranga's son, was anxious to give battle to the rebels at the first opportunity. Muttu Virappa Nayaka saw at this crisis no reason why he should not espouse the rebel cause and shake off once for all the effects overlordship of the emperor of Vijayanagar. There was no point in sending tribute amounting to one-third of the revenues to an overlord who could give nothing in return for the defence of his kingdom. He, therefore, allied himself with Jaggaraya, while the Nayaka of Tanjore allied himself with Yachama Nayaka. In the battle of Toppur that took place (1616) Muttu Virappa Nayaka was defeated and Jaggaraya was killed. Close upon this defeat Raja Wodaiyar, the ruler of Mysore, came and occupied some parts of the Kongu country and harassed the province of Dindigul. The Raja's

[1] *History of the Nayaks of Madura* by R. Sathyanatha Aiyar, 1924, pages 89–97. *The Kongu Country* by M. Arokiaswamy, 1956, pages 355–356.

army, it is said, was beaten off by the palayakars of Virupakshi and Kannivadi, but it is not said whether the Kongu country was completely freed from its occupation.[1]

The position, so far as the Kongu country was concerned, became even worse during the rule of Tirumala Nayaka (1623-1659), the younger brother of Muttu Virappa Nayaka. Tirumala was great alike in war and peace; he was, in fact, the greatest among the Nayakas of Madurai. He strengthened the defences of his kingdom, constructed fortresses on its frontiers, raised an army of 30,000 men, shifted his capital from Tiruchirappalli back to Madurai, which was, indeed, less vulnerable and better defensible, and refused to pay tribute to the Vijayanagar emperor, being convinced that loyalty to the emperor meant nothing more than a perpetual drain on his treasury. He knew that the emperor had become a mere shadow, incapable of doing anything to protect Madurai either from internal or from external dangers. He knew that these dangers were then increasing and he prepared to meet them, if necessary, single-handed. The Travancore country having failed to pay him its usual tribute, he attacked it and brought it under his subjection. The Marava country having plunged itself into a civil war, he dragged it out of that war and appointed over it as its ruler, Raghunatha Setupati an energetic, loyal and capable man. When the Vijayanagar emperor, Sri Ranga, who had by now lost everything save a small territory round Vellore, came to attack him, he made alliances with the Nayakas of Tanjore and Gingee and defied him; and when these allies failed him at the last moment, he induced the Sultan of Golconda to attack the emperor's territories and thereby compelled the emperor to rush to the north for the protection of his dominions. When, again, the Golconda forces proved treacherous and attacked Gingee, he sought and obtained the aid of Bijapur against Golconda and flew to the relief of Gingee. And, finally, when the Bijapur forces too betrayed him, joined the Golconda forces, took Gingee and came to attack him, he put up a stiff resistance and eventually turned them out of his dominions. But in spite of all this, he could not drive away the Mysore forces from parts of the Kongu country which it had occupied. Early in his reign, Chamaraja Wodaiyar, the ruler of Mysore, sent his General Nandi Raja to invade the Madurai country. Nandi Raja passed through Kongu as far as Dindigul and suffered a defeat at the hands of Tirumala's Generals, Dalavay Ramappaya and Raghunatha Nayaka, the palayakar of Kannivadi. But towards the end of this reign, there came another Mysore invasion, this time launched by Kantirava Narasa Raja,

---

[1] *History of the Nayaks of Madura* by R. Sathyanatha Aiyar, 1924, pages 98-109.

the new ruler of Mysore. Hampaiya, the Mysore General, marched to Satyamangalam and from there to the very gates of Madurai, perpetrating the most horrible outrages on the people. It is said that his army cut off the noses of all people, men, women and children that came on its way. Tirumala was then on his sick-bed. But he sent his faithful vassal, Raghunatha Setupati, to repel the invasion. Raghunatha collected a large army and not only defended Madurai but also, after a pitched battle, carried the war into the Mysore country perpetrating the same cruelty of cutting off the noses of the Mysoreans. Nevertheless, Mysore, it would appear, did not relinquish its hold on its possessions in the Kongu country.

The loss of the Kongu country is the only blot on the escutcheon of Tirumala, and he would have wiped it out, perhaps, if he had lived a few years longer. But destiny never pays any attention to the cares and anxieties of man. It snatched Tirumala away at a critical moment, but it could not snatch away the glory that was rightfully his, the fruits of the lifelong labours of a wise and benevolent ruler. By this admirable foresight and tenacity he preserved his kingdom more or less intact from the perils of disunity and destruction; and by his inimitable passion for all that is, beautiful and noble in art, architecture and religion, he left an imperishable name behind. His splendid monuments, such as his palace, are the artistic wonders not only of his age but also of all ages. And the numerous temples, mantapams, gopurams, etc., which he built all over his kingdom, mark him out as a pious man solicitous of the material welfare of his subjects and that he made it a point to frequently tour his dominions in order to redress the grievances of the people.[1]

Tirumala was succeeded by his son Muttu Virappa Nayaka who ruled only for about a few months (1659). But in these few months he did much. As soon as he ascended the throne he threw all subservience to the Muslims to the winds and made rapid preparations to attack the Nayaka of Tanjore for his infidelities to Tirumala. Vijayaraghava, the Nayaka of Tanjore, became desperate and appealed to the Sultan of Bijapur for aid. The Sultan despatched a large army under 'Sagosi' father of Shivaji and 'Mulla' (Mustafa Khan)[2], but this army instead of helping Tanjore attacked it and conquered it and drove away Vijayaraghava into the jungles. Tanjore, Vallam, and Mannargudi fell one after another

1 *History of the Nayaks of Madura* by R. Sathyanatha Aiyar, 1924, pages 110–149.

Madura District Manual by J. H. Nelson, 1868, Part III, pages 121–142.

Gazetteer of the Madura District by W. Francis, Vol. I, 1906, pages 44–50.

2 *The Nayaks of Tanjore* by V. Vridhagirisan, 1949, Index–Pages 21 and 31.

into the hands of the Muslims, but Madurai stoutly held out. Muttu Virappa offered stiff resistance and the Muslim army harassed by famine and the Kallars came readily to terms with him and walked off with whatever they could get.[1]

During the reign of Chokkanatha Nayaka (1659–1682), the son of Muttu Virappa Nayaka, Madurai's hold on Kongu become precarious. Chokkanatha is an enigma in history. For a time he showed himself as a bold, energetic and capable ruler. Though only sixteen years of age when he ascended the throne, he broke up the cabal of his Pradhani, the Rayasam and the Dalavay who had usurped all power to themselves. Soon afterwards he marched twice against Vijayaraghava Nayaka of Tanjore, once for his having sided with the cabal, and a second time for his having instigated the Bijapur General ' Vannamian ' to attack Madurai, and during the second campaign he captured Vallam and humbled the pride of Tanjore. He also attacked and captured several important forts of the Setupati who had failed to assist him in his fight against ' Vannamian'. He transferred his capital from Madurai to Tiruchirappalli with a view to renewing hostilities against Tanjore and eventually launched an invasion against Tanjore, captured Tanjore and appointed one of his own men, Muddalagiri Nayaka, as its Governor. But, from this time onwards, he behaved in a manner at once strange and inexplicable. For, he now showed foolishness, pusillanimity and helplessness. He left first Muddalagiri to become practically independent and then allowed him to be attacked and defeated by Ekoji and thus lost Tanjore for ever to the Marathas. Subsequently he opened his eyes and declared war against Tanjore, but failed to attack Ekoji when he was returning utterly discomfited after his disgraceful defeat by Santaji, the Governor of Gingee. Nor is this all. He allowed himself to be shortly afterwards superseded by his younger brother, Muttulinga Nayaka (1678) and to be made captive by Rustum Khan, a Muslim adventurer. Although the fates rescued him from captivity, although he was again reinstated on the throne by Kilavan Setupati and some of his palayakars, he made no attempt to reassert his authority with vigour. The result was Mysore lost no time in occupying large parts of his possessions in Kongu. From about 1670 the inscriptions of Devaraya Wodaiyar and Chikkadeva Raya are found in the Coimbatore and Salem districts. A few years later, Chikkadeva Raya fought against him a decisive battle at Erode and conquered, it is said, large parts of his territories. The Mysore menace became even greater towards the end of his reign. Dalavay Kumarayya, the Mysore General, came and occupied

---

1 *History of the Nayaks of Madura* by R. Sathyanatha Aiyar, 1924, pages 150–153.

his capital itself. It was only with the aid of Ekoji and Arasumalai, the General of Gingee, that he drove the Mysoreans from his kingdom. But Arasumalai proved treacherous to him and attacked Tiruchirappalli. This was too much for him to bear, and he died of heart-failure.[1]

His son and successor, Ranga Krishna Muttu Virappa Nayaka (1682–1689), had great difficulty in re-establishing his authority in his kingdom. The Mysoreans, the Marathas of Tanjore and Gingee, and the Setupati of Ramanathapuram, had by then come and squatted on large parts of his kingdom. Fortunately for him, however, they quarrelled among themselves or found themselves faced with their own troubles. Sambaji, the ruler of Gingee, declared war on Mysore and compelled the Mysore army to withdraw from Madurai. Chikkadeva Raya, the king of Mysore, at the same time, encountered a rebellion of his subjects. Ekoji, the ruler of Tanjore, found his kingdom distracted by a serious discontent caused by the failure of his domestic policy, while the Setupati faced a revolt in his own country stirred up by his Dalavay. These factors enabled Ranga Krishna to recover most of his dominions, including some parts of the Kongu country. He was a frank, jovial, good-natured king noted for his impartiality and strict sense of justice.[2]

A few months after his death, his wife Muttammal gave birth to a male child and committed suicide. The child was named Vijayaranga Chokkanatha and crowned when three months old, his grandmother, Mangammal (Chokkanatha Nayaka's wife), becoming the regent during his minority (1689–1706). Mangammal who had seen a great deal of adversity during her husband's life now ruled with not a little tact and sagacity. She had difficult times to contend with. It was then that Aurangazib, after extending the Mughal supremacy in the Deccan, began periodically despatching his Generals to the south for collecting tribute. It was then also that the Marathas began sending lightning expeditions to the south for collecting chouth. She bowed down to both, gave tribute to the one and chouth to the other, and thus warded off the dangers from both. But she could not ward off her other enemies, the rulers of Travancore, Ramanathapuram and Mysore. She has to send annual expeditions to Travancore to collect the tribute due to her. She had to hold in check the aggressive actions of Shahji, the ruler of Tanjore. She had to try her best to curb the increasing power and influence of the Setupati. And,

1 *History of the Nayaks of Madura* by R. Sathyanatha Aiyar, 1924 pages 154–190.

Madura District Manual by J. H. Nelson, 1868, Part III, pages 182–204.

2 *History of the Nayaks of Madura* by R. Sathyanatha Aiyar, 1924, pages 191–203.

finally, she had to defend whatever possessions she had in the Kongu country against the invasions of Chikkadeva Raya, the king of Mysore. Chikkadeva, it is said, invaded her territories in Coimbatore and Salem and was driven back not so much by her forces as by the sudden appearance of the Marathas in Mysore. In spite of all her troubles, however, she proved to be a benevolent ruler. She showed tolerance to the Christians as well as the Muslims, made liberal donations to the temples, granted many agraharams and built numerous choultries and water pandals.[1]

On her death, Vijayaranga Chokkanatha (1706–1732) assumed the reigns of Government. But his rule was marked by nothing but sheer negligence. He left everything in the hands of his Dalavay Kasturi Rangayya and Pradhani Venkata Krishnayya and they and their minions oppressed the people with impunity. Moreover Madurai now entered into Marava politics which very soon robbed her of all her glory. She also now lost all her possessions in the Kongu country. Dodda Krishna Raja of Mysore came and occupied them without expending the life of a single soldier.[2]

In the reign of Minakshi (1732–1736), the wife of Vijayaranga, nothing was left for her to govern in the Kongu country. But the sun was then setting not only over the Kongu country but also over the whole of the Nayaka kingdom of Madurai. Bangaru Tirumala, the father of her adopted son, started a rebellion and sought the aid of Safdar Ali and Chanda Saheb, the son and son-in-law of Dost Ali, the Nawab of the Carnatic. Safdar Ali hesitated to act, but Chanda Saheb acted at once. He came with a large army and by threats and cajolery entered Tiruchirappalli, made Minakshi prisoner and occupied her throne. Minakshi committed suicide, and with her death the whole of the Madurai kingdom passed into the hands of the Muslims.[3]

We may pause at this stage to give an account of the Nayaka rule under which the Kongu country remained for nearly two centuries from the time of Viswanatha to the time of Vijayaranga Chokkanatha. The Nayaka, as the Chola king of old, was autocratic. He was the unquestioned head of the army, the executive and the judiciary. He could appoint or dismiss any officer. His word was law or a command which had to be implicitly

---

1 *History of the Nayaks of Madura* by R. Sathyanatha Aiyar, 1924, pages 204–222.

Madura District Manual by J. H. Nelson, 1868, Part III, pages 205–238.

2 *History of the Nayaks of Madura* by R. Sathyanatha Aiyar, 1924, pages 223–231.

3 Idem, pages 232–234.

Madura District Manual by J. H. Nelson, 1868, Part III, pages 239–264.

obeyed. But his authority was tempered, even restrained, by tradition and custom. None of the Nayakas, not even the great Tirumala, dared to ride rough-shod over Hindu traditions or Hindu customs sanctioned by the Sastras and followed by the majority of his subjects. The truth is, tradition and custom constituted in those days the essence of public opinion, and this public opinion, stronger than any modern law or modern public opinion, put an effectual curb on the autocracy of the Nayaka.

Moreover, the Nayaka was in practice, upon all important matters, assisted by the advice of a council of high officers or ministers. And if, in any case he set aside their advice, he did so at his own peril. This council normally consisted of the Dalavay, the Pradhani, the Rayasam, the Kanakkan and the Stanapati. The Dalavay was both the Prime Minister and the Commander-in-Chief. He wielded immense power alike in the military and in the civil administration of the realm. He was responsible for the organization of the army, for the conduct of war, for the control of foreign policy, as well as for the maintenance of public peace. The Pradhani was the Finance Minister. He was responsible for the collection of revenue and its expenditure. The Rayasam was the Chief Secretary, the head of the whole administrative machinery. The Kanakkan was the Accountant in charge of the audit department, while the Stanapati was the Foreign Secretary, the accredited agent of the king in his dealings with foreign powers.

We have hardly any precise information about the constitution of the various departments of the Government. It would, however, appear that under the Dalavay there were provincial governors, each in charge of a province consisting of two or more palayams. Below these governors came the palayakars, such as the Ghetti Mudaliyar of Omalur and Taramangalam and others, and some of the bigger palayakars exercised control over the smaller palayakars. The palayakars, as has already been seen, supervised both the civil and military administration of the palayams, paid one-third of the revenue as tribute to the Nayaka and maintained and furnished a specified number of troops for the defence of the kingdom. The kingdom was protected from invasion by a number of forts well-built and well-garrisoned at strategic places like Dindigul, Dharapuram, Coimbatore, Satyamangalam, Erode, Karur, Namakkal, Sendamangalam, Salem, Melur, and Attur. Besides these forts there were the famous fortresses of Madurai and Tiruchirappalli which were considered impregnable and garrisoned by the pick of the troops. The seventy-two bastions of the Madurai fortress, it is said, were garrisoned by the best contingents supplied by the seventy-two palayakars. Each fort or fortress was in charge of a commander and all the commanders were under the immediate supervision and control of the Dalavay. The army of the Nayaks consisted of the infantry, the cavalry and the elephantry. The chariots had by their time completely fallen into disuse, but instead of them, artillery was fast becoming popular. Guns, swords, lances, bows and arrows and shields formed their chief weapons of offence and defence.

As to the civil administration, each province or palayam was divided into a number of nadus, seemais, or maghanams. The smallest division was obviously the village, variously called the gramam, the mangalam, the samudram, the kudi, the ur, the puram, the kulam, the kurichi or the patti. We do not know who were the officers in charge of each of these sub-divisions and what their duties were. But we know that the brunt of the administration fell on the villages themselves which enjoyed a large measure of local autonomy. The village assembly consisting of the representatives of the people still played a vital part. This assembly had its village headman who maintained peace and order through village watchmen. It had its revenue officer, maniyakarar or ambalakarar who collected the land revenue of the village. It had its kanakku pillai who kept revenue accounts. And it had its panchayats and arbitrators who decided all civil and criminal cases. Over these officers there seem to have been other corresponding officers of the larger territorial divisions. The Nayaka himself, it is stated, constituted the highest court in the realm and decided all cases impartially after consulting his chief officers. All these officers, whether the king's officers, or the village officers, were paid mostly in 'maniums' or grants of land; and such of them as rendered meritorious services were also periodically rewarded by presents of money.

The chief source of the revenue of the Nayakas, as of the Cholas, was, of course, land. It is, however, not known what portion of the produce was claimed by the State; some say it was half the gross produce while others say it was half the net produce. Whatever it is, there is nothing to show that the assessment pressed hard on the people and led to any disturbances or migrations. There is, on the other hand, ample evidence to show that agriculture was encouraged, that large tracts of waste and forest lands were systematically brought under cultivation by the Nayakas and their palayakars, that irrigation works were undertaken and that the crown lands which formed no small part of the cultivated lands of the kingdom were considered rich and fertile. It would seem that the assessment was fixed on the village and that the ryots shared it among themselves. It would also seem that tenancy was known and practised.

Next to land revenue came the tribute paid by the palayakars and next to tribute the various profession taxes, import and export duties, transit duties, receipts from fines and royalties from the pearl and chank fisheries. The Nayakas seem to have collected a large amount of revenue from all these sources and utilized the surplus revenues over the renovations of old temples, building of new temples and the erection of splendid works of art such as the Tirumala Nayakan Palace. This they could very well afford to do, since they had not much to spend over their general administration. The palayakars maintained the army, the civil as well as the military officers were paid mostly in 'maniums', and the villages bore all the expenses connected with their administration.

The Nayakas, however, did little towards the encouragement of trade. They maintained no navy and they allowed the foreign trade to slip entirely into the hands of the Portuguese and the Dutch. The ancient ports, which in the glorious days of the Cholas and the Pandyas controlled both the western and eastern trade routes, fell into decay. The exports of cloth, etc., became restricted and the import of luxury goods negligible. Pearl and chank alone continued to be exported, but this was done not by the Indian merchants but by the Portuguese and the Dutch. Internal trade also showed signs of decline; we do not hear of any powerful merchant guilds like that of the Nanadasis of old days in the Nayaka period. The roads were generally unsafe, infested as they were by thieves and robbers.

In the field of religion, however, the Nayakas did all that was needed to place Hinduism on a firm footing. Like the Vijayanagar kings and generals before them, they took a great deal of interest in renovating and building temples, in granting endowments to them and in creating agraharams. They professed Vaishnavism and encouraged the Vaishnavaites to come and settle down in their dominions, but they showed no antipathy to Saivism and did nothing to wound the feelings of the Saivites. Indeed, they showered their benefactions equally on the Saivite and Vaishnavite temples and on the Saivite and Vaishnavite Brahmins. They also encouraged several of the Telugu communities such as the Kammalars, the Kaikolars, the Khammas, the Reddis, the Sourashtras, etc., to come and settle down in their dominions, but there is nothing to show that they did this to the detriment of the existing communities of their realm. No religious or communal quarrels or disturbances took place during their rule and temple worship and public feasts and festivals were enjoyed by all Hindus of all denominations without any hindrance.

Under their rule, society continued in its traditional pattern; the varnasrama dharma was observed and the Brahmins, the vedas and the dharmasastras were respected. Toleration was extended to Christians and Muslims alike, but any excessive missionary zeal which resulted in unfair methods of proselytisation was resented and resisted. Education was imparted in the hundreds of temples and maths endowed by royal grants. Nobili tells us that in Madurai alone there were 10,000 students distributed in several classes of two or three hundred and that splendid foundations had been made for their maintenance. It would appear that besides Sanskrit, Tamil and Telugu were encouraged by the Nayakas. Nothing is known about the ordinary life of the people, but it is known that the Nayakas and their nobles kept harems and tolerated sati[1].

It has already been seen how Coimbatore or the Kongu country was gradually acquired by the Mysore rulers from the Nayakas until at last, just before the fall of the Nayaka kingdom into the hands of Chanda Saheb, it became a part of Mysore. Save for very short intervals it remained under Mysore from about 1730 to 1799 when it became a part of the British possessions. During this whole period it had no separate existence, its political and administrative history being bound up with that of Mysore. We have, therefore, to trace the history of Mysore to show how it shared the glories as well as the tribulations of Mysore.

Dodda Krishna Raja (1714—1732) under whose rule Mysore finally absorbed Coimbatore was by no means a sagacious ruler. It was not his political sagacity as that of his ministers who controlled him and the weakness of the Nayaka ruler that decided the fate of Coimbatore. But, although Mysore secured Coimbatore, it found itself exposed to other dangers that threatened it. At this time Sadatulla Khan who was till then the governor of the whole of the Muslim possessions in the south—of the Balaghat (Mysore tableland) as well as Payanghat (the Carnatic)—was appointed as the Nawab of Arcot with Payanghat as his jurisdiction, while Amin Khan was appointed as the Nawab of Sira, with Balaghat as his jurisdiction. Mysore came naturally under the jurisdiction of Amin Khan. But Sadatulla Khan, who was longing for the riches accumulated at Mysore and who resented the removal of that State from his control, formed an alliance with the Pathan Nawabs of Cuddapah, Kurnool and Savanur and the Maharashtra chief of Gooty and marched towards Mysore. Finding, however, that Amin Khan had already forestalled him, he patched up his quarrels with him and both forced Dodda Krishna to contribute a crore of rupees as tribute. This was but the beginning of further exactions. Two years later, the Maharashtras appeared before

[1] *History of the Nayaks of Madura* by R. Sathyanatha Aiyar, 1924, pages 235—262.

Madura District Manual by J. H. Nelson, 1868, Part III, pages 143—170.

The Kongu Country by M. Arokiaswamy, 1956, pages 342—369.

Seringapatam and levied another contribution. In order to replenish these drains upon the treasury, the Mysore ministers in whose hands the Raja was but a puppet attacked the chief of Magdi and captured and plundered his wealthy capital Savan-durga[1].

The ministers who did all this were Deva Raj and his cousin Nanja Raj. Both were able but unscrupulous and both usurped all power the moment Dodda Krishna died in 1732. Deva Raj became the Dalavoy (Commander-in-Chief) and Nanja Raj became the Sarvadikari (Finance Minister) and the Pradhani (Privy Councillor). They selected and appointed Chama Raja, a scion of the royal family, as king and, when he proved troublesome, they seized him and sent him to die as a prisoner at Kabbaldurga under its deadly climate. They passed over the younger brother of the deceased Raja, simply because he had too much talent to be submissive and placed on the throne Chikka Krishna Raja (1734–1765), a child of five years of age, hailing from a distant branch of the royal family. They continued to administer as before, except that they separated the office of Pradhani and conferred it first upon their tool called Venkatapati and then upon his death, six years later, upon their relation called Karachuri (the younger brother of Deva Raj). At this time Dost Ali Khan, still greedy and still jealous of the control exercised by the Nawab of Sira (now Tahir Khan) over Mysore, sent a large army to Seringapatam in order to exact another instalment of tribute; but Deva Raj, who was an able commander, won over it a signal victory. Nanja Raj then carried on a successful expedition into Coimbatore against the palayakar of Dharapuram who was becoming restive, leaving the charge of the revenue and finances to Deva Raj. It was at this time that Nazar Jang, the son of Nizam-ul-Mulk, the Subadar of the Deccan, came south to Seringapatam for demanding a tribute from Mysore. Deva Raj gave him the tribute and sent him back. Soon afterwards, on return from Coimbatore, Nanja Raj gave his daughter in marriage to the nominal Raja and launched an attack on Devanahalli, against its refractory chieftain. The siege of Devanahalli lasted for nine months and, at last, its chieftain was reduced. This siege is memorable in that it brought to the notice of Nanja Raj, an obscure private, Hyder Ali, who was soon destined to outshine all other rulers of Southern India. Hyder, who in a private capacity accompanied his elder brother Shabaz, the commandant of a small body of Mysore horse and foot, showed such calmness and courage during the hostilities that Nanja Raj immediately gave him the command of 50 horse and 200 foot with freedom to recruit and augment his corps and appointed him to the

1 *History of Mysore by* Mark Wilks, Vol. I, 1869, pages 141—143.
Mysore by B. L. Rice, Vol. I, 1897, pages 369—370.

charge of one of the gates of Devanahalli, then a frontier fortress of Mysore [1].

All this time great events were happening in the Carnatic. Dost Ali had two sons, Safdar Ali and Hasan Ali, and several daughters. One of the daughters was married to Chanda Saheb and another to Murtaz Ali, both kinsmen of the Nawab. In 1736, as we have already seen, Chanda Saheb seized the throne of Madurai. In 1740, the Marathas, instigated by the Nizam (the Subadar of the Deccan), overrun the Carnatic and routed and killed Dost Ali and his younger son Hasan Ali. Safdar Ali then lost no time in proclaiming himself as the Nawab and bought off the Marathas and induced them to attack Tiruchirappalli where Chanda Saheb had become independent. In 1741 Tiruchirappalli surrendered to the Marathas, and Chanda Saheb, upon his failing to pay the ransom was taken as prisoner to Satara. The disappearance of Chanda Saheb strengthened the hands of Safdar Ali, but he still felt his position insecure, since Nizam-ul-Mulk had refused to recognize him as the Nawab. He, therefore, sought and obtained the aid of the English, sent his family to Madras and proceeded to Vellore to seek the aid of Murtaz Ali, its killedar. Murtaz Ali, one of the craftiest chieftains of those turbulent times, gave him a warm reception, but in October 1742 suddenly assassinated him and proclaimed himself as the Nawab. The army, however, obliged him to fly and proclaimed Safdar Ali's son, Saheb Jedda, as the Nawab under the title of Muhammad Said. The English recognized him as the Nawab, but the Nizam did not. In 1743 Nizam-ul-Mulk arrived at Arcot and when the young Nawab visited him, promptly made him a prisoner. He promised to consider the boy's claim when he reached the man's estate and in the meantime appointed Kwaja Abdulla Khan as the Nawab and, upon the latter's sudden death, Anwar-ud-din Khan as the Nawab, and specially recommended Sahib Jedda to his care. But Murtaz Ali, apparently at the instigation of Anwar-ud-Din, assassinated the boy [2].

Close on the heels of these kaleidoscopic changes came the news of a declaration of war between France and England and this led to the establishment of a closer bond of union between the English and the Nawab. Anwar-ud-Din received overtures from the English as well as the French and secretly rejoiced at the capture of Madras by the French. But his days were numbered and his son, Muhammad Ali, was very soon compelled to seek the English aid. On the death of Nizam-ul-Mulk, in

---

1 *History of Mysore* by Mark Wilks, Vol. I, 1869, pages 143—148.
Mysore by B. L. Rice, Vol. I, 1897, pages 370—372.

2 *Studies in Madras Administration* by Dr. B. S. Baliga, Vol.I, 1949, pages 262—263.

1748, both his son Nazar Jang and his grandson Muzafar Jang, claimed the title of Nizam and Muzafar Jang, in order to strengthen his claims, came to the south with an army, allied himself with Chanda Saheb—lately released by the Maharashtras—and Duplex and, with the aid of a picked French force, attacked, defeated and killed Anwar-ud-Din in the battle of Ambur (August 1749). This led to the arrival of Nazar Jang to the south with a large army. He allied himself with the English, called for a contingent of Mysore troops (which incidentally included Hyder and his men) and attacked Muzafar Jang and took him prisoner. But very soon the French became victorious and through the treachery of the Nawabs of Cuddapah, Kurnool and Savanur, assailed Nazar Jang and slew him in battle. In the confusion that ensued, Hyder secured two camel loads of coins belonging to Nazar Jang and safely sent them to Devanahalli. The French then took Muzafar Jang in triumph to Pondicherry and from there, with Chanda Saheb, marched to Tiruchirappalli where Muhammad Ali had entrenched himself. Muhammad Ali now frantically applied to the English and Mysore for help promising the latter the cession of Tiruchirappalli itself after the war. The English sent him a strong force to repel the attack and in the war that followed Clive defended Arcot against the army of Chanda Saheb. Deva Raj hesitated and counselled prudence, but Nanja Raj, tempted by the promise, threw prudence to the winds and taking Hyder and his troops flew to Tiruchirappalli. The French were reduced to great straits and Chanda Saheb was compelled to seek refuge with the English ally, the Raja of Tanjore, by whom he was murdered. Eventually, the war was terminated by the Anglo-French treaty of 1754. Muhammad Ali having now become secure in his position easily broke his promise and Nanja Raj had to return home with Hyder (1755) empty handed, notwithstanding all his intrigues with the French and the Nawab's officers. He would have, indeed, gone on hammering at the gates of Tiruchirappalli but for the fact that he received a summons from Deva Raj to return at once to face the financial crisis caused by his wars and the sudden appearance of the Nizam, Salabat Jang, with a strong force under Bussey to demand arrears of tribute. Nanja Raj could do nothing. Deva Raj had to sell even the plate and jewels belonging to the temples and the Raja's household and prevail on the bankers to give adequate security in order to satisfy the Nizam and send him home[1].

---

1 *Studies in Madras Administration* by Dr. B. S. Baliga, Vol. I, 1949, page 263
History of Mysore by Mark Wilks, Vol. I, 1869, pages 149—207.
Mysore, by B. L. Rice, Vol. I, 1897, pages 371—374.
Haidar Ali, by N. K. Sinha, 1949, pages 16—19.

Soon afterwards Hyder, in recognition of services rendered at Tiruchirappalli, was appointed as the Faujdar of Dindigul which had been ten years back conquered by Mysore, but which was still giving not a little trouble owing to the intrigues of Muhammad Ali with its palayakars. Here came Hyder with his Beder peons and Pindari horsemen augmented by the troops he had recruited from among those discharged by Nanja Raj after his Tiruchirappalli expedition. He had with him about 5,000 regular infantry, 25,000 horses, 2,000 peons and 6 guns and with the help of these he rapidly restored order. He also plundered the chiefs in the neighbourhood, established an arsenal under the superintendence of French artificers obtained from Pondicherry and thus laid a secure foundation for his future ascendancy. And all this time his interests in Mysore were looked after by his able manager and agent, Khande Rao, who never failed to sing his praises in the ears of Nanja Raj [1].

About this time (1756) the young Raja entered into a plot for confining his ministers and taking all power into his own hands. The plot was discovered. Deva Raj was not inclined to take harsh measures against the plotters; but Nanja Raj, who had by now more than once offended Deva Raj by his rashness, stormed the palace and in the presence of the Raja himself cut off their ears and noses. This disgusted Deva Raj and he consequently retired and settled down at Satyamangalam in Coimbatore and revoked the assignments made to Hyder, in order to meet his own expenses. Upon this Khande Rao advised Hyder to return to Seringapatam at once, but before he could return, the Marathas came under Balaji Rao, demanding a large contribution. Seringapatam was besieged and reduced to extremity and Nanja Raj had to pay 32 lakhs of rupees, partly in cash and partly in assignments of land. The Marathas then departed leaving their agents and part of their troops in the pledged districts. But the moment Hyder returned, he induced Nanja Raj to withhold payment of revenue to the Maharashtras and going to Satyamangalam secured from Deva Raj his own revenues that had been resumed as well as a promise of 3 lakhs of rupees for the expenses he had incurred in sending an expedition to Malabar just before his return. He, however, surrendered his claims to the military contributions from Malabar and Deva Raj accordingly sent thither Hari Singh, a brave Rajput commander and rival of Hyder, to realise them. Hyder then departed to Dindigul only to be called back again to suppress a mutiny of the Mysore army. The army having not been paid for months, clamoured for their arrears

---

1 *Haidar Ali and Tipu Sultan*, by L. B. Bowring, 1893, pages 25—27.
History of Mysore, by Mark Wilks, Vol. I, 1896, pages 216—219.
Mysore, by B.L. Rice, Vol. I, 1897, pages 374-375.

of salary and threatened Nanja Raj. Hyder first effected a reconciliation between Nanja Raj and Deva Raj and then by firmness and tact completely silenced the clamours of the mutineers by a settlement of their just claims. This was one more feather in his cap. Deva Raj died within a few days and Nanja Raj became more and more dependant on Hyder. Hyder, however, still feared Hari Singh's ascendancy and planned to remove him with his characteristic ruthlessness. He sent a force to encounter Hari Singh who was then returning from Malabar and this force fell upon the brave Rajaput at night while he was encamping in Coimbatore at Avanashi and massacred him and a great part of his troops. Hyder also received at this time from Nanja Raj an assignment on the revenues of Coimbatore in lieu of the three lakhs promised by Deva Raj. This made his position still more strong.[1]

It became much more strong a little later. Early in 1759 the Marathas invaded Mysore under Gopal Rao Patvardhan and, after reoccupying all the pledged districts, suddenly invested Bangalore and sent a detachment to surprise Channapatna. Hyder was now appointed to the chief command of the army to repel the invasion. He relieved Bangalore and Channapatna, put up a stubborn resistance and compelled Gopal Rao to come to terms. It was arranged that the Marathas should relinquish all claim to the districts formerly pledged to them and that Mysore should pay 32 lakhs of rupees in discharge of all demands, past and present. Sixteen lakhs were paid in cash by imposing a forced levy on all people and for the rest Hyder gave his personal security to the Maratha bankers on the understanding that he should have the management of the restored districts in order to realise the amount. The Maharashtras then withdrew to their own country and Hyder returned in triumph to Seringapatam where he was received by the Raja in a splendid durbar and given the title Fatte Hyder Bahadur.[2]

Within a short time he reached the highest position in the State, the position occupied by Nanja Raj himself, by a combination of fortuitous circumstances. The pay of the troops again fell into arrears and he was

1 *History of Mysore* by Mark Wilks, Vol. I, 1869, pages 219–228.
Mysore by B.L. Rice, Vol. I, 1897, pages 375–376.
Haidar Ali and Tipu Sultan by L.B. Bowring, 1893, pages 28–29.
Haidar Ali by N. K. Sinha, 1949, pages 19–22.
Military Despatch to England, dated 6th June 1757, paragraphs 17–22.
Military Despatch to England, dated 13th March 1758, paragraph 16.

2 *History of Mysore*, by Mark Wilks, Vol. I, 1869, pages 228–230.
Mysore by B. L. Rice, Vol. I, 1897, pages 376–377.
Haidar Ali and Tipu Sultan by L.B. Bowring, 1893, pages 28–30.
Haidar Ali by N. K. Sinha, 1949, pages 23–25.

again called upon, this time by the Raja, to satisfy their demands. He said that he would gladly undertake this task provided Nanja Raj was pensioned off and sent into retirement. And when this was done, not without however some difficulty, he secured fresh assignment on lands covering almost half the kingdom, appointed Khande Rao as his pradhani and, through his skilful management, met the demands of the troops. Having thus practically become supreme, he entered into an alliance with the French promising them assistance against the English and Muhammad Ali on condition of their promising to cede to him Tiruchirappalli, Madurai and Tirunelveli, after the conclusion of the war. And true to his word he forthwith took possession of Baramahal and Anekal, occupied Tiagadurg (yielded by the French) and sent Makhdum Ali with his troops into the Carnatic. Makhdum Ali won an unexpected victory at Tiruvadi, but the ambitious prospects which this opened up were blighted by a royal plot to overthrow Hyder. The royal party now headed by Khande Rao, who had deserted Hyder, and assisted by a Maratha force under Visaji Pandit, very nearly caught Hyder when he was encamped at Seringapatam; but he managed to escape to Anekal and thence to Bangalore and to send word to Makhdum Ali to return at once. Makhdum Ali, hard pressed by the Marathas on this return march, found it impossible to join forces with Hyder. Hyder's position became critical, but at the last moment fate saved him. The famous battle of Panipat which took place at this time laid low the Marathas everywhere. Visaji anxious to return home expressed willingness to negotiate and, on the payment of 3 lakhs of rupees and a promise of cession of Coimbatore and Salem, withdrew to the north. The moment Visaji turned his back, however, Hyder refused to cede Coimbatore and Salem, despatched thither Makhdum Ali to secure the revenues and himself proceeded against Khande Rao to whom place after place was yielding. He had a small army and Khande Rao had no difficulty in defeating him in an open action. But shortly afterwards he returned with a considerable army having induced Nanja Raj to lend his name as well as his household troops to put down the rebellion. Even this did not give him superiority over Khande Rao who was then camping with his whole army at Katte Malvadi. He, therefore, fabricated letters in the name and with the seal of Nanja Raj to the principal officers of Khande Rao's army directing them to deliver up the rebel at once. This ruse worked. Khande Rao, thinking himself betrayed, mounted his horse and fled to Seringapatam. And, as soon as Hyder came to know this, he fell upon the royal forces and routed them. He then descended the ghats, took all forts in Salem and Coimbatore that had declared for the rebels and returning to Seringapatam with a large force crushed Khande Rao and his army and prevailed upon the Raja to resign the entire management of the kingdom into his hands. He imprisoned Khande Rao, once his friend and now his enemy, in an iron cage like a parrot.[1]

His usurpation was now complete (1761). He became supreme in Mysore and tried to become supreme in South India. At that time Salabat Jang had been imprisoned by one of his own brothers, Nizam Ali Khan, while his other brother, Basalat Jang, who was in charge of Adoni, had been meditating the reduction of Sira, then in the hands of the Marathas. Basalat Jang finding Sira impregnable advanced upon Hoskote, another Maratha stronghold not far from Bangalore, but here also he met with stubborn opposition. Hyder now saw his opportunity. He opened negotiations with Basalat Jang as a result of which the latter, in return for a gift of three lakhs of rupees, invested him with the office of the Nawab of Sira, styling him in the deed of investiture as 'Hyder Ali Khan Bahadur'. He then speedily united his forces with those of Basalat Jang and captured Hoskote, Dodda Bellapur and Sira. At Sira, Basalat Jang left Hyder, being called to the north by the hostile movements of Nizam Ali who had now proclaimed himself as the Subadar of the Deccan. But Hyder pushed on his conquests, attacking and reducing Ckikka Bellapur, defeating Morari Rao of Gooty who had come for its relief and capturing one after another the possessions of Morari Rao, Kodikonda, Penukonda and Madakasira. Returning then to Sira he received the submission of the chiefs of Rayadurga and Harpanahalli and forced the submission of the chief of Chitaldurg[2].

While he was encamped near Chitaldurg his assistance was solicited to replace on the throne of Bednur an individual who gave himself out to be the legitimate heir to the throne of Bednur—a small kingdom in the Malnad in the hilly country of the west coast whose king had died a short while ago. His opportunism made him embrace the cause of the pretender at once. In 1763 he divided his troops into four columns and, having seized Shimoga, proceeded to Kuneri. Here he found the imprisoned minister of the late king who readily undertook to be his guide through the wild country between Kuneri and Bednur. On his approach, the widowed Rani, affrighted, twice offered him large sums of

---

[1] *History of Mysore* by Mark Wilks, Vol. I, 1869, pages 230–267.
Mysore by B.L. Rice, Vol. I, 1897, pages 377–381.
Haidar Ali and Tipu Sultan by L. B. Bowring, 1893, pages 31–34.
Haidar Ali by N. K. Sinha, 1949, pages 27–36.
Military Despatch to England, dated 3rd November 1760, paragraphs 13–16.

[2] *History of Mysore* by Mark Wilks, Vol, I, 1896, pages 268–275.
Mysore by B.L. Rice, Vol. I, 1897, page 381.
Haidar Ali by N. K. Sinha, 1949, pages 37–40.

money to return, but he pressed onwards rejecting all overtures. He took the Rani by complete surprise and collected from her palace, which had been set on fire, a huge booty valued at 12 million sterling. He made short work of her and her lover by arresting and sending them both as common prisoners to the hill fort of Madhugiri. He also, at the same time, despatched detachments which captured the fortified island of Basavaraj-durga, as well as Honavar and Mangalore on the west coast.

This conquest of Bednur, characterised by daring and ruthlessness, was always spoken of by Hyder as the foundation of all his subsequent greatness. He at first thought of making Bednur, which he now named Hydernagar, his capital, and made plans for building there a palace, an arsenal and a mint, besides a dockyard on the coast. He tried to build a navy on the west coast which could command the western sea and protect his western dominions. But a severe attack of illness and a conspiracy in which some 300 persons were implicated frustrated these projects. He hanged all the conspirators, suppressed all signs of revolt and, after conquering the small territory of Sunda, north of Bednur, returned to Mysore.[1]

He now deemed it prudent to appease the Marathas and the Nizam, the former for the seizure of Sira and the possessions of Morari Rao and the latter for accepting the title of Nawab from his brother, and sent embassies and gifts to both. Nizam Ali was pacified, but the Marathas could not be reconciled. He, therefore, resolved to anticipate a Maratha invasion, conquered Savanur and carried the Mysore frontier almost right up to the Krishna. When Gopal Rao, the chief of Miraj, was sent with a considerable force to attack him, he defeated him, but when Madhav Rao, the greatest of the Peshwas, crossed the Krishna with an immense army, he found his position becoming precarious. Madhav Rao inflicted severe defeats upon him in the open field at Rattihalli and Anavatti, retook all his recent conquests in the north, drove him to Bednur and forced him to sue for peace. According to a treaty which was then concluded (February 1765), the Marathas retired on the restoration of all places taken from Morari Rao of Gooty and the chief of

[1] *History of Mysore* by Mark Wilks, Vol. I, 1869, pages 275–281.
Mysore by B. L. Rice, Vol. I, 1897, pages 381–382.
Haidar Ali and Tipu Sultan by L. B. Bowring, 1893, pages 34–39
Haidar Ali by N. K. Sinha, 1949, pages 40–45.

Savanur and the payment of 32 lakhs of rupees. Sira was, however, left in Hyder's hands.[1]

But even this severe blow failed to affect his spirits. He could always face adversity with courage and rise above it. During these wars his recent acquisitions on the east had blazed up in a flame of rebellion. He now sent thither his brother-in-law, Mir Ali Reza, to restore his authority. The palayakar of Chikka Ballapur was starved out on Nandi-durga, was forced to surrender and sent as a prisoner with his family first to Bangalore and then to Coimbatore. Nor was this all. He planned a conquest of Malabar when Ali Raja, the Mopla chieftain of Cannanore, a feudatory of the Kolatiri Raja, applied to him for assistance. After leaving a force at Basavapatna for the security of the north, he, with his whole army, descended into Malabar early in 1766. He subdued the northern chiefs of Malabar in spite of the stiff resistance put up by their Nayar troops and in spite of the wooded nature of the country, and then coming south reduced the Zamorin and, after receiving the submission of the Rajas of Cochin and Palghat, proceeded to Coimbatore. When these Malabar chieftains rebelled in less than three months of his departure, he marched back to Malabar again, despite the inclemencies of weather, subdued them once more and, in order to strike terror into the insurgents, beheaded or hanged some prisoners and deported the rest wholesale to the plains of Mysore where thousands of them perished from hunger and misery[2].

During these operations, the pageant king, Chikka Krishna Raja, had died and Hyder had sent instructions to install the Raja's eldest son, Nanja Raja, then eighteen years of age, in his place. On arriving at the capital in 1677 he discovered that the new Raja was by no means disposed to remain subservient. He, therefore, immediately resumed the three lakhs of pagodas allowed to the Raja, plundered the palace of every article of value, and placed over it his own guards. But fresh difficulties now began to assail him. The Marathas having formed a coalition with the Nizam and the English for the purpose of invading Mysore, came down and, although he endeavoured to arrest their progress by sending an envoy to negotiate terms, Madhav Rao, the Peshwa, advanced steadily forward with a large army. Hyder resorted to the scorched earth

---

1 *History of Mysore* by Mark Wilks, Vol. I, 1869, pages 281–287.
Mysore by B. L. Rice, Vol. I, 1897, page 383.
Haidar Ali and Tipu Sultan by L. B. Bowring, 1893, pages 40–41.
Haidar Ali by N. K. Sinha, 1949, pages 46–52.

2 *History of Mysore* by Mark Wilks, Vol. I, 1869, pages 287–294.
Mysore by B. L. Rice, Vol. I, 1897, pages 383–384.
Haidar Ali and Tipu Sultan by L. B. Bowring, 1893, pages 42–46.

policy; he broke down the embankments of the reservoirs, poisoned the wells and drove away the peasantry into the woods. But Madhav Rao overcame all these obstacles, arrived at Rayadurga and marched to Sira. Here Mir Sahib, Hyder's brother-in-law, betrayed his trust and surrendered Sira in return for Gurramkonda, the possession of his ancestors. Hyder now made strenuous efforts to treat with the Marathas who had overrun all the east and, at length, through the skilful diplomacy of his envoy, Appaji Ram, induced Madhav Rao to withdraw on receiving 35 lakhs of rupees, half of which sum was to be paid down on the spot and the remainder to be realised later from the district of Kolar. On Nizam Ali's arrival soon afterwards with an English contingent, Hyder persuaded him into an alliance with himself against the English. Meanwhile discovering that Nanja Raj, the old minister, was intriguing with the Marathas and the Nizam, he enticed him to come to Seringapatam on the plea that his advice was needed at that crisis and, when he came, promptly made him prisoner and reduced his allowances to the barest necessaries of life.[1]

And now began his wars with the English, who had ever since the capture of Pondicherry from the French (1761) became the supreme masters in the Carnatic. By this time Muhammad Ali, the Nawab of Arcot, having owed everything to them, had practically become their dependant. They had also by then allied themselves with the Marathas and the Nizam and planned a joint invasion of Mysore. It was this plan that had brought the Marathas and Nizam Ali into Mysore. It has already been shown how Hyder had detached them both from the English. He now joined forces with Nizam Ali, and suddenly descending the ghats, attacked Colonel Joseph Smith who was in command of the English troops on the frontier. Smith was taken by surprise, but he repulsed Hyder in an action which took place at Changam, and shortly afterwards joining forces with Colonel Wood defeated him again in the battle of Tiruvannamalai (September 1767). But Hyder captured Tirupathur and Vaniambadi and besieged the strong fort of Ambur until it was relieved by Smith. The English then attacked him at Vaniambadi which he evacuated. But learning that a convoy with large supplies was on its way to join the English forces, he made a desperate attack upon it at Singarapetta in which he narrowly escaped being shot, a shot having hit and killed his horse. Just at this moment, his treacherous ally, Nizam Ali, having received intimation that the English had sent a force to attack his own territory, deserted him, made peace with the English (Treaty of 22nd

1 *History of Mysore* by Mark Wilks, Vol. I, 1869, pages 294–310.
Mysore by B. L. Rice, Vol. I, 1897, page 384.

March 1768) and marched northwards leaving him to fight the English alone. Hyder having now heard that an English fleet had been sent from Bombay for capturing his ports on the West Coast, marched with all haste to that coast, retook Mangalore, Honavar, and Basavaraj-durga which had all fallen to the English, and after levying heavy contributions on Bednur and Malabar for having assisted the English, returned quickly to Mysore. During his absence, Wood captured all places in Salem and Coimbatore up to Dindigul, while Smith, after capturing the stronghold of Krishnagiri, advanced into the Mysore plateau and took Mulbagal, Kolar and Hosur. Seringapatam itself was now in danger. At this crisis, divided counsels in Madras and the Nawab's inability to furnish supplies, prolonged the operations and saved Mysore, although the English had by this time succeeded in inducing Morari Rao to join them with his Maharashtra troops. As soon as Hyder returned he made a desperate attempt to surprise the camp of Morari Rao, but failed. Then sending off his family and treasure to Savandurga, he tried to prevent Wood from joining Smith. In this also he failed. Everything looked dark and ominous. But he never lost courage and resourcefulness. With a brilliant brain wave he passed rapidly by a circuitous route, east and north, to Gurramkonda, induced Mir Saheb to return to his allegiance, and with the latter's troops returned reinforced towards Kolar. But still fearing the probable investment of Bangalore, he made overtures for peace to the English offering to cede Baramahal and to pay 10 lakhs of rupees. The Madras Government, however, egged on by Muhammad Ali, made extravagant demands which Hyder refused to comply with[1].

Hostilities thereupon began again. Hyder took Mulbagal, then garrisoned by the Nawab's troops, and repulsed Wood who came to its relief. But very soon, thinking that Smith had come to reinforce Wood,

---

1 *Military Despatch to England*, dated 22nd January 1867, paragraphs 67–77.
Idem, dated 21st March 1767, paragraphs 1–4.
Idem, dated 5th April 1767, paragraphs 1–4, 9.
Idem, dated 21st September 1767, paragraphs 1–23.
Idem, dated 8th October 1767, pragraphs 1–2.
Idem, dated 5th March 1768, paragraphs 1–14.
Idem, dated 11th May 1768, paragraphs 1–14.
Idem, dated 8th September 1768, paragraphs 1–10.
Idem, dated 1st November 1768, paragraphs 39–49.
Idem, dated 16th November 1768, paragraphs 1–4.
Secret Despatch from England, dated 25th March 1768, paragraphs 21–45.
Idem, dated 23rd March 1770, paragraphs 6–21.
History of Mysore by Mark Wilks, Vol. I, 1869, pages 311–338.
Mysore by B. L. Rice, Vol. I, 1897, pages 384–385.
Haidar Ali and Tipu Sultan by L. B. Bowring, 1893, pages 49–53.
Haidar Ali by N. K. Sinha, 1949, pages 70–86.

he retired. When, however, he learnt that he was mistaken he resumed the charge but was driven back by Wood, both sides suffering heavily. When Smith soon afterwards joined Wood, Hyder disappeared with his army and refused to be drawn into a regular engagement. He was here, there and everywhere, harassing the English with his cavalry and easily evading pursuit, but all the same, cutting off all their supplies. Just then Smith was recalled because of his failure to force Hyder into a general action and Wood was given the command. Hyder at once beseiged Hosur, attacked Bagalur and compelled Wood to withdraw to Hoskote and finally to Kolar. Wood was now recalled and replaced by Colonel Lang, who, however, could achieve nothing. Hyder then went southward towards Coimbatore, and retook Salem, Attur, Namakkal, Erode and Dindigul, in short all Wood's conquests in addition to Karur. From Coimbatore he descended into the Carnatic and marched towards Cuddalore and Madras, carrying fire and sword into the enemys' country. This movement so alarmed the Madras Government that they despatched Captain Brooke to offer terms of peace. In the interview which ensued Hyder showed a desire to arrange matters seeing clearly that the friendship with the English would be more advantageous to him than their hostility, but he resolutely set his face against any concessions to the treacherous and selfish Nawab of Arcot, whom he detested. As, however, the influence of the Nawab was then predominant in the counsels of the Madras Government, the negotiation proved fruitless and hostilities were resumed again. Hyder now, with that indomitable energy that characterised him, sent off the main body of his army to retire westward through the Attur Pass, and himself with a chosen army of 6,000 horses and a very small infantry, made a sudden appearance at St. Thomas Mount and threatened Madras. Here he practically dictated his own terms to the English. They were not, however, harsh. They were finally embodied in the treaty of 29th March 1769. This treaty prescribed that in case either of the contracting parties should be attacked by other powers mutual assistance should be rendered to drive the enemy out. It also prescribed that a mutual restoration of conquered districts and an exchange of prisoners should be made. Thus ended what is known as the First Mysore War. Hyder then returned leisurely to Kolar and thence to Bangalore[1].

---

[1] *Military Despatch to England*, dated 8th March 1769, paragraphs 1–26.
Idem, dated 26th June 1769, paragraphs 2–30.
Separate Letter, dated 27th June 1769, paragraphs 1–4.
History of Mysore by Mark Wilks, Vol. I, 1897, pages 338–372.
Mysore by B. L. Rice, Vol. I, 1897 pages 385–386.
Haidar Ali and Tipu Sultan by L. B. Bowring, 1893, pages 53–58.
Haidar Ali and Tipu Sultan by N. K. Sinha, 1949, pages 70–86.

He was, however, soon again in the field to meet the impending Maratha invasion. As a preliminary measure, after obtaining the tacit assent of Nizam Ali, he moved north-east, levied contributions on the Nawabs of Cuddapah and Kurnool and awaited the arrival of the Marathas and, as soon as they invaded his territory, he applied to the English for assistance in accordance with the treaty of 1769. But the English sent him no assistance, thus clearly violating the terms of the treaty, and left him alone to bear the brunt of the Maratha attack. Knowing his inability to meet the foe in the open field, he retreated southwards to his capital, laying waste the country as he retired ; but finding his position still precarious, he sent an envoy to treat for terms. Madhav Rao demanded a crore of rupees; Hyder would offer only 12 lakhs. Hostilities, therefore, were re-commenced. Madhav Rao conquered the whole of the north and east of the country, his progress being checked only by a gallant defence of the little fort of Nijagal which was at last taken by the palayakar of Chitaldurg who had joined the Marathas. But Madhav Rao soon fell ill and returned to Poona, leaving Trimbak Rao in command. Emboldened by this change Hyder took the field, but met with no success and, while he was retreating through the Melukote hills, was attacked by the Marathas and routed at Chinkurali (March 1771). He then fled on horseback to Seringapatam where Tipu, who was supposed to have been lost, came and joined him. This was another dark hour in his life. But the Marathas instead of pushing home the attack, wasted their time in dividing the spoils and finally, when they invested Seringapatam, agreed to depart on his proposing to pay at once 15 lakhs of rupees and a like sum afterwards on the security of some of his districts (June 1772). During the course of these hostilities, having found out that Nanja Raja, the king, had been in secret communication with the enemy, he ordered him to be strangled and substituted for him, his brother Chama Raja[1].

---

1 *Military Despatch to England*, dated 16th September 1769, paragraphs 2–6.
Idem, dated 21st November 1769, paragraph 2.
Idem, dated 6th April 1770, paragraph 2.
Idem, dated 4th June 1770, paragraph 1.
Idem, dated 10th September 1770, paragraphs 1–2.
Idem, dated 29th September 1770, paragraphs 1–10.
Idem, dated 21st January 1771, paragraphs 19–20.
Idem, dated 6th February 1771, paragraphs 1–31.
Idem, dated 20th July 1771, paragraphs 10–11.
Idem, dated 9th October 1771, paragraph 11.
Idem, dated 28th February 1771, paragraph 14.
Idem, dated 4th July 1772, paragraph 4.
History of Mysore by Mark Wilks, 1869, pages 373–384.
Mysore by B. L. Rice, Vol. I, 1897, pages 386–387.
Haidar Ali and Tipu Sultan by L. B. Bowring, 1893, pages 59–63
Haidar Ali by N. K. Sinha, 1949, pages 95–113.

Madhav Rao died in November 1772 and his successor Narayana Rao was killed in August 1773 and Raghunatha Rao, or Raghoba then usurped the power of the Peshwa. The elevation of Raghoba was vehemently opposed by the famous Balaji Janardhan, commonly called Nana Farnavis, the Finance Minister of Madhav Rao, who supported the claims of Narayana Rao's posthumous son. Hyder took full advantage of these troubles. He sent an embassy to Madras to form an alliance with the English, despatched Tipu to the north to recover the places ceded to the Marathas and, interfering in a succession dispute in Coorg, suddenly invaded that country and reached its capital, Mercara. The Coorgs who were entirely unprepared were surrounded by his troops and massacred ; the landholders were confirmed in their possessions on a moderately increased rent ; a fort was erected at Mercara ; and Devaiya, the Raja who had fled, was captured and sent to Seringapatam. This done, Hyder despatched a force through Wynad to Calicut and speedily achieved the reconquest of Malabar which had shown symptoms of independence. By this time Tipu had been equally successful in the north so that, by the beginning of 1774, Hyder completely recovered all the territory he had lost. He next made a treaty with Raghoba—little caring who the rightful claimant was—by which he engaged to support Raghoba's pretensions in consideration of the tribute payable from Mysore being reduced to six lakhs. Shortly afterwards a serious insurrection broke out in Coorg owing to the oppressive exactions of his revenue officials, but he marched there again with a strong force and suppressed the rebellion, hanging without remorse all its leaders. He returned to Seringapatam early in 1775 and, as his negotiations with the English had come to nothing on account of the intrigues of Muhammad Ali, he turned towards an alliance with the French[1].

In 1776 the young king of Mysore died and was succeeded by another young king, Chama Raja IX, selected and appointed by Hyder. In the meantime Hyder had been fomenting dissensions in all the neighbouring countries through his Brahmin agents. Some of these agents succeeded in Bellary, the palayakar of which place renounced allegiance to the Nizam and, being attacked by Basalat Jang and the French under Lally, applied to Hyder for assistance. Hyder marched to his relief in the incredibly short space of five days, fell upon the besiegers before they

1 *Military Despatch to England*, dated 15th March 1774, paragraph 4.
Idem, dated 9th December 1775, paragraphs 12–13.
History of Mysore by Mark Wilks, Vol. I, 1869, pages 385–399.
Mysore by B. L. Rice, Vol. I, 1897, pages 387–388.
Haidar Ali and Tipu Sultan by L. B. Bowring, 1893, pages 64–68.
Haidar Ali by N. K. Sinha, 1949, pages 114–120.

new that he had left his capital and completely routed them, the commander being killed and Lally escaping with difficulty. But he promptly took their place in the batteries and forced the chief to surrender the fort to himself at discretion. He then proceeded to demand a heavy contribution from Morari Rao of Gooty and, when refused, besieged and took Gooty, stripped him of all his possessions and sent him as a prisoner first to Seringapatam and then to Kabbaldurga where he shortly afterwards died[1].

Meanwhile Raghoba's power had met with a reverse which caused him to fly to Surat and to enter into a treaty with the English to aid him in recovering his authority. Strengthened by this alliance (March 1775) he proposed to Hyder to occupy all the Maharashtra possessions up to the Krishna. Hyder lost no time in executing this plan. He summoned all the palayakars in the north to attend with their troops and overran Savanur; but the monsoon having by this time begun, he was compelled to return to Seringapatam. The result of this was that the Poona ministers and Nizam Ali declared war against him. They sent four chiefs in advance to clear Savanur of his troops, but his general Muhammad Ali skilfully and completely defeated them at Saunsi, taking two of them prisoners. The main armies of the confederates now arrived, the Maratha troops under Parasuram Bhau and the Nizam's troops under Ibrahim Khan. Hyder waited for them at Gooty, but Parasuram Bhau on hearing of the defeat of the advanced corps fell back beyond the Krishna for reinforcements, while Ibrahim Khan, either being afraid or being bribed, also retired beyond the Krishna. The rains then set in and hampered their movements, but Hyder marched to 'Chitaldurg to punish its palayakar who had deserted him and joined his enemies. Before, however, he could reduce Chitaldurg, hearing that the Marathas were approaching, he made peace with the palayakar and retired on receiving 13 lakhs of pagodas.

In the mean time the Maratha army commanded by Haripant, after waiting in vain for the Nizam's army to join it, crossed the Tungabhadra and encamped at Raravi where Hyder advanced to meet it. He had previously bribed Manoji Sindhia, an influential chief, to abandon Haripant at the decisive moment and to draw off his troops. But

1 *Military Despatch to England*, dated 9th December 1775, paragraphs 19–21.
Idem, dated 14th February 1775, paragraph 2.
History of Mysore by Mark Wilks, Vol. I, 1869, pages 393–396.
Mysore by B. L. Rice, Vol. I, 1897, page 388.
Haidar Ali and Tipu Sultan, by L. B. Bowring, 1893, pages 68–69.
Haidar Ali by N. K. Sinha, 1949, pages 121–123.

finding this wavering he directed demonstrations to be made in the form of pretended communications with him. This convinced Haripant of Manoji's treachery and he, therefore, overwhelmed him by a mass of cavalry and drove him off the field. He then retired across the river, effecting his retreat in good order although harassed by incessant assualts from Hyder's army. Hyder now proceeded to seize all the territory between the Tungabhadra and the Krishna, reducing the stronghold of Kopal and Gajendragarh with minor posts and capturing Dharwar after a long siege. All the local chiefs then tendered him their submission and, having made arrangements for the permanent occupation of the country, he returned to Mysore to wreak his vengeance on the palayakar of Chitaldrug who had failed to co-operate with him in his recent struggle. The palayakar, in spite of his gallant resistance, was reduced by treachery and sent to languish in prison at Seringapatam, and about 20,000 of his subjects, the Bedars, were also deported to Seringapatam. The young boys among the Bedars were afterwards converted and trained in the use of arms, forming what were called the Chela battalions. Hyder, next, took Cuddapah, put down sternly a conspiracy hatched there to slay him in his tent at night, and attacking Sidhout where the Nawab had taken refuge, reduced it and sent him as a prisoner to Seringapatam. He, however, married the Nawab's beautiful sister and placed her at the head of his seraglio under the title of Bakshi Begum[1].

His authority now having been firmly established, he commenced a scrutiny into several departments of the State. He appointed Mir Muhammad Sadik as his Finance Minister and Shamaiya as the head of police with powers not only to prevent crime but also to extract by force, if necessary, the ill-gotten gains of his revenue officers. Shamaiya organised an efficient espionage as well as a postal system but sometimes went to excesses, extorting money not only from the officials but also from the bankers. Hyder also gradually introduced, for what reason it is not known clearly, a system of payment called das mahi, or ten months pay to the troops in the year, instead of twelve months pay. About this time (1799) he arranged a double marriage with the family of the Nawab of Savanur, whose eldest son was united to Hyder's daughter. The ceremonies were celebrated with great pomp at Seringapatam and accompanied with the gift of the unrestored half of Savanur to the Nawab[2].

---

1 *History of Mysore* by Mark Wilks, Vol, I, 1869, pages 400–412.
Mysore by B. L. Rice, Vol. I, 1897, pages 389–391.
Haidar Ali and Tipu Sultan by L. B. Bowring, 1893, pages 69–77.

2 *History of Mysore* by Mark Wilks, Vol. I, 1869, pages 412–417.
Mysore by B. L. Rice, Vol. I, 1897, page 391.
Haidar Ali and Tipu Sultan, by L. B. Bowring, 1893, pages 79–89.

During the progress of these festivities an ambassador arrived at Seringapatam with proposals from the Poona Durbar that he should join the Marathas and the Nizam in expelling the English from South India. The Marathas had cause to resent the action of the Bombay Government in upholding the rights of Raghoba. The Nizam had cause to resent the action of the Madras Government in acquiring the Guntur Circar without his consent from Basalat Jang. Hyder too had cause to resent the manner in which he had been treated by the Madras Government. He had not been supplied with English aid in accordance with the treaty of 1769 when he had applied for it during the invasion of his territories by the Marathas. He had more than once sought an alliance with the Madras authorities but, every time, his advances had been repulsed, owing to the insidious influence exercised at Madras by Muhammad Ali, the Nawab of Carnatic. As if all this was not enough, when the war had broken out between England and France and Pondicherry had been captured from the French in 1778, the English had seized Mahe which he considered to be under his protection, in spite of his protests and threat that in the event of Mahe being attacked, he would retaliate by invading Arcot. And when the Guntur Circar was acquired, they had sent troops to occupy it, through his territory, without obtaining his permission for the passage of troops. To Schwartz, the well-known missionary, who had come as a trusted envoy from Sir Thomas Rumbold, the Governor of Madras, he had frankly recalled all that has passed and expressed his wish to maintain friendly relations with the English, if possible. But the Madras Government had promised no reparation. He, therefore, treated Mr. Gray, another envoy sent by the English to get the release of some prisoners, with scant courtesy and accepted the proposals of the ambassador sent by the Poona Durbar. These prescribed mutual co-operation on the part of the Marathas, the Nizam and Hyder, confirmed the possession of the territory held by Hyder up to the Krishna and fixed the tribute payable by him at 11 lakhs of rupees. The plan was that the Marathas were to invade Bedar, Central and Northern India, while Nizam Ali was to subjugate the Circars and Hyder was to conquer the Carnatic. The coalition was a formidable one and, when aided by the French, threatened the very existence of the British power in India[1].

---

1 *Military Despatch to England*, dated 13th March 1779, paragraphs 5–9.
Idem, dated 29th April 1779, paragraphs 2–4.
Idem, dated 14th October 1779, paragraph 23.
Idem, dated 12th February 1780, paragraph 5.
Idem, dated 3rd April 1780, paragraphs 14–15.
History of Mysore by Mark Wilks, Vol. I, 1869, pages 417–446.
Mysore by B. L. Rice, Vol. I, 1897, pages 391–392.
Haidar Ali and Tipu Sultan by L. B. Bowring, 1893, pages 80–86.
Haidar Ali by N. K. Sinha, 1949, pages 136–143 and 164–183.
A comprehensive History of India by H. Beveridge, Vol. II, 1867, pages 472–478.

Thus began the Second Mysore War. After prayers for success in both mosques and temples, Hyder left his capital and descended the Ghats in July 1780 with a force of 83,000 men, unequalled perhaps in strength and efficiency by any army that had ever been assembled in South India. French officers of ability guided its operations and the commisariat was under the management of Purnaiya, one of the Ministers of Finance. A choice body of horse under his second son Karim Sahib was sent to attack Porto Novo, while a larger body of horse and infantry proceeded towards Madras carrying destruction everywhere, up to St. Thomas Mount. Hyder himself proceeded to invade Arcot, but hearing of the movement of the British troops under Sir Hector Munro, the English Commander -in-Chief, he abandoned the siege. Munro was then camping at Kanchipuram awaiting the arrival of a force from Guntur under Colonel Baillie. Baillie reached the Corteliar, and although harassed by Tipu's cavalry, managed to join forces with Colonel Fletcher but as he reached Pollilur, both Hyder and Tipu fell upon him and, in spite of his gallant resistance, forced him to capitulate. This was a great victory and was commemorated at Seringapatam by a painting on the walls of the Darya Daulat Garden, where it is still to be seen.

Meanwhile Warren Hastings, the Governor General, who had seen how the British interests were suffering in the south, had despatched Sir Eyre Coote to Madras with full powers to prosecute the war. Hyder now besieged Arcot and tried to reduce the other forts of the English. But all of them held out except Ambur, and Coote having relieved Chingleput and occupied Karunguli, dislodged the enemy from Wandiwash which they were besieging. The sudden appearance of the French fleet off Madras at this time made it impossible for him to receive supplies by sea or to move to the north and so, after relieving Peramakoil (Perumalkoil), he moved towards Pondicherry with the object of preventing the French boats from landing. In this he was unsuccessful; nor was he successful in reducing the fortified temple of Chidambaram. A few days afterwards when the English fleet under Sir Edward Hughes arrived in Madras, Coote took the field. His movements were closely watched and harassed by Hyder, but at Porto Novo he attacked Hyder and inflicted a heavy defeat upon his forces. He then effected a junction with a force sent from Bengal, compelled Tipu to raise the siege of Wandiwash, captured the fortress of Tirupasur, and encountering Hyder on the very ground which had witnessed the disaster that had be fallen Colonel Baillie in the previous year, fought an engagement with him and compelled him to withdraw. Hyder now took up a strong position in the pass of Sholinghur to prevent the relief of Vellore which had been reduced almost to extremities; but he was again attacked by Coote and again compelled to withdraw. Vellore was saved and the palayakars of Chittoor now came over to the English. Hyder, indignant at their desertion, detached some troops to lay waste their country, but these were driven out by Coote. About the same time Colonel Braithwaite, then commanding a field force at Tanjore, took Nagapattinam occupied by Hyder's troops, but Tipu very soon attacked and defeated him and took him prisoner[1].

Hyder had naturally hoped that the Nizam and the Marathas would carry out their undertakings, but both these allies of his were won over to the English side by Warren Hastings. Hastings disavowed the transaction of the Guntur Circar and by ordering the immediate restitution of the Circar to the Nizam, disarmed his hostility. He, at the same time, by a mixture of force and diplomacy induced the Poona Durbar to enter into an important treaty with the English (the treaty of Salbai, 17th May 1782). The English by this treaty sacrificed much territory and gave up the cause of Raghoba but gained a great advantage over Hyder in asmuch as it detached the Marathas from him and provided for the restoration by him of all the conquests he had made from the English and the Nawab of Arcot. He was thus made to stand alone against the English.

Hyder, although deserted by his allies, unsupported by the French and threatened by rebellion in his western possessions—Malabar, Coorg, etc.—was not the man to abandon himself in despair. Having despatched Makhdum Ali to re-establish his authority in the west, he was about to leave the low country himself when he received the news of the landing at Porto Novo of the French troops he had long expected. Unfortunately for him the convoys bearing this succour, having been twice intercepted and mostly captured by the British men-of-war, the number of the troops that acutally landed was but small. Several actions took place between the rival English and French fleets in the Indian waters without any decisive results. The French troops, however, captured Cuddalore and after forming a junction with his troops carried Peramakoil (Perumalkoil) and returned to Pondicherry. Coote now marched towards Arni to attack

[1] *Military Despatch to England,* dated 1st October 1780, paragraphs 2–7.
Idem, dated 29th October 1780, paragraph 6.
Idem, dated 9th January 1781, paragraphs 19–55, 72–98, and 150.
Idem, dated 30th October 1781, paragraphs 10–38 and 59–62.
Idem, dated 22nd June 1781, paragraphs 1–30.
History of Mysore by Mark Wilks, Vol. I, 1869, pages 447–504.
Mysore by B. L. Rice, Vol. I, 1897, pages 392–394.
Haidar Ali and Tipu Sultan by L. B. Bowring, 1893, pages 87–99.
Haidar Ali by N. K. Sinha, 1949, pages 185–213.
A Comprehensive History of India by H. Beveridge, Vol. II, 1867, pages 479–499.

Hyder. Tipu and Lally harassed him while Hyder by his rapid movements evaded him. Hyder, however, managed by an ingenious ambuscade to decoy his mainguard and inflict upon it severe losses. Then came the monsoon when the English returned to Madras and Hyder to Arcot. Meanwhile, on the other coast, the troops sent to Malabar were completely defeated by Colonel Humberstone and the troops despatched from Bombay. In November, Tipu, on Hyder's orders and assisted by Lally, proceeded by forced marches to Malabar to retrieve the situation. The English were then preparing for the siege of Palghat. On his approach they retreated to Ponnani and here a battle was fought in which he sustained a reverse. Just at this time Hyder, who had for some time been suffering from a cancer in his back, died in his camp at Narasingarayanapet near Chittoor (December 7, 1782)[1].

Thus died a great ruler of whom not only Mysore but also all parts of his dominion, including Coimbatore, may be proud. He took the whole of South India as his field of action, fighting now here, now there, now everywhere, from the east to the west coast. When we think of him, we think of vast spaces over which he marched at the head of his cavalry with exceptional rapidity and celerity[2]. He was not quite successful in the open field. Whenever he met the Marathas under a great leader like Madhav Rao, he suffered defeats and whenever he met the English he refused to be drawn into a general action[3]. Nor was he quite successful in diplomacy, partly because he was too frank to conceal his intentions, partly because he was too powerful, too dangerous to be trusted, and partly also because he hated the Nawab of Arcot too strongly to make friends with the English[4]. He, however, knew where his interests lay and sought for an English alliance; but, as the English under the influence of

---

1 *Military Despatch to England*, dated 29th January 1782, paragraphs 8–16, 40–42, 44–61 and 69–91.

Idem, dated 26th March 1782, paragraphs 14–29.

Idem, dated 5th September 1782, paragraphs 41–44, 75–85, 125–165, 180, 200, 209 and 261.

Idem, dated 31st October 1782, paragraphs 41 and 104–105.

Idem, dated 29th January 1783, paragraphs 2–4.

History of Mysore by Mark Wilks, Vol. II, 1869, pages 1–33.

Mysore by B. L. Rice, Vol. I, 1897, page 395.

A Comprehensive History of India by H. Beveridge, Vol. II, 1867, pages 499–507.

2 *Haidar Ali and Tipn Sultan* by L. B. Bowring, 1893, pages 107–108.

Haidar Ali by N. K. Sinha, 1949, page 262.

3 This is clear from what has been stated above. *See* also.

Haidar Ali by N. K. Sinha, pages 265–266.

Haidar Ali and Tipu Sultan by L. B. Bowring, 1893, page 107.

4 This also has been already made clear.

the Nawab distrusted him and even repudiated the treaty of 1769 concluded with him, he turned to the French alliance[1]. He hoped that in his final struggle with the English, the French, the Marathas and the Nizam would stand by him firmly; but actually, while the French did little to assist him, the Marathas and the Nizam deserted him at the last moment and left him to face the English alone[2]. Nothing, however, daunted his valiant heart, nothing could overawe him, and he could almost always rise superior to circumstances, never desponding in defeat. A born soldier, an excellent rider, a good swordsman, a dead shot, he was brave, daring, reckless of personal danger and possessed of inexhaustible energy. These qualities, joined to his tenacity, resourcefulness and skill in military tactics, made him a great commander, always to be dreaded and never to be trifled with[3]. He excelled in cavalry tactics and by this weapon managed to inflict sudden and severe losses upon his enemies. Cool, collected and sagacious on the battlefield he knew how and where to strike with the greatest effect[4]. He relied mostly on cavalry but he did not neglect his infantry. He, in fact, sought to improve his army in every way. He employed French Officers and, through their help, tried to master the science of artillery, sieges and fortifications. He sought to build a navy to protect his western dominions from the insults and invasions of the European powers[5]. And given some years of peace, he would, indeed, have become very formidable, if not invincible.

In administration he was a conservative in various ways. He maintained the fiction of the rule of the Wodeiyars, never wishing to offend the feelings of his subjects. He issued coins (pagodas), copied from the coins of the Vijayanagar Emperors, retaining on many even the figures of the Hindu deities. He continued the central administrative machinery created by Chikkadeva Raja, consisting of eighteen departments such as the Atthavanam (Revenue Department), Kandacharam (Military Department), Sunkam (Customs Department), Devastanam (Religious Endowments Department), etc., infusing, however, into them a vigour unknown before. He employed the Brahmins, as before, to run most of the civil departments. He retained the palayakar and the kavali systems, purging them of most

---

1 *See* also page 92.

2 *See* above. *See* also *Haidar Ali and Tipu Sultan* by L. B. Bowring, 1893, page 113.

3 *History of Mysore* by Mark Wilks, Vol. II, 1869, page 376.
Mysore by B. L. Rice, Vol. I, 1897, page 396.
Hyder Ali and Tipu Sultan by L. B. Bowring, 1893, pages 107 and 113.

4 *Hyder Ali and Tipu Sultan* by L. B. Bowring, 1893, page 107

5 *See* above.

of the evils to which they were exposed by his efficient system of police and spies[1]. In revenue administration alone, as is clear from the system followed in Coimbatore during his time, he made some radical changes. He abolished the duties of the palayakars in the matter of land revenue collection and entrusted those duties to the Amildars. He abolished also the ancient system of division of produce and the payment of revenue in kind and introduced the system of survey and money assessment[2], and thereby paved the way for the ryotwari system under the British. These were obviously salutary changes, but we are told that his assessments were heavy and that they led to oppression. In other ways he, like his predecessors undertook irrigation works, constructed roads and tried to encourage trade[3]. He maintained the village system intact, making use of the services of the patels, the karnams and the talayaris, but there is nothing to show that he employed the panchayat system[4]. His Amildars combined in themselves the revenue, judicial as well as magisterial and police functions, and set the pattern for the early British Administration under the Collectors.

In person, he was of medium height, dark complexion, with an aquiline nose, small eyes, a mellow voice, a rather long neck and broad shoulders. His face was clean shaven, his countenance expressed a mixture of sternness and gentleness and his dress exhibited no jewelry or vanity but dignity. He ordinarily wore a long robe, and a scarlet turban but, while on the field, a uniform of white satin with gold flowers, yellow drawers, yellow velvet boots, and a white silk scarf round his waist[5]. Although he was unable to read and write any language, he spoke fluently Hindustani, Kannada, Marathi, Telugu and Tamil. He was besides a good conversationalist and an accurate appraiser of men. The only instance in which his judgment went wrong was in placing his trust in his treacherous manager, Khande Rao. He was endowed with an excellent memory and an admirable capacity for work. He had the gift of giving attention to several subjects at one and the same time so that he could hear a letter read, dictate his orders, talk to an ambassador or witness a theatrical

---

1 *Hyder Ali* by N. K. Sinha, 1949, pages 233–242.

2 *Manual of the Coimbatore District* by F. A. Nicholson, 1887, pages 93–94.

3 *Coimbatore Manual*, 1865, pages 173–174.
Hyder Ali by N. K. Sinha, 1949, pages 251–253.

4 *Hyder Ali* by N. K. Sinha, 1949, pages 250–251.

5 *History of Mysore* by Mark Wilks, Vol. II, 1869, pages 375–376.
Mysore by B. L. Rico, Vol. I, 1897, page 396.
Hyder Ali and Tipu Sultan by L. B. Bowring, 1893, page 110.
History of Mysore by C. Hayavadana Rao, Vol. II (1945), pages 269–272.

exhibition all at once, without being distracted by any of these occupations[1]. When he was not engaged in war he used to sit in public durbar from morning till past midday; at noon he used to take some rest for an hour or two and then return to public business either superintending the work of the various departments or issuing orders till far into the night. He could not tolerate inefficiency or oppression of his subjects by his officers. He could be abusive, rough and even very severe at times whenever his orders were disobeyed by his officers or whenever they misused their powers. He had them whipped soundly and made them disgorge their ill-gotten gains[2]. He organised a secret service which none could escape and of which everyone was afraid. He never showed any mercy or tenderness to the rivals, rebels or enemies. He placed them in irons, imprisoned them or ruthlessly suppressed them or transported them wholesale to his capital to be punished or trained as soldiers and made use of for his own purposes[3]. There was in him a streak of sternness which made him feared and respected; and possibly this was his asset since without it, he would have lost all power on more than one occasion. In religion he was entirely free from bigotry. He offered prayers in mosques as well as temples believing, as he did, that all religions proceed from one God and that all are equal in the eyes of God[4]. He showed not the least ill feeling to Hinduism, continuing as he did, the agraharams and the Brahmadeva and the devadanam inams[5]. In accordance with the custom of his age he often drank wines and liquors and kept a large harem; but he never went to excesses and never allowed either wine or women to interfere with the affairs of State[6].

The death of Hyder was concealed from the army by his ministers Purnaiya and Krishna Rao and while his body embalmed in a chest was sent secretly to Kolar, express messengers were despatched to the west coast to convey the news to Tipu. The moment he heard the news, Tipu broke up his camp near Ponnani, proceeded by forced marches to Kolar and, after performing the funeral ceremonies joined the main army which was then halting along with the French forces between Arni and Vellore (2nd January 1783). Within a week, however, he was suddenly called to

1 *History of Mysore* by Mark Wilks, Vol. II, 1869, page 376–377.

2 *History of Mysore* by Mark Wilks, Vol. II, 1869, pages 376–377.
Hyder Ali and Tipu Sultan by L. B. Bowring, 1893, page 108.
History of Mysore by C. Hayavadana Rao, Vol. III (1946), pages 500–501, 522–528.

3 *See* above.

4 *History of Mysore* by Mark Wilks, Vol. II, 1869, page 378.

5 *Hyder Ali* by N. K. Sinha, 1949, pages 243–245.

6 *History of Mysore* by Mark Wilks, Vol. II, 1869, page 376.
Mysore by B. L. Rice, Vol. I, 1897, page 396.

the west coast to regain his possessions. For, during his absence from that coast, General Mathews sent from Bombay had captured Hyderghar, Bednur, Honavar and Mangalore. Mathews' task had been rendered easy by the treachery of Shekh Ayaz, the Governor of Bednur, who, fearing Tipu, had surrendered the country to the English and fled with whatever treasure that could be siezed to Bombay. Tipu divided his army into two columns, with one retook Kavale-durga and Hyderghar and with the other Anantpur; and, cutting off all communications to the coast, invested Bednur, forced the English garrison to surrender and marched off, both officers and men, as prisoners to Seringapatam. He next invested Mangalore and, although the French deserted him at this time in accordance with the peace concluded between France and England, he pushed on the siege with vigour and compelled the English garrison to surrender. Meanwhile the English had entered into a plot with Tirumal Rao, and emissary of the Mysore Rani, for restoring the imprisoned Raja and an English Force under Colonel Fullarton had captured Palghat and Coimbatore. But the fruits of these victories were thrown away by the treaty of Mangalore which Tipu now forced upon the English. By this treaty (January 1784) which prescribed mutual restitutions of possessions seized and the surrender of prisoners, Tipu recovered possession of all the territory held by Hyder in Kanara and Malabar and regained Palghat and Coimbatore. This was a triumph to him; and, before returning to the upper country, he signalized his zeal for Islam by deporting from the west coast to Mysore a large number of Christians. All these were converted into Muslims and called 'Ahmadi' or praiseworthy and such of them as could be utilized for the army were formed into battalions of 500 each. About the same time he succeeded in killing a plot hatched by Shamaiya, for seizing the capital and restoring the Hindu Raj; the Raja was deposed, Shamaiya and his brother were confined in iron cages in which they perished and the rest of the conspirators were dragged at the feet of elephants. A revolt in Coorg next year led to the deportation of large number of its inhabitants to Mysore and their conversion to Islam, the occasion being marked by Tipu's assumption of the title of Nawab.[1]

---

1 *Military Despatches to England*, dated 29th January 1783, paragraphs 5–12, and 21–22.
Idem, dated 13th August 1783, paragraphs 13–18, 23–32, 43–56, 86–87, 99–102, 107, 135–198, 282–300, 340–480, and 512–513.
Idem, dated 30th September 1783, paragraphs 3, 9–18.
Idem, dated 14th October 1783, paragraphs 14–16, and 19–34.
Idem, dated 24th January 1784, paragraphs 8–28, and 35.
Idem, dated 1st February 1784, paragraph 3.
Idem, dated 8th June 1784, paragraphs 6, 9–17, 19, 26–27, 35–52.
Idem, dated 20th September 1784, paragraphs 3, 58–95, 123.
Idem, dated 13th December 1784, paragraphs 2–29.
History of Mysore by Mark Wilks, Vol. II, 1869, pages 33–97.
Mysore by B. L. Rice, Vol. I, 1897, pages 397–399.
Hyder Ali and Tipu Sultan by L. B. Bowring, 1893, pages 117–130.
A Comprehensive History of India by H. Beveridge, Vol. II, 1867, pages 507–527.

On returning from Coorg, Tipu tried to recover the territories formerly held by Hyder lying between the Krishna and the Tungabhadra. He attacked these territories which had now come under Maharashtra sway and also laid claim to Bijapur from the Nizam. This led to an alliance between the Nizam and the Marathas and, in the beginning of 1786, their joint forces came to invade Mysore. The Marathas were commanded by Haripant and the Nizam's forces by Tohavar Jang. They attacked Badami and took it, while Tipu suddenly dashed to Adoni and, in spite of the gallant resistance of the defenders captured it and, after joining forces with the Bednur division under Burhan-ud-din, proceeded to meet his enemies in the vicinity of Savanur. After many a desultory engagement he dislodged his enemies from their position and captured Savanur, the Nawab having previously fled to the Maratha camp. Early in 1787, however, he made peace with the Maharashtras agreeing to pay 45 lakhs of rupees as arrears of tribute, 30 at once and 15 after a year, and agreeing also to give up Badami, Adoni, Kittur and Nargund[1].

Returning shortly afterwards to his capital by way of Harpanahalli and Rayadurga, he directed the destruction of the old town and fort of Mysore, in order to obliterate all its associations with the deposed Raja. In January 1788 he descended on Calicut issued a proclamation denouncing the practice of polyandry and, after making many conversions, marched to Coimbatore and Dindigul and subdued the refractory palayakars. He then retuned in triumph to his capital and occupied himself in reforming his army. A rebellion having now occurred in Malabar on account of the oppression of Mir Ibrahim, his governor, he marched thither through Coorg and suppressed it with a stern hand, hanging the Raja of Chirakkal and offering the rebel Nairs the alternative of either conversion to Islam or deportation to Seringapatam. He divided Malabar into smaller units and placed over each of these units officers charged with the duties of collecting revenue, numbering the productive trees and giving religious instruction to the Hindu converts. He had by this time sent out embassies to Constantinople and Paris; and Louis XVI, the French King, had promised to support him in his struggles with the English. He now aspired to become supreme in South India and began his wars with the English by attacking Travancore[2].

---

1 *History of Mysore* by Mark Wilks, Vol. II, 1869, pages 98–118.
Mysore by B. L. Rice, Vol. I, 1897, page 400.
Hyder Ali and Tipu Sultan by L. B. Bowring, 1893, pages 131–134.

2 *History of Mysore* by Mark Wilks, Vol. II, pages 119–133.
Mysore by B. L. Rice, Vol. I, 1897, pages 400–401.
Hyder Ali and Tipu Sultan by L. B. Bowring, 1893, pages 135–138.

The Raja of Travancore had been an ally of the English and any attack upon him was bound to lead to a war with the English. But Tipu found that there was sufficient reason to teach a lesson to the Raja. In 1759 when the Zamorin of Calicut had overrun the territories of the Raja of Cochin, the Raja of Travancore had come to the aid of the latter and, after having driven out the former, had secured certain districts from Cochin. Over these districts he had erected a line of fortresses and, in order to complete this line had obtained from the Dutch the forts of Ayakota and Cranganore. Tipu now claimed that all these districts as well as the Dutch forts belonged to him as the overlord of Cochin and when the Raja of Travancore refused to acknowledge his claim, immediately attacked Travancore (29th December 1789). And, although he was first repulsed, and he narrowly escaped capture, having fallen into a ditch and lost his seals, rings and personal ornaments to the enemy, he finally collected all his forces, compelled the Travancore forces to retreat, demolished the whole line of fortifications and carried fire and sword into parts of Travancore[1].

The English had by then begun to realise full well the danger of allowing him to continue his conquests unopposed. Lord Cornwallis, the new Governor-General, had come to believe that he should be subdued at all costs. Cornwallis, therefore, brushed aside all excuses made by Tipu, entered into treaties with the Marathas and the Nizam binding them to unite against Tipu on the basis of an equal division of conquests and declared war against him. Thus began the Third Mysore War. The first stage of this was mostly confined to operations in Coimbatore and Salem, conducted under General Medows, the new Governor and Commander-in-Chief of Madras. The plan of the English campaign was that the main division under Medows, after taking all the forts of Coimbatore and Palghat, was to ascend to the tableland by the Gazzalhatty Pass, while another division under Colonel Kelly was to invade Baramahal (Salem). Medows took Karur, Dharapuram, Coimbatore, Dindigul and Erode besides several minor places. But, when a division under Colonel Floyd established itself at Satyamangalam, Tipu, leaving his heavy baggage at the top of the Ghat descended the Gazzalhatti Pass with a large body of cavalry and attacked it and forced it to retreat. Floyd's detachment arrived safely at Velladi where Medows met it having

---

1 *Political Despatch to England*, dated 5th January 1790, paragraphs 67–144.
Idem, dated 12th February 1790, paragraphs 20–21.
Idem, dated 16th September 1790, paragraphs 74–80, 88, 109–114.
History of Mysore by Mark Wilks, Vol. II, 1869, pages 134–155.
Mysore by B. L. Rice, Vol I, 1897, pages 401–402.
Hyder Ali and Tipu Sultan by L. B. Bowring, 1893, pages 139–144.

returned from Dannayakankottai on the way to Gazzalhatti. Tipu then imagining that Medow's march was a manoeuvre to get between him and Seringapatam retired across the Bhavani, while the English troops returned to Coimbatore. They were there joined by Colonel Stuart's division which had captured Palghat. The main object of this enterprise, the invasion of Mysore through the Gazzalhatti Pass, having been successfully frustrated by Tipu, he now marched rapidly southwards taking Erode, Dharapuram and other places. Then, hearing of the invasion of Baramahal by Colonel Maxwell who had succeeded Kelly, he proceeded thither with the greater part of his army and prevented him effectually from surprising Krishnagiri. During this inroad into Coimbatore and Salem the English troops pursued him in vain, being baffled by the rapidity of his movements, while his cavalry always hovering about, harassed them much.

Tipu now succeeded in carrying the war into the enemy country and drawing them off in pursuit of him. He made rapid marches to Tiruchirappalli and, threatening that place, plundered Srirangam. On Medow's approach he went northward burning and plundering along his route and, although he was repulsed in an attempt to take Tiyagar (a village in the South Arcot District) he took Tiruvannamalai and Perumalkoil and then despatched an envoy to Pondicherry, hoping to get French aid to defeat the English. But the Governor of Pondicherry gave no aid. Nor did the king of France to whom Tipu appealed to give any aid. In the meantime, although he had frustrated the English plan to invade Mysore, he lost all his dominions on the West Coast to the English. The allies of the English also now began to take part in the operations; the Marathas besieged Dharwar and the Nizam's army Kopal, and after protracted sieges took them[1].

But a greater danger was yet to come. At the end of January 1791 Lord Cornwallis personally assumed the command of the English army then stationed at Vellore and determined to invest Bangalore. Tipu, on hearing of his advance towards the Mysore country, hastened to prevent his ascending the ghats from Baramahal, but Cornwallis by a feigned march on Ambur took the main army first north and then due east to the Mogili Pass. Here he found the ascent easy and marched to Bangalore,

---

1 *Political Despatch to England,* dated 21st January 1791, paragraphs 149–185.
Secret Despatch from England, dated 31st July 1788.
Idem, dated 17th February 1789.
A Comprehensive History of India by H. Beveridge, Vol. II, 1867, pages. 582–593.
History of Mysore by Mark Wilks, Vol. II, 1869, pages 155–181.
Mysore by B. L. Rice, Vol. I, 1898, pages 402–403.
Hyder Ali and Tipu Sultan by L. B. Bowring. 1893, pages 145–151.

taking Kolar and Hoskote on the way. Tipu tried to harass his movements in vain and Bangalore capitulated to the English on 21st March 1791. By 13th May 1791 Cornwallis, having effected a junction with the Nizam's troops, came within nine miles of Seringapatam. But Tipu now put up a stubborn resistance, cut off the enemy's supplies and compelled Cornwallis to fall back on Bangalore, notwithstanding the fact that the Marathas under Haripant and Parasuram Bhau then came and joined the English. Intending to resume the operations soon after the rains, Cornwallis arranged that the English should take possession of the hill forts and places in the east, that the Marathas aided by a loan of 13 lakhs of rupees should proceed to Sira under Parasuram Bhau and operate to the north-west—Haripant remaining with the English camp—and that the Nizam's force should operate to the north-east against Gurramkonda. Between July 1791 and January 1792 the English having taken Hosur, Rayakota and all places to the east, succeeded in capturing also the hill forts of Nandidrug and Savandrug, deemed impregnable, as well as Hatridrug, Ramigiri, Sivagiri and Huliyurdrug. The Marathas went on plunder, after placing a corps in Dodda Ballapur and one near Madhugiri and making some fruitless attempts against Chitaldrug, marched towards Bednur at the time when they should have, according to the plan, marched to Seringapatam. They took Hole Honnur and worsted the Mysoreans near Shimoga ; but the Mysoreans under Kamar-ud-din defeated them at Madhugiri and compelled them to evacuate Dodda Ballapur. In the south, Maxwell failed to take Krishnagiri, while Kamar-ud-din took Coimbatore and marched off the English garrison as prisoners to Seringapatam in violation of the terms of capitulation. Cornwallis, however, marched into the heart of Mysore and on 5th February 1792, encamped six miles north of Seringapatam and, without waiting for the arrival of the Bombay forces under General Abercrombie which were then at Periyapatna, resolved to attack the Mysore capital at once. On the 6th night the English forces entered the Mysore lines. Tipu did his best to dislodge them but it was of no use. He then opened negotiations with Cornwallis but was told that the release of prisoners taken at Coimbatore in violation of promises was indispensable as a preliminary. He, therefore, set free the officers and sent offers of peace. Meanwhile, Abercrombie had joined the main army, and the siege was pushed on. Tipu was at the same time informed of the terms of the allies. They were these. He should cede to the allies the countries adjacent to theirs comprising one half of his dominions; should pay 3 crores and 30 lakhs of rupees, one half of the sum immediately the remainder in three instalments within the year; should release all prisoners taken from the time of Hyder; and, finally, should deliver two of his sons as hostages. After a great mental struggle, Tipu agreed to these terms and surrendered his two sons, one aged ten and the other eight as prisoners. The English obtained Malabar, Coorg, Dindigul and Baramahal; the Maratha boundary was extended to the Tungabhadra; and Nizam Ali recovered his possessions to the north of that river and Cuddapah to its south. Thus ended the Third Mysore War. Cornwallis was not disposed to go to extremes partly because the Directors of the East Indian Company were not in favour of conquests and partly because he believed that Tipu had been rendered harmless[1].

Tipu was, however, not the man to take things lying down. He began earnestly and consistently to build up the resources of his country. He punctually discharged the large sums due under the treaty. He improved the fortifications of Seringapatam. He began to increase his cavalry and infantry and to introduce discipline into his whole army. He punished the refractory palayakars and encouraged the cultivation of his country. And, all the time, he endeavoured to form a coalition for the expulsion of the English from India. He despatched an embassy to Zaman Shah, the Afghan ruler, to seek his aid against the Marathas and the English. He began to foment misunderstandings between the Peishwa, the Sindhia and the Nizam, and, when the war broke out between France and England, he did his best to obtain French assistance. He sent an embassy to Maurutius (1798) and hoped to get French aid not only from there but also from Paris. But Malartic, the French Governor of Mauritius, sent him only a handful of soldiers and, at the same time, injured his cause by issuing a proclamation to the whole world that he was only waiting for

---

1 *Political Despatch to England*, dated 28th January 1791, paragraph 14.
Idem, dated 16th February 1791, paragraphs 2–3.
Idem, dated 17th February 1791.
Idem, dated 14th April 1791, paragraphs 2–20.
Idem, dated 29th April 1791, paragraph 2.
Idem, dated 21st June 1791, paragraphs 1–24.
Idem, dated 19th September 1791, paragraphs 16–22.
Idem, dated 21st February 1792, paragraphs 1–15.
Idem, dated 15th February 1792, paragraphs 1–8.
Idem, dated 24th March 1792, paragraphs 1–9.
A Comprehensive History of India by H. Beveridge, Vol. II, 1867, pages 594–623.
History of Mysore by Mark Wilks, Vol. II, 1869, pages 182–262.
Mysore by B. L. Rice, Vol. I, 1897, pages 403–408.
Hyder Ali and Tipu Sultan by L. B. Bowring, 1893, pages 151–172.

French assistance to declare war against the English and to expel them from India[1].

This afforded a justification for Lord Wellesley, the new Governor-General, who had just arrived, to embark on an attack on Mysore. Wellesley's original intention was to declare war at once against Tipu, to annex all the maritime territory still belonging to him on the West Coast, to march on Seringapatam, to extort a war indemnity, to compel him to maintain a British Resident at his court and to expel all Frenchmen from his dominions. But Wellesley could not carry out this plan since the Madras Government were utterly unprepared for war. He, therefore, formed alliances with the Nizam and the Maharashtras, ordered Madras to make preparations without delay and wrote to Tipu warning him of his dealings with the French and asking him to receive Major Doveton, who would explain the English point of view. Tipu delayed the answer and finally sent an evasive reply explaining away the embassy to Mauritius as being only the trip of a merchantman that carried rice thither. On December 31st, 1798 Wellesley came to Madras, took over the military affairs into his own hands from Lord Clive the Governor and sent another letter to Tipu once more calling upon him to receive Doveton and ending with the warning that ' dangerous consequences ' were likely to result ' from the delay of arduous affairs '. He sent a third letter to Tipu immediately afterwards enclosing a communication from the Ottaman Sultan which warned him that the French were the enemies of Islam and which protested against the French attack on Egypt. Tipu answered once more evasively and Wellesley at once retaliated by declaring war. Two armies converged upon Seringapatam, one under General Harris of Madras in conjunction with the Nizam's army nominally under Mir Alam but really commanded by Arthur Wellesley (later the conqueror of Napoleon and the Duke of Wellington) from Vellore in the east, and the other under General Stuart of Bombay accompanied by Vira Raj, the Raja of Coorg, from Cannanore in the west. Tipu struck one blow at the western army and one at the eastern but, both having failed, retired within Seringapatam. On 6th

1 *Political Despatch to England*, dated 20th January 1797, paragraphs 2–16.
Idem, dated 16th October 1798, paragraphs 146–147.
Idem, dated 15th October 1798, paragraphs 2–3.
Secret Despatch from England, dated 18th June 1798.
Idem, dated 19th September 1798.
A Comprehensive History of India by H. Beveridge, Vol. II, 1867, pages 675–681.
History of Mysore by Mark Wilks, Vol. II, 1869, pages 295–314.
Mysore by B. L. Rice, Vol. I, 1897, pages 410–411.
Haidar Ali and Tipu Sultan by L. B. Bowring, 1893, pages 172–178.
India under Wellesley by P. E. Roberts, 1929, pages 41–44.

March he was repulsed at Saduseer, 45 miles west of the capital, by a part of Stuart's forces, and turning eastwards he was defeated by Harris at Malvelly, 30 miles east of the capital. The remaining operations were carried out rapidly. Tipu had expected the attack on the capital to come from the northward but Harris unexpectedly crossed the Cauvery at Sosilayy and attacked from the south-west. Everything became suddenly critical. Tipu now realised that the sun was setting on Mysore. As a last resort he attempted negotiations but revolted from the conditions offered him which demanded within twenty-four hours his promise to cede half his dominions, to pay an indemnity of £. 20,00,000, and to surrender four of his sons and four of his ministers as hostages. He steeled his mind to fight and spurned these humiliating conditions preferring 'to die like a soldier than to live a miserable dependent on the infidels in the list of the pensioned rajas and nabobs'. And like a soldier he died fighting when Seringapatam was stormed and taken on the 4th May 1799 [1].

There is something grand as well as pathetic in the character of Tipu. He was, like Hyder, a brave soldier, an excellent horseman, a capable commander and an expert in military tactics [2]. He fought in the thick of the battles on several occasions, notably in the war against Travancore and in the final siege of Seringapatam, never even caring for his personal safety, infusing courage and vigour at crucial moments into his army. [3] He showed unusual strategic and tactical ability, particularly in his success over Colonel Braithwaite, in his campaigns against the Marathas and the Nizam in 1786 and in his operations against General Medows [4]. In his earlier campaigns he showed much ability in the celerity and quickness

---

1 *Secret Despatch from England*, dated 18th June 1799, paragraphs 1–10.
Political Despatch to England, dated 2nd January 1799, paragraphs 8–11.
Idem, dated 12th August 1799, paragraphs 1–3.
Military Despatch to England, dated 11th May 1799.
A Comprehensive History of India by H. Beveridge, Vol. II, 1867, pages 681–704.
History of Mysore by Mark Wilks, Vol. II, 1869, pages 315–374.
Mysore by B. L. Rice, Vol. I, 1897, pages 411–415.
Hyder Ali and Tipu Sultan by L. B. Bowring, 1893, pages 174–200.
Memoirs of the Marquis of Wellesley by R. Pearse, Vol. I, 1846, pages 172–247 and 292–317.

A Selection from the Despatches, etc., of the Marquis of Wellesley by J. Owen 1877, pages 1–132.

Marquis of Wellesley's Despatches by M. Martin, Vol. I, 1837, contains most of the correspondence relating to Mysore.

India under Wellesley by P. H. Roberts, 1929, pages 45–57.

2 *History of Mysore* by Mark Wilks, Vol. II, 1869, pages 380–382.
Mysore by B. L. Rice, Vol. I, 1897, page 417.
Hyder Ali and Tipu Sultan by L. B. Bowring, 1893, page 208.

See above.

4 *Hyder Ali and Tipu Sultan* by L. B. Bowring, 1893, page 208.

of his movements and in the sharpness and suddenness of his attacks upon his enemies. But, in his later campaigns, he lost mobility as well as striking power chiefly because he failed to make good use of his cavalry and came to rely more and more on his infantry [1]. In diplomacy he did not exhibit any marked ability. He made no determined efforts to detach the Maharashtras and the Nizam from the English and sought the French aid at a time when the French, though willing, were unable to render it effectually. He failed to obtain what was near and sought to secure what was distant and the result was that he lost the substance and caught the shadow and was left alone to fight the English [2].

In administration too he exhibited some good and some bad qualities. Like Hyder and even more than Hyder, he paid great attention to the affairs of State, worked from morning till midnight without even a break for mid-day rest, mastered the workings of all departments and issued instructions on every conceivable subject, military, civil and commercial [3]. He had a lofty conception of the State ; he called the State 'khudadad' or God-given government. He enjoined economy in every department and introduced Persian as the language of administration. He organised his army into five divisions and twenty-seven regiments and set up three establishments of cavalry regular, voluntary and predatory. He improved the fortifications of Seringapatam. He established a Board of Admiralty (1796) and planned the creation of a navy of twenty-nine battleships and twenty frigates. At one time he prohibited imports and exports in order to protect domestic trade ; at another time he established a Board of Trade with seventeen foreign and thirty home factories to carry out under detailed instructions an import and export trade by land and sea. He made banking and money lending a Government monopoly and contemplated the establishment of a State Bank. He interdicted the growth of poppy and prohibited the sale of all kinds of alcoholic drinks in his dominions. All these measures surely deserve to be commended and not condemned as some of the historians have condemned them.[4]

---

1 *India under Wellesley* by P. E. Roberts, 1929, page 59.
Hyder Ali and Tipu Sultan by L. B. Bowring, 1893, page 208.

2 *See* above.

3 *History of Mysore* by Mark Wilks, Vol. II, 1869, pages 263–294.
Hyder Ali and Tipu Sultan by L. B. Bowring, 1893, pages 210–211.
India under Wellesley by P. E. Roberts, 1929, page 57.

4 *History of Mysore* by Mark Wilks, Vol. II, 1869, pages 263–274, 279–282, 380, 382–383.
Hyder Ali and Tipu Sultan by L. B. Bowring, 1893, pages 209, 213–214.
Mysore by B. L. Rice, Vol. I, 1897, page 409.
India under Wellesley by P. E. Roberts, 1929, pages 58-59.

But he also introduced some other measures which may be criticised as being too chimerical to be beneficial. He issued a new coinage with high sounding superscriptions. He introduced a new calendar with all sorts of names for months and years. He adopted a new scale of weights and measures. He altered the names of forts, towns, offices, civil as well as military, and even went to the extent of demolishing the existing irrigation works built by the Hindu Rajas and rebuilt new ones in his own name. He came under the influence of the passion for innovations engendered by the French Revolution. But he never subscribed to the ideals of that revolution, namely, Liberty, Equality and Fraternity. He always acted like a despot, rarely if ever took the advice of even his ministers, distrusted his own officers and alienated the sympathies of the Hindus who formed the majority of his subjects by showing extreme partiality to Muslims, by withholding almost all offices in administration from the Hindus, and by confiscating, wherever possible, the endowments enjoyed by the Hindu temples[1].

But taking all in all, it must be stated that, while some historians like Wilks have little favourable to say about his administration, others like Mill have much to commend it. It must also be stated that some of his contemporaries were very much impressed by his administration. Mill declared that ' as a domestic ruler he sustains an advantageous comparison with the greatest princes in the East ' and that his country was ' the best cultivated and its population, the most flourishing in India '.[2] Sir John Shore, the Governor-General and a great authority in revenue matters, gave a most favourable verdict that ' the peasantry of his dominions are protected and their labours encouraged and rewarded '.[3] Two of the British Officers, who actually took part in the war against him, have nothing but praise for his rule. Moore said that his kingdom was ' well cultivated, populous with industrious inhabitants, cities newly founded, commerce extending, towns increasing and everything flourishing so as to indicate happiness '.[4] Dirom observed that ' his country was found everywhere full of inhabitants and apparently cultivated to the utmost extent of which the soil was capable; while the discipline and fidelity of his troops in the field, until their last overthrow, were testimonies equally

---

1 *History of Mysore* by Mark Wilks, Vol. II, 1869, pages 275–278, 381–382.
Hyder Ali and Tipu Sultan by L. B. Bowring, 1893, pages 209–210.
Mysore by B. L. Rice, Vol. I, 1897, page 409.
India under Wellesley by P. E. Roberts, 1929, page 58.

2 *History of India* by J. Mill, Vol. VI, page 105.

3 *History of India* by J. Malcom, Vol. II, Appendix II, page lx–lxi.

4 *India under Wellesley* by P. E. Roberts, 1929, pages 59–60.

strong of the excellent regulations which existed in his army. His Government, though strict and arbitrary, was the despotism of a polite and able sovereign '[1]. So far as Coimbatore was concerned, he continued the land revenue system of Hyder and even tried to improve it in some respects. He abolished the large amildaris and divided the country into smaller amildaris. He fixed a standard rent roll for each village and made the ryots pay for all arable lands in the village whether they cultivated them or not. And, though his assessments were high, they were never really collected in full so that they never seem to have pressed heavily on the ryots.[2]

In personal appearance he was neither so tall nor so robust as Hyder. He had a clean shaven face but for the moustache, a dark complexion, a prominent nose, large eyes, a rather thick neck, delicate hands and feet, and a body somewhat inclined to stoutness. He spoke Hindustani, Kannada and Persian fluently and wrote also with some fluency, in Persian[3]. His mind was always restless and energetic and his tastes were wide and varied. He took an ardent interest in many subjects such as religion, ethics, science, politics and administration[4]. He had indeed the fervour of a saint but, also unfortunately, the shortcomings of a bigot. His dress was usually simple as becoming an orthodox Muslim, and it was only on occasions that he put on a dignified dress, a cloth of gold with a red tiger streak embroidered on it and a green turban[5]. His tastes were equally simple; he took plain food, eschewed alcohol, evinced little interest in the pleasures of the harem and slept in his later days, on a coarse canvas, instead of a bed[6]. He had a great love for Islam and all that Islam implies; but this love sometimes degenerated into a blind passion which warped his mind and made him insensible to the virtues of all other religions. He took the tiger as his emblem and like the tiger, at times, exhibited a ferocity which does little credit to his statesmanship. He was harsh, sometimes unreasonably harsh, to the weak and the fallen; he

---

1 *India under Wellesley* by P. E. Roberts, 1929, page 60.
History of Mysore by C. Hayavadana Rao, Vol. III (1946), pages 1027–1064.

2 *Coimbatore Manual*, 1865, page 174.
Manual of the Coimbatore District by F. A. Nicholson, 1887, pages 94–95.

3 *History of Mysore* by Mark Wilks, Vol. II, 1869, pages 379–380.
Mysore by B. L. Rice, Vol. II, 1897, page 416.
Hyder Ali and Tipu Sultan by L. B. Bowring, 1893, page 222.

4 *See* above—also *India under Wellesley* by P. E. Roberts, 1929, pages 57–58.

5 *History of Mysore* by Mark Wilks, Vol. II, 1869, page 380.
Mysore by B. L. Rice, Vol. I, 1897, page 416.
Hyder Ali and Tipu Sultan by L. B. Bowring, 1893, page 223.

6 *History of Mysore* by Mark Wilks, Vol. II, 1869, page 380.
Hyder Ali and Tipu Sultan by L. B. Bowring, 1893, page 224.

sullied the grandeur of his victories by forcibly converting or deporting large numbers of Hindus and Christians of Malabar, Kanara and Coorg and meting out needlessly severe treatment to the English prisoners[1].

Upon his death, Wellesley made a series of political arrangements. His sons and dependants were pensioned off. The ancient Hindu Raj was revived under Krishna Raja Wodeiyar in Mysore within a more confined territory and the rest of the Mysore territories were divided between the allies. The British share comprised the whole of Kanara, Wynaad, Coimbatore and Dharapuram, the greater part of Salem and not only the base of the ghats but also the heads and forts of all the passes leading from the tableland to the British possessions and the town and island of Seringapatam. The Nizam's share consisted of the districts of Gooty and Gurramkonda and part of the district but not the fort of Chitaldrug. The territory to the north-west lying between the northern part of Kanara and of the lands ceded to the Nizam, consisting of the districts of Harpanahally and Soonda was offered to the Peishwa but ultimately divided between the Nizam and the British. It was by this division of Mysore territory that Coimbatore came into the possession of the British[2].

---

[1] *A Comprehensive History of India* by H. Beveridge, Vol. II, 1867, pages 704–705.
History of Mysore by Marks Wilks, Vol. II, 1869, pages 381–383.
Hyder Ali and Tipu Sultan by L. B. Bowring, 1893, pages 218–224, 226–227.

[2] *Political Despatch to England*, dated 13th August 1799, paragraphs 1–3.
Idem, dated 19th October 1797, paragraphs 2, 4, 7, 15, 18–26.
A Comprehensive History of India by H. Beveridge, Vol. II, 1867, pages 707–714.
History of Mysore by Mark Wilks, Vol. II, 1869, pages 383–387.
Hyder Ali and Tipu Sultan by L. B. Bowring, 1893, pages 203–205.
Mysore by B. L. Rice, Vol. I, 1897, pages 417–418.
India under Wellesley by P. E. Roberts, 1929, pages 63–69.

CHAPTER IV.

NATIONALISM AND INDEPENDENCE.

In Coimbatore, as in several other districts in this State, nationalism began to make itself felt only with the rise of the Home Rule, the Non-Co-operation and the Khilafat movements. These movements which came in the wake of the First World War of 1914-1918 shook off the political lethargy into which the people had sunk for over a century, and struck at the very foundations of the British rule itself. Everywhere the people began to think and, in many places they began to act as well, fired by the ideals and aspirations of our great national leaders like Mrs. Annie Besant and Gandhiji.

The credit for broadcasting the ideals of the Indian National Congress for the first time in our State goes in a large measure to Mrs. Annie Besant. Within a year of the declaration of the First World War, she started in Madras, as the Government themselves have avowed it, ' a red hot agitation ' for Home Rule (Self Government or Swaraj) which soon began to spread like wild fire from district to district. She commenced her campaign in March-April 1915 in a series of articles on Home Rule published in her newspaper ' New India '. India, she declared, asked to be governed by her own men freely elected by herself, to make and break ministers at will, to have her own army and navy, to levy her own taxes, to frame her own budget, to educate her own people in her own way, in short, to become a sovereign nation within her own borders owing only allegience to the Imperial Crown. And so long as this Swaraj was not attained, all her crying problems like the poverty of the masses, unemployment, the decay of industries and so forth would remain unsolved. In order to attain Swaraj, she organised a Home Rule League and preached everywhere about swadeshi, boycott of foreign goods, temperance, national education, labour welfare and responsible government, ideals similar in essence to those propounded by the Indian National Congress since 1885. In vain the Governor sent a friendly remonstrance to Mrs. Besant to dissuade her from her course. In vain also the Government of Madras proposed to the Government of India that ' drastic steps should be taken to check her activities which were fraught with danger to the public peace '. In vain too she was compelled to deposit security for her press and, shortly afterwards, subjected to the penalty of forfeiting this security. She continued her agitation with unabated vigour, attacked the Press Act, appealed to the High Court, and thereby gained an immense popularity because, though that court decided against her, it adjugded at the same time that, out of the 14 extracts of her articles which had been considered as seditious by the Government, only two were really seditious. She then, with the help of Mr. G. S. Arundale, the Organising Secretary of the Home Rule League, began to enthuse the students and enlist their aid and sympathy. She condemned the existing educational system as being backward, reactionary and unpatriotic; hailed the students as the rising hope of India who were destined to secure for the country freedom from foreign yoke, instituted Home Rule classes for them, formed Boy Scouts and Volunteer troops for them and took up their cause on every occasion. Nor was this all. She turned the Theosophical Society, of which she was the President, into a political organisation, believing as she did that 'all great national movements in India are rooted in religion' and that the Home Rule Movement could not, therefore, be an exception to this rule; and by this single act, more than anything else, brought into the national arena hundreds of teachers, government servants, social workers and other intellectuals. Her Home Rule League, which she looked upon as an auxiliary to the Indian National Congress, now began to carry on an extensive political propaganda. Speeches were delivered and pamphlets were issued in English as well as in the regional languages which greatly disconcerted the Government.[1] All this agitation naturally caught Coimbatore in its sweep. The ten theosophical lodges of the district became ten potential centres of politics, and its hundreds of political workers held several political meetings and signed the Home Rule Pledge.[2]

But this was only the beginning. The moment Mrs. Besent and her associates, Mr. Arundale and Sri Wadia were interned in the Nilgiris (16th June 1917) under the Defence of India Rules, Coimbatore became one of the most active centres of Home Rule agitation. Protest meetings were held in the district, speeches were made demanding Home Rule, and leaflets in Indian languages as well as picture post cards on Home Rule were widely distributed. There is evidence to show that Mrs. Besant had the largest following among the Brahmins, especially among the Brahmin Vakeels of the district, and that they conveyed a largely attended Home Rule Conference at Coimbatore on 19th August 1917, on the very

1 G.O. No. 744, Public (Confidential), dated 7th June 1917.
Fortnightly Reports (Confidential), dated 18th June 1917; 2nd July 1917.

2 G.O. No. 842, Public, dated 15th September 1918, page 4, 23-26.

day on which the fete in aid of the War Fund was celebrated [1]. A few days afterwards, Coimbatore was honoured by the arrival of Mrs. Besant herself. Her health for sometime had been failing in Ootacamund. Her presence at Ootacamund had also been causing not a little anxiety to the Government since her residence, ' Olcott Lodge [2], was becoming a centre of pilgrimage for all sorts of intellectuals and political workers. Thither were continually going for instruction and inspiration men like Dr. C. P. Ramaswami Ayyar and Dr. Pattabhi Sitharamayya. So that, when for reasons of health Mrs. Besant elected to fix her residence at Coimbatore the Government gladly acquiesced. But her residence at Coimbatore too was not without its effect, it made the entire district, ' a centre of special Home Rule activity,' [2] And when, for instance, the Home Rule flag hoisted on her residence soon after her arrival was pulled down under the orders of the District Magistrate, a wave of resentment against the Government swept over the whole district. Many political workers also from outside the district came to see her and some, like Sri Jamnadas Dwarakadas, editor of ' Young India ', organised political meetings and delivered inspiring speeches, sowing far and wide the seeds of Home Rule among the young and the old alike.[3] Then came her release and the release of her associates (18th September 1917), but these events did not by any means damp the Home Rule activities. Home Rule meetings continued to be held in Coimbatore ; Home Rule volunteers continued to carry on propaganda in towns as well as villages ; and the Home Rule Movement petition which roused the whole State was signed by numerous people, including the ryots, of the district.[4]

The Home Rule Movement very soon merged itself into the two greater movements of All-India importance, namely, the Non-Co-operation and the Khilafat Movements. These movements took the whole country by storm and, by identifying themselves with the Indian National Congress and utilising its whole machinery for effective propaganda, gave a permanent character to nationalism. They arose during the war and went on gaining momentum even after the war, even after the introduction of the Montague-Chelmsford Reforms of 1919. They owed their origin to various causes but they owed their inspiration, their force and vitality essentially to one towering personality, Gandhiji. After having successfully carried on the campaign of passive resistance for improving the lot of Indians in

1 Fortnightly Reports (Confidential), dated 17th July 1917 ; 17th August 1917.

2 Secret File No. 8 on Home Rule, pages 2, 85.
Fortnightly Reports (Confidential), dated 17th August 1917 ; 1st September 1917.

3 Fortnightly Reports (Confidential), dated 1st September 1917 ; 18th September 1917.

4 Fortnightly Report (Confidential), dated 19th November 1917.

South Africa, Gandhiji returned to India in 1915, and almost immediately started political propaganda, took up the cause of the tenants of Bihar against the oppressions of the planters and organised passive resistance in the Kaira district of Bombay against the land revenue exactions of the Government. He then supported the extremist sections of the Indian National Congress, and induced the Congress to join the Muslim League and the Muslim agitiation against England and her allies when they endangered the suzerainty of the Khalifa, the Sultan of Turkey, and occupied the holy places of the Muslims in Asia Minor and Arabia. Nor was this all. He assailed the Government when they curtailed the liberty of the people by arming themselves by the Rowlatt Acts with powers of arrest and detention without trial of persons suspected of anti-Government activities and condemned the Reforms of 1919 as being utterly inadequate to satisfy Indian aspirations. It is under these circumstances that he launched in February 1919 the Non-Co-operation and Khilafat agitation; and his sincerity, his spiritual insight and his political sagacity made him at once a great leader, a 'Mahatma', beloved and respected by both the Hindus and Muslims. This agitation which is called the Satyagraha Campaign or the Civil Disobedience Movement, stirred the hearts of millions all over India and, in pursuance of it, national leaders and political workers preached everywhere non-co-operation with the Government and passive resistence to the Government with unprecedented vigour.[1] In August 1920, Gandhiji himself came down on a propaganda tour to the South accompanied by the two notable Muslim leaders Sri Shaukat Ali and Muhammed Ali, and delivered a number of speeches in Madras City and in the districts. In these speeches he emphasised that civil disobedience signified the force of truth or the force of the soul, that its acceptance involved the rejection of all physical violence as well as the implementation of all policies laid down by the Congress such as the resignation of titles and posts in Government service, the boycott of Legislative Councils and foreign goods, and the encouragement of khaddar, swadeshi goods, national education, temperance, labour unions, etc. He also emphasised that the Hindus and Muslims should unite together, and fight for their common cause, Swaraj, for the redressal of Khilafat grievances, for the reparation of the Punjab atrocities and for the withdrawal of the Rowlatt Acts.[2]

---

1 *Histories of the Non-Co-operation and Khilafat Movements* (Confidential) by P. C. Bamford, 1925, pages 1–20.

2 The Non-Co-operation and Khilafat Movements in the Madras Presidency (Confidential), pages 4–7.

G.O. No. 222, Public (Confidential), dated 24th April 1919.

See also Newspaper cuttings in the Government Order.

All this agitation naturally produced repercussions in Coimbatore. Early in 1920, a Mill Workers' Labour Union was formed at Coimbatore and a Railwaymen's Labour Union was formed at Podanur. Both were promoted by local leaders, Sri N. S. Ramaswami Ayyangar and Sri C. V. Venkataramana Ayyangar, the Secretary and the President respectively of the Home Rule League. As soon as the Non-Co-operation resolution was passed at the Khilafat Conference and Sri Shaukat Ali visited Madras (April 1920), a series of Non-Co-operation and Khilafat meetings were held in the district. At Erode, the lead was taken by Sri E. V. Ramaswami Naicker, the ex-Chairman of the Municipal Council. He was described by the District Magistrate as ' the most troublsome man in the district '. Outside Congress, leaders like Sri S. Satyamurthy came in May, Mrs. Besant in July and others from time to time to fan the flame. In September the movement received a fresh impetus from Gandhiji's visit. Enthusiasm went up high, meetings were held at Erode, Jambai (near Bhavani), Coimbatore, and other places at which the non-co-operation programme was explained to large audiences. In 1921, the agitation assumed a more serious complexion. The anti-drink campaign was started, picketing of arrack and toddyshops was carried on and the arrack sales fell considerably. Labour strikes broke out in two textile mills, organised by Sri N. S. Ramaswami Ayyangar and Sri V. O. Chidambaram Pillai of Tirunelveli. Early in April, a Muslim Conference was held at Erode at which about 6,000 people came to extend welcome to Sri Shaukat Ali and Sri Muhammed Ali; and many local leaders made violent speeches attacking the Government. The strength of the agitation can be gathered from the fact that an Anti-Non-Co-operation meeting held at Pollachi a few days afterwards, though presided over by one of the leaders of the Justice Party in the State, the Hon'ble the Raja of Panagal, failed to produce any impression. It can also be gathered from the fact that in July, the Non-Co-operators (the Congress) obtained a majority in the Municipal Council at Erode and from then on till 1923 passed a number of anti-Government resolutions. In August 1921, the picketing of liquor shops was intensified, spathes of trees were cut, and as a result toddy sales fell by 30 per cent. Most of the members of the Legislative Council in the district took part in the anti-drink campaign. In September Gandhiji's visit to Coimbatore and Erode gave a great fillip to the movement, and in consequence, repressive measures were resorted to by the Government. Public meetings were prohibited in Coimbatore, men like Sri V. O. Chidambaram Pillai were prosecuted and over a hundred persons were sent to jail. In 1922, the repressive measures were continued. But Sri E. V. Ramaswami Naicker, the moment he came out of the prison, organised a successful hartal at Erode on 13th January, the date on which the Prince of Wales visited Madras. Similar hartals, however, organised at Coimbatore, Pollachi and other places were scotched or suppressed by means of orders passed under section 144 of the Criminal Procedure Code. Then came the strike at Stanes Mills organised by Sri V. O. Chidambaram Pillai (March), the visit of the Civil Disobedience Committee (July), the holding of the Tamil Nadu Conference at Tiruppur (November) and the re-election of Sri E. V. Ramaswami Naicker as the Secretary of the Tamil Nadu branch of the Congress. All these kept up the agitation in the district even after the close of 1922.[1]

Meanwhile, the awakening of the political consciousness of the country led to the introduction of the Montague-Chelmsford Reform of 1919. By the Morley-Minto Reforms of 1909 the Madras Legislative Council, which was then the Executive Council supplemented by additional members for making laws, had been enlarged, the number of its additional members having been raised from 20 to 42 of whom 19 were to be elected. The official majority in the Council had been surrendered and the members had been given the rights of moving resolutions on the budget as well as on matters of general public importance and of asking supplementary questions on reply to their interpellations. But nevertheless its resolutions had not been binding on the Executive Government, nor had it any control over any department of the Government. By the Montague-Chelmsford Reforms, the Legislative Council ceased to be the Executive Council supplemented by additional members appointed or elected for the purpose of making laws. It became a separate body of which the members of the Executive Council became ex-officio members. Its members, including the proportion of elected members, were also increased. There were to be now 98 elected members and not more than 30 nominated members of whom only 15 might be officials. The Governor no longer presided over it, though he had a right to address it. Its powers too were enlarged. It had the powers of discussing and voting on the budget, of moving resolutions on matters of general public importance, of interpellation, of putting supplementary questions and of moving the adjournment of business to discuss a definite matter of urgent public importance. The constitution of the Executive Government was at the same time modified. A system of dyarchy was introduced. Provincial subjects were classified as ' Reserved ' or ' Transferred ' and while the former were administered by the Governor-in-Council, the latter were administered by the Governor

[1] Secret File No. 407, dated 6th May 1923, on Non-Co-operation, pages 265-267. Fortnightly Reports (Confidential), dated 18th April 1921 ; 6th October 1921 ; 6th December 1921 ; 6th January 1922 ; 3rd July 1923 ; 5th December 1923.

acting with Ministers appointed from and responsible to the Legislative Council.[1]

The introduction of the Montague-Chelmsford Reforms of 1919 brought about a split in the ranks of the Indian National Congress. The group led by Mahatma Gandhi, Vallabhai Patel and Sri Rajagopalachari opposed the entry of the Congress into the Legislature envisaged under the Reforms of 1919. This group was known as " Party of No-charges ". Against this leadership there was the Swarajya Party led by Sri C. R. Doss, Pandit Motilal Nehru and Sri S. Srinivasa Iyengar. Eventually this Party entered the Imperial Legislature at Delhi under the Reforms of 1919. Sri R. K. Shanmugam Chetty of Coimbatore was selected by the Swarajya Party leadership for the very important post of Chief Whip in the Legislative Assembly. The Swarajya Party under the able leadership of Pandit Motilal Nehru (Leader), Sri S. Srinivasa Iyengar (Deputy Leader) and Sri R. K. Shanmugam Chetty, won many momentous victories in the Legislature and impressed the English administrators about the high abilities of Indians to bear the responsibilities of administration.

When these reforms were on the anvil, a new party entered into the political arena This was the Non-Brahmin party which came to be called the South Indian Liberal Federation or the Justice Party. It was by no means, as is sometimes supposed, a thoroughly reactionary party. It was not anti-nationalist in its outlook. It was only more moderate than the Congress Party and it sought to attain its goal of full responsible Government through constitutional methods. It came into existence in this State towards the end of 1916 and gathered strength gradually during the Home Rule, the Non-Co-operation and the Khilafat Movements.

Its first pillars were Sri P. Theagaraya Chetty, President of the South Indian Chamber of Commerce, the oldest member of the Corporation of Madras and an ex-member of the Legislative Council, and Dr. T. M. Nair, both of whom enjoyed the confidence of large sections of Non-Brahmins. In December 1916, Sri P. Theagaraya Chetty issued a manifesto attacking the Home Rule Movement in trenchant language, charging it with being a scheme devised by the Brahmins who were not content with having secured the practical monopoly of political power and high Government appointments, and calling upon all the Non-Brahmins to assert and press their claims against the domination of the Brahmins. The party thus ushered into this State was backed by a journal called ' The Non-Brahmin ' and, shortly afterwards, by a newspaper of its own called ' The Justice ' with Dr. T. M. Nair as editor and

[1] *Madras Presidency*, 1881–1931 by G. T. Boag, 1933, pages 6–7.

Sri Theagaraya Chetty as Publisher.[1] It lost no time in making propaganda. Thus in August 1917, it held a Non-Brahmin Conference at Coimbatore presided over by the Raja of Panagal at which Sri P. Theagaraya Chetty and Dr. T. M. Nair and others attacked the Home Rule Movement and explained its own programme.[2] In October 1918 it held another Non-Brahmin Conference at Palladam at which it urged that, in the coming reforms, communal representation by communal electorates as well as communal representation in public services should be introduced. It also protested at this conference against the nomination of Sri V. S. Srinivasa Sastry on the Franchise Committee and urged in his stead the nomination of either Dr. T. M. Nair or some other Non-Brahmin leader.[3] Indeed, what gave the Justice Party its strength was the appeal which it made to the entire Non-Brahmin community that the predominance of the Brahmin leaders in the Home Rule and the Congress movements and the over representation of the Brahmins in the services were matters demanding the serious notice of all Non-Brahmins. When the Reforms of 1919 were introduced, although they were not palatable to it, it accepted office and tried to work them. And during the Non-Co-operation and the Khilafat agitations it tried its best to counteract them, though in vain.[4]

Amidst this agitation and counter agitation, the Non-Co-operation and Khilafat movements suddenly came to an end. The Congress split over the question of Council entry and the Muslims beheld with dismay the abolition of the Khalifa by Kemal Pasha. But the agitation for swaraj, though much abated, was continued, while Gandhiji took to constructive work planning, as he said, to start the Civil Disobedience Movement at the proper opportunity.[5]

From then onwards till the time of the Civil Disobedience Movement of 1930–31, interest in the Congress creed was kept alive in Coimbatore

---

1 Fortnightly Reports (Confidential), dated 17th May 1917 ; 31st May 1917.

2 Fortnightly Report (Confidential), dated 1st September 1917.

3 Letter No. 1049, Public, dated 9th November 1918.

4 G.O. No. 339, Public, dated 17th April 1918.
G.O. Nos. 854–855, Public, dated 19th September 1918.
G.O. No. 980, Public, dated 31st October 1918.
G.O. Nos. 1019–1020, Public, dated 7th November 1918.
G.O. No. 142, Public (Confidential), dated 28th February 1920.
G.O. No. 155, Public, dated 6th March 1920.
Fortnightly Reports (Confidential), dated 1st January 1917, 1st March 1917. 2nd April 1917, 19th April 1918 and 1st May 1918.

5 *Histories of the Non-Co-operation and Khilafat Movements* by P. C. Bamford 1925, pages 98–99, 185–210.

by the peaceful but persistent propaganda carried on by the Congress workers. It was this propaganda that now and again started the anti-drink campaign and collected many purses for Gandhiji's Khaddar Fund.[1] It was this propaganda that led to a serious situation in Coimbatore in August 1927 when over 5,000 workers of almost all textile mills of the town struck work and refused to leave the mills.[2] It was also this propaganda combined with the propaganda of Thanjavur and Tiruchirappalli that commenced the strike in the South Indian Railway Workshops in June 1928 at Podanur, Nagapattinam and the Golden Rock which developed rapidly into a general strike of the South Indian Railway and gave an immense amount of trouble to the Government.[3]

Close upon this came the Civil Disobedience Movement forged by Gandhiji and introduced at the Lahore Session of the Congress in 1929. The Resolution on this movement framed by Pandit Jawaharlal Nehru, the rising leader of India, and issued on behalf of the Congress Working Committee, charged the British Government with having not only deprived the Indian people of their freedom but also 'ruined India economically, politically, culturally and spiritually' and declared in emphatic terms that 'India must', therefore, 'sever the British connection and attain Purna Swaraj or complete independence'. The way to Swaraj, it further declared, was not through violence but through civil disobedience, including non-payment of taxes.[4] A manifesto like this issued to the numerous Congress organizations throughout India and a movement like this led by no less a leader than Gandhiji could not but be expected to produce widespread political agitation. A wave of nationalism, the like of which had never been witnessed before, spread over the whole of India and the Congress leaders everywhere began to organize mass meetings, salt satyagraha, no-tax campaigns, boycott of the Government and village servants, boycott of British goods, boycott of liquor shops, the seducing of troops and police from loyalty to the Government and anti-Government propaganda[5]. The Government for the first time realised the national significance of the movement and introduced a series of repressive laws to meet the extraordinary situation.[6]

---

1 Fortnightly Reports (Confidential), dated 5th December 1923 and 2nd March 1927.

2 Fortnightly Reports (Confidential), dated 2nd September 1927.

3 Fortnightly Reports (Confidential), dated 5th July 1928; 6th August 1928.

4 The Civil Disobedience Movement (India), 1930–1934 (Confidential), pages 29–30.

5 *Idem*.

6 *Idem*, pages 4–8, 15–16.

In consequence of this movement Coimbatore witnessed a great deal of national agitation, almost throughout 1930. But this agitation true to the teachings of Gandhiji never here, as in some other districts, degenerated into violence, save in a few instances. Salt Satyagraha was a physical impossibility in the district, and yet, attempts at making salt were made at Tiruppur and Erode in April and May under the influence of the Congress Committees. Volunteers also went from the district and joined the famous Vedaranyam Salt Satyagraha Campaign launched by Sri C. Rajagopalachari. Dr. T. S. S. Rajan and Sri Swaminatha Sastri from Tiruchirappalli contributed not a little to keep up interest in this activity in the district. Hartals were at the same time organized in several towns, especially at Coimbatore, on a large scale on 7th May. A Congress Committee was formed at Coimbatore under the presidentship of Sri Balaji Rao in June. A series of public meetings were held at various places at which passages from prescribed books were read and the Congress creed was explained to large audiences. On 25th June 1930 an intensive picketing of toddy shops was started in Coimbatore town. The situation became so grave that the District Magistrate passed orders prohibiting picketing within the town limits for two months, and served notices on all Congress leaders prohibiting their participation in processions and meetings. A large number of arrests were made and many persons were sent to jail. But this created only a temporary lull in the activities. In the first week of July the boys of the Government High School in Coimbatore went on strike and even the women came out to take part in the movement. In the last week of June, picketing of toddy shops again broke out in Coimbatore which resulted in a lathi charge, and in the serving of orders on the leaders again, prohibiting them in any manner from doing civil disobedience work for two months. In the subsequent months, especially in September and October, a virulent campaign against drink was carried on by enforcing a form of social boycott known as the '*Urukattumanam*', a method by which social rules were sometimes enforced in the villages. All this time, in other places, in the Pollachi and Udumalpet taluks, toddy shop bidders were intimidated, obstructed or sometimes even beaten. The consequence was that the toddy revenue in the district fell by $1\frac{1}{4}$ lakhs of rupees. It was not till the end of the year when about 300 persons had been sentenced to imprisonment that the movement was brought under control.[1]

Shortly afterwards by a settlement reached by Gandhiji, on behalf of the Congress, with Lord Irwin, the Viceroy, on behalf of the British Government, the Congress agreed to participate in the Round Table

[1] Civil Disobedience Movement, 1930–1931 (Confidential), pages 95–97.

Conference held in London. The Government now withdrew all repressive ordinances banning the Congress bodies, etc., and released all political prisoners while the Congress called off the Civil Disobedience Movement. But this truce remained in force only for a time. The Civil Disobedience Movement was started again by the Congresss early in January 1932 on account of the repressive ordinances passed by the Government to put down agitation in the North-West Frontier Province, in the United Provinces and in Bengal.[1] Immediately afterwards the Congress workers in Coimbatore defied the ban on meetings and processions in spite of the steps taken by the police to prevent them. For example one of the processions taken out by the Desabandu Youth League of Tiruppur on 11th January 1932 carrying national flags and singing national songs was dispersed by a severe lathi charge in the course of which Sri O. K. S. R. Kumaraswami Mudaliar, popularly known as 'Tiruppur Kumaran' was fatally wounded.[2] The Congress workers also organized new Congress Committees, enrolled new Congress members and began to concentrate on the constructive programme of Gandhiji, such as the encouragement of khaddar, the uplift of Harijans and so on. And when Gandhiji visited the district in February 1934, all people of the district extended to him a warm welcome. Large crowds, it is said, greeted him, venerated him and treated him 'like an avait of god' and contributed large sums to his Harijan Fund. It is of interest to note that Coimbatore contributed the highest amount to the Harijan Fund. While the contributions from the eight districts that he visited came to Rs. 68,000, the contributions from Coimbatore alone came to Rs. 25,000.[3] Enthusiasm for the Congress did not subside even when the Civil Disobedience Movement was called off by Gandhiji in April-May 1934.[4] Thus, for instance, when Bulabhai Desai, Secretary to the Congress Parliamentary Board visited the district in July and when the Tamil Nadu Provincial Conference presided over by Sri C. Ralagopalachari, was held at Coimbatore in September 1934, opportunity was taken to enroll more Congress members and to carry on an intensive propaganda for putting up Congress candidates for the forthcoming general elections.[5]

---

[1] The Civil Disobedience Movement (India), 1930–1934 (Confidential), page 16.

[2] G.O. No. 340, Public (General), dated 27th February 1932.
Fortnightly Report (Confidential), dated 18th July 1934.

[3] Secret File No. 877, dated 1st March 1934. *See* the District Magistrate's Reports from Coimbatore, dated 8th February 1934 and 9th February 1934.
Secret File No. 862, dated 20th February 1934.

[4] G.O. No. 609, Public, dated 11th June 1934.

[5] Fortnightly Reports (Confidential), dated 18th July 1934 ; 4th October 1934.

During all this time, from the end of the Non-Co-operation Movement to the end of the Civil Disobedience Movement, other parties in the State were not idle. The Justice Party, although it co-operated with the British in running the dyarchy under its leaders like the Raja of Panagal and Sri A. P. Patro, very soon began to lose all faith in dyarchy. It happened like this. In 1926 it was defeated in the general elections by the Swaraj Party, the party of the Congress which believed in council entry. But the Swaraj Party, though it had a majority, refused to form the Ministry and, as a result, an Independent Ministry under Dr. P. Subbarayan, having the support of the Swaraj Party was formed. The moment this Ministry was formed, the Justice Party started an agitation against it, against the British Government itself and attempted to undermine the Congress. It convened a meeting of the Non-Brahmin Federation at Coimbatore on 2nd July 1927 attended by prominent Justicites like the Raja of Panagal, Sri A. P. Patro, Sri R. K. Shanmugam Chetty, Sri A. Ramaswami Mudaliar, Sri O. Thanikachalam Chetty and presided over by Sri S. Kumaraswamy Reddiar and, at this meeting, passed three important resolutions. The first of these permitted the individual members of the Justice Party to enter the Congress with the object of swamping the Congress and working on the feelings of the Non-Brahmins inside the Congress. The second condemned dyarchy as being a system utterly unworkable and demanded full provincial autonomy from the British Government. The third advocated a vote of no-confidence in the Legislature to unseat the Ministry.[1] Soon after this meeting several prominent members of the Justice Party joined the Congress.[2] A vote of no-confidence was also brought in the Legislative Council, but the motion was defeated by the members of the Swaraj Party. This did not upset the Justice Party, and at the general elections of 1930, the Congress (both the Congress Party and the Swaraj Party) having refused to contest the elections, it easily obtained a majority and again formed a Ministry, this time headed by Sri B. Muniswami Naidu. This Ministry was succeeded in 1932 by the Ministry of the Raja of Bobbili. The Justice Party now felt itself quite safe, and finding from the elections that the Non-Brahmins had little to fear politically from the Brahmins, threw open its membership to the Brahmins so as to strengthen its organization. But its position was really by no means safe. This was clearly shown by the general elections of 1934. The Justice Party was now completely defeated by the Congress Party, the Congress having lifted

1 Fortnightly Reports (Confidential), dated 19th July 1927.

2 Fortnightly Reports (Confidential), dated 4th August 1927.

the ban on Council entry.[1] The Congress, however, did not accept office and accordingly a Justice Party Ministry was again formed under the Raja of Bobbili. But the sands of this party were running fast. Thereafter disunity in its ranks, the lack of effective party machinery and, above all, the want of a dynamic nationalist policy, ruined all its chances of success.[2]

During the same period, two new parties, namely, the Self Respect and the Communist Parties, came into existence. Both opposed the Congress and both demanded radical social, economic and political reforms. The Self Respect Party was started by Sri E. V. Ramaswami Naicker who, as we have seen, had played a no inconspicuous part in Coimbatore during the Non-Co-operation and Khilafat agitation. After that agitation, however, he left the Congress believing that the only way to improve the condition of the people was to abolish all caste distinctions, to banish all religion and to introduce some sort of Communism.[3] In 1933–34 he toured the Tamil districts, including of course his own district Coimbatore, attacking all religions, Hinduism, Islam and Christianity alike, denouncing the Brahmins for being the authors of caste distinctions, condemning all forms of private property and advocating the establishment of 'the Russian form of Government' as being the best suited to the country.[4] By his hatred of Brahmins he won the support of the Non-Brahmins or the Justice Party, and by his love of the Soviet System, he earned the sympathy of the Communist Party. Wherever he went, he formed associations of Self Respecters and his Self Respect Party, because it promoted class hatred, caused some anxiety to the Government and, because it attacked the Congress, caused some annoyance to the Congress Party. It contributed a succession of intemperate articles in some Tamil newspapers, violently abused the Brahmins and the Congress and organized some demonstrations even against Gandhiji when he came on his southern tour to Coimbatore and other districts in 1934.[5]

---

1 Fortnightly Reports (Confidential), dated 16th July 1923; 19th July 1927; 4th July 1927; 4th October 1934; 20th November 1934.

2 *Idem*, dated 20th November 1934; 3rd December 1934.

3 *Idem*, dated 2nd June 1923; 20th July 1933; 9th October 1933; 19th June 1934 and 18th July 1934.

4 *Idem*; dated 20th March 1933; 2nd June 1933; 17th May 1933; 3rd July 1933; 3rd August 1933; 5th September 1933; 9th October 1933; 19th June 1934; 18th July 1934; 18th December 1934.

5 Secret File No. 877, dated 1st March 1934—*See* the report of the District Magistrate of Coimbatore, dated 8th February 1934.

But it was the Communist Party that caused real concern to the Congress and much anxiety to the Government. This party received a fillip by the visit of Sri Saklatwala, a prominent labour leader and a member of British Parliament, to Madras in 1927 and gave rise to several associations of workers. It refused to have anything to do with the Congress and denounced the Congress as 'the stronghold of landlordism, capitalism and private ownership'. The Congress found it impossible to conciliate the Communists (or 'Socialists' as they called themselves) who organized a spate of strikes in Madras and elsewhere.[1] Indeed, they grew from strength to strength in all parts of India. It was therefore no wonder that in July 1934 the Communist Party and its organizations were banned by the Government of India on the ground that they constituted a danger to public peace. The Government of India stated that a close investigation of all Communist activities, and especially the Meerut Conspiracy case had revealed to them that the Party aimed at nothing less than the violent overthrow of the existing order of society. Its aims, they said, were hatred of God and all forms of religion, the destruction of private property, the enforcement of absolute social and racial equality, the annihilation of all forms of responsible Government including civil liberties such as freedom of speech and trial by jury, and the establishment of the dictatorship of the proletariat by means of a world revolution. Its objects, they observed, were the achievement of complete independence of India by the violent overthrow of British rule, the cancellation of all national debts, the establishment of a Soviet Government, the abolition of the Indian States, the confiscation without compensation of all the lands, forests and other properties of the ruling princes, the landholders. And it sought to secure these objects, they remarked, by developing a general strike of workers culminating in a political strike, by developing a peasant movement for the non-payment of rents and taxes into an All-India Agrarian Revolution, and by organizing a nation wide movement for political independence by attaching to it all the workers, peasants and petty bourgeois and by spreading revolutionary propaganda in the army and the police and inciting them to revolt against British rule.[2]

As a result of this, in Madras, the Government declared unlawful the Young Workers' League (November 1934) which had for its avowed object, the overthrow of British Imperialism and which was in no sense a bonafide trade union and was in touch with the Communist

1 Madras Presidency Administration Report for 1926-1927, pages XIII—XV.

2 G.O. No. 621, Public, dated 17th April 1935 and G.O. No. 2111, Public, dated 18th December 1936.

International.[1] All this created a storm of protests in the left wing press[2] and a great deal of uneasiness in the Self Respect Party which had, as has been seen, imbibed some of the Communist ideas. Sri E. V. Ramaswami Naickar lost no time in announcing that his party was not a Communist Party, that it was only a Socialist Party, that it worked always within the bounds of law, that violence had no place in it, and that its aim was the establishment of the British system of administration and failing that alone, 'a Communist system of administration'.[3] His party, however, was not banned. Nor were the other socialist organizations in the State banned, although some of them, like the All-India Congress Socialist Organization, agitated for complete independence, non-compromise with British Imperialism, the elimination of the princes, landlords and other classes of exploiters and the redistribution of lands to the peasants.[4]

The banning of the Communist Party did not by any means put a stop to their activities in this State. They formed what was called the Labour Protection League and steadily spread Communist ideas among the workers.[5] In Coimbatore, however, their activities, as yet, did not extend beyond fomenting labour discontent and organizing a few strikes in the textile mills.[6] It was only when the Congress Government came to power in 1937 that they started a widespread agitation in the whole State.

In the meantime the Government of India Act of 1935 was passed which gave a further instalment of reforms. So far as this State is concerned, it abolished dyarchy and, with certain exceptions, granted provincial autonomy. The State Government was given exclusive authority over provincial subjects and concurrent jurisdiction over certain other subjects. The Government of India was precluded from interfering in State administration save when the Governor-General proclaimed an emergency or considered interference necessary for ensuring the peace and tranquillity of India. The Governor, like the Governor-General, was also entrusted with certain discretionary powers and special responsibilities which he could discharge without consulting the Ministers. Thus, under his discretionary powers, he could nominate certain members to the Legislative Council, appoint and dismiss Ministers

1 G.O. No. 621, Public, dated 17th April 1935, page 7.

2 G.O. No. 324, Public (Confidential), dated 23rd February 1935, pages 13, 31, 60, etc.

3 *Idem*—pages 25–27.

4 G.O. No. 324, Public (Confidential), dated 23rd February 1935, page 101.

5 Fortnightly Report (Confidential), dated 5th September 1935.

6 *Idem*, dated 18th November 1935 and 3rd February 1936.

and members of the Public Service Cómmission, summon, prorogue or dissolve the Legislature, stop the proceedings of a bill which affected peace and tranquillity, return a bill to the Legislature for reconsideration with suggestions for amendment, veto a bill or reserve it for the consideration of the Governor-General, pass an act or promulgate an Ordinance when immediate action was necessary or assume to himself all the powers of the State Government and the Legislature in the event of a breakdown of the Constitution. Under his special responsibilities he was authorised to prevent any grave menace to public peace, to safeguard the legitimate interests of the minorities and the public servants, to administer the Partially Excluded Areas, to protect the rights of the rulers of Indian States and to execute the orders or directions issued to him by the Governor-General. Subject to these restrictions, the Ministers were invested with full powers over all other subjects relating to State administration. The Governor was to appoint the leader of the party or the parties commanding a majority in the Legislature as the Chief Minister and also other Ministers chosen by the Chief Minister generally from among the members of the Legislature. If a Minister chosen was not a member of the Legislature he had to become one within six months or resign. All the Ministers were to be responsible to the Legislature and were to resign if the Legislature passed a vote of no-confidence. The Governor was to preside over the Council of Ministers. The Legislature was to consist of a Legislative Council and a Legislative Assembly. The Council was to consist of 46 members of whom a certain proportion were to be elected and a certain proportion to be nominated by the Governor. It was to be a permanent body, one-third of whose members were to retire every three years. The Assembly was to consist of 215 members elected by voters arranged in separate electorates. It was to sit for five years, unless sooner dissolved by the Governor. The Council was to have no power to vote on the demands for grants or to sanction expenditure; it could only discuss the budget. Such powers were to be exercised only by the Legislative Assembly in which all money bills were to be first introduced. In case of difference of opinion between the two houses, the Governor was to summon a joint sitting to decide the disputed measure.

This Act came into force on 1st April 1937, but long before that date, strenuous efforts were made by the Congress and the Justice Parties throughout the whole State, including Coimbatore, to increase their strength and to carry on an effective propaganda for the forthcoming elections. On the Congress Party's side the propaganda was carried on by Madras leaders like Sri S. Satyamurthy and Sri C. Rajagopalachari and leaders from other States like Sri Vallabhai Patel and Pandit Jawaharlal Nehru.[1] No leader, however, attracted a larger audience and none produced a greater impression than Pandit Jawaharlal Nehru, who arrived in Madras on 5th October 1936 and immediately afterwards started on a whirlwind tour of the Tamil districts. Wherever he went in Coimbatore as also in other districts he was given an enthusiastic reception. In almost every village on his route, the villagers gathered and cheered him on his arrival; in more important villages, welcome arches were erected, festoons were hung and Congress slogans were displayed. He was received with flowers, fruits and music sometimes with 'vedis' fired in his honour. In towns in which he halted, very large crowds assembled, consisting of both townsmen and villagers of the surrounding areas. They did not mind any inconvenience; they waited for hours to have his 'darsan'; and they brushed aside the feeble hostile demonstrations carried on in some places by the members of the Self Respect Party. They presented him addresses of welcome and purses and thanked him for his campaign against poverty and unemployment. Indeed, he literally achieved mass contact and became exceedingly popular by frequently stopping his car while passing through the villages, by talking freely with all who came to see him, by mixing freely with them, by showing extreme solicitude for their welfare and, by distributing the flowers and fruits presented to him to the women and children. He arrived in Coimbatore district on 11th October accompanied by Sri S. Satyamurthy and Sri Avanashilingam Chettiar and toured through Bhavani, Erode, Gobichettipalayam, Satyamangalam, Avanashi, Tiruppur, Palladam, Sulur, Coimbatore, Pollachi and Udumalpet. And everywhere he went he delivered speeches laying emphasis on the prevailing poverty and unemployment in India and attributing them largely to the policies followed under British Imperialism. He remarked that, so long as British imperialism remained, the masses could not hope to better their condition, and that, therefore, it must be brought to an end. He pointed out that to achieve this object all classes should strengthen the hands of the Congress which was the only powerful, organized and disciplined body in India. He asked the people to vote for the Congress and he invariably wound up by saying that the Congress was working for independence and that once independence was gained, the problems of poverty and unemployment could be solved by introducing socialism in the country.[2]

---

[1] Fortnightly Reports (Confidential), dated 21st July 1936; 5th August 1936; 2nd September 1936; 19th October 1936; 3rd November 1936 and 5th January 1937.

[2] Secret Files Nos. 981 and 982, dated 10th January 1937. In Secret File No. 982—*see* the transcripts of his speeches delivered at Pollachi, Palladam, Tiruppur, Coimbatore and Avanashi on 11th October 1936.

Pandit Nehru's tour strengthened not a little the electioneering campaign of the Congress Party. The Justice Party's campaign lost all vigour. By this time, new parties such as the People's Party and the Madras Provincial Scheduled Castes Party have come into existence. As the Provincial Branch of the Muslim League having been revived, the opponents of the Congress fondly hoped to undermine its strength.[1] In the general elections held in 1937, however, the Congress Party won a decisive victory over the other parties. The fact that the anti-Congress vote was split made little or no difference and the Congress Party secured 159 out of the 215 seats in the Legislative Assembly and 26 out of the 46 seats in the Legislative Council.[2] The Congress Party, however, having refused to accept office without securing assurances against the interference in the day to day administration by the Governor's discretionary and special powers under the new Constitution, an Interim Ministry was formed under Sri K. V. Reddy.[3] But in the first half of July, the Congress Party being satisfied with the assurances given by the Viceroy accepted office and formed a Ministry under Sri C. Rajagopalachari.[4]

Of all the measures introduced by Sri C. Rajagopalachari's Ministry none came in for so much opposition from his political opponents as the introduction of Hindustani (Hindi) compulsorily in certain schools as an experiment. The opposition to this measure came mostly from the Self Respect Party led by Sri E. V. Ramaswami Naicker, but it was backed alike by the Justice Party, the Muslim League and the Scheduled Castes Federation.[5] Meetings were held by the Self-Respect Party in Madras and in the Tamil districts, including Coimbatore, at which speeches were made attacking the Brahmins and alleging that the introduction of Hindi was an attempt to impose Aryan influence on Dravidian culture to perpetuate Brahmin domination.[6] Black flag demonstrations were made by this party during the visits of Ministers. And, above all, picketing by successive batches of volunteers was conducted by this party before the Premier's residence and before certain schools. More than a thousand arrests were made in the city and most of the picketers were convicted. Sri E. V. Ramaswami Naicker himself was arrested, convicted

1 Madras Administration Report for 1935–1936, pages VIII–IX.

2 Fortnightly Report (Confidential), dated 4th March 1937.

3 G.O. No. 835, Public, dated 16th May 1938.

4 Fortnightly Reports (Confidential), dated 5th May 1937 ; 23rd July 1937.

5 *Idem,* dated 10th June 1938 ; 24th June 1938 ; 9th August 1938 ; 29th August 1938.

6 *Idem* dated 6th July 1938 ; 20th July 1938 ; 5th September 1938.

and sentenced to one year's imprisonment.[1] But still the agitation went on. It ended only when the Congress Ministry laid down office in 1939 and the succeeding Government abolished the teaching of Hindi and released all anti-Hindi prisoners.[2] Meanwhile, in December 1938, Sri E. V. Ramaswami Naicker was elected as the President of the Justice Party, although he was then in jail.[3]

It was not, however, so much the open agitation of the Self-Respect Party or the Justice Party as the underground agitation of the Communist Party which was rapidly becoming powerful, that caused much concern to the Congress Government. It was at this time that many of the Communists under the guise of Socialists formed unions 'embracing all branches of industry and husbandry' and began to foment labour troubles.[4] Between 1937 and 1939, during the period of the Congress Ministry, a spate of strikes occurred everywhere in the State. In Coimbatore, labour in the textile mills became exceedingly restive and resorted to a series of strikes. Thus, in September 1937 there were strikes in two mills near Coimbatore.[5] In October a serious strike began in the Sarada Mills, Coimbatore, and spread to eight other textile mills.[6] In December a hunger strike was staged in the Lakshmi Mills, Coimbatore.[7] In February 1938 another strike occurred in the Sarada Mills[8] and in February-March, a more serious strike broke out in the Saroja Mills, Coimbatore.[9] In July five textile mills in Coimbatore and one textile mill in Tiruppur struck work[10], and in October, the Murugan Mill workers of Coimbatore went on strike.[11] In January 1939 there was a strike in the Kaleswara Mills at Coimbatore and another in the Coimbatore Spinning and Weaving Company 'A' Mills.[12] In February-March strikes took place in two mills in Tiruppur.[13] In some of these

---

1 He was, however, released after six months on medical grounds.

2 Fortnightly Reports (Confidential), dated 20th July 1938 to 16th March 1940.

3 Fortnightly Report (Confidential), dated 4th January 1939.

4 G.O. No. 835, Public, dated 16th May 1935 and the Report of the Inspector-General of Police.

Fortnightly Reports (Confidential), dated 5th October 1937; 8th October 1937; 8th December 1937; 21st December 1937; 16th March 1939; 4th March 1939.

5 Fortnightly Report (Confidential), dated 5th October 1937.

6 *Idem*, dated 19th November 1937.

7 Fortnightly Report (Confidential), dated 21st December 1937.

8 *Idem*, dated 23rd February 1938.

9 *Idem*, dated 5th March 1938.

10 *Idem*, dated 6th July 1938; 20th July 1938; 5th August 1938, 19th August 1938.

11 *Idem*, dated 19th October 1938.

12 *Idem*, dated 19th January 1939.

13 *Idem*, dated 16th February 1939; 4th March 1939.

strikes; the workers employed violence, put forth unreasonable demands, spurned every attempt made by the Government to settle their grievances and could be controlled only by police intervention.

In September 1939, the Second World War broke out and opened a new chapter in the history of the struggle for independence. The Congress having decided not to participate in the war, Sri C. Rajagopalachari's Ministry resigned in October and the Government was carried on by the Governor with the aid of Civilian Advisers.[1] As soon as this took place and individual satyagraha was permitted by the Congress, Coimbatore once more became the scene of Congress activities. Congress committees were formed in the district, Satyagraha pledges were taken, anti-war speeches were made, anti-war slogans were shouted, and anti-war posters were displayed in prominent places ; and all this anti-war propaganda led to a large number of arrests. Here, as elsewhere, not only Congress leaders but also a large number of persons courted imprisonment, with the result that the Government were eventually compelled to ignore all but the leaders and arrest only such as wielded any influence. It was only when the Satyagraha movement was withdrawn by the Tamil Nadu Congress Committee in January 1942 that things quietened down everywhere.[2]

But very soon events moved to a crisis. The interminable waiting for the fulfilment of the pledges by the British, the failure of the Cripps's Mission, the danger of the conversion of India into a theatre of war by Britain and her Allies, all these, induced Gandhiji and the Congress to make an all out effort to get rid of British rule. The nation having waited in vain could wait no longer for independence. The Civil Disobedience Movement, or the Quit India Movement, as it was called, was fashioned by Gandhiji in May-June 1942, was put into shape by the working committee by the Wardha Resolution in July and was launched by the All-India Congress Committee by its Bombay Resolution on 8th August. This Resolution which was a long one, demanded, in short, the immediate withdrawal of Britain from India, the setting up of a Provisional Government representing all the parties, the pooling of all resources

---

1 Madras Administration Report for 1939–1940, page 1.

2 Appendix II to Fortnightly Reports (Confidential), dated 17th January 1940 ; 4th April 1940 ; 3rd May 1940 ; 5th August 1940 ; 19th August 1940 ; 4th September 1940 ; 19th September 1940 ; 4th October 1940 ; 18th October 1940, 4th November 1940 ; 2nd December 1940 ; 20th December 1940 ; 4th January 1941 ; 21st January 1941 ; 3rd February 1941 ; 25th May 1941 ; 4th March 1941 ; 18th March 1941 ; 3rd April 1941 ; 3rd May 1941 ; 18th May 1941, and 21st March 1942.

for fighting the struggle for freedom against the aggression of Nazism, Fascism and Imperialism and thereby strengthening the cause of the United Nations and, after the war was over, the establishment of a World Federation of Free Nations. And, in order to secure the preliminary step, the immediate withdrawal of Britain, it sanctioned a nation-wide non-violent mass movement under the leadership of Gandhiji.[1]

This clarion call was no sooner made, than Gandhiji and a large number of prominent Congress leaders were arrested and imprisoned and all the Congress organizations throughout India were banned.[2] This was a signal for the outbreak of a national uprising throughout India, in which violence was freely used side by side with non-violence to paralyse the activities of the Government. The British Government held the Congress responsible for the violent outbreaks stating that the Congress must have known that the incitement to mass action on such a wide scale was bound to lead to violence, but the Congress held the Government responsible stating that it was the arrest of the leaders and the repressive policy of the Government that was responsible for violence.[3] So far as Madras was concerned, Sri C. Rajagopalachari having by this time resigned from the Congress on the issue of Pakistan before the passing of the Bombay Resolution, and the other leaders having been imprisoned, the people were more or less left to themselves and their resentment in many places resulted in acts of violence.

In Coimbatore both peaceful and violent methods were employed by the people. Meetings were held, hartals were observed, strikes were organized, and at the same time acts of sabotage and arson were also resorted to. The movement began on the 9th August 1942 with a protest meeting held at Coimbatore. From then onwards till the 11th, students, (including the students of the Agricultural College) picketed schools and colleges, and people observed hartals and held meetings and processions in defiance of the prohibitory orders of the District Magistrate. On the 11th, eleven mills in Coimbatore and three mills in Udumalpet went on strike and Sri N. G. Rangaswamy, a member of the Legislative Assembly, and some other persons were arrested. On the 14th, the situation became grave. A ban on meetings and processions was declared at Tiruppur and Udumalpet.

[1] *History of the Indian National Congress* by Sri Pattabhi Sitaramayya, Vol. II, 1947, pages 343–346.

[2] G.O. No. 2541, Public, dated 9th August 1942.
G.O. No. 2543, Public, dated 9th August 1942.

[3] Congress Responsibility for the disturbances 1942–43. Correspondence with Mr. Gandhi, August 1942—April 1944.

On the same day, telegraph wires were cut around Coimbatore and an ammunition train from Cochin consisting of two engines and forty-four wagons was derailed by sabotage between Podanur and Singanallur railway stations. The fishplates and spikes having been removed, both the engines ran down an embankment and capsized with eleven wagons. Thereafter there was a lull in activity in the district for a few days except for strikes in some schools, the defying of ban on meetings and some lathi charges and the cutting of telegraph wires between Gobichettipalayam and Bhavani. On the 19th Sri P. Subbiah and Sri Avanashilingam Chettiar, the two local Congress leaders, were arrested. From then onwards till the end of the month the situation became serious. On the same day a mile of telegraph wires were cut at Erode and an attempt was made to set fire to the Government timber Depot at Pollachi. On the 20th public meetings were held at Coimbatore, Erode and Dharapuram in defiance of the ban on such meetings and several persons were arrested. On the 21st an attempt was made to derail a train near Pollachi and the village chavadi at Karnalur in Avanashi taluk was attacked and damaged. On the 22nd a serious stay-in-strike broke out in the Pankaja Mills, Coimbatore, which involved violence and ended in lathi charges and firings by the police. Two persons were killed by the firing and several were injured. On the 23rd an attempt was made to remove fish plates on the Erode-Tiruchirappalli railway line near Chavadipalayam. On the 24th ten mills went on strike at Singanallur and telephone wires were cut at Erode. On the 25th and 26th several toddy shops were burnt at Singanallur, Irugur and Pallapalayam. And on the 27th at about 2 a.m. a batch of 200 persons left Coimbatore, went to the Sulur R.A.F. Aerodrome and set fire to the thatched sheds, destroying the sheds completely and also 22 motor lorries kept inside them.

Thereafter only sporadic attempts were made. Thus in the first half of September, an attempt was made to burn the Revenue Divisional Office at Erode, some toddy and arrack shops were burnt in Pasur and Kariampalayam, threatening letters to the police and other officials were written at Erode and picketing was carried on before the toddy shops and Government offices in some places. In the second half of September, some toddy shops were burnt, and telegraph wires were cut in some places and a virulent propaganda by pamphlets, leaflets, letters as well as speeches was carried on everywhere against the Government. In November telephone wires were cut in some places, and an attempt was made to break the Electricity Department tower at Tudiyalur. The total number of persons detained up to 31st December in connection with the Civil

Disobedience Movement was 28 and the total number convicted 73. Besides this, collective fines amounting to Rs. 35,410 were imposed on certain villages and the Coimbatore Municipal Council was suspended for a period of six months for having passed resolutions at its meeting held on 26th September, supporting the Civil Disobedience Movement and condemning the repressive policy of the Government.[1]

From this time onwards there was no Congress agitation on any extensive scale in the district or in the State or in India. The political atmosphere in India continued for a time to remain dark and sullen, what with the detention of the Congress leaders in jail and the unhelpful attitude shown by the Viceroys, Lord Linlithgow and Lord Wavell, and Sri M. A. Jinnah, the implacable leader of the Muslim League. The Viceroys insisted on the solution of the communal and minority problems as a preliminary to the consideration of the grant of any reforms while Mr. Jinnah insisted on Pakistan. Gandhiji having been released in May 1944 tried his best to solve the tangle but in vain. From 1945, however, the sky began to clear. The formation of the Labour Government in Britain, the end of the Japanese war, Lord Wavell's visit to England for consultation with the Labour Government, the arrival first of the Parliamentary Delegation and then of the Cabinet Mission to hammer out a Constitution for India, all these led to a succession of rapid political changes. Then it was that the ban on the Congress was lifted, the Congress leaders were released and they resolved to accept the reforms offered in good faith by the British. This speedily led to the holding of the general elections, the formation of the Interim Government at the centre consisting of Indian leaders drawn from major political parties (1946), the convening of the Constituent Assembly, the decision of the British to withdraw from India by June 1948, the arrival of the new Viceroy, Lord Mountbatten (March 1947), the partition of India into India and Pakistan and the declaration of independence (July 1947 with effect from August 15th 1947).

With the attainment of Independence by India on 15th August 1947, the whole country was pulsating with new life. In the place of irresponsive and irresponsible administration at Delhi, a Cabinet form of Government responsible to the Parliament was organized. Pandit Jawaharlal Nehru was the head of the First Cabinet of the Independent India and the

---

1 District Calendar of Events of the Civil Disobedience Movement, August—December 1942—Secret, pages 34–39.

Fortnightly Reports (Confidential), dated 25th August 1942; 7th September 1942; 5th October 1942; 23rd October 1942; 7th November 1942; 21st November 1942; 5th December 1942; 21st December 1942; 7th January 1943.

Prime Minister of the land. He collected around himself a team of able men to run the administration of the newly independent country. Sardar Vallabhai Patel was the Deputy Prime Minister. In order to fill up the post of the Finance Minister in the First Cabinet, the Prime Minister Jawaharlal Nehru was able to think of none else except Sri R. K. Shanmugam Chetty who in the course of his parliamentary career beginning from 1927 has achieved notable success as the President of the Central Legislative Assembly in 1932, as the able representative of Indian view point at the Ottawa Conference for Imperial Preference for the British Empire Goods, as the Dewan of Cochin between 1935–43, as the Indian Member of the Purchase Mission (1943-46) and as the President of the Tariff Board, 1947. Sri R. K. Shanmugam Chetty during the very first year of his Finance Ministership was able to solve successfully the problem of repatriation of the sterling balances. His policies generally encouraged the industrial classes of the country to increase production. That Sri R. K. Shanmugam Chetty of Coimbatore was chosen as the First Finance Minister of India was considered to be a coveted honour for a citizen hailing from the district.

In Madras the Governor's rule which, as has been seen, was established in 1939 continued till the end of March 1946 when the Congress having contested and won in the general elections accepted office again. During this period from 1939 to 1946 when the Congress Party was fighting for freedom the other parties co-operated with the British Government and tried to strengthen their own position. Sri E. V. Ramaswami Naicker, now the recognized leader of the Justice Party, offered ' unconditional support of Tamilians in the prosecution of the war ' as a ' counterblast to the Congress attitude.''[1] He also courted the Muslim League, supported the scheme for Pakistan, inveighed against the Congress and continued to stir up anti-Brahmin feelings in Coimbatore and other Tamil districts.[2] His violent anti-Brahmin attitude, however, sometimes annoyed the Government. For, he threatened to start another agitation like the anti-Hindi agitation for the removal of caste and social distinctions in temples, restaurants, railway-refreshment rooms, etc.[3] Nor was this all. He convened a Justice Party Conference at Kancheepuram for urging the establishment of Dravidanad and at this Conference unveiled a map of Dravidanad ' comprising the areas where Tamil, Telugu, Kannada and Malayalam were spoken '.[4] But, fortunately for the Government, his

1 Fortnightly Report (Confidential), dated 19th October 1939.

2 Fortinightly Reports (Confidential), dated 18th June 1941 ; 4th August 1941; 18th June 1942 ; 9th September 1944.

3 *Idem*, dated 16th March 1940 ; 4th January 1941.

4 *Idem*, dated 19th June 1940.

position in the Justice Party was soon challenged when he and his followers, among whom the most prominent was Sri C. N. Annadurai, began to insist on changing the name of the Justice Party into ' The Dravidian Association ' or ' The Dravida Kazhagam ' and calling upon all title holders to surrender their titles. The orthodox Justicites now promptly assailed him, repudiated his leadership and met and elected first Sri B. Ramachandra Reddy and then Sri P. T. Rajan, as their leader.[1] But he was not discomfited, he continued to canvass support for the Dravida Kazhagam, holding meetings in Coimbatore and other Tamil districts.[2]

During the same period, the Communist Party, under its leaders like Sri Mohan Kumaramangalam, Sri P. Ramamoorthy, Sri M. R. Venkataraman and Sri K. Anandan Nambiar, cast its net wider and tried its best to secure a more permanent hold over the workers and the kisans. It found the time and circumstances eminently propitious for its propaganda. In July 1942 the ban on the Communists was removed [3] and in August 1942, as we have seen, the ban on the Congress was imposed. This gave the Communists a free field to carry on their activities, and their activities bore abundant fruit amidst the economic distress caused by the war, amidst the rise in prices and the scarcity of food-stuffs. The ban on the Communists was removed by the British Government in the hope that they would fully co-operate with the war effort since Russia, the home of Communism, had by then become a firm ally of Britain. In this hope the Government were not disappointed. The Communists rendered wholehearted support to the British in their war effort. Thus, at a meeting held in July 1942 by the Madras and Southern Mahratta Railway Employees' Union, Perambur, Sri Mohan Kumaramangalam said that, though the attitude of Britain towards Communism had until recently been hostile, it was now the duty of Indians to co-operate actively, in the war; that, if Japan conquered India it was not the British Imperialism but Indians that would suffer most, and that, therefore, the people should join the army in large numbers.[4] This co-operation in war effort, however, did not prevent the Communists from strengthening their hold upon the workers. They carried on an extensive underground propaganda, tried to seduce as many workers as possible from the Congress into the Communist fold, and in order to show how lively an interest they took in the cause of labour, they instigated the workers to make all sorts of demands and to go on strikes

1 Fortnightly Report (Confidential), dated 9th September 1944; 25th September 1944; 9th October 1944; 22nd May 1945.

2 *Idem*, dated 9th October 1944; 6th November 1944; 10th May 1946; 1st June 1946.

3 G.O. No. 2152, Public, dated 23rd July 1942.

4 Fortnightly Report (Confidential), dated 7th August 1942.

if their demands were not complied with[1]. In Coimbatore they organised the Mill Workers' Union as opposed to the Congress controlled Textile Workers' Union[2] and started strikes in the Vasantha Mills,[3] the Madukarai Cement Factory[4] and the Kaleshwara Mills, Coimbatore.[5] They also started scavengers' and sweepers' strikes in Coimbatore,[6] formed a Hotel Workers' Union at Coimbatore and instigated the hotel workers in the district to start an agitation for weekly holidays, minimum wages, etc.[7]

The secret as well as the open propaganda which they carried on everywhere against the Congress and the ruthless manner in which they tried to seize control over the workers, the kisans and the students compelled the Congress in 1945 to expel them from the Congress Party. The Congress Party in Madras now attempted to recover its lost ground and to consolidate its position by forming associations called Samithis for dealing with problems connected with the workers, kisans, students, food, etc., and by making intensive propaganda in all districts. But the Communists put up a stiff fight in Coimbatore as well as elsewhere.[8]

Then came the general elections, and Sri C. Rajagopalachari having by this time left the Congress on account of his differences with the Congressmen over the Pakistan issue, the leadership in Tamil Nadu passed into the hands of Sri Kamaraj Nadar, the President of the Tamil Nadu Congress Committee. There is plenty of evidence to show that he wielded at this time the most powerful influence in the Tamil districts.[9] He inaugurated a National Youth Federation in Madras for co-ordinating the activities of all Youth Organisations with the object of carrying on the constructive programme of the Congress.[10] And, as soon as the Congress High Command decided to contest the elections, he and his followers

---

1 Fortnightly Report (Confidential), dated 5th October 1942; 5th December 1942; 21st December 1942; 25th January 1943; 6th February 1943; 22nd February 1943; 24th July 1943; 21st December 1943; 6th March 1944; 9th October 1944; 21st January 1945; 9th April 1945; 22nd May 1945; 8th September 1945; 26th January 1946.

2 *Idem*, dated 9th September 1944.

3 *Idem*, dated 6th March 1944.

4 *Idem*, dated 23rd March 1944.

5 *Idem*, dated 22nd May 1945.

6 *Idem*, dated 8th June 1945.

7 *Idem*, dated 9th July 1945.

8 *See* for instance—Fortnightly Reports (Confidential), dated 8th November 1943; 22nd February 1943; 22nd May 1945; 25th October 1945; 26th November 1945.

9 Fortnightly Reports (Confidential), dated 9th October 1945; 25th October 1945; 8th November 1945; 11th January 1946; 26th January 1946; 7th March 1946.

10 *Idem*, dated 25th October 1945.

conducted strenuous tours in all the Tamil districts, including Coimbatore, addressing numerous meetings, explaining the Quit India Resolutions, etc., and creating enthusiasm everywhere for the Congress.[1] The opposition parties now more or less disappeared from the field, save the Communist Party. Throughout the election campaign the Communists kept the labour situation tense and restless everywhere. In Coimbatore they organized strikes in the Sarada Mills, Coimbatore,[2] in the ' B ' Mills of the Coimbatore Spinning and Weaving Mills[3] and in the Madukarai Cement Factory.[4]

In spite of all this, however, the Congress obtained an overwhelming majority in the general elections held in March 1946, securing 164 seats out of the 215 seats in the Legislative Assembly and 32 seats out of the 56 seats in the Legislative Council.[5] Sri T. Prakasam, who was now chosen as the leader of the Parliamentary Party, formed a ministry in April 1946. In April 1947, his ministry was succeeded by that of Sri O.P. Ramaswami Reddiar and this ministry was in April 1949 succeeded by that of Sri P. S. Kumaraswami Raja. Sri P. S. Kumaraswami Raja's ministry continued till the general elections of 1952 when it was succeeded by the ministry of Sri C. Rajagopalachari. And Sri C. Rajagopalachari's ministry was followed in April 1954 by the first ministry of Sri K. Kamaraj Nadar. Sri K. Kamaraj Nadar's ministry continued till the general elections of March 1957, the date at which we propose to close this chapter. During this whole period Sri Archibald Nye, who had become Governor in May 1946 continued to hold office even after the declaration of Independence till September 1948, when he was succeeded by the Maharaja of Bhavanagar. The latter was succeeded by Shri Sri Prakasa in March 1952 and Shri Sri Prakasa was succeeded by Sri A. J. John in December 1956.

The whole period from the time of the general elections of 1946 to the time of the general elections of 1952 was marked by momentous events in India. It was during this period that the New Constitution of India was hammered out and introduced (January 1950). It was also during this period that political agitation and political disturbances broke out everywhere consequent on the formation of Pakistan, the integration of the Indian States and the economic distress caused by the War and the bad seasons. Freedom was born in travail and had to be protected against all sorts of exceptional dangers. Pakistan created communal hatred

---

1 Fortnightly Reports (Confidential), dated 7th September 1945 ; 8th October 1945 ; 25th October 1945.

2 *Idem*, dated 25th January 1946.

3 *Idem*, dated 8th April 1946.

4 *Idem*.

5 Madras Administration Report 1946–1947, Part II, page 5.

among the Hindus and Muslims, and gave rise to All-India Movements like the Rashtriya Sevak Sangh directed against the Muslims and provincial movements like the Razakars in Hyderabad directed against the Hindus. The Dravida Kazhagam created a violent communal agitation in Madras against the Brahmins, the Aryans and the North Indians and gave rise to continual, unceasing, propaganda against the Government. The economic distress created everywhere high prices, hoarding and black-marketing and unusually hard times to the poor and gave rise to widespread activities of the Communists to capture labour and thereby to capture power, if possible. The situation was at the same time rendered worse by the death of Gandhiji, the only man who might have opposed Communism with vigour, and the birth of the Praja Party which caused a split in the Congress. No wonder, therefore, that Madras passed through troubled times during this period.

As we describe the political events that agitated Coimbatore during this period, we may indicate the changes introduced in Madras by the New Constitution. This Constitution declared India a sovereign democratic republic and defined the powers of the Government of India and the State Governments drawing freely from the Government of India Act of 1935. Now Madras became a Part A State and her Governor came to be appointed by the President of India for a period of 5 years. The Governor as the executive head of the State, was empowered to appoint as before, the Ministers and other high officials. He was to appoint the leader of the party or the parties commanding a majority in the Legislature as the Chief Minister and other persons chosen by the Chief Minister from among the members of the Legislature, as Ministers. He was to exercise, as before, special functions in relation to the scheduled areas and scheduled tribes subject to the control of the Government of India. He was also to exercise, certain discretionary powers without even consulting the Ministers. In all other matters he was to act on the advice of the Council of Ministers. All decisions of the Council of Ministers relating to the administration of the State and all proposals for legislation were to be communicated to him. He was to summon and prorogue the Legislature and he had the right to dissolve the Legislative Assembly. He might, as before, address or send messages to the Legislature, might give his assent to, or veto, a bill passed by the Legislature or send it back to the Legislature with amendments for its reconsideration. If, however, the Bill was again passed by the Legislature with or without amendments, he was not to withhold his assent to it, but he might, if it related to a subject in the concurrent list, reserve it for the consideration of the President. He was also to reserve for the consideration of the President bills relating to certain matters like the compulsory acquisition of property, the imposition of a tax on the sale or purchase of commodities considered by the Parliament to be essential for the life of the community, and bills which derogate from the powers of the High Court so as to endanger its position or impose any tax in respect of water or electricity under any inter-state river or river valley scheme. Nor was this all. He might promulgate an ordinance during the recess of the Legislature. But such an ordinance was to be laid before the Legislature when it reassembled and was to cease to operate at the end of six weeks or earlier if the Legislature were to disapprove it. And no demand for grant of money and no money bill was to be introduced in the Legislature except on his recommendation.

The Ministers were to hold office at the pleasure of the Governor. They were to be, as before, normally chosen from among the members of the Legislature, and if any Minister was not a member of the Legislature, he was to become one within six months or resign. All the Ministers were to have the right to attend the meetings of the Legislature, even though they might not be its members. They were to be collectively responsible to the Legislative Assembly. The Legislature was to consist of a Legislative Council and a Legislative Assembly; the former was to have 72 members and the latter 376 members. One-third of the members of the Council were to be elected by the municipalities, district boards and other local bodies, one-twelfth by graduates of at least 3 years' standing, one-twelfth by teachers of at least 3 years' standing in secondary schools, one-third by the members of the Legislative Assembly, while the remainder was to be nominated by the Governor from among persons possessing special knowledge in arts, science, etc. The Council was to be a permanent body not subject to dissolution, but one-third of its members were to retire every year. It could be abolished by a resolution passed by the majority of the total members of the Assembly or by a majority of no less than two-thirds of the members of the Assembly present. The Assembly members were to be elected by the voters on the basis of adult franchise. The Assembly was to sit for 5 years unless sooner dissolved by the Governor ; and it was to elect a Speaker and a Deputy Speaker. Meetings of the Legislature were to be summoned at least twice a year, and, for ten years from 1950 there was to be representation of minorities in the Assembly, seats being reserved for Scheduled Castes and Scheduled Tribes. The Legislature was to have the power to make laws on matters relating to the State list and the concurrent list. Normally its power to legislate with regard to the State list was to be unfettered; but, if theCouncil of State was to declare by two-thirds vote any matter included in the State list to be of national interest, the Union Legislature was to have the power to legislate with regard to that matter. Moreover, the President might issue a proclamation of emergency and might authorise the Union Legislature to make laws on subjects included in the State List. In regard to concurrent subjects, usually any laws made by the Union Legislature or any existing Union laws on the subject were to over-ride the laws passed by the Legislature. But, if the State laws had been reserved to the President and had been assented to by him, those laws were to prevail over the Union laws on the subject. The Legislature could not pass any laws on matters considered by the Governor to come within his discretionary powers. Nor could it pass any laws on matters relating to Scheduled areas unless such laws were assented to by the Governor. As to the relative powers of the Council and the Assembly, money bills could be introduced only in the Assembly. After such bills were passed by the Assembly they were to be sent to the Council, and they were to become Acts on being assented to by the Governor 14 days after the receipt of the bills by the Council, whether the Council approved them or not. Only the Assembly was to have the power to vote upon demands for grants of money. All other bills might be introduced in either house and must be approved by both of them. If, however, a bill passed by the Assembly was rejected by the Council or was amended in such a way that the Assembly could not accept it, or if more than three months were to elapse without the Council doing anything about it, the Assembly could pass it a second time and send it to the Council. It would then be taken to have been passed by both the houses after the lapse of a month whatever the Council might do with it.

The Constitution, of course, proved to be no remedy for the political distempers of the time. Those distempers, as has already been stated, manifested themselves in all their virulence from 1946. All the political parties now came forward to fight with the Congress Party in Power, and none gave the Congress Government more anxiety than the Communist Party, the Dravida Kazhagam and the Praja Party.

The Communists vowed to discredit the Congress, to capture labour and to keep up a sustained agitation against the Government even before the results of the general elections of 1946 were announced.[1] And soon after Sri T. Prakasam formed his Ministry, they demanded nationalisation of all industries, opened a parliamentary office in Madras to collect statistics about the grievances of the workers and organized a general strike in the South Indian Railway.[2] When this strike was scotched, they openly accused the Government of being capitalistic, tried to capture labour in all fields, formed labour unions in the city as well as in the

1 Fortnightly Report (Confidential), dated 20th April 1946.

2 *Idem*, dated 8th June 1946 ; 21st September 1946.

districts, set up village food committees, came into violent clashes with the Congressmen, fomented a series of strikes in mills, factories, dockyards and essential services and, what is more, incited agricultural labourers making it thereby difficult for the authorities to maintain law and order over wide and dispersed areas.[1] The anarchy let loose by the Communists compelled the Government to take stringent measures to preserve public peace and safeguard public interests. Early in 1947 the Government issued the Madras Maintenance of Public Order Ordinance (Ordinance No. I of 1947)[2] and followed it up by the Madras Maintenance of Public Order Act (Act I of 1947)[3]. In this Act, in order to deal with subversive activities, they provided for preventive detention, imposition of collective fines and censorship, control of meetings, processions, camps, drills and parades, requisitioning of property and control of essential services. This Act was amplified and amended in 1948[4] and re-enacted in 1949 (Act XXIII of 1949).[5] Besides this, in September 1949, the Communist organisations were banned under the Criminal Law Amendment Act[6] and when this act was declared *ultra vires* of the Constitution by the High Court[7], the drive against the Communists was continued under the Preventive Detention Amendment Act (India Act IV) of 1951.[8] Without these special laws passed against them, it was quite evident that their activities would have assumed very serious proportions and led to utter chaos in the fields of kisan and industrial labour. But it is worth remarking that the Government, though they took stringent measures to put down Communist activities, did not show any undue harshness towards the Communists. Their action in most cases of detention under the Acts mentioned above, was upheld by the Advisory Boards set up to review such cases. And yet, they released all detenus who gave an undertaking not to take part in subversive activities.[9] They granted allowances to the families of many

---

1 Fortnightly Reports (Confidential), dated 20th April 1946 ; 10th May 1946 ; 1st June 1946 ; 8th July 1946 ; 24th July 1946 ; 9th August 1946 ; 30th August 1946 ; 21st August 1946; 27th August 1946; 30th October 1946; 19th November 1946 ; 23rd November 1946 ; 11th December 1946 ; 28th January 1947 ; 12th February 1947.

2 G.O. No. 13, Legal, dated 22nd January 1947.

Fortnightly Reports (Confidential), dated 12th February 1947 ; 25th February 1947.

3 G.O. No. 26, Legal, dated 12th March 1947.

4 G.O. No. 199, Legal, dated 29th December 1948.

5 G.O. No. 173, Legal, dated 15th October 1949.

G.O. No. 188, Legal, dated 29th October 1949.

6 Fortnightly Report (Confidential), dated 13th October 1949.

7 *Idem*, dated 26th September 1950.

8 *Idem*, dated 14th March 1951.

9 G.O. No. 2339, Public, dated 19th July 1949.

of the detenus and they also released on parole several detenus to attend on their sick relations, to perform obligatory ceremonies, etc.[1]

In Coimbatore, the Communists tried to capture mostly mill labour and, in so doing, came into violent clashes with Congressmen which sometimes culminated even in murders. Through their Mill Workers' Union they organized a series of strikes in the textile mills. Thus in 1946 they started ' a wave of strikes ' in the district, the most serious of which was the strike of the ' A ' and ' B ' Mills of the Coimbatore Spinning and Weaving Company. In this strike the strikers insisted that only Communist labourers should be recruited, and attacked all loyal workers with stones and soda water bottles and called for the intervention of the police which ended in the police opening fire and killing 7 and injuring 20 persons.[2] In 1947 they organized even more serious strikes in the district. These strikes began early in January in the Asher and Dhanalakshmi Mills, Tiruppur,[3] and developed first into lock outs in the Balasubramaniam Mills, Singanallur, and in the Madukarai Cement Factory, and then, into a general strike in all the mills, except three, in the district (February). Over 35,000 workers struck work and a number of persons were arrested for attacking loyal workers and resorting to arson. It was not till the Chief Minister and the Minister for Labour came upon the scene and started negotiations that the strike was called off.[4] This happened under Sri T. Prakasam's Ministry.

The position in the district did not by any means improve under Sri O. P. Ramasami Reddiar's Ministry. The Communists now widely criticised the Maintenance of Public Order Act as an Act aimed at the suppression of civil liberties and organised what is called ' the Basic Demands Day '.[5] To begin with, they launched a succession of short strikes in the various textile mills in Coimbatore and came into violent clashes with the labourers of the Congress controlled Textile Workers'

---

1 G.O. No. 1346, Public, dated 6th May 1947.
G.O. No. 2492, Public, dated 7th October 1948.
G.O. No. 1797, Public, dated 23rd July 1948.
G.O. No. 1944, Public, dated 17th August 1948.
G.O. No. 4613, Public, dated 28th December 1949.
G.O. No. 5, Public, datod 3rd January 1950.

2 Fortnightly Reports (Confidential), dated 27th September 1946 ; 19th November 1946 ; 23rd November 1946.
G.O. No. 2701, Public, dated 14th December 1946.

3 G.O. No. 2701, Public, dated 28th January 1947.

4 Fortnightly Reports (Confidential), dated 12th February 1947 ; 25th February 1947 ; 14th March 1947 ; 24th March 1947.
G.O. No. 864, Public, (Confidential), dated 18th March 1947.

5 *Idem*, dated 17th April 1947.

Union at the Sarada, Mahalakshmi and Radha-Krishna Mills.[1] At the last mentioned mill an open fight between the two parties resulted in injuries to 41 persons, bobbins, iron-rollers and stones being freely used.[2] Then came the strikes in the Kaleswara Mills and in the seven cigar factories in Erode as well as bitter and sometimes fatal contests between the Communists and the Congressmen which necessitated the promulgation of an order under Section 30 of the Police Act over the Coimbatore area (June 1947), and the intervention of the police in Tiruppur and Udumalpet. All this ended in several arrests.[3] The situation became no better in 1948. The Communists continued to stir up strikes. In the beginning of the year they organsied strikes lasting for more than three months in all the mills except one in Coimbatore when retrenchment was effected by the mill owners on the recommendations of the Textile Standardization Committee. They opposed all attempts made by Sri Kamaraj Nadar to effect a settlement and it was with great difficulty that the Government at last brought about a settlement between the mill owners and the labour unions.[4] Shortly afterwards they started the scavengers' strike in Coimbatore, Pollachi, Dharapuram and Erode and a strike in the A.B.T. Bus Service.[5] All the time they also tried to strengthen their party in the district; they trained youths in army drills, collected funds to keep the leaders underground, and mercilessly assailed the Government both in the press and on the platform.[6] Early in 1949 they threatened a strike in the South Indian Railway, but this was scotched by a large number of arrests in the district and elsewhere.[7]

They did not in the least abate their activities when Sri P. S. Kumaraswami Raja formed his Ministry. They now turned their attention, for a time, to the police in Coimbatore as well as other districts and tried their best to seduce them. They distributed leaflets entitled ' Policemen, the struggle for labourers and kisans is your struggle—Those who oppose the people are sure to be ruined ', and in these leaflets they played upon the feelings of the police by emphasizing their poor pay and service conditions

---

1 Fortnightly Report (Confidential), dated 30th April 1947.

2 *Idem*, dated 30th April 1947

3 Fortnightly Reports (Confidential), dated 3rd September 1947; 28th June 1947; 29th June 1947; 11th October 1947; 13th November 1947; 22nd December 1947; 15th January 1948.

4 *Idem*, dated 14th February 1948; 30th March 1948; 2nd April 1948; 21st April 1948; 10th May 1948; 14th May 1948; 9th July 1948.

5 Fortnightly Reports (Confidential), dated 2nd April 1948; 18th June 1948.

6 Fortnightly Reports (Confidential), dated 30th March 1948; 2nd April 1948; 31st August 1948.

7 Fortnightly Reports (Confidential), dated 22nd February 1949; 4th March 1949; 13th March 1949.

and appealing to them not to obey their superiors.[1] They went on making at the same time, a ceaseless propaganda among labourers and stirred up strikes in the Somasundara and Kaleswara Mills, Coimbatore, and in a knitting factory at Tiruppur.[2] They then issued secret instructions to build up their party on the proletariat basis, to enforce rigorous discipline, to form village committees, to organise the unemployed, to adopt guerilla tactics when attacked, and to do everything possible to achieve mass support.[3] They committed in many places, including Coimbatore, murder, sabotage and arson, criticised the Congress policies, demanded the release of political prisoners, issued pamphlets captioned 'Congress Prisons are Hitler's Cells' and menaced the authorities with reprisals.[4] They organised the Martyrs' Day in the District on 5th September 1949 and, on the 7th September, some 30 of them, armed with sticks and spears, entered the Railway Colony at Erode and stabbed the vice-president of the Congress controlled South Indian Railway Workers' Union.[5]

Acts such as these committed not only in the Coimbatore district but also throughout the State, in spite of the Maintenance of Public Order Act, soon exhausted the patience of the Government. In September 1949, therefore, the Government declared the Communist Party and other important organisations under its control in the State, unlawful under the Criminal Law Amendment Act.[6] This very much improved matters. The Communists indeed, for some time, continued to indulge in acts of violence in Coimbatore as well as in other districts and denounced the ban as 'a monstrous attack on democracy'[7]. But gradually they were compelled to slow down their violent activities so that, in 1950, the District became comparatively calm. But then a new difficulty suddenly arose. The High Court held the ban *ultra vires* of the Constitution. The Government appealed to the Supreme Court, but, in the meantime, the ban having become ineffective, the Communists at once revived their activities everywhere.[8] They stirred up labour troubles in Coimbatore again early in 1951.[9] But, very soon, the passing of the Preventive Detention

---

1 *Idem*, dated 25th April 1949.

2 Fortnightly Reports (Confidential), dated 11th June 1949; 12th July 1949; 4th August 1949.

3 Fortnightly Reports (Confidential), dated 12th July 1949.

4 Fortnightly Reports (Confidential), dated 30th August 1949; 14th September 1949.

5 Fortnightly Reports (Confidential), dated 27th September 1949.

6 *Idem*, dated 13th October 1949.

7 Fortnightly Reports (Confidential), dated 13th October 1949; 28th October 1949.

8 *Idem*, dated 26th September 1950; 15th November 1950.

9 *Idem*, dated 16th January 1951; 25th January 1951.

Amendment Act (India Act IV) of 1951 enabled the Government to muzzle their violent activities.[1] This Act piloted successfully by Sri C. Rajagopalachari as Home Minister in the Central Legislature, came in for a great deal of criticism at the hands of the Communists. They denounced it as an 'undemocratic' measure, dubbed the Home Minister, as a 'Dictator' and warned him to give up 'the idea of carrying on the administration at the point of the bayonet'.[2] But the Act, none the less, came really as a blessing. All moderate public opinion voiced by the newspapers like 'The Hindu' welcomed it. The drive against the Communists was intensified and law and order were more or less restored in Coimbatore and elsewhere.

All this time, side by side with the Communist agitation, communal agitation was carried on at full blast by the Dravida Kazhagam. Soon after the accession of the Congress Government in 1946, Sri E. V. Ramaswami Naicker, the leader of the Kazhagam, began to agitate for the establishment of Dravidasthan, in all the Tamil districts, including Coimbatore.[3] He won the sympathy of the Muslim League for his move and never tired of repeating that Tamil Nadu should be freed from 'the domination of Britishers, Aryans and other exploiters.[4] When the Black Shirts, which was a militant off-shoot of the Kazhagam, was declared by the Government an unlawful association along with the other militant association like the Khaksers and the Rashtriya Sevak Sangh, be kept up a continual barrage against the Government.[5] Black shirts, he said, were worn only to show the present degradation of the Dravidians by the Aryans, and that they would continue to be worn until a castless society was established.[6] He appealed to the people to observe 1st July 1948 as a Dravidanad Separation Day, criticised the policy of the Government to make Hindi compulsory in schools, exhorted the Tamilians to oppose the measure, recruited more than 10,000 volunteers in the State to start an Anti-Hindi agitation and appointed Sri C. N. Annadurai as the first Anti-Hindi Dictator for picketing schools in Madras.[7] Actual picketing was started in Madras in September 1948. In some places even women volunteers wearing black saris took part in the agitation. When the police removed one batch of picketers and left them outside the City, another batch came forward to take its place, until at last the picketers had to be

---

1 Fortnightly Report (Confidential), dated 14th March 1951.

2 *Idem*, dated 14.h Marth 1951.

3 *Idem*, dated 25h June 1946; 14th March 1947.

4 *Idem*, dated 11th August 1947; 11th October 1947; 14th February 1948.

5 *Idem* dated 25th February 1948.

6 *Idem*, dated 2nd April 1948; 21st April 1948; 14th May 1948.

7 *Idem*, dated 21st July 1948; 31st August 1948.

arrested and convicted.[1] Sri E. V. Ramaswami Naicker himself had to be arrested when he defied prohibitory orders in Tanjore.[2] As soon as he was released, however, he started ' the Anti-Repression Day ' meetings in Coimbatore as well as other Tamil districts and launched again Anti-Hindi agitation in Madras early in 1949.[3] This was not all. He held a Kural Conference in Madras, and urged the Dravidians to discontinue the study of Aryan literature and to stop the patronage of Aryan newspapers like ' The Hindu ' and ' The Indian Express ' and, soon afterwards, started similar propaganda throughout Tamil Nad.[4] He addressed meetings at several places in the Coimbatore district, received a welcome address from the Municipal Council of Udumalpet, and courted arrest by holding a public meeting in defiance of prohibitory orders.[5] And wherever he went, Erode, Anamalai, etc., he whipped up communal feelings, by condemning Brahmanism and idolatry, and by expatiating on the alleged oppression and exploitation of the Dravidians by the Aryans.[6]

Shortly afterwards it looked as if the Kazhagam would cease to be a menace. Sri E. V. Ramaswami Naicker married the lady who was the editor of the ' Viduthalai ' despite the opposition of Sri C. N. Annadurai and several of his followers and thereby created a split in his party (July 1949).[7] Sri C. N. Annadurai, Sri K. Neelamegam and others walked out of the Dravida Kazhagam and formed a new party called the *Dravida Munnetra Kazhagam* (the Dravidian Progressive Party). The new party was duly inaugurated on 16th October 1949.[8] But very soon it became evident that this split, instead of abating the Anti-Brahmin and the Pro-Dravidasthan propaganda, actually intensified it. For, instead of one party two parties now came to conduct this propaganda. Branches of the new party were opened in Coimbatore and other Tamil districts, and by December 1949, the party could boast of no less than 350 branches.[9] In 1950 both the old and the new party started their campaign in Coimbatore as well as other Tamil districts with renewed vigour. Both demanded Dravidasthan, both showed Communist leanings, both characterised the

---

1 Fortnightly Reports (Confidential), dated 29th September 1948; 12th October 1948; 13th December 1948.

2 Fortnightly Reports (Confidential), dated 21st January 1949.

3 *Idem*, dated 2nd February 1949.

4 Fortnightly Reports (Confidential), dated 22nd February 1949; 13th March 1949.

5 Fortnightly Reports (Confidential), dated 13th May 1949.

6 *Idem*, dated 11th June 1949.

7 Fortnightly Reports (Confidential), dated 12th July 1949; 4th August 1949; 12th August 1949.

8 *Idem*, dated 27th September 1949; 13th October 1949; 28th October 1949.

9 Fortnightly Reports (Confidential), dated 27th December 1949.

Congress as a Capitalistic organisation, both courted Muslim support, both appealed to the Tamilians to observe the Republic Day as a day of mourning and both asserted that the advent of the New Constitution meant the complete domination of South India by North India, of Dravidians by the Aryans.[1] Both of them began to write books and stage dramas inciting class hatred and both started Anti-Hindi agitation in the whole of Tamil Nad, holding Anti-Hindi meetings and condemning the policy of the Government.[2] Sri E. V. Ramaswami Naicker characterised the Government ' as a reign of dacoits ' under which, men were shot down like birds '.[3] When the Government introduced the compulsory study of Hindi and English as second and third languages in schools and organised the ' Tamil Valarchi Conference ' in Coimbatore in May 1950, Sri C. N. Annadurai organized the 'Muth Tamil Valarchi Conference' as a counter blast at the same place in the same month. This conference attacked the Government policy and passed resolutions urging the Government to make Tamil a compulsory subject in schools and the State language in Tamilnad.[4] Both the Kazhagams now raised the cry that the Tamil language was in danger, until the Government withdrew Hindi as a compulsory subject from schools and made Tamil or mother tongue and English as compulsory subjects.[5] Sri E. V. Ramaswami Naicker, in the meanwhile, began to solemnize marriages without marriage ceremonies, criticizing the ceremonies as being Brahminic, Aryan, and therefore foreign to Dravidanad.[6]

Nor was this all. About the middle of 1950, the High Court, on a petition filed by two Brahmin students, considered that the procedure laid down by the Government for the admission into Government colleges—a procedure by which seats were reserved for certain communities in a certain order—was inconsistent with Articles 15 (1) and 22 (2) of the Constitution.[7] This at once created a storm of protests from both the Kazhagams, and both now started a virulent agitation for reversing the High Court judgment. They launched a hartal on 14th August, insisted on the retention of the ' Communal G.O. ' regarding admissions and intensified their propaganda against Brahmins and North Indians.

---

1 Fortnightly Reports (Confidential), dated 3rd February 1950 ; 9th February 1950 ; 27th February 1950 ; 13th March 1950.

2 *Idem*, dated 13th March 1950 ; 18th April 1950 ; 24th April 1950 ; 8th March 1950 ; 22nd May 1950.

3 Fortnightly Reports (Confidential), dated 6th June 1950.

4 Fortnightly Reports (Confidential), dated 6th June 1950 ; 24th June 1950 ; 10th July 1950.

5 *Idem*, dated 10th July 1950 ; 31st July 1950 ; 10th August 1950.

6 Fortnightly Reports (Confidential), dated 24th June 1950.

7 *Idem*, dated 10th August 1950.

They staged black flag demonstrations on the occasions of visits of North Indian Ministers, criticised the practice of giving welcome addresses to North Indian Leaders or naming public places after them and preached the boycott of Brahmin coffee hotels and Brahmin owned newspapers. And when both Sri E.V. Ramaswami Naicker and Sri C. N. Annadurai were sentenced to pay fines or undergo imprisonment for publishing the objectionable books ' Ponmozhigal ' and ' Arya Mayai ', the Kazhagamites held a spate of public meetings everywhere, including Coimbatore, and read passages from both the books at those meetings.[1] It was at this time that the Munnetra Kazhagam started a journal of its own called ' the Dravida Nadu ', under the aegis of Sri C. N. Annadurai.[2] And it was from this time that both the Kazhagams determined to defy law and order on a large scale. They now advised the people to take to ticketless travel on trains, to boycott North Indian goods, to picket North Indian shops and Brahmin hotels, to enter into temples and desecrate the idols, to efface Hindi names from railway station sign-boards, to sell prohibitory literatures and to violate prohibitory orders.[3] They also now began to indulge in cheap ridicule against the Ministry. In one of their public meetings in Coimbatore they called the Ministry as ' the tail of the Central Government '.[4]

Towards the end of 1950, their activities went beyond the bounds of law. They held public meetings in many places defying the ban on such meetings. They wrote a series of objectionable articles in their newspapers. Sri E. V. Ramaswami Naicker himself wrote a number of articles in the ' Viduthalai ' urging his followers to continue the agitation against the Brahmins and North Indians despite the opposition of the Government. In Madras certain selected hotels and cloth shops run by the North Indians, were picketed. In the districts, the Brahmin hotel keepers were intimidated and the word ' Brahmin ' on the name boards of Brahmin hotels was tarred. So also were tarred the Hindi names on the sign-boards in railway station. And everywhere an insistent demand was put forward for the establishment of Dravidasthan and for the retention of the ' Communal G.O. ' Many arrests and convictions followed. Sri Kamaraj Nadar and the Ministers went about condemning the anti-social activities of the Kazhagams. But still the Kazhagamites continued their activities. They also now indulged in

[1] Fortnightly Reports (Confidential), dated 28th August 1950; 26th September 1950; 12th October 1950; 27th October 1950.

[2] Fortnightly Reports (Confidential), dated 27th December 1950.

[3] Fortnightly Reports (Confidential), dated 27th October 1950; 15th November 1950.

[4] Fortnightly Reports (Confidential), dated 27th October 1950.

violent attacks on the food policy and yarn policy of the Government, especially in Coimbatore, where the scarcity of food and yarn was causing some distress among the people.[1]

Then came the time for the commencement of propaganda for the general elections. Although the elections were actually held early in 1952, the election propaganda was started by all the parties early in 1951 itself. Not only the Communists and the Kazhagamites but also the Socialists, the Muslim leaguers, and the Justicites now entered into the political arena. New parties were also formed like the Tamil Nad Toilers' Party and the Democratic Party, and the position of the Congress was rendered all the more difficult by the defection of some of its members. Acharya Kripalani raised the standard of revolt in the North and formed a new party called the Praja Party or the Kisan Mazdoor Praja Party, and to this party joined eagerly some dissatisfied Congress leaders in the South, like Sri T. Prakasam and Sri N. G. Ranga in the Andhradesa, Sri Adityan in Tamilnad and Sri Kelappan in Malabar.

The Communists now practically withdrew from subversive activities and concentrated their attention solely on the elections and the improvement in the law and order situation. The Government not only released almost all Communist detenus but also permitted them to take part in election propaganda. This consider helped the Communist election campaign.[2] Sri A. K. Gopalan visited a number of Communist centres in the Tamil districts and addressed several election meetings. In Coimbatore he exhorted all labour to rally round the Communist flag and promised that in case his party came to power, it would confiscate all foreign possessions, nationalise all key industries and divide all land among the landless tillers. He also invited all leftist parties, including the Socialists and Congressmen opposed to the Government, to unite with the Communists so as to build up a broad-based United Front against the ruling party.[3] The Communists. besides, staged dramas in Erode and other places and brought leaders like Dr. Kitchlew, Sri Mohan Kumaramangalam, Sri S. A. Dange and Mrs. Aruna Asaf Ali to address public meetings in Coimbatore.[4] These leaders asserted at the propaganda meetings, that the independence achieved by India was a mockery,

---

[1] Fortnightly Reports (Confidential), dated 15th November 1950; 21st November 1950 ; 26th December 1959 ; 16th January 1951 ; 25th January 1951 ; 7th February 1951 ; 27th February 1951 ; 27th March 1951

[2] Fortnightly Report (Confidential), dated 15th October 1951.

[3] *Idem*, dated 11th March 1951.

[4] Fortnightly Reports (Confidential), dated 28th July 1951 ; 30th August 1951; 14th September 1951 ; 19th November 1951 ; 29th November 1951.

since British capitalism continued to keep the country under economic bondage; that the existing shortage of food and cloth was the result of maladministration by the Congress; that the Congress was really Fascist and controlled by capitalists, that the Government was contaminated by corruption and nepotism and that, if only the Communists were returned to power, there would be great prosperity similar to that prevailing in China, Czechoslovakia and Rumania. They also stressed the need for a United Front of all democratic parties to defeat the Congress.[1] As the election time approached they intensified their campaign, organising jathas, processions and drama, holding public meetings as well as street corner meetings, and going about from village to village collecting funds and distributing Communist pamphlets.[2]

Neither of the Kazhagams contested the elections, but they tried their utmost to undermine the Government by constantly attacking it, and the Dravida Kazhagam, in particular, by asking people everywhere to vote for the Communist Party candidates and, failing them, the Independents. Thus, Sri E. V. Ramaswami Naicker vehemently criticised the Supreme Court Judgment which upheld the judgment of the Madras High Court on the ' Communal G.O. ' demanded the immediate resignation of the Madras Ministers on that issue, and organised black flag demonstrations in almost every place which the Ministers visited.[3] Sri C. N. Annadurai joined hands with Sri. E. V. Ramaswami Naicker, and, in addition to organising black flag demonstrations, staged anti-Brahmin dramas of Sri M. R. Radha and his troupe in several places.[4] Thus black flag demonstrations were made when a State Minister visited Gobichettipalayam[5] and an anti-Brahmin drama was staged at Coimbatore in which Sri C. N. Annadurai himself took the role of Ravana.[6] In May 1951 an ' Exploitation, Prevention and Communal Rights Conference ' was held at Erode at which Sri E. V. Ramaswami Naicker, Sri Guruswami and others accused the Madras Ministry of playing into the hands of the Union Ministry against the interests of Dravidians. Both the Kazhagamites harped on Dravidasthan especially at Coimbatore where they wished to make capital out of the plight of the handloom weavers.[7] On the near approach of elections Sri E. V. Ramaswami Naicker addressed a public

---

1 Fortnightly Reports (Confidential), dated 29th November 1951.

2 Fortnightly Reports (Confidential), dated 11th December 1951; 31st December 1951; 1st February 1952.

3 *Idem*, dated 26th April 1951; 11th May 1951; 14th June 1951.

4 *Idem*, dated 26th April 1951; 11th May 1951.

5 Fortnightly Reports (Confidential), dated 29th May 1951.

6 *Idem*, dated 14th June 1951.

7 *Idem*, dated 29th May 1951.

meeting at Erode and held a Communal Rights Conference at Tiruppur and exhorted the people not to vote for the Congress.[1] And, at a meeting in Coimbatore, he said that Dravidasthan could be achieved by the Dravidians in much the same way as Pakisthan was achieved by the Muslims[2]. Sri C. N. Annadurai, at the same time, pointed out that when the cry for the formation of the Andhra State which was then raised, was at its height, the Dravidians should put forth all their strength and demand Dravidastan [3]. From about October 1951 the Dravida Kazhagam persistently appealed to the people to vote for the Communist Party[4], while the Dravida Munnetra Kazhagam, although it refused to pledge its full support to the Communist Party unless it subscribed to the demand for Dravidasthan, indirectly helped that party not a little by carrying on Anti-Congrees propaganda.[5]

Some of the other parties that entered the election contest can be disposed of in a few words. The Socialist Party had from the beginning some status in Madras, and now it tried to improve its position by holding frequent propaganda meetings. Early in June it observed a Construction Week in various centres including Coimbatore. During this week it not only held public meetings but took out processions and presented the so called ' Peoples Charter ' to the Collectors containing the demands that the lands should be divided among the tillers of the soil, that the factories and workshops should be nationalised, that foodstuffs should be made available at low prices, that an All-Party Government should be set up, and that the maximum and the minimum incomes should be fixed at Rs. 1,000 and Rs. 100 respectively. [6] These and other socialistic principles it preached in many places and at the near approach of the elections, invited Sri Jai Prakash Narain to come to the south to carry on propaganda. He toured Coimbatore and some other districts, holding public meetings, collecting funds and observing that, while the Congress had outlived its usefulness and ceased to be an organisation of the common man, the Communists had determined to bring the country under the dictatorship of Stalin.[7] The Muslim League Party showed no marked activity either in Coimbatore or elsewhere. It hesitated at first as to

---

1 Fortnigbtly Reports, dated 28th July 1951.

2 Fortnightly Reports (Confidential), dated 30th August 1951.

3 *Idem*, dated 26th September 1951.

4 Fortnightly Reports (Confidential), dated 15th October 1951; 19th November 1951 ; 31st December 1951; 18th January 1952 ; 1st February 1952.

5 *Idem*, dated 15th October 1951 ; 19th November 1951 ; 31st December 1951 ; 18th January 1952 ; 1st February 1952.

6 Fortnightly Reports (Confidential), dated 22nd June 1951.

7 *Idem*, dated 11th December 1951.

whether to join the Congress or to fight the elections independently and eventually decided to contest the elections only in constituencies where the Muslims were in a majority.[1] The Justice Party contested the elections but showed no marked activity in Coimbatore or other districts. The Tamilnad Toilers' Party, a new party organised by Sri S. S. Ramaswami Padayachi, appealed only to the Vanniyakulakshatriyas and confined its activities mostly to South Arcot.[2] Another new party known as the Democratic Party formed by Sri M. Ratnaswami, a former Vice-Chancellor of the Annamalai University appealed to all democrat in the Tamil districts. Its leader pointed out that the Congress party had been tried and found wanting, that the Praja Party was nothing but an inferior edition of the Congress, that the Muslim League and the Hindu Mahasabha were communal bodies and that the Justice Party was moribund.[3] But it showed hardly any life in Coimbatore or other districts.

The greatest activity was, however, shown by the rebels from the Congress and the leaders of the Kisan Mazdoor Praja Party, Sri T. Prakasam, Sri N. G. Ranga, Sri Adityan and Sri Kelappan. They went from place to place gathering followers and making public speeches not a little damaging to the reputation of the Congress[4]. Sri N. G. Ranga, it is true, subsequently left the Praja Party, but then it was only to form a new party known as the Krishikar Lok Party; and he and his party began to co-operate with the Congress Party only after the elections were over and the new Ministry was formed. Sri T. Prakasam, in particular, took a bitter attitude towards the Congress and brought charges of corruption and nepotism against it.[5] Sri Adityan, the leader of the Tamilnad branch of the Praja Party, held a Convention in Madras in August 1951 at which Acharya Kripalani, the architect of the party itself, indulged in a tirade against the Congress Government.[6] A little later the Acharya spurned an appeal issued by Pandit Nehru to all the dissidents to come back and rejoin the Congress and formed an electoral alliance with the Socialists (with their leader Sri Jai Prakash Narain) at Madras.[7] Sri Adityan then toured the Tamil districts, including Coimbatore, carrying on propaganda, blaming the Congress Government for its corruption and mismanagement

---

1 Fortnightly Reports (Confidential), dated 26th September 1951 ; 25th October 1951 ; 29th November 1951.

2 Fortnightly Report (Confidential), dated 29th November 1951.

3 *Idem*, dated 28th July 1951.

4 Fortnightly Reports (Confidential), dated 29th May 1951 ; 14th June 1951 ; 22nd June 1951 ; 30th August 1951.

5 *See*, e.g., Fortnightly Report (Confidential), dated 29th May 1951.

6 *See*, e.g., Fortnightly Reports (Confidential), dated 14th September 1951 ; 26th September 1951.

7 *See*, e.g., Fortnightly Reports (Confidential), dated 15th October 1951.

and charging it with being solely responsible for the scarcity of food and cloth. He, as well as his colleagues, predicted that, if the Congress were returned to power, a violent revolution would take place and that the only way to avert this impending doom was to vote for the Praja Party which guaranteed to carry on administration ' on Gandhian principles '[1].

The Congress entered the lists against all these parties hoping to succeed by virtue of their solid achievements. Even from April 1951, Sri Kamaraj Nadar, the President of the Tamil Nad Congress Committee, and other leading Congressmen began to address a number of public meetings.[2] In the same month Dr. Rajendra Prasad, the President of the Republic, himself came down to Madras and appealed to the public to safeguard India's hard-won freedom by preserving unity and putting down all fissiparous tendencies.[3] Throughout May, June and July, Sri Kamaraj Nadar and some of the Ministers addressed a large number of public meetings in Coimbatore as well as other districts, explaining the difficulties facing the Government and the efforts made to overcome them with a view to removing the hardships of the people. They deplored the split caused in the Congress and pointed out that, if the Congress had become impure, it was for the dissidents to remain in the Congress and remove the impurities and not to form a new rival party. They deplored the anti-social activities of both the Kazhagams and condemned them in no uncertain terms. They deplored also the differences that had arisen between the Town Congress Committee and the District Congress Committee in Coimbatore and tried to patch them up.[4] In August Sri Kamaraj Nadar and some Ministers once more toured Coimbatore and other districts and once more condemned the activities of the Kazhagams.[5] Thereafter they intensified their propaganda everywhere and pointed out that unless the Congress Party came to power, there would be an end of the democratic rule in the country.[6] Pandit Nehru came to Madras on 27th November to give a fillip to the election campaign. Public meetings were now held throughout the State at which not only the State Ministers but also the Union Ministers addressed the people and warned them not to be misled by the malicious propaganda of interested parties. They charac-

---

[1] Fortnightly Reports (Confidential), dated 29th November 1951; 11th December 1951.

[2] Fortnightly Reports (Confidential), dated 15th April 1951.

[3] *Idem*, dated 26th April 1951.

[4] Fortnightly Reports (Confidential), dated 14th June 1951 ; 22nd June 1951; 9th July 1951 ; 28th July 1951.

[5] *Idem*, dated 30th August 1951 ; 14th September 1951.

[6] *Idem*, dated 26th September 1951 ; 15th October 1951 ; 19th November 1951 29th November 1951 ; 11th December 1951.

terised the Communists as the satellites of Russia whose policy was one violence and destruction, and the Kazhagamites as the authors of anti-social activities. They also emphasized that the Congress was the only organization which had a sound economic programme calculated to improve the lot of the common people. [1]

It was in the midst of all this ebullition that the general elections were held in January 1952. The results of these elections proved not a little disappointing to the Congress. In the State sphere, the Chief Minister Sri Kumaraswami Raja and five other Ministers, Sri B. Gopala Reddi, Sri Kala Venkata Rao, Sri M. Bhakthavatsalam, Sri K. Madhava Menon and Sri K. Chandramouli were defeated. In the Union sphere, Sri K. Santhanam, the Minister for Transport and Railways, Dr. P. Subbarayan, India's former Ambassador to Indonesia and Mrs. Subbarayan, sitting member of Parliament, were defeated.[2] Nor were the results wholly palatable to the dissidents of the Congress Party. Both Sri T. Prakasam and Sri N. G. Ranga were defeated, although their parties secured a good number of seats.[3] The results proved heartening only to the Communist Party. A very large number of Communists were returned to the Assembly and among them were Sri P. Ramamoorthy, and Sri M. Kalyanasundaram and Sri K. T. Raju, the two important labour Union leaders.[4] However, the Congress Party, though it lost the absolute majority, still remained the largest single party in the Assembly. The position of the major parties in the Assembly stood as follows : Congress 132 members, Communists 61, Kisan Mazdoor Praja Party 35, Tamil Nad Toiler's Party 19, Krishak Lok Party 15, Socialists 13, Independents 63, and others 17.[5] The Congress at the same time gained 34 seats in the Council.[6]

The uneasiness created by this position in Congress circles was increased by the frantic efforts made by the non-Congress Parties, especially the Communist Party and the Praja Party, to form a United Democratic Front in the Legislature against the Congress Party. The United Front received also the blessings of the Dravida Kazhagam and the Dravida Munnetra Kazhagam.[7] The Congress Party now began to seriously take stock of the situation. Some of its members felt that the set back in the

1 Fortnightly Reports (Confidential), dated 31st December 1951 ; 18th January 1952 ; 1st February 1952.

2 *Idem*, dated 1st February 1952 ; 15th February 1952.

3 Fortnightly Reports (Confidential), dated 16th February 1952.

4 *Idem*, dated 16th February 1952.

5 *Idem*, dated 4th March 1952.

6 Madras in 1952, Part I, Page 4.

7 Fortnightly Reports (Confidential), dated 4th March 1952 ; 17th March 1952.

elections was due to their failure to follow the teachings of Gandhiji and to maintain a close contact with the masses. Others felt that it was due to the difficult economic situation in the country for which the electorate, without much thinking, held the Congress responsible. Some others felt that it was due to the defection of some of their party leaders.[1] But all agreed that a strong, capable leader commanding respect not only from the Congress Party but also from other parties and the general public, should be chosen to form the Ministry. All eyes now turned to Sri C. Rajagopalachari and he was unanimously elected as the leader of the Congress Legislature Party[2]. But Sri T. Prakasam, who had now been elected to the Council and elected also as the leader of the United Democratic Front, lost no time in writing to the Governor, Shri Sri Prakasa, that the United Front had a membership of 166 legislatures and therefore, as the leader of the largest single party in the Assembly, he should be called upon to form a Ministry[3]. The Governor, however, distrusted the stability of the United Front, and asked Sri C. Rajagopalachari as the leader of the majority party in the Legislature to form the Ministry. The new Ministry was sworn in on 10th March 1952, amidst the fulminations of the Praja Party, the Communists and the Kazhagamites, and the *jubilations* of the Congressmen and the general public. The Chief Minister was hailed in the press and cheered on the platform. He was given an ovation by a mammoth gathering assembled to hear him at a public meeting in Madras soon after he assumed office[4]. He was, it may be stated here, first nominated and subsequently elected to the Council. Meanwhile Sri T. Prakasam staged a walk-out, the moment the Governor opened the inaugural session of the Legislature. Sri C. Rajagopalachari threatened to bring a censure motion against him, but subsequently dramatically dropped it, thereby depriving the United Front of what might otherwise have afforded some material for propaganda against the Ministry[5]. From that time onwards the United Front began to crumble. The Praja Party and the Socialist Party, it is true, now combined to form a Praja Socialist Party[6] ; but this combination very soon split over the issue of disciplinary action against Sri Adityan.[7] The Dravida Kazhagam as well as the Dravida Munnetra Kazhagam, finding that the United Front was by no means disposed to fight for Dravidastan, withdrew their

---

1 Fortnightly Reports (Confidential), dated 4th March 1952.

2 *Idem*, datod 17th April 1952.

3 *Idem*, dated 17th April 1952.

4 *Idem*, dated 26th April 1952.

5 *Idem*, dated 10th May 1952 ; 11th June 1952.

6 *Idem*, dated 29th September 1952.

7 *Idem*, dated 6th January 1952.

support for it[1]. The Tamil Nad Toilers Party which till then co-operated with the United Front now came forward to co-operate with the Congress Party[2]. The Krishikar Lok Party too promised support to the Ministry[3]. And thus the dream of the Communists and the Praja Party men to isolate the Congress Party by means of the United Front came to nothing.

Though the United Front crumbled, neither the Communists, nor the Kazhagamites, nor the Praja Socialists, relaxed their opposition to Sri C. Rajagopalachari's Ministry. The Communists and the Kazhagamites in particular carried on a regular vendetta against his ministry, while the Praja Socialists tried their utmost to discredit it, though with little effect. The other parties, however, did not give any trouble. The Muslim League confined its activities to Malabar and even thought of joining the Congress.[4] The Rashtriya Swayam Sevak Sangh and the Hindu Maha Sabha only carried on their usual activities[5].

The Communists did all that they could to strengthen their own position and to undermine the Congress. They shifted the Central Headquarters of their Party, the Central Polit Bureau, from Bombay to Madras, brought out newspaper like the " Cross Roads " and the " Jana Sakti " and intensified their propaganda, though by the end of 1952, they had to shift their Central Polit Bureau to Delhi[6]. They made special efforts to collect funds for their party, formed Secret clubs, held study classes in Marxism and opened kisan and labour fronts everywhere, including the Coimbatore district[7]. Two of their leaders, Sri P. Ramamurthy and Sri K. T. Raju, toured Coimbatore criticising the Chief Minister and holding out a threat that, if he were to attempt to put down their party, he would have to be prepared to share the fate of Hitler, Mussolini and Tojo[8]. A third one, Sri A. K. Gopalan, followed them in the District stimulating the formation of Kisan Sanghams.[9]

In fact, the Communists here, as elsewhere, assailed the Congress Government from every direction. They supported the agitation of the

---

1 Fortnightly Reports (Confidential), dated 29th September 1952.

2 *Idem*, dated 14th November 1952.

3 *Idem*, dated 17th April 1952.

4 *Idem*, dated 2nd January 1953.

5 *Idem*, dated 2nd January 1953; 13th June 1953; 12th August 1953; 24th February 1954; 8th March 1954.

6 *Idem*, dated 13th October 1952.

7 *Idem*, dated 17th April 1952; 12th August 1953.

8 *Idem*, dated 11th June 1952.

9 *Idem*, dated 1st Juy 1952.

Madras City Police Constabulary for higher emoluments, stirred up sympathetic strikes of labour and, when the Government handled the situation with tact and firmness, condemned the manner in which the agitation had been put down.[1] They characterised everywhere the First Five-Year Plan which had just then been introduced, as an unpractical plan designed only to help the capitalists and the Anglo-American powers.[2] They demanded the extension of the Tanjore Tenants and Pannaiyals Protection Act to the entire State, started kisan troubles in several districts, blamed the Government for the scarcity prevailing in the country and led hunger marches to the local revenue officials in every district requesting the opening of more fair price shops and more relief centres and the granting of more loans and remissions.[3] They took credit for the Ordinance issued by the Government for declaring a moratorium for the agriculturists and demanded its extension for a period of three years. They attributed the growing unemployment to the policies of the Congress, organised unemployment protest days and appealed to the workers to unite under Communist leadership so as to fight for the improvement of their living conditions. They criticised the Elementary Education Scheme for rural areas drawn up by the Chief Minister, a scheme designed to avoid wastage, eliminate plural class teaching and impart occupational training. They demanded again and again the release of Communists prisoners.[4] And, at a special party conference held at Perur in November 1953 and attended by their top ranking leaders, they resolved to fight for the confiscation of foreign capital in India for the abolition of large holdings in land and for the adoption of Tamil as the State language for administration after the formation of the new States.[5]

The Dravida Kazhagam as well as the Dravida Munnetra Kazhagam carried on a virulent propaganda against the Chief Minister and the Congress throughout Tamilnad. They continued to sing unceasingly the hymn of hatred against the Brahmins and the North Indians,[6] and

1 Fortnightly Reports (Confidential), dated 2nd January 1953.

2 *Idem.*

3 *Idem*, dated 6th February 1953; 5th March 1953; 15th April 1953; 9th May 1953; 25th May 1953; 25th June 1953; 10th July 1953: 25th July 1953: 12th August 1953.

4 *Idem*, dated 12th August 1953: 28th August 1953; 14th September 1953. 29th October 1953; 27th November 1953; 10th December 1953; 9th January 1954: 27th January 1954; 2nd October 1954; 24th February 1954; 8th March 1954; 22nd March 1954.

5 *Idem*, dated 23rd December 1953.

6 For their early agitation *See* Fortnightly Reports (Confidential), dated 26th April 1952; 10th May 1952; 26th May 1952; 1st July 1952; 14th July 1952; 29th August 1952; 29th September 1952; 13th October 1952; 27th November 1952; 6th January 1953.

lost no opportunity to condemn the actions and policies of the Government. They charged the Government with callousness to the sufferings of kisans, tried to form kisan sanghams, and championed the cause of the handloom weavers, of the city police constabulary and of the Tamils against the Andhras[1]. They objected to the Andhras having their capital and their High Court in Madras City even temporarily, when the formation of the Andhra State came to be considered[2], and conducted black flag demonstrations raising anti-Andhra slogans when the President of India visited Madras in February 1953[3]. They pressed for legislation for the eradication of caste and advocated inter-caste marriages[4]. The Dravida Kazhagam in particular launched a wide spread campaign against the Brahmins. In May 1953, Sri E. V. Ramaswami Naicker toured the Tamil districts, including Coimbatore condemning the Hindu religion and the Puranas and advocating the breaking of clay idols of Hindu Gods. This campaign, however, proved to be a flop; it only served to rouse the latent religious feelings of the people who everywhere retaliated by burning the effigies of Sri E. V. Ramaswami Naicker. But the "Viduthalai" immediately attributed the failure of the campaign "to the machinations of the Chief Minister and other Brahmins," called upon the Dravidians to drive out the Brahmins from Tamilnad and threatened to start a new campaign for burning the effigies of the Chief Minister[5]. Hardly had this agitation died down, when the Dravida Kazhagam started an anti-Hindi agitation. Its members blacked out with tar the Hindi letters on the name boards of railway stations all over Tamilnad and came into frequent clashes with the members of the Congress Youth Leagues who systematically came to remove the tar[6]. About the same time the Dravida Munnetra Kazhagam also started an agitation against North Indians in Tamilnad. Its members insisted on changing the name 'Dalmiapuram' to 'Kallakudi' and persistently pasted Tamil posters bearing the latter name over the former on the name board of the railway station and attempted to hold up trains in several places. In attempting to stop trains in some places they attacked police parties and this led to police firing and the

---

1 For their early agitation *See* Fortnightly Reports (Confidential), dated 2nd January 1953 ; 25th June 1953.

2 *Idem*, dated 5th March 1953; 28th March 1953.

3 *Idem*, dated 12th March 1953.

4 *Idem*, dated 15th April 1953.

5 Fortnightly Reports (Confidential), dated 25th May 1953 ; 13th June 1953 ; 25th June 1953 ; 10th July 1953.

6 *Idem*, dated 10th July 1953 ; 25th July 1953 and 28th August 1953.

killing of some persons. This also led to many arrests and convictions including the arrest and conviction of Sri C. N. Annadurai[1].

As time went on, the opposition of both the Kazhagams to the Chief Minister and the Congress became more and more bitter. Both attacked everywhere the Elementary Education Scheme for rural areas devised by the Chief Minister. The Dravida Kazhagam characterised it as a scheme based on " Varnasharama dharma " intended to perpetuate caste evils and communal differences[2]; and at a conference held at Erode in January 1954, Sri E. V. Ramaswami Naicker warned the Chief Minister that, unless the scheme was withdrawn, an all out agitation against it would be started[3]. The Dravida Munnetra Kazhagam took out unlicensed processions in Madras City and attempted to stage demonstrations in front of the Chief Minister's residence[4]. Leaders of both the Kazhagams now began to indulge in inflammatory speeches against the Chief Minister, against the Brahmins, against Hinduism and against the Congress. When the Prime Minister of India visited Madras, Coimbatore and Malabar in October 1953, they organised black flag demonstrations.[5] When they saw a rift growing in the Tamilnad Congress Party between the Chief Minister's supporters and others, they tried to widen this rift by working upon the feelings of the Non-Brahmins in the Congress Party.[6] In their public speeches as well as in their newspapers, " Viduthalai " and " Nam Nadu ", they made downright personal attacks upon the Chief Minister. They saw in him a Brahmin, out to appoint only Brahmins to high posts and out to perpetuate Hindu religion and the caste system. And they not only assailed him but also assailed Hinduism. Sri E. V. Ramaswami Naicker said that Hinduism with its numerous gods and superstitious customs and practices was responsible for the domination of Brahmins and the degradation of others and that this domination could be got rid of only by burning the Shasthras, the Vedas and the Puranas and by breaking the idols of Rama, Krishna etc. Nor was this all. Both parties now continually clamoured for the establishment of Dravidasthan at all costs, [7] and Sri E. V. Ramaswami Naicker went to extremes. At a public

---

1 Fortnightly Reports (Confidential), dated 25th July 1953 ; 12th August 1953 ; 29th September 1953.

2 *Idem*, dated 14th September 1953.

3 *Idem*, dated 10th February 1954.

4 *Idem*, dated 12th August 1953.

5 *Idem*, dated 29th October 1953.

6 *Idem*, dated 10th December 1953.

7 *Idem*, dated 13th November 1953; 27th November 1953 ; 10th December 1953 ; 23rd December 1953 ; 9th January 1954; 27th January 1954 ; 10th February 1954 ; 24th February 1954 ; 8th March 1954

meeting held at Coimbatore in March 1954, he delivered an inflammatory speech declaring that Dravidasthan, by bloodshed[1].

The Praja Socialists refrained from indulging in such rancourous denunciations. But all the same, until the formation of the Andhra State (October 1953) they kept up a continual barrage of criticism against the Congress in Coimbatore as well as other districts. They held a series of public meetings, assailed the policy of assigning lands to political sufferers, demanded the extension of Tanjore Pannaiyals ProtectionAct, to the whole State, and advocated the nationalisation of all key industries. They also took up the cause of the kisans against the landholders, and of the Madras city police constabulary against the Government. Above all, they severely criticised the First Five-Year Plan, urged the formation of the Madras City into a Part C State and insisted on the location of the Andhra capital in it[2]. After the formation of the Andhra State, and the defection of Sri T.Prakasam who joined the new Andhra Ministry, their position became somewhat weak in Tamilnad. But they tried to strengthen their position by inviting their All India leaders to visit this State to carry on propaganda. Thus, Acharya Kripalani, the Chairman of the All India Praja Socialist Party, visited Madras more than once towards the end of 1953 and the beginning of 1954, and severely criticised the Congress policies[3].

All this time the ministry was not idle. Sri C. Rajagopalachari took every possible measure to nullify the effect of the opposition parties. He organized frequent public meetings in many places in the various districts, including Coimbatore, for explaining Congress policies and for condemning Communists as well as communal propaganda. He showed a judicious mixture of lenity and sternness in dealing with the Kazhagamites and the Communists. So long as they did not violate law and order, he allowed them perfect liberty to preach their doctrines, but whenever they violated law and order, he did not hesitate to take action against them[4]. Had there been no opposition from his own camp, he would perhaps have more effectively dealt with his political opponents.

1 Fortnightly Report (Confidential), dated 22nd March 1954.

2 Fortnightly Reports (Confidential), dated 2nd January 1953; 6th February 1953; 5th March 1953; 28th March 1953; 15th April 1953; 13th June 1953; 25th June 1953; 14th September 1953.

3 *Idem*, dated 12th October 1953; 29th October 1953; 23rd December 1953; 27th January 1954; 24th February 1954.

4 *See* the Fortnightly Reports (Confidential) mentioned already in connection with the activities of the other parties.

But very soon opposition from his own camp began to assert itself, and he felt himself powerless against it. From about the middle of 1953 serious differences of opinion arose between him and some of the Tamilnad Congress leaders, and, even the Congress High Command attempted in vain to smoothen them. They became acute after the formation of the new Andhra State and compelled him to resign in April 1954[1].

Sri K. Kamaraj Nadar was now chosen as the leader and called upon to form a Ministry. His first ministry which thus came into being continued till the general elections of March 1957 the date at which we propose to close this chapter.

Sri K. Kamaraj Nadar was for years the President of the Tamilnad Congress Committee and as such has shown himself as a strong, silent man of ability and resourcefulness. He had served the party faithfully through many a crisis, notably through the Quit India Agitation, and had by persistent work, uncommon capacity for organisation and selfless devotion to duty, built up for himself a no small reputation in Congress circles. And having, at the same time, risen from the masses, he had come to understand their psychology better than any one else, and had established a firm hold upon their affection. He was not eager to become the Chief Minister, but having become so, he did his best to implement the various policies of the Congress. And this was no easy task. For, it was during his regime that the States Reorganization Scheme was hammered out and implemented and the merger of the French possessions with the Indian Union was effected. It was during his regime that the First Five-Year Plan was completed and the Second Five-Year Plan was begun. It was during his regime that the memorable session of the All India Congress was held at Avadi (January 1955) at which the aim of the Congress Party was declared to be no other than the establishment of a Socialistic pattern of society. It was during his regime again, that new alignments were made by old parties, that some new parties were formed and that the Congress Party itself was reorganized and brought under strict discipline and control. All this naturally produced a great deal of agitation in the whole State including Coimbatore.

Throughout his ministry, the Communists never ceased their activities and even tried to consolidate their position. But all their efforts led them nowhere near success. The Congress activities as well as the Congress policies, especially the avowed policy of the socialistic pattern of society, took the wind out of their sails and eventually left them stranded in this

1 Fortnightly Reports (Confidential), dated 25th May 1953; 29th September 1953; 27th November 1953; 10th December 1953; 23rd December 1953; 8th March 1954; 12th April 1954 and 26th April 1954.

State. The Dravida Kazhagam, seeing in the Chief Minister none but a Non-Brahmin bound to serve the cause of Non-Brahmins, hailed him as their own champion; and Sri E. V. Ramaswami Naicker loaded him with encomiums. But, all the same, neither Sri E. V. Ramaswami Naicker, nor his Kazhagam, relaxed in any way the rigour of their communal campaign. They not only carried on this campaign with full vigour but also started another campaign, a linguistic campaign for including every bit of Tamil-speaking area in the Madras State when the States Reorganization Scheme came on the anvil. The Dravida Munnetra Kazhagam actively participated in both these campaigns and went even a step further. Unlike the Dravida Kazhagam, it showed little faith in the Chief Minister and under the leadership of Sri C. N. Annadurai and others boldly came out as a political party and attacked all Congress policies. Rapidly gathering strength, especially from among the younger generation, it became a party to be reckoned with by the Congress. The Praja Socialist Party lost much of its strength, faced as it was then with an internal crisis which culminated in the emergence of a new party called the Socialist Party. Another new party that now emerged into the lime light was the Tamil Arasu Kazhagam with Sri M. P. Sivaganana Gramani as its leader. It had sprung from the Congress Party and it now failed to see eye to eye with the Congress in several matters, particularly those relating to the States Reorganization Scheme. One other important new party which came upon the scene was the Congress Reforms Committee. Composed also of the dissidents mostly of the Congress Party, it raised its head just before the general elections of 1957 and began to assail the Government. But the other parties like the Muslim League, the Rashtria Swayam Sevak Sangh and the Hindu Maha Sabha never gave any serious headache to the Government.

In Coimbatore, as elsewhere, the Communists busied themselves in organizing kisan sanghams, in arranging kisan jathas to meet the Chief Minister, in demanding 75 per cent of the varam for the kisans and in creating kisan troubles with the landlords[1]. They held a special kisan conference at Pollachi at which they condemned the levy of a betterment tax, and demanded the extension of moratorium on agricultural debts and of the provisions of the Tanjore Tenants and Pannayals Act to the entire State[2]. They also stirred up everywhere, including Coimbatore a series

1 Fortnightly Reports (Confidential), dated 26th April 1954; 8th May 1954; 24th May 1954; 10th June 1954: 25th June 1954; 16th August 1954; 18th October 1954; 10th March 1955; 12th July 1955 and 22nd June 1956.

2 *Idem*, dated 26th July 1954.

of small strikes again and again in mills and factories[1]. They criticised the Government and put up a candidate to oppose the Chief Minister when the latter stood for a bye-election in the Gudiyatham Constituency; but this only brought upon them an ignominious defeat and the criticism of their own All India leaders[2]. They were however not discomfited. They put up candidates for the District Board Elections and once more suffered defeats everywhere except in Malabar[3]. They encouraged the Bank Employees Strike against the modification made by the Government of India in the Bank Tribunals' award and condemned the action of the Government of India[4]. They held an All India Congress for Peace and Asian Solidarity in Madras City in December 1954 and praised Russia and China for their achievements[5]. When, however, the All India Session of the Indian National Congress was held at Avadi soon afterwards, they blamed the Government for having wasted over it huge sums of money and belittled the resolution on the socialistic pattern of society[6]. And when they suffered a severe defeat at the hands of the Congress Party in the general elections in the new Andhra State, they attributed the success of the Congress Party to the adoption of questionable methods like the tampering with ballot papers and boxes[7].

Indeed, feeling their position day by day weakening, they started making frantic collections for converting their propaganda organ "Jana Sakti" into a daily newspaper, assailed all Congress policies and criticised the Government for not hastening with the land reforms[8]. They demanded the fixation of ceiling on landholdings, minimum wages for agricultural labourers, fair prices for agricultural products, a ceiling on all forms of distributed profits and ridiculed the Second Five-Year Plan[9]. They contested the municipal elections but lost heavily to the Congress in Coimbatore as well as other districts[10]. When the States Reorganisation Scheme came up for consideration, they opposed the move for Dakshina Pradesh and joined in the agitation started by the

---

1 *Idem*, dated 24th May 1954; 10th June 1954; 17th July 1954; 18th October. 1954; 8th January 1955; 28th January 1955; 19th April 1955 and 20th July 1955.

2 Fortnightly Reports (Confidential), dated 26th August 1954 and 13th September 1954.

3 *Idem*, dated 1st October 1954; 1st November 1954; 13th November 1954 and 8th December 1954.

4 *Idem*, dated 18th October 1954.

5 *Idem*, dated 8th January 1955.

6 *Idem*, dated 28th February 1955.

7 *Idem*, dated 23rd March 1955.

8 *Idem*, dated 19th April 1955; 6th June 1955; 21st June 1955.

9 *Idem*, dated 14th September 1955.

10 *Idem*, dated 25th October 1955 and 22nd November 1951.

opposition parties for including certain areas, Devikulam, Peermedu and some portions of the Shencottah taluk, in the Madras State instead of in the Kerala State and for naming the Madras State as Tamilnad State[1]. Nor was this all. They perpetually criticised the Government for not taking effective steps to bring down the prices of essential commodities, or allowing foreigners to invest capital in India under the Second Five-Year Plan and for failing to tax the huge profits made by Indian capitalists[2]. They invited their All India leaders to come and do propaganda in this State; and as a result of this, several of these leaders visited this State. Thus for instance, Professor Hiren Mukerji, Deputy Leader of the Opposition in the Lok Sabha, visited Coimbatore in May 1956 and inaugurated the Second Annual Conference of National Federation of Posts and Telegraph employees[3]. They also lent their support to the Non-Gazetted Government Officers' agitation for increased pay, etc., which again and again popped up to embarrass the Government[4].

From about the middle of 1956 they started intensive party propaganda in Coimbatore as well as other districts for the forthcoming general elections[5]. They now severely blamed the Government for the prevailing increase in prices, demanded land reforms, especially the Fair Rent Bill, whipped up the kisans everywhere to ventilate their grievances and organised kisan demonstrations and kisan agitations in the various districts ; and when the Fair Rent Act was passed, they took all the credit for its passing[6]. They tried their utmost to seek the co-operation of the leftist parties for forming a United Front against the Congress to contest the elections[7]. They inaugurated " Jana Sakti " as a daily from August 1956, and resolved to maintain an intimate contact with the workers and kisans in general and the middle class and students in particular[8]. They formed Steering Committees and Elections Dispute Committees in Coimbatore as well as other districts, opened a ten lakh election fund and organized a series of propaganda meetings all over the State[9]. Their leaders like Sri P. Ramamurthy, Sri P. Jeevanandam,

1 *Idem*, dated 12th October 1955 ; 5th December 1955 and 24th February 1956.

2 *Idem*, dated 23rd April 1956 and 15th May 1956.

3 *Idem*, dated 23rd May 1956.

4 *Idem*, dated 15th June 1956 ; 22nd June 1956 ; 23rd August 1956 ; 7th February 1957 and 27th March 1957.

5 *Idem*, dated 5th July 1956 and 24th July 1956.

6 *Idem*, dated 24th July 1956 ; 23rd August 1956 ; 27th November 1956 ; 24th December 1956.

7 *Idem*, dated 13th August 1956 ; 8th September 1956 and 10th October 1956.

8 *Idem*, dated 8th September 1956 and 21st September 1956.

9 *Idem*, dated 16th October 1956 ; 26th October 1956 and 7th November 1956.

Sri Kalyanasundaram and Sri Mohan Kumaramangalam, now made extensive tours in the districts for canvassing support for their party. They emphasised in essence that the aim of the Communist Party was to create a strong democratic opposition. They condemned the repressive measures of the Congress Government; and they characterised the Government as pro-capitalist[1]. All this however produced no encouraging result in the elections. Of the 55 seats of the State Assembly which they contested they won only 4 seats. This was a great blow to their prestige and this showed that, in spite of all their propaganda, they were quickly losing ground in this State.

Turning to the Dravida Kazhagam and the Dravida Munnetra Kazhagam, the activities of both these parties continuously harassed the Government in Coimbatore as well as in other districts. It is true that the Dravida Kazhagam felt exceedingly happy over the accession of Sri K. Kamaraj Nadar to power and jubilant over the decision taken by him to withdraw the scheme of elementary education for rural areas[2]. It is also true that Sri E.V. Ramaswami Naicker preached everywhere including Coimbatore that here was a Chief Minister in whom the Dravidians could implicitly place their trust and that here was a Ministry composed purely of Non-Brahmins of which all the Non-Brahmins could be proud[3]. It is true that both Sri E. V. Ramaswami Naicker and his party warned the Dravidians that the fall of Sri K. Kamaraj Nadar's Ministry would mean the rise of Sri C. Rajagopalachari and that, as such, they should give every support to the Chief Minister[4]. But all this did not in the least deter Sri E.V. Ramaswami Naicker or his party from continually preaching hatred, and sometimes violent hatred against the Brahmins, the North Indians and the Hindu Religion.

Beginning from 1954 the Dravida Kazhagam was active on various fields such as opposition to caste system, compaign against sacred religious literature like Ramayana, Mahabaratha, Kandapuranam, etc. The Kazhagam made use of the services of talented actors like Sri M. R. Radha to enact on the stage dramatic performances which graphically depicted the ideas of the Party about things secular and sacred. Besides, the performers went to an extent and questioned the propriety of the Dramatic Performances Act of 1954 which was passed with a view

---

1 *Idem*, dated 29th January 1957; 14th March 1957 and 22nd February 1957.

2 *Idem*, dated 10th June 1954 and 16th July 1954.

3 *Idem*, dated 26th July 1954.

See also the references given later under the opposition of the Dravida Kazhagam to the Dravida Munnetra Kazhagam.

4 *Idem*, dated 22nd February 1957 and 27th March 1957.

to ensure proper control of the stage in the State. Sri E. V. Ramaswami Naicker was using his eloquence not only for vilifying Ramayana but also against religious intolerance in general. His followers were throwing themselves wholeheartedly in his Anti-Rama campaign and the campaign for erasing the names of railway stations in Hindi characters on the railway platforms. This emotional upsurge of Dravida Kazhagam caused a powerful reaction. Sri Vibhoothi Veeramuthu, an active propagandist for religious revival and Sri V. Muthuramalinga Thevar, a Member of Parliament from Ramanathapuram District opposed the move of the Kazhagam. Parties like Rashtria Swayam Sevak Sangh and Hindu Maha Sabha put in their weight against the Dravida Kazhagam, not to speak of the main opposition led by the Congress Party.

The Dravida Munnetra Kazhagam also showed not a little hostility towards the Brahmins and Hinduism. Again and again it warned the Brahmins to give up their religion and fall in line with the Dravidians. Again and again it advocated the establishment of a casteless society. And again and again it attacked Hinduism considering it utterly unsuited to modern times. But in the mode of showing this hostility it exercised restraint and rarely went beyond bounds. Thus, for instance, it refused, to join the Anti-Rama campaign launched by the Dravida Kazhagam. And the reason for this is obvious. Whereas the Dravida Kazhagam remained essentially a communal party bent on establishing social and economic equality and justice, the Dravida Munnetra Kazhagam became essentially a political party bent on capturing power. It is this which explains the cautious tone of its communal propaganda especially from about the middle of 1956 when it decided to contest the coming general elections.

Nor was this all. Both the Dravida Kazhagam and the Dravida Munnetra Kazhagam never ceased harping on the exploitation of the South Indians by the North Indians. Both also were never tired of attacking the Government for betraying the interests of Tamilnad. Thus, when it was mooted by the All India Congress that Hindi should be made the language for All India examinations, both started an Anti-Hindi agitation[1]. And when it was decided to reorganize the States, both condemned the move for the formation of a Dakshina Pradesh, both pressed for the naming of Madras State as Tamilnad, and both insisted upon the inclusion of Tamil-speaking areas of Devikulam, Peermedu and a portion of the Shenkottah taluk in the Madras State. Sri E. V. Ramaswami Naicker declared that the formation of a Dakshina Pradesh would

1 Fortnightly Report (confidential), dated 21st May 1955; 6th June 1955; 9th August 1955 and 20th January 1956.

spell disaster to the Tamilians, inasmuch as it would result in swamping Tamilnad with Malayalees, Kannadigas, Andhras, etc., in all walks of life. It is amusing to note that, when the agitation for Dakshina Pradesh was at its height, he gave up his slogan for Dravidanad and pressed for the formation of Tamilnad, but the moment this agitation died down he again demanded Dravidasthan. Sri C. N. Annadurai, however throughout demanded Dravidasthan[1]. This Dravidasthan they had in view was something like Pakistan, a State independent of the Indian Union. Seeing however that it was to be composed, of the very States which came within the orbit of Dakshina Pradesh[2], it is difficult to reconcile their attraction for the former with their repulsion to the latter.

Whatever it is, the Dravida Munnetra Kazhagam, in particular, made Dravidasthan a vital weapon in its contest with the Congress. The idea indeed gave it an immense scope to condemn Aryan exploitation, to resurrect Dravidian aspirations and, in the process of so doing, to attack all policies of the Government. It is of not a little interest to observe that, after the Kazhagam decided to contest the elections, Sri C. N. Annadurai and his henchmen mercilessly used this weapon against the Congress policies. They condemned the Five-Year Plans; they alleged that under these plans all important projects for industrial development were located in Northern India; and they raised a cry that South Indian were being bled, being drained of all their wealth and money, to fatten the North Indians[3]. A propaganda like this at once political, regional, as well as communal, could not but have some effect on the masses. In the general elections of 1957, the party contested 112 seats of the Legislative Assembly and won 15 seats. It thus became the largest single opposition party in the Legislature.

Seeing that the Dravida Kazhagam and the Dravida Munnetra Kazhagam agreed on so many points, it may be asked why they did not combine together and form a strong single party or put up a united front to oppose the Congress. In fact, the possibilities of such a combination struck some politicians. Towards the close of Sri C. Rajagopalachari's

---

[1] *Idem*, dated 16th August 1954; 1st October 1954; 18th October 1954; 12th October 1955; 22nd November1955; 8th February 1956; 24th February 1956; 24th March 1956; 9th April 1956; 23rd April 1956; 15th May 1956; 15th June 1956; 13th August 1956; 21st September 1956 and 26th October 1956.

[2] *Idem*, dated 26th July 1954.

[3] Fortnightly Report (confidential), dated 10th March 1955; 13th April 1955; 15th May 1956; 24th July 1956; 13th August 1956; 8th September 1956; 7th January 1957; 22nd January 1957 and 14th March 1957.

regime, some of the members of the Legislature had formed themselves into new party called the Dravidian Parliamentary Party[1]. They had imbibed the views of both the Kazhagams and they now came forward to unite the Kazhagams. Their representatives more than once met the leaders of the Kazhagams to discuss the possibilities of a combination but their scheme was wrecked by Sri E. V. Ramaswami Naicker. He had no faith in Sri C. N. Annadurai and had complete faith in Sri K. Kamaraj Nadar; he, therefore, refused to link his party with Sri C. N. Annadurai's party[2]. And during the election campaign, he even roundly condemned Sri C. N. Annadurai and his party dubbing them as traitors and advised all people to vote for Sri K. Kamaraj Nadar and his Congress candidates, even if those candidates happened to be Brahmins[3].

Coming to the Praja Socialist Party, the Praja Socialists felt themselves elated by their success in the general elections of Travancore-Cochin State held early in 1954, which enabled them to form a Ministry in that State about the same time when Sri K. Kamaraj Nadar formed his Ministry in this State[4]. And, in the first flush of their enthusiasm they tried to do many things. They tried to align themselves with the Dravida Munnetra Kazhagam[5]. They held a number of public meetings in Coimbatore and some other districts, demanded land reforms, incited troubles among the kisans[6], decided to contest the District Board elections and stressed the need for the formation of a Separate Tamilnad. They charactercised the Congress Government as pro-capitalist, and condemned the Communist Party for its violence and the Dravida Kazhagam for its class hatred[7]. They started a Bhoodan Movement in some districts, organized demonstrations before the Legislative Assembly and presented a memorandum to the Chief Minister demanding legislation for securing fixity of tenure, economic holdings, distribution of land to the landless poor, etc.[8] They criticised the modification of the Bank Award by the Government of India and organized, in this connection with the help of other parties, strikes and processions in many places.[9] And, now and again they brought

---

[1] Fortnightly Reports (Confidential), dated 9th January 1954.

[2] *Idem*, dated 23rd March 1955; 13th April 1955 and 19th April 1955.

[3] *Idem*, dated 16th October 1956; 26th October 1956; 7th November 1956; 24th December 1956; 29th January 1956; 22nd February 1956; 14th March 1956 and 27th March 1956.

[4] *Idem*, dated 26th April 1954.

[5] *Idem*, dated 8th May 1954.

[6] *Idem*, dated 24th May 1954 and 16th August 1954.

[7] *Idem*, dated 10th June 1954.

[8] *Idem*, dated 26th August 1954.

[9] *Idem*, dated 18th October 1954.

their leaders like Sri H. V. Kamath, Dr. B. Menon and Sri Pattom Thanu Pillai, the Chief Minister of Travancore-Cochin State, to give a fillip to their activities. But very soon their position deteriorated. They lost heavily in the District Board elections of 1954.[2] They found themselves robbed of their principles by the Avadi Resolution of the All India Congress on the socialistic pattern of society. Feeling their position shaky they tried to prop it up by inviting their All India leader, Sri Ashok Metha to come to Madras and conduct propaganda. He visited Madras, Coimbatore and some other districts and preached that the fundamental aim of socialism was the break up of monopolies and that this meant the redistribution of land, diffusion of property, decentralization of production, division of authority, etc. He also severely criticised the Congress policies including the Second Five-Year Plan which, he said involved the giving of loans to big capitalists like Tatas and Birlas[3]. But all this proved to be of no use. The party position became still more shaky by the split which occurred in it about the middle of 1955. For, it was at this time that Dr. Ram Manohar Lohia, one of their All India leaders came out of the Praja Socialist Party and formed a new party called the Socialist Party in Madras[4].

Thereafter, neither the Praja Socialist Party nor the Socialist Party had much chance in this State. Both these parties created a great deal of effervescence in Coimbatore as well as other districts by their recriminations and counter recriminations and both suffered in the process[5]. Both therefore had to rely upon their All India leaders to invigorate them. Thus Sri Acharya Kripalini and Sri H. V. Kamath of the Praja Socialist Party and Dr. Ram Manohar Lohia of the Socialist Party had to come, more than once to Madras to conduct propaganda[6]. Both however did not desist from opposing the Government. The Socialist Party staged state wide demonstrations to focus the attention of the Government on what were called the basic demands of the people[7] and held its First Tamilnad Conference at Coimbatore,[8] while Sri Jai Prakash Narain, the All India leader of the Praja Socialist Party, came to conduct a Bhoodan

1 Fortnightly Reports (Confidential), dated 13th September 1954; 18th October 1954.

2 *Idem*, dated 1st October 1954; 1st November 1954 and 13th November 1954.

3 *Idem*, dated 21st May 1955 and 20th July 1955.

4 *Idem*, dated 9th August 1955.

5 *Idem*, dated 14th September 1955; 24th September 1955; 12th October 1955 and 22nd November 1955.

6 *Idem*, dated 22nd November 1955; 1st December 1955; 8th February 1956; 24th February 1956.

7 *Idem*, dated 22nd November 1955.

8 *Idem*, dated 5th December 1955.

movement in Coimbatore and some other districts[1]. Both also decided to contest the general elections of 1957, and carried on brisk propaganda. Sri Jai Prakash Narain, Sri H. V. Kamath and Sri Acharya Kripalini on the one hand and Sri B. Adityan, Sri Anthony Pillai and Dr. Ram Manohar Lohia on the other, blamed the Government for everything[2]. Thus, at a conference held at Udumalpet in January 1957 the Praja Socialist Party made a bitter attack on the Congress administration charging it with corruption and nepotism and scoffing at its ideal of socialistic pattern of society by calling it "political hambug"[3]. All this however did not improve matters. The Praja Socialist Party won only 2 Assembly seats out of the 22 which it contested ; and the Socialist Party won only 2 Assembly seats out of the 8 seats which it contested.

As to the other opposition parties, namely the Tamil Arasu Kazhagam and the Congress Reforms Committee, the Tamil Arasu Kazhagam had even during Sri C. Rajagopalachari's Ministry carried on some agitation for the transfer of certain Tamil speaking areas of the Chittoor district of the Andhra State to the Madras State[4]. It now continued this agitation with more and more vigour and courting banishment from the Congress fold, came out to criticise the Government. Led by Sri M. P. Sivagnana Gramani, it posed as the champion of Tamil culture when the States Reorganization Scheme came to be considered and continually demanded the inclusion of the Tamil speaking areas of the Kerala State in the Madras State, and insisted on the naming of the Madras State as Tamilnad. It also opposed the formation of Dakshina Pradesh and pressed for the introduction of Tamil as the State language and as the medium of instruction in colleges[5]. And in January 1956, as soon as the decision of the States Reorganization Commission, not to include Devikulam, Peermedu and the western part of the Shenkottah taluk in the Madras State became known, it started with the help of the Dravida Kazhagam and Dravida Munnetra Kazhagam, a wide spread agitation to mark the protest of Tamilians against that decision. All over Tamilnad, including Coimbatore, demonstrations and hartals were

---

1 Fortnightly Reports (Confidential), dated 20th January 1956.

2 *Idem*, dated 22nd June 1956 ; 5th July 1956 ; 23rd August 1956 ; 8th September 1956 ; 21st September 1956 ; 16th October 1956 ; 7th November 1956 ; 27th November 1956 ; 7th February 1957 ; 22nd February 1957 and 14th March 1957.

3 *Idem*, dated 7th February 1957.

4 *Idem*, dated 25th July 1953.

5 *Idem*, dated 16th July 1954 ; 26th July 1954 ; 16th August 1954 ; 13th September 1954 ; 1st October 1954 ; 18th October 1954 ; 13th November 1954 ; 26th November 1954 ; 8th February 1955 ; 20th July 1955 ; 12th October 1955 ; 5th December 1955 ; 20th January 1956 ; 23rd April 1956 ; 21st September 1956 ; 16th October 1956 and 27th October 1956.

organized, strikes in schools and colleges were staged, public meetings were held, black flag demonstrations were made and, in some places even passenger trains were stopped and public offices were picketed. But this storm passed off without any serious incidents[1]. The party, however, continued to carry on anti-Government propaganda and though it did not contest the general elections it advised the people to caste their votes to the Independents and the Congress Reforms Committee candidates[2]. It may be stated here that in spite of its strong linguistic leanings, the party kept completely aloof from all communal propaganda. The Congress Reforms Committee came into existence only just on the eve of the general elections. Consisting mostly of the radical dissidents of the Congress it carried on intensive propaganda against the Government, contested 50 Assembly seats and won 14 seats. It thus became, next to Dravida Munnetra Kazhagam an important opposition party in the Legislature.

Such were the activities of the various political parties during Sri K. Kamaraj Nadar's first ministry. All these, aimed as they were against Congress policies and Congress administration, had to be watched and counteracted where necessary. And for counteracting them the Government relied solely upon publicity and propaganda and not upon any form of repression. The Chief Minister, the other Ministers as well as the President of the Tamilnad Congress Committee, now made it a habit of frequently touring the various districts (including of course, Coimbatore) for explaining the Congress policies like the Five Year Plans, the States Reorganization Scheme, and the socialistic pattern of society[4]. They also now and again invited prominent men like the President of the Republic, the Prime Minister, and the President of the All India Congress, to come here to get into touch with the people[5]. They moreover started Sarvodaya and Bhoodan Movements in the State and extended a warm welcome to Acharya Vinoba Bhave, when he came to give a fillip to these movements; and the Acharya visited Coimbatore and some other

---

[1] Fortnightly Reports (Confidential), dated 8th February 1956; 24th February 1956.

[2] *Idem*, dated 22nd February 1957; 14th March 1957; 27th March 1957.

[3] *Idem*, dated 7th February 1957; 22nd February 1957; 16th April 1957.

[4] *Idem*, dated 8th May 1954; 24th May 1954; 8th December 1954; 10th March 1954; 13th April 1954; 21st May 1955; 21st June 1955; 12th July 1955; 20th July 1955; 9th August 1955; 25th August 1955; 14th September 1955; 22nd December 1955; 20th January 1956; 24th March 1956; 24th July 1956; 14th March 1957.

[5] *Idem*, dated 28th January 1955; 8th February 1955; 6th June 1955; 12th October 1955; 25th October 1955; 1st December 1955; 5th December 1955; 7th January 1956; 15th May 1956; 22nd February 1957,

districts in 1956 and achieved considerable success[1]. Above all, they concentrated on purifying the Congress Party by rejecting from it all dissidents like the members of the Tamil Arasu Kazhagam and the Congress Reforms Committee and by selecting only tried party men as candidates for the 1957 elections[2]. The result was as might be expected. The Congress party secured an overwhelming majority at the elections. Out of the 201 Assembly seats which it contested it won 151 seats. This was most encouraging to the party, and this brought again Sri K. Kamaraj Nadar to power.

---

[1] *Idem,* dated 3rd November 1954 ; 10th March 1955 ; 12th July 1955 ; 14th September 1955 ; 23rd May 1956 ; 22nd June 1956 ; 5th July 1956 ; 13th August 1956 ; 23rd August 1956 ; 8th September 1956.

[2] *Idem,* dated 26th August 1954 ; 21st September 1956 ; 16th October 1956 ; 15th December 1956 ; 29th January 1957 ; 22nd February 1957.

CHAPTER V.

THE PEOPLE.

Coimbatore has a population of 3,154,296. It is distributed in the nine taluks of the district as follows: Coimbatore has over five hundred and fifty thousand people; Erode has over four hundred thousand; Gobichettipalayam, Palladam and Pollachi have over three hundred and fifty thousand; Dharapuram has over three hundred thousand; Avanashi has over two hundred and fifty thousand; Bhavani has over two hundred thousand and Udumalpet has over one hundred and fifty thousand[1]. The density of population in the district is 523 persons per square mile[2]. During the decade 1941 to 1951 the population has registered an increase of 17·2 per cent as against 14·4 per cent for the State and 14·9 per cent for the district in the previous decade. This is because the execution of the Lower Bhavani Project in Gobichettipalayam taluk, the tea and coffee estates in Pollachi taluk and the industrial development, mostly textile mills and associated industries in Coimbatore municipality and its suburbs, have attracted large numbers of labouring classes to these areas[3].

Of the total population of 3,293,204 (including the Kollegal taluk which has lately been transferred to the Mysore State), Tamil is spoken by the majority, by no less than 2,160,054 persons; Telugu is spoken by 663,159, Kannada by 367,288, Malayalam by 57,348 and Hindustani by 30,308 persons. The remaining persons speak Hindi; Marathi, Gujerati, English, Lambadi, etc.[4] Details of the distribution of population according to language in rural and urban areas are given at the end of this chapter. In regard to the distribution of population on the basis of religion, the Hindus constitute the bulk of the population, numbering as they do, 3,134,144. The Muslims come next with 83,806 persons, the Christians number 74,493, while the rest consist of a few Sikhs, Jains, Buddhists, Zoroastrians, etc.[5]

In a book like this it is not possible to describe the philosophical tenets of the various religions. All that can be done is to give a general account of the people who profess these religions and a particular account

1 1951 *Census Handbook, Coimbatore District*, 1953, page 4.

2 *Census of India (Madras and Coorg)*, Part I, page 43.

3 1951 *Census Handbook, Coimbatore District*, 1953, pages 4–5.

4 *Idem*, page 198.

5 *Idem*, pages 210–211.

of their castes, where such castes exist, and their customs. It may, however, be stated here that we have no up-to-date statistics showing the number of persons belonging to different castes, inasmuch as such information was not collected during the last two censuses. Even in the 1931 census all the castes were not enumerated. It is only in the 1921 census that the castes were enumerated in detail. The castes dealt with in this chapter are those mentioned in the Census report of 1921.

The social and religious customs of the people have remained the same through centuries in this as in the other districts, although latterly they have been undergoing some important changes in matters like untouchability, temple entry, etc. Several of the people who live in towns have caught a veneer of European manners and customs in dress and behaviour and some of those who live in villages too have, to some extent, become affected by it. But the great mass of the people, whether living in towns or in villages, still continue to follow the ancient customs and usages in matters like dress, and behaviour. And almost all people, whether townsmen or villagers, still continue to adhere to their ancient religions, customs and practices, in matters like marriages, funerals and festivals, etc. Modern amenities, however, such as the motor cars, buses, radio and newspapers, are enjoyed by all who can afford them and the towns have naturally become the centre of these amenities. In the towns also people of all castes and persuasions, irrespective of their castes or hereditary occupation, have taken to all sorts of avocations. Here are to be found among them lawyers, doctors, officials, merchants, artisans and so on. Here again they wear all kinds of dresses, European as well as Indian ; the hat, the coat, the trousers and shoes are as commonly seen here as the turban or the cap, the dhoti and the chappals. This is, however, not so in the villages. There the caste distinctions are more marked. There the Brahmin, the Non-Brahmin and the Harijan quarters are more clearly distinguished. There the caste avocations are more rigidly followed. There decent houses are possessed by only a chosen few, and the small houses and huts are commonly met with. And there the people wear mostly the traditional South Indian dress.

In conformity with this traditional dress, the men everywhere wear white dhotis; the more respectable among them, the long dhotis in the form of *panchakacham* or *mulakacham* while the others, the short dhotis tied round their waists. The former put on also shorter cloths or towels over their shoulders or wear shirts. The boys wear small under-cloth and a waist cloth or put on shirts and shorts. The girls wear pavadai. The women usually wear handloom sarees or silk sarees of various colours and patterns, six to nine yards in length.

Among the Non-Brahmin castes, the saree is passed round the waist and a knot is tied to keep it in place and then a fold (*kusavum*) is made in front or on a side over the hip for ornamental purpose. The saree is then passed tightly round the waist and the end of it is brought up in front of the breast, thrown over the left shoulder and tucked into the waist behind. The higher caste women show only a little of the ornamental fold, the rest being concealed beneath the saree, while the lower caste women let it drop round the hip to the length of about a foot. All the Brahmin women pass the saree between their legs, but some of them, like the Kannada Brahmin women, do this by passing one corner of the ornamental fold above the lower part of the saree, pulling this up to show a part of their legs and leaving the portion of the saree passing between the legs visible; all others conceal this portion by bringing the saree again round the waist. The Smartha Tamil women make the ornamental fold on the left side, the Vaishnava Tamil women do not have it at all, and the others put it in front. The Pallar and Paraiyar women wear the saree a little above the ankle. The Brahmin widows who shave their heads ordinarily wear white sarees and always bring the end of the saree over their heads. Most of the younger women nowadays wear choli, bodice and petticoats. Tattooing was formerly common among some castes, but now it is fast disappearing. All Hindu women of whatever castes, or sect, except widows, wear a *tilakam* of kumkum, while the girls prefer *tilakams* of " Chandu ". They are also fond of jewellery. The high castes go in for a variety of ornaments like neck chains, pendants, girdles, bangles, ear-rings, nose-screws, etc., made of gold and often studded with diamonds, rubies or other precious stones. The lower classes go in for similar cheaper jewellery of silver or guilded silver and artificial stones. All women love flowers and all of them, except widows, adorn their hair with them on almost all occasions. The Christian and Muslim women do not put on the *tilakam*.

The food of the mass of the people consisted formerly of ragi, cholam and cumbu; but nowadays rice has become popular except in villages where paddy is not grown and where the staple food continues to be ragi, cholam and cumbu. All Brahmins and some of the higher caste Non-Brahmins such as Vaisyas and Saiva Vellalars abstain from meat. Some of the lower castes eat beef and pork. The other Non-Brahmins, the Christians and the Muslims generally eat mutton, fish and the ordinary edible birds, and the Muslims eat beef in addition. The grown-ups among the Brahmins and other higher castes generally take two meals a day, one at mid-day and the other at night, but they supplement these meals by tiffin and coffee or tea in the morning and in the afternoon. The meals among the well-to-do classes commonly consist of rice, ghee, dholl, *rasam sambar* made of vegetables, appalams, pickles, curds or butter milk. On festive occasions these are supplemented by sweet and special savoury dishes and fruits. Orthodox Brahmin widows do not take meals at night, but take only light food like cakes of rice and blackgram. The lower classes take usually three meals, breakfast in the morning of cold rice, a lunch at mid-day of hot or cold rice and a dinner at night of hot rice, meat, soup or curry. Cold rice at breakfast is nowadays widely replaced by coffee.

A variety of indigenous games are played by the young and old of all castes and communities. The children play with dolls of different kinds and at odd and even. The boys and girls play the blindman's buff, the otti (tossing up and catching tamarind seeds), the kattam (a game played with pieces on a board), the pachaikudirai (a kind of leap frog), the balchitangadu (catching while holding breath), marbles, kite-flying, etc. The girls play in addition, kolattam and do dancing of various kinds. The women play various games with cowries on a board and the men play chess and cards. As to pastimes in the hot weather, when all agricultural operations are at a standstill, the villagers take delight in dramatic performances conducted by the local companies of players, the performances are held at night in improvised theatres, usually on the village maidan. They constitute mostly scenes from the Ramayana, the Mahabharatha, etc. The women seldom act, the female parts being taken by the younger and more comely men.

The Hindus observe a variety of festivals. The most important of these, common to almost all castes and sects, are the New year's Day, the Vinayaka Chathurthi, the Saraswathi or Ayudha Puja, the Deepavali and the Sankaranti or Pongal. The New Year's Day for Tamilians falls generally in the middle of April and for the Telugu and Kannadigas in the latter part of March. Vinayaka Chathurthi falls in September and on that day most of the Hindus worship God Vinayaka or Ganesa by installing his image in clay in their houses. The Saraswathi Puja falls in October and is dedicated to Saraswathi, the Goddess of Learning. On this day students offer worship to the books and others to their tools and instruments. The Deepavali which commemorates the destruction of the demon Narakasura by Lord Krishna falls in October or November. It is observed by having an oil bath in the early morning, by putting on new clothes and by firing crackers and other fireworks. The Sankaranthi or Pongal is the day on which the sun passes from Dakshinayana to Uttarayana, i.e., from Sagitarius to Capricorn. It comes in the middle of January. On this day Pongal or sweetened rice is offered to the Sun and other gods. The day following this festival is called the Mattupongal, or the festival of cows and oxen. On this day the animals are washed and decked with flower garlands and their horns are painted. Of the other festivals which are observed by many may be mentioned the following: Sri Rama Navami, the birthday of Sri Rama which falls in the end of March or in the beginning of April, is usually celebrated by all Vaishnavaites. Upakarmam or Avaniavittam which comes in August or September is observed by all Brahmins; on this day they have to renew their sacred thread. Sri Jayanti, the birthday of Sri Krishna which comes in the latter half of August, is observed by all Vaishnavites. The festival of Navarathri and Vijaya Dasami which occur in October and last for ten days and which commemorate the victory of the Goddess Durga over the demon Mahishasura are observed mostly by the Brahmins. It is celebrated by the display of dolls and by the puja to Durga. The first or third Saturday of the Tamil month of Purattasi (September-October) is sacred to all Vaishnavaites. Lord Venkateswara is worshipped on this day. Karthikai which occurs in the Tamil month of Karthikai (November-December) is celebrated by many Tamilians by decorating the front of the houses by numerous tiny oil lamps. Vaikunta Ekadasi which falls in December and which is sacred to all Vaishnavites, is observed by most classes of the people also by fasting and prayer. Maha Sivarathri which falls in the beginning of March and which is sacred to all Saivites is likewise observed by other classes as well by fasting and prayer. Besides these festivals there are also several other temple festivals observed by the people, and these will be described in the chapter on XVII.

The orthodox Gods of the Hindus, as is well-known, are Siva, Vishnu and the whole hierarchy of lesser gods who form the Hindu pantheon. These Gods, as is equally well-known, are worshipped in the shape of images as the visible symbols of an invisible Supreme. They need no description here. An account of such of them, however, as are usually worshipped in the famous temples at Avanashi, Bhavani, Kodumudi, Perur, Thirumuruganpundi, Karaimadai, Tirumurthimalai, is given in the chapter XVII. But here we may give a descriptión of the popular gods, the minor deities or the evil spirits which are commonly worshipped by the people.

Among these unorthodox deities Draupadi, Aiyanar, Muniappan and Mariamman occupy a prominent place in the district. Draupadi, the wife of the famous Pandava brothers, is the special favourite of the Palliars. Her image is invariably accompanied by the image of Dharmaraja, the eldest of the Pandava brothers, and her temples are, therefore, commonly known as Dharmaraja kovils. They are very numerous and the priests in them are generally Palliars by caste, and all Palliars take a leading part in the temple ceremonies. Outside the temple there is often a figure of Pothuraja, or ' the king of buffaloes', a person of ferocious aspect who holds a dagger in his right hand and a human head in his left. Festivals to Draupati always involve two forms of ritual, the recital or acting of part of the Mahabharatha which lasts for several days and a fire-walking ceremony. The first of these is usually done by the Palliars; the second of these is done by others as well, and has been introduced at the festivals to some other goddesses also.

Aiyanar is even more popular with the masses. There is, indeed, hardly a village in the district which has not a shrine to him. Even the Brahmins venerate him and give him an Aryan descent, calling him Hariharaputhra. His temple is either a rude shrine or a spot marked by trident or an image in a grove. It is heinous to remove even a twig from these grove. He is supposed to keep watch over the villages by riding on horses and other animals at night. It is, however, considered unlucky to meet him when he is so engaged and in consequence his shrine is always erected at some little distance from the village. Muniappan is also called Muniswami, Muniandi, Pandi Muni, Jatamuni, etc., and he is said to possess young girls and married women. He is worshipped during ear-boring and hair-cutting ceremonies. Yet another deity who is worshipped by many is Mariamman, the goddess of small-pox whose temples are scattered in numerous places. The most important of these is the Kottaimariamman Kovil of Kolanalli near Unjalur, where on the full moon day of Panguni (March) a large number of sheep, buffaloes and fowls are offered by the ryots, who in holiday attire crowd in from all parts of the Kongu Country[1]. Other minor deities are Kongaliamman, Kaliamman, Ponnammal, Muttammal, Gangammal, and the Sapta Kanniyar. There are also several devils who are worshipped by some people and which go by the general name of ' pisasu ' or ' pei '. Some of these which are said to possess women are exorcised by professional exorcists who are often the pujaries of the shrine of the local goddesses.

Tree worship and cobra worship are also not uncommon. Among the trees and plants, the margosa and the tulasi are commonly worshipped in the district. The margosa is considered sacred and worshipped as the abode of Mariamman. The tulasi, as is well-known, is worshipped by all Brahmin women. As to the cobra, the higher castes consider it a sin to kill it, believing as they do that the man who does so will have no children. Childless wives also take a vow to install a cobra (naga) if they are blessed with offspring. And the ceremony of installation and

1. *Coimbatore District Manual*, page 49.

worship consist in having a figure of a cobra cut on a stone slab, placing it in a well for six months, ' giving it life ' by reciting mantrams and performing certain rites over it and then setting it up under a pipal tree which has been ' married ' to a margosa tree. Worship, by going round the tree 108 times, is then performed for 45 days. The child which is supposed to be born by performing this worship is, in this as in other districts, given a name bearing reference to serpants, such as Seshachalam, Seshamma, Nagappa, Nagamma and so on. Earth, cattle and water are likewise worshipped. Cattle worship is done not only at the time of the Pongal but also sometimes when the ploughing begins and the treading is done. The earth is worshipped when the seed is sown and the first ploughing of the year is begun. Water is worshipped when the first floods arrive and so are the rivers on the eighteenth day of the month of Adi when they rise. The latter festival is called the *Padinettamperukku*.

Besides worship, vows play a large part in the life of the people. Vows are made to Gods as well as minor deities and they take various forms. Parents desiring offspring make a vow that, if a child is born, they will perform the ceremony of the first shaving of its head in the temple of the deity which granted the boon. Sometimes they vow that, if a child is born, they will hang a miniature cradle in the temple. Similarly when a child is ill, they vow that, if it recovers, its jewels will be presented to the deity. More often when a person falls ill, he vows to brand his body or to go round the temple a certain number of times, sometimes by himself rolling over and over on the ground, after he recovers. Vows are also taken in anticipation of boons, in which case, until the boon is granted the devotee undertakes to forego salt in food or to offer models of the affected limb in silver or other metal.

More numerous than vows are the superstitious beliefs of the people. Thus an owl or a vulture brings ill-luck to the house on which it perches; a tortoise in a house or in a field which is being ploughed is inauspicious. The cawing of a crow on a house indicates the arrival of a guest. The dream of a temple car in motion or burglary foretells the death of some near relation. To hear some one sneezing, or to be questioned as to the business on which one is going, is bad omen. So is the catching sight of either one Brahmin or two Non-Brahmins or a widow or oil, or a snake, or a huntsman or a *Sanyasi*. It is good omen to hear a bell ringing, a cannon sounding, an ass braying, a garuda flying, or on first leaving the house, to catch sight of a married women, a corpse, flowers or water. Evil spirits can be warded off by talisman; and houses and persons haunted or possessed by evil spirits can be exorcised by professional sorcerers. A clay-wasp-building-fly's nest in the house predicts the birth of a child ;

if a jungle lac nest, of a male child, if a mud nest, of a girl. The going out of lights during a meal or on auspicious occasions foreshadows evil. The hissing noise of the oven indicates the arrival of a guest. The entrance of a viper inside the house or in the field is an ill omen. The fighting of crows in front of the house foretells news of death. The effects of an evil eye can be warded off by adorning houses in the course of construction by some object to attract it.

Nor is this all. In several places stone slabs may be seen set up on the outskirts of the villages. These are thought to be able to ward off sickness and other harm which threaten to enter the villages and are reverenced accordingly. Some of these slabs are quite blank, others have letters cut on them, while some others again bear the rude outline of a deity and are accordingly given the names such as *Pidari* or *Ellaimman* (the goddess of the boundary). To these last, periodical worship is performed by breaking coconuts, burning camphor and placing a light on the slab. Again, at cross roads may sometimes be seen pieces of broken pots, saffron, etc. They too are thrown there at dead of night to ward off diseases. Further, amulets are worn by many villagers and rain is invited by some by burning the effigies of sinners upon the earth.

Coming now to the principal castes of the district, the Brahmins, though they constitutes a very small percentage of the population, occupy a conspicuous position in society. They numbered 39,389 in 1921[1]. They are the repositories of Vedic knowledge, priests, purohits, astrologers, etc. They are also the persons who have made much headway in modern education and taken to all sorts of professions such as medicine, law and government service with considerable facility and success. They are primarily divided into two well-known religious sects, the Saivites and the Vaishnavites. The Saivites are either the Saivites proper or the Smarthas. The Saivites proper believe that there is only one God Siva who is self-existent and that he is not liable to lose his personality. The Smarthas, on the other hand, recognize the Trimurtis, Brahma, Vishnu and Siva, as equal manifestations of the Supreme Spirit and believe that the soul of man (Jiva) is only a portion of the infinite spirit (Atman) and that it is capable of being absorbed in the atman. Among the Vaishnavites there are two principal sects in the south, those who are the followers of Sri Ramanuja and who call themselves Sri Vaishavites, and those who are the followers of Sri Madhvacharya and who call themselves as Madhvas. All Brahmins, whether Vaishnavites or Saivites, have, according to the sutras, to go through the following Samskaras (rites) : Garbhadanam,

1 The strength of this caste in 1931 was 37,816.
Figures for later years are not available.

Pumsavanam, Simantham, Jatakaranam, Namakaranam, Annaprasanam, Choulam, Upanayanam and Vivaham. These rites are believed to purify the body and spirit, but not all of them are in practice performed at the present day. The Garbhadana or impregnation ceremony should be performed on the fourth day of the marriage ceremonies. But if the bride s a young girl, it is omitted, only Vedic texts are repeated. The Pumsavanam and Simantham are performed together during the seventh or the ninth month of the first pregnancy. The Jatakaranam, Namakaranam (naming ceremony), Annaprasanam (food-giving ceremony) and Choulam (tonsure ceremony) are ordinarily celebrated one after the other on the Upanayanam day. The Upanayanam is essentially a ceremony of initiation. From the orthodox point of view, it should be performed before the age of eight, but in practice it is performed much later. The wearing of the sacred thread is a sign that the boy has gone through the ceremony. The Vivaham, or the marriage ceremony, resembles even to-day, that of the Vedic times in all essentials. All sections of Brahmins closely follow the Grihya Sutras relating to their Sakha. In addition to these ceremonies, all Brahmins perform funeral ceremonies and the annual Sradha (memorial rites). The Brahmins are all expected to perform the Ahnikams (or daily observances) such as the bath, the sandhya prayers, Brahma Yagna, Deva Puja, Tarpana (oblations of water), etc.[1]

The Tamil Brahmins are mostly Smarthas and Vaishnavas. Each of these sects is divided and sub-divided into a number of smaller groups based on sectarian, occupational, territorial, ritualistic and other differences. Among the smartha subdivisions may be mentioned the Vadama (the northerners), the Brahacharanam, the Asthasahasram, the Vattima or the Maddhima, the Kaniyalar, the Choliya, the Viliya, the Kesika, the Prathamasaki and the Gurukkal. The Vadamas claim to be superior to the other classes, they worship both Siva and Vishnu but follow the Smartha customs in every way. The Brahacharanams are more Saivite and more orthodox than the Vadamas. The Ashtasahasrams are considered to be inferior to the Vadamas and the Brahacharanams ; they are, however, like the Brahacharanams, more Saivite than the Vadamas. The Vattimas are said to be noted for their economical habits and for their sense of corporate unity. The Kaniyalars are mostly temple servants and wear Vaishnva marks. The Choliyas are mostly temple priests and temple servants. The Villiyars are supposed to be descended from an ancestor who offered his eye to Lord Siva for want of flowers. The Kesikas or Hiranyakesikas, as they are sometimes called, closely resemble the Vadamas but are an

1. *Castes and Tribes of Southern India* by Edgar Thurston, 1909, Vol, I, pages 269–278.

exclusive endogamous unit and are highly orthodox. The Prathamasakis follow the White Yajur Veda; they are also sometimes called Katyayanas and are considered inferior by the other sects. In regard to the Vaishnavas or Sri Vaishnavas, as they are sometimes called, to distinguish them from the Madhavas, they are all supposed to be converts from Smarthas. There are two distinct groups of Vaishnavas, the Vadagalais (northerners) and the Tengalais (southerners) who are easily distinguished by the marks on their foreheads. The Vadagalais put on a U shaped mark and the Tengalais as Y shaped mark. Each one of these groups is divided into the Vaikhanasas, the Pancharatras[1] and the Hebbars. The Tengalai group also consists of the Mandyas. The orthodox Sri Vaishnavas are very exclusive and hold that they co-existed as a separate caste of Brahmins with the Smarthas. All Vaishnavites are expected to undergo a ceremony of initiation into Vaishnavism, after the Upanayanam ceremony. There are various points of differences between the Tengalais and the Vadagalais which sometimes lead to bitter quarrels in connection with temple worship and temple processions[2].

There are also the Telugu Brahmins, the Kannada Brahmins and the Tulu Brahmins. The first are divided into two sections, the Niyogis and the Vaidiks; the second are divided into two other sections, the Smarthas and the Madhvas, while the third are divided into six sections, the Shivallis, the Kotas, the Kandavaras, the Haviks, the Panchagramis and the Koteswars[3]. It is not necessary to say more about these Non-Tamil Brahmins as they are not many in number in the district.

The marriage rites in vogue among the Brahmins resemble those of the Vedic times in all essentials; and, as has already been stated, each section of the Brahmins closely follow the Grihya Sutras relating to their Sakha. A marriage is usually arranged only if the horoscopes of the boy and the girl agree, and if they do not belong to the same gotra, and if the girl is not older than the boy. The horoscopes are examined by professional astrologers. In former days, it was usual for the bridegroom to pay a small sum of money as a bride price, but now-a-days the opposite practice of paying a handsome dowry by the bride's father to the bridegroom has become the rule. The marriage ceremony is performed in the bride's house and the bride's father generally bear all the expenses. Formerly the ceremony invariably used to last for four or five days, but now-a-days it is completed even in a day.

---

1. According to J. N. Farguhar, the Pancharatras and the Vaikhanasas refer to the mode of worship in the Sri Vaishnava temples.

2. *Castes and Tribes of Southern India* by Edgar Thurston, Vol. I, pages 333–349.

3. *Idem*, pages 365–386.

The ceremony begins with the (Nischayatharatham) or betrothal and is followed by the performance of various Vratams consisting of oblations to the sacred fire by the bridegroom. He then dresses himself like a married man and proceed on a mock pilgirimage called Paradesapravesam or Kasiyatra and is met and brought back by the bride's father. The bride is now brought out, decked in her wedding clothes and the pair are brought face to face and made to exchange garlands. Formerly they used to be taken up on the shoulders of their maternal uncles for the purpose of exchanging garlands. The couple then sit on a swing and married women goround them thrice carrying water, light, fruits and betel. After this, the couple are conducted into the house and seated on the marriage dais. The ceremony proper now begins with the proclamation of the gotras of the bride and bridegroom so as to ensure that they do not belong to the same gotra. The bridegroom does puja to Ganapathi if he is a Saivite and to Vishwaksena, if he is a Vaishnavite. He then performs the Ankurarpana (the seed sowing ceremony). Four earthen pans are arranged in the form of a square, east, west, north and south and a fifth pan is set down in the centre of the square. The pan to the east represents Indra, that to the west Varuna, that to the South Yama and to the north Soma. In each of these pans are placed nine kinds of grain soaked in water and the Devatas are invoked.

The next stage is the tying of the wrist thread. Two cotton threads are laid on a vessel representing Varuna and, after the recitation of Vedic verses, the bridegroom takes one of the threads and, after dipping it in the turmeric paste, holds it with his left thumb, smears some of the paste on it with his right thumb and forefinger, and ties it on the left wrist of the bride. The purohit ties the other thread on the right wrist of the bridegroom who facing the assembly proclaims, " I am going to take the bride ". He then invokes the gods-Indra, Surya and Bhaga to bless the marriage. The fathers of the bride and the bridegroom now wash each other's face with milk and water, after which the bride sits on her father's lap and her mother stands at her side. The father then places the bride's hand in that of her bridegroom and both the father and mother pour water over the united hands of the couple, the father reciting the sloka " I am giving you a virgin decorated with jewels to enable me to obtain religious merit " This is called the Dhara (pouring water) ceremony. It forms the binding portion of the marriage ceremony among Telugu Brahmins and some Non-Brahmin castes. The couple then sit in front of the sacred fire and the bride's father after pouring ghee as an oblation and reciting some mantras, pours some water over the hands of the bridegroom and offers him a mixture of honey, plantain fruit and ghee and, afterwards a coconut and plantains. The bride next sits on a heap or a bag of paddy and the bridegroom invokes the gods to bless her. A yoke is now brought and one end of it is placed on the head of the bride and some mantras pronounced. The bridegroom then gives a new and costly silk cloth (Kurai) to the bride who puts it and sits on her father's lap. This is followed by the bridegroom tying the *tali* on the bride's neck when all the Brahmins bless the couple by throwing rice and flower over their heads. A waist band made of darbha grass is passed round the waist of the bride, and the couple now perform a *homan*. The bridegroom takes hold of the bride's right wrist and pressing the fingers passes his hand over the united fingers three times. This is called *Panigrahanam*. The next item is sapthapadhi or the taking of the seven steps which is generally considered the most binding part of the ceremony. In this the bridegroom lifts the left foot of the bride seven times repeating certain mantras. A *homam* is then made. The bride then treads on a stone thrice and some fried paddy is put into the sacred fire each time. The darbha girdle is now removed from the bride's waist when everybody disperses.

Towards evening, the bride and bridegroom sit before the sacred fire while the Brahmins recite the Vedic mantras. A male child which has not lost his brothers or sisters is now made to sit on the lap of the bride and given a plantain fruit and the bridegroom invokes prosperity and progeny to bless the house. The couple are then shown *Dhruva* (the Polar Star) and Arundhathi (smaller star, Ursa major) and these are worshipped. The Stalipaka Ceremony is afterwards performed In this the bride should cook some rice and the bridegroom should offer it as an oblation to the sacred fire. In practice, however, some food is brought and placed in the fire. The purohit now decorates a ficos stick with darbha grass and gives it to the bridegroom. It is placed in the roof or somewhere inside the house near the seed pans.

On the second and third days, *homams* are performed in the morning and evening and the *nalangu* ceremony is gone through. In this ceremony, the couple sit before trays containing betal leaves, areca nuts, fruits, flowers and turmeric paste, and the women sing songs. Taking a little of the turmeric paste mixed with chunam the bride makes marks by drawing lines over the feet (*nalangu idal*) of the bridegroom. *Arathi* is then offered followed by the distribution of *tambulam* (*pansupari*). On the fourth day, the Brahmin priests make the couple sit beside them and after the recitation of Vedic verses, bless them. The shoulders of the couple are then smeared with turmeric paste made red with chunam and a mark is made with the same paste on their foreheads. This is called *Pachai Kalyanam*. It is peculiar to Tamil Brahmins, both the Smarthas and the Vaishnavas. The bride and bridegroom are then made to exchange garlands. Towards the evening a procession called *Amman kolam* is got up at the expense of the maternal uncle of the bride. The bride is dressed up as a boy and another girl is dressed up as the bride. They are taken in procession through the streets and, on their return, the pseudo bridegroom is made to speak to the real bridegroom in somewhat insolent terms and some mock play is indulged in. The real bridegroom is sometimes treated as a thief. Among Sri Vaishnavas, after the *Pachai* ceremony, the bridal couple are made to roll a coconut to and fro across the dais amidst the chanting of songs of Andal by the assembled Brahmins. *Tambulam* (of which a little together with some money is set apart for Andal) is then distributed to all. The family priest now calls out the names and *gotras* of those who have become related to the couple; and, as each person's name is called out, he or she is supposed to make a present of clothes, money, etc., to the couple. Among Telugu and Kannada Brahmins, instead of the *Pachai Kalyanam* another ceremony called *Nagavalli* is performed. In this ceremony, thirty-two lights and two vessels representing Siva and Parvathi are arranged in the form of a square. Unbleached thread soaked in turmeric paste is passed round the square and tied to the *pandal*. The couple sit in front of the square and after doing puja cut the thread and take their seats within the square. The bridegroom then ties a *tali* of black beads on the bride's neck symbolically in the presence of all the gods which are here represented by a number of small pots round the fire. Close to the pots are designed the figures of two elephants one in rice grains and the other in salt. After going round the pots the couple bargain as to the prices of the animals. This is followed by a burlesque on domestic life and the introduction of the bride to her new relations by marriage and the making of the present of *tambulam* and turmeric.

A mock marriage is occasionally celebrated among the Brahmins when a person marries a third wife. As the third marriage is considered inauspicious, as the bride thereby is believed to become a widow, the man is first made to marry the Arka (*Erukku* plant) and then the bride so that his real marriage becomes the fourth. In orthodox fashion, it is celebrated on a Sunday or a Monday when the constellation Hastham is visible. The bridegroom accompanied by the priest and another Brahmin repairs to the place where the Arka plant is growing. The plant is decorated with cloth and a piece of string and invoked by the bridegroom to avert the evils of a third marriage. The bridegroom then asks the plant to marry him and become his third wife. After this, all the ceremonies such as the *homam*, *tali*-tying etc., are performed by the Brahmins as at a regular marriage. The plant is then cut down and the marriage is considered to be over[1].

As to the funeral ceremonies among the Brahmins when a person is about to die, he is removed from his bed and laid on the floor. If he dies on Danishtapanchami (inauspicious) day, he is taken out of the house and placed in the court-yard or the pial. Some prayers are then uttered and sometimes a cow is presented to the Brahmin priest (*godanam*) so as to render the passage of life through the various parts of the body as easy as possible. As soon as he is dead, his body is washed, religious marks are made on the forehead and parched paddy and betel leaves are scattered over and around it by the son. The sacred fire is then lighted, rice is cooked in a new earthen pot and a new cloth is thrown over the corpse. A simple bier of bamboos and straw is then prepared and four bearers are selected. To each of the bearers darbha grass is given in token of his office to carry the corpse to the burning ground. The eldest son who is the funeral celebrant and his brothers if any are shaved and the last respects are paid by the widow and the female relations by going round the corpse three times. The funeral procession then starts consisting of men alone, preceded by the eldest son carrying a mud pot containing fire. On the way to the burning ghat, the corpse is usually placed on the ground and some mantras are recited and cooked rice offered to propitiate evil spirits. At the burning ground certain mantras are again recited and rites performed after which the body is placed on the funeral pyre and the pyre set fire to by the eldest son. He then carrys a pot filled with water having a hole at the bottom through which water trickles out on his shoulders, three times round the corpse and at the end of the third round, throws it down and breaks it. Sometimes in the case of respected elders, the son and all the relations present scatter darbha grass repeating certain Vedic verses. The son then pours a little water on a stone and sprinkles himself with it and the rest follow him. After this they pass through a bundle of darbha grass held aloft by the priest and gaze for a moment at the sun. Everybody then goes to a tank and bathes. All these rites are performed and the corpse is cremated in the course of a few hours. No food is cooked in the house on the day of death.

On returning home, the son performs the rites of *Nagna Sradham* and *Pashana Sthapanam*, the former by presenting clothes, lamp and money to a Brahmin and offering balls of cooked rice to the spirit and the latter by setting up two stones, one in the house and the other on the bank of a tank. For ten days libations of water mixed with gingelly seeds and balls

---

1 *Castes and Tribes of Southern India* by Edgar Thurston, Vol. I, 1909, pages 278–298.

of cooked rice are offered to the stones. On the day after cremation, the relations assembled at the cremation ground for performing the ceremony called *Sanchayanam* which consists in extinguishing the burning embers and removing the fragments of bones from the ashes. These bones are taken away in a mud vessel and later thrown into a sacred river or buried in the ground. On the tenth day a large quantity of food is cooked and heaped on plantain leaves when all the female relations go round it wailing. The food is thrown into a tank and the *tali* of the widow is then removed. In former days her head used to beclean shaved on that day; but now-a-days most of the widows do not undergo this ritual. All the agnates should be present on the tenth day to perform *tarpanam* or oblation of water. After a bath a *homam* is performed. On the eleventh day a Brahmin is fed after going through *Sraddha* rites. On the twelfth day an important *Sraddha* like ceremony is performed; and, at the close of this ceremony six balls of cooked rice are offered to the ancestors. The balls are arranged in two rows with some space between them and some cooked rice is placed between them. This is divided with darbha grass into three portions and each portion is arranged close to the balls of rice. A cow is now sometimes presented to a Brahmin to render the crossing of the river Vaitarani easy for the departed soul. On the thirteenth day a feast is held and domestic worship is carried out at the close of which verses composed in praise of the deceased called *Charama Slokas* are read. In the course of the year following the death, twelve monthly and four quarterly *Sradhas* are performed by the son. Annual *Sraddhas* are performed thereafter; but, if the son performs the *Sraddha* at *Gaya*, it is not obligatory upon him to perform the annual *Sraddha*. The annual *Sraddha* consist of *homam*, offering of cooked rice to the pitris (manes) and the feeding of one or two or three Brahmins.[1]

Turning to the Non-Brahmins who form the bulk of the population of the district, we may first say something in general about their customs and then describe separately the peculiar customs followed by each caste. Usually, among the Non-Brahmins, a boy should not marry the daughter of his maternal aunt or his paternal uncle, but he has a right to marry the daughter of his sister, his maternal uncle or his paternal aunt. Ordinarily an eldest son should not marry an eldest daughter nor should a boy marry a girl older than himself. The bride's mother is paid a bride's price, (*parisappanam* or *mulaippal kuli* or the price of suckling) by the bridegroom. Usually the dead are cremated; a few castes bury the dead. And, usually the *Karumantaram* ceremony takes place on the

1 *Castes and Tribes of Southern India* by Edgar Thurston, Vol. I, 1909, pages 299–305.

sixteenth day. With these few general remarks we may enter into the description of the various castes.

The Vellalars, the famous cultivating classes of the Tamil country, form an important community in the district. They numbered 694,906 in 1921[1]. The word Vellalar is derived from *Vellanmai* (*vellam* or water plus *anmai* or management), meaning cultivation or tillage. Essentially a peace loving and industrious people, they have taken to the cultivation of rice, betel and tobacco with excellent results. Among them are to be found also merchants, shop-keepers, Government servants, etc., but they do not generally take up any degrading avocation. They are considered to occupy the first place in the social scale among the Non-Brahmins. They call themselves Pillais, Chettiars and Mudaliars. There are among them four main divisions named after the tract of the country in which the ancestors of each originally resided; the Tondaimandalam or the dwellers of the Pallava country (Chingleput and North Arcot districts), the Solia (or Sozia) or men of the Chola country (Thanjavur and Tiruchirapalli districts), the Pandya or the inhabitants of the Pandyan Kingdom (Madurai and Tirunelveli districts) and the Konga or the residents of Kongu country (Coimbatore and Salem districts). The Konga Vellalars are subdivided into the Sendalais (red headed men), the Padaitalais (leaders of armies), the vellikkai (the silver hands), the Pavalamkatti (wearers of coral), the Malaiyadi (foot of the hills), the Tollakadu (ears with big holes), etc. The Tondamandalam Vellalars are subdivided into the Tuluvas who came from the Tulu country; the Poonamallee (or Pundamalli) Vellalars who came from Poonamallee; and the Kondaikatti who tie their hair with a knot. The Solia Vellalars are subdivided into the Vellalar Chettiars (merchants), the Kodikkals (grower of betel vine), the Kanakkilinattar or inhabitants of Kanakkilinadu. The Pandya Vellalars are subdivided into the Karkattars or the Karaikattars who, notwithstanding the legends about their origin, are probably a territorial subdivision named after a place called Karaikadu; the Nangudis and the Panjais whose origin is not clear; the Arumburs and the Sirikudis, so called from the villages of those names; the Agamudaiyars who are probably recruits from the caste of that name; the Neerpusis, meaning the wearers of sacred ashes; and the Kotai Vellalars or Fort Vellalars. In addition to these divisions and subdivisions of the Vellalar caste proper, there are now-a-days many groups who, though they belong to quite distinct castes, pretend to be Vellalars.

The Vellalars whatever division and subdivision they belong to, observe in common some essential customs. Their marriage ceremonies

1 Figures for later years are not available.

are usually performed in the puranic fashion with the Brahmins officiating as priests (except among the Konga Vellalars). They all burn their dead, observe fifteen days pollution and perform the *Karumantaram* ceremony to remove the pollution on the sixteenth day. Each division of them contains both the Vaishanvaites and the Saivites, and contrary to the rules among the Brahmins, the differences of sects among the Vellalars are not of themselves any bar to intermarriage. Each division has pandarams or priests recruited from among its members who officiate at funerals and minor ceremonies and some of these wear the sacred thread, while the other Vellalars wear it only at funerals. All the Vellalars perform *Sraddhas* and observe the ceremony of invoking their ancestors on the *Mahalaya* days. All of them abstain from alchohol and refuse to eat in the houses of any but the Brahmins. All of them may dine together but no member of any one of the four main divisions and the various subdivisions may marry into another division or subdivision. The Karaikat Vellalars are said to have some peculiar customs. It is said that they associate freely with the Kunnavar and eat food dressed by them; but if a Kunnavar is invited to the house of a Karaikat Vellalar, he must not touch the cooking utensils or enter the kitchen. It is also said that they observe a ceremony called *Vilakkidu Kalyanam* or the auspicious ceremony of lighting the lamp. It is performed by girls in their seventh or ninth year or later but before marriage and it consists in worshipping Ganesa and the Sun at the house of the girl's parents. At this ceremony the girl's maternal uncle gives her a necklace of gold beads and coral and a new cloth, while the other relatives make other presents. The girls wear this necklace called *kodachimani* (hooked jewel) even after marriage.

Some Vellalars observe the Brahminical custom with regard to second and third marriages. A man marrying a second wife, after the death of his first, has to marry a plantain tree and cut it down before tying a *tali* and, in the case of third marriage, he has to tie a *tali* first to the *Erukkan* plant. The idea is that the second and third wives do not prosper and the tree and the plant are therefore made to take their places. Some Vellalar women observe a ceremony called *Sevvai* (Tuesday) Pillayar or as it is sometimes called *Avvai Nombu,* because the famous poetess Avvai observed it. The ceremony takes place twice in a year, once on a Tuesday in the month of Thai (January-February) and again on a Tuesday in the month of Adi (July-August). It is held at midnight and no males, even babies in arms, are allowed to witness it. A number of women join together and provide the rice required, and at the house where the ceremony is to be performed, it is pounded into flour and mixed with leaves of *Pongamia glapra* and *margosa.* The mixture is then made into cakes, some flat and some conical to represent Pillayar and the rites are performed with these cakes and flowers, fruits, betel, turmeric, comb, kumkum, etc [1].

The Konga Vellalars differ strikingly from the rest of the Vellalars in many of their customs. They have an elaborate caste organization and their country is divided into twenty-four nadus, each comprising a certain number of villages and possessing recognized headquarters, which are arranged into four groups under the villages of Palayakottai, Kangayam, Pudur and Kadayur, all in the Coimbatore district. Each village is under a Kottukkaran, each nadu under a Nattu-Kavundan or Periyatanakkaran, and each group under a Pattakkaran. The last is treated with considerable respect and is only occasionally called in to settle caste disputes. Both at wedding and funeral ceremonies, the Konga Vellalars employ priests of their own caste called Arumaikkarans and Arumakkaris who must be married people with children. The most desirable match for a boy is his maternal uncle's daughter. The betrothal ceremony takes place at the house of the future bride in the presence of both the uncles, and consists in tying fruit and betel leaf in the girl's cloth. On the wedding day the bridegroom, after taking a bath, goes on horseback to a stone called nattukal planted for the occasion, carrying some fruit and a pestle and worships it. The stone is supposed to represent the Kongu country and the pestle the villagers, and the whole ceremony is said to be a relic of a custom of the ancient Kongu people, which required them to obtain the sanction of the king for every marriage. On his return from nattukkal, balls of white and coloured rice are taken round the bridegroom to ward off the evil eye and his mother gives him three mouthfuls of food. The barber then blesses him and he repairs on horse back to the bride's house where he is received by one of her party similarly mounted. His ear-rings are put in the bride's ears and the pair are then taken to the nattukal. On their return thence, an Arumaikkaran touches them with a betel leaf dipped in oil, milk and water and ties the *tali* on the neck of the bride, after it has been worshipped and blessed. Then, after an elaborate blessing by a barber and a *Pulavar* (bard among Kaikolars), the fingers of the contracting parties are linked together, anointed with milk and then separated. The death ceremonies of Konga Vellalars are not peculiar except that the torch for the pyre is carried by a Pariar and not, as among most castes, by the chief mourner, and that no ceremonies are performed after the third day. On that day after the bones are collected and thrown into the water, the barber pours a mixture of milk and ghee over a green

1 *Castes ad Tribes of Southern India* by Edgar Thurston, 1909, Vol. VII, pages 361–389.

tree, crying *poli* and *poli*. The caste has its own beggars called Mudavandies[1].

The Komatiars or the Arya Vaisyas form the great trading caste of this State and are to be found in almost all the districts. They numbered 6,354 in this district in 1921[2]. They speak Telugu but they are conversant with Tamil and Kannada in the Tamil and Kannada districts. They have caste headmen and caste panchayats. They have also several sub-divisions such as the Gavara, the Kalinga, the Trinika, the Lingadurai, etc., and many septs which are strictly exogamous. The septs are based on totems and are variously termed *gotram*, *vamsam* and *kulam*.

A Brahmin purohit officiates at their marriages and each purohit has a number of houses attached to his circle. On the first day of their marriage ceremony, when what is called the ' puranoktha ' ceremonial is in vogue, the ancestors are invoked. On the second day, the astavarga is observed, according to which the bride and the bridegroom worship eight of the principal gods of the Hindu patheon. On this day the marriage pandal is erected. On the third day, the mangalyam is tied, sometimes by the officiating Brahmin purohit, and sometimes by the bridegroom. On the fourth day, the Brahmins of the place are honoured and on the following day, in most places, a festival is held in honour of the goddess Kannika Parameswari. The bride and bridegroom's mother then go to a tank or river with copper vessels and bring back water at the head of a procession. The vessels are placed in a special pandal and worshipped with flowers, turmeric powder, etc., and finally coconuts are broken before them. On the next day, or on the same day, a festival is held in which five boys and girls are bathed, decked with jewellery and taken in procession to the local temple whence they are conducted to the bride's house and fed. On the following day, the ceremony called ' *thotlu puja* ' is perfomed, a doll is placed in a cradle connected with two poles and rocked to and fro. The bridegroom then hands over the doll to the bride saying that he has to go on a commercial trip. The bride, however, hands it back to him with the remark that she has to attend to her kitchen work. On the next day, the bridal couple are taken in procession which brings the marriage ceremony to a close. According to another form of marriage ceremonial called ' the Vedokta ' the contracting couple, on the first day, have an oil bath and the bridegroom goes through the

[1] *Castes and Tribes of Southern India* by Edgar Thurston, Vol. III, pages 417–421.

Manual of the Coimbatore District, 1876, pages 56–60.

[2] The strength of this caste in 1931 was 11,451. Figures for later years are not available.

Upanayanam ceremony. He then pretends to go off to Kasi (Banares) and is met by the bride's party who takes him to the bride's house, where the mangalam is tied by the bridegroom before the homam (sacrificial fire). On the second day, the homam is continued and a caste dinner is given. On the third day the gotra puja is performed. On the fourth day the homam is repeated and, on the following day, the pair are seated on a swing and rocked to and fro. Presents are made to the bridegroom and no bride-price is paid.

Widow re-marriage is not permitted among any sections of the caste; and, except among the Saivites, a widow is not compelled to have her head shaved, or to give up wearing jewellery or chewing betel. The Vaishnava widows always retain their hair.

The Komatiars wear the sacred thread and utter the Gayatri and other sacred mantrams. There are among them Saivites as well as Vaishnavites. The Saivaites daub themselves with ashes; the Vira Saivites or Lingayats wear the Linga in a silver casket, and the Madhvas put on the sect mark of the Madhva Brahmins. In bygone days Komatiars used to take part in the faction fight known as the right and left hand caste disputes. They belong to the former caste. They venerate, as has already been stated, the deified virgin Kannika Parameswari, and worship also other gods and goddesses. They employ the Brahmins for the performance of their ceremonial rites and recognized the Brahmin Guru, Bhaskaracharya. The dead among them are cremated, except in the case of the children and the Lingayats, and their death ceremonies closely resemble those of the Brahmins. They are, as is well known, not only traders, but also money lenders[1].

The caste Chettiars belong to several groups and their occupation is generally trade. Of these, Beri Chettiars claim to be superior to Komatiars. They numbered 46,240 in 1921[2]. They are said to have come from Kavaipuram near Kumbakonam in the Tanjore district. They have a number of endogamous divisions, but they all belong to the left hand section. They have also caste panchayats presided over by a headman called Periathanakkaran. Some of them worship Siva, and some Vishnu and some of them are Lingayats. Some of them bury, while others burn their dead. All of them wear the sacred thread and do not tolerate widow re-marriage. Some of them follow the pure Vellalar customs and abstain from animal food[3].

---

1 *Castes and Tribes of Southern India* by Edgar Thurston, Vol. III, 1909, pages 306–348.

2 Figures for later years are not available.

3 *Castes and Tribes of Southern India* by Edgar Thurston, Vol. I, pages 211–218.

There is a lot of controversy over the origin and status of the Palliars or the Vanniyars or the Padayachis as they are commonly called. They numbered 70,793 in 1921[1]. The name Palliar is said to denote their Pallava origin and the name Vanniyar is said to denote Vannikula Kshatriyas which means Kshatriyas of the fire or Agnikula race. Some of them also claim descent from the solar or lunar race. They regard themselves as superior to all other Non-Brahmin communities and some of them wear even the sacred thread. They are also known by several names such as Nayakar, Varma, Nayanar, Odayar and Gounder. Some of them claim to belong to the Chola race and call themselves Chemiars. These names, however, do not denote sub-divisions or sects and all the Palliars freely inter-dine and inter-marry. They are said to be strict in matters of caste and social customs. Their occupation is generally agriculture and trade.

They have among them several sub-divisions such as Rudra Vanniar, Krishna Vanniar, Sambu Vanniar, Brahma Vanniar, Indra Vanniar, the Agamudaiyars, the Agni, the Arasu, the Nagavandam (Cobra head or ornament of that shape), the Nattumar, the Pandamuthu, the Perumal and the Kallaveli. It is stated that the wives of the Palliars side with the left hand section. They are either Saivaites or Vaishnavites, but they also worship demons like Mutyalamma, Mariamma, Aiyanar, Muneswara and Ankalamma. During the festivals the goddesses are frequently represented by a pile of seven pots, called Karagam, decorated with garlands. They have their caste beggars called Nokkars who receive presents at marriages, funerals, etc.

Among some of the Palliars at the betrothal ceremony, the future bridegroom goes to the house of the prospective father-in-law, where the headman of the future bride is present. The bridegroom's headman or his father then hands over betal and flowers, the bride's price (Pariyam) the milk money (*Mulapal kuli*) and a coconut to the father or headman of the bride saying " the money is yours, the girl is mine ". The bride's father or headman, while receiving them, says, " the money is mine, the girl is yours ". This performance is repeated thrice and afterwards thambulam is distributed first to the maternal uncle and then to others. The marriage ceremony follows close on the betrothal; but if, in the interval, the girl's prospective husband dies, she may marry some one else. A girl normally, however, may not marry without the consent of her maternal uncle and, if he disapproves of a match, he has the right to carry her off even when the marriage ceremony is in progress and to marry her to a man

1 The strength of this caste in 1931 was 63,855. Figures for later years are not available.

of his selection. Among some Palliars, the bride after her betrothal, is asked to touch the bow and sword of the bridegroom.

For the marriage ceremony the bridgroom goes with much pomp, sometimes mounted on horseback, to the bride's house. In ordinary cases the ceremony is performed in a day but in some cases it is spread over three days and performed with the puranic form of ritual. On the day preceding the wedding day, the bride is brought in procession to the house of the bridgroom and the marriage pots are purchased. On the morning of the wedding, the pots, the milk post and the light are placed on the marriage dias. The bride and bridegroom then go separately through the nalangu ceremony. They sit on a plank, while five women smear them with oil and afterwards with green gram paste. Coloured water is then waved before them to avert the evil eye. They then go to bathe and, when they are bathing, five small cakes are placed on their head, knees, shoulders, etc. When the bridegroom is about to leave the bathroom, cooked rice is waved before him and thrown away. The couple then go three times round the dais and offer pongal to the village gods, house gods and the ancestors. The tying of tali is next performed before the milk post or the handle of a plough which has been set up, in the midst of a grindestone, a large pot and two lamps called Kudavilakku (pot light) and alankara vilakku (ornamental light). The Brahmin purohit ties the threads (kankanam) round the wrists of the bride and the bridegroom. The tali is now passed round to be blessed by the assembled persons and handed to the bridegroom who ties it on the bride's neck, while his sister holds a light called Kamakshi Vilakku by his side. All this is done amidst music and the blowing of conches. The couple then change their seats and the ends of their clothes are tied together and blessing rice is showered on them. They next go round the dais and the milk post and at the end of the second turn, the bridegroom lifts the bride's left foot and places it on the grindstone. At the end of the third turn, the brother-in-law places the bridegroom's foot on the grindstone and puts on a toe ring, for which he is paid a golden ring some money and betel. The couple are then shown the pole star and Arundhati and milk and fruit are given to them. In the evening after their wrist threads are removed, they proceed to a tank for a mock ploughing ceremony and afterwards worship Pillayar. They remain in the bride's house for about a week and then go to the bride-groom's house. Before they enter the house, coloured water and coconut are waved in front of them and, as the bride steps into her new house, she is made to touch pots containing rice and salt with her right hand.

The dead are sometimes burnt and sometimes buried by them. As soon as a person dies, his son goes round the corpse three times, carrying an iron measure (marakkal) in which a lamp rests on paddy. The corpse is then washed, while the widow bathes in such a way as to make the water fall upon it. The dead man and the widow then exchange betel three times, after which, the corpse is carried to the burning or burial ground on a bamboo stretcher. On the way thither it is set down near a stone representing Harischandra, the guardian of the burial and cremation grounds, and puja is offered to the stone. By some Padayachis a two anna piece is placed on the forehead and a pot of rice is placed on the breast of the corpse; and these are taken away by the officiating barber and Paraiyar respectively[1].

The Agamudaiyars are another cultivating class. They numbered 26,408 in 1921[2]. The word Agamudaiyar means a house holder or a land-lord. The more important sub-divisions among them are said to be the Aivali, the Nattu, the Kottaipattu, the Malainadu, the Nattumangalam, the Rajabhoja, the Rajakulam, the Rajavasal, the Kallar, the Maravar, the Tuluvar and the Servaikarar. They have no exogamous septs or Kilais.

Their marriage ceremonies are generally very simple. The sister of the bridegroom goes to the house of the bride on an auspicious day accompanied by a few women carrying cloth, jewels, flowers, etc. The bride is then dressed up in the cloth and seated on a plank close to the wall, facing east. Betel, arecanuts and flowers are presented to her by the bridegroom's sister who also places round her neck the turmeric dyed string or garland amidst the din of conches. On the same day, the bride is conducted to the home of the bridegroom and a feast is held. The more prosperous Agamudiyars, however, celebrate their marriages according to the puranic fashion with, of course, some variations.

The dead are either buried or cremated and as the Agamudaiyars are Saivites, pandarams assist at their funeral ceremonies. On the third day after death, the son and the others go to the spot where the corpse was buried or burnt, offer food to the deceased and leave a pot of water behind. Those who are particular about performing the death ceremonies on an elaborate scale offer cooked food to the deceased until the fifteenth day and carry out the death ceremonies on the sixteenth day. Presents

---

1 *Castes and Tribes of Southern India* by Edgar Thurston, Vol. VI, 1909, pages 1-28.

2 Figures for later years are not available.

are then distributed to the Brahmins, and after the death pollution has been removed by sprinkling holy water, a feast is given to the relatives.[1]

The Vaniyars are the oil pressers or oil mongers among the Tamils. For some reason, Manu, classed oil pressing as a base occupation. They are hence held in small esteem in some places, but in consequence of their services in lighting lamps in temples, they are held in considerable esteem in several places. They numbered 10,887 in the district in 1921[2]. Their caste contains four sub-divisions called Kamakshiamma, Visalakshiamma, Ac-chu tali and Toppa tali, the first two referring to goddesses worshipped by each, and the last two to the peculiar kinds of talis worn by their women. There is nothing peculiar in their customs. They employ the Brahmins as priests, prohibit widow re-marriage, usually burn their dead and decline to eat in the houses of any caste below that of a Brahmin[3].

The Kammalars, or the Viswa Brahmins, as they are now called, are made up of five occupational sections, namely, the Thattar (goldsmith), the Kannar (brass smith), the Thachar (carpenter), the Kal-Thachar (stone mason) and the Kollar or Karumar (blacksmith). The name panchala which is sometimes used by the artisan classes has reference to these five-fold occupations. The five sections intermarry but, it is said the gold-smiths have, especially in towns, ceased to intermarry with the blacksmiths. There are also three endogamous tribal groups among them, the Pandya, the Sozia (the Chola) and the Kongar. The Pandya Kammalars live principally in the Madurai and Tirunelveli districts, the Sozias live in Tiruchirappalli Tanjore, South Arcot, Chingleput and North Arcot districts, while the Kongas are found chiefly in Salem and Coimbatore districts. They numbered 54,037 in the district in 1921[4].

The Kammalars have adopted Brahminical gotras and the five sections among them have five gotras called the Visvagu, the Jungha, the Ahima, the Janardhana and the Ubhendra (the Upendra). Each of these gotras, it is said, has twenty-five subordinate gotras. In their marriages they closely imitate the Brahminical ceremonies and their marriage ceremonies last for three or five days. But contrary to the Brahminical custom the

---

1 *Castes and Tribes of Southern India* by Edgar Thurston, 1909, Vol. I, pages 5–16.

2 The strength of this caste in 1931 was 3,619. Figures for later years are not available.

3 *Castes and Tribes of Southern India* by Edgar Thurston, Vol. VII, 1909, pages 312–314.

4 The strength of this caste in 1931 was 50,423. Figures for later years are not available.

bride's money is paid among them and their widows are allowed the use of ordinary jewellery and betel and are not required to make the usual fast.

Their dead are as a rule buried in a sitting posture but cremation is now-a-days more and more coming into vogue among them. Death pollution among them, as among the other non-Brahmin castes, is observed for sixteen days. It is usual for a *pandaram* to officiate at their death ceremonies. On the first day, the corpse is anointed with oil and given a bath. On the third day, five lingams are made of mud and of these four are placed on the four corners at the spot where the corpse is buried and the fifth is placed in the centre. On the fifth day, food is distributed to the pandarams and the castemen. Some of them observe also sraddha ceremonies.

They profess the Saiva faith and hold Pillayar in great reverence, but their special goddess is Kamakshi Amma who is commonly spoken of as a Vriththi Daivam. She is worshipped by all the subdivisions and female children are frequently named after her. On auspicious occasions the first betel and dakshina are set apart in her name and sent to the pujari of the local temple dedicated to her. Oaths are taken in her name and caste disputes are settled before her temple. Besides Kamakshi Amma, they worship also various village goddesses (grama devatas) such as Saptha Kanniar (Seven virgins), Kochade Periyandavan (Vishnu) and Periyar Nayanar (a manifestation of Siva). They claim to be descended from Visvakarma, the architect of the gods, and on that account they consider themselves superior to Brahmins, and call the latter as Co-Brahmins and themselves as Visva-Brahmins. Visvakarma is said to have had five sons named Manu, Maya, Silpa, Trashtra and Daivatha; and these are said to be the originators of the five castes among the Kammalars. Accordingly some of them who do smithy work are called Manus; some who do carpentry work are named Mayas; some who do stone carving are known as Silpas; some who do metal work style themselves as Trashtras; and some who do jewellery work call themselves Visvagnas or Daivagnas. According to another story, however, the Kammalars are the descendants of a Brahmin and a Beri Chettiar woman. They belong to the Left Hand as opposed to the Right Hand faction. Sometimes they call themselves Achari and Paththar which are equivalent to the Brahmin titles Acharya and Bhatta and claim a knowledge of the Vedas. Their pandarams officiate at their marriages, funerals and other ceremonies. They wear the sacred thread and most of them claim to be vegetarians. Their women unlike those of the other castes, throw the end of their sari over the right shoulder.

The Kammalars are a highly organized caste. Each of their five sub-divisions has at its head a Nattanmaikarar or headman and a Karyasthar or Chief Executive Officer under him, who are elected by the members of the sub-division. Over them all is Anjivittu Nattanmaikarar (also known as Andi vittu Periyathanakkarar or Anjjati Nattamaikarar) who is elected by lot by the representatives chosen from among the five sub-divisions[1].

The Kaikolars or the Sengundars are a caste of Tamil weavers. The word Kaikolar is said to be the Tamil equivalent of the Sanskrit Virabahu, a mythical hero from whom the caste is supposed to have sprung. It is also said to be derived from Kai (hand) and Kol (shuttle). The Kaikolars are also called Sengundar (red dagger). They consider the different parts of the loom to represent various devatas and rishis. There are among them several sub-divisions. In religion, most of them are Saivites and some of them have taken to wearing the lingam; but there are also Vaishnavites among them. Their hereditary headman of the caste is called Perithandakaran or pattakaran and is, as a rule, assisted by two subordinates entitled Sengili or Gramani and Ural. It is said that every Kaikolar family was formerly expected to set apart one girl to be dedicated as Deva-Dasi to a temple. The Kaikolars are said to belong to the Left Hand section but Dasis, save those engaged to the Beri Chettiars and the Kammalars, were said to belong to the Right Hand faction. In 1921, they numbered 83,000 in the district [2].

Some of the Kaikolars observe a peculiar method of selecting a bride, called 'siru tali kattu' (tying the small tali). A man who wishes to marry his maternal uncle's or paternal aunt's daughter has to tie a tali; or simply a bit of cloth torn from her clothing round her neck and report the fact to his parents or the headman. If the girl eludes him, he cannot claim her, but should he succeed, she belongs to him. In some places the consent of the maternal uncle to a marriage is signified by his carrying the bride in his arms to the marriage pandal. The live post is used in the wedding ceremony; and, after the tali has been tied, the bridegroom has to lift the bride's leg and place it on a grinding stone. Widows are allowed to re-marry if they have no issue, but not otherwise. On the final day of the death ceremonies among them, a small hut is erected and inside it stones brought by the barber are set up and offerings are made to them[3].

---

1 *Castes and Tribes of Southern India* by Edgar Thurston, 1909, Vol. III, pages 106–125.
Census of India, 1901, Vol. XV, Part I, pages 159–160.

2 In 1931, they numbered 66,444. Figures for later years are not available.

3 *Castes and Tribes of Southern India* by Edgar Thurston, 1909, Vol. III, pages 31–44.

The Lingayats (anglicised form of Lingavants) are immigrants from the Kannada country and in 1921 they numbered 23,312 in the district[1]. They are supposed to be the followers of Basava who lived in the 12th century and founded a new sect. They acknowledge only one God, Siva, and reject Vishnu and Brahma. They reverence the Vedas but disregard the latter commentaries on which Brahmins rely. They deny the supremacy of Brahmins and pretend to be free from caste distinctions although caste is in fact observed among them. The cardinal principle of their faith is an unquestioning belief in the efficacy of the lingam which they always carry on their persons. Men and women, old and young, rich and poor, all alike wear this symbol of their faith and its loss is regarded as spiritual death. They are strict disciplinarians in the matter of food and drink and abstain from meat and drink. This Puritan simplicity has made them very conservative. Their priests are called Jangams and are revered highly. As they have originally been formed out of several communities they have several occupations, but they are chiefly priests or traders or agriculturists [2].

Besthas are a Telugu caste, the hereditary occupation of which is hunting, and fishing, but they have largely taken to agriculture and other occupations involving physical labour. In the Coimbatore district they speak Kannada and are called Siviyars denoting that they were palanquin bearers. They numbered 4,988 in 1921[1]. They are supposed to have migrated from Mysore in the times of the Muslim usurpation. The Besthas are divided into two sub-castes, the Telaga and the Parigirti. The latter trace their descent from Suta, the expounder of Mahabharata. Besthas employ Brahmins and Satanis for their domestic ceremonies and imitate the Brahmin customs, prohibiting widow remarriage and worshipping Siva and Vishnu as well as the village deities[3].

The Kavarais are Balijas, a Telugu trading caste who have settled in the Tamil country. In 1921, they numbered 28,344 in the district.[1] The name is said to be a corrupt form of Kauravar, the descendants of Kuru of the Mahabharatha, or Gauravalu, the sons of Gowri. There are several exogamous septs among them like tupakki (gun), jetti (wrestler), pagadala (coral), bandi (cart), etc. Their common titles are Chettis and Nayakars. Their marriage customs are similar to those of many Telugu castes[4].

---

1 Figures for later years are not available.

2 *Castes and Tribes of Southern India* by Edgar Thurston, 1909, Vol. IV, pages 236–291.

3 *Idem*, Vol. I, pages 218–222.

4 Vol. III, pages 263–266.

The Gollas are the great pastoral caste of the Telugu people. In this district they numbered 10,366 in 1921 [1]. They claim to be the descendants of Sri Krishna. Some of them claim to belong to the Go-Vaisya division. Their title is Mandadi, but it is not commonly used. Their social status is fairly high, for they are allowed freely to mix with Kapu, Kamma and Balija castes. Some of them are Vaishnavites while others are Saivites. Their hereditary occupation is the tending of sheep and cattle and the selling of milk. They are a quiet, inoffensive and honest people. In the last century they were employed largely in transporting treasure from one place to another.[2]

The Kammas are supposed to be the immigrants from the Telugu country during the Vijayanagar times. Originally, soldiers by profession they are now mainly agriculturists and traders. There are several sub-divisions among them. Those found in Coimbatore district generally belong to the Vaduga subdivision. They numbered 53,569 in 1921.[3] Some Kammas are Vaishnavites while others are Saivites. A Brahmin priest officiates at their marriages and funerals. The dead are cremated.[4]

The Kapus or Reddis are also immigrants from the Telugu country, who are chiefly engaged in agriculture. They have a partiality for the black cotton soil. They, like the Kammas are called Vadugans in Coimbatore. They numbered 8,529 in 1921.[3] There are several sub-divisions among the Kapus. Those in the Tamil districts belong to the Panta Reddi sub-division and follow a Brahminical form of marriage, and adopt the funeral ceremonies in vogue among the various Tamil castes. They are both Vaishnavites and Saivites and worship also numerous other deities like Thallamma, Puttamma, Ankamma, etc.[5]

The Okkiliyars or Vakkaligars are a large Kannada caste of cultivators who have migrated from Mysore. They numbered 48,228 in the district in 1921[3]. There are numerous subdivisions among them. In the Coimbatore district some of them called Kiraikarars are stated to be Kempati Okkiliyans, that is, those who came from Kempampatti in Mysore. The hereditary headman of the Okkiliyans at Coimbatore is called Pattakaran.

---

1 The strength of this caste in 1931 was 3,157. Figures for later years are not available.

2 *Castes and Tribes of Southern India* by Edgar Thurston, 1909, Vol. II, pages 284–296.

3 Figures for later years are not available.

4 *Castes and Tribes of Southern India* by Edgar Thurston, 1909, Vol. III, pages 94–105.

5 *Idem*, pages 222–249.

He has under him a chinna (little) Pattakaran. He presides over the caste council meetings, settles disputes and inflicts fines and other forms of punishment. In some places there is a headman for the village called Uru Goundan who is subject to the authority of the Nattu Goundan. Several nadus each composed of a number of a villages are subject to a Pattakar who is assisted by a Bandari. All these offices are hereditary. A Brahmin priest officiates at their marriages. The dead are buried. The death ceremonies last for four days and pollution for 10 days.[1]

The Devangas are a caste of Kannada and Telugu weavers of the Tamil districts. They are also called Senniars and Sedars. In 1921, they numbered 53,105 in the district[2]. The name Devanga menas 'body of the Gods' and the caste people say that they originally sprang from a Brahmin Rishi called Devalar or Devanga. They employ generally their own caste men as priests, but some of them also employ Brahmin priests. Some of them wear also the sacred thread. The title is usually Chetti; but some of them call themselves by the Brahminical titles of Sastri and Aiyar. They have several endogamous as well as exogamous septs. The majority of them are Saivites and wear the lingam. They belong to the Left Hand faction and have their own dancing girls called Seda Dasis. They have also a class of beggars of their own called Jatipillais.

Their tribal Goddess is Chamundeswari; a form of Kali or Durga, who is worshipped annually at a festival in which the entire community takes part either at the temple or at a house or grove specially prepared for the occasion. Their headman is called Pattagar. Their marriage ceremonies are either carried out according to the puranic ritual or performed with some modifications to it. The ceremony usually commences with the distribution of tambulam and Vigneswara worship. The bride is then presented with a new cloth and sits on a three legged stool, or cloth roller (dhonige) when her maternal uncle puts round her neck a bondhu (strings of unbleached cotton) dipped in turmeric. On the first day of the actual wedding ceremony a milk pot is set up and various rites are performed, which include tonsure, upanayanam, padapuja kasiyatra, dharadattam (giving away the bride) and Mangalya-dharanam (tying the tali or bottu). The proceedings then conclude with pot searching. A pap-bowl and ring are put into a pot. If the bride picks out the bowl, her first born will be a girl, and if the bridegroom gets hold of the ring, it will be a boy. On the fifth day a square design is made

---

1 *Castes and Tribes of Southern India* by Edgar Thurston, 1909, Vol. V, pages 438–443.

2 Figures for later years are not available.

on the floor with coloured rice grains and, between the couple and the square, a row of lights is placed. Four pots are set, one at each corner of the square and eight pots are arranged along each side of it. On the square itself two pots representing Siva and Uma are placed with a row of seedling pots near them. A thread is wound nine times round the pots representing the Gods and Goddesses and tied above to the pandal. After the pots have been worshipped this thread is cut and worn with the sacred thread for three months. This ceremony is called Nagavalli. The dead among them are generally buried in a sitting posture. Before the grave is filled in, a string is tied to the hair knot of the corpse and by its means the head is lifted. Over it a lingam is set up and worshipped throughout the death ceremonies.[1]

The Idaiyars or the Yadavas are the great shepherd caste of the Tamils. In 1921, they numbered 14,811 in this district [2]. This caste has many sub divisions of which the Kalkatti and Pasi Idaiyars are so called from their custom of wearing sixteen glass beads on either side of the tali; the Semban Idaiyars take their name from Sambu or Siva; the Kallar Idaiyar take their name from the Kallars; the Podumattu Idaiyars claim to have come to Coimbatore from Tirunelveli; and the Pancharamkatti Idaiyars derive their name from the custom prevalent among their women of wearing a neck ornament called Pancha-haram or Pancharam. Among the Pancharamkatti Idaiyars widow marriage is practised and this is because it is said Sri Krishna used to place a similar ornament round the neck of the Idaiyar widows of whom he was enamoured, in order to transform them from widows into married women. The Idaiyars take a higher social position than they would otherwise do owing to the tradition that Sri Krishna was brought up by their caste and to the fact that they are the only purveyors of milk, ghee, etc., and so are indispensable to the community. All the Brahmins, except the most orthodox, drink butter-milk and eat butter brought by them. In some places they enjoy the privilege of breaking the butter pot on Sri Krishna's birthday; and for doing this, they are given a new cloth and paid some money. They eat in the houses of Vellalars, Palliars and Nattamars. They either burn or bury their dead. They assume titles like Kone, Konar, Pillai, Pongadan and Karaiyalar. They consider Saturday as a holy day and being Vaishnavites, they brand themselves like the Vaishnava Brahmins and observe Sri Jayanti as their important festival.

---

1 *Castes and Tribes of Southern India* by Edgar Thurston, 1909, Vol. II, pages 154–166.

2 The strength of this caste in 1931 was 13,865. Figures for later years are not available.

Among some Idaiyars, a man has a right to marry his paternal aunt's daughter. But, if the woman's age is much greater, she is usually married to her cousin or someone else in the maternal side of her family. A Brahmin priest officiates at their weddings and the sacred fire is used, but the bridegroom's sister ties the tali; caste affairs are settled by a headman called the Nattanmaikaran. This headman has the management of the caste fund which is generally utilized in the celebration of the festivals of the larger temples of the district. Some Idaiyars again observe an uncommon rule of inheritance according to which a woman who has no male issue at the time of her husband's death has to return his property to his brother, father or maternal uncle. She is, however, allotted a maintenance, the amount of which is settled by caste panchayat. According to another odd form of inheritance observed by others among them, a man's property descends to his sons-in-law who live with him and not to his sons. The sons merely get maintenance until they are married.

In this district when a marriage between two persons is contemplated, a red and white flower tied up in separate betel leaves, are thrown before the idol at a temple. A little child is told to pick up one of the leaves, and, if she selects the one containing the white flower, the omens are considered auspicious, and the marriage will be arranged with the consent of the girl's cousins (maternal uncle's sons) who have a right to marry her. On the marriage day a Brahmin purohit makes homam and places a cowdung Pillayar (Ganesa) in the pandal. The relations of the bride and bridegroom fetch from the potter's house seven pots called adukupanai and place them in front of a platform made of earth, after filling them with water and placing a small bit of gold in each. The bridegroom then goes to a Pillayar temple and, on his return, the bride's brother washes his feet, and puts rings on his second toe. The Kankanams (wrist-threads) are tied on the wrists of the couple and the bridegroom takes his seat within the pandal, to which the bride is carried in the arms of one of her maternal uncles, while another carries a lighted torch placed on a mortar. The bride takes her seat by the side of the bridegroom and the torch light is set in front of them. The tali is taken round to be blessed by those assembled and handed to the bridegroom who ties it on the bride's neck. The right hand of the bridegroom is placed on the left hand of the bride and their hands are tied together by one of the bride's maternal uncle's sons. The bride is then carried into the house in the arms of an elder brother of the bridegroom. At the threshold she is stopped by the maternal uncle's sons, who may beat the man who is carrying her. The bridegroom pays them each four annas and the couple are allowed to enter the house. On the seventh day, the ends of the cloths of the newly married couple are tied together, and they bathe in turmeric water. When the wrist threads are removed, they rub oil over each others heads and bathe in a tank. They then perform the pot searching ceremony and the ceremony of touching the grindstone and looking at the star Arundathi.

On the death of a married Idaiyar in this district, the male relations put on sacred threads which are thrown on the pyre when the son sets fire to it. On the third day after death the smouldering ashes are extinguished with water, and the fragments of the bones are collected and placed on a leaf. A miniature plough is made, and the spot on which the body was burned is ploughed, and the nine kinds of grain are sown. On the sixteenth day, a Brahmin makes a human figure with holy grass, which has to be worshipped by the chief mourner not less than twenty-five times, and he must bathe between each act of worship. The bones are then carried in a new earthen pot, and floated on a stream. At night food is cooked and worshipped with a new cloth. A cock is tied to a sacrificial post called Kazhukumaram set up outside the house, to which rice is offered. One end of the thread is tied to the post, and the other end to a new cloth, which is worshipped inside the house. The thread is watched till it shakes and then broken. The door is closed, and the cock is struck on the pointed tip of the post and killed. An empty car is carried in procession through the streets, and alms are given to beggars. When a grown up, but unmarried male or female dies, a human figure made out of holy grass, is married to the corpse, and some of the marriage rites are performed.

In some districts the Idaiyars observe some peculiar customs in performing their marriages and funerals. It is said that, when a bride enters the room decorated for the marriage ceremony, her followers pay to the sister of the bridegroom, the money called the 'Bride's room gold' ; and that when the bridegroom goes to the house of his mother-in-law, his young companions arrest him on the way and do not release him until he pays a piece of gold. On the third day of the marriage ceremony when the sprinkling of saffron water on the guests is over, the whole party repair to the village tank. Here the friend of the husband brings a hoe and a basket and the husband fills three baskets with earth from the bottom of the tank, while the wife takes them away and throws out the earth. The couple then say " We have dug a ditch for charity ". At their funerals, it is said, a Maravar who styles himself " the father of the grand-father " comes amidst the assembly and addresses it in the following enigmatical words: " the slave who intrudes himself of his own accord spreads his foot over the way and will throw a spear into the breast of the strong "[1].

The Tottiyars or Kambalattars are a caste of Telugu cultivators whose ancestors were probably poligars and soldiers of the Nayakkan Kings of Vijayanagar. In 1921, they numbered 28,505 in the district[2]. They claim to be descended from the Gopis associated with Sri Krishna. Most of them are Vaishnavites, some of whom employ Brahmin priests, but the majority are guided by their own Gurus called Kodangi Nayakkars. Each family has its own family deity which appears to be a sort of representation of departed relations, chiefly women who have committed Sati. The Pongu tree is the sacred tree of the caste. Remarriage of widows is discouraged. The dead are generally burnt. Both men and women are supposed to practise magic and are consequently feared by the other people. They are also supposed to be one of the nine Kambalam castes so called because of their practice of spreading at caste council meetings a Kambli (blanket) with a decorated pot of water on it.[3]

The Vettuvans are an agricultural and hunting caste. In 1921, they numbered 34,499 in the district.[4] According to a tradition their ancestors were invited from the Chola and Pandya countries by the Kongu Kings to assist them against the Keralas. Another story says that they helped the Chola King Aditya Varma to conquer the Kongu country during the latter part of the ninth century. There are several endogamous subdivisions among them. Besides the Hindu gods they worship the seven Kannimars (Virgins). Widow marriage is forbidden. The dead are buried or burnt. They are ordinarily called Kavandans.[5]

The Shanars (called Nadars or Gramanis) were formerly the toddy-drawing caste of the Tamil country. Most of them, however, do not follow this calling now but have taken to trade in which they are generally successful. In social position they are placed above the Pallars and the Parayars and were formerly regarded as a polluting caste. There are several sub-divisions among them. In Coimbatore some Shanars engaged as shop keepers have adopted the name of Chetti and some are

---

1 *Castes and Tribes of Southern India* by Edgar Thurston, 1909, Vol. II, pages 352–366.

Census of India, Vol. XV, Part I, 1902, page 155.

2 Figures for later years are not available.

3 *Castes and Tribes of Southern India* by Edgar Thurston 1909, Vol. VII, page 183–197.

4 Figures for later years are not available.

5 *Castes and Tribes of Southern India* by Edgar Thurston, 1909, Vol. VII, pages 394–395.

called Muppans meaning headmen.[1] They numbered 72,923 in the district in 1921.[2]

Andis are a class of beggars composed of many low castes. They numbered 33,707 in the district in 1921. They are divided into several sub-divisions, the chief of which are Jangam, Komanandi, Lingadari, Mudavandi and Uppandi. They go out every morning begging for alms, singing ballads or hymns, beating a gong and blowing a conch. Some of the Andis are engaged in other occupations like brick laying, temple service and cultivation. They employ Brahmin priests at their ceremonies. Widows and divorcees remarry. The dead are buried.[3]

The Pallars are mostly agricultural labourers. In 1921, they numbered 28,910 in the district.[4] Their name is said to be derived from Pallam, a pit, in which low place they were said to be standing when the castes were originally formed. It is also said to be derived from low-ground or wet cultivation in which they were experts. Some say that they were the descendants of a Sudra and a Brahmin; others say that they were created by Devendra for the purpose of labouring on behalf of the Vellalars. They themselves trace their lineage to Indra and in token thereof their brides, like the Kallar brides, wear a wreath of flowers. They consider themselves superior to the Paraiyars and Chakkiliyars, as they do not eat beef.

They have a number of sub-divisions such as the Aiya (father), the Amma (mother), the Anja (father), the Atta (mother), the Devendra (Indra), the Kadaiyar (lowest or last), the Konga, the Managanadu, the Sozhia and the Tondaman. These subdivisions are endogamous. The Aiya and the Amma Pallars are said to have exogamous septs or kilais which, like those of the Maravars and the Kallars, run in the female line. Children belong to the same kilai as that of their mother and maternal uncle and not of their father. The headman of the Pallars is called Kudumbar and he is assisted by a Kaladi and sometimes by a caste called Variyar whose business it is to summon people to attend to caste meetings, marriages, funerals, etc. An ex-communicated man among the Pallars is strictly dealt with and deprived of the services of even the barber and the washerman. Restoration to caste is done by a purification ceremony.

---

1 *Castes and Tribes of Southern India* by Edgar Thurston, 1909, Vol. VI, pages 363–370.

2 Figures for later years are not available.

3 *Castes and Tribes of Southern India* by Edgar Thurston, 1909, Vol. I, pages 44–47.

4. The strength of this caste in 1931 was 29,706. Figures for later years are not available.

In one form of marriage among them the bridegroom's sister goes to the house of the bride with a tali, a new cloth, betel, flowers and fruits and ties the tali round the bride's neck. The bride then goes round the milk post [1] and afterwards to the house of the bridegroom. Here the couple sit together on a dais when coloured water or coloured rice balls with lighted wicks are waved round them. They then go thrice round the dais with linked fingers and the ceremony comes to an end. In another more elaborate form of ceremonial, on the occasion of the betrothal, the parents and maternal uncle of the bridegroom go to the bride's house with rice, fruits, plantains, coconuts, sandal paste and turmeric and hand over these articles with the bride's money to the Kudumbar or Kaladi of her village. On the wedding day a booth is erected, a milk post is set up by the maternal uncles of the bride and bridegroom, a marriage dais is made and the couple, after being bathed and tied with wrist threads (kankanam) are made, to go round, four betel leaves and areca nuts placed at each corner of the dais three times, saluting the betel as they pass. They then sit on the dais, while two men stretch a cloth over their heads. The kudumbar or kaladi pours a little water on the palms and heads of the couple and waves the water vessel before them, while the maternal uncle, the headman and others garland the couple. The bride is now taken into the house and given a new cloth by her maternal uncle, and, as soon as she is dressed, she is lifted by him in his arms and carried to the dais and seated beside the bridegroom. After this the fingers of the couple are linked together beneath a cloth held by the maternal uncle. The tali is then placed on the neck of the bride by the bridegroom to be tightly tied thereon by his sister. Just before the tali is tied, the headman cries out, " May I look into the bride's money and presents ? " and on being answered " Yes " he says thrice, " Seven bags of nuts, seven bags of rice, etc., have been brought." In some places the bridegroom is required to steal some thing from the bride's house when they return home after the marriage.

The Pallars, it is said, are nominally Saivites but in reality devil worshippers who perform pujas to grama devatas. Formerly they used to indulge in animal sacrifices. Their common titles are generally Muppar, Kudumbar and Mannadai.[2]

---

1 A live branch of either the Arasu (ficus religiosa) or Banian (ficus bengalensis) or Athi (Bauhinia tomentosa) is tied to a small fresh green bamboo. It is erected in the marriage booth in front of the seats of the bride and the bride groom.

2 *Castes and Tribes of Southern India* by Edgar Thurston, 1909, Vol. V, pages 472–486.

The Kusavars are the Tamil potters. In 1921, they numbered 25,625 in the district [1]. The name Kusavar is said to be derived from the Sanskrit word 'ku' signifying earth, the material in which they work, and 'avar' a personal termination. They wear the sacred thread and profess both Saivism and Vaishnavism. Their ceremonies are somewhat like the ceremonies of the Vellalars. Some of them have priests of their own caste, while others employ Brahmin priests. They have usually Velan as their title. They are divided into three territorial sections, Chola, Chera, and Pandya and they say that they are descended from the three sons of Kulan, the son of Brahma. Kulan, they say, prayed to Brahma to be allowed, like him, to create and destroy things daily and Brahma accordingly made him a potter.

A Kusavar can claim the hand of his paternal aunt's daughter. The bride's price is paid and the tali is tied by the bridegroom's sister. The marriage ceremonies last for three days and one of the curious ceremonies consists in the bridegroom's sister sowings seeds in a pot. On the last day of the wedding, the seedlings which have sprouted are taken with music to a river or tank and thrown into it. When the bride attains maturity, their caste priest conducts a ceremony and consummation follows on the next auspicious day. Both divorce and widow marriage are normally forbidden among them. Their special deity is Aiyanar. [2]

The Ambattars are the Tamil barbers who have for ages been also village medicine men, surgeons and musicians. In 1921, they numbered 30,485 in the district [3]. Their women used to act as the village midwives. They have adopted Brahmin ceremonies to a large extent and at their marriages a Brahmin priest officiates. On the first two days of the marriage ceremony a *homam* is made. On the third day the tali is placed on the circular silver or brass tray and touched with the forefinger of the right hand, first by the presiding Brahmin and then by other Brahmins men of superior castes and the caste men headed by the Perithanakkaran or the headman. It is then, amidst much music, tied to the bride's neck before the sacred fire. During the ceremony no widows are generally permitted to be present. The relations of the bride and the bridegroom bless the couple by pouring rice from their hands in a stream in front of them. This rice is afterwards given to the Perithanakkaran. The Brahmin receives as his fee some money and

---

1 Figures for later years are not available.

2 *Castes and Tribes of Southern India* by Edgar Thurston, 1909, Vol. IV, pages 188–197.

3 The strength of this caste in 1931 was 15,103. Figures for later years are not available.

a pair of silk bordered cloths. He receives also the first pansupari, plantains and coconuts. During the fourth and fifth days, the *homam* is completed and *shadangu* or merry-making between the bride and bridegroom before the assembled people takes place, in which the bride sings songs. On the fifth day the removal of the kankanam, or the threads which have been tied round the wrists of the bride and bridegroom is done. Widow marriage is forbidden.

The dead among them are cremated, with the exception of children who are buried. Their death ceremonies are conducted by a Brahmin priest who is remunerated for his services with money and a cloth. Gifts of money and cloth are made to other Brahmins as well when the days of pollution are over. They also perform *sraddhas*.

They are either Saivites or Vaishnavites. The Vaishnavites among them who have been branded by their Brahmin guru with the Chank and Chakram, abstain from meat. Intermarriages between the two sections is allowed and commonly practised. They belong to the Right Hand faction.[1]

The Vannars are the washermen of the community. In 1921, they numbered 26,706 in this district.[2] The name is said to be rather an occupational term than a caste title. The Pandya Vannars or Vannars proper, include the Vaduga Vannars ' northern washermen ', or washermen of the Telugu country and the Palla, the Pradara and the Tuluka Vannars who wash for the Pallars, the Paraiyars and the Muslims respectively. The Pandya Vannars have a headman called Periamanushar (big man) who has the usual powers and privileges. As to their marriage customs, a man can claim the hand of his paternal aunt's daughter and at the weddings the bride's price is paid, the bridegroom's sister ties the tali and the Nambis officiate. Divorce is allowed among them on payment of twice the bride's price and the divorcees may marry again. Their caste God is Gurunathar and they have their own pujaris. They generally burn their dead and observe the sixteenth day ceremony.

The Oddas or Voddas have been described as the ' navvies of the country, quarrying stone, sinking wells, constructing tank bunds and executing other kinds of earthwork more rapidly than any other class so that they have almost a monopoly of the trade '. They are Telugu speaking people who came originally from Orissa. In the

---

[1] *Castes and Tribes of Southern India* by Edgar Thurston, 1909, Vol. I, pages 32–41.

[2] The strength of this caste in 1931 was 29,981. Figure for later years are not available.

Coimbatore district they numbered 72,817 in 1921.[1] They are employed to dig the numerous irrigation wells which on account of the hard nature of the sub-soil demand the labour of strong men accustomed to the use of the crowbar, pick-axe and manual power. They are of good physique. Their caste titles are Nayakan and Boyan. They are divided into two branches, the Kallu (stone) and the Mannu (earth) Oddas, between whom there is no social intercourse of any kind or intermarriage. The marriage ceremony is simple, the bride and bridegroom walking three times round a stake placed in the ground, but some of them in the Coimbatore district adopt a more elaborate form in imitation of the Balijas. The Oddas are Vaishnavites in some places and Saivites in other places. They also worship minor deities like Ellamma, Ankamma, etc. The dead are generally buried and the funeral ceremonies are simple but here also those in Coimbatore sometimes adopt a more elaborate form in imitation of the Balijas.[2]

The Paraiyars, some say, derive their name from parai which means a drum, since certain sections of the Paraiyars act as drummers at marriages, funerals, festivals, etc. Others, however, question this derivation remarking that it is only some of the Paraiyars, and not all, who act as drummers. The term Paraiyar is said to be not found in ancient Tamil literature; instead, the term used in those days is said to be Pulayar or Eyinar. In ancient times they are said to have held a higher social status but today they rank low in society and are employed as agricultural labourers, grave diggers, village watchmen, scavengers, etc. They are most numerous in the district and in 1921 they numbered 73,363.[3]

It is usual among them to give the father's name when distinguishing one person from another; as, for instance, Tamburan, son of Kannan. They also delight in giving nick-names such as Nondi (lame), Kallan (thief), Kullan (dwarf), etc. There are some occupational subdivisions among them such as the barbers, the washermen, the play-actors, the priests and the scavengers and outside these subdivisions any Paraiyar may marry any Paraiyar girl. They generally live in a poor quarters away from other communities. They belong to the Right Hand faction, have priests of their own called Valluvars and a few important individuals known as Panakkarars (monied men). The Panakkarars form a committee

1 Figures for later years are not available.

2 *Castes and Tribes of Southern India* by Edgar Thurston, 1909, Vol. V, pages 422–436.

3 The strength of this caste in 1931 was 74,647. Figures for later years are not available.

or council to decide ordinary quarrels and caste disputes, and exercise the rights of imposing fines, dissolving marriages, passing sentences of ex-communications, etc. The ex-communicated Paraiyars are said to go to a mythical place called Vinnamangalam.

Among the Paraiyars it is usual for a man to marry his paternal aunt's daughter or his maternal uncle's daughter. Marriage contracts are generally made by parents and marriage presents, such as clothes, jewels, rice, etc., are exchanged between the families of the bride and bridegroom. Their actual marriage ceremony is very simple. A lucky day is fixed by the Valluvar, their priest. A bride price of varying amount is paid. A part of the marriage ritual consists in setting up a pole of the *Odina Wodier* tree at the place appointed for the ceremony and afterwards planting it near the house and nursing it to grow. The bride and the bridegroom having been dressed—the latter wearing a thread in the Brahmin fashion—the Valluvar hands the tali to the bridegroom who ties it round the bride's neck. A series of feasts are then given to all the relatives of both the parties by the parents of the couple. The rites at the marriage of a widow are far simpler and are performed inside the house and sometimes at night. The removal of the tali of a widow is effected in a curious manner. On the sixteenth day after the husband's death, another woman stands behind the widow who stoops forward and unties the tali in such a way that it falls into a vessel of milk placed below to receive it. Adoption ceremonies are also odd. The adoptees' feet are washed in turmeric-water by the adopter, who then drinks a little of the water. Adoption is accordingly known as 'manjinir kudikkiradu' or the drinking of turmeric-water and the adopted son as the 'manjanirpillai' or the 'turmeric-water boy'.

The dead are as a rule buried, but sometimes they are burnt. As for their funeral rites, these are also very simple. The corpse is carried on a litter of palm-leaf mats and bamboos, wrapped in a new cloth and, on the third or fifth day after death, a milk ceremony, pal sadangu is performed when some milk is poured out by the relatives as an offering to the spirit of the deceased. The spirit is then supposed to depart to a place of respite of the soul till it is reborn. This ceremony is accompanied by a family feast. On the fifteenth day, the final ceremony is held. Occasionally, for some months after death, a few flowers are placed on the grave and a coconut is broken over it.

The Paraiyars are nominally Saivites or Vaishnavites but in reality are devil worshippers. They acknowledge the existence of a supreme, omnipresent, spiritual being, the source of all, whom they call Kadavul (he who is). But Kadavul possesses no temples, nor is he worshipped. The devatas whom they generally worship are called Ammas (mothers). Sometimes the Ammas are worshipped as virgins (Kanniyamma) or the Seven Virgins. Some stones representing the Seven Virgins are placed on a little platform under a margosa tree sheltered by a wattle hut or a small brick temple. This temple is called Amman Koil. More usually they worship in a similar temple one particular mother called Grama Devata, such as Ellamma, Mungilamma, Padaiyattal or Pidariyamma. The Goddesses whom they specially revere as titular deities are Gangammal and Mariyattal. The former is considered the Goddess of small-pox. Festivals are held in her honour whenever Cholera or small-pox makes its appearance. Besides these Goddesses, they worship also a number of ghosts and goblins.[1]

The Valluvars, as has been already stated, are the priests of the Parayars. Tiruvalluvar, the famous Tamil poet and author of the Kural, is believed to this caste. In 1921, they numbered 4,187 in this district.[2] They include in their ranks both the Vaishnavites and the Saivites; the former are called Valluva Tadans and the latter are Valluva Pandarams. The two classes, however, inter-marry and dine together. The Saivites, both men and women, wear the lingam.

At their betrothal ceremony, the bride's money (pariyam), betel, jewels, flowers and fruits are placed on the future bride's lap. The bridegroom's party also pays fees for a feast to the relatives. On the wedding day, the milk post consisting of a green bamboo pole is set up and a number of pots are placed near it. On the dais are set four lamps—an ordinary brass lamp, a Kudavilakku (pot light), an alankaravilakku (ornamental light) and paligaivilakku (seedling light). The bride and bridegroom bring some sand, spread it on the floor near the dais and place seven leaves on it. Cotton threads dyed with turmeric are tied to the pots and the milk post. On the leaves are set cakes and rice and the contracting couple worship the pots and the family Gods. The priest then ties the kankanams (threads) on their wrists. They are then led into the house and garlanded with jasmine or 'Nariam' flowers. The pots are now placed on the dais, and while one of them is planted with seedlings by the female relations, four others are filled with water by the bridegroom's party. A small quantity of seedlings is usually wrapped in a cloth and placed over the seedling pot. Next morning the bundle is untied and

1 *Castes and Tribes of Southern India* by Edgar Thurston, 1909, Vol. VI, pages 77–139.

2 The strength of this caste in 1931 was 3,981. Figures for later years are not available.

examined to see if the seedlings have germinated. If they are so, the bride is considered a worthy one; if not, the bride is considered unworthy or liable to premature death. The usual Nalangu ceremony is then performed, the bride and bridegroom being anointed with oil and smeared with *Phaselous Mungo* paste. This is followed by the offering of food on eleven leaves to the ancestors and house gods. Towards the evening, the couple sit on planks kept on the dais, and exchange betel and paddy nine or twelve times, and rice twenty-seven times. The priest then kindles the sacred fire, and pours some ghee into it from a mango leaf. The bridegroom is now asked thrice whether he sees Arundhati (Ursa Major) to which he replies in the affirmative. The tali is then shown to the sky, smoked over burning camphor and placed on a tray together with a rupee. After being blessed by those present, it is tied round the bride's neck by the bridegroom. On the second day, there is a procession through the village and, on the third day, the wrist threads are removed.

The Saivite lingam wearers bury their dead in a sitting posture. After death has taken place, a coconut is broken and camphor is burnt. The corpse is washed by the relations who bring nine pots of water for the purpose. The lingam is then tied to the head and a cloth bundle containing a rupee, seven bilva leaves and nine *leucas aspara* flowers, is tied to the right arm. The corpse is then carried to the grave on a cart surmounted by five brass vessels, After it is buried, the priest is given a fee for his services. On the third day after death, the female relations of the deceased pour milk into a vessel which is taken by the male relatives to the burning ground and offered at the grave. A lingam is then worshipped here. The final death ceremonies are celebrated on the seventeenth day.[1]

The Chakkiliyars are the shoe-makers of the Tamil districts. In 1921, they numbered 206,162 in the district [2]. They appear to be immigrants from the Telugu or Kannada districts and a very large proportion of them speak Telugu or Kannada. In social position, they occupy the lowest rank, though there is much dispute on this point among them and the Paraiyars. The avaram plant, the bark of which is a tanning agent, is held in much veneration by them and the tali is tied to a branch of it as a preliminary to marriage. Their marriage ceremonies closely resemble those of Paraiyars. Their widows can remarry. Divorce can be obtained among them by the payment of a certain sum to the other in the presence of the local head of the caste. The men among them belong to the right

---

1 *Castes and Tribes of Southern India* by Edgar Thurston, 1909, Vol. VII, pages 303–310.

2 The strength of this caste in 1931 was 235,366. Figures for later years are not available.

hand faction, while the women belong to the left hand faction. Nominally they are Saivites but are in reality devil worshippers. Their gods include Aiyanar, Madurai Veeran, Mariamman, Muniswara, Draupati and Gangamma. [1]

The Vedars [2] are a Tamil speaking, labouring and hunting caste, the members of which were formerly soldiers. The name means a hunter. Among them, widows may marry their late husband's brothers or agnates. They either burn or bury their dead. They claim a descent, like the Ambalakarars, from Kannappa Nayanar, one of the sixty-three Saiva Saints. Their title is generally Nayakkar. [3]

The Malasars who are described as a forest tribe are classified into three grades, viz., those who live on the hills, those who live on the slopes near the foot of the hills and those who live on the plains. In 1921, they numbered 4,928 in this district [4]. In this district, they are found chiefly in the Anaimali hills, in the low jungles of Pollachi and Udumalpet taluks and in the Bolampatti jungles. They live by hill cultivation and day labour as baggage coolies, while some are employed as agricultural labourers or in collecting honey. They are proverbially lazy and will take a week's wages in advance from their landlord but put in only three or four days work in the week. They are good at game-tracking, and very handy with their axes, with the help of which they will construct a bamboo house for the wandering sportsman in a few hours. They are also employed in the operations connected with the catching and training of wild elephants. They eat and drink almost anything except vermin and cobras. Like the hill tribes they dig up yams, when food is scarce. It is said that Kadars and Eravalars are admitted into the Malasar caste. But, while the Kadars abstain from eating the flesh of the bison and the cow, the Malasars will eat the carrions of these animals. On the hills, their dwelling huts are made of bamboo matting thatched with grass and teak leaves, while on the plains the walls are made of mud and are roofed with grass and bamboo.

The Malasars reside in hamlets known as padhais or pathis, each of which has a headman, who exercises the usual authority with the assistance

---

1 *Castes and Tribes of Southern India* by Edgar Thurston, 1909, Vol. II, pages 2–7.

2 Figures relating to the strength of this caste are not available

3 *Castes and Tribes of Southern India* by Edgar Thurston, 1909, Vol. VII, pages 331–335.

4 The strength of this tribe in 1931 was 4,719. Figures for later years are not available.

of a panchayat. One of the punishments inflicted by panchayats, it is said, is to make the culprit carry a heavy load of sand for some distance, and then stand with it on his head and beg for forgiveness. The Malasar who live in the plains consider *Ficus glomerala* (Athi, country fig) tree sacred, and worship it once a year. At least, a branch of this tree should be used in the construction of their marriage pandal and the menstrual hut. They also avoid the use of the *Pongamia gladra* (Pungam, Indian Beech) tree for any purpose. The hill Malasars worship, among other deities, Pullarappachi (Ganesa), Kaliamma and Ponnalamman (Mariamman) and sacrifice to the last deity pigs and buffaloes once a year. The Malasars of the plains worship Mariayi (Mariamma), at whose festival a stake is fixed on the ground and eventually shaken by the Malasars, and removed by Paraiyars. But the special deity of the Malasars is said to be Manakadatta to whom they sacrifice fowls and sheep in the month of Masi (February-March). A man of the tribe acts as a priest on these occasions, and keep the heads of the offerings as his perquisites. The Malasar women of the plains wear glass bangles only on the left wrist, as Paraiyar women do. If a Malasar woman puts such bangles on both wrists, it is taken as an insult by the Paraiyars, who, it is said will break the bangles and report the matter to the headman who is expected to fine the woman.

The Malasars observe peculiar customs in performing their marriages and funerals. The Malasars of the plains perform the marriage ceremonies at the home of the bride on a Monday which is considered to be an auspicious day. On the previous day, the contracting couple stand on a pestle and are anointed. Two balls of cooked rice are placed in a tray with two lighted wicks of the same height stuck into them. The lights are waved in front of the bride and bridegroom to ward off the evil eye. After bathing, the couple are seated on a dias within the marriage pandal and the bridegroom ties the tali on the neck of the bride, which consists of a brass disc tied to a string dyed with turmeric. Their hands are then joined by the headman and the ceremony comes to an end with the couple eating from the same leaf or plate. In the case of hill Malasars, the bridegroom goes on a Wednesday to the bride's house and takes her to his home on the following day for performing the marriage ceremony. He generally presents his mother-in-law with a cloth with an eight anna coin tied in its skirt. Before commencing their ceremonies, cooked rice and the flesh of the fowl are offered to the ancestors on seven leaves.

When a girl reaches maturity, she occupies a separate hut for seven days. On the seventh day she bathes and goes to the dwelling hut before which a measure and a lamp are placed. The girl goes over them with her right foot foremost, then steps backwards and then again goes over them before entering the hut.

The dead are usually buried. If the dead person was an elder, his personal effects, such as pillows, walking-stick and clothes are buried with him, or the corpse is cremated. Sometimes, the dead are buried in a sitting posture in a niche excavated on one side of the grave. In the case of the Malasars of the plains, the widow chews betel leaf and arecanuts and spits the juice over the eye and neck of the corpse. On the third day after the death, cooked rice and meat are offered to the soul of the deceased on seven arka leaves. The male members of the family then eat from the same leaf.[1]

The Irulas are a forest tribe with very dark skins and platyrhine noses. They speak a corrupt form of Tamil. They numbered 5,288 in 1921 in the district.[2] They are generally worshippers of Vishnu under the name of Rangaswami, whose principal shrine is at Karamadai. They mostly work on coffee and tea estates on the Nilgiris, and also collect forest produce like honey, bees-wax, gall-nuts, soap-nuts, sheekoy, deer's horns, etc., besides cultivating ragi, samai, maize, plantain, limes, oranges, jack fruits, etc. Their marriages are usually very simple affair. When an Irula dies, two Kurumbas come to the village and one shaves the head of the other. The shorn man is then fed and presented with a cloth which he wraps round his head. This is supposed to bring good luck to the deceased. Outside the hut where the body is kept, men and women dance to a rude band. The dead are buried in a sitting posture.

The Kadars are a forest tribe inhabiting the Anaimalai hills. They are short and dark-skinned and have platyrhine noses. Both men and women are in the habit of chipping off their front teeth. Women wear a bamboo comb in the back hair. Men have the lobes of the ear adorned with brass ornaments and the nostril pierced and plugged with wood. The ear-lobes of the women are widely dilated with palm leaf rolls or huge wooden discs and they wear ear-rings, brass or steel bangles and finger-rings and bead necklets. They speak a Tamil patois or a mixture of debased Tamil and Malayalam. They possess little or no knowledge of cultivation. They are handy with their bill hooks and their huts are neat structures of bamboo thatched with leaves of the teak tree and bamboo. Each hut is divided into a verandah and some compartments by bamboo partitions. They are nomadic in habits, living in small communities and shifting from place to place in the jungle. When wandering in the jungle they make a rough lean-to shed covered over with leaves and keep a small

---

1. *Castes and Tribes of Southern India* by Edgar Thurston, 1909, Vol. IV, pages 394–405.

2. *Census of India*, 1901, Vol. XV, Part I, 1902, page 166. Figures for later years are not available.

fire burning through the night to keep off bears, elephants, tigers and leopards. They are good hunters. They collect minor forest produce like wax, honey, cardamoms, myrobalams, ginger, turmeric, dammer, deer's horns, elephants' tusks and rattan and sell it to the Government through contractors. They are experts at collecting honey and climb tall trees and giddy precipices with the help of chains made of bamboo or rattan. Very often the honey is collected on dark nights. They eat succulent roots, bamboo seeds, sheep, fowls, rock snakes, deer, porcupines, rats, wild pigs, monkeys, etc. They are also said to eat the carcases of wild beasts which they come across in the forest. The mealy portion of the seeds of the cycas tree which flourishes in the lower slopes of the Anaimalais is also eaten by them. In its raw state the fruit is said to be poisonous, but the Kadars cut it into slices, thoroughly soak the slices in running water and dry afterwards and grind them into flour and make cakes or bake in hot ashes. They also prepare a kind of sago flour from the pith of the wild sago palms.

In regard to their marriage practices, a Kadar youth who wishes to marry goes to the village of his bride-elect and gives her a dowry by working there for a year. On the wedding day a feast is given by the parents of the bridegroom to which the Kadar community is invited. The bride and bridegroom stand beneath a pandal or arch decorated with flowers erected outside the bridegroom's house while men and women dance separately to the music of drum and fife. The bridegroom's mother or sister ties the tali of gold or silver round the bride's neck and her father puts a turban on the head of the bridegroom. The contracting parties link together the little fingers of their right hands as a token of their union and walk in procession round the pandal. Then sitting on a reed mat they exchange betel *. The marriage can be dissolved for incompatibility of temper, disobedience on the part of the wife, adultery, etc. A council of elders pronounces judgment in such cases. Polygamy is permitted. Widows are not allowed to remarry, but may live in a state of concubinage. Special huts are maintained for women during menstruation on the parturition. When a girl reaches puberty a special hut is erected for her and the event is celebrated by a feast. All girls change their names when they reach puberty.

The religion of the Kadars is a crude polytheism. They worship Paikuttatha (a projecting rock overhanging a slab of rock on which are set up two stones on end), Athuvisariamma (a stone enclosure ten to fifteen

* M.W. M. Yeats says in his Census of India, 1931, that the marriage ceremonies are the simplest that exist and that all that happens is that the two persons eat from the same plate.

feet square almost level with the ground and containing a representation of the goddess), Vanathavathi (a god with no shrine), Ayyappaswami (a stone set up beneath a teak tree) and Masanyatha (a goddess depicted in stone on a masonry wall near the village of Anamalai). She has a high repute for her power of detecting thieves and rogues. Chillies are thrown into the fire in her name and the guilty person is expected to suffer from vomitting and diarrhoea. The Kadars also worship Kali and offer to her a pudding of rice and vegetables cooked in honey by a number of virgins. They are said to be good exorcists and trade in Mantravadam or magic.

The dead are buried in a grave, but when death occurs in the depth of the jungle, the corpse is placed in a crevice between the rocks and covered over with stones. A band of music, consisting of drum and fife, plays weired dirges outsides the hut of the deceased and whistles are blown when the corpse is carried away. The old clothes are placed under the corpse and a new cloth is put on it. It is then completely tied up in a mat and carried to the burial ground on a bamboo stretcher. As it leaves the hut rice is thrown over it. The corpse is laid with its head to the east (north, according to Mr. Yeats) and protected on all sides with bamboo mats so as to prevent its touching the earth on any side. Well-to-do families perform the final death ceremonies on the eighth day. But poorer families have to wait for a year or more till they have collected sufficient money. On the day of the ceremonies rice called ' polli chor ' is cooked at cock-crow and piled up on leaves in the centre of the hut. Cooked rice or ' Tullagu chor ' is then placed in each of the four corners of the hut to propitiate the spirit of the dead person and the gods. At a short distance from the hut rice called ' Kanal chor ' is cooked for all Kadars who have died. The relations of the deceased then begin to cry and make lamentations and proclaim the good qualities of the deceased. Everybody then adjourn to the hut and partakes of the food after throwing up a pinch from each of the heaps as a gift to the gods.[1]

Muduvars [2] are a tribe of hill cultivators found in some parts of the Anamalai hills. They have a tradition that thier ancestors were Vellalars living in Madurai until they were forced by the disturbances caused by some of the kings to seek refuge in the hills. They exhibit in their physical features a mixture of the East Coast and West Coast races. They live in

---

1. *Castes and Tribes of Southern India* by Edgar Thurston, 1909, Vol. III, pages 5-29.

2. Figures relating to the strength of this hill tribe are not available.

huts but occasionally change their quarters from one part of the hills to another. Disputes among them are settled by an informal panchayat of the men of the village. References are also occasionally made to a Muppan or Sub-headman of the tribe. When a boy or girl reaches puberty the parents give a feast to the village. A man may not marry the daughter of his brother or sister; he ought to marry his uncle's daughter. Marriages are arranged by the friends and more often by the cousins on the mother's side of the bridegroom, who request the hand of a girl or woman from her parents. If they and the near relatives agree, a day is fixed and the couple leave the village to live a few days in a cave by themselves. On their return they announce whether they would like to go on with it or not. In the former case the man publicly gives ear-rings, a brass bangle, a cloth and a comb to the woman and takes her to his hut. In the latter case the marriage does not take place and the man and the woman are at liberty to try again with some one else. Remarriage of widows is permitted and the widow by right belongs to her deceased husband's maternal aunt's son and not under any circumstances, to any of his brothers. Divorce is permitted but only rarely. The tribe follows the West Coast or Marumakkatayam law of inheritance with a slight difference, the property descending to an elder or younger sister's son. The Muduvars profess to be Hindus and worship Palaniandi (the God of Palani) and Minakshi and Chokkanatha (the God and Goddess of Madurai). They also worship numerous malevolent deities. Priests of other castes are not employed. The dead are buried lying down, face upwards and placed north and south. The grave has a little thatched roof put over it. Two heavy stones are placed at the head and the foot. Totemism does not exist, but, in common with other jungle tribes, the tiger is called the jackal. The men generally wear a leg cloth and a turban. A blanket is invariably carried and put on when it rains. Ear-rings, finger and tow rings and bangles are also worn. The women go in for beads, strings of them adorning their necks. They also wear rings on the ears, fingers and toes, and anklets and bangles. Their cloth, often being brought round the waist and tucked in there, is carried over the body and the two corners are knotted over the right shoulder. The Muduvars believe that they were originally cultivators of the soil and they still raise some ragi or hill rice in the clearing of the jungle. They are, however, now chiefly hunters and trappers. They use several kinds of straps, blow pipes and darts and also guns. They eat all animals except cattle, dogs, jackals and snakes and all birds except kites and vultures. They also collect honey from the crevices of rocks by descending the rocks with the help of ropes or creepers[1]

1. *Castes and Tribes of Southern India* by Edgar Thurston, 1909, Vol. V, pages 86–103.

Turning to the Non-Hindus, the Muslims, as has already been stated, come second in the matter of population, their number being 83,806. The recent census reports do not show the various sects to which they belong, but there is some evidence in the earlier reports to show that the bulk of them are Tamil speaking Labbais or Malayalam speaking Moplas and that the rest are the Hindustani speaking Saiyids or Sheikhs or Pathans or Moghuls. The word Labbai seems to be of recent origin; formerly the Labbais were called Sonagan, meaning natives of Sonagam (Arabia). They are of mixed blood, partly the descendants of Arab traders or refugees who married with the women of the east coast and partly the descendants of the Hindus who were forcibly converted to Islam by Tippu Sultan and the previous Muslim invaders. They belong to the Shafi sect and their mother-tongue is Tamil. In their domestic ceremonies, in their customs of inheritance and in their methods of dress, manners, etc., they follow the Hindus. Their marriage ceremony closely resembles that of the lower caste Hindus, the only difference being that they cite passages from the Koran and their women do not appear in public even during marriages. Some of the Labbais set up a bamboo post at marriage and tie a tali round the neck of the bride while the Nikkadim is being read.

The Mappillas or Moplahs are a hybrid Muslim race of the adjacent district of Malabar now in the Kerala State. They are the descendants of Arab traders by the women of the country. Their strength was greatly increased by forcible conversions during the reign of Tippu Sultan. Voluntary conversion, especially from lower castes, is still going on. The exact origin and significance of the word Mapilla is not known. Some think that it was a title of honour bestowed on the early immigrants, both Muslim and Christians. The former were called Jonaga Mappillas, Jonaka standing for Yavanaka or Greek. The word has also been derived from Maha or Mohai (Mocha) and pilla or child, that is the natives of Mocha, and from the Arabic Muflih (from the root fallahic to till the soil).

The chief characteristics of Mappillas are their enthusiasm for religious practices. This enthusiasm has on numerous occasions led to fanatical uprisings in Malabar, attended with the massacre of non-Hindus. They are generally petty traders and shop-keepers. The dress of the men is a mundu or cloth generally white with a purple border, but sometimes orange or green or plain white. This cloth is kept in position by a waist string. A small knife is worn at the waist. The head is covered by a small cap of white or white and black round to which an ordinary turban or a bright coloured scarf is tied. The women wear a mundu of some coloured cloth, generally dark blue, and a white loose bodice and veil or scarf on the head. Among the higher classes they are kept shrouded and their faces are covered when they go out. They wear numerous ornaments.

The marriage ceremony consists of the nikka or formal conclusion of contract before two witnesses and the Kazi. The dead are buried with the legs pointing to the east. Widows may remarry some months after the death of their husbands.[1]

The Christians of the district comprise Roman Catholics as well as Protestants. Christianity was first introduced into the district by the Jesuit fathers of the Madurai Mission who had a chapel at Dharapuram, so early as 1608. Father Robert de Nobili first started evangelisation at Satyamangalam among a colony of weavers, having proceeded to that place from Moramangalam in the Salem district where he had converted Ramachandra Nayaka, the exiled Palayakar of Sendamangalam and his family to Christianity. The Palayakar of Satyamangalam supported the mission till his death in 1647 when the Christians began to be persecuted. However, by 1652 there were fifteen churches attached to the Satyamangalam Station. By 1656 there were in the same area 130 Christian villages or hamlets round 23 churches under the protection of the Raja of Mysore. Subsequently Karumathampatti and Andiyur became headquarter stations. In 1739 the Pope prohibited certain Hindu customs which were being followed by the Christians. This led to dissentions and desertions. The Christians were now placed under the Archbishops of Cranganore and Cochin. When the Society of Jesus was suppressed by the Pope in 1773 missionary work in the district was taken up by the mission Entrangere (the Society of Foreign Missions) of Paris. One of the new missionaries was the well-known Abbe'Dubois whose field of activity extended to Coimbatore from 1790 to 1823. In 1846 the district was separated from Pondicherry and became a district Vicariate Apostollic, with Karumathampatti as its headquarters and Koduveri, Satyamangalam and Dharapuram as sub-stations. The headquarters was subsequently moved to Coimbatore which in 1887 was raised to the status of a see.

The London Mission started work in Coimbatore in 1830 on the suggestion made by the Collector of the district, Mr. John Sullivan, to a travelling deputation from the Society in London. As the work developed especially among the Harijans near Erode who were converted in large numbers, that place was made a separate headquarters. The followers of the mission

---

1 *Castes and Tribes of Southern India* by Edgar Thurston, 1909, Vol. IV, pages 455–501.

have joined the South India United Church which unites Christians belonging to the Congregational, Presbyterian and Reformed Lutheran Missions in South India.

The Leipzig Evangelical Lutheran Mission started work in the district in 1856 and continued to function till the outbreak of the first World War of 1914–1918, when the Church of Sweden Mission took over its work.

The American Madurai Mission had a small congregation in Kumaramangalam in the Udumalpet taluk, but withdrew from the district after some years.[1]

The Christians, generally follow the Hindus in the matter of food, clothing, etc. As for their religious practices there is nothing peculiar to the Christian inhabitants of the district. They are the practices followed by the Christians everywhere.

---

[1] *Gazetteer of the Coimbatore District*, 1933, Vol. II, pages 116–120.

Population according to languages.

Language.	Total.	*Rural.* Kollegal taluk.	Gobichettipalayam taluk.	Bhavani taluk.	Avanashi taluk.
(1)	(2)	(3)	(4)	(5)	(6)
Tamil	2,160,054	10,920	214,224	175,130	120,032
Telugu	663,159	6,932	84,765	33,247	47,823
Kannada	367,288	96,072	45,764	12,950	49,378
Malayalam	57,348	446	1,938	214	401
Hindustani	30,308	3,657	2,474	881	881
Hindi	5,096	744	368	257	79
Marathi	3,571	231	182	7	30
Gujarathi	1,246	349	16	..	..
English	1,203	8	36	3	..
Lambadi	882	544	57	281	..
Sindhi	823	..	..	..	..
Konkani	579	14	..	..	..
Tulu	554	1	23	67	..
Yerukula	462	..	35	..	100
Sourashtra	278	..	2	..	..
Punjabi	88	..	..	..	4
Bengali	70	..	..	..	..
Coorgi	38	7	2	..	..
Badaga	34	..	..	..	..
Arabic	33	..	..	..	..
Marvari	32	..	1	..	..
French	13	3	2	..	..
Swedish	11	..	..	..	..
Sinhalese	8	..	..	..	..
Portuguese	7	..	6	..	..
Oriya	5	..	..	..	..
Burmese	3	..	..	..	..
Nepali	2	..	..	..	1
Pushtu	2	..	..	..	..
Chinese	1	..	..	..	..
Russian	1	..	..	..	..
Malayan	1	..	..	..	..
Italian	1	..	..	..	..
Dutch	1	..	..	..	..
Spanish	1	..	..	..	..
Swiss	1	..	..	..	..

Population according to Languages—cont.

Language.			Rural.			
			Erode taluk.	*Coimbatore taluk.*	*Palladam taluk.*	*Dharapuram taluk.*
			(7)	(8)	(9)	(10)
Tamil	..	..	330,721	156,741	204,110	250,132
Telugu	..	..	44,478	76,345	62,333	33,880
Kannada	..	..	5,182	44,388	13,654	14,049
Malayalam	..	..	849	4,896	942	454
Hindustani	..	..	618	495	386	801
Hindi	..	..	201	154	82	..
Marathi	..	..	..	126	18	28
Gujarathi	..	..	..	10	11	..
English	..	..	15	33	..	..
Lambadi	..	..	..	..	..	..
Sindhi	..	..	1	..	..	..
Konkani	..	..	..	53	..	..
Tulu	..	..	..	24	9	..
Yerukula	..	..	..	327	..	..
Sourashtra	..	..	..	4	..	..
Panjabi	..	..	..	13	..	..
Bengali	..	..	..	5	8	..
Coorgi	..	..	..	18	..	..
Badaga	..	..	..	2	..	..
Arabic	..	..	..	5	..	..
Marwari	..	..	..	..	..	..
French	..	..	..	3	..	..
Sweedish	..	..	..	..	..	..
Sinhalese	..	..	..	2	..	..
Portuguese	..	..	..	..	..	..
Oriya	..	..	..	4	..	..
Burmese	..	..	..	..	..	..
Nepali	..	..	..	1	..	..
Pushtu	..	..	..	..	..	..
Chinese	..	..	..	..	..	..
Russian	..	..	..	1	..	..
Malayan	..	..	..	..	..	..
Italian	..	..	..	..	..	..
Dutch	..	..	..	1	..	..
Spanish	..	..	..	..	..	..
Swiss	..	..	..	..	..	..

Population according to Language—cont.

Language.	Rural.		Urban.	
	Pollachi taluk.	*Udumalpet taluk.*	*City.*	*Non-city.*
	(11)	(12)	(13)	(14)
Tamil	189,194	102,409	178,489	217,952
Telugu	75,567	56,716	68,489	72,784
Kannada	22,186	6,977	21,903	34,785
Malayalam	16,044	503	22,595	8,066
Hindustani	905	437	8,895	9,878
Hindi	747	32	1,655	767
Marathi	200	7	2,048	6,921
Gujarathi	7	..	779	74
English	..	4	879	225
Lambadi	..	..	..	..
Sindhi	..	..	822	..
Konkani	..	..	481	31
Tulu	20	..	354	56
Yerukula	..	..	..	..
Sourashtra	..	48	224	..
Panjabi	..	..	69	2
Bengali	..	..	35	22
Coorgi	..	..	11	..
Badaga	25	..	7	..
Arabic	..	..	14	14
Marwari	..	..	31	..
French	..	..	5	..
Sweedish	..	..	..	11
Sinhalese	..	..	5	..
Portuguese	..	..	1	..
Oriya	..	..	1	..
Burmese	..	..	3	..
Nepali	..	..	..	..
Pushtu	..	..	2	..
Chinese	..	..	1	..
Russian	..	..	..	..
Malayan	1	..	..	..
Italian	..	..	1	..
Dutch	..	..	..	..
Spanish	..	..	..	1
Swiss	..	..	1	..

CHAPTER VI

AGRICULTURE AND IRRIGATION.

Coimbatore, though an industrial district, plays a no small part in agriculture. Of its total area of 3,855,782 acres, an extent of 2,181,346 acres is cultivated with food and other commercial crops. This gives it a percentage of 56·5 of occupied area to the total area, a percentage which places it fourth in the State, the first three places being taken by Tanjore, South Arcot and Tiruchirappalli.[1] Its food crops occupy 65·1 per cent of the total area cultivated, the rest of the cultivated are being devoted to the cultivation of non-food crops.[2] A quinquennial statement showing the area cultivated with the chief food and non-food crops and their yield during 1920—21 to 1950—51 is appended at the end of the chapter.

Of the food crops, the chief cereals grown in the district are paddy, cholam, cumbu, ragi, tenai, samai and varagu. Paddy and varagu occupy only a small area when compared to the other districts; paddy normally occupies 122,000 acres and varagu 6,600 acres and their normal yield amounts to 79,000 tons and 1,500 tons respectively. Cholam, cumbu, ragi, tenai and samai, on the other hand, occupy large areas. Cholam normally occupies 495,000 acres and yields 146,000 tons; cumbu occupies 314,000 acres and yields 61,000 tons; ragi occupies 83,000 acres and yields 41,100 tons; tenai occupies 31,003 acres and yields 8,203 tons; and samai occupies 92,600 acres and yields 17,000 tons. Of these, cholam, cumbu and tenai occupy the highest acreages in the State. But while the yield of cholam and tenai is the largest in the State. The out-turn of cumbu stands second in the State. Samai occupies the second highest acreage in the State but its yield stands third in the State. The chief pulses grown in the district are redgram, blackgram, horsegram, bengalgram and greengram. Of these redgram normally occupies 12,000 acres and yields 1,600 tons; blackgram occupies 5,000 acres and yields 600 tons horsegram occupies 134,000 acres and yields 10,000 tons; bengalgram occupies 2,000 acres and yields 300 tons; and greengram

[1] *Season and Crop Report for* 1956–57, *page* 29.

[2] *Idem*—page 41.

[3] *Idem*—pages 32, 33, 45 and 46.

occupies 11,000 acres and yields 800 tons. Bengalgram occupies the highest acreage and yields the largest tonnage in the State, while horsegram occupies the second highest acreage and yields the second largest tonnage in the State, the highest acreage and yield of this crop being found in Salem [1]. The chief condiments and spices grown in the district are betelnuts, cardamoms, chillies, turmeric and coriander. Betelnuts occupy 1,400 acres, cardamoms 2,000 acres, turmeric 4,000 acres and coriander 3,000 acres, but figures of their normal yield are not available. Chillies occupy 10,000 acres and yield 7,300 tons. Betelnut and turmeric occupy the highest acreages in the State and cardamom the second highest acreage in the State, the highest acreage in the case of the latter being found in Mȧdurai [2]. The chief sugar crop of the district is sugarcane and the chief fruit crops, the banana or the plantain. Sugarcane normally occupies 17,000 acres and plantain 3,000 acres,but figures of their normal yield are not available[3]. In fact, in the matter of foodgrains and food crops, the district stands fourth in the State, the first, second and third places being taken by Salem, Tiruchirappalli and Thanjavur [4]. In spite of its occupying this important place in the matter of food grains the district is deficit both in rice and dry grains; in rice it is deficit to the tune of 113,000 tons and in millets and other cereals to the tune of 19,000 tons [5].

Of the non-food crops, the most important crops grown in the district are cotton, groundnut, castor, tobacco, coconut and fodder crops. Cotton normally occupies 300,000 acres and yields 112,500 bales; groundnut occupies 282,000 acres and yields 118,900 tons ; castor occupies 3,200 acres and yields 520 tons and tobacco occupies 32,000 acres and yields 17,700 tons. As for coconut and fodder crops they occupy11,000 acres and 5,000 acres respectively, but figures of their normal yield are not available. The district takes easily the first place in the State both in the area grown under cotton and tobacco and in their normal yield, the second place in cotton being taken by Tirunelveli and in tobacco being taken by Madurai. It occupies a third place both in the area grown under groundnut and in its normal yield, the first two places being taken by North Arcot and South Arcot [6].

Paddy is largely grown under the Bhavani, Amaravathi and Aliyar river channels in the Gobichettipalayam, Dharapuram, Udumalpet and Pollachi taluks, and, under the Noyyal in the Coimbatore taluk. The

1 *Idem* pages 33, 47.
2 Season and crop Report for 1956–57, pages 33, 47.
3 *Idem*—page 34.
4 *Idem*—page 40.
5 *Idem*—Information furnished by the Director of Statistics, Madras.
6 Season and Crop Report for 1956–57, pages 36, 38, 48.

kar paddy, a crop of three months duration, is generally raised as a first crop in June-July and harvested in September-October. It is also raised occasionally as a second crop when it succeeds ragi. The ground is prepared in June—July in the usual way by swamping, cross ploughing, manuring and levelling with the beam, and the seedling raised from a separate nursery are transplated. In the fourth week the land is weeded, and the crop irrigated by flooding the field. The second crop paddy is either kuruvai (short crop) or samba paddy of five months duration. With good irrigation sources, as in Erode under the Cauvery channels, or under the Amaravathi channels, and in good seasons, samba is, as a rule, the second crop. It is usually transplanted from nurseries in September-October. Three crops of it are raised under the Kuduveri and Kalingarayan channels of the Bhavani and the Amaravathi river systems. The cultivation in such cases is from April to February.[1] Except in the Gobichettipalayam taluk, there is a first crop to utilize the available water before the samba is sown. Samba crop sometimes succeeds ragi or other dry first crop, as for instance, under the lower Amaravati channels. Paddy is sown on dry lands in parts of the Pollachi taluk where the south-west monsoon brings good rains. Here, the paddy is generally broadcast in June and reaped in September-October.

As a result of the various experiments made for the evolution of better strains at the Paddy Breeding Station at Coimbatore since 1913, several new strains of paddy have been introduced into the district. In olden days the chief varieties of paddy used for the kar or the three months crop were kuruvai, annathanam, and aruvatham kodai; for the samba, or five months crop samba, kalingarayan samba, kartigai samba and moligai semmoligi; and for the dry crop suvarna valle.[2] Today many new strains have become popular. The most popular of these are G.E.B. CO 1, CO 2, CO 3, CO 19, CO 25, T.K.M. 6, etc. The harvesting of G.E.B. 24 is done in the first week of December, and the longer duration varieties are harvested later and proceed on to end of January. The harvest of late planted varieties may extend to third week of February. G.E.B. 24, CO. 19 and CO. 25 are popular samba varieties in the district. CO.13 can be raised both as a first and as a second crop in June-September and February-May. T.K.M. 6 can be raised both as a first and as a second crop in June-October and November-March.[3]

---

1 *Notes on Irrigation in Coimbatore District* by V. N. Kudva, dated 4th March 1953.

Manual of the Coimbatore District by F. A. Nicholson, 1887, pages 214–215.

2 *Idem*—page 214.

3 *Memoirs of the Department of Agriculture, Madras,* No. 36, 1954, pages 120–122.

Rice is by no means the staple food of the people of the district. Half of the population eat rice while the remaining half eat millet [1].

Cholam, which is a principal food crop of the district, is grown in the Palladam, Dharapuram, Pollachi, Coimbatore and Udumalpet taluks. Its importance lies in its being the heaviest yielder of both grain and straw among all the rain-fed cereal crops. It can be grown in a variety of soils but it thrives best on soils supplied with lime. Under irrigation or garden cultivation it is usually sown in March and reaped in June-July or sown in October-November and reaped in January-February. The soil is manured mostly with cattle manure or by sheep penning, the manure being well ploughed in when the rains commence. The seed is then broadcast and ploughed in, after which, beds are formed for irrigation. Irrigations are given at 10 to 15 days intervals depending on rainfall. About three weeks after sowing, the crop is hoed and thereafter watered about once in 10 or 15 days till harvest. The irrigated crop grows high, stout and healthy with splendid heads full of grain, in contrast to the dry crop which is low, thin and with poor heads. The dry crop is sown in two seasons. The first, called the kar, is sown in May, June or July and reaped from three to four months later, while the second called the paruvam is sown in September-October and cut in February. The kar crop is usually mixed with castor and pulses. The paruvam crop is not usually mixed. When mixed, castor and pulses are sown in lines and other cereals are broadcast with cholam. The pulses crop is reaped in January, the castor crop is harvested in February-March. Cholam is sometimes grown also as a fodder crop in the hot weather, especially in the Kangayam division of Dharapuram. It is grown then thickly and cut at flowering [2].

Since the opening of a separate Millets Breeding Station at Coimbatore a number of high yielding strains of cholam have been introduced into the district suited for both irrigated and rain-fed conditions. They are CO. 1 to CO.13; and all of them have become popular, yielding as they do from 10 to 15 per cent above the local varieties. CO. 1 periamanjal cholam, and CO. 2 and CO. 3 talaivirichan cholams are rain-fed crops. CO. 4 sencholam, CO. 5 chinnamanjal, CO. 6 chitravellai cholam, CO. 7 ennai vellai cholam, and CO. 9 kesari are all irrigated crops. CO. 11 is both an irrigated and a rain-fed crop of fodder variety. CO. 12 evolved from uppam or mottai cholam and CO.13 evolved from ennai vellai cholam

1 Information furnished by the Director of Agriculture, Chepauk, Madras-5.

2 *Notes on Irrigation in Coimbatore District* by U. N. Kudva, dated 4th March 1953.

Memoirs of the Department of Agriculture, Madras, No. 36 of 1954, pages 127–128.

Manual of Coimbatore District by F. A. Nicholson, 1887, pages 216–217.

are irrigated crops [1]. Co. 18 is a short duration vellai cholam which has become very popular and is rapidly replacing the earlier CO. strains.

Cholam grain intended for food is stored in underground pits under the belief that it improves in quality when so stored for two or three months. These pits are usually rectangular and narrow at the top and wide below, ranging in size from 2 feet across and 4 feet deep to 8 feet across and 9 feet deep. The sides and bottom of the pits are lined with cholam straw before the grain is put into it. The mouth of the pit is closed with planks or stones on the top of which a thick layer of mud is plastered to exclude air. Grain intended for seed however is usually stored in gunny bags or sometimes in bamboo receptacles or in twisted straw bundles [2].

Cumbu is another staple food crop. It is grown to a great extent in the Gobichettipalayam, Erode, Dharapuram and Bhavani taluks, to a considerable extent in the Pollachi and Palladam taluks and to some extent in the Udumalpet taluk. It is shorter in duration than cholam and is grown both as a pure crop and as a mixed crop with cotton, castor and pulses. It is cultivated on a wide variety of soils, black, red, loamy, gravelly and even sandy soils. As an irrigated crop it is usually sown in April and harvested in June-July. As a rain-fed crop it is generally sown in July-August and harvested in November-December though, in some parts, it is sown earlier with the May rains. When properly cultivated, the land is ploughed in April and May after having been manured in the usual way. In July-August it is again ploughed and the seed, mixed with pulses and castor is sown broadcast. After three weeks the crop is interploughed and occasionally weeded. In November-December cumbu is reaped by cutting off the ears as they ripen. The pulses are gathered gradually up to February, leaving cotton when sown and castor only on the ground. Castor seeds are gathered up to February-March while cotton gives its first flush in March-April. As in the case of cholam new strains of cumbu have been evolved at the Millets Breeding Station and these have been introduced into the district. Of these strains CO. 1 is both an irrigated and a rain-fed crop ; CO. 2 is a rain-fed crop and CO. 3 is an irrigated crop [3].

Ragi is the third principal food crop. It is raised largely in the Gobichettipalayam, Dharapuram and Coimbatore taluks. There are

---

1 *Memoirs of the Department of Agriculture, Madras*, No. 36 of 1954, page 146.

2 *Idem*, page 150.

3 *Notes on Irrigation in Coimbatore District*, by V. N. Kudva, dated 4th March 1953.

Memoirs of the Department of Agriculture, Madras, No. 36 of 1954, pages 153-154.

Manual of the Coimbatore District, by F. A. Nicholson, 1887, pages 218–219.

considerable tracts under it also in the Palladam taluk and some parts under it in the Pollachi and Udumalpet taluks and on the dry lands near the hills in the Bhavani taluk. It can be grown in practically all the months of the year, but, in practice, it has two chief cultivation seasons; the main season is May-June and the other season is November to the middle of January. Sometimes in wet lands it is grown in December-January after the harvest of a paddy crop. In dry lands it is grown in June-July. It can be grown in a wide variety of soils from the very poor to the very fertile, but it thrives best on arable land where the soil is a well drained loam or clay loam. In wet lands the land is prepared after the harvest of the previous crop by giving two or three ploughings, applying manure and ploughing it in. After bringing the soil to the proper tilth, the bunds and channels are formed, the fields thrown into beds 10 to 12 feet square and levelled. The seedlings prepared in nurseries are then transplanted. The seedlings are raised in carefully prepared nurseries which receive heavy dressings of cattle manure and wood ashes. The seed beds are slightly raised to facilitate good drainage. The seeds are sown thinly and lightly stirred in, and water is let in carefully to prevent the seeds getting washed off. In dry lands the seed is generally sown broadcast evenly, after the receipt of the first rains and covered by a light ploughing. A brush harrow or a log of wood is also dragged along the surface for levelling it and packing the surface soil. Three improved strains of ragi have been introduced into the district in consequence of the experiments carried out at the Millets Breeding Station, namely, CO. 1, CO. 2 and CO. 3, and all these are suitable for both irrigated and rain-fed crops.[1]

Tenai is grown in several parts of the district, both as a rain fed and as an irrigated crop. As a rain-fed crop it is sown in November-December and as an irrigated crop it is sown in March-July. It is cultivated on a wide variety of soils, though it thrives best on good black or red loams. It is sown either pure or mixed with cotton. Its improved strains introduced into the district are CO. 1, CO. 2 and CO. 3. CO. 1 is both an irrigated and a rain-fed crop; CO. 2 is an irrigated crop and CO. 3 is a rain-fed crop.[2] Samai is raised mainly as a dry crop on poor soils like

---

1 *Notes on Irrigation in Coimbatore District*, by V. N. Kudva, dated 4th March 1953.

Memoirs of the Agricultural Department, Madras, No. 36 of 1954, pages 163–164.

Manual of the Coimbatore District by F. A. Nicholson, 1887, page 220.

2 *Note on Irrigation in Coimbatore District* by V. N. Kudva, dated 4th March 1953.

Memoirs of the Department of Agriculture, Madras, No. 36 of 1954, pages 171–172.

red gravel in the Dharapuram taluk. Sometimes it is also raised as a garden crop when the season is unfavourable. The chief season for sowing it is August-September but, in the Pollachi taluk it is sown in May-June. It is either grown alone, or as is usually the case, mixed with redgram[1]. Varagu, which is generally cultivated on poor soils, is grown in the Coimbatore, Udumalpet and Dharapuram taluks as a garden or dry crop[2]. Besides these cereals, wheat is sown as a garden crop in October-November and reaped in February-March in the Coimbatore taluk and the adjoining portions on the borders of the Palladam taluk[3].

The area under horsegram is more than half the extent under all other pulses in the district. It is largely raised in the poorest soils in the Dharapuram, Udumalpet and Palladam taluks and in all taluks, except the Avanashi, Gobichettipalayam, Bhavani and Erode taluks, under the north-east monsoon rains. It is also raised as a substitute for cumbu when the south-west monsoon is too late for it. It is mostly cultivated as a second crop in the western portion of the Pollachi taluk which is under the influence of the south-west monsoon. Blackgram is grown on dry lands or garden lands as a separate crop in August-September and harvested in December-January. Bengalgram is grown as a separate crop or as a mixed crop with cotton and korra on black soils. Redgram, greengram and beans(mochai)are grown as mixed crops chiefly with cumbu, cholam or cotton. The area under the pulses is largest in the Palladam taluk and next in the Dharapuram taluk, and these are essentially dry taluks lacking in irrigation facilities[4].

The area under condiments and spices is the largest in the Erode, Bhavani, Gobichettipalayam and Udumalpet taluks. Chillies are chiefly grown in Erode, Dharapuram and Pollachi taluks; and those of Pollachi are superior to others. Garlic is chiefly grown in gardens. Onions are grown as a garden crop either separately or mixed with chillies. Turmeric is grown under channels or other plentiful sources of water-supply, chiefly in the Erode and Udumalpet taluks; it is usually sown as a mixed crop with vegetables, onions and castor. Cummin seeds are sown as a two or three months crop in the Udumalpet taluk and its borders.

---

1 *Note on Irrigation in Coimbatore district* by V. N. Kudva, dated 4th March 1953.

Memoirs of the Agricultural Department, Madras, No. 36 of 1954, page 177.

2 *Note on Irrigation in Coimbatore district* by V. N. Kudva, dated 4th March 1953.

3 *Idem.*

4 *Idem.*

Manual of the Coimbatore district by F. A. Nicholson, 1887, pages 222–224.

Coriander is grown mixed with cotton in the black soil tracts and occasionally also as an early garden crop[1].

Sugarcane is an important crop of the district. It is grown chiefly in the Coimbatore, Dharapuram and Udumalpet taluks. It is also grown to some extent in the other taluks. It is usually grown on wet lands and occasionally on dry lands. In wet lands, it is sometimes rotated with paddy, leaving an interval of at least two years. Thus, in the first year there would be the sugarcane crop, in the second year, the sugarcane ratoon crop, in the third and fourth years paddy followed by pulses or fodder and in the fifth and sixth years again sugarcane and ratoon. In garden lands it is rotated with other garden crops. Thus, in the first year there would be the sugarcane crop, in the second year the ratoon crop and in the third and fourth years, ragi, cholam, vegetables or fodder crops[2].

Formerly the chief varieties of sugarcane grown were white (vellai or rastali), striped (namam) and red or purple cane. The first was possibly the Mauritius cane introduced by the Government in 1840[3]. All these varieties of cane have come to be gradually replaced by purer strains that have been evolved. The dominant strains now grown in the district are CO. 419, CO. 421, CO. 413, CO. 449 and CO. 527. As is well known, sugarcane is an exhausting crop. It thrives best in fertile soils with good drainage facilities but it can be grown on a variety of soils, even on red loams and sandy loams, provided it is properly manured and looked after. Soon after the harvest of the previous crop, the land is ploughed a number of times fairly deep until the required tilth is obtained. Both wooden and iron ploughs are used for ploughing. The main planting season is March-April but in some parts, it commences even earlier. The crop is heavily manured by bulky as well as concentrated manures. Cattle manure is the common basal dressing given before planting. After two or three deep ploughings, the manure is applied to the land. Where cattle manure is not available, sheep penning is adopted or compost manure is used. Green-leaf manure is also applied wherever possible; this is sometimes done by growing a sunnhemp crop before the sugarcane crop. These manures are now-a-days supplemented by oil-cakes and nitrogenous fertilizers, either alone or in suitable combinations. The oil-

---

1 *Note on Irrigation in Coimbatore district* by V. N. Kudva, dated 4th March 1953.

2 *Note on Irrigation in the Coimbatore district* by V. N. Kudva, dated 4th March 1953.

Memoirs of the Agricultural Department, Madras, No. 36 of 1954, pages 427 and 431.

3 *Manual of the Coimbatore district* by F. A. Nicholson, 1887, pages 235–236.

cakes used are commonly those of groundnut, neem or castor, and the fertilizer used is commonly the sulphate of ammonia[1].

Cotton is the foremost among the industrial crops in all the taluks of the district. The chief varieties of cotton grown are the Cambodia and the Karunganni, the Uppam and other varieties like the Bourbon and the Nadan are found in small pockets here and there. Cotton is grown in the black soils of the Coimbatore taluk under both the monsoons. There are also considerable tracts of it in the Dharapuram and Palladam taluks, large areas of it in the Erode taluk and some areas of it in the Pollachi, Udumalpet, Avanashi, Bhavani and Gobichettipalayam taluks. The Cambodia cotton crop in the Avanashi taluk has a very high reputation and merchants from all mill centres in the country visit Tiruppur to buy this first class cotton in the season. Cotton is also grown on red gravelly soils but its quality is not good[2].

In order to prevent deterioration in the quality of cotton due to ravages of insects and adulteration by the mixture of inferior grades, as well as to regulate its ginning and pressing and buying and selling and to control its price and ascertain its stock, legislation has been undertaken and Coimbatore has naturally come under this legislation. The Madras Pests and Diseases Act of 1919 (and its later amendments) applies to two insect pests *playedra gossypella* and *Pemperulus affinis* attacking *Cosstpium hirsutum* under which the Cambodia and panchandam varieties are included. It requires that all cotton plants in the notified districts (of which Coimbatore was one) should be pulled off the ground and allowed to wither before 1st August every year, so as to starve the pests altogether. The Cotton Transport Act (Act III) of 1923 provides for the restriction and control of the transport of cotton in certain well-defined zones so that the quality and reputation of the cotton grown in such protected zones may be maintained. Coimbatore comes within the protected zone for Cambodia cotton. The Act prohibits the transport of cotton 'kapas', ginned cotton or cotton waste to a station in any protected area from any station outside the protected area by road, rail and river; and it has been helpful in a large measure in checking the practice of mixing inferior with quality cottons. The Ginning and Pressing Factories Act (Act XII) of 1925 has for its object the better regulation of cotton ginning and pressing factories in the whole of India. It requires the owner of every cotton ginning and pressing

---

1 *Memoirs of the Agricultural Department, Madras,* No. 36 of 1954, pages 425–427, 430–431 and 477.

2 *Note on Irrigation in Coimbatore District* by V. N. Kudva, dated 4th March 1953.

Memoirs of the Agricultural Department, Madras, No. 36 of 1954, page 485

factory to maintain a register in the prescribed form showing dates, names of persons for whom ginning and pressing is done with details regarding the quantity ginned or pressed. It also requires the owner to cause every bale pressed to be marked in a prescribed manner and to submit weekly returns for each season to the Director of Agriculture. It moreover provides for the standardization of weights and measures for cotton transactions in all places; and it has recently been amended to prevent adulteration of varieties, deliberate watering and mixing of seed, leaf and foreign matter. The Madras Commercial Crops Market Act (Act XX) of 1933 (and its further amendments) provides for the better regulation of the buying and selling of commercial crops and for that purpose, establishes a reliable market for the same. It has been applied to the cotton and groundnut crop of the Coimbatore district and the Market Committee set up under the Act consists of not more than twelve members elected from the growers and traders. This Committee has powers to enact bye-laws with a view to regulate market charges to fix commission, trade allowances, standard weights, etc., and to check the scales and weights. The Madras Cotton Control Act (Act VII) of 1932 is intended to prohibit the cultivation and possession of low grade ' pulchai ' cotton either in a pure or mixed form. It empowers the officers of the Agricultural Department to seize ' pulchai ' cotton from any place where it is being mixed or grown and to prosecute the offender. Since 1943, in order to control the soaring price of cloth, the Government of India have fixed the floor and ceiling prices of various types of cotton after consultation with all interested parties. And finally, the Madras Cotton (Trade Stocks), Census Act (Act XLVII) of 1949 has been passed with a view to collecting reliable data relating to the stocks of Indian raw eotton. The Act requires every trader and every owner of cotton and owner of a ginning or pressing factory to declare the stocks of Indian raw cotton held by him on 31st January and 31st August each year to the Director of Agriculture[1].

Groundnut which is another important commercial crop of the district is grown on a large scale in the Pollachi taluk and on a considerable scale in the Avanashi, Bhavani, Coimbatore and Gobichettipalayam taluks. The variety cultivated is mostly the Coromandel, also known as the local Mauritius or the Mozambique Mauritius. It is a long duration (4½ months) spreading variety. The other two varieties cultivated are the Spanish Peanut and the Pollachi red; they are short duration (3½ months) bunch type varieties. In recent years, the department has introduced new strains TMV1, TMV2 and TMV3, and these are fast becoming popular.

---

[1] *Memoirs of the Agricultural Department, Madras*, No. 36 of 1954, pages 562–565.

The groundnut crop is mostly raised under rain-fed conditions from June-July to December-January, the time of sowing depending upon the receipt of rains. It is sometimes cultivated as a summer crop under irrigated conditions from February-March to June-July. The sowing of the seeds is done either in lines behind a country plough or by means of a seed drill. Normally two inter-cultivations are given. The crop is harvested when the vines begins to turn yellow and the inside of the shell turns dark. The short duration bunch type is harvested by pulling out the plants by hand, while the long duration spreading type is harvested by digging out the plants with a spade[1].

Gingelly is universally grown in wet, dry and garden lands. It is largely raised after the regular crop in the Dharapuram taluk. It is also raised as a third crop from March to June after ragi and paddy in the same taluk. It is raised as a mixed crop with cotton and redgram in the Kangayam division of that taluk. It is usually raised before the regular crop at the tail-end of the Kalingarayan channel and as a garden crop in some taluks with the kar rains in dry lands. The department has introduced improved strains of gingelly into the district; and these are TMV 1, TMV 2 and TMV 3[2].

The area under castor is the largest in the Pollachi taluk. It is also grown in the Udumalpet, Bhavani and Avanashi taluks. In the Pollachi taluk it is grown in dry lands near the hills. In the northern part of the Dharapuram taluk it is usually grown as a mixed crop with cereals and pulses. It is sometimes grown as a garden crop with ragi or as a shade for turmeric[3].

The area under tobacco is large in the Dharapuram, Palladam and Gobichettipalayam taluks. Tobacco is grown mostly in lands under well irrigation and its varieties are named locally according to the shape of the leaf such as yerumaikappal (broad and large) vattakappal (round) and usikappal (narrow). All these are dark brown to almost black in colour and are mostly used for chewing or cherroots. The usikappal is a superior quality having a mild flavour and is used as fillers in cheroots. The best type of chewing tobacco is grown in Meenampalayam, which is characterized

---

1 *Note on Irrigation in Coimbatore district,* by V. N. Kudva, dated 4th March 1953.

Memoirs of the Department of Agriculture, Madras, No. 36 of 1954, pages 215-216 and 218.

2 *Note on Irrigation in Coimbatore district* by V. N. Kudva, dated 4th March 1953.

Memoirs of the Agricultural Department, Madras, No. 36 of 1954, pages 233–237

3. *Note on Irrigation in Coimbatore district* by V. N. Kudva, dated 4th March 1953.

by a special flavour of its own. Tobacco is sown in nurseries in September-October, transplanted in the fields in November-December and cut down in February-March. It grows extremely well where there is brackish water charged with lime. For preparing nurseries the soil is liberally manured, then ploughed, formed into beds and covered by ashes and sieved compost. After a fine tilth is obtained, the seeds are sown. The nurseries are carefully watered daily for the first week, every alternate day during the second week and twice a week thereafter until the seedlings are transplanted. The seedlings are transplanted into well prepared fields formed into beds by ridges and furrows and thereafter watered twice a week. They are hoed three or four times in the first two months, topped at the end of the third month, suckered four times and harvested in about four months. It is usual to leave the crop in the field the first night after cutting. It is then heaped for two days and on the third day hung up to dry for twelve or fifteen days. It is again heaped to sweat for some days, the heaps being shifted occasionally and weights being kept upon the heaps. The leaves are then bundled and sold[1].

The extent under fruit trees is the largest in the Palladam taluk; next comes the Pollachi taluk. Plantains are grown on wet lands in Erode and, to a large extent, in the gardens in some villages in the same taluk and in the Palladam taluk. Limes are grown near Bhavani taluk, pomegranates in the vicinity of Perundurai, Utukuli, Tiruppur and Avanashi. Coconuts are found in large topes near Coimbatore. Palmyra is largely seen especially in the Erode, Dharapuram and Palladam taluks. Betel is grown chiefly near Coimbatore and in the Pollachi and Bhavani taluks. Coffee to a small extent and tea to a great extent are grown in the estates on the Anaimalai hills and in a few estates on the hills of the north Coimbatore forests. Cardamoms, rubber and cinchona are grown on the Anaimalais[2].

In general, the agricultural practices of the district are of a high order. The fields are usually well fenced with shrubby perennials like Mullikiluvi and *Euphordia tricalli*, Prickly-pear, once popular, has practically disappeared after the introduction of the cochinial insect. An uncultivated border of 2 to 3 yards around fields and along the fence is common in most of the garden and dry land holdings. These patches afford grazing for cattle and other live-stock when the fields are occupied by crops. The special features of the district is that the ryots in garden lands practically live on the holdings. Preparation of lands for the crop is done

---

1 *Note on Irrigation in Coimbatore district* by V. N. Kudva, dated 4th March 1953.; *Memoirs of the Department of Agriculture, Madras*, No. 36 of 1954, page 667.

2 *Note on Irrigation in Coimbatore district* by V. N. Kudva, dated 4th March 1953.

by ploughing with the country plough, or by the iron plough advocated by the Agricultural Department. When the fields are foul with ' hariali ', they are dug with crow-bars.Deep ploughing is, however, seldom practiced. Manuring is ordinarily done before cropping except for special crops like sugarcane, plantain, betel-vine leaves and tobacco. Cattle-manure, tank silt, municipal rubbish, green leaves (erukkan, kolinji, etc.) and other bulky organic manures are largely used for the garden and wet lands. The dry lands are, however, not adequately manured. Penning sheep and cattle is very common in all classes of farming. In many places the cattle are tied in the open field during the off season and the tether is shifted daily and the droppings are ploughed in. Tannery refuse is largely used for coconut and plantain. Farm-yard manure is stored in pits to which tank silt or soil is copiously added. On the advice of the Department many have taken to using the silt or soil with waste fodder as bedding in the byre before adding them to the pit. Green manuring with sesbania, daincha, sunnhemp, kolinji and horsegram has become popular in the wet land tracts. Among the artificial fertilizers, the use of ammonium sulphate is common and large quantities of it are used for paddy and sugarcane instead of oil-cakes. Seeds for sowing are saved large from their own crops by the ryots. Improved strains evolved by the department have, as has already been seen, become very popular. Line sowing has however not become so popular but the reduced seed rate for paddy recommended by the Department is adopted over large areas. The principle of sowing crops by rotation, as has also been seen, is well understood by the ryots. Irrigation is done by flooding the wet lands where, on account of sharp slopes, the fields are small and often terraced. In garden lands water from the wells is lifted by the common bullock ' mhote ' (kavalai) where however, the wells are deep, oil engine pumps and electric-motors have been installed[1].

The agricultural improvements in this, as in other districts, are to be ascribed in no small measure to the growth of the Agricultural Department and its activities. Official interest in agriculture was shown in Madras for the first time in 1863 when the Governor, Sir William Dennison, stressed the need for improving the prevailing agricultural practices[2]. Some agricultural implements were then obtained from England and an Agricultural Farm under the management of some enthusiastics was established at Saidapet to demonstrate improved methods of cultivation to the ryots. In 1871, the management of this farm was assumed by the

---

1 *Statistical Atlas of the Madras Presidency, Coimbatore district for* 1940–41, pages 3–4.

2 G. O. Nos. 63–66, Revenue, dated 6th November 1863.

Government and in 1876 an Agricultural School was started at Saidapet. In 1878, this school was raised to the status of a College. In 1884, the control of this college was transferred from the Board of Revenue to the Director of Public Instruction. In 1885, the farm at Saidapet—except for a small portion of it which remained attached to the college—was abolished and thereafter, the Superintendent of the farm, who was made an Assistant to the Commissioner for Agriculture, was directed to devote all his time to the business of famine analysis, to the tabulation of village statistics and to enquire on various agricultural or economic subjects. Much of the Saidapet land was kept as a dairy farm; and district farms were opened for investigating special problems. It was, however, not till the opening years of this century that more and more attention came to be paid to agriculture. It was not till 1905 that, on the recommendation of the Famine Commission of 1901, and the initiative of Lord Curzon, the Viceroy, reorganization and expansion of the Agricultural Department were undertaken everywhere in India. In 1906, a whole-time Director of Agriculture was appointed in Madras and an Agricultural College as well as an Agricultural Research Institute were established at Coimbatore, the Saidapet College being closed and the control over the new college being vested in a Director of Agriculture[1].

Since then, the Department has gone on expanding rapidly in the sphere of teaching, research as well as demonstration. The teaching and research work, as will be shown presently, are done mostly at Coimbatore. Extension and demonstration of improved methods evolved by research are entrusted to the Agricultural Extension Officers, the District Agricultural Officers, the Deputy Directors and Agricultural Demonstrators. The propaganda methods adopted by them consist of demonstration in ryots' fields, publicity through departmental journals such as village calendars, journals, press notes, radio talks and posters, exhibitions and shows, and contacts with ryots through village and taluk agricultural demonstrations. There used to be an Agricultural Demonstrator for each taluk assisted by a staff of fieldmen and maistries. Fieldmen have been provided for every two or three firkas and maistries for each firka. With the coming in of Community Development and National Extension Services, Agricultural Extension Officers have been appointed to cover one or two firkas. Depots have been provided at the rate of one for each Block for stocking and selling agricultural requirements like improved seeds, manures and implements. The Demonstrators and Agricultural Extension Officers work under the District Agricultural Officers and the latter work in close co-operation with the Revenue Department and are responsible

---

1 *Memoirs of the Department of Agriculture, Madras*, No. 36 of 1954, Page 3.

to the Deputy Directors who have been appointed for groups of districts called circles. The District Agricultural Officers were formerly called Assistant Directors of Agriculture. The Assistant Directors came to be appointed from 1916, one for every two or three districts, but in 1941 their number was increased so as to provide one officer for each district and their designation was changed to District Agricultural Officers.[1] Coimbatore is now under a Deputy Director of Agriculture who has his headquarters at Coimbatore and jurisdiction over Coimbatore, the Nilgiris and Salem districts. The District has also a District Agricultural Officer with headquarters at Coimbatore and a large number of specialists in different subjects relating to agriculture stationed at the Agricultural College and Research Institute.

The District is indeed fortunate in having at Coimbatore the two premier agricultural institutions of this State, namely the Agricultural College and the Agricultural Research Institute. As has already been mentioned, agricultural education in this State was first imparted in the School of Agriculture, started at Saidapet in 1876, a school which was raised to the status of a college in 1878. In 1881, the college was provided with a separate building. It had then two courses of studies, one of three years working up to a diploma, and the other of a shorter period leading up to a certificate, in agriculture. In 1890, the certificate course was abolished and in 1902-1903, the Government decided to shift the college to Coimbatore. In 1906, the foundation for the college building was laid by Sir Arthur Lawley, the Governor, on a site of about 400 acres situated within three miles of Coimbatore town. The building was opened by him in 1909. In 1913, the courses of studies were reorganized. A two-year certificate course, largely practical in character and capable of imparting a working knowledge of agriculture to 40 students at a time and a higher course of scientific training intended for the select few for a further period of twenty months leading up to a diploma, were instituted. In 1920, the control of agricultural education was passed on to the Madras University and this led to the affiliation of the college to the University and to the introduction of a B.Sc. degree course in agriculture. The certificate and the diploma courses were then abolished.

---

[1] G.O. No. 1545, Development, dated 28th September 1927.

G.O. No. 452, Development (Confidential), dated 10th March 1941.

G.O. No. 1432, Development, dated 9th August 1941.

G.O. No. 2256, Development, dated 9th December 1941.

G.O. No. 1254, Development, dated 26th June 1942.

Memoirs of the Department of Agriculture, Madras, No. 36 of 1954, pages 1–13 and 109–130.

Madras Presidency by G.T. Boag, 1933, pages 85–90.

Rural Problems in Madras, a Monograph by S. Y. Krishnaswami, 1947.

The college had, in the beginning, facilities for training only 20 students in each of the three classes of the degree course. Provision was made for admitting 48 students from 1926 when a separate and commodius building was erected for housing the college. The new building called the 'Freeman Building' was opened by Lord Willingdon, the Governor on 9th July 1926. In 1944, under the Post-War Reconstruction Scheme, the admission to the college was raised from 48 to 96. In the meanwhile, in 1932, the syllabus of the B.Sc. course was revised in accordance with which candidates possessing a pass in the Intermediate Examination with Chemistry and two other science subjects as optional subjects alone were admitted and these candidates were obliged to sit for the University Examination at the end of each year of the course. The syllabus and the scheme of the examinations were further revised in 1953 so as to provide for a practical training of six months during the third year of the course. With the increasing demand for trained agricultural personnel to carry on the programmes under the Five-Year Plans, the annual admissions to the B.Sc. course have been raised to 168.

Ever since 1933-1934, the University has recognized the facilities available at the Research Institute for doing research leading up to M.Sc. and Ph.D. degree courses and has amended the regulations suitably for enabling the degree holders of the college to qualify themselves for M.Sc. and Ph.D., by research. In recent years, new courses have been introduced. A post-graduate diploma course in horticulture, which had been for sometime run departmentally, has been affiliated to the University (1953) and the control of this course has been vested in the Principal of the Agricultural College and the Research Institute. A provision has been made for admitting 35 candidates each year for the course from all the States in India. A short course in practical agriculture lasting from June to March every year has also been run to meet the needs of young men who have attained more or less the S.S.L.C. standard and who cannot undergo the University course in agriculture. A refresher course for young farmers has likewise been instituted at the Central Farm of the College, designed to give practical training in Tamil to 20 young men desirous of going back to land at the end of the course. Another short course not exceeding two months, has also been opened for the B.Sc. students of the college for acquiring sufficient knowledge of the working and maintenance of tractors and allied machinery. The college, it may be stated, is a residential college with a hostel attached to it. It has a Central Farm of about 316 acres covering all types of soils and lands—

dry, garden and irrigated—and an excellent library consisting of more than 60,000 publications.[1]

Adjoining the college is situated the Agricultural Research Institute where fundamental and applied Research is being done by a number of specialists in various stations or sections. The Paddy Breeding Station was started in 1913 and here pure lines are being isolated particularly with a view to increasing the yield, inducing non-lodging habit, adjusting duration of growth and imparting resistance to diseases. Types showing desirable characteristics are used for hybridization experiments in an attempt to combine all desirable characteristics in one plant. Attempts are also being made to induce mutations by chemicals, X-ray, etc. A limited number of trials are also being conducted on problems connected with manuring, methods of cultivation, seasonal effects of sowing and so on. A collection of nearly 2,300 types obtained from all over the world and, including those of this State, is being maintained here and most of the materials for hybridization work is drawn from this collection. The Cotton Breeding Section was opened in 1922. The main work of this section is directed towards the improvement of cambodia, karungani and uppam cotton grown in the various districts of this State with a view to increasing the yield and improving the quality of local cotton. Better strains are being synthesized by planned hybridization work to reduce loss arising from pests, diseases and adverse factors. Fundamental and genetical research work are also being undertaken in order to understand the inter-relationship between yield and other characters in cotton. A separate Millet Section was formed in 1921 for the better breeding of millets and a scheme for the improvement of pulses sanctioned in 1943 was merged with this section in 1953. Every attempt is being made here for the improvement of such crops as cholam, cumbu, ragi, tenai, samai, varagu, and pulses. Exploitation of hybrid vigour in cumbu for increasing production and breeding of cholam for striga resistance are being undertaken in addition to the improvement of millets and pulses through selection and hybridization. The oil seeds section was started in 1930 with the object of tackling problems connected with a variety of oil yielding crops like groundnut, gingelly, castor and coconut. In this section, several improved strains having desirable economic and commercial characteristics have been evolved and methods for proper cultural and manurial practices are being studied. Here are also studied some of the minor oil-seeds like safflower, sunflower, niger and linseed and since recently, the prospects of introducing exotic varieties of oil-seed crops.

1 *Handbook of Rules and Regulations relating to the Agricultural College, Coimbatore*, 1954, Pages 1–3, 5–6.

A Sugarcane Breeding Station was opened in 1912 and its work was expanded by the introduction of hybrid types raised from seed. This gave a wide range of material from which varieties suited to the various conditions and tracts over the whole of India could be selected. An account, however, of the importance of the sugarcane work done here to the vast sugarcane tracts lying outside the State, the Government of India have taken over the control of the Sugarcane Breeding Station since 1925. At this station, work on the evolution of new types of hybrid canes, trials of improved types and yield studies are being undertaken. The Horticultural Section was formed in 1941 for the improvement of horticultural crops. Here, an orchard and a vegetable area have been set apart. Mango, sapota, guava and papaya are the main fruits raised and studied, besides about forty varieties of banana. Here also are tackled problems such as the hybridization in sapota and banana, improvement of vegetables like brinjal and bhendai through selection and breeding, and varietal trials in other vegetables. The Botany Section has the Herbarium which was founded in about 1874 and which now contains about two lakhs of plant specimens representing the flora of the different parts of India, including particularly those of this State. This Herbarium is one of the important centres of botanical education both for students and specialists. The section is engaged in the study of fodder grasses and legumes, soil conservation plants, cover crops, green manure plants, essential oil producing plants and medical plants, and has a small but well maintained botanical garden containing a representative collection of species. It has a wing for Cytogenetics and another for Plant Physiology ; the former for aiding the breeders in solving problems involving cytogenetical studies and the latter for making research on weedicides, hormones and pre-treatment of seeds for increasing production. The Mycology section was created in 1910 primarily for investigating such diseases as palmyra bud-rot and the 'mahali' disease of arecanuts. Later on, its work has expanded to deal with all important diseases like the smut on cholam, the 'blast' on rice, the mosaic and the red-rot on sugarcane, the mildew on grapes and the wilt disease on groundnut. It has also developed methods for the preparation of 'food yeast' and the manufacture of 'ergot' of rye. The Entomology Section was started in 1912. Its preliminary work was devoted to the study of the life histories of insect pests on crops and the remedial measures to be taken against them. Subsequently, it studied measures for the control of the pink-ball worm and the stem weevil of cotton. Later on, it did research to control such important crop-pests as the swarming caterpillar, the stem borer and the bug on rice, the borers on sugarcane, the thrips on chillies, the mango hopper, the fruit-sucking moth, the caterpillar and the beetle on coconut, the hairy caterpillar and the 'surul' on groundnut and the pests on stored products. Besides protective and remedial measures, the section has introduced biological methods of control by insect parasites. The section also runs a well-equipped apiary for purposes of research, demonstration and propaganda on honey bees and provides short courses on bee-keeping for the benefit of those who are interested in agro-industry.

Nor is this all. There is the Chemistry Section which was started as early as 1909, and which since then has been considerably expanded. The main work of this section is the study of the soil of this State in all its aspects, including its origin and properties. The problems of soil fertility and manuring of crops by combining laboratory investigations, pot culture experiments and field trials are being extensively studied by the section and the results obtained are passed on to the ryots for adoption. Numerous samples of soils, manures, irrigation water, dairy products fodder, feeding stuffs, grains, industrial products and bye-products, etc., are analysed every year. Suitable advice is also given to the ryots on the methods of nutrient status of the soils, suitability of water for irrigation purposes and judicious manuring of crops. A recent development is the institution of rapid soil testing techniques by which farmers could quickly get opinion on the fertility status of their soils to adopt a correct manuring programme. Side by side, fundamental investigations are conducted on the bio-chemistry of the soils, studies on the effect of light and heavy irrigations on the salt movement in black soils, physico-chemical problems of soils relating to the effect of green manure and differently manured soils, soil erosion on the Nilgiris, study of the microflora in relation to the maintenance of soil fertility, the best way of building up soil fertility by green manure crops, the improvement of marginal lands and the determination of the nitrogen and phosphorous requirements of the paddy soils of Thanjavur, etc. Finally, there is the Agricultural Research Engineering Section which was started in 1928 on the recommendation of the Royal Commission on Agriculture, to investigate the possibilities of improving the indigenous implements and farm machinery used by the ryots, to design new agricultural and allied equipment required for special purposes and to test other mechanical appliances advocated for the field and the farm. A large variety of implements, machines and water-lifts are tested to determine the types and makes best suited for the several tracts, and those found satisfactory are recommended and demonstrated by the Department. A representative collection of the different types of indigenous implements, improved appliances and farm machines are kept in the section. A repair unit, called the Tractor Workshop, is also attached to the section for servicing, repairing and maintaining tractors and bull dozers of all types working in the zone.[1]

Besides this important Agricultural Research Station at Coimbatore, there is an Agricultural Demonstration Farm at Satyamangalam and an Agricultural Station as well as a Basic Agricultural Training School at Bhavanisagar. The Satyamangalam Farm was originally started as a research station in 1951 to conduct experiments for finding out suitable methods of improving the fertility and the physical texture of the soils by the application of green leaf manure, cattle manure, and compost in different doses. Cotton and millets were grown in the soil by ploughing them *in situ* in order to find out which of them, under what conditions, produced the best yield. The Research Station, having been closed in 1955, a Demonstration Farm has been set up in its place. The Bhavanisagar Basic Agricultural Training School was opened in 1954 for training each year 50 village-level workers under the National Extension Service Scheme. The Bhavanisagar Agricultural Research Station was started in the Community Project Area in 1955. Since then, it has reclaimed much land and conducted several experiments for cultivating cereals, millets, oilseeds and cotton.[2]

The agricultural prosperity of the district has been considerably increased not only by the measures taken for demonstration, propaganda, teaching and research, but also by the Grow More Food Campaign started during the Second World War and the Five-Year Plans introduced after the Independence. The Grow More Food Campaign was launched in 1942 in order to overcome the scarcity of foodgrains produced by the cessation of imports of rice from Burma, Siam and Indo-China. The problem was how to meet this shortage so as not only to enable the State to become self-sufficient but also to enable it to supply the needs of the neighbouring States by some short-term planning. And the planning that was devised took two directions, first that of bringing under food-crop cultivation all areas lying uncultivated or cultivated with commercial crops and of increasing double-crop cultivation during the off-season, and secondly that of encouraging intensive cultivation by the use of improved seeds and better manuring. For achieving these objects the Government

---

1 *Handbook of Rules and Regulations relating to the Agricultural College, Coimbatore*, 1954, pages 6–10.

Memoirs of the Department of Agriculture, Madras, No. 36 of 1954, pages 3–10.

See also *A Popular account of the progress of the work of the Madras Agricultural Department*, 1922–25.

Administration Report of the Agricultural Department, 1953–54, pages 133, 191, 192.

Idem, 1954–55, pages 11, 121–122.

introduced a series of measures. Free or concessional cultivation of unoccupied Government lands, such as poramboke, village or town sites, lands in panchayats and reserved forests, tank-beds and railway lands, was permitted. Temporary assignment of lands reserved for public purposes were made. Compounds of Government offices quarters and institutions, and backyards of houses were allowed to be cultivated. Reductions in water rates were made and penalties for technical infringement of irrigation rules were waived. Loans were advanced on a liberal scale for bringing new lands under cultivation, for purchasing seeds, manures and implements and for deepening existing wells and digging new wells. The assessment of water rate on land irrigated by such wells was remitted for three years. Seeds of improved strains of paddy, millets, pulses, groundnut and green manure crops were produced regardless of expenses and sold to the ryots at fair rates. Oil-cakes were produced from the presses under legal enactments and chemical fertilizers were obtained from the Government of India and both were distributed at fair prices to the ryots. The preparation of compost from town refuse, waste vegetable matter, etc., was subsidised and encouraged. The movement of manure was controlled to prevent export outside the State. Agricultural implements and steel and iron required for agricultural purposes were distributed at cost price. Pump-sets run by oil engines, petrol or electricity were supplied in large numbers for irrigating fields with sub-soil water. Tractors were hired out for clearing, levelling and ploughing lands and making them fit for cultivation. Restriction on the cultivation of commercial crops like cotton was imposed and the export of cotton seeds was banned. Numerous crops were cultivated departmentally to demonstrate the efficacy of improved methods of cultivation. Every encouragement was given to intensive cultivation by the distribution of prizes to those who produced the best results. Every opportunity was taken at fairs and festivals to hold agricultural exhibitions. Every effort was made to encourage the growing of vegetables and fruits and the production of eggs and milk through co-operative societies. The slaughtering of sheep and goats was controlled and the export of these as well as cattle and cattle food was banned. Schemes for the increased production of fish were undertaken. Power was taken under the Defence of India Rules for acquiring uncultivated lands. Power was also taken under the Madras Estates Land Temporary Amendment Act of 1944 for permitting tenants in estates to cultivate waste lands without their acquiring occupancy rights wherever the zamindars were not permitting such lands to be cultivated for fear of conferring such rights on the tenants. Power was likewise taken under the Madras Irrigation Works (Repairs, Improvement and Construction) Act of 1943 to repair or improve at

Government cost any irrigation work lying neglected in private ownership and to recover the cost from the persons concerned. And everywhere land reclamation co-operative societies were subsidised and encouraged.[1]

Coimbatore enjoyed all these as well as some special benefits. On the Anaimalais the insistence on the cultivation of plantation products as a condition of assignment of certain lands was relaxed in favour of vegetables up to a certain percentage. The beds of the big tank and the Valunkalam tank in Coimbatore Town were permitted to be cultivated with vegetables that are not consumed raw, subject to the condition applicable to the temporary cultivation of tank-bed lands. And the ban on the extension of irrigation under the Bhavani channels in the district was lifted as a temporary measure.[2]

The cessation of the war did not by any means put an end to the Grow More Food Campaign. The war had shown how precarious the conditions in India could become, if she were to rely on other countries for the import of food grains. The moment the National Government took up office, therefore, they formulated a Five-Year Plan to be enforced from 1947–48 to 1951–52, the object of which was to produce an additional annual four million tons of foodgrains in India by the end of that period. The Government of India generously came forward to bear a portion of the cost of the scheme in all the States and fixed a target of production of six and a half additional lakhs of tons of foodgrains for Madras. The Government of Madras thereupon propounded a Five-Year Plan for this State. They found that, of the total arable area of 364 lakhs of acres, nearly 334 lakhs of acres were already under crops of several kinds and that the real problem was not so much that of increasing the cultivable area as of increasing the food and fodder crops in the areas already under cultivation. They accordingly fixed certain targets for the production of foodgrains for each year in the-five year period and sanctioned several schemes for achieving an allround improvement. Under wells and irrigation schemes they sanctioned the digging of over 60,000 wells, the construction of about 5,000 private tanks and of about 240 minor irrigation works. Under the works schemes, they sanctioned schemes for contour-bunding in certain districts and for the supply of tractors and bulldozers for land clearance and reclamation and pumping installations for lift irrigation. Under supply schemes they subsidised compost making from town refuse and waste vegetable matter by municipalities and panchayats for providing cheap manures; they requisitioned the

1 *See* the Grow More Food Pamphlets of 1942 to 1947.

2 Grow More Food Pamphlet of 1947, pages 8–9.

groundnut cake from oil presses and sold it to the ryots at subsidized prices; they obtained ammonium sulphate from the Government of India and distributed it; they adopted a scheme for the increased distribution of phosphatic manures, such as super-phosphate and bone meal; they introduced a comprehensive scheme for the multiplication and distribution of improved seeds of paddy, millets, pulses, groundnut and green manure to the ryots at subsidized prices ; and they continued the scheme for the distribution of iron and steel required for agricultural purposes. Under miscellaneous schemes they provided for the distribution at cost price of chemicals and sprayers to control pests and diseases of food crops and continued the free distribution of manures and seeds to the poor ryots. Under protective food production schemes, they took special steps to increase the production of vegetables, particularly in urban areas, and for the popularization of poultry farming, bee-keeping and production of fish, milk and eggs. And finally, under service schemes, they sanctioned the creation of an adequate supervisory staff, provided for the training of more agricultural graduates and fieldmen and aimed at the appointment of an agricultural demonstrator for each firka.[1]

Very soon a greater tempo was given to the whole plan. In March 1949 the Government of India announced their decision to stop all imports of food grains from foreign countries from the end of 1951 and asked the State Governments to still further intensify their food production schemes in order to achieve self-sufficiency. This Government then appointed a Cabinet Sub-Committee for Food Production and a Member of the Board of Revenue as Commissioner of Food Production for co-ordinating the activities of the different departments engaged in food production. They also introduced a Two-Year Plan to intensify the several schemes sanctioned under the Five-Year Plan. The Two-Year Plan hoped to achieve the target of an additional production of 4·71 lakhs of tons of rice and millets by the end of 1949–50 and 5·87 lakhs of tons by the end of 1950–51. This Two-Year Plan was shortly afterwards converted into a Three-Year Plan which fixed the targets at 2·09 lakhs of tons in 1949-50, 3·63 lakhs of tons in 1950–51 and 5·38 lakhs of tons in 1951–52.[2]

[1] *See* the Printed Five-Year Plan for Food Production in Madras in G.O. Nos. 2535–2536, Development, dated 9th June 1947.

[2] G.O. No. 2723, Development, dated 20th May 1949.
G.O. No. 3694, Development, dated 11th July 1949.
G.O. Nos. 868 and 869, Food and Agriculture, dated 2nd September 1949.
G.O. No. 1182, Food and Agriculture, dated 18th October 1949.
G.O. No. 1192, Food and Agriculture, dated 9th October 1949.
Madras in 1950, page 23.

This Three-Year Plan was merged into the Five-Year Plan formulated by the Planning Commission so that the final year of the Three-Year Plan, namely, 1951–52, became the first year of the Five-Year Plan.[1] This Five-Year Plan, which is called the First Five-Year Plan, fixed the targets to be achieved by 1955–56 for this State at 8·90 lakhs of tons of food, 1·80 lakhs of bales (392 lb. each) of cotton, 1·0 lakh of tons of oilseeds and 0.80 lakh of tons of sugar (gur). Since then, the Second Five-Year Plan has been drawn up for this State for the years 1956–57 to 1960–61. This plan envisages, a balanced development of agriculture and an all round increase in production in food as well as cash crops, recognizing, as it does that, without such an all round development, there can be no appreciable increase in national income. It was originally proposed under this plan to increase the production of cereals by 7 lakhs of tons or 15 per cent over and above the production achieved by the First Five-Year Plan ; but it is now being realized that there is scope for stepping up the production in cereals up to 40 per cent. It is hoped to achieve this end by introducing schemes for the increased distribution of improved seeds, by the opening of about 400 seed farms, each about 25 acres in extent capable of serving as a seed store and seed testing laboratory. The plan provides for the production and distribution of not only 2,000 tons of improved paddy and 400 tons of improved millets, but also 2,000 tons of improved groundnut, 1,000 tons of improved cotton and 40 million setts of sugarcane. It also provides for the Japanese method of cultivation of paddy as well as millet, cotton and sugarcane, for the intensive manuring of seed-beds, for the treatment of seed to eliminate chaff and disease and for the thin sowing of seed-beds and planting in lines followed by systematic interculture and top dressing. Nor is this all. It proposes to benefit 36,000 acres in the plains and 26,000 acres in the hilly regions by soil conservation measures, 80,000 acres of virgin land and 1,00,000 acres of current fallows by tractor ploughing, 30,000 acres by filter point tube-wells, 3,000 acres by pumping units and, what is more, 23,00,000 of acres by major and minor irrigation schemes. It proposes to distribute 1.75 lakhs of tons of ammonium sulphate to cover an area of 42 lakhs of acres and 4 lakhs of tons of urban compost to cover an area of about a lakh of acres. It proposes to popularise the growing of green manure crops, like *Sesbania* and *glyricidia* in no less than 25 lakhs of acres. And lastly, it proposes to conduct special campaigns for the better cultivation of cotton, tobacco, tea, coffee, groundnut, coconut, arecanut, fruits, etc.[2]

---

[1] *Administration Report of the Agricultural Department for* 1951–52, page 1 of Government Order.

[2] *The Second Five-Year Plan—A Symposium* 1956, pages 7–11.

It remains now to recount the results produced under the First Five-Year Plan and the results hoped to be produced under the Second Five-Year Plan in Coimbatore. Under the First Five-Year Plan, the increase in paddy cultivation in the district went up from 112,718 acres in 1950, which is taken as the base year, to 132,158 acres in 1955–56 and in paddy production from 56,000 tons to 70,000 tons. Under the Second Five-Year Plan it is hoped to increase the extent under paddy by 20,000 acres by implementing the major and minor irrigation works and to step up production by 94,000 tons by using improved seeds, green manure, chemical manure, etc. Under the First Five-Year Plan the extent of millets cultivation was increased from 905,899 acres to 1,287,422 acres as a result of the execution of the Lower Bhavani Project and production was increased from 226,500 tons to 322,000 tons. Under the Second Five-Year Plan it is hoped to bring in an additional extent of 300,000 acres under millets cultivation and to step up production by 37,000 tons by the distribution of good seed and manure. It is also hoped to secure an additional production of 2,500 tons of millets by extending the contour bunding scheme, which has been introduced in a small area in the Dharapuram taluk, to the whole of that taluk. Under the First Five-Year Plan the area under pulses was increased by 4 per cent. Under the Second Five-Year Plan it is hoped to increase the area by another 10 per cent by applying improved seeds to an extent of 26,000 acres. Under the First Five-Year Plan the area under cotton was increased from 212,847 acres to 291,332 acres by the provision of irrigation facilities in the Lower Bhavani Project area. Under the Second Five-Year Plan it is hoped to bring in another 20,000 acres under cotton in the Lower Bhavani Project area, and this would increase production from 72,883 tons to 83,750 tons. Under the First Five-Year Plan the area under sugarcane, instead of increasing, fell from 18,750 acres to 14,112 acres owing to adverse seasonal conditions. Under the Second Five-Year Plan it is hoped to increase the area by 5,000 acres in the Amaravathi Project area. It is also hoped to effect an additional production of about 2 lakhs of tons and thereby to increase the production to 560,000 tons by the application of chemical manures and the extent of area under cultivation. Under the First Five-Year Plan the area under tobacco was increased from 24,233 acres to 26,516 acres. Under the Second Five-Year Plan there is no scope to extend this area but there is scope to increase the yield from 13,758 tons to 15,258 tons by the use of chemical manures. Under the First Five-Year Plan, the extent of area cultivated under groundnut, instead of increasing, fell from 296,353 acres to 205,297 acres owing to the diversion of the area under groundnut to millets and other crops in the Lower

Bhavani Project area. Under the Second Five-Year Plan it is hoped to bring in an additional acreage of 60,000 acres under improved strains of groundnut and thereby step up production by 12,600 tons. It is also hoped to check the ravages of the hairy caterpillar which attacks the groundnut crop by suitable plant protection measures. In regard to other matters it has been proposed under the Second Five-Year Plan to popularise papayas, guavas, lemons, mangoes, and sapotas by supplying weedicides to the ryots at half the cost price and induce them to grow fruit trees around the irrigation wells and backyards of their houses. It has also been proposed to supply the seeds of indigenous and exotic vegetables at half the cost price to the ryots. It has likewise been proposed to supply to the ryots annually 15,000 tons of chemical manure in addition to the 7,500 tons now annually used by them, under the rural credit system. And finally, it has been proposed to upgrade the Agricultural College, Coimbatore.[1]

As to animal husbandry, a quinquennial statement showing the number of livestock population and poultry during 1920–21 to 1950–51 is appended at the end of this chapter. At present, there are 981,641 cattle (371,573 males; 356,759 females; 253,309 calves), 230,844 buffaloes (8,985 males; 125,689 females; 96,170 calves), 931,209 sheep, 336,631 goats and 789,920 poultry in the district.[2]

Of the four chief breeds of cattle found in the district the most famous is the Kangayam breed. The Kangayam bull is generally grey in colour with darker grey merging into black on the head, neck, rump and hump. He is a well shaped, short, compact animal with a well sprung barrel and fine bone. His head is short with a broad level forehead and his horns are fairly long and pointed and curve slightly backwards and inwards. His dewlap is not so pendulous as in the Ongole variety and it extends just between the forelegs while his sheath is tucked well up to the body. His tail is long, fine and tapering with a good switch of hair. Although he is of a fiery nature he makes an excellent work animal. His feet are small and hard which enable him to stand any amount of road work. The Kangayam cow is generally white in colour with black markings on and below the knee of the forelegs. Her average milk yield ranges from 1,500 to 2,000 lb. and in a few exceptionally good cows, the yield is 5,000 lb. She is thus a fair milker.[3] Both the bulls and the cows are bred and reared in the tract around Dharapuram and Kangayam and fed

---

1 *Second Five-Year Plan, Madras State, Coimbatore District* by P. K. Nambiar, 1955, pages 13–15.

2 *Season and Crop Report for* 1956–57, pages 62 and 63.

3 *Gazetteer of Coimbatore District,* Volume II, 1933, page 164.

on Kollukottai grass (*Cenchrus ciliares*) which is rich in protein, calcium and other minerals and which is grown on large areas in the Dharapuram taluk, especially in the Kangayam area. The Pattagar of Palayankottai specialises in breeding Kangayam cattle and some ryots of the tract also keep them on their own holdings. They are purchased by dealers from the neighbouring districts at the breeding centres or at the cattle fairs held at Avanashi and Tiruppur. The Bargur cattle found in the hills of Bhavani and its neighbourhood though small in size are a compact, well built and strong breed. The Kollegal cattle, bred not only in the Kollegal taluk which has now been transferred to the Mysore State, but also all over the central parts of the district are well fitted for the purposes of road draught. The Alambadi or the Mysore cattle are also bred and reared, mostly in the forests ; they are found in the wild country on the Coimbatore side of the Cauvery.[1]

In recent years, in order to encourage the breeding of better cattle, the Government have taken several measures in this, as in other districts. Pedigree bulls are now being distributed under three main schemes. Under the first scheme, called the premium scheme, introduced in 1916, Government grants are given to owners of approved stud bulls subject to certain conditions laid down for ensuring their efficiency. Under the second scheme, introduced in 1935, the district board is given a grant for purchasing stud bulls and distributing them to the ryots, panchayat boards and co-operative societies ; the animals become the property of the latter after three years, provided they are maintained in proper condition and used as stud bulls. Under the third scheme, introduced in 1942, the Animal Husbandry department purchases and distributes young breeding bulls to the ryots and pays them a subsidy of fifty rupees per bull for a period of two years or until they commence serving. In addition to this, stud bulls are kept in veterinary institutions and in selected firkas under the National Extension Service for the use of the ryots.[2]

From 1942, the Kangayam Cattle Improvement Scheme sponsored by the Indian Council of Agricultural Research has been working in the district for improving the milking qualities of the Kangayam cows without impairing the draught qualities of the males by selection breeding and balanced feeding.[3] In 1950, an artificial insemination centre was opened

[1] *Note on Irrigation in the Coimbatore District* by V. N. Kudva, dated 4th March 1953.

[2] *Rural Problems in Madras* by S. Y. Krishnaswami, 1947, pages 203–205.
See also for example, *Administration Report of the Animal Husbandry department* for 1953–54, pages 81, 91–92, 187, 202–203.

[3] *Administration Report of the Madras Animal Husbandry Department for* 1954–55, page 57.

in Coimbatore so as to meet the shortage of pedigree bulls.[1] Its object was to carry out the technique of artificial insemination started successfully at the Madras Veterinary College in 1948. Under this technique there is no necessity to worry about the size of the breeding bull with reference to the size of the cows; nor is there any necessity to have a large number of breeding bulls. The semen from one bull can be utilized to impregnate at least 40 cows and it can also be made easily available to the cattle owners by quick transmission.[2] Recently four insemination centres have been opened, three in the Kangayam breeding tract at Vellakoil, Kangayam and Anamalai (Malayandipatnam) and one in the Scindhi breeding tract at Anamalai (Cinchona) under what is called the Key Village Scheme.[3] This scheme sponsored by the Government of India aims at livestock improvement in compact and contiguous areas by the castration of all scrub bulls by the enforcement of the Madras Livestock Improvement Act and by having an artificial insemination centre with a few sub-centres round about it and by the distribution of pedigree bulls in the area for natural service. The key centres are mainly located in the breeding tracts of distinct breeds so that the first generation of bull calves can be utilized for further distribution as pure bred bulls in due course. Other problems, such as the development of fodder resources milk recording, progeny testing and co-operative marketing of milk are also to be tackled in these centres in due course.

Nor is this all. In order to create an incentive to cattle breeders to rear calves up to maturity (and not to sell them away) a subsidy of Rs. 10 per calf from the date of weaning to the date of maturity is being paid.[4] In order to develop the local non-descript sheep of both the mutton and woolly variety, to make them yield more meat and wool by mating them with improved breeds of sheep, a sheep shearing demonstration unit has been started in Coimbatore since 1942. It trains the professional sheep breeders in the improved methods of shearing and grading wool by practical demonstration and teaches them also in the scientific methods of breeding, feeding and management of sheep.[5] And in order to treat all cattle diseases and to do castration work, the department maintains 5 Veterinary hospitals at Coimbatore, Erode, Tiruppur, Udumalpet and Pollachi and 19 veterinary dispensaries in the district. There is a District Veterinary Officer and there are 26 Veterinary Assistant Surgeons in charge of the

---

1 *Idem*, for 1949–50, page 30.

2 *Madras Information*, *July* 1956, page 17.

3 *Administration Report of the Madras Animal Husbandry department for* 1954–55, page 61.

4 *Madras Information*, *July* 1956, pages 17–18.

5 *Idem*, page 18.

several veterinary institutions of the district. In 1956-57, for instance, these institutions treated 66,506 animals and castrated 9,223 animals. Under the Second Five-Year Plan it is proposed to upgrade the existing dispensaries and to provide each taluk with a veterinary hospital and each planning area with one dispensary and two first aid centres. It is also proposed to start 41 poultry units and 6 artificial insemination centres, to open 1 dairy farm, 1 salvage depot and 2 livestock farms for the Kangayam and Bargur breeds, to improve the existing verterinary hospitals and the livestock, and to install a pasturization unit at Coimbatore.[1]

Turning to irrigation, the principal sources of irrigation of the district are the rivers Cauvery, Bhavani, Noyyal, Amaravati and Aliyar, a number of rain-fed tanks and a large number of wells. The numerous streams that carry the drainage of the local valleys during the north-east and the south-west monsoons are not very useful for irrigation, except in very favourable years. Roughly speaking all the rivers of the district are those of the south-west monsoon and irrigation therefore begins with that monsoon. The rain-fed tanks and jungle streams are fed generally by the north-east monsoon which is capricious in the extreme. But the wells, which are chiefly fed also by the north-east monsoon, rarely go dry and constitute the most valuable source of irrigation.[2]

Taking the rivers one by one, there is hardly any direct irrigation under the Cauvery in the district. The reason for this is that this river flows in a rocky bed with a rapid fall till it passes Erode and, even beyond Erode where its fall is lighter and its bed is smoother. There is irrigation under its channels only in the Salem and Tiruchirappalli districts.[3] Recently, however, the river has been tapped at the Mettur Dam to irrigate large areas both in this and the Salem district under what is called the Mettur Canal Scheme. This scheme was taken up under the Grow More Food Campaign in 1943, investigated in 1946 and sanctioned by the National Government in 1949. Costing as it did about 2·67 crores of rupees, it was treated as a major development scheme under the First Five-Year Plan. In accordance with this scheme a weir has been constructed across the high level supply channel from the Mettur Reservoir 490 feet below the toe of the dam and provision has been made to draw the

---

1 *Second Five-Year Plan, Coimbatore District,* by P. K. Nambiar, 1956, page 20. Information supplied by the Director of Animal Husbandry, Madras.

2 *Note on Irrigation in Coimbatore District* by V. N. Kudva, dated 4th March 1953.

Manual of Coimbatore District by Harold A. Stuart, Volume II, 1898, pages 190–191.

3 *Note on Irrigation in Coimbatore District* by V. N. Kudva, dated 4th March 1953.

supply from low level vents when the level in the reservoir falls below the high level sluices. The main canal has been designed to serve 45 acres per cusec. It starts from the high level supply channel of the Mettur Dam and runs on a falling contour more or less at the foot of the hills. For two miles and three furlongs it passes through the Public Works department lands managed by the Mettur Township Committee and at 4 miles and 3 furlongs, it bifurcates. One branch of it continues to flow on the right side of the Cauvery while the other branch crosses the river by a pressure (syphon) aqueduct and flows into the Tiruchengode taluk of the Salem district. The former is called the West Bank Canal and the latter the East Bank Canal. The course of the West Bank Canal is, at its commencement, parallel and more or less very close to the river up to a distance of 11 miles from the dam. The canal then takes a south-westerly direction enclosing a greater and greater area between it and the river. Its total length is 26 miles and 5 furlongs and its tail end is about 3 miles north-west of Urachikottai which is about 3 miles north of Bhavani town. A field bothi from the dam at the tail end takes the surplus to the Bhavani near Jambai. The canal irrigates 800 acres in the Omalur taluk in the Salem district and 17,200 acres in Jambai, Kibavi, Poonadhi, Ammapettai, Nerinjipetta and Chinnapallam villages in the Bhavani taluk. It has been completed and the entire length of it has been opened for irrigation from 1st August 1955 covering the full ayacut of 18,000 acres. The East Bank Canal which is 39 miles and 1 furlong long is intended to irrigate about 27,000 acres in the Omalur and Tiruchengode taluks of the Salem district. It is now being completed.[1]

It is proposed to classify the area under both the canals as dry and to charge a water rate of Rs. 15 per acre for paddy, Rs. 7-8-0 for millets and Rs. 10 for groundnut, gingelly, etc., into two zones under each canal. Zone 'A' will be wet and Zone 'B' will be dry in the first year and Zone 'A' will be dry and Zone 'B' will be wet in the second year and so on.[2]

There is an old anicut known as the Nerinjipetta anicut, on the Cauvery within the limits of Aryagoundanur village in the Bhavani taluk. It is said to have been constructed in former times by a Raja of Mysore and is said to have irrigated lands from two channels from either side. It is however, now in ruins; huge boulders are found lying loosely on either side of it more or less in a straight line across the river. Some of the boulders have been washed away by the floods with the result that there

---

1 *Note on Irrigation in the Coimbatore District* by V. N. Kudva, dated 4th March 1953.

A Short Note on the Mettur Canal Scheme, 1956.

2 Information supplied by the Chief Engineer for Irrigation, Madras.

is hardly any stagnation of water. In 1947-49, a regulator known as the Jederpalayam Bed Regulator was constructed at mile 17/6 from the Erode railway bridge; but this is an irrigation scheme not of this district but of the Salem district.[1]

The Bhavani, the most important river, is a perennial stream which affords the best irrigation in the district. Its water is fully utilized from its several anicuts for irrigating large tracts of lands. The principal old anicuts across it were till recently two, the Kanniyampalayam anicut in the Avanashi taluk and the Kodiveri anicut in the Gobichettipalayam taluk. The former which was 12 miles below Mettupalayam and which was irrigating some 400 acres, has since been submerged with its ayacut by the Lower Bhavani Project. The latter has recently been improved. It was originally constructed some 370 years ago. In view of the difficulty of feeding its two channels when the supplies in the river are low sand bags were formerly put over its crest to raise the level of water. Since 1950 falling shutters, two feet high, have been installed in concrete broken stone without altering the crest of the anicut and the gap between the shutters has been sealed with flat iron. By so doing, an area of about 8,000 acres has been brought under second crop cultivation. Of the two channels of the anicut, the Tadapalli channel takes off on the right and irrigates 19,332 acres while the Arakkankottai channel takes off on the left and irrigates 6,000 acres. Masonry sluices have been provided to the channels and other improvements have been made to economize the use of water and extend irrigation. In addition, a channel called the Mewani distributary channel has been excavated from mile 8-3½ of the Kugalur branch channel of the Tadapalli channel to stabilize 29 acres of existing ayacut and to irrigate 263 acres of new ayacut in Mewani and Ammayapalayam, and another channel called the Perumugai Atani channel, nearly 6 miles long branching from mile 17-1½ of the Arakkankottai channel and running through Perumugai in the Gobichettipalayam taluk and Athani in the Bhavani taluk, has been excavated at a cost of about 14 lakhs of rupees to irrigate nearly 2,000 acres of new ayacut. All these works have been undertaken under the Grow More Food and Intensive Cultivation Schemes.

The Bhavani has also other channels and some tributaries. There is the Kalingarayan channel in the Erode taluk which takes off on the right at the Kalingarayan anicut near the Bhavani Bridge just above the junction of the Bhavani and the Cauvery, which is 62 miles long and which irrigates about 12,800 acres. There is the Orakkarai Venkatrama Chettiar anicut

[1] *Note on Irrigation in the Coimbatore District* by V. N. Kudva, dated 4th March 1953.

in the Avanashi taluk put up across the Tekkampatti vari which falls into the Periyapallam flowing into the Bhavani on the right and its channel which irrigates a few acres. As this anicut and its channel are in ruins it has been proposed to construct a new masonry anicut with head sluices, etc., and to restore the channel to irrigate about 300 acres at a cost of 6 lakhs of rupees. Then there are the rivers Coonoor, Kallar and Elerumalaipallam, all tributaries of the Bhavani, which irrigate some lands in the Avanashi taluk. There is also the river Gandaipallam which rises in the Nilgiris and flowing through the Avanashi taluk past Gandai falls into the Bhavani on the left (north) within the limits of Sirumugai. It receives freshes every year from September to February and it has three channels taking off from it which irrigate 240 acres. There is next the Moyar which flows along the boundary of the Coonoor taluk, enters the Gobichettipalayam taluk and falls into the Bhavani at 10 miles east of the Gazalhatti Pass. And finally, there is the Chickarasampalayam which falls into the Bhavani just before it flows into Satyamangalam. It has been proposed to put up a reservoir across the stream 4 miles from Chickarasampalayam to irrigate 250 acres.[1]

Nor is this all. Two projects on the Bhavani of supreme importance to the district have been considered and one of them has just been executed. The idea of utilizing the surplus waters of the Bhavani by constructing one or more reservoirs for the extension of irrigation in the district is more than a century old. It was again and again considered in the last century, in 1834, 1857, 1866, 1880 and 1897. In 1905 it was proposed to construct two reservoirs on the Bhavani, one at the junction of the Siruvani and the Bhavani and the other just below the junction of the Kundah and the Bhavani for an irrigated dry scheme. It was also proposed at the same time to construct one reservoir on the Bhavani a little lower down below the junction of the Moyar and the Bhavani, 10 miles above Satyamangalam for an irrigated wet scheme. The former, which was called the Upper Bhavani Project, was intended to irrigate by means of a high level canal and a high level branch, a vast tract of lands in the Pollachi, Coimbatore, Erode, Gobichettipalayam, Palladam, Dharapuram and Udumalpet taluks. The latter, which was called the Lower Bhavani Project, was intended to irrigate by means of a canal a smaller extent of lands in the Gobichettipalayam, Bhavani and Erode taluks. In 1906 Mr. Charles Innes was appointed as a Special Revenue Officer to investigate the revenue aspects of the projects and in 1908 it was decided to drop the Upper Bhavani Project on the ground of cost and to proceed only with

1 *Note on Irrigation in the Coimbatore District* by V. N. Kudva, dated 4th March 1953.

the investigation of the Lower Bhavani Project. Subsequently, however, the investigation was ordered to lie over pending the decision on the Cauvery-Mettur Project which was then under consideration. As the gaugings taken over a long term of years showed that there would be sufficient supply for one or more storage reservoirs on the Bhavani in addition to the one at Mettur, on the Cauvery, the original proposals regarding both the Upper and the Lower Bhavani projects were re-examined in 1925. In 1926 the Government appointed a special officer to investigate in detail the revenue aspects of the proposed Upper Bhavani Project before deciding finally as to whether that project or the Lower Bhavani Project was to be taken up; and in 1928 as a result of the Special Officer's report, they ordered that the Upper Bhavani Project should be dropped in favour of the Lower Bhavani Project. In 1932 they decided that the Lower Bhavani Project should be revised as an irrigated dry scheme.

The Lower Bhavani Scheme then drawn up contemplated the construction of a reservoir with an effective capacity of 17,740 million cubic feet across the Bhavani at the place formerly selected, namely, 10 miles upstream of Satyamangalam, and the excavation of a main canal 74 miles long from the reservoir to irrigate 207,000 acres of dry crops—117,000 acres in the first crop zone (June to September) and 90,000 acres in the second crop zone (October to December) in the taluks of Gobichettipalayam, Bhavani and Erode. This scheme, the cost of which was estimated at Rs. 233 lakhs, was sanctioned by the Government in 1933. Its estimates were revised and the cost was increased to Rs. 247 lakhs in 1936. In 1937, however, on the Special Deputy Collector's report, the Government ordered a more detailed examination. The Chief Engineer for Irrigation now sent up an alternative proposal to irrigate the entire area of 207,000 acres in the second crop season from October to February and to abandon altogether both the division into zones and the attempt to supply water during the first crop season. The main advantage claimed for this proposal was that it would allow the ryots over the entire area to grow cotton if they wished to do so and would enable a water-rate to be charged to give the necessary return. This, however, involved an increase in reservoir capacity to 20,720 million cubic feet and an increase in cost to 267 lakhs of rupees. When this scheme was being considered, some representations were received from the District urging the desirability of reconsidering the Upper Bhavani Scheme in preference to the Lower Bhavani Scheme on the ground that it would benefit the taluks where the rainfall was lower and more uncertain. The First Congress Government then while tentatively approving the modified Lower Bhavani Scheme, ordered also the re-examination of the Upper Bhavani Scheme. The Chief Engineer then proposed for the Upper Bhavani Project to construct only one reservoir with a dam high enough to secure the required storage for an ayacut of 125,000 acres, either just below the junction of the Kundah with the Bhavani or at a few miles lower down the river at Nellithorai about 5 miles above Mettupalayam. The former site, he pointed out, had these advantages that the dam would be shorter in length and that the reservoir would command the area between the Noyyal and the Amaravati, an area considered to be most liable to famine. But it had, he remarked, the disadvantages of requiring three tunnels for its canal and of making the canal run along hill slopes for the first 15 miles of its course. The latter site, he observed, would avoid these disadvantages and would also possess the advantage of having a shorter canal running in more open country. But, it had, he stated, this disadvantage that it would command only the area between the Noyyal and the Bhavani rivers. The Lower Bhavani Reservoir, he felt, could be built at the site originally proposed, i.e., 10 miles above Satyamangalam, to irrigate an ayacut of 120,000 acres in the taluks of Gobichettipalayam, Bhavani and Erode. The Upper Bhavani Project, he estimated, might cost Rs. 498 lakhs and the Lower Bhavani Project Rs. 267 lakhs; and considering the high cost of the former, he thought it difficult to justify its execution. The Government thereupon abandoned the Upper Bhavani Project and ordered that the detailed investigation of the Lower Bhavani Project should be taken up after the Tungabhadra Project was considered.[1]

Nothing was done till 1947. In that year, however, the Lower Bhavani Project was sanctioned by the National Government for execution. The project was shortly afterwards included in the First Five-Year Plan and completed by August 1955. Under it, a dam of capacity of about 28,000 m.cft. has been constructed across the Bhavani about a mile below the confluence of the Moyar river and a canal has been cut from the dam on the right flank to irrigate an extent of 207,000 acres of dry irrigated crops, half the area for growing cotton and the other half for raising food crops in rotation in the Gobichettipalayam, Bhavani and Erode, as well as Dharapuram taluks. The project is expected to yield 33,000 tons of food-

---

1 G.O. No. 971–972, Public Works (Irrigation), dated 2nd September 1904.
G.O. No. 1234, Public Works (Irrigation), dated 14th December 1905.
G.O. No. 1341, Public Works (Irrigation), dated 25th September 1926.
G.O. No. 47, Public Works (Irrigation), dated 7th January 1928.
G.O. No. 959, Public Works (Irrigation), dated 29th April/1st May 1953.
G.O. No. 2710, Public Works and Labour (Irrigation), dated 12th December 1933.
G.O. No. 675, Public Works (Irrigation), dated 31st March 1937.
G.O. No. 2202, Public Works (Irrigation), dated 13th October 1938.
G.O. No. 1889, Public Works (Irrigation), dated 29th July 1939.

grains and 14,700 tons of cotton. The dam consists of a central masonry portion across the river for a length of 1,523 feet and earth dams on either side, for a length of 15,250 feet on the left flank and 12,069 feet on the right flank. The total length of the dam is five and a half miles. Commencing from the left end of the masonry section, for a length of 357 feet there is the non-overflow or the bulk head section of the dam. The next 396 feet from the overflow section, expected to flow with a depth of 20 feet over the crest. This is followed by the river sluices section of 200 feet length having 9 river sluices of 6 feet by 10 feet; the penstock section having four numbers of 8 feet diameter penstock pipes in a length of 140 feet for producing a seasonal electric power of 10,000 k.w. at a later stage; and the canal sluices section 137 feet long with 5 canal sluices of 6 feet by 10 feet on the right flank there is the non-overflow section 293 feet long similar to that on the left flank. The masonry dam is 204 feet high over the deepest foundation to the top of the dam and 140 feet above the river-bed level and it carries a road-way 22 feet wide. The earth dam on either side of the masonry dam rises to a height of 110 feet in certain portions. It is of the zone type and consists of seven parts built according to the latest practices in earth dam design. Its rocky layer has been drilled and cement slurry has been forced under pressure to fill in all the crevices within the rocks so as to prevent water from getting underneath the dam. And it has been provided with a road-way 25 feet wide with parapet walls on either side. The area of the reservoir is 30·41 square miles and four villages have been completely, and five partly, submerged by it. The length of the canal that takes off from the right flank of the masonry dam is 124 miles with a bed width of 111 feet, at head. Being a contour canal, irrigation is only on its left side, and as it traverses an undulating country, it has to cross several spurs and valleys. The maximum depth of cutting in the spurs is about 45 feet at the 49th mile and the maximum height of the embankment in the valley is about 30 feet. As the canal intercepts a number of natural drainages about 190 cross drainage works, drainage culverts, aqueducts, syphons and super passages have been constructed. In addition, 105 bridges, 6 regulators and a number of direct and head-sluices have been provided. The total length of the distributaries of the canal is about 500 miles, excluding field bothies involving about 6,000 masonry works. The total cost of the works, the dam and the canal, come to about 9·5 crores of rupees. All the items of works in the masonry dam have been completed (1955-56), except the finishing of architectural towers on either end of the spillway. All canal works have also been completed and supply has been let down for irrigation to an extent of 167,400 acres during 1955–56. The entire ayacut was thrown open for cultivation during the year 1956–57. The areas actually cultivated are 10,400 acres in 1953–54; 92,500 acres in 1954–55 and 124,000 acres in 1956–57. The credit for the successful execution of the project goes in a large measure to Sri A. R. Venkatachari, the former Chief Engineer for Irrigation.[1]

Some works have been constructed on the Siruvani, an important tributary of the Bhavani. The Siruvani is a perennial stream which rises in the Attapadi valley 25 miles west of Coimbatore town and fed by the Muthikulam waterfalls and also by some streams, flows north and falls into the Bhavani. At one time the question of a combined water supply and hydro-electric scheme for supplying drinking water and electricity to Coimbatore town by constructing a dam on the Siruvani was considered, but the hydro-electric scheme was abandoned after the Pykara Scheme was taken up. For supplying drinking water, however, a dam was subsequently constructed to a height of 23 feet at a cost of Rs. 2,17,725 across the Siruvani just below the confluence of the Gopiar on its left at a place where it runs in a narrow gap on a rocky bed to form a small lake. A little water that surpluses over the dam flows into the old course of the Bhavani. A channel takes the water from the lake through a tunnel 6 feet by 8 feet and 4,800 feet long cut at a cost of Rs. 8,60,180 through hills which form the watershed between the Bhavani and the Noyyal. The tunnel ends in the Bolampatty range in the eastern slope on the Coimbatore side of the hills and water is taken through it into two settling tanks constructed at a cost of Rs. 80,250 at Adivaram at the foot of the hills in the Anaiyar valley. The surplus water from the settling tanks is let into the Anaiyar which falls on the left into the Periyar, a tributary which falls on the right into the Noyyal. After the water settles down in the tank for about three hours, it is sent down through 18 inch diameter gravitation mains (for a length of about 22 miles) into the service reservoir in Coimbatore town. The distribution system involves a length of 30 miles. The cost of the gravitation main, the service reservoir and the distribution system came to Rs. 16,84,380, Rs. 1,04,560 and Rs. 7,15,280 respectively. Recently, under the Grow More Food Campaign, the dam has been raised by 4 feet to divert the available water supplies in the Siruvani into the Noyyal for a better supply into the existing Noyyal channels at a cost of Rs. 52,000 for works and Rs. 67,660 for direct

---

[1] Lower Bhavani Dam.

Lower Bhavani Project—Canals Brochure.

Opening of the Lower Bhavani Dam Spillway Gates—Note on the Project by the Chief Engineer, 1955.

Administration Report of the Public Works Department (Irrigation) for 1955–56.

and indirect charges (1950) [1]. Since then, under the Second Five-Year Plan it has been proposed to put up a reservoir at a cost of Rs. 30.05 lakhs for diverting still further the surplus waters of the Siruvani into the Noyyal so as to irrigate 3,000 acres in the Palladam taluk. This scheme is called the Noyyal Scheme [2].

The Noyyal, as has already been stated, is a jungle stream whose freshes are noted for their brief duration, for their violence and for their capriciousness. The irrigation under its channels has consequently been supplemented by tanks which it fills up along its course. It has specially enriched the neighbourhood of Coimbatore by its channels and tanks. Its water, however, is not quite sufficient for the tanks which depend upon it and it barely fills the upper tanks in the south-west monsoon. All the same, its water is fully utilized for irrigation in the Coimbatore and Palladam taluks. No less than 13,213 acres are irrigated under its 8 anicuts in the Coimbatore taluk. Of these anicuts, the Neeli anicut irrigates 1,030 acres on the right; the Padukkadu anicut 585 acres on the left; the Kuniamuthur anicut (or the Perur anicut) 1,037 acres plus 1,747 acres on the right; the Coimbatore anicut 143 acres plus 2,327 acres on the left; the Kuruchi anicut 60 acres plus 452 acres on the right; the Vellalore anicut 338 acres plus 331 acres on the right; and the Singanallur anicut 455 acres plus 845 acres on the left. Besides this, 3,062 acres are irrigated under its 17 anicuts in the Palladam taluk, but the extent of cultivation under these anicuts is small, except under the Oddarpalayam anicut which irrigates 634 acres plus 129 acres. One of these anicuts also irrigates some acres in the Dharapuram taluk and a channel from another of these anicuts supplies water to the Sulur tank in the Palladam taluk. The increased violence and fitfulness of the freshes of the Noyyal as well as the decrease in its underground flow is attributed to the denudation of the Bolampatty forests at its source to supply the immense fuel and timber demands of Coimbatore town and its neighbourhood . Its spring channels which were formerly found to be very useful in supplementing the irrigation under its channels in the Palladam taluk have of late been found to be practically useless owing to their poor underground flow [3].

1 *Note on Irrigation in the Coimbatore District* by V. N. Kudva, dated 4th March 1953.

2 *Second Five-Year Plan, Madras State, Coimbatore District* by P. K. Nambiar, 1955, page 24.

3 *Note on Irrigation in the Coimbatore District* by V. N. Kudva, dated 4th March 1953.

The Nallar which is a tributary of the Noyyal and which flows through the Avanashi and Palladam taluks has channels taking off from the Alavati and Marudavali anicuts across it. These channels irrigate two villages in the Avanashi taluk. The Vannathankaripallam, which is a drainage course and which is taking its source from the north of Coimbatore town and passing through the Coimbatore, Avanashi and Palladam taluks falls into the Noyyal near the Vanjipalayam railway station in the Avanashi taluk, receives freshes only for a few days in the south-west monsoon to be of any use for irrigation [1].

We may now pass on to the Amaravathi. It is a river of not a little importance which is fed mostly by the south-west monsoon. Its banks are low and its water is fully utilized for irrigation of a good quality throughout its course over an almost continuous, though narrow, belt of land to the south and east of Dharapuram taluk. It has numerous anicuts and korambus across it and even baling is a little resorted to on its course. It irrigates 7,317 acres through channels from eight anicuts in the Udumalpet taluk and 9,156 acres under six anicuts in the Dharapuram taluk as shown below :

Taluk.	*Names of the anicut.*	*Area irrigated.*
Udumalpet	1 Kallapuram	1,444 acres on the right.
	2 Komaralingam ..	1,237 Do.
	3 Kannadipattur ..	600 acres on the left.
	4 Sholamadur	536 Do.
	5 Kadathur	1,108 acres on the right.
	6 Kaniyar	376 acres on the left.
	7 Karatholuvu	582 Do.
	8 Ramakolam (a private anicut).	1,384 acres on the right.
Dharapuram ..	1 Alangium	1,039 acres on the right.
	2 Dalvoipatnam ..	865 Do.
	3 Dharapuram	3,409 Do.
	4 Kolingivadi	3,196 Do.
	5 Nanjaithalaiyur ..	387 Do.
	6 Sundakampalayam ..	260 Do.

It may be stated that the Kadathur and Kaniyar anicuts are no more than Korambus, that the Dharapuram channel runs through the Dharapuram town, that most of the lands irrigated by the anicuts are double crop lands and that some of the anicuts mentioned above have been improved under the Grow More Food Scheme [2].

1 *Note on Irrigation in the Coimbatore District* by V. N. Kudva, dated 4th March 1953.

2 *Idem.*

Very recently the Government have taken up what is called the Amaravati Reservoir Project. The idea of building a reservoir on the Amaravati is, however, an old one. The earliest investigation for constructing a reservoir on the river at the foot of the hills near Kallapuram, was undertaken in 1901. A more detailed investigation was ordered in 1902. A scheme was actually prepared in 1905 but it was abandoned in 1913 owing to its excessive cost and provision of large surplus discharges. In 1918, however, another investigation was ordered, but in 1921 the scheme was once more abandoned in view of its low return. In 1946 a fresh investigation was again ordered in view of the need for obviating famines such as the one which visited the Udumalpet and Dharapuram taluks in 1939. The scheme then prepared was included in the First Five-Year Plan and continued in the Second Five-Year Plan. Its aim is to stabilize irrigation in about 32,000 acres of existing ayacut under river channels and to irrigate 21,000 acres of new ayacut of which 18,000 acres will be for dry crops and 3,000 acres for sugarcane in the Udumalpet and Dharapuram taluks, and thereby to contribute to an additional production of about 5,788 tons of rice and 2,156 tons of millets. The reservoir will be constructed about half a mile below the Kombu forest bungalow and about 14 miles south-east of Udumalpet town. The dam will be about 120 feet high above the river bed and 3,594 feet long, 2,527 feet being earth dam and 1,067 feet being masonry dam. In the masonry portion there will be an overflow section over the river bed 396 feet long and at both ends of it a non-overflow section 671 feet long. The overflow section will discharge a maximum flood of 78,000 cusecs. The storage capacity of the reservoir will be 3,600, m.c. feet and there will be sluices in the dam for both old and new irrigation. The length of the canal will be nearly 40 miles. The total cost of the scheme will be Rs. 296.71 lakhs.[1]

It was originally proposed, under the Grow More Food Scheme, to put up a dam across the Uppar and to construct a reservoir on the Vattamalakarai, two of the tributaries of the Amaravati, in order to benefit lands in the Dharapuram taluk. The site of the dam across the Uppar was fixed at a place one furlong above Kandiamankoil of Marudur and two furlongs above the Kundadam-Pannavaram Road, and this scheme was intended to provide irrigation for dry irrigated crops on

1 *The Amaravathi Reservoir Project—Note on the Project*, by the Special Chief Engineer for Irrigation 1953.

The Amaravathi Reservoir Project, Coimbatore District—a Pamphlet.

Administration Report of the Public Works Department (Irrigation) for 1955–56 and Information furnished by the Chief Engineer for Irrigation, Madras.

3,000 acres. The site of the reservoir on the Vattamalakarai was fixed near the hill temple of the place and this scheme was intended to provide irrigation for 900 acres of dry land. But both these schemes have been abandoned in view of their high cost and poor return.[1]

The next river of some importance is the Aliyar which rises in the Anaimalais and, after passing through the Pollachi taluk and receiving the Uppar on the left near Anaimalai town and the Palar a little further down, enters the Kerala State. It has five anicuts across it in the Pollachi taluk. One of these anicuts, the Pallivalangal anicut, situated 40 miles west of Kottur, has a channel on the left flank which directly irrigates 650 acres of which 462 acres are double crop lands and the rest single crop lands. Another of these anicuts, the Ariyapuram anicut, has a channel 8 miles long on the right which directly irrigates 1,143 acres of which 695 are double crop wet and the rest single crop wet lands. The third, the Karanpatti anicut, has a channel 7 miles long on the left which irrigates 732 acres of which 587 acres are double crop lands. The fourth, the Perianai (the big dam), has a channel 11¼ miles long on the right which irrigates 1,912 acres of which 833 acres are double crop lands. And the fifth, the Vadakkalur anicut, has a channel 6 miles long on the left which irrigates 1,140 acres of which 745 acres are double crop and about 250 acres are dry lands. There was a proposal to construct a dam and to form a storage reservoir across the Aliyar near Chickajapari about 1¼ miles below the Vannathorai bridge in order to stabilize the existing irrigation and also to provide new irrigation to 5,000 acres in the Palladam taluk ; but this scheme has now been merged in the Parambikulam Reservoir Scheme. There is an anicut across the Uppar and another across the Palar. The former and its channel directly irrigate 116 acres and indirectly through a tank, 288 acres. The latter, which is called the Somandurai anicut, supplies water through a channel to the Elavakkarai tank.[2]

The Parambikulam Reservoir Scheme is one of the most important projects of the Second Five-Year Plan, for diverting, with the consent of the Kerala State, the waters of the rivers flowing waste into the Arabian Sea in the west into the Coimbatore district in the east. The Parambikulam-Chalakudi River has its origin in the Western Ghats near Ramalakshmanmalai with the name Periyar. This river, after flowing 12 miles in the Coimbatore district, enters the Kerala State. Just about three miles below the boundary of the Coimbatore district and the Kerala

---

[1] *Note on Irrigation in the Coimbatore District,* by V. N. Kudva, dated 4th March 1953.

[2] *Idem.*

State, where it is called Parambikulam, it is proposed to construct a dam and a reservoir with a catchment area of 88 square miles. It is proposed also to divert the water stored in this reservoir through a tunnel about 6 miles long cut through mountains and to use it for irrigation in the Pollachi,Udumalpet and Dharapuram taluks with the help of six reservoirs, one erected across the Aliyar, one erected across the Palar, two erected across the Sholaiar, one erected across the Themakudam and one erected across the Tekkadi, and all linked to the Parambikulam reservoir. By this arrangement, as has been stated already, the Aliyar reservoir scheme has been merged in this bigger project. The whole scheme would irrigate a new area of not less than 320,000 acres and enable the raising of second crops on 27,000 acres, besides producing 120,000 k.w. of electric power. The estimated cost of the scheme is the huge sum of 32 crores of rupees.[1]

So much about irrigation under the rivers. Among other sources of irrigation there are some spring channels in the Pollachi and Udumalpet taluks which benefit by both the monsoons and which have a good supply, a low lift and a natural drainage. Valuable crops are grown in the lands on their banks. There are also some tanks in the District. They are, however, more or less isolated and only a fifth of them receive supplies from the channels. The Coimbatore, Udumalpet and Erode taluks have comparatively a larger number of them than the other taluks. The big tanks in the Coimbatore taluk are the Perur Periyakulam, the Coimbatore large tank, the Valankulam tank and the Singanallur tank. The Perur tank gets some of its supplies from an escape in the left bank of the channel from the Kuniamuthur anicut across the Noyyal. It has two weirs with two vents and four sluices and it irrigates 860 acres. The Coimbatore large tank, situated south of the town and west of the railway line, receives some supply from a channel, from the Coimbatore anicut across the Noyyal and surpluses into the river and it irrigates 1,436 acres. The Valankulam tank situated south-east of Coimbatore also gets its supply from the Coimbatore anicut channel and surpluses into a jungle stream; it has an ayacut of 878 acres. The Singanallur tank receives some supply from the Singanallur anicut channel and from the Singanurpallam through a road culvert; it has an ayacut of 845 acres. There is a tank in the Palladam taluk called the Sulur large tank which is fed by a channel from an anicut across the Noyyal and which surpluses into the Sulur-Sunkalam tank. It irrigates 542 acres. There are two series of jungle stream-fed tanks. Of these, the Appakudal series of tanks in the Bhavani taluk are

[1] *Second Five-Year Plan, Madras State, Coimbatore district,* by P. K. Nambiar, 1955, page 24.

Administration Report of the Public Works Department (Irrigation) for 1955–56.

fed by various jungle streams from the Bargur hills and they usually fill in the north-east monsoon. The other series called the Dhali series of tanks are in the Udumalpet taluk; they extend from Dhali to Udumalpet and are fed by jungle streams from the Anaimalais. Of the former series, the chief tank is the Ennamangalam tank which irrigates 114 acres; and of the latter series, the chief tank is the Periakulam tank which irrigates 1,163 acres. The Periakulam tank situated on the right side of the road from Udumalpet to Dhali is fed by a channel from the Dhali anicut across the Palar; it has a bund 2¾ miles long and 8 sluices. In general it must be said that most of the tanks are rainfed and much silted and that cultivation under them is precarious, owing to the scarcity of rainfall, when it is not supplemented by wells. Some of the old tanks in the Bhavani taluk have been restored under the Tank Restoration Scheme, and some of the tanks in the Palladam, Pollachi and Dharapuram taluks have been restored under the Grow More Food Scheme. Among the tanks so restored, the principal ones are the Nilambur tank in the Palladam taluk, the Kothavadi tank in the Pollachi taluk and the Kathangani and Surianallur tanks in the Dharapuram taluks.[1]

It is, however, not for tank irrigation but for well irrigation that the District is famous. From early days wells have been the chief source of irrigation. Even during the Great Famine of 1877–78 the majority of them are stated to have held out and yielded splendid returns to their owners. One officer, Mr. Clogstoun, has observed that they are ' the chief mainstay of the revenue ' another, Mr. Stuart, has remarked that they are ' the chief mainstay of the ryot ' ; and a third Mr. Thomas, has stated that they are ' the heart and life of the district '[2]. In a district of scanty rainfall like Coimbatore it is no wonder that the wells are of incalculable value.

The gradual slope of the country in the district is very favourable for well cultivation. Besides the wells in wet lands there are a number of wells in dry lands. These wells situated in the little valleys and hollows are a peculiar feature of cultivation in the district. The wells are usually large and on an average irrigate 3¾ acres. They are mostly situated on tank-fed lands to supplement, as has already been stated, the precarious supply of the tanks. They are in many cases more than 60 feet deep sunk into apparently solid rock which, however, is more or less fissured. There are over 400 oil engines, mostly in the Coimbatore and Palladam taluks,

---

1 *Note on irrigation in the Coimbatore district* by V. N. Kudva, dated 4th March 1953.

2 *Manual of the Coimbatore district* by Harold A. Stuart, Volume II, 1898, page 191.

and some in the Avanashi, Dharapuram and Bhavani taluks, for lifting water from the wells for irrigation. Electric motors are gradually replacing oil engines on the electricity line from Coimbatore to Erode and some of the wells worked by electric power irrigate over 100 acres. The well known Coimbatore gardens are irrigated by wells fitted with electric motors.[1]

Over 54·3 per cent of the irrigated lands in the District are under wells. There are 86,223 wells in the District. The chief supply of water to the wells is brought by the north-east monsoon but the kar rains of April and May also replenish them to some extent in the dry weather. Two crops are invariably raised under them and sometimes a third, the chief crops raised being paddy, sugarcane, plantain, cotton, cholam, ragi and tobacco.

Statement showing the area cultivated with the Chief food and non-food crops and their yield during 1920–21 *to* 1950–51

	1920–21.		1925–26.		1930–31.
	Area in acres Normal.	*Normal yield in Tons.*	*Area in acres Normal.*	*Normal yield in Tons.*	*Area in acres Normal.*
(1)	(2)	(3)	(4)	(5)	(6)
Paddy	95,200	80,190	108,400	91,520	99,600
Cholam	534,000	204,500	573,700	224,500	478,000
Cumbu	512,200	104,900	427,000	93,100	427,000
Ragi	195,350	112,900	204,000	120,700	152,000
Korra or Tenai ..	22,650	7,100	19,600	6,100	27,000
Varagu or Arika ..	7,850	2,100	7,800	2,100	10,000
Samai	121,250	21,700	95,000	17,000	75,000
Bengal Gram ..	6,050	1,350	4,600	1,000	4,000
Horse Gram ..	..	..	229,400	20,500	222,000
Sugar cane ..	9,700	32,600	9,800	32,800	8,000
Cotton	287,000	12,600	300,000	97,900	336,000
Groundnut ..	77,400	38,700	89,000	44,500	158,000
Gingelly	22,450	2,800	23,500	2,900	40,000
Castor	22,200	4,000	15,700	2,800	9,000
Tobacco .. .. (Yield in dry leaf)	31,800	17,000	31,000	16,600	33,000

Contd.

[1] *Note on Irrigation in the Coimbatore district* by V. N. Kudva, dated 4th March 1953.

Season and Crop Report of the Madras State for 1956–57.

Statement showing the area cultivated with the Chief food and non-food crops and their yield during 1920–21 *to* 1950–51—cont.

	1930–31.	1935–36.		1940–41.	
	Normal yield in Tons.	*Area in acres Normal.*	*Normal yield in Tons.*	*Area in acres Normal.*	*Normal yield in Tons.*
	(7)	(8)	(9)	(10)	(11)
Paddy	83,670	101,010	84,940	99,600	84,210
Cholam	183,000	492,000	188,900	521,000	192,000
Cumbu	92,300	387,100	85,600	335,200	77,100
Ragi	84,800	151,500	86,300	149,200	84,900
Korra or Tenai ..	8,440	27,800	8,690	19,000	5,940
Varagu or Arika ..	2,680	9,600	2,570	5,000	1,340
Samai	13,400	72,900	13,000	70,000	12,500
Bengal Gram ..	900	5,260	1,170	3,930	880
Horse Gram ..	19,800	218,000	19,500	168,000	15,000
Sugar cane ..	26,800	7,340	24,600	7,140	27,900
Cotton	109,400 (in Bales)	348,000	113,310 (in Bales)	379,000	133,810 (in Bales)
Groundnut ..	79,000	158,000	79,000	175,000	87,500
Gingelly	5,000	38,100	4,760	36,000	4,500
Castor	1,600	9,090	1,620	8,170	1,460
Tobacco .. .. (Yield in dry leaf)	17,700	30,300	16,200	30,000	20,100
				(farm-cured leaf)	

	1945–46.		1950–51.	
	Area in acres Normal.	*Normal yield in Tons.*	*Area in acres Normal.*	*Normal yield in Tons.*
	(12)	(13)	(14)	(15)
Paddy	128,320	95,200	141,330	95,780
Cholam	546,000	160,800	466,000	105,490
Cumbu	297,400	62,600	263,000	45,520
Ragi	174,600	92,600	155,000	67,670
Korra or Tenai ..	26,800	7,220	25,400	5,510
Varagu or Arika ..	6,810	1,550	9,390	1,770
Samai	71,100	10,900	60,200	7,450
Bengal Gram ..	2,920	550	3,370	550
Horse Gram ..	198,000	13,600	197,000	9,600
Sugar cane ..	10,800	38,700	15,190	52,410
Cotton	333,000	143,900 (in Bales)	241,680	113,180 (in Bales)
Groundnut ..	184,000	79,800	224,000	93,470
Gingelly	46,200	5,110	36,600	3,530
Castor	6,650	1,070	5,800	900
Tobacco .. .. (Yield in dry leaf)	27,900	17,100	27,700	15,210
		(farm-cured leaf)		

Statement showing the number of Livestock and poultry in the district during the period 1920–21 *to* 1950–51.

(1)	1920–21. (2)	1925–26. (3)	1930–31. (4)	1935–36 (5)
Cattle—				
Males	435,467	452,637	430,510	422,522
Females ..	400,311	344,584	368,822	405,750
Young stock (calves)	269,301	211,867	204,544	359,738
Buffaloes—				
Males	9,957	9,453	9,626	9,230
Females ..	86,662	94,698	121,202	121,090
Young stock (calves)	54,081	59,342	68,405	134,335
Sheep	907,602	877,955	1,012,361	1,124,539
Goats	413,623	525,066	534,889	430,761
Poultry ..	..	..	..	..

	1940–41. (6)	1944–45. (7)	1950–51. (8)
Cattle.—			
Males	365,539	405,503	408,642
Females	355,646	396,469	401,902
Young stock (calves)	263,100	273,748	313,524
Buffaloes.—			
Males	3,277	6,260	12,719
Females	101,490	112,016	135,591
Young stock (calves)	67,349	77,804	104,241
Sheep	1,244,698	935,701	999,054
Goats	409,346	356,186	396,609
Poultry	822,875	701,640	774,016

* Figures taken from Season and Crop Reports for the respective years

CHAPTER VII.

FORESTS.

Coimbatore is one of the few districts of this State which has some dense forests as distinguished from patches of scrub jungle of small trees in other districts. These forests can boast of having teak, sandalwood and rosewood besides a variety of other valuable forest trees. They have been, for administrative purposes, included in two divisions, called the North Coimbatore Forest Division and the South Coimbatore Forest Division. The North Coimbatore Forest Division comprises the forests of the Erode, Bhavani and Gobichettipalayam taluks while the South Coimbatore Forest Division comprises the forests of the Avanashi, Coimbatore, Pollachi, Udumalpet and Dharapuram taluks. The former division is sub-divided into six ranges, namely, the Bhavani, the Bargur, the Andhiyur, the Satyamangalam, the Satyamangalam Sandal Depot and the Talamalai ranges, while the latter division is sub divided into eight ranges, namely, the Mettupalayam, the Mettupalayam Irrigated Plantations, the Bolampatty, the Tunacadavu, the Pollachi, the Pollachi Depot, the Punachi and the Udumalpet ranges. The forests of the district cover 2,272 square miles of reserved forests and 24 square miles of private forests. In 1927–29 some forests of the district comprising about 50 square miles were handed over to the Panchayats, but, as they were mismanaged, they were taken back by the Forest Department in 1951.

The forests of the North Coimbatore Division comprise those situated on the Bargur and the North Coimbatore plateaux which form the southern extension of the Mysore plateau. The Bargur plateau which rises steeply from the bank of the Palar and reaches a height of 3,000 feet and in some places up to 6,000 feet is cut up into numerous ravines.[1] The north Coimbatore plateau which rises to a height of 2,500 to 3,000 feet is bordered on the south by a chain of lofty hills (over 3,600 feet) some of which have peaks rising over 5,500 feet.[2]

The Bargur forests can be divided into two types; sub-montane forests from 800 to 1,200 feet above sea level extending as a narrow strip at the

[1] *Working Plan for the Kollegal Forest Division* 1942–43 *to* 1957–58 by V. S. Krishnaswami, pages 1–3.

[2] *Working Plan for the North Coimbatore Forest Division* 1932 *to* 1942 by C. R. Ranganathan, page 1.

foot of the Bargur hills and the forests on the plateau situated on higher altitudes. The sub-montane forests consist of a degraded scrub with thorny species, stunted, open and almost xerophytic (excessively dry). Their soil is generally shallow, hard and stony, and they have commonly blanks. Their chief species are *Acacia latronam* (Kodavelam), *Acacia leucophloea* (Velvalem), *Acacia sundra* (Karungali), *Albizzia amara* (Unjal), *Azadirachta indica* (Vepam), *Balsamodendron berryi* (Kiluvai), *Cordia monoica* (Salle), *Chloroxylon suietenia* (Porasu), *Commiphoyra cauoata* (Pachavuluvai), *Canthium didymum* (Theranai), *Dichrostachys cinerea* (Vedathalan), *Erythoroxylon monogynum* (Sembulichan), *Gyrocarpus jaquini* (Thanakku), *Harwickia binata* (Valambiri), *Morinda tinctoria* (Manjavathi), *Zizyphus jujuba* (Elandai), *Zizyphus trinervia* (Karakatan) and *Zizyphus xylopyrus* (Rotti, kottai). The common undergrowth met with in them are *Carrissa caran las* (Kilakkai), *Cassia auricalata* (Avaram), *Dodonaea viscosa* (Virali), *Grewia hirusta* (Kalunnu, Tavidu), *Pterolobium indicum* (Indu), *Randia dumetorum* (Madu karai), *Solanum pubescens* (Sundai), *Toddalia garcilis* and *Zizyphus oenoplia* (Chooraimullu). The forests on the outer slopes of the plateau in higher altitudes contain the following chief species; *Aldizzia amara* (Unjal), *Acacia leucopholoea* (Velvelam), *Anogeissus latifolia* (Vellanagai), *Atalantia monophylla* (Kattelumichai), *Bambusa arndinacea* (Perumoongal), *Careya ardorea* (Ayma), *Cochlospermum gossypium* (Kongilavam), *Dendrocalamus strictus* (Kalmoongal), *Grewia tiliaefolia* (Thadasu), *Harwickia dinata* (Valambiri) *Pterocarpus marsuipium* (Vengai) *Terminalia chebula* (Kadukkai) and *Zizyphus zylopyrus* (Rotti, Kottai). Their undergrowth consist mainly of *Acacia intsia* (Ingai), *Acacia pennata* (Kari Indu), *Grewia hirsuta* (Kalunnu, Tavidu), *Phoenix acaulis* (Icham), and *Randia dumetorum* (Madukarai).[1]

The forests on the plateau in altitudes of 2,000 to 3,600 feet contain sandal. The species met with in the sandal zone are *Acacia leucopholoea* (Velvelam), *Acacia sundra* (Karungali), *Albizzia amara* (Unjal), *Albizzia lebbck* (Vagai), *Albizzia Odoritissima* (Salevagai), *Anogeissus latifolia* (Vellanagai), *Atalantia monophylla* (Kattelumichai), *Bambusa aruddinacea* (Perumoongal), *Bauhinia racemosa* (Athi), *Canthium didymum* (Theranai), *Chloroxylon swietenia* (Porasu), *Dendrocalamus strictus* (Kalmoongal), *Dichrostachys cinerea* (Vedathalan), *Diospyros melanoxylon* (Karumthumbi), *Diospyros montana* (Vakkanai), *Erythroxylon monogynum* (Sembulichan), *Elacodendron glaucum* (Kannir Maram), *Feronia elephantum* (Velam), *Gmelina arborea* (Kumil), *Grewia tilaefolia*(Thadasal),

1 *Working Plan for the Kollegal Forest Division* 1942–43 to 1957–58 by V. S. Krishnaswami, pages 2–3.

Holoptelea integrifolia (Aya), *Ixora parvifolia* (Sulundurvaram), *Mimusops hexandra* (Kanupala), *Polyalthia creasoies* (Nedunnari), *Pongamia glabra* (Pungam), *Prejna tomentosa* (Kolakattai teku), *Pterocarpus marsupium* (Vengai), *Sapinus emarginatus* (Naikottai), *Soymida febrifuga* (Soma), *Strychnos potatorum* (Tettan maram), *Vitex altssima* (Mailaei) and *Zizyphus xylopyrus* (Rotti, Kottai). The undergrowth which occurs in the sandal zone is mainly *Acalypha fruticosa* (Chinni), *Argyreia* species, *Capparis* species, *Cariassa carandas* (Kilakkai), *Cassia* species, *Chomelia asiatica* (Therani), *Cipadessa baccifera* (Savattu chedi), *Dodonaca viscosa* (Usali), *Flueggca leucopyrus* (Veppalam), *Indigofera pulchella* (Avari), *Lantana camara* (Arippu), *Pterolobium indicum* (Indu), *Randia dumetorum* (Madukarai), *Scutia indica* (Thoratti) and *Zizyphus Oenoplia* (Chooraimullu). The present condition of the sandal trees in these forests is not very satisfactory; the spike disease is seen in the Thattakerai and Tamarakerai plateaux of the Bargur range; and especially near Ondani and Eratty enclosures, the disease has practically exterminated sandal.[1]

Generally between 2,000 and 4,500 feet on the plateau a miscellaneous type of growth is met with. This may be divided into two sub-types, namely, the superior deciduous type or the timber type (altitude 3,000 to 4,000 feet) and the inferior deciduous type (altitude 2,000 to 3,500 feet), mostly open scrub degenerating into the bush type of formation with occasional trees. Teak, which belongs to the superior deciduous type, is found near Naikerai and around Tamarakerai, Talakerai and Dolli enclosures as well as the Athimalai enclosure with a mixture of *Pterocarpus* marsupium and *Dalbergia latifolia* (Itti), but the trees are, as a rule, stunted, unsound and misshapen due to repeated injuries by natural and other agencies. The inferior deciduous type occurs on the lower slopes of the hills and in the villages. The growth in this type is very often degenerating into bushes interspersed by large blanks with occasional trees. The forest floor is bare, stony and with no humus and little depth in the soil. The trees are poor in height and girth. These forests usually serve as grazing grounds and most of the fuel series have been laid out only in this type. The common species of this type are *Albizzia amara* (Unjal), *Albizzia lebbek* (Vagai), *Albizzia Odoratissima* (Salevagai), *Acacia intsia* (Ingai), *Acacia leucophloea* (Velvelam), *Acacia sundra* (Karungali), *Anogeissus latifolia* (Vellangai), *Atalantia monophylla* (Kattelumichai), *Azadirachta indica* (Vepam), *Balsomodendron berryi* (Kiluvai), *Bambusa arundinacea* (Perumoongal), *Bauhinia racemosa* (Athi), *Boswellia serrata*

[1] *Working Plan for the Kollegal Forest Division* 1942–43 *to* 1957–58 by V. S. Krishnaswami, page 3.

(Kungiliam), *Bridelia retusa* (Mullu vengai), *Cassia auriculata* (Avaram), *Cassia fistula* (Konnai), *Canthium didymum* (Theranai), *Chloroxylon swietenia* (Porasu), *Cochlospermum gossypium* (Kongilavam), *Dalbergia latifolia* (Ithi), *Dalbergia paniculata* (Panchalan), *Dendrocalamus strictus* (Kal-moongal), *Dichrostacys cinerea* (Vedathalan), *Dodonaca viscosa* (Virali), *Diospyros melanoxylon* (Karumthumbi), *Diospyros montana* (Vakkanai), *Erythroxykon monogynum* (Sembulichan), *Flacourtia* species, *Fleggea leucopyrus* (Veppalam), *Gmelina arborea* (Kumil), *Govotia rottleriformis* (Buthala), *Hardwickia binata* (Achan), *Helicteres isora* (Valambiri), *Holoptella integrifolia* (Aya), *Kydia calycina* (Vandai), *Magnifera indica* (Mamaram), *Morinda citrifolia* (Nona), *Opuntia dillenii* (Sapathi Kalli), *Phoenix acaulis* (Icham), *Phyllanthus emblica* (Nelli), *Premna tomentosa* (Kolakkattai teku), *Protium caudatum* (Mala Kiluvai), *Pterolobium indicum* (Indu), *Pterocarpus marsupium* (Vengai), *Randia* species, *Rhus mysorensis* (Chippamaram), *Semecarpus anacardium* (Sarengottai), *Scheleichera trijuga* (Puvam), *Soymida febrifuga* (Soma), *Stephegyne parvifolia* (Nir Kadambe), *Tamarindus indica* (Puliyan maram), *Terminalia bellerica* (Thani), *Terminalia chebula* (Kadukkai), *Terminalia paniculata* (Pillamarudu), *Terminalia tomentosa* (Karimarudu), *Tectona grandis* (Thekku), *Vitex altissima* (Mailadi), *Wrightia tinctoria* (Palai), *Zizyphus jujuba* (Elandai), *Zizyphus Oenoplia* (Chooraimullu), and *Zizyphus xylopyrus* (Kottai, Kotti). *Shorea talura* (Jalari maram), is confined to higher elevations, *Hardwickia binata* (Achan) occurs in elevations below 2,500 feet on the fireswept low hill slopes, while bamboo (both *Dendrocalamus strictus* (Kal-moongal) and *Bambusa arundinacrea* (Perumoongal) is found generally in elevations below 3,500 feet. The Bargur range has 48,189 acres of bamboo. [1]

On higher altitudes between 4,000 and 6,000 feet lie the shola or evergreen type of forests. They lie on the Bodamalai and Kardianaioddu of the Bargur range and generally present the following species : *Acrocarpus fraxinifolias* (Malankonnai), *Amoora rohituka* (Vella Kongu), *Artocarpus integrifolia* (Pila), *Bischofia javanica* (Milachadayan), *Canarium strictum* (Karun Kungilium), *Cedrela toona* (Madagiri Vembu), *Cinnamomum litseaefolium*, *Cinnamomum sulphuratum*, *Elaeodendron glaucum* (Kannirmaram), *Eleocarpus* species, *Garuga pinnata* (Arunelli), *Ligustrum roxburghii*, *Ligustrum decaisnei*, *Litsea floribunda*, *Litsea ligustrine*, *Macaranga roxburghii* (Vatta), *Machilus macrantha* (Kollai mavu), *Mesua ferrea* (Nangu), *Michelia champaca* (Shanbagam), *Nephelium longana* (Shampuvan), *Olea glandulifera* (Kundai), and *Palaquium ellipticum* (Palvadinjan).[2]

---

[1] *Working Plan for the Kollegal Forest Division* 1942–43 *to* 1957–58 by V. S. Krishnaswami, pages 3–4.

[2] *Idem*, page 4.

The North Coimbatore plateau forests are, as a whole, composed of mixed deciduous species of poor growth and height. In a few favoured and naturally protected localities, however, they attain the density and dimensions of high forests; and the abundant occurrence of sandal in them redeems them from insignificance. They may be divided into three types, namely, sub-montane forests occupying the ' bays ' of plains, intruding into the hill ranges locally known as ' combais ' or foot-hills and margins of the plains; the forests on the outer slopes; and the highland forests which exhibit in themselves several types. The sub-montane forests (800 to 1,200 feet elevation) extend in a narrow strip along the foot-hills of the plateau and in the ' combais ' from the Moyar basin on the west to the Palamalais of the Salem district on the east. They adjoin the cultivation on the plains and are at various points close to the towns of Satyamangalam, Anthiyur, Bhavani and Gobichettipalayam. They contain all the fuel-felling series and nearly all their accessible area is under fuel working. They are also intensively grazed over, with the result that their soil has become exposed and barren in patches, as well as hard and caked, a condition inimical to the germination of seed and natural regeneration. Their soil is also shallow, often stony and of poor quality unfit for cultivation. They are, in fact, degraded, almost xerophytic, open scrub of low density and stunted growth. Along the numerous stream beds that traverse them, a denser but still stunted semi-evergreen type of vegetation is found, consisting of *Mangifera indica* (Mamaram), *Terminalia chebula* (Kadukkai), *Vitex altissima* (Mayiladi), *Tamarindus indica* (Puliyamaram), *Elaedendron glancum* (Kanniramaram), *Eugenia jambolana* (Naval), etc. Their chief species are *Albizzia amara* (Unjal), *Acacia latronum* (Anaimullu), *Acacia leuocophloea* (Velvelam), *Gyrocarpus americanus* (Thanaku), *Balsamodendron berryi* (Mulkilavai), *Dichrostachys cineria* (Vedathalai), *Zizyphus trinervia* (Kottai-elandai), *Atalantia monophylia* (Kattelumichai), *Cordia monoica* (Narivalli), *Ziziphus xylopyrus* (Kottaielandadi), *Ziziphus jujuba* (Elandai), *Melia Azadirachta* (Veppam), *Sapindus emarginata* (Naikottai), *Chloroxylon swietenia* (Porasu), *Pterocarpus marsupium* (Vengai), *Acacia Catechu, Erythroxylon monogymum* (Sembulichan), *Protium caudatum* (Pachakiluvai), *Morinda tinctoria* (Nona), *Hardwickia binata* (Acha), *Strychnos nux-vomica* (Etti), *Mangifera indica* (Mamaram), *Tamarindus indica* (Puliyamaram), *Terminalia arjuna* (Nirmaddi), *Eugenia jambolina* (Naval), *Dalbergia paniculata* (Porapatchalai), *Elaeodendron glaucum* (Kannirmaram), *Vitex altissima* (Mayiladi), *Grewia asiatica* (Palica), *Premna tomentosa* (Kolakkattaitheku), and *Ailanthus malabarica* (Mattipal). Of these, *chloroxylon swietenia*

(Porasu) is illicitly and heavily felled as it is prized by the ryots for agricultural implements. *Hardwickia binata* (Acha) which generally favours higher elevations (1,500 to 2,000 feet), occurs in these lower elevations only here and there, as, for instance, in the Moyar Valley and the slopes facing Dodda Combai in Talamalai. Sandal is present here in a very limited quantity; it is mostly young, rarely more than 15 inches in girth and has evidently recently spread from the plateau to these areas. Tamarind is fairly common everywhere in this type, but in the Bhavani range, especially in Peria Combai, it is almost gregarious, large numbers of trees being found in compact areas. Besides grasses, the undergrowth of this type is almost entirely of throny kind. It chiefly consists of *Opuntia dillen* (prickly pear), *Randia dumetorum* (Karai), *Zizyphus oenoplia* (Churaimullu), *Capparis* species, *Solanum pubescens* (Sundai), *Acacia intsia* (Indu), *Pterlobium indicum* (Karu Indu), *Grewia hirsuta* (Kalunnu, Tavidu), *Lantana camara* (Puchedi), *Toddalia aculeata* (Kattumilagu), *Dodonae viscosa* (Virali), *Cassia auriculata* (Avaram), and *Fluggea leucopyrus* (Veppula). Prickly pear is a serious pest in these forests.[1]

The forests on the outer slopes of the plateau (1,200 to 4,000 feet elevation) constitute an extensive, rocky, ill-protected and unproductive zone. In the neighbourhood of Galidimbum, the slopes consist of a series of steep stony cliffs with hardly any vegetation except grass; the growth is here confined to the margins of stream beds and is of no importance. Further west, beyond the Ramarakandi Malais, the slopes become more gradual and carry a somewhat denser jungle; but generally speaking, the growth steadily improves only as we go towards the east. The poverty of the growth in the greater part of the outer slopes is due to the prevalence of fires. These areas are burnt wilfully every year; and the steeper the slope, the more extensive has been the damage done by fires. The soil is here generally very shallow and often absent, there being numerous outcrops of bare rock. The chief species occurring on the outer slopes are *Albizzia amara* (Unjal), *Acacia leucophloea* (Velvalem), *Anogeissus latifolia* (Vellanagai), *Terminalia chebula* (Kadukkai), *Cochlospermum gossypium* (Kongilavam), *Gyrocarpus americanus* (Thanaku), *Boswellia serrata* (Kungiliam), *Hardwickia binata* (Achan), *Elaeodendron glawcum* (Kannirmaram), *Dichrostachys cinera* (Vedathalam), *Balsomodendron berryi* (Kiluvai), *Protium caudatum* (Malakiluvai), *Zizyphus xylopyrus* (Rotti, Kottai), *Pterocarpus marsupium* (Vengai), *Phyllanthus emblica* (Nelli), *Kydia calicina* (Vendai), *Erioloena quinquelocularis* (Vatta unam), *Dalbergia paniculata* (Panchalan), *Atalantia*

1 *Working Plan for the North Coimbatore Forest Division* 1932 to 1942 by C. R. Ranganathan pages 15-17.

monophylla (Kattelumichai), *Zizyphus jujuba* (Elandai), *Acacia catechu*, *Buchanania latifolia* (Saraiparuppu), *Givotia rottleriformis* (Boothalai), *Wrightia tinctoria* (Palai), *Moringa concanensis* (Kari murungai), *Erythrina indica* (Murukku), *Dendrocalamus strictus* (Kal-moongal), *Bambusa arundinacea* (Perumungal), and *Stereospermum suaveolens* (Padiri), *Hardwickia binata* (Achan) occurs at elevations between 1,500 and 2,000 feet in more or less gregarious patches in many places on the outer slopes. The slopes facing the Periacombai in the Bhavani range carry a fair growth of these species of which trees over 4 feet in girth and 25 feet in height are common. Bamboos are absent as a rule from the outer slopes of the Talamalai range. They, however, occur at elevations above 2,000 feet on the slopes of the Periapallam near Kavalur and on the Periacombai slopes in the Bhavani range. The undergrowth of these forests is often only grass (*Andropogan* species and *Symbopogan* series). In denser areas *Zizyphus oenoplia* (Chooraimullu), *Acacia pennata* (Vellai Indu), *Acacia intsia* (Indu), *Phoenix acaulis* (Icham), *Grewia hirsuta* (Kalunnu, Tavidu) and prickly pear are found.[1]

The highland forests range in elevations from 2,000 to 5,000 feet and form an extensive tract carrying a diversified flora. They can be divided into the following specific types ; the *Anogeissus* type, the sandal type, the shorea talura type, the semi-evergreen type, the teak type, the high forest type, the shola type and the bamboo type. The *Anogissus* type occurs extensively at elevations between 2,500 and 3,500 feet on the flat or undulating country and on the lower slopes of hills on the plateau. In character and composition it closely resembles the sandal type, except that sandal is absent in it on account of frequent fires. It follows therefore that, given fire protection, the *Anogeissus* areas will become sandal bearing areas in due course. These forests form a fringe around the sandal zone and can be found nearly everywhere on the plateau. They mark a stage between the sandal zone and the semi-evergreen type which are both comparatively immune from fire. In the Talamalai range they occur chiefly on the low range of hills which divide the Talamalai-Higgalur plain from Tiganarai, Kalbandipuram, etc. They are to be seen also to the north of the *Shorea talure* (Kungiliam) area around Onnaithittu in the old Gerhatti and Vanavasi Dodelis. As they occupy the lower slopes of hills and adjoin villages, they are subject to heavy grazing. Their crop is open scrub, often degenerating into sparse bushes and occasional trees composed of a variety of species. Their soil is without a layer of humus and their trees are rarely over four feet in girth ; and yet these trees serve

1 *Working Plan for the North Coimbatore Forest Division* 1932 *to* 1942 by C. R. Ranganathan, pages 17–18.

well for agricultural implements in the neighbouring villages. The species commonly met within them are *Anogeissus latifolia* (Vellanagai). *Terminalia chebula* (Kadukkai), *Zizyphus xylopyrus* (Rotti, Kottai), *Acacia leucophloea* (Velvelam), *Canthium didymum* (Theranai), *Chloroxylon sweitenia* (Porasu), *Pterocarpus marsupium* (Vengai), *Albizzia odoratissima* (Salevagai), *Erythroxylon monogynum* (Sembulichan), *Premna tomentosa* (Kolakattaiteku), *Dalbergia paniculata* (Panchalan), *Randia dumetorum* (Karai), *Diosphros montana* (Vakkanai), *Eloeodendron glaucum* (Kaannira-maram), *Buchanania latifolia* (Saraiparuppu), *Bridelia retusa* (Mullu-vengai), *Albizzia amara* (Unjal), *Bassia latifolia* (Iluppai), *Kydia calycina* (Vendai), *Gardenia gummifera* (Kambili), *Erioloena quinquelocularis* (Vatta unam), *Grewia tilioefolia* (Thadachi), *Soymida febrifuga* (Sombu-pattai), *Dalbergia sissoides*, *Albizzia lebbek* (Vagai), *Diospyros melanoxylon* (Karumuthumbi), *Chlospermum rottleriformis*, *Terminalia belerica* (Thani), *Pongamia glabra* (Pungam), *Vitex altissima* (Mailadi), *Terminalia tomentosa* (Karimarudu), *Wrightia tinctoria* (Palai), *Cassia fistula* (Konnai), *Semecarpus anacardium* (Serangottai), *Schleichera trijuga* (Puvam), *Schrebera swietenioides* (Magalingam), *Dendrocalamus strictus* (Kalmoongal), *Bambusa arundinacea* (Perumoongal), and *Acacia Catechu*. The undergrowth of these forests consists of *Dodonoea viscosa* (Virali), *Grewia hirsuta* (Kallunnu, Tavidu), *Helicteres isora* (Valambiri), *Fleggea leucopyrus* (Veppalam), *Flacourtia* species, *Jasminum angustifolium* (Kattumalligai), *Zizyphus oenoplia* (Chooraimullu), *Pterolobium indicum* (Indu), *Phoenix acaulis* (Icham), *Urena lobata* (Ottatti), *Cassia auriculata* (Avaram), *Gymnosporia montana* (Kattangi) and grass.[1]

The sandal type forests occur chiefly on the flat or undulating plateau at elevations between 2,500 and 3,200 feet. Sandal is also found on the Geddesal-Mavahalla-Kotadai plateau at 4,000 feet elevation as well as at much lower altitudes, for example, in the Moyar valley. Its main habitat where the optimum conditions for its growth and spread are found is the Talamalai—Higgalur plain, the Hassanur valley, and the Yekkatur and Gundri plateau. It occurs in a fringe round villages and clearings and tends to become more and more scarce as we go further from the enclosures. It grows in patches of varying density and size, in almost all types of soil and under different conditions of rainfall. The main factors which operate as effective check to its spread are grazing and repeated fires. *Lantana* (Unni) and *Scutia indica* (Kokkimullu) are found to be excellent nurses for its seedlings. Birds and flood waters of the streams are undoubtedly important agents for its dispersal. The species that occur

---

1 *Working Plan for the North Coimbatore Forest Division* 1932 *to* 1942 by C. R. Ranganathan, pages 18–19.

in the sandal zone are, *Canthium didymum* (Thuanai). *Chloroxylon swietenia* (Porasu), *Erythroxvlon monogynum* (Sembulichan), *Premna tomentosa* (Kolakkattaiteku), *Zizyphus xylopyrus* (Rotti, Kottai), *Acacia leucophloea* (Velvelam), *Atalantia monophylla* (Kattelumichai), *Strychnos potatorum* (Thethankottai), *Ixora parviflora* (Sulundu), *Pterocarpus marsupium* (Vengai), *Bridelia retusa* (Mullu Vengai), *Pongamia glabra* (Pungam), *Grewia* species, *Albizzia Odoritissima* (Salevagai), *Anogeissus latifolia* (Vellanagai), *Terminalia chebula* (Kadukkai), *Polyalthia cerasoides* (Nedunarai), *Linociera malabarica* (Porumbolu), *Feronia elephantum* (Velam), *Randia dumetorum* (Karai), *Limonia acidissima* (Kattelumichai), *Buchanania latifolia* (Saraiparuppu), *Acacia ferruginea* (Parambai), *Acacia catechu*, *Albizzia amara* (Unjal), *Dalbergia paniculata* (Panchalan), *Bambusa arundinacea* (Perumoongal), *Diospyros montana* (Vakkanai), *Vitex altissima* (Mailadi), *Holoptelea integrifolia* (Aya), *Soymida febrifuga* (Soma), *Lagerstrolmia parviflora* (Paikadukkai), *Albizzia lebbek* (Vagai), *Eloedendron glancum* (Kanniramaram), *Diospyros melanoxylon* (Karumthumbi), *Gmelina arborce* (Kunnil), *Pittosporum floribundum* (Kattusampangi), *Olea dioica* (Idalai), *Ligustrum* species, *wendlandia notoniana* (Kadambam), *Mimusops hexandra* (Kanupala), *Gardenia gummifera* (Kambili), and *Zizyphus jujuba* (Elandai), The undergrowth here consists of *Toddalie aculeata* (Milagucharanai), *Webera corymbos.* (Therani), *Opuntic dillenii* (Sapathikalli), *Laptane camara* (Aruppu), *Pterolobium indicum* (Indu), *Gymnosporia montana* (Kattangi) *Grewia hirsuta* (Kalunnu, Tavidu), *Fiuggea leucopyrus* (Veppalam), *Flacourtia* species, *Acalypha fruticosa* (Chinni), *Argyreia* species, *Dodonoea Viscosa* (Virali), *Indigofera pulchellu* (Narinchi), *Carissa* species, *Capparis* species, *Memecylon edule* (Kayan, Kayala, Kasan), *Cipadessa fruticosa* (Savattuchedi), *Jatrophe cureas* (Katamanakku) *Cassia* species, *Barleria buxifolia* (Kattumulla), *Euphorbia tirucalli*, (Tirucalli), *Sarcostemme brevistigma* (Kodikalli), *Secamone emetica* (Angaravalli), *Hipatage madablota* (Karipakkukodi), and *Scutia indica.*[1] (Kokkimullu, Thoratti).

The condition of the sandal trees is different in different localities. In the Talamalai reserve, sandal is found in large numbers, but the trees are generally unhealthy. Around the Talamalai enclosure many of the trees have been reduced to extreme stages of stagheadedness ; the crown is generally poorly developed and the leaves are small and yellowish green in colour. To the south of the Jeeragahalli rest house, the trees are stagheaded and attacked by borers. To the north of Jeeragahalli, near Varadabetta and adjoining Kalabandipuram, the trees are healthy and

1 *Working Plan for the North Coimbatore Forest Division* 1932 to 1942 by C. R Ranganathan, page 21.

well grown. In the neighbourhood of Higgalur enclosure, though the trees grow well and densely, they are attacked by spike. In the eastern half of the Akkurjorai reserve, which is a small island of forest surrounded on all sides by cultivation, the trees grow dense and healthy ; so also do they grow well in the unreserves along its eastern and south-eastern boundaries. In the Satyamangalam range, well grown sandal is found in the Hassanur valley, but this area has been repeatedly ravaged by spike. On the Geddesal plateau where sandal was artificially introduced in 1904, the tree grows luxuriantly with thick, large, dark-green leaves and big fruits; this area has been free from spike till now. On the Kotadai plateau however where there is natural growth, the trees are unhealthy and extensively attacked by spike. On the Yekkatur plateau, the trees near Karumbur, Yekkatur, Karlia and Ullepalayam are often stagheaded, but the growth is on the whole better than the Talamalai sandal trees. Near Kadahatti towards the north-east and Attiyur, towards the south-west, the tree grows very well. Along the Haleruhalla some very fine sandal is to be found; and the Gundri plateau is remarkable for its fine, well grown healthy sandal.[1]

Generally the natural regeneration of sandal is adequate. In the Barabetta reserve and in portions of the Cutialattur reserve near Kotadai and Hassanur, the regeneration is profuse. It is believed that the germination of sandal seed takes place most freely on freshly turned loam, that the presence of humus or manure acts adversely on germinating seeds, that the seedlings grew well in the shelter of thorny bushes and that the trees standing in the open or patta lands bear heavier seed crop than those in the reserve. As to the production of heartwood or scented wood, the outturn of such wood from trees of the same girth shows marked variations from place to place, and even within the same place. Trees of 24 inches in girth have sometimes been found to be pure sapwood. It may, however, be stated as a general rule that proportionately more heartwood is found in elder trees growing on poor, dry, rocky soils and under adverse conditions than in younger trees of the same girth in moist and favourable localities and in trees with a thick, *suberized* (cork-like) fissured bark, *exfoliating* (peeling) in patches, than in trees with a smooth bark.[1]

The *Shorea talura* (Kungiliam) type forests occur on steep slopes at elevations between 3,000 and 4,000 feet, generally above 3,000 feet in localities which are heavily and frequently fired. The species grows in gregarious patches of varying but small size over an area of 3,000 acres on the hill slopes around Onnaithittu the south-easterly slopes of the

1 *Working Plan for the North Coimbatore Forest Division*, 1932 to 1942 by C. R. Ramanathan, pages 22–23.

Surabarbetta, the easterly slope towards the Odurkuttaihalla and the slopes rising from the Alamarahalla and Dasarihalla. The species is practically confined to the Talamalai range. A few trees are, however, found on the top of Araikanbetta,north of Hassanur in the Satyamangalam range and near Karimathanboli in the Bhavani range. Several of the *Shorea* patches are pure dense 'stands', notably the patch on the Surabarbetta, and the one near Mavanatham. Elsewhere the species forms about a third of the tree crop and is associated with *Pterocarpus* marsupium (Vengai), *Terminalia chebula* (Kadukkai), *Anogessus latifolia* (Vekkali, Namai), an occasional teak, *Albizzia odoratissima* (Karu Vagai, Sila Vagai), and *Buchanania latifolia* (Saraiparuppu). The undergrowth of these forests consists of *Phoenix acaulis* (Ichampal), grass, and *grewia hirsuta* (Kalunnu, Tavidu). The *Shorea* regeneration is very good in all areas. Fire evidently helps the regeneration while killing the parent trees, possibly because the seeding takes place after the fire season and the seeds fall on a good, well-burnt, germinating bed. The species is, however, badly attacked by a Longicorn borer.

The semi-evergreen type of forests appears at 3,500 to 4,000 feet elevation. It is characteristic of the region round Onnathittu which abounds in undulating hills traversed by numerous streamlets. These forests are generally dense with a more or less complete canopy and a humus soil forming a mass of climber-bound tanglewood. In their open portions grass grows abundantly. The species of the *Oleaceae* (*olea, Ligustrum*) occur in them commonly. Big trees of *Pterocarpus marsupium* (Vengai) are to be found in them here and there and associated with it are *Canthium didymum* (Navugu), *Canthium neilgherrense Vitex altissima* (Mayiladi), *Eugenia jambolina* (Naga, Nava, Naval), *Mangifera indica* (Mamaram), *Albizzia odoratissima* (Karu vagai), *Grewia tilioefolia* (Thadachi), *Trema Orientalis* (Amparuthi), *Terminalia chebula* (Kadukkai) and *Anogeissus latifolia* (Vekkali). *Gmelina arborea* (Kumalan), occurs in them occasionally. The undergrowth in them is chiefly grass and *Lantana* (Puchedi, Arippu, Unni), and *Pgoenix acaulis* (Ichampul), patches.[2]

The teak type of forests occurs on elevations between 3,200 and 3,600 feet. Teak is found in deciduous scrub forests on the ridges and on the gentle hill slopes of the plateau. It is also found near Tattavadi and Karaipalayam in the Satyamangalam range. It is likewise found here and there near Hulikerai west of Hassanur and on the hills round

---

1 *Working Plan for the North Coimbatore Forest Division*, 1932–42 by C. R. Ranganathan pages, 23.

2 *Idem*.

Onnai-thittu. But in none of these places is it plentiful enough to be commercially significant. A somewhat better type of teak is found in the Bhavani range on the Yethnibetta near Talakerai. The species is fire-hardy and is associated with other fire hardy species like *Buchanania latifolia* (Saraiparuppu), *semecarpus anacardium* (Serankottai, Shenkottai), *Terminalia chebula* (Kadukkai), *Phyllanthus emblica* (Nelli), *Bridelia retusa* (Mulvengai), *Anogessue latifolia* (Vekkali), *Shorea talura* (Kungiliam), *Pterocarpus marsupium* (Vengai) and *Gmelina* (Kumalan). It is rarely found in localities where the crop tends to close up and form high forest. It exhibits, however, splendid powers of natural regeneration. In the Tattavadi locality, for instance, teak regeneration is superb, but it never comes to anything on account of the regular fires that sweep the area.[1]

The high forest type, excluding the sholas which are separately described, is found in the Minchiguli Valley (elevation 4,000 feet) and parts of the area between the Tattavadihalla and the Mysore State frontier in the Gutialattur reserve. It consists of the following species ; *Terminalia tomentosa* (Karimarudu), *Dalbergia latifolia* (Itti), *Pterocarpus marsupium* (Vengai), *Grewia tilaoefolia* (Thadachi) *Phylanthus emblica* (Nelli), *Kydia calycine* (Vendai), *Albizzia Odoratissima* (Karu Vagai), *Stereospermum chelonoides* (Padiri), *Terminalia belerica* (Thani), *Terminalia chebula* (Kadukkai), *Bridelia retusa* (Mulvengai), *Agnogeissue latifolia, Michilus maerantha, Cinnamomum zeylanicum* (Lavangam), *Eugenia jembolina* (Naga, Nava), *Atalantia monophylla* (Kattuelimichai), *Mallotus philippinensis* (Kamala), *Magnifera indica* (Mamaram), *Cedrula toona* (Mala Vembu) *Bischofia javanica* (Milachadayan), *Michelia champaca* (Shanbagam), *Ixora parviflora* (Sulundu), *Strychnos potatorum* (Thethankottai), *Bombax malabaricum* (Elavamaram) and *Careya arborea* (Ayma). The undergrowth of this type of forest is, for the most part, a rank growth of sword grass often 15 feet high which chokes all other young vegetation. Under the dense groups of trees the floor is free from weeds and is covered with a wholesome layer of humus. In places where the tree growth is not too dense are found *Solanum giganteum* (Sambalkiluvai), *Grewia hirsuta* (Kalunnu), *Strobilanthes* (Kurunji), *Toddalia aculeata* (Milagacharani), *Rubus lasiocarpus* (Kolalindu), *Clerodendron infortunatum* (Vattakanni), and *Hiptage madablota* (Karipakkukodi). Bracken comes up gregariously after a fire but the tall grass soon overtakes and swamps it.[2]

---

1 *Working Plan for the North Coimbatore Forest Division*, 1932–42 by C. R Ranganathan, pages 23–24.

2 *Idem*, page 23.

The shola type of forests is met with almost exclusively in the Satyamangalam range, especially on the slopes of the Biligirirangans. Patches of them occur on the Kugavubetta and the ridge continuing therefrom and on the slopes of the Aiyangiribetta and Kanisiribetta around the Minchiguli valley. They are surrounded by extensive belts of grass land which is burnt almost annually. The crop is generally composed of the following species : *Eugenia jambolina* (Naga, Nava), *Machilus macrantha* (Kolarmavu), *Pittosporum floribundum* (Kattu Sampangi), *Cinnamomum zeylanicum* (Lavangam), *Mallatus philippinensis* (Kamala), *Bischofia javanica* (Milachadayan) *Cedrela toona* (Mala Vembu), *Mangifera indica* (Mamaram), *Atalantia monophylla* (Kattuelimichai), *Ligustrum walkeri*, *Olea dioica* (Idalai), *Celtis tetrandra* (Kuviya), *Albizzia marginata* (Nir usil), *Meliosnea wightii* (Todc), *Heynea trijuga* (Karikaru-Vilangam), *Salix ichnostachya*, Canthium didymum (Navugu), *Wendlandia notoniana* (Kadambam), *Acrocarpus fraxinifolius* (Malankonnai), *Eloeocarpus tuberculatus* (Pathrachi), and *Erythrina indica* (Murukku). The undergrowth of this type of forest consists of *Strobilanthes* (Kurunji), *Toddalia aculeata* (Milagucharani), *Cocculus laurifolius*, *Solanum giganteum* (Sambalkiluvai), *Pavutta indica* (Pavattai), *Callicarpa lanata* (Vettilai Batta), *Clerodendron infortunatum* (Vattakanni), *Citrus aurantium* (Narangam), *Rubus lasiocarpus* (Kolalindu), *Allophylus cobbe* (Sirusalle), *Acacia concinna* (Siyakayi), bracken and grass.[1]

The bamboo type of forests are very wide spread. The densest growth of bamboo is to be found on the outer slopes of the North Coimbatore plateau between 1,500 feet and 3,000 feet elevations. The main bamboo species is *Dandrocalamus strictus* (Kalmungil) but a proportion of *Bambusa arundinacea* (Peru mungil), is also found in most localities, more especially as a narrow fringe along streams and in swampy ground. The species associated with the bamboos are practically the same as those described in other types. The main bamboo areas are Vadaparai, Gundri plateau, Gutialattur enclosure and the Hassanur basin in the Satyamangalam range and Talamalai-Higgalur plain, Matam enclosure, Varuttu pallam watershed and Doddakombai in the Bhavani range.[2]

So much is about the forests of the North Coimbatore Division. The forests of the South Coimbatore Division comprise the forests of the Nilgiri slopes and the Thadagam hills, and the forests of the Bolampatty and Thadagam valleys in the west as well as the forests of the Anaimalais

1 *Working Plan for the North Coimbatore Forest Division*, 1932-42 by C. R. Ranganathan, pages 24–25.

2 *Idem*, page 25.

in the south. The forests of the Nilgiri slopes and the Thadagam hills demand no separate description, as the description already given for the forests of the North Coimbatore plateau is applicable to them also. The only additional point that need be mentioned here is that these forests of the Mettupalayam range contain sound sandal trees unattacked by spike as well as bamboo.

The forests of the Bolampatty and Thadagam Valleys, however, demand a separate description. In the Bolampatty Valley, the Coimbatore-siruvani road runs along the watershed which separate the streams that rise in the high south-western range of hills (5,500 to 6,500 feet) from those originating in the distinctly lower northern hills (4,000 to 5,000 feet). The forests to the south of this road are of a more moist type than those to its north. At the lower elevations to the south-west of the road is found a good growth of mixed deciduous species of superior quality. The more important of these species are *Albizzia lebbek* (Vagai), *Albizzia odoratissima* (Karu Vagai), *Albizzia procera* (Vel Vagai), *Terminalia paniculata* (Pillamarudu), *Grewia tiliaefolia* (Thadachi), *Pterocarpus marsupium* (Gengai), *Dalbergia latifolia* (Itti), *Lagerstroemia lancelata* (Venthekku), *Anogeissus latifolia* (Vellanagai) and on occasional teak. The soil is here light and deep and keeps moist for a longer period than in the area to the north of the road. The slopes up to about 3,500 feet support a similar type of forest, but with more teak, *Pterocarpus marsupium* (Vengai), *Anogeissus latifolia* (Vellanagai), *and Dalbergia latifolia* (Itti). Between 3,500 feet and 5,000 feet the tropical rain forest type prevails in which *Cullenia excelsa* (Vedipila), *Palaquium ellipticum* (Palvadinjan), *Galophyllum elatum* (Kattupinnai), *Acrocarpus fraxinifolius* (Malankonnai), *Vaterla macrocarua* and *Mesua ferrea* (Nangu), occur among other species. Above an elevation of 5,000 feet the vegetation degenerates into the high level shola (sub-tropical evergreen) of the comparatively stunted type. *Lantana* (Pucheddi) often forms an inpenetrable mass in many places and suppresses regeneration badly. Woody climbers such as *Spatholobus roxburghii*, *Butea superba* and *Derris* species stifle the growth in moist places. *Bambusa* of all sizes is the predominent bamboo but *Dendrocalamus* is found near rocky places. In the area to the North of the Coimbatore–Siruvani road, the prevailing species are the same but their height is considerably poorer and *Dendrocalamus* is the predominent bamboo. *Albizzia lebbek* (Vagai), *Albizzia odoratissima* (Salevagai) and *Terminalia paniculata* (Pillamarudu) gradually yield place to more teak, *Grewia, Tamarind, Melia indica, Erythroxylon monogynum* (Sembulichan), *Acacia latronum* (Odasithai), *Pterocarpus marsupium* (Vengai), *Zizyphus* species, and *Albizzia amara* (Unjal), *Mesua ferrea* (Nangu), *Calophyllum elatum* (Kattupinnai) and *Vateria macrocarpa* are among the chief species met with in these comparatively dry sholas from which *Palaquium* is practically absent.[1]

In the Thadagam Valley which is dry, the growth on the lower slopes consist of moderate sized trees of the deciduous fuel type, the chief species being *Albizzia amara* (Unjal), *Atalantia monophylla* (Kattuelimichai) *Ixora parvifolia* (Sulundu), *Canthium didymum* (Theranai), *Mundulea suberosa* (Pullavaram), *Chloroxylon swietenia* (Porasu), *Zizyphus* species, *Protium caudatum* (Malakiluvai), *Balsamodendron* species, *Euphorbia, Givotia* and *Gyrocarpus jacquini* (Thanaku). The quality degenerates as we proceed eastwards until at last it dwindles into thorny shrub, *Euphorbia* and *Dodonaca viscosa* (Virali). The middle slopes contain stunted fire-scarred trees of *Anogeissus latifolia* (Vekkali), *Pterocarpus marsupium* (Vengai), *Buchanania latifolia* (Saraiparuppu), *Dalbergia latifolia* (Itti) and *Termilnala chebula* (Kadukkai) among other species, with an under-growth of tall coarse grass. No bamboo of any kind is known to occur here. On the highest points a few patches of high level shola still survive the inroads of almost annual fires from the surrounding grass-land. The largest of these surrounds Perumalmudi peak and there is another patch of considerable size near the Melmudi Rangaswami temple. *Machilus, Litsea, Eugenia, Diospyros, Garcinia, Cinnamomum, Elaeocarpus, Calophyllum, Symplocos* and reed are here the most common genera. Beyond the western extremity of the valley, the ground rises to a plateau with a general elevation of about 2,500 feet and here the growth improves to a better type of mixed deciduous forest. Here are found *Anogeissus latifolia* (Vellanagai), *Albizzia lebbek* (Vagai), *Albizzia odoratissima* (Salevagai), *Albizzia amara* (Unjal), *Acacia leucophloea* (Velvelam) *Pterocarpus marsupium* (Vengai), *Terminalia chebula* (Kadukkai), *Atlantia monophylla* (Kattuelimichai) and a few badly grown teak. *Bambusa* and *Dendrocalamus* are both found, but more in the south than in the north *Lantana* and *Strobilanthes* form the chief undergrowth on the low slopes while coarse grass is common on the upper.[2]

The other forests of the Southern Division comprise mostly those the Anaimalais and are distributed in the Tunacadavu, Pollachi, Udumalp and Punachi ranges. Situated as they are in a tract exhibiting a wi variety of terrain and climate, with elevations ranging from 1,200 to on 8,000 feet and rainfall from 20 to over 200 inches, they bear a vegetatian of equally wide and striking variation. They vary from the luxury

---

1 *A Revised Working Plan for the forests of the Walayar, Bolampatty and Thada Valleys, Palghat Forest Division*, 1937–46 by T. V. Venkateswara Ayyar, page

2 *Idem*, pages 8–9.

tropical wet evergreen forests on the hills of the Punachi range to the tropical thorn forests (Scrub jungle) on the plains of the Udumalpet and Pollachi ranges. Some of them, such as those in the Gundran and Thorakadavu valleys, have suffered not a little by fires caused by abundance of high grass, while others have benefited by occasional fires, that have destroyed all offensive insect and fungus life. Some again have deteriorated on account of excessive grazing, lopping, unrestricted felling and shifting cultivation. It is to these destructive effects of man that we must trace the disappearance of dense forests which were said to be existing about two centuries ago on the plains of the Pollachi and Udumalpet taluks. The forest that now exist may be classified into the following types, the tropical wet evergreen forests, the southern tropical moist deciduous forests, the southern tropical dry deciduous forests, the southern wet temperate forests and the southern tropical thorn forests.[1]

The tropical wet evergreen forests are mainly confined to the Punachi range. In the Tunacadavu range they are found only in a few compact, isolated, patches in the Palakadavu, Ulandi and Mount Stuart blocks, the most accessible of these being Karianshola touching Topslip colony. In the Punachi range, they once occupied an area of about 150 square miles in a continuous stretch between 1,500 and 5,000 feet elevations, but half of them have now been cleared for planting tea. In some of them cinchona plantations are also now being raised by the Cinchona Department. Most of these forests usually occur in regions with elevations from 2,000 to 5,000 feet and with rainfall well over 80 inches. In exceptional cases, however, as for instance in the Karianshola near Topslip, they are found even in localities with an annual rainfall of 70 inches. The species that occur in them are numerous and the dominants attain a height of 150 feet or more. Canopy is extremely dense and there is a certain differentiation in it into layers and tiers. Some of the species such as *Poeciloneuron indicum* (Puthangali), exhibit typical blank buttresses. Epiphytes are numerous, especially aroids, ferns, mosses and orchids. Generally speaking, the chief species occuring in the top storey are *Mesua ferrea* (Nangu), *Poeciloneuron indicum* (Puthangali), *Palaquium ellipticum* (Palvadinjan), *Hopea parviflora* (Vellaikongu), *Cullenia excelsa* (Vedipila), *Calophyllum elatum* (Kattupinnai), *Vateria indica* (Vellaikundrikaru), *Heritiera papilio* (Soundalaiunnu), *Aglaia roxburghiana* (Vegulachokla), *Dysoxylum malabaricum* (Vellagil), *Eugenia* species, *Cedrela toona* (Malavembu), *Artocarpus integrifolia* (Pila), *Bombax malabaricum* (Elavamaram) *Canarium strictum* (Karunkungiliam), *Polyalthea* species, *Amoora*

[1] *Working Plan for the Coimbatore South Forest Division from* 1954–55 *to* 1968–69 by Sri K. A. Bhoja Shetty, Part I, paragraphs 21–22.

canarana (Karaqil) and many species of *Elaeocarpus*. In the second storey *Adenochlaena indica, Acronichia laurifolia* (Vidukanalai), *Cyclostemon macrophyllus Gomphandra polymorpha, Lasium anamalayanum* (Santhanaviri), *Macaranga* species, *Nephelium longana* (Shempuvan), and many species of *Litsaea* and *Myristica* are among the more prominent. The understorey is composed of *Laportea crenulata* (the devil's nettle), (Ottapila), *Psychotria* species, *Eugenia* species, *Calamus* species, Cardamom and reeds in most places and several species of *strobilanthes*. Different associations of the predominating species may be noticed in the topmost tier of the evergreen forests. Basing on such associations three more or loss distinct sub-types may be distinguished in the evergreen forests. The first of these sub-types is the comparatively dry type of Tunacadavu and Ulandi Blocks in which *Hopea parviflora* (Vellaikongu) and *Mesua ferrea* (Nangu), occur in appreciable quantities. The second is the intermediate type found in portions of the Punachi range in which *Mesua ferrea* (Nangu) and *Palaquium ellipticum* (Palvadinjan) predominate. The third is in the wet shola regions, as in the Italiar Valley of the Punachi range, in which *Poeciloneuron indicum* (Puthangali) with a small admixture of *Cullenia excelsa* (Vedipila) occurs in abundance. The natural regeneration of the timber species of these forests is generally plentiful, but usually remains suppressed for lack of opening of the canopy and proper tending. In the *Hopea-Meusa* association, natural regeneration of *Hopea parvifolia* (Vellaikongu) is dense and *Mesua ferrea* (Nangu) free. In the *Palaquium-Mesua* association natural regeneration of *Palaquium ellipticum* (Palvadinjan) is more prolific than that of *Mesua ferrea* (Nangu). In the *Poeciloneuron cullenia* association there is always a dense mass of natural regeneration of *Poeciloneuron indicum* (Puthangali). The undergrowth of these forests is generally sparse. In some patches a carpet of *Strobilanthes* and other ferns occur, in others canes, screw-pine, cardamoms and curcuma.[1]

The southern tropical moist deciduous forests are the most remunerative forests of the south and are mostly confined to the Tunacadavu range. They are distributed in regions with elevations ranging from about 1,500 feet to 3,500 feet and rainfall from 40 inches to 100 inches. They are high forests with trees over 100 feet in height. Their dominant species are mostly deciduous, and their understorey is composed mainly of evergreen shrubs. They contain timber trees of great economic value. Their top canopy consists of *Tectona grandis* (Thekku) which is of excellent development wherever the soil is suitable, and other species such as *Terminalia*

1 *Working Plan for the Coimbatore South Forest Division from* 1954–55 *to* 1968–69 by Sri K. A. Bhoja Shetty, Part I, paragraph 23.

tomentosa (Karimarudu), *Terminalia paniculata* (Pellamarudu), *Lagerstroemia lanceolata* (Venthekku), *Dalbergia latifolia* (Itti), *Pterocarpus marsupium* (Vengai), *Grewia tiliaefolia* (Thadachi), *Adina cordifolia* (Manjakadambai), *Xylia xylocarpa* (Irul), *Stereospermum Xylocarpum* (Kalpadiri), *Stereospermum chelonoides* (Padiri), *Stephegyne parvifolia* (Nirkambai), *Albizzia odoratissima* (Salevagai), *Schleichera trijuga* (Puvam), *Anogeissus latifolia* (Vekkali), *Bombax malabaricum* (Elavamaram), and *Dillenia pentagyna* (Naiteku). The understorey of these forests consists of plenty of *Bambusa arundinacea* (Perumungil) and *Zizyphus oenoplia* (Churaimullu), *Zizyphus xylopyrus* (Kottai), *Bauhinia malabarica* (Mandarai), *Bauhinia racemosa* (Athi), *Cassia fistula* (Konnai), *Macaranga roxburghii* (Vatta), *Sterculia villosa* (Kottaithanuku), and *Wrightia tinctoria* (Palai). Their undergrowth abounds in Lantana and elephant grass, especially in the teak plantations, both of which are a scourage, and also other species such as *Caesalpinia mimosoides* (Pulinakkagonnai) and species of *Desmodium, Hibiscus lampas* (Kattuparuthi), *Narvelia zylanica, Impatiens chinensis, Crotolaria dubia* and *glycosmis pentaphylla* (Anam). Artificial regeneration of teak in these forests is confined to moist deciduous regions and the bulk of the plantations lie in the Tunacadavu range, and only a small area in the Punachi range. The subsidiary species occurring naturally in the teak plantations are *Dalbergia latifolia* (Itti), *Lagerstroemia lanceolata* (Venthekku), *Grewia tiliaefolia* (Thadachi), *Terminalia tomentosa* (Karimaruthu), *Terminalia paniculata* (Pillamaruthu), *Xylia xylocarpa* (Irul) and *Bambusa arundinacea* (Perumungil). The undergrowth of the plantations mostly consists of low weeds and short grass.[1]

The southern tropical dry deciduous forests occur along the foot of the hills in the Pollachi range adjoining Sethumadai and in the lower Punachi and Thorakadavu blocks in the Punachi range. Both the upper and lower canopies of these forests consist mainly of deciduous species; and the canopies being rather open, there is usually considerable growth of grass. In the upper canopy is to be found *Tectona grandis* (thekku) with its common associates *Anogeissus latifolia* (Vekkali), *Terminalia tomentosa* (Karimarudu), and *Terminalia chebula* (Kadukkai). Other usual species met with here are *Terminalia belerica* (Thani), *Pterocarpus marsupium* (Vengai), *Lannea grandis* (Odiyamaram), *Bridelia retusa* (Mulvengai), *Dalbergia latifolia* (Itti), and occasionally *Bombax Malabarica* (Elavamaram). In the understorey both *Bambusa arundinacea* (Perumungil) and *Dendrocalamus* strictus (Kalmungil) occur, but the latter is

---

1 *Working Plan for the Coimbatore South Forest Division from* **1954–55 to 1968–69** **by Sri K. A. Bhoja Shetty, Part I, paragraphs 24–25.**

more common. Other species met with are *Cassia fistula* (Konnai), *Cleistanthus collinus* (Oduvan), *Butea frondosa* (Elaiporasu) and *Mallotus philippinensis* (Kamala). *Lantana* forms a dense undergrowth in certain localities while in others there is usually heavy grass.[1]

The southern wet temperate forests commence at about 5,000 feet elevation and are characteristic of the landscape of the Nilgiri, Anaimalai, Palni and other hill ranges of South India. In this district these forests are mostly confined to the upper reaches of the hills in the Punachi and Udumalpet ranges. They consist typically of vast stretches of grassland interrupted by numerous, isolated, compact small woods of evergreen trees. The trees are mostly short, boled and branchy; their heights are relatively low, rarely exceeding 50 to 60 feet. Their crowns are usually very dense and rounded with *coriaceous* leaves which tend to be red to a varying degree when young. These forests are exposed to winds and to fires from grass. The species commonly met with in them are *Bugenia* species, *Michelia nilgirica* (Kattushanbagam), *Elaeocarpus ferrugineus* (Pathrachi), *Euonymus indicus* (Nallakakidi), *Rhododendron arboreum* (Pumaram), *Mahonia leschenaultii* (Mullukadambu), *Eurya japonica* *Cinnamomum wightii* (Vettadu) and *Symplocos* species. Their undergrowth consists of *Strobilanthus* species, *Gaultheria fragrantissima*, *Impatiens* species, *Rebus* species and species of hill bamboos *Arundinaria wightiana* and *Oxytenanthera thwaitesii*; and their ground flora consists of a great wealth of ferns and mosses. It may be stated that over 5,000 feet in elevation, there are extensive grasslands and that in these grasslands are sometimes found scattered stunted shrubs like *Gaultheria fragrantissima* (Kolakkai), *Osbeckia* species and *Rhodomyrtus tomentosa* (Thavuttu Koyya).[2]

The southern tropical thorn forests, commonly known as scrub jungles, are confined to the plains portion of the division. Most of these are on flat ground or on low undulating hills and plateaux with elevations of 1,000 to 1,500 feet, in the eastern portion of the Pollachi range and over a large portion of the Udumalpet range. Their usual height is 20 to 30 feet and their lower stories consist of smaller trees and large shrubs mostly spiny and often with other *xerophytic* characters. Their soil is meagre and their undergrowth consists of light grasses like *Aristida* and *Hoterpogen*. Their species are mostly thorny trees like *Acacia latronun* (Odasithai) *Acacia leucophloea* (Velvelam), *Acacia arabica* (Karuvelam) *Dichrostachys*

---

1 *Working Plan for the Coimbatore South Forest Division from* 1954–55 *to* 1968–69 by Sri K. A. Bhoja Shetty, Part I, paragraph 26.

2 *Idem*, paragraphs 27–28.

cinerea (Vedathalam), *Azadirachta indica* (Veppam), *Gyrocarpus jacquini* (Thanaku), *Givotia rottleriformis*, *Hardwickia binata* (Acha), *Albizziaamara* (Unjal), *Zizyphus juba* (Elandai), *Zizyphus oenoplia* (Churaimullu), *Protium caudatum* (Pachakiluvai) and *Anogeissus latifolia*.[1]

Turning to the injuries to which the forests of the District are liable, the forests of both the Northern and the Southern divisions present the following picture. The Bargur forests are subject to high winds which have a dessicating effect on seedlings, to drought which dry up shoots of big trees as well as seedlings and to troublesome climbers like *Pterolobium indicum* (Karu Indu) and *acacia pennata* (Vellai Indu) which specially affect sandal. They are also subject to parasites like *Loranthus*, and *Cusent refloxa*, to the spike disease of sandal, to the overgrazing of cattle, to the free browsing of sambur, spotted deer, jungle sheep and hares, and to the fire and thefts of man.[2] The forests of the North Coimbatore plateau do not suffer much from high winds but they suffer much from drought and injuries caused by insects, climbers, spike, animals and man. In these forests, drought is the probable cause of the stagheadedness and retarded growth of sandal. The insect Jal borer attacks a large percentage of trees, especially the *Shorea talura* (Kungilium) in the Talamalai range. Several species of defoliators and borers attack sandal; several types of climbers also attack sandal, but the most virulent disease that attacks sandal is spike which kills trees outright within a period of two years of the attack. Cattle grass extensively, harden the soil, make it unsuitable for seed-bed, browse down tender seedlings or kill them by trampling. Elephants do damage to young trees in the Tattavadi and Minchiguli Valleys and around Makkampalayam and Gundri by pulling them down and breaking them. Bisons destroy young rosewood plants in the Minchiguli Valley. Sambur and deer eat away sandal leaves and rub off the bark from the young sandal trees. Hares nibble and destroy sandal seedlings, while rats, squirrels and fowls eat sandal fruit and minimise sandal regeneration. Man is, however, barring the spike, the worst sinner. He burns many portions of the forests either for cutting up forest paths, or for rendering the collection of minor produce (such as gall-nut and deer horn) easy,or for procuring a flush of young grass in burnt areas, or, again, for facilitating shooting by shikaris. He also resorts to illicit fellings for obtaining firewood or timber for making ploughs and agricultural implements. The fires caused by him have not only killed valuable

---

1 *Working Plan for the Coimbatore South Forest Division from* 1954–55 *to* 1968–69 by Sri K. A. Bhoja Shetty, Part I, paragraph 29.

2 *Working Plan for the Kollegal Forest Division* 1942–43 *to* 1957–58 by V. S. Krishnaswami, page 5.

trees like sandal but completely wiped out regeneration; and the thefts made by him have not only depleted the forests of valuable species like *Chloroxylon swietenia* (Porasu), *Acacia sundra* (Karungali) but also greatly hampered their regrowth.[1]

As to the Southern Division, what has been stated about the injuries to the forests of the North Coimbatore plateau applies to the forests of the Nilgiri slopes and the Thadagam hills also. The forests of the Bolampatty and Thadagam Valleys, however, have somewhat different problems to contend with. They are not subject to high winds or drought. Their plain portions are also generally free from fire, but their hill portions are subject to fires caused by graziers and collectors of minor produce. They are, besides, free from insects, but are infested by *lantana* and thorny climbers. Some of them are suffering from heavy grazing and some from the havoc caused by wild animals. Elephants knock down cairns, pull up coups stones, tear up teak poles and strip the bark off teak, *Grewia* and some other species, while sambur and spotted deer nibble away the young shoots of *Pterocarpus marsupium* (Vengai). Man, as usual, commits theft of timber and fuel; he illicitly fells and removes teak, *Dalbergia latifolia* (Itti), *Pterocarpus marsupium* (Vengai) and Mesua ferrea (Nangu).[2] The Anaimalai forests are subject to many kinds of injuries, to thefts and damage by wild animals, insect pests, *lantana*, bamboos, climbers, grass, *strobelanthes*, fungi and wind. Fires damage considerably valuable species like teak and rosewood. Illicit removal of timber, fuel, bamboos and other forest produce, lead to degradation of forests in the Pollachi and Udumalpet ranges. Such removals are, however, rare in the Tunacadavu range and negligible in the Punachi range. Wild elephants destroy seedlings, break saplings and strip off the bark in teak plantations. Bison, sambur and spotted deer browse down several valuable species, while porcupines, bats, squirrels, monkeys and rats consume large quantities of seeds and fruits of shola trees. Insects like defoliators and skeletonizers play havoc in teak plantations. *Lantana,* particularly in elevations between 2,000 and 3,000 feet, effectually suppresses seedling regeneration and proves a real menace to teak plantations. Bamboos (*Bambusa arundinacea*) often grow densely and severely affect seedlings of valuable tree species. Climbers do a great deal of damage in the deciduous forests and plantations. Elephant grass proves inimical to tree growth and cause frequent fires. Various species of *strobelanthes* cover the ground thickly

---

1 *Working Plan for the North Coimbatore Forest Division,* 1932–42 by C. R. Ranganathan, pages 27–28.

2 *A Revised Working Plan for the forests of the Walayar, Bolampatty and Thadagam Valleys, Palghat Forest Division,* 1937–46, pages 9–11.

in several parts of the evergreen forests and hinder the growth of natural seedlings of trees. Fungi sometimes attack the leaves of teak in young plantations. And finally, high winds now and again spread fires in dry months and up-root trees in the south-west monsoon season.[1]

As may be expected, the main requirements of the people from the forests are grazing and penning facilities, certain species of wood for making agricultural implements and small timber, fuel and bamboos. In the Bargur forest areas grazing and penning are popular, species like *chloroxylon swietenia* (Porasu), *Azadirachta indica* (Veppam), *acacia arabica* (Karuvai), *acacia leucophloea* (Velvelam) and *Albizzia amara* (Unjal) are utilized for agricultural implements and teak, *Acacia sundra* (Karungali), *Grewia tilliaefolia* (Thadachi), *Chloroxylon swietenia* (Porasu) and *Pterocarpus marsupium* (Vengai) are commonly used for posts, beams, etc. Bamboos (*Dendrocalamus strictus*) are used as rafters and fuel is obtained both from reserves and unreserves and patta fields.[2] In the North Coimbatore plateau and the Nilgiri slopes and the forest areas of the Thadagam hills, grazing and penning are very popular, agricultural implements are commonly made out of *chloroxylon swietenia* (Porasu), *Anogeissus latifolia* (Vekkali) *Acacia leucophloea* (Velvelam), *Acacia sundra* (Karungali)and *Grewia tiliaefolia* (Thadachi), but the fuel and timber requirements of the people are not much, those being met mostly from unreserves.[3] In the Bolampatty and Thadagam Valley forest areas the demand for grazing, small timber, and other trees for agricultural implements is not so great; but here there is a great demand for firewood on account of the vicinity of Coimbatore town.[4] In the Anaimalai forest areas there is a good demand for timber, fuel and certain species for agricultural implements. The chief species of timber in demand are *Tectona grandis* (Thekku), *Dalbergia latifolia* (Itti), *Pterocarpus marsupium* (Vengai), *Terminalia tomentosa* (Karimarudu), *Terminalia paniculata* (Pillamarudu), *Xylia xylocarpus* (Irul), *Lagerstroemia lanceolata* (Venthekku), *Grewia tilaefolia* (Thadachi), *Adina cordifolia* (Manjakadambai), *Hopea parviflora* (Vellaikongu), and *Mesua ferrea* (Nangu). There is also here a fair demand for grazing and minor forest produce such as honey, wax,

---

1 *Working Plan for the Coimbatore South Forest Division*, 1954–55 *to* 1968–69 by K. A. Bhoja Shetty, Part I, paragraphs 30–37.

2 *Working Plan for the Kollegal Forest Division* 1942–43 *to* 1957–58 by V. S. Krishnaswami, pages 5–6.

3 *Working Plan for the North Coimbatore Forest Division*, 1932 to 1942 by C. R. Ranganathan, pages 36–39.

4 *A Revised Working Plan for the forests of the Walayar, Bolampatty and Thadagam Valleys, Palghat Forest Division*, 1937 to 1946 by T. V.V enkateswara Ayyar, page 11.

cardamoms, tamarind, soapnuts and manure leaves, especially the leaves of *Wrightia tinctoria* (Palai).[1]

As to the markets and marketable products, all important products of the forests find a ready sale in the local markets and some even attract outside and foreign markets. The entire output of sandalwood of the Bargur forests is sold at the Satyamangalam Sale Depot where the principal buyers are merchants of Bombay and the distillers of sandalwood oil of Kuppam, Kanouj, Mangalore and Mettur. Sandalwood from there is also exported to Madras where it is used on a small scale for carving and for making sandal paste and from where it is exported to foreign countries, chiefly to the United States of America. Bamboos of these forests are carted down to Andhiur, whence they are exported to Tiruppur, Karur, Tiruchirappalli and the coastal centres. Tanstuff of these forests, like *chibulic myrabolam*, konnai (*Cassia fistula*) bark and Avaram (*Cassia auriculata*) bark are absorbed by the tanning centres of the State. Stone and tree moss of these forests find a market in Bangalore while honey and wax, which are now departmentally collected, have both local and outside markets. Tamarind of these forests is mostly locally consumed; so also are locally consumed date leaf, korai grass, soapnuts, pungam seeds and fruits of *Saspinus emarginatus* (Naikottai).[2] The forests of the North Coimbatore plateau, the Nilgiri slopes and the Thadagam hills have their principal markets at Satyamangalam, Gobichettipalayam, Andhiyur, Bhavani, Mettupalayam and Erode. Andhiyur, Bhavani, Erode and Mettupalayam are recognized markets for their bamboos. Coimbatore and Gobichettipalayam are the nearest markets for their timber. All the towns and villages of the plains consume all their firewood. The Satyamangalam Sandalwood Depot sells in auction all their sandalwood; and, as has already been stated, this sandalwood is exported also to Madras and from there to foreign countries. Their gall nuts find a sale chiefly in Madras and also in Erode and Coimbatore, Tiruchirappalli and Bangalore. Their avaram bark and Konnai bark are consumed in Erode and Tiruchirappalli. Their stone and tree moss are exported to Bangalore and from there to Bombay and Germany where, it is said, they are used for making litmus paper. Their deer and sambur horns are exported to Madras. Their tamarind, date leaves, kora grass, neem seeds and soapnuts are consumed locally. Almost the whole output of the Bolampatty and Thadagam Valley forests, both major and minor produce,

---

[1] *Working Plan for the South Coimbatore Forest Division*, 1954–55 to 1968–69 by K. A. Bhoja Shetty, Part I, paragraphs 40–42.

[2] *Working Plan for the Kollegal Forest Division*, 1942–43 to 1957–58 by V. Krishnaswami, pages 6–8.

is absorbed by Coimbatore town. The Coimbatore market thus attracts all their timber, all their firewood and almost all their bamboos. The rest of their bamboos go to Palghat, Tiruchirappalli, Madurai and other places. Next to Coimbatore, Ondiputhur near Singanallur is an important market for their teak poles. Their minor produce like tamarind, avaram bark, soapnuts, honey, wax and gall-nuts are collected by the lessees and sold mostly in Coimbatore.[1] The entire output of the Anaimalai forests, timber, fuel, bamboos as well as minor produce, finds a market chiefly at Pollachi, Udumalpet and Dharapuram, and also at Chalakudi in the Kerala State.[2]

The lines of export vary in different forest areas. Some of the Bargur forests are served by the railway passing through Mettur, but the rest are not only not served by any railway, but ill served by roads.[3] The North Coimbatore Plateau, and the Nilgiri slopes and the Thadagam hills forests are poorly served by railways. The broad gauge system from Mettupalayam to Erode and Madras via Coimbatore is the only line of export by rail for their produce; and, except at Mettuplayam, the railway is never near enough to the forests to influence their working materially. The Cauvery and the several bridges across the Bhavani help transport to some extent. Roads serve these forests fairly well, but there are, however, large tracts of forests where no communications, save footpaths, exist.[4] The Bolampatty Valley forests are served by the Coimbatore-Siruvani road and another road running from Coimbatore to Narasapuram. The Thadagam Valley forests are served by the Anaikatty-Coimbatore road and the Thadagam Valley cart track.[5] The Anaimalai forests are served by the metre gauge railway connecting Pollachi and Udumalpet with Palghat and Coimbatore and three main roads, the Chinnar-Udumalpet road, the Valparai-Pollachi road, and the Sethumadai-Pollachi road.

---

1 *Working Plan for the North Coimbatore Forest Division*, 1932 to 1942 by C. R. Ranganathan, pages 39–44.

A Revised Working Plan for the Forests of the Walayar, Bolampatty and Thadagam Valleys, Palghat Forest Division, 1937 to 1946 by T. V. Venkateswara Ayyar, pages 11–12.

2 *Working Plan for the Coimbatore South Forest Division*, 1954–55 to 1968–69 by K. A. Bhoja Shetty, Part I, paragraphs 43–44.

3 *Working Plan for the Kollegal Forest Division*, 1942-43 to 1957–58 by V. S. Krishnaswami, page 8.

4 *Working Plan for the North Coimbatore Forest Division*, 1932 *to* 1942 by C. R. Ranganathan, page 44.

5 *A Revised Working Plan for the Forests of the Walayar, Bolampatty and Thadagam Valleys, Palghat Forest Division*, 1937–46 by T. V. Venkateswara Ayyar, page 12.

They are also served by some 13 forest roads and the Travancore-Cochin Forest Tramway.[1]

In regard to labour supply unskilled labour is available in plenty during the non-agricultural seasons in the Bargur forests. Sholagas are chiefly employed here for sandal extraction and Wodders for road work. Some Sholaga Settlements have been formed in the North Bargur forests.[2] Labour supply is not plentiful in the North Coimbatore plateau forests. Sholagas and, to some extent, Badagas and Sivachars are employed here for sandal extraction and routine work.[3] Nor is the labour supply satisfactory in the Nilgiri slopes and Thadagam hills forests and in the Bolampatty and Thadagam Valley forests. In all these forests, therefore, Sholaga and Irular Settlements have been formed.[4] In the Anaimalai forests too the labour supply is by no means satisfactory. Here, the labour of the local hill tribes like the Kadars, the malasars, the Malaimalasars, the Mudavars and the Pulaiyars has to be supplemented by the labour of the workers brought from outside places. Thus the axemen have to be brought from Malabar for felling trees in the Thunacadavu range and wodders from the plains for road-works. Some settlements of hill tribes have also been formed here, and the chief of these is the Sircarpatty Settlement near Sethumalai for Malasars.[5]

It remains now to trace the general history of the forests and their past and present systems of managements. The whole district with all its forests came into the hands of the British in 1799 after the capture of Seringapatam and the fall of Tipu. It would appear that Tipu appreciated the value of sandal trees of the North Coimbatore forests; he treated them as ' royal trees ' and recognized in them no private rights. It would also appear that during the early days of British rule, gangs of robbers (Moplas and Kurumbers) used to come and plunder these forests and convey all sandalwood to the West Coast for sale.[6]

---

1 *Working Plan for the Coimbatore South Forest Division*, 1954–55 *to* 1968–69 by K. A. Bhoja Shetty, Part I, paragraphs 45–50.

2 *Working Plan for the Kollegal Forest Division*, 1942–43 *to* 1957–58 by V. S. Krishnaswami, page 11.

3 *Working Plan for the North Coimbatore Forest Division*, 1932–42 by C. R. Ranganathan, pages 58–60.

4 *Idem*, pages 58–60.

A Revised Working Plan for the forests of the Walayar, Bolampatty and Thadagam Valleys, Palghat Forest Division, 1937 to 1946, pages 15–16.

5 *Working Plan for the Coimbatore South Forest Division*, 1954–55 *to* 1968–69 by K. A. Bhoja Shetty, Part I, paragraphs 66–73.

6 *Working Plan for the North Coimbatore Forest Division*, 1932 *to* 1942 by C. R. Ranganathan, page 60.

Taking first the North Coimbatore forests, for about half a century no attempts were made by the British to exploit these forests. In 1856, however, the Forest Department was for the first time organised in these areas under Dr. Cleghorn, the Conservator of Forests, and the Satyamangalam, the Talamalai and the Bhavani (including Bargur) forests were placed in charge of Captain Morgan with his headquarters at Ootacamund. The departmental exploitation of sandalwood was first begun in Talamalai in 1860–61, in Bargur in 1864 and in Satyamangalam in 1865. It was, however, not successful; the fellings being done mostly by local supervisors, the forests were continually and indiscriminately exploited. North Coimbatore was constituted into a forest division in 1879–80. In 1880 the Anaimalai forests which were known as the South Coimbatore Division forests were amalgamated with the North Coimbatore forests and the united division was called the Coimbatore Division. In 1883 this was split up again into the North and South Coimbatore Divisions. In 1884 the North Coimbatore Division came to comprise three ranges, the Kollegal, the Satyamangalam and the Bhavani ranges, each in charge of a ranger assisted by a forester and some guards. The Talamalai range then formed part of the Satyamangalam range, but, in 1892, it was constituted into a separate range under a ranger. In 1909 the North and the South Coimbatore divisions were further split up into four divisions, North, South and Central Coimbatore and Kollegal. The North Coimbatore Division now consisted of the Satyamangalam, the Talamalai and the Bhavani ranges. In 1910 the Bhavani range was divided into two ranges namely, the Bhavani range consisting chiefly of the ghat faces and the Bargur range consisting of the plateau portions. On the abolition of the Central Coimbatore Division in 1921, the Mettupalayam range was transferred to North Coimbatore and the Bargur range was included in the Kollegal range. Meanwhile the Nilgiri Eastern Slopes reserved forest had been transferred to the Nilgiri Division in 1909–10, but it was re-transferred to the North Coimbatore Division in 1920[1]. Since the transfer of the Kollegal taluk to the Mysore State in 1956, the Bargur range has been included in the North Coimbatore Division.

Coming to the past systems of management of the northern forests in the Bargur range, regular extraction of sandalwood was for the first time made under Mr. Lushington's Working Scheme of 1895–96. This was made in 27 square miles, divided into 10 coupes; but spike very soon upset the whole programme. In 1917–18 Mr. Hodgson prepared a working scheme for the tract according to which, dead and spiked sandal

1 *Working Plan for the North Coimbatore Forest Division*, 1932 *to* 1942 by C. R. Ranganathan, pages 61–62.

trees were extracted on a felling cycle of 3 years. In 1921, when the Bargur range was transferred to the Kollegal Division, a revised working scheme was drawn up for the range by Mr. Dupre Thornton. A 5-year felling cycle confined only to the spiked areas was adopted and extraction was made of dead sandal trees alone. From 1923–24, Sri Sadasiva Ayyar's working scheme for three years came into effect, according to which also spiked and dead sandal trees alone were extracted. But large-scale theft of sandal upset this scheme and the annual quota of sandal had to be made up by extraordinary fellings. When this scheme expired in 1926–27, spiked and dead sandal trees were removed without any system or order. In 1928, Sri Shani's consolidated working scheme was introduced but its prescriptions relating to sandal management being of a general nature, random and unsystematic fellings continued, as before, unabated. Then came in 1933 the Working Plan for the Kollegal Division prepared by Sri Ranganathan and Sri Krishnaswami under which, two Sandal Working circles were constituted, one for the reserves and the other for the unreserves and patta fields. These were called the Reserve Sandal Working Circle and the Village Sandal Working Circle. The Reserve Sandal Working Circle was constituted on the basis of detailed stock maps prepared after actually counting all sandal trees above the height of man in units of 5 acres each in areas where the sandal growth was dense and in units of 10 acres each in areas where the sandal growth was scattered. The incidence of spiked trees was determined, but, since it was low though wide-spread, it was not taken into account while constituting the felling cycle. 9 felling series were constituted and exploitation was confined to the uprooting of dead sandal trees only and the felling cycle was fixed at 6 years. The Village Sandal Working Circle included all the villages of the division which contained sufficient sandal in their unreserves or patta lands to make annual exploitation worthwhile. Here also the enumeration of the trees was made but 12 felling series were constituted and the felling cycle was fixed at 3 years, as it was considered desirable to work the coupes on the shortest possible felling cycle so as to prevent theft and smuggling. Sandal trees of certain girth standing in all patta fields where the Government were entitled to sandal were recognized as Government property and those in other fields to which the Government could lay no claim were acquired[1].

So far as timber is concerned there have been no working plans for the Bargur forests. Nor have there been any working plans relating to fuel in the same forests till the introduction of the present working plan of

[1] *Working Plan for the Kollegal Forest Division*, 1942–43 *to* 1957–58 by K. S. Krishnaswami, pages 12–14.

1942–43. In 1917, a working scheme was prepared for the bamboos in the Bargur and Bejalatty blocks and a felling cycle of 5 years was prescribed. In 1923, a revised working scheme was prepared for working the bamboos of the Kollegal and Bargur ranges. Six series were formed in the Bargur range and worked on contract system. In 1928–29, however, on account of the semi-gregarious flowering of the bamboos, felling and coupe restriction were removed. In 1933 the coupe system was again restored. Under the 1933 working plan several bamboo felling series were formed. Under the same plan, grazing and minor produce were also regulated and a demonstration grazing plot was opened near Tattakerai[1].

The Working Plan at present followed in the Bargur forests is the one that was drawn up for the Kollegal Division in 1942 by Sri V. S. Krishnaswami. According to it, sandal is supplied from the Reserve and Village Sandal Working Circles; firewood is supplied from the Fuel Working Circle; regeneration of useful tree crops is conducted in the Regeneration Working Circle; grazing is controlled by the issue of permits; and minor forest produce is leased out in suitable farms.

The Reserve Sandal Working Circle includes nine felling series in the Bargur range. Under the natural selection system prescribed, only dead sandal trees are exploited. The felling cycle is six years. Each felling series is divided into six coupes and one coupe is worked each year in each of the series. All exploitation is done departmentally. No general tending is done for natural sandal and no special methods of fire-protection are undertaken. The Village Sandal Circle comprises such of the villages as contain in their unreserves and patta fields significant numbers of sandal trees over which the Government have any right and which lend themselves to economical working. This circle comprises three series of the Bargur range. It aims at the exploitation of Government-owned sandal trees occurring in patta fields and unreserves, protection of such trees, and the purchase of privately owned sandal trees, both green and dead, for immediate extraction. Normally only dead sandal belonging to the Government is extracted but there is no such restriction in regard to private sandal. A three-year felling cycle is prescribed and one coupe in each series is worked every year[2].

The fuel Working Circle includes three felling series of the Bargur range. The method of treatment is simple coppice, but the contractor is not required to fell growth which he does not want to remove. Sandal is

---

1 *Working Plan for the Kollegal Forest Division,* 1942–43 *to* 1957–58 by K. S. Krishnaswami, pages 15–18.

2 *Idem,* pages 23–35.

reserved and no tending is prescribed. The rotation is fixed at 40 years. Working is regulated by area and coupes and one coupe in each year, in each series, is sold to contractors. The Regeneration Working Circle includes 312 acres of the Bargur range which are capable of being improved by concentrated methods of regeneration. The silvicultural system is clear felling followed by artificial regeneration mainly by the Kumri method. The species generally selected for regeneration are *Acacias*, especially *Acacia ferruginea* (Parambai), *Albizzia, prosopis juliflora, Zizyphus jujuba* (Elandai) and Casuarina plantations in 11 years, but for other plantations, it may vary. Regeneration areas are demarcated and sold one year in advance of regeneration to contractors or Kumridars. They are clear-felled before they are regenerated by the Kumri method. They are also fire-protected by external fire lines 20 feet wide and by the annual clearing of internal boundaries between plantations to a width of 12 feet[1].

The Bamboo Working Circle includes several series in the Bargur range. Felling rules are prescribed and the felling cycle is fixed at three years. Normally coupes are to be sold to contractors but, in exceptional cases, departmental exploitation may be undertaken. Leases are either annual or triennial. The Grazing Working Circle includes all the reserves of the Bargur range, except areas which may be closed for any reason. Grazing and penning is regulated by the issue of permits subject to the usual conditions at the rates sanctioned by the Government. The grazing fee at present is four annas per cow and the grazing year is 1st September to 31st August. The penning rate at present is Rupee one per owner of 100 cattle or less. Deferred and rotational grazing is in vogue. The minor Forest Produce Working Circle includes the Bargur range. The system prescribed in it is generally the contract system, save for certain minor items like deer and sambur horn and honey which are collected departmentally[2].

As regards the past systems of management of the other northern forests of the district, until 1896 it does not appear that any system of exploitation of sandalwood was followed in the North Coimbatore plateau forests. In that year, Mr. Lushington introduced a provisional working scheme for 62 square miles, the estimated extent of the sandal bearing tracts in the Guttialattur reserve and the unreserves in the enclosures within it. In 1900 a working plan for the Guttialattur Working Circle was sanctioned, but it was little more than a rough table of fellings according to which the whole area was divided into 13 annual and unequal

---

1 *Working Plan for the Kollegal Forest Division*, 1942–43 *to* 1957–58 by K. S. Krishnaswami, pages 35–39.

2 *Idem*, pages 39–59.

coupes to be worked over till 1909. It prescribed extraction under the system of selection of roots and stumps left from the former fellings of dead trees, of dying trees and of trees over 32 inches in girth at breast height. A similar working scheme dividing the sandal area in the Talamalai range into ten annual coupes was introduced in 1896–97. A provisional scheme for the extraction of sandalwood from the Bhavani and Bargur ranges was sanctioned in 1895–96; but, as has already been stated, the onset of spike upset the working of this scheme The scheme was therefore, abandoned in 1961. In the same year, the prescriptions regarding the felling of living sandal trees in the Guttialattur Working Circle were cancelled. In 1917–18 Mr. Hodgson drew up a provisional working scheme for extracting all spiked and dead trees in the spiked localities of the Satyamangalam range. He prepared similar working schemes for the Talamalai, Bargur and Bhavani ranges. His scheme for the Talamalai range was based on a cycle of two years and covered only the areas affected by spike; that for the Bhavani and Bargur ranges (which latter was then included in the North Coimbatore Division) was based on a joint working scheme on a cycle of three years for the extraction of dead and spiked trees from the entire sandal bearing areas, including unspiked areas. All these schemes of Mr. Hodgson having expired in 1921, revised schemes were prepared by Mr. Dupre Thornton in that year for the Satyamangalam, Talamalai and Bargur ranges. These schemes were based on a three-year cycle (three year cycle for the Bargur range) and covered the entire sandal bearing areas, including unreserves, in the Talamalai range and only the spiked areas in the Satyamangalam and Bargur ranges. The Talamalai sandalwood working circle was divided into two felling series of three coupes each. Provision was made for climber cutting and freeing of suppressed stems in each coupe in the year previous to its working in the Talamalai range. The basis of working was different in the three ranges. In the Talamalai range the scheme prescribed the extraction of dead, dying and spiked trees; in the Satyamangalam range dead and spiked trees alone were to be removed; and in the Bargur range only dead trees were to be extracted. In 1925–26 similar working schemes covering the spiked areas of the Satyamangalam and Talamalai ranges were sanctioned (the Bargur range having been in 1921 transferred to the Kollegal Division). As the prescription relating to the extraction of dying and spiked trees was much abused by the subordinates, it was decided in 1927 that, for the future, only actually dead sandal trees should be extracted, whether occurring in spiked or unspiked areas[1].

---

1 *Working Plan for the North Coimbatore Forest Division*, 1932 *to* 1942 **by C. R. Ranganathan, pages 62–65.**

Timber is not produced at present in the Northern forests. In the early years of the department, however, a small revenue was realized by unregulated fellings on licence of *Pterocarpus marsupium* (Vengai) and *Tectona grandis* (Thekku) in the plateau forests. In 1906–07 it was recorded that a disastrous felling of rosewood from the Minchiguli Valley and Geddasal was made by a contractor of Malabar. From 1924 to 1928 a few acres of teak and rosewood near Karaipalayam were clear-felled for experimental purposes. In 1928 Mr. Law prepared a simple scheme for the extraction of all *Dalbergia latifolia* (Itti) teak, *Pterocarpus marsupium* (Vengai) and *Albizzia odoratissima* (Karuvagai) trees over 6 feet in girth from the area east of the Suvarnavati river between the Tattavadi river and the northern boundary of the division; but this scheme was not sanctioned. In 1912, Mr. Richmond drew up a rough working scheme for extracting dead *Shorea talura* (Kungiliam) and *Pterocarpus marsupium* (Vengai) trees from the Darrihalla Valley near Onnaithittu and in 1923, Mr. Stileman drew up another working scheme for the same valley. But both the schemes broke down for want of demand. Some haphazard exploitation of teak was made in 1923–24 in the south Bargur reserve forest of the Bhavani range through the agency of a contractor. In 1924, Mr. Mitchell sought to regularize the working in the Bhavani range by drawing up a scheme for timber extraction. An area to the south of Talakkarai was divided into 10 annual coupes from which dead and dying teak, *Pterocarpus marsupium* (Vengai), *Dalbergia latifolia* (Itti) and *Albizzia Odoratissima* (Karuvagai) were marked and sold. But the scheme failed for want of demand. The working plan for the Mettupalayam range sanctioned in 1917 created two timber working circles, one embracing the whole of the Kallar reserved forest and the other situated in the upper slopes of a portion of Jakkanare reserved forest. The growing stock consisted of small-sized trees of *Pterocarpus marsupium* (Vengai), *Dalbergia latifolia* (Itti), *Albizzia lebbek* (Vagai), *Anogeissus latifolia* (Vekkali) and *Prosopis spicigera* (Vanni) mixed with other valuable species. In order to improve the existing stock and to utilize all dead and deteriorating trees, improved fellings on a felling cycle of fifteen years were prescribed in both the working circles. But the prescriptions were not regularly carried out and, as a result, the scheme was abandoned in 1923[1].

Free removal of fuel and other forest produce—except teak, *Dalbergia latifolia* (Itti), *Pterocarpus marsupium* (Vengai), sandalwood and tamarind was permitted in the early years of forest administration. In 1868 the indiscriminate removal of forest produce was regularized by the issue

1 *Working Plan for the North Coimbatore Forest Division,* 1932 *to* 1942 by C. R. Ranganathan, pages 65–66.

of free permits for all species, except the five mentioned above, for agricultural and domestic purposes only. For other purposes a charge of Rs. 3–12–0 per tree was made, while for teak, *Dalbergia latifolia* (Itti) and *Pterocarpus marsupium* (Vengai), the rate was fixed at Rs. 7 per tree, sandalwood being not allowed to be cut. These rules were framed under the Jungle Conservancy Department and monigars of villagers were appointed as permit issuing officers, the permits being supplied by Tahsildars. Firewood permits were issued at 3 pies per head-load and 5 annas per cart-load and bamboo permits were issued at 6 pies to 1 anna per head-load and 8 annas to one rupee per 100 bamboos. Some changes were made in these rates and in the system of issuing permits in the subsequent years. In 1904 departmental exploitation was started in the Satyamangalam range, but it met with considerable opposition. No purchasers came forward for the fuel in the coupes and it was not till depots were opened in Satyamangalam and Gobichettipalayam that any success was met with. In 1909 the depots were abolished, felled fuel in the coupes was disposed of to the contractors and the contractors were asked not to sell fuel above certain fixed maximum rates. In 1912 the restrictions on selling rates were withdrawn. It was, however, not till 1915 that the system of leasing the coupes to contractors became general[1].

The fuel working circles are all situated in the ' terais ', in the ' combais ' and on the foothills of the Nilgiris, the Thadagam range of hills and the North Coimbatore plateau. On the plateau itself there are no fuel coupes, although there are numerous villages of varying size. In 1923, Mr. Stileman opened a fuel working circle consisting of three felling series in the Talamalai range in order to supply certain villages with firewood and small timber for agricultural needs. The system adopted was simple coppice on a rotation of 40 years, with reservation of sandalwood, *Terminalia chebula* (Kadukkai), tamarind and *Feronia elephantum* (Velam). But the experiment soon ended in failure owing to the general unwillingness of the villagers to work the fuel coupes. In 1927, the felling of indicator areas was ordered in all fuel coupes in advance of their sale in order to ensure the realization of adequate prices and to exercise a check on the contractor's return of yields. The fuel obtained from the indicator areas was auctioned separately in 1928–29 and 1929–30, but from 1930–31 it was sold with the fuel coupe concerned[2].

[1] *Working Plan for the North Coimbatore Forest Division*, 1932 *to* 1942 by C. R. Ranganathan, pages 66–67.

[2] *Idem*, pages 67–68.

For the Mettupalayam range, a preliminary working plan was prepared by Mr. Faulkes in 1902. Six fuel working circles and a 'compensation' working circle were formed. The coupes were worked under the coppice with standard system on a rotation of 25 years. A revised working plan for the whole range (with the exception of Thadagam reserve) was prepared by Sri Habibullah in 1917. This plan created seven fuel working circles, two timber working circles and a sandalwood working circle; and of these seven, four, namely, Modur, Odanthorai East, Odanthorai West and Nellimalai, were transferred to panchayat management in 1926–27. The method of treatment prescribed was coppice with standards on a rotation of 30 years; but in 1920 this method was changed into simple coppice. The plan prescribed an elaborate scheme for the eradication of prickly pear and lantana in all the fuel working circles, but the scheme, having been found to be costly as well as unsuccessful, was abandoned in 1919[1].

The Thadagam reserve of the Mettupalayam range was worked under the permit system for fuel and timber till 1905. Mr. Foulkes' working plan proposed to divide certain areas into some fuel working circles and prescribed rest for the remaining areas. The coupes were opened in 1905 but the prescription soon broke down entirely on account of the high cost of extraction of prickly pear and the barreness of ground in some places. A few new series of fellings were opened subsequently. A revised working plan for the reserve drawn up by Sri Habibullah was sanctioned in 1917. This formed two working circles in the Mettupalayam range, prescribed the system of coppice with standards and 30 years rotation. The Nilgiri Eastern slopes reserved forest included in the Mettupalayam range in 1920 had no working plan for fuel till 1915 when a provisional working scheme for three years was introduced. According to this, permits for the removal of bamboos but not fuel or timber, were issued. The method of treatment prescribed was simple coppice with reservation of sandal, tamarind and *Dalbergia latifolia*. This scheme was, in some respects, revised by Mr. Law[2].

The fuel working plan of the Satyamangalam range was prepared by Mr. Lushington in 1908. It created three working circles and prescribed fellings on a rotation of 20 years under coppice with standards. It recommended the clearing of prickly pear and thorny undergrowth wherever necessary in advance of felling. It was revised in some respects

1 *Working Plan for the North Coimbatore Forest Division*, 1932 *to* 1942 by C. R. Ranganathan, pages 68–69.

2 *Idem*, pages 69–70.

in 1918 by Mr. Hogdson, and in other respects subsequently. In the Bhavani range six fuel felling series were formed under an unsanctioned working scheme drawn up by Mr. Hogdson in 1919. In order to supply the Shanars of the Bhavani range with firewood for the manufacture of jaggery, a cottage industry, working plans were drawn up in 1928 by Mr. Law and in 1929 by Mr. Wilson[1].

Provision for grazing has always been the major obligation of the northern forests. On the plateau, cattle breeding is an important industry and in several villages the grazing revenue amounts to a considerable sum. Nearly everywhere large herds of cattle are kept by the villagers for the sake of manure, without which the soil, which is generally shallow and stony, cannot be made to yield them a living. In order to regulate the incidence of grazing, the system of grazing blocks was introduced in 1917. The Satyamangalam, Talamalai and Bhavani ranges were divided into four blocks each. In 1921 the Mettupalayam range consisted of as many as 32 blocks. The grazing fee was fixed at 4 annas per cow, 8 annas per buffaloe and 2 annas per sheep. The fee for penning licence was fixed at Re. 1 per 100 cattle or less. In 1909 the penning fee was increased to Rs. 2 per 100 and in 1910 to Rs. 2–8–0 per 100. In the Mettupalayam range the grazing fee per cow was fixed at 3 annas. In 1910 the Bhavani range was split up into the Bhavani and Bargur ranges and each of the two ranges was divided into six grazing blocks in 1911. In the same year (1911) a detailed grazing scheme for the Talamalai range was prepared by Mr. Richmond. Under this scheme the grazing area in the range was divided into 29 blocks and a block was assigned to each village or a group of villages. It was proposed to exclude sheep altogether from the reserves and to quadruple grazing fee for cows. But the scheme was considered impracticable and dropped. The Mettupalayam range working plan of 1917 prescribed a grazing scheme on similar lines. This scheme was, however, worked for 11 years and cancelled in 1929 when the system of issuing permits was reverted to. In 1918–19 the grazing fees were doubled and the penning fee was raised to Rs. 12–8–0 per one hundred or less. The Forest Advisory Committee appointed in 1921, suggested remedies for the grievances of the grazers. Several changes were made. The block system of grazing, then prevalent, was abolished, except in the Mettupalayam range Each range was treated as a grazing unit and cattle licensed to graze in one range were permitted to enter the adjoining range to a distance of half a mile without trespass. The license fee on

[1] *Working Plan for the North Coimbatore Forest Division*, 1932 *to* 1942, by C. R. Ranganathan, pages 70–74.

penning amounting to Rs. 12–8–0 per 100 cattle was abolished, and free penning was permitted. The department was also required to increase the grazing facilities by providing water for cattle and facilities for the passage of cattle through closed coupes. Permission to carry knives was granted to grazing permit holders. And finally, the period of closure of worked fuel coupes was reduced from fifteen years to five years. In 1929, consequent on the reclassification of the forests and the transfer of 'local' or 'ryots' forests to panchayats, the grazing position was revised by the Government. It was then decided that the grazing fee should be raised, that the Forest Department should encourage the cutting of grass, that, as an experiment in certain places, cattle might be kept confined in pens supplied with grass cut from the forests and that, where particular areas of forests had to be protected, such areas might be closed to cattle[1].

Bamboos were exploited under the lease system according to which a coupe was leased to a contractor every year for extraction. In 1927–28, the mode of fellings was to thin the bamboo clumps according to the silvicultural conditions embodied in the agreements with the contractor. Bamboos were for the first time sold standing in located coupes in the Bhavani range in 1908–1909. In 1909–10, the system was extended to the Satyamangalam and Talamalai ranges. In the Mettupalayam range bamboo coupes were worked though no working scheme was formally introduced.

In pursuance of the recommendations of the Forest Advisory Committee (1922), an Agricultural Implements Working Circle was opened in 1923 in the Satyamangalam range to meet the needs of the villagers. It consisted of four felling series worked on a felling cycle of ten years each. The ryots were permitted to select their own trees for felling and this led to mismanagement and closure of the circle in 1927. In the Bhavani and Mettupalayam ranges, the requirements of the people were met by fuel coupe contractors and no special provision for the supply of agricultural implements was found to be necessary. In the Talamalai range a fuel working circle was opened in 1923 for the supply of small timber and agricultural implements to the villagers[2].

Until the end of 1915 the collection of gallnuts, honey, wax, deer horns, sambur horns and soapnuts was carried out departmentally. The

---

1 *Working Plan for the North Coimbatore Forest Division*, 1932 *to* 1942 by C. R. Ranganathan, pages 74–76.

2 *Idem*, page 79.

produce was stored in sale depots at Satyamangalam and Bhavani and sold in auction periodically. From 1916 it was leased out to the contractors. In 1930–31 the collection of gallnuts was made departmentally in the Satyamangalam, Talamalai, Mettupalayam and Bhavani ranges, but this experiment ended in a failure owing to the general trade depression with the result that, the practice of exploiting gallnuts through the agency of contractors was again reverted to in 1931–32. The leasing of the right to collect deer horns and sambur horns was stopped in 1930–31, as the practice led to poaching and destruction of game. Horns then began to be collected and sold departmentally. Honey and wax were, however, left to be collected through the agency of the contractors. Avaram bark was leased out annually and konnai bark was leased out on a five-year rotation. All items of minor produce occurring in the unreserves except tamarind were leased out; and Sholagas in forest settlements were allowed the free use of the minor produce found in their settlements[1].

Fire protection of the reserves as a systematic annual operation was commenced in 1895. The method adopted was to fire-trace a net work of fire lines, the more frequented footpaths and roads being selected as fire lines. It is not clear whether all the fire lines in the various ranges were burnt every year. In 1916 the net-work of fire lines in the Satyamangalam and Talamalai ranges was revised and the general tracing of all important paths was abandoned as being ineffective and expensive.[2]

The present working plan of the North Coimbatore plateau forests of the Northern Division as well as the Nilgiri slopes and the Thadagam Hills forests of the Southern Division was drawn up by Sri C. R. Ranganathan in 1932. It covers also the Palamalai forests which are situated in the Salem district. Save for a few modifications, this plan continues to be in force, even today. It covers the Satyamangalam, Talamalai, Bhavani and Mettupalayam ranges of the district. Its objects are to exploit fully, subject to silvicultural principles, the resources of the forests in sandalwood, firewood, bamboos and minor forest produce, to provide facilities for pasture and small timber to the local population and to conserve and improve the forest. Speaking generally, the exploitation is regulated in the case of sandal, fuel and bamboos on the area basis, the annual coupes being so devised as to ensure sustained yields in perpetuity. Attempts are made on a modest scale to supplement the natural reproduction of sandal and fuel species. Grazing is, as before, controlled by the

---

1 *Working Plan for the North Coimbatore Forest Division*, **1932** *to* **1942, by C.R. Ranganthan, pages 79–80.**

2 *Idem*, **pages 80–82**

issue of permits and the areas set apart for the production of wood are closed entirely for cattle. The supply of agricultural timber is regulated in such a way that the annual needs of the people are fully and cheaply met. The exploitation of minor produce is carried out on large units of area. In addition, experiments in artificial regeneration of *Dalbergia latifolia* (Itti) in conjunction with field crops, and in the growing of lac so as to initiate a new village industry, are prescribed. With the exception of sandal which is worked departmentally, the ideal aimed at is to exploit all produce through the agency of contractors. This rule is, however, departed from in some respects in the case of Shanars. In pursuance of these objects the plan has constituted ten working circles; the Sandal Working Circle, the Village Sandal Working Circle, the Fuel Working Circle, the Shanar Pollard Working Circle, the Bamboo Working Circle, the Grazing Working Circle, the Small Timber Working Circle, the Minor Produce Working Circle, the Podu Regeneration Working Circle and the Lac Working Circle.[1]

The Reserve Sandal Working Circle includes all sandal areas in the Satyamangalam, Talamalai, Bhavani and Mettupalayam ranges. Its area is 2,09,683 acres. Sandal has been stock-marked over all these ranges on an objective basis, the trees occurring over small units of area having been counted. Tree densities, namely, dense, sparse and scattered, have been distinguished in the stock maps. The Working Circle is divided into sixteen felling series. The method of treatment prescribed is called the natural selection system which consists in the removal of trees killed by natural causes and in the maintenance of growing stock through natural regeneration assisted by artificial protection, tending and propagation. A felling cycle of six years is adopted and each felling series is divided into six annual and approximately equi-productive coupes. One coupe in each felling series is completely exploited every year in the order prescribed. All operations connected with the exploitation of sandal are carried out departmentally. The removal of dead trees to a minimum girth of 3 inches is prescribed. Discretion is given to the Conservator to raise the minimum girth to 6 inches in special cases. The tending of sandal trees is done on a six year felling cycle; it is carried out every year in the coupes under exploitation. Five sandal propagation centres annually in non-sandal areas are prescribed. An experiment in the artificial regeneration of sandal in strips over an area of 5 acres every year near Hassanur is also prescribed. A selected area of not less than 10 acres in each coupe under working

1 *Working Plan for the North Coimbatore Forest Division*, 1932 *to* 1942, by C. R. Ranganathan, pages 114–115.

which contains little or no sandal is to be dibbled with sandal in bushes. Collection of seeds from healthy trees is suggested and localities from which seeds are to be collected are indicated. Provision is made for the retail sale of sandal billets for domestic use at Coimbatore, Satyamangalam Mettupalayam and Bhavani. The working circle as a whole is open to grazing. All regeneration areas, except those where sandal is dibbled in bushes are, however, closed to grazing[1].

The Village Sandal Working Circle embraces all sandal bearing areas in the four ranges. It includes both patta lands and unreserves. Its area is 96,956 acres. It is divided into 14 felling series. In it complete enumeration of sandal trees over 6 inches in girth has been made. All survey fields containing sandal are brought under exploitation. In the case of fields where the trees belong to the landholder, the right to exploit is acquired by purchase. In all cases only dead trees are extracted. A felling cycle of three years is prescribed. Each felling series is divided into three annual and approximately equi-productive coupes, each coupe consisting of both patta and unreserve fields intermixed[2].

The Fuel Working Circle includes all areas in the marginal forest on the lower outer slopes of the North Coimbatore plateau and the Nilgiris. Its area is 65,340 acres. It is divided into 26 felling series and its method of treatment is simple coppice with reservation of sandal, tamarind, *Terminalia chebula* (Kadukkai) and *Dalbergia latifolia* (Itti). A rotation of forty years is adopted and one coupe in each series is felled every year. Generally the coupes are worked through the agency of contractors. All trees, except certain species which it is desirable to eradicate, are to be felled at a height not exceeding 6 inches from the ground; and undesirable species are to be cut at a height not less than 2 feet and the bark pulled off. The eradication of pricklypear in fuel coupes by means of the cochineal insect is prescribed. Artificial regeneration of fuel species by the method of 'rab' sowings are to be carried out in all coupes. Collection of various seeds in the appropriate season is suggested. There is to be no weeding, but tending may be done by the removal of excess plants once in 5 or 6 years or earlier. The entire fuel circle is closed to grazing and penning, but cutting and removal of grass, except in coupes under regeneration, is freely permitted. Each felling series is protected from fire by fire-tracing a line 66 feet wide just above the highest point of the series.

---

1 *Working Plan for the North Coimbatore Forest Division*, **1932** *to* **1942, by C. R. Ranganathan, pages 116–136.**

2 *Idem*, **pages 136–165.**

Maintenance of a minimum stock of timber for agricultural implements and its sale at fixed rates is prescribed[1].

The Shanar Pollard Working Circle is specially constituted for supplying branchwood fuel to the Shanars for the manufacture of palmyrah jaggery. It comprises an area of 885 acres in the Ennamangalam reserved forest adjoining the Shanar villages. It is worked on the pollarding system. A felling cycle of 8 years is adopted. One coupe in the working circle is worked every year under the permit system. The circle is permanently closed to grazing and penning[2].

The Bamboo Working Circle includes all areas in the ranges where bamboos occur in workable quantities. Its total area is 1,49,615 acres and it is divided into two sections, the Commercial Section (1,29,788 acres) and the Village Section (19,827 acres). The Commercial Section is divided into Nineteen felling series and the Village Section into six felling series. The system of management is the selection thinning of bamboo clumps. A felling cycle of three years is adopted and each felling series is divided into three coupes one of which is worked every year. In the Commercial Section, the fellings are made through the agency of contractors. In the Village Section the agency of felling is not prescribed. The entire felling series to be sold in auction once in three years on a lease of three years. No restriction on grazing is prescribed in the circle[3].

The Grazing Working Circle comprises all the reserved forests, some 4,58,000 acres, with the exception of certain areas which are specially closed to grazing. Grazing is regulated by the issue of permits subject to the usual conditions. Permits are sold at the following rates; sheep 4 annas per head, cows and bulls 8 annas per head and buffaloes, Re. 1 per head. Penning of cattle in the reserves is regulated by the issue of permits on payment of a minimum fee to be fixed by the Conservator. Fodder grass is leased out as an item of minor produce. Free removal of grass in head-loads from closed areas is permitted. Experiments in rotational grazing and the introduction of fodder grasses are prescribed[4].

The Small Timber Working Circle consists of forest areas adjoining cultivation, irrespective of whether sandal occurs in them or not. Its area is 60,792 acres. It is divided into 22 felling series arranged with reference to the convenience of a group of hamlets or villages. The

---

1 *Working Plan for the North Coimbatore Forest Division,* 1932 *to* 1942, by C.R. Ranganathan, pages 165–181.

2 *Idem,* pages 181–183.

3 *Idem,* pages 183–195.

4 *Idem,* pages 195–201.

method of treatment is selection-coppice of marked trees and regrowth is depended upon for regeneration. The trees to be felled are to be marked and numbered after careful selection; and they are to be individually sold on permits to the ryots who are to coppice the trees they fell. No tree below 15 inches in girth-height is to be felled. A felling cycle of ten years is prescribed. The selection and marking of trees are carried out departmentally in consultation with experienced local ryots. No restriction on grazing is proposed.[1]

The Minor Forest Produce Working Circle embraces all the reserves as well as the unreserves adjoining or enclosed in the reserves. Tamarind in unreserves, however, is to be worked by the Revenue Department. The circle covers an area of 5,32,398 acres. It is divided into nine gall-nut and ten tamarind farms for the exploitation of gallnuts and tamarind. For other items of minor produce, a range is the unit of working. Exploitation through the agency of contractors is the rule. Minor items of produce, such as tree moss and deer and sambur horns, the collection of which by contractors might lead to damage to the forests, are to be collected departmentally. The right to collect gallnut is to be leased out annually for each farm; the right to collect avaram is to be leased out annually for each range. Konnai bark is to be worked on a rotation of five years, each range, including unreserves, being treated as a unit of sale. The collection of tamarind is to be leased out for each farm annually. The right to collect fodder is to be leased out for each range for one year.[2]

The Podu Working Circle is situated in the Minchiguli Valley. It covers 40 acres and is divided into four equal biennial regeneration areas. The method of treatment is clear felling with artificial regeneration. The regeneration is carried out by 'podu cultivation' a method which consists in raising of a tree crop with agricultural crops. The cultivation is to be effected through the agency of Sholagas from the Sholaga Settlement of Minchiguli. The species proposed for introduction are *Dalbergia latifolia* (Itti), *Pterocarpus marsupium* (Vengai) and other suitable associates of *Dalbergia latifolia*.[3]

The Lac Working Circle is experimental and confined to the four patches of *Shorea talura* (Kungiliam) along the *Odurkottaihalla* near

1 *Working Plan for the North Coimbatore Forest Division*, 1932 *to* 1942, by C.R. Ranganathan, pages 201–210.

2 *Idem*, pages 210–214.

3 *Idem*, pages 214–228.

Mavanatham in the Talamalai range. It covers an area of 479 acres and is permanently closed to grazing.[1]

The working plan also suggests the utilization of the perennial rivers of the Mettupalayam range for the creation of irrigated teak plantations. Teak may be mixed with *Dalbergia latifolia* (Itti) *Pterocarpus marsupium* (Vengai) and other suitable associates of teak. The experiment may be conducted in the area of the forest in Hulikaldrug reserve which lies to the west of the Pykara transmission line and close to the Mettupalayam-Coonoor road. Water from the water channel in existence near the site may be used for the irrigated plantations.[2] It is in accordance with this suggestion that irrigated teak plantations have been raised in Mettupalayam area.

The Bolampatty Valley and the Thadagam Valley forests which are now included in the South Coimbatore Division have a history of their own. The Bolampatty Valley came under systematic management in 1887. A working plan prepared by Mr. Gass in 1896 was followed here with some modifications till 1915. Coupes were worked under the coppice with standard system on a twenty year rotation. More felling series were added in 1924 and 1925. The next working plan (1926—35) prescribed three working circles, the Ponam Working Circle under which coupes averaging 28 acres each were clear-felled and regenerated annually with teak and other timber species; a coppice working circle consisting of three felling series to be worked under the simple coppice system for the production of firewood; and a Bamboo Working Circle of one series consisting of three coupes only. Minor produce was leased out and grazing was permitted on payment. In the Thadagam Valley local fuel fellings were started near Mangarai in 1906-1907. Sri Habibulla's plan of 1917 prescribed a Fuel Working Circle under coppice with standards consisting of Mangarai and Veerapandy series. Simple coppice was however, ordered to be followed from 1920. Then came Sri Krishnaswami's Working Plan (1930-39) which prescribed three fuel series in this valley and one in the Bolampatty Valley on a thirty year rotation under the simple coppice system. The coppice regeneration was to be cleared, but no artificial regeneration was to be undertaken[3]. The present working plan drawn up by Sri T. V. Venkateswara Ayyar which was introduced in 1937 and which is still being followed with some

---

1 *Working Plan for the North Coimbatore Forest Division*, 1932 *to* 1942, by C. R. Ranganathan, pages 218-223.

2 *Idem* page 231.

3 *A revised Working Plan for the forests of Bolampatty and Thadagam Valleys, Palghat Forest Division*, 1937 to 1946 by T. V. Venkateswara Iyyer, pages 16-35.

modifications, relates not only to the Bolampatty and Thadagam Valley forests but also to the Walayar forests which have now been transferred to the Kerala State. It provides for seven working circles, namely, the Pole Working Circle, the Ponam Working Circle, the Fuel Working Circle, the Bamboo Working Circle, the Minor Forest Produce Working Circle, the Protection Working Circle, and the Grazing Working Circle.[1]

The total area of the Pole Working Circle is 3,671 acres out of which 2,706 acres lie to the west of the Walayar river (now in the Kerala State) and the rest to its east. There is only one felling series. The object is to grow poles of teak and other species as well as firewood and the method of treatment in simple coppice assisted by artificial regeneration of areas insufficiently stocked with teak or coppice regeneration. The rotation is forty years. The coupes may be leased out or worked departmentally and the fuel leased out afterwards. Teak is the principal species to be introduced, but *Terminalia tomentosa* (Karimaruthu), *Terminalia paniculata* (Pillamaruthu) and *Pterocarpus marsupium* (Vengai) and other species may be planted in other localities. Weeding is to be undertaken and *lantana* is to be uprooted and bamboo and other regrowth is to be cut. The coupes are closed to grazing for five years but grass cutting in them is allowed.[2]

The area of the Ponam Working Circle is 1,800 acres practically all of which lie to the south of the Coimbatore-Siruvani road. It has two felling series. Its object is to convert the existing crop to plantations of teak, *Pterocarpus marsupium* (Vengai) and other valuable species. The method of treatment is clear felling followed by artificial regeneration in combination with field crops (ponam). Rotation is forty years. The coupes are leased out for felling and afterwards regenerated artificially by the ' ponam ' method. They are to be closed to grazing for five years after felling, but grass cutting in them is to be permitted.[3]

The area of the Fuel Working Circle is 19,961 acres. It extends over all the three valleys. It has fifteen felling series—Eleven commercial and four village series. The silvicultural system is the simple coppice system, but sandal and tamarind are not to be cut. One coupe in each commercial series is felled every year. In the village series, felling is governed by the demand. Felling is generally done through the agency of contractors, the period of the lease being one year. Felled coupes are regenerated by

---

1 *A Revised Working Plan for the forests of the Bolampatty and Thadagam Valleys, Palghat Forest, Division,* 1937 to 1946, by T. V. Venkateswara Ayyar, pages 45–57.

2 *Idem*, pages 50–61.

3 *Idem*, pages, 61–66.

the 'rab' or the 'ponam' method or by a combination of both. The species suggested for regeneration are *Cassia siamea* (Ponavarai), *Cassia ferrugenea, Acacia planifrons* (Odai), *Albizzia amara* (Unjal), *Albizzia Odoratissima* (Karuvagai) and *Melia indica*. Felled coupes are normally closed to grazing for five years after exploitation.[1]

The Bamboo Working Circle includes all localities in the area where both kinds of bamboos, *Bambusa arundinacea* and *Dendrocalamus strictus* occur in workable quantities. The grass area of the working circle is 47,021 acres, but the net bamboo bearing area is 28,710 acres. Bamboos are exploited on a felling cycle of three years under carefully controlled rules. There are eight 'commercial series' and one 'experimental series'. The normal agency of felling is the contractor but departmental felling may be undertaken.[2]

The Minor Forest Produce Working Circle covers the whole of the working plan area and, for the sale of avaram bark only, the unreserves and margins of local fund roads in the Erode and Palladam taluks. The chief minor produce is avaram bark, 'peypodal', tamarind, catechu and korai grass. Exploitation is done normally through the contractors, but departmental collection may be resorted to where necessary.[3] The Grazing Working Circle comprises all the reserves, except the areas temporarily closed to grazing for silvicultural reasons. All animals, except goats, are admitted to graze in the reserved forests at sanctioned rates and free grazing of cattle by Irulars is controlled by the issue of free permits. The penning of cows is allowed and a penning fee at the rate of Rs. 2–8–0 per 100 cows or less is charged. Fodder grass is allowed to be removed free in head-loads. Some experimental plots are opened for the study of fodder grasses under controlled grazing.[4] The Protection Working Circle consists of 24,400 acres. Grazing and penning of licensed cattle and the collection of minor produce in it is permitted. Parts of the tropical rain forests in certain compartments may be worked for *Mesua ferrea* (Nangu), *Palaquium ellipticum* (Palvadiajan), *Colophyllum tomen-tosum* and *Acrocarpus fraximifolias* (Malankonnai). Parts of the semi-evergreen may also be worked for *Dalbergia latifolia* (Itti).[5]

---

1 *A Revised Working Plan for the forests of the Bolampatty and Thadagam Valleys, Palghat Forest Division*, 1937 to 1946, by T. V. Venkateswara Ayyar, pages 67–79.

2 *Idem*, pages 80–84.

3 *Idem*, pages 84–86.

4 *Idem*, pages 86–89.

5 *Idem*, page 89.

We now come to the southern forests. For tracing their general history and past systems of management, they may be divided for convenience into (*a*) the Mount Stuart forests comprising the Mount Stuart, Ulandi and Palakadavu forest blocks and (*b*) the remaining Anamalai forests of the Pollachi taluk and the forests of the Udumalpet and Dharapuram taluks.

The early history of the Mount Stuart forests is shrouded in obscurity. It is probable that these forests were, in early times, exploited through contractors. It is, however, certain that they were preserved from over-exploitation mostly on account of their comparative inaccessibility. Towards the close of the eighteenth century they were exploited for supplying timber to the Naval Dockyard at Bombay and the Madras Arsenal. About the middle of the last century the increasing shortage of teak induced the Government to appoint Major Cotton to investigate teak supplies. He reported in 1849 that there was an almost unlimited supply of teak in these forests and that a special officer might be employed to exploit the trees. Captain Michael, the Special Officer so employed, reported that there were over 18,000 exploitable trees. He was subsequently appointed as the Superintendent of these forests to supervise their protection and working. Under his supervision, large quantities of teak were felled and exported, so much so that, in 1866, it was reported that no large trees were left in the forests. Fellings, however, were continued till 1885 when they were stopped on Mr. Gamble's recommendation. This officer for the first time stressed the necessity for the preparation of a regular working plan to control exploitation and to provide for regeneration. Mr. Porter was accordingly appointed for the purpose. Mr. Porter divided the area into several compartments of which some were considered unexploitable and the others exploitable. He fixed a rotation of 120 years and divided this period into four periods of thirty years each during which the whole forest was to be worked over once. Although the timber extracted under his plan fell far below the estimated quantities, so much timber remained felled and unremoved in 1915 that, all fellings were suspended for three years, during which a new working plan was ordered to be prepared. Mr. Wood prepared such a plan. His prescriptions briefly were that certain forest areas should not be exploited for teak, that certain other areas were to be given rest for 25 years and that the Mount Stuart forests should be worked for timber annually, the rotation being fixed at 150 years. Some attempts were also made for regeneration. The Ulandi block, which had not been worked for years on account of its inaccessibility, contained, in the beginning of this century, the finest stand of natural teak in India. In 1906 Mr. Arbuthnot prepared a working plan for the Vangoli Valley area of this block which was divided into ten annual coupes, each to be felled annually through the agency of contractors.[1]

In 1926 Mr. Laurie drew up a working plan for all the Mount Stuart forests. He divided the forests into several working circles : (1) the Conversion Working Circles for teak in which a rotation of 100 years was fixed divided into four periods of 25 years in which clear felling and regeneration were prescribed; (2) the Selection Felling Working Circle for deciduous trees, including the Ulandi and Mount Stuart felling series; (3) the Karian Shola Working Circle for certain species of evergreen timber; and (4) the Bamboo Working Circle. Then came the working plan of Sri Venkateswara Iyer of 1951 covering all the forests of the division. Although the period of this working plan was only ten years, its prescriptions, fellings and regeneration programmes were prepared for fifteen years. Mr. Laurie had taken up only the best areas for conversion into teak. Sri Venkateswara Iyer, however, considered that it was preferable to raise artificial teak plantations of even low quality, than to depend solely on natural regeneration in selection forest. He, therefore, transferred certain areas from Mr. Laurie's Selection Felling Working Circle to the Conversion Working Circle. He also reduced the conversion rotation to 80 years. He similarly reduced the deciduous selection felling cycle of Mr. Laurie, but made no important changes in the Karian Shola Evergreen Working Circle and the Bamboo Working Circle.[2]

As to the history of the other forests of the south, in 1886 rosewood and *Pterocarpus marsupium* were exploited through a contractor in the Punachi range. In 1908, a scheme for exploiting timber from the Punachi deciduous forests was prepared by Mr. Arbuthnot and this remained in force till 1925. This was revised first by Mr. Code in 1925 and later by Sri Sarma in 1935. Sri Venkateswara Iyer, in 1951, brought this whole area under his Conversion Working Circle. As to the evergreen forests the earliest attempt at marketing evergreen timber was made in 1903–1905 when *Mesua ferria, Colophyllum tomentosum, Dysoxylum malabaricum, Artocarpus integrifolia* and *Cedrula toona* were felled departmentally in the Andiparai Shola near Iyerpadi and some scantlings were transported to Anamalai and sold. In 1896, the Government began to grant forest areas for raising coffee, tea and cardamoms and very soon large areas of evergreen forest were rapidly taken up for plantations. In 1927 an area

1. *Working Plan for the Coimbatore South Forest Division,* 1954–55 to 1968–69, by K. A. Bhoja Shetty, Part I, paragraphs 74–88.

2 *Idem*, paragraphs 89–93.

of 23,000 acres of virgin evergreen forests of the Kallar Valley was set apart for planting cinchona and, in 1951, an area of 8,800 acres was handed over to the Cinchona Department for planting cinchona. Some departmental exploitation of Shola timber was also made in the Kallar Valley forests between 1925–30 and 1935–40, mostly for supplying sleepers to the South Indian Railway.[1]

Localised fellings for fuel under the simple coppice system was started in the Sethumadai area of the Pollachi range as early as 1890. In 1896 Mr. Gass prepared a scheme for the working of the Ayerangal felling series departmentally under the coppice with standard system, the coppice rotation being 25 years. In 1889 Mr. Porter drew up a scheme for working an additional 2,400 acres in the same area under the simple coppice system, the rotation being 12 years. This was subsequently revised by Mr. Bryat, but neither scheme was sanctioned. In 1902 Mr. Foulkes prepared two schemes for regulating fuel working, one for the Pollachi range and the other for the Udumalpet range. Coppice rotation was fixed at 20 years and the system of working coppice with standards was prescribed. In 1920, Mr. Crowthers drew up a ' summary of prescriptions for fuel working in the Pollachi range and this was embodied in a regular scheme by Mr. Dyson in 1923. The rotation was fixed at 35 years and the simple coppice system was prescribed. Subsequently Sri Sarma's working plan raised the area of the fuel working circle to 20,200 acres with twelve felling series of which seven were in the Pollachi and five in the Udumalpet range. Coupes were worked on the simple coppice system and the rotation was fixed at thirty years for the five western series and 40 years for the seven remaining series. Sri Venkateswara Iyer's working plan of 1951 constituted a fuel working circle of 20,775 acres divided into 12 felling series in the Pollachi and Udumalpet ranges. It did not change either the rotation period or the silvicultural system. The same working plan created eleven felling series of bamboos, six in the Pollachi range, four in the Udumalpet range and one in the Punachi range.[2]

The present working plan of the Mount Stuart forests and the forests of the Pollachi, Udumalpet and Dharapuram taluks was prepared by Sri K. A. Bhoja Shetty in 1954 and sanctioned in 1956. Its main objects are the protection, conservation and improvement of forests on steep slopes and high ranges, the securing of maximum annual yield of timber, fuel and bamboos, the artificial regeneration of valuable species wherever

1 *Working Plan for the Coimbatore South Forest Division*, 1954–55 to 1968–69, by K. A. Bhoja Shetty, Part I, paragraphs 94–98.

2 *Idem*, paragraphs 99–101.

possible, and the disposal of minor forest produce in a profitable manner. In order to achieve these objects, it has created six working circles, namely, the Teak Plantation Working Circle, the Deciduous Selection Working Circle, the Evergreen Selection Working Circle, the Fuel Working Circle, the Bamboo Working Circle and the Minor Forest Produce Working Circle.[1]

The Teak Plantation Working Circle consists of all existing teak plantations as well as areas considered suitable for artificial regeneration of teak. Its area (including the Tekkadi reserved forest area now transferred to the Kerala State) is 16,375 acres. It is divided into three felling series, the Mount Stuart felling series, the Ulandi felling series, and the Punachi felling series. The system prescribed is clear-felling followed by concentrated artificial regeneration. All species saleable at profit are exploited. Teak is the primary species to be regenerated, but areas tending towards swampiness are to be planted with *Eucalyptus robusta.* Rotation is fixed at 80 years. Material left after extraction of all saleable timber is to be sold in auction. A fire line is to be cut all round the regeneration area and scarped and burnt well. Kumri cultivation in the regeneration area by the ryots is to be encouraged. Local seeds should be used in raising the nursery and they should be collected only from mature, sound and straight grown trees of clear bole. One or two year old stumps may also be used for planting. Casualties should be replaced promptly and weeding and tending should be done.[2]

The Deciduous Selection Working Circle comprises the moist deciduous forests of the Tunacadavu and Pollachi ranges which are not covered by the Plantation Working Circle and excludes areas containing open stunted crop. Its area is 12,999 acres. It is divided into three felling series, the Tunacadavu felling series, the Ulandi felling series and the Villoni felling series. The system is selection felling of all saleable species of prescribed girth. The rotation is 160 years. The felling cycle is forty years and the fellings are regulated by area. The coupes in the Tunacadavu range are to be worked departmentally while the rest are to be worked through contractors.[3]

The Evergreen Working Circle comprises some of the wet evergreen forests of the Tunacadavu and Pollachi ranges which are economically

1 *Working Plan for the Coimbatore South Forest Division*, 1954–55 to 1968–69, by K. A. Bhoja Shetty, Part II, paragraphs 141–150.

2 *Idem*, paragraphs 151–208.

3 *Idem*, paragraphs 209–231.

considered exploitable. Its area is 5,027 acres and it is divided into two felling series, the Karainshola felling series and the Punachi felling series. The minimum exploitable girth limit is 7 inches at breast height for all species. All species marketable at profit are to be marked for felling. The system prescribed is the selection system. The rotation is 150 years and the felling cycle is thirty years. Exploitation is through the agency of contractors. Areas required by the Cinchona Department for the extension of its plantations are to be fully exploited by the Forest Department without adhering to girth limits or felling rules, before they are handed over to the Cinchona Department.[1]

The Fuel Working Circle comprises 20,783 acres and included the forests along the outer slopes of the hills which can be exploited. It is divided into twelve felling series. The simple coppice system with reservation of certain specified species is prescribed. Rotation is fixed at thirty and forty years according as the areas are better or inferior. The coupes are to be worked through contractors. The kumri method of regeneration is to be followed where possible; in other areas, departmental exploitation is to be undertaken. Felled coupes are closed to general grazing for five years, but restricted rotational grazing may be allowed after three years.[2]

The Bamboo Working Circle includes all the bamboo bearing areas. Its system of management is selection thinning of bamboo clumps. A felling cycle of three years is prescribed and fourteen felling series are formed. Coupes are annually leased to contractors. The circle is open to grazing.[3] The Minor Produce Working Circle comprises the entire area of the forests. Ivory and horns are to be collected departmentally while other items of produce are to be leased to contractors, save the items of the Tunacadavu range which are to be leased out to the Co-operative Society of the hill tribes of that range.[4]

The Working plan prescribes a uniform grazing fee of 4 annas per cow. It also prescribes rotational grazing where necessary. It does not prescribe any fee for penning, which is free. It gives instructions for obtaining good broad lac and suggests the possibility of artificial regeneration of evergreen softwood species of the Punachi range.[5]

1 Working Plan for the Coimbatore South Forest Division. 1954–55 to 1968–69, by K. A. Bhoja Shetty. Part II, paragraphs 232–255.

2 *Idem*, paragraphs 256–282.

3 *Idem*, paragraphs 283–296.

4 *Idem*, paragraphs 297–307.

5 *Idem*, paragraphs 311, 316–317, 346–352, 353–359.

Since this working plan was drawn up the Second Five-Year Plan has given special importance to the artificial regeneration of the forests with valuable timber trees and softwood species. Attention has also been given by this plan to the afforestation of low hill areas to prevent soil erosion, the raising of valuable timber trees on river margins and the provision of facilities for starting forest industries such as basket and mat making. A road at a cost of Rs. 7 lakhs has been proposed to be constructed from Seechali road to Palakadavu for facilitating the exploitation of inaccessible forests and for planting teak in that area.[1]

Such is the history of the forests of the district. In regard to other forest matters, there is a Forest College at Coimbatore station in the early years of this century. The question of imparting instruction and practical training in forestry, not only to the forest rangers of this State but also to the forest rangers of the adjoining Indian States engaged the attention of the Government as early as 1905. It was then felt that the Forest College at Dehra Dun was far away from Madras, and that the training and instruction given in it, relating as it did to the North Indian forests, was not quite suited to South Indian conditions. But it was not till 1912 that the Madras Forest College, Coimbatore, as it was then called came into being.[2]

The College with a Principal at its head was placed under the administrative control of the Commissioner of Forests, assisted by a Board of Visitors consisting of the four Conservators of the State. Admission to it in the first year was restricted to the students of this State, but admissions thereafter were thrown open to other States as well, including the then existing Indian States. The College course extended over a period of 21 months and the subjects taught comprised forestry, mathematics, physical science, botany, zoology, drawing, surveying and estimating, forest engineering, forest law, and forest accounts and procedure. Three kinds of certificates were granted to those who passed the examination at the end of the course, viz,, Honours, Higher Standard and Lower Standard, depending upon the marks obtained by them at the examination. A library, a museum and an arborium were attached to the college.[3] But within a few years, the College went under a cloud. It worked at a considerable loss to the Government and, as a result, the question of closing

[1] *Second Five-Year Plan, Madras State, Coimbatore District*, 1955, by P. K. Nambiar, page 21.

[2] G.O. No. 788, Revenue, dated 16th March 1912.
G.O. No. 2780, Development, dated 13th December 1937.
The Southern Forest Rangers' College Magazine, 1955, page 185.

[3] G.O. No. 1271, Revenue, dated 30th April 1912.

it was again and again considered, in 1923, 1932, 1934, 1936 and 1939. The First Congress Ministry took the final decision and closed the college in July 1939.[1] Though it was once more re-opened in October 1945, it was soon handed over to the Government of India to be run as a Central Government institution from 1948.[2] As soon as the Government of India took up the institution, they transferred the Officers' (Superior Forest Service) Course from Dehra Dun to Coimbatore; and for a time both the Officers' and the Forest Rangers' Course were continued in the College.[3] But in 1951, owing to the poor demand for the Officers' course, that course was abolished.[4] Since then, however, the Forest Rangers' Course has been supplemented by a Regional Foresters' School Course (1952) for training foresters deputed by Southern States, and this course extends over a period of one year. The subjects taught for this course are forestry (including silviculture, forest protection and preservation of wild life, forest utilization, forest law, forest mensurations and mathematics and forest management) botany, engineering, surveying, drawing, geology, accounts and procedure, and first aid and hygiene. The College is now called the Southern Forest Rangers' College.

The forests of the district are administered by two District Forest Officers. The District Forest Officer in charge of the North Forest Division has his headquarters at Coimbatore, while the District Forest Officer in charge of the South Forest Division has his headquarters at Pollachi. The latter is assisted by an Assistant Conservator of Forests. All these officers are under the control of the Conservator of Forests, Coimbatore Circle, who has his headquarters at Coimbatore. The Conservator is subordinate to the Chief Conservator of Forests.

[1] G.O. No. 2780, Development, dated 13th December 1937.
G.O. No. 2879, Development, dated 17th December 1940.

[2] G.O. No. 2949, Development, dated 2nd June 1948.
G.O. No. 878, Development, dated 7th March 1950.

[3] Progress Report of the Madras Forest College, Coimbatore, 1948–49.

[4] Progress Report of the Madras Forest College, Coimbatore, 1951–52.

CHAPTER VIII.

INDUSTRIES AND TRADE.

Next to Madras, Coimbatore is the most highly industrialised district in this State, in which a large proportion of the population, about 47 per cent, lives by industries, trade and other avocations. This is however, by no means surprising, seeing that it has a large general trade and that it possesses a large textile industry, both textile mills and hand-looms.[1]

The development of textile industry on a large scale is mainly due to the abundant growth of cotton in this district. This industry is mostly concentrated around Coimbatore. In fact, Coimbatore is considered as one of the most important textile centres in the Indian Union comparable only to Bombay and Ahmedabad. It is undoubtedly the most conspicuous example of an industrial town in this State, for the concentration of major industrial units[2]; for there are no less than 36 cotton spinning and weaving mills situated within a radius of 7 miles from the heart of the town. Among these mills the most well-known are the Kothari Textile Mills, Singanallur, with an authorised capital of 100 lakhs of rupees and an installation of 300 looms and 43,000 spindles and the Lakshmi Mills, Coimbatore with an authorized capital of 100 lakhs of rupees and an installation of 200 looms and 59,988 spindles. Next to these come the Sri Venkatesa Mills, Coimbatore, with an authorized capital of 50 lakhs of rupees and an installation of 268 looms and 47,444 spindles, the Radhakrishna Mills, Peelamedu, with an authorized capital of 30 lakhs of rupees and an installation of 300 looms and 51,664 spindles and the Vasantha Mills, Singanallur, with an authorized capital of 30 lakhs of rupees and an installation of 270 looms and 44,424 spindles. Then follow the other mills; the C. S. & W. Mills, Coimbatore, with an authorized capital of 25 lakhs of rupees and 407 looms and 72,832 spindles; the Sivananda Mills, Coimbatore, with an authorized capital of 25 lakhs of rupees and 18,816 spindles; the Coimbatore Pioneer Mills, Peelamedu, with an authorized capital of 25 lakhs of rupees and 24,466 spindles ; the Pankaja Mills, Coimbatore, with an authorized capital of 25 lakhs of rupees and 30,790 spindles; the Combodia Mills,

1 *Census of India*, 1951, *Madras and Coorg*, Part I, Report page 109.

2 *Idem*, page 70.

Coimbatore, with an authorized capital of 25 lakhs of rupees and 38,110 spindles; the Coimbatore Cotton Mills, Singanallur, with an authorized capital of 25 lakhs of rupees and 30,824 spindles; and the Janardhana Mills, Coimbatore, with an authorized capital of 25 lakhs of rupees and 23,784 spindles. Besides the 36 textile mills concentrated in the Coimbatore area, there are also about 10 weaving and spinning mills in the taluks of Erode, Palladam, Pollachi and Udumalpet. The most well-known among them are the Dhanalakshmi Mills with an authorized capital of 25 lakhs of rupees and an installation of 201 looms and 34,708 spindles situated at Tiruppur, and the Premier Mills with an authorized capital of 25 lakhs of rupees and an installation of 20,736 spindles situated at Udumalpet[1]. All the 45 mills of the district employ about 46,000 workers; and it is said that the workers engaged in the mills in the Coimbatore area form almost 75 per cent of the labour class people in the town. These mills were depending upon steam power in the initial stage and were so till about 1933, when Pykara Hydro-Electric Power was made available at cheap rates.

The concentration of a large number of textile mills in the Coimbatore area has led to the establishment of a large industrial unit called the Textool Company Limited which is situated at a distance of three miles from Coimbatore on the road leading to Satyamangalam. This industrial unit manufactures almost all textile machineries required in the spinning, carding and reeling sections of textile mills. It employs about 1,200 workers. Another industrial unit which manufactures textile machinery is the Ramakrishna Industrial (Private) Limited, Peelamedu, Coimbatore. This unit employs 210 workers. A third large industrial unit is the P.S.G. and Sons' Charities Industrial Institute, Peelamedu, which produces electrical motors, centrifugal pumps, agricultural machineries and other small machines and tools. This unit employs about 1,200 workers. Besides these industrial units, there are about 25 foundaries in Coimbatore, which manufacture mainly electric motors, centrifugal pumps and textile machinery spare parts. They employ 7,500 workers. At Madukkarai, 7 miles west of Coimbatore, there is a cement manufacturing unit established in 1934 by the Associated Cement Company Limited. It employs about 1,500 workers and manufactures daily 800 to 1,000 tons of cement, which is the largest output in South India. At Mettupalayam there is a bleaching unit, called the United Bleachers, which has been established by the joint efforts of all the mill owners in the district. It engages 700 workers. There is another industrial unit in this place for the manufacture of synthetic gems. This factory which is the first of its kind

---

[1] Based on the information furnished by the Director of Industries and Commerce.

in India was started in 1956 with the collaboration of a Swiss Team headed by Mr. R. R. J. Hoffer, with a capital investment of Rs. 22 lakhs. It has the maximum capacity of 40 kilo a day and employs 30 workers. With the technical collaboration of Sri G. D. Naidu, one Radio Manufacturing Unit and one Radio Assembly Unit at Coimbatore and one Carbon Ink Factory at Podanur have been started and these units employ 23, 22 and 20 workers respectively [1]. The rest of the large scale industries consist of 141 cotton ginning and pressing establishments, 10 knitting mills, 16 textile dyeing and printing works, 15 starch works, 15 tanneries, 18 beedi factories, 4 tobacco beedi factories, 16 transport equipment works 4 coffee curing works, 30 tea factories, 3 rubber and its products works, a glass factory and a sugar manufacturing plant and these employ altogether about 7,512 persons.[2]

Turning to cottage industries, hand spinning is the most ancient industry of the district. It still flourishes here on a large scale because of the abundance here of Karunganni variety of Cottons and the systematic efforts made here by the All-India Spinners' Association to develop the industry. It is found in the Palladam, Avanashi, Dharapuram and Gobichettipalayam taluks, the chief centres being in and around Tiruppur, Avanashi, Kangayam and Puliampatti. Thousands of charkas are at work in these centres and are fed by ginned cotton supplied by the branches of the All India Spinners' Association and the Tiruppur Khadi Vastralayam. The yarn produced from these charkas are used for weaving cloths of varying widths of single and double threads. In spite of the advent of power spinning and the production of cheaper, finer, as well as larger quantities of mill-made yarn, the industry still retains its hold on a large section of the agricultural population as a subsidiary occupation in the off season.[3]

Handloom weaving also has been an important occupation here, of a large number of people from time immemorial. In olden days it depended upon the handspun yarn, but today it depends on the mill-made yarn. It is, however, a full-time occupation and it now engages no less than 63,700 persons in the district and in the Dharapuram taluk alone over 18,000 [4]. It is chiefly dependant upon big merchants or sowcars who

---

1. Based on the information furnished by the Assistant Director of Industries and Commerce (General), Coimbatore.

1951 *Census Handbook, Coimbatore District*, 1953, page 8.

2. *Idem*, pages 7–8.

3. G.O. No. 2211, Development, dated 13th December 1929—*See* the Report on the Survey of Cottage Industries in the Coimbatore District, pages 2–3.

G.O. No. 2296, Development, dated 26th September 1940, page 13.

4. 1951 *Census Handbook Coimbatore District* 1953, page 13.

engage weavers and pay them wages. They issue yarns and take off the stuffs woven, charging more for the former and paying less for the latter. The chief communities engaged in this occupation are Devangas and Kaikola Mudaliars with a few Seda Chettis, Jangama Andis and Catholic Christians here and there. Almost all the looms in the district are fitted either with fly shuttle or fly shuttle slay. Warping is done by means of small rotary mills made of split bamboos and sizing is done generally in streets with the usual rice gruel.

The principal centres of weaving in the district are Coimbatore, Ondipudur, Bhavani, Sennimalai, Sivagiri, Satyamangalam, Dharapuram, Puliampatti, Jalathur and Kundadam. Of these, Coimbatore and Dharapuram are important centres of silk weaving. Here saris of pure and mixed silk 16 to 18 cubits long and 45 to 54 inches wide are woven with elaborate designs in lace in the body and kongu. In both the varieties the lace is introduced in such a lavish scale that, at times, the cost of the lace employed in a fabric is much more than that of the silk used. In order, therefore, to keep down the cost of the saris, Surat lace, which is cheaper than the French lace, is used for the borders, while superior lace is used for the Kongu. The weaving is particularly skilful and lace is so interwoven as to appear on one side only. Fretwork of all kinds with figures of parrots are finely woven with lace in richer varieties. All the silk required for weaving is obtained from Kollegal in Mysore and dyed in Coimbatore with fleeting colours which give brightness and glaze to the silk saries. Fast colours are not purposely used, as the Coimbatore saris are mostly exported to Bombay and Poona where the weavers have a fancy to change colours as often as possible. The usual colours employed are red, orange, yellow, blue and pink and a mixture of these colours to produce other light shades. Weaving of mixed silk saris of Kornad fashion with black yarn and silk is done at Dharapuram where both yarn and silk are obtained ready dyed. The yarn used are 80s and 100s and these are imported from Madras and Bombay.

The silk saris, however, have been thrown into the background with the advent of art silk and mercerised yarn. Saris woven of art silk in the weft and mercerised yarn in the woof have become the order of the day and their cheapness, brightness and glaze have created a roaring demand for them among the middle and poorer classes. The important centres where these saris are produced on a large scale are Sowripalayam, Negamam, Marianallur and Mantripalayam. The art silk required for weaving is imported from Madras and Bombay ready dyed and distributed to the various centres. In Marianallur and Somanur, coating, shirting, and gown cloths, both in mercerised yarn and art silk, are produced by

Roman Catholic weavers to supply the needs of Christians and Anglo-Indians. The weavers here get the art silk dyed from Madurai and themselves dye the yarn with sulphur black and naphthol red. The increasing use of art silk has made it necessary for many silk weavers adapt themselves to the changed conditions.

The most common variety of cloths produced in the district are the coarse coloured saris. They are woven from yarns of 20s to 30s and measure 14 to 18 cubits long and 42 to 45 inches wide with 18 to 20 punjams. The chief centres of producing these coloured saris are Negamam, Jalathur, Pulavadi, Malayandipatnam, Bhavani, Kangayam, Kundadam, Mantripalayam, Periyapalayam, Ammapalayam, Sennimalai and Sivagiri. Most of the yarn consumed is obtained from local mills, while coloured yarn, especially red, is imported from Madurai ready dyed. Dyeing with other colours is done at Tiruppur, Kangayam, Sennimalai, Bhavani and Mantripalayam where the agents of the Havero Trading Company supply the colours and instruct the dyers in the process of dyeing. Besides these coarse saris, grey saris of finer counts of Pullampetta pattern are also produced in Satyamangalam for export to the Northern Circars.

The district is famous for its fine rumals or turban cloths of both cotton and silk. They are produced chiefly in Coimbatore, Satyamangalam and Malayandipatnam. They measure from 80 to 104 inches square and are woven both in silk and yarn of finer counts with lace peta for kongu and border. The loom, being too long for a single weaver, has to be worked invariably by two persons assisted by a boy in cases where strings are to be pulled for peta work in the border. Fine upper grey and lace cloths are manufactured from superior yarns of 100 to 150s in Satyamangalam, Jalathur, Pulavadi and Erode, while red upper cloths of Bangalore pattern with yarn and art silk combined are made in Kangayam, Satyamangalam, Dasayyagoundenpudur, Puliampatti, Arasur, Sadumagai and other places. White and grey cloths and towels of 20s and 30s are produced at Kangayam, Avayapalayam and Modacheri and exported largely to Ceylon. As regards khader cloths, they are produced from spun yarn in and around Tiruppur where a large number of looms are engaged in weaving them. The price of this cloth is regulated by the All India Spinners' Association who fix it according to the price of cotton prevailing in the market.[1]

---

[1] G.O. No. 2211, Development, dated 13th December 1929—*See* the Report on the Survey of Cottage Industries in the Coimbatore District, pages 3 to 15.

G.O. No. 2296, Development, dated 26th September 1940, pages 13 to 16.

Printing on grey cloths is done by Kshatriyas in Tiruppur where the khader depots get their khader cloths block-printed at the borders. It is also done at Sennimalai where the cloths are supplied by the merchants who get them from Coimbatore. Before the cloths are block-printed, they are bleached and washed, and after printing at the borders, they are calendered by being beaten with club on a wooden surface in order to give them a finish. These printed cloths are exported to Burma and Ceylon for sale.[1]

The town of Bhavani was once famous for the manufacture of fine cotton carpets which were in great demand in all parts of India and in some foreign countries where they were very much appreciated. In fact they won a first prize in the exhibition held in Madras in 1883. But this industry is not very flourishing now. It is under the control of merchants who engage weavers and pay them wages according to the size of the carpets woven. Formerly only Jangama Andis were engaged in this work, but now other caste people including agriculturists have taken to this occupation. The yarns used are 8s and 3-20s and are obtained from Madurai, Bangalore, Mysore and Bombay. They are dyed by the local Devanga Chettis who use mostly aniline dyes, especially for yellow, red and orange colours, and sulphur black for black colour. Besides cotton carpets, carpets of Agra, pattern and of artificial silk are also produced here. Good carpets are also made by some Pandarams in Sennimalai for export to Burma and Ceylon.[2]

The extraction of fibre from sunn-hemp and the weaving of gunnies with it is a subsidiary occupation of Telugu Chettis of Avayapalayam, Nallannaickenpalayam, and other villages of the Gobichettipalayam taluk. They do not grow the sunn-hemp, but buy it from the ryots who grow it. The stems are soaked in running water for more than five days and then fibres are separated by splashing the stalks over the surface of water and again beating them against a hard surface or stone. The fibre thus separated is spun into yarn. The spinning is done mainly by women and the weaving is done by men. A patti of 16 cubits long is stitched into two gunny bags of 4 cubits long and 1 foot wide. These gunnies being stronger than those made of jute are in great demand among agriculturists for marketing their produce.[3]

---

[1] G.O. No. 2211, Development, dated 13th December 1929—*See* the Report on the Survey of Cottage Industries in the Coimbatore District, page 16.

[2] *Idem*, pages 23–24.
G.O. No. 2296, Development, dated 26th September 1940, pages 9–12.
Manual of Coimbatore District, Vol. II, page 161.

[3] G.O. No. 2211, Development, dated 13th December 1929—*See* the Report on the Survey of Cottage Industries in Coimbatore District, pages 24–26.

Metal industry is carried on in Anuparapalayam, three miles from Tiruppur where Kannar Chettis are engaged in the manufacture of vessels of different descriptions, such as, *jodu thabalai, vanachatti, chembu, kudam*, dish plates, etc. The industry is said to have been started about a century ago by a group of workmen who came from Mysore and settled down in these parts. Brass is the metal largely used and the workers are either master-workmen who obtain metal sheets from capitalists and engage men for making them into articles or actual labourers who work for wages under the capitalists. The workers have specialised in making certain kinds of articles and they confine themselves to the manufacture of those articles only. To a small extent bell metal and bronze wares are also manufactured have for local consumption. In making wares of bell metal, copper and tin are mixed in the proportion of 40 : 14 and in the case of bronze wares, brass and zinc are mixed in the proportion of 6 : 1 or, if the alloy is made of copper and zinc, in equal proportion. The industry was once in a flourishing condition, but it is now gradually dwindling owing to the competition of porcelain and aluminium vessels and other machine-made articles which are sold at comparatively cheap prices[1].

Basket making is carried on extensively in Mettupalayam, Satyamangalam, Pollachi and other places. This is the occupation of a class of people, called ' Medars ', who are professional workers in bamboos in almost every part of the State. They obtain bamboos from coupe contractors who bring them from the Anaimalai and Thalamalai Hills and from the lower regions of the Nilgiri Hills. Besides ordinary baskets, special baskets are made in Pollachi for handling groundnuts in decorticating factories. These baskets are fitted with iron brackets at the bottom, so that they may not easily give way under the pressure of the weight of the seeds. In slack seasons, when there is no demand for special makes, the workers are engaged in making winnows, mats and other ordinary varieties for domestic and agricultural use. They also make nursery baskets for cinchona plantations, bamboo being supplied free by the Government.

There is a great demand for fruit baskets in Mettupalayam where fruits and vegetables grown on the Nilgiri Hills are brought and packed. These baskets are made by Kavara Nayudus and sent to Madras, Mangalore and Bombay for packing fruits and vegetables. There is also a considerable demand here for nursery baskets for coffee and tea plantations. The making of these baskets is practically a monopoly of the

---

[1]. G.O. No. 2211, Development, dated 13th December 1929—*See* the Report on the Survey of Cottage Industries in Coimbatore District, pages 26–28.

[2]. G.O. No. 2296, Development, dated 26th September 1940, pages 5–6

Kavara Nayudus who, unlike the other rural workers, have been intelligent enough to organize themselves so as not to be exploited by traders.

At the beginning of each year they auction the right of monopoly to the person who offers the highest bonus and he is made the sole purchaser of their nursery baskets for the year. The bonus amount is distributed among the workers so as to bind them to supply the monopolist and is not repaid. This is one of the very few cottage industries in which the workers by their organization and united action are able to extract a fair portion of the profits of the merchants as bonus without getting into their clutches.[1]

The extraction of palmyra fibre from sheaths of palmyra palms is carried on extensively by Shanars and also by Chucklers to some extent. The chief centres where the fibre is prepared are Sivagiri, Perundurai, Kunnatturu, Kanakkapuram, Vedakkurur, and adjoining villages. The sheaths are obtained practically free, as they are to be removed periodically for cleaning the trees and for tapping. The uncleaned fibre is collected by merchants who clean and sort it into various varieties for supply to European firms at Calicut from where it is said to be exported to Hamburg in Germany for making brushes, etc. The industry is carried on only for six months, i.e., from June to November, as during the rest of the year the workers are engaged in tapping trees for sweet toddy. Though it is of recent origin, it provides employment for half the year to a large class of people.[2]

Manufacture and sale of both palmyra and cane jaggery engages a large number of people in the district. The former is carried on by the Shanars in the Gobichettipalayam, Avanashi and Erode taluks, while the latter is carried on by agricultural ryots. The palmyra jaggery is a very coarse product, containing as it does much invert sugar and greatly discoloured by the crude process of manufacture. Generally sweet toddy is drawn from November to May, the male trees yielding juice from November to January and the female trees from January to May. Pots, in which the toddy is collected, is coated inside with lime and attached to the shoots in which an incision has been made. The yield from a tree is about one to two measures in the first ten days and it diminishes gradually during the next twenty days. The daily yield from ten trees is ordinarily a pot of 16 measures and this can be converted into jaggery within three hours by the simple process of boiling in open earthen pots

1 G.O. No. 2211, Development, dated 13th December 1929—*See* the Report on the Survey of Cottage Industries in Coimbatore District, pages 28–32.

2 *Idem*, pages 32–33.

over a smoky wood fire. While the toddy is boiling, some quantity of castor seeds or oil is put into it, so that the liquid may not foam. When it turns thick, it is poured into moulds and allowed to cool. This jaggery is very largely used by the poorer classes and it is brought in hundreds of baskets to village shandies where they are purchased by the agents of Parry and Company for the preparation of spirits, sugar and sweets. Besides the jaggery, candy and sugar are also made out of the palmyra toddy. Jaggery is also produced from coconut toddy; but as it is not used by all classes, this industry is not in a flourishing condition. The palmyra jaggery industry, on the other hand, affords a substantial additional income to the workers, when they are free from agricultural work.[1]

The spinning and weaving of wool into cumblies is done by the Kurumbars in a few places in the district. The chief centre for them is Kalangal in the Palladam taluk where the work is done mostly by women. Most of the weavers have their own flocks and shear wool from them once in a year, i.e., in May. Before they are sheared, the sheep are well cleaned; and generally 100 sheep are sheared in four days, yielding about 40 lb. of wool. Carding is done by a stringed bow and spinning is done on laps with the help of spindles. Only white cumblies are made with a thin stripe of black wool or coloured yards at the borders. They are of a rough variety ordinarily used by the poor class of people. A cumbly is 5 cubits long and 3 cubits wide, but made of two or three patties stitched together. The woollen patties are also stitched into small bags which orthodox Brahmins use for keeping ' madi ' cloths against pollution.[2]

Coir yarn is made in the district mostly by Pallas and Pariahs and to some extent by Nayakars, Koravas and Thotkars of villages on river margins where there are coconut trees. Coconut husks are purchased from tope owners and retted in pits in the river bed for a period of six to eight months. They are then taken out and beaten into fibres. The yield of fibre from 1,000 husks is generally 10 maunds or 250 lb. of fibres; but, when cleaned, it will weigh only 7 to 8 maunds. The fibre is twisted into yarn by the following simple process. At the ends of a small piece of bamboo two threads are attached and they are joined together to form a triangle with the bamboo piece as the base. To this base a small handle is attached for turning it round. The fibre is fed at the vertex

1 G.O. No. 2211, Development, dated 13th December 1929—*See* the Report on the Survey of Cottage Industries in Coimbatore District, pages 33–34.

G.O. No. 2296, Development, dated 26th September 1940, pages 17–18.

2 G.O. No. 2211, Development, dated 13th December 1929—*See* the Report on the Survey of Cottage Industries in Coimbatore District, pages 34–35.

and is spun into yarn as the handle revolves. Generally three such yarns are twisted into one rope. Twisting into a rope is done by a simple machine which consists of a block of wood to which three hooks are attached. To another block of wood which is mounted on a wheeled stand, a single hook is attached. Three strands of yarn which are to be twisted into a rope are attached each at one end, while the other ends of all the three are attached to the single hook on the other block which is opposite to the first one. When the three hooked machine turns, yarn is twisted into rope, the sliding apparatus being taken nearer and nearer to the other instrument in the opposite direction. Besides ropes of three strands, ropes of nine strands are also made and all these ropes are brought to the Pollachi shandy for sale. This is one of the few industries which could be practised as a subsidiary occupation by many classes of people, since no large capital is required or elaborate machinery used for the manufacture of ropes.[1]

Oil pressing from gingelly, castor and groundnut seeds is done by Vaniyars in almost every important village in the district. It is carried on as usual with very little variance either in the method adopted or the profits realized. Margosa oil, however, is extracted on a fairly large scale in Kangayam and other adjoining places where there is a large growth of margosa trees. The seeds are collected by women and children of the poor classes and are dried and sold to merchants. The outer shell of the seeds is removed by beating the dry seeds and the kernal is put in ghannies or wooden mills and crushed for oil. The cake is used as manure for coffee and tea plantations, while the oil is sent to Madurai, Dindigul, Devakottai and other places in Chettinad where it is used by the poorer classes for bathing and hair dressing.[2]

Dharapuram is famous for the building of spring carts for travelling and heavy-wheeled carts for carrying goods. It supplies the carts to almost all the bordering districts of Tiruchirappalli, Madurai, etc. They are remarkable for their strength and durability. The chief kinds of wood used for them are Irumbagam, Tadash and Purusa which are obtained from Palghat in Malabar. Generally Teak is used for spokes and felloes, Purusa for naves, Irumbagam for side frames and centre pole and Venteak or Taddsh for yoke. About 100 spring carts and over 150 heavy load carts are made in a year. They are taken to cattle shows at Tiruppur and

[1] G.O. No. 2211, Development, dated 13th December 1929—*See* the Report on the Survey of Cottage Industries in Coimbatore District, pages 36–37.

[2] *Idem*, page 37.

other places and offered for sale. The industry still continues to survive in spite of the heavy influx of motor buses and trucks.[1]

Crystal works such as spectacles, glass beads and various kinds of ornaments, lingams and other sacred images are made by a few families of Jangam caste at Settipalayam near Tiruppur. The crystals are procured locally or from Vallam in the Thanjavur district. The process is exceedingly simple, but the work turned out is neat and well finished. The crystals are ground on emery discs which are prepared locally by mixing corundum and lac. The discs are attached by a little lac to the ordinary lathe which is worked with a bow. With his right hand the worker turns the lathe and with his left he works on the stone attached to the end of a small piece of wood by a little lac. The discs are kept wet, while the crystals are being ground. A stone obtains complete polish after being turned on three lathes, the last of which is the copper one. But lingams and beads made out of Vallam pebbles require to be polished on five lathes, the last of which is a wooden one. The workers are wholly engaged in this industry, but sometimes they work on precious stones. They likewise purchase imitation stones from Tiruchirappalli and polish and convert them into imitation rubies. As a class they are industrious and make a decent living from their profession.[2]

In olden days iron was smelted near Sennimalai, Mulanur and other places in the district. Solid iron ore was never used; what was used was only black sand which is found in the beds of surface streams after the rains are over. This was smelted with an enormous proportion of charcoal on a crude conical furnace urged by the common country bellows. The iron was never completely melted so as to run, but was taken out as a white hot bloom, and at once cut nearly in two by blows from an axe. But this industry is no more.[3] Some new industries which have now come into existence on a small scale are poultry-breeding at Ramanathapuram and bee-keeping at Avanashi, Coimbatore and Ramanathapuram. There is also some scope for manufacturing paper from grass, bamboo, etc., available from the reserved forests in the Udumalpet taluk.[4]

Several of these cottage industries are suffering from one drawback or another. Some need finance, some organisation, some improved technical

---

1 G.O. No. 2211, Development, dated 13th December 1929,—*See* the Report on the Survey of Cottage Industries in Coimbatore District, page 38.

2 *Idem*, pages 39–40.

3 *Manual of Coimbatore District*, Vol. II, page 158.

4 G.O. No. 2211, Development, dated 13th December 1929—*See* the Report on the Survey of Cottage Industries in Coimbatore District, page 40.

G.O. No. 2296, Development, dated 26th September 1940, pages 5 and 21.

knowledge, and some greater facilities for procuring raw materials, storing finished goods and marketing them. The Government have been quite alive to these drawbacks which are existing not only in this district but also in all other districts. They have been trying to set them right through the Industries, Co-operative and Rural Welfare Departments. What the Co-operative and Rural Welfare Departments have done will be shown in the chapters on Co-operation and Welfare Schemes. But what the Industries Department has done may be indicated here.

The first attempt at developing the industries in this State was made in 1906 by the appointment of Mr. Chatterton as the Director of Industrial and Technical Enquiries. In 1908 as a result of an Industrial Conference held at Ootacamund, endeavours were made by the Government to re-organize the Industries Department, but these were frustrated by Lord Morley, who was then the Secretary of State for India. It was not till 1914 that the Department of Industries, which is now called the Department of Industries and Commerce, was reorganised and a Director of Industries with an adequate number of officials under him were appointed. Since then this department has made many attempts to improve the cottage as well as the large scale industries in the State, by organizing periodical exhibitions, by instructing the weavers and other cottage industry workers in improved methods, by opening industrial and commercial museums and technical trading institutes for groups of districts, by rendering financial assistance to private industrial schools and by giving grants in aid to industries under the State Aid to Industries Act of 1922. This Act which has been amended several times provides now for the grant of financial aid to new or nascent industries, cottage industries, and even old industries (for special reasons). The aid may take the form of loans, guarantee of cash credit, over draft, or fixed advance with a bank, subscription of shares or debentures; and guarantee of a minimum return on part of the capital in the case of a Joint Stock Company and also subsidies which in the case of cottage industries may be given for any purpose and in the case of other industries for the conduct of research or purchase of machinery. The maximum value of the loans is 50 per cent of the net value of the assets of the industrial enterprise. Other forms of aid may consist of grants of land on favourable terms, and supply of raw materials, firewood, water, or electricity at concessional rates. The Act has provided for a statutory Board of Industries whose business it is to advise the Government in the matter of granting of loans. Loans upto Rs. 500 in the case of cottage industries, however, can be granted by the Director of Industries and Commerce.[1]

Coimbatore, like other districts, has been benefited by all these measures. Till 1951 it had a District Industries Officer, but since then it has been placed under a new officer, the Assistant Director of Industries and Commerce, who has his headquarters at Coimbatore. He is assisted by an Inspector of Industries, two District Inspectors of Cottage Industries and a Village Industries Officer.[2]

The department has, in Coimbatore, a Polytechnic and an Industrial and Commercial Museum. The Polytechnic is one of the five institutions started on a regional basis under the Five-Year Plan in order to meet the growing need for technicians. It was established with the generous help of Sri G. D. Naidu, Managing Director for United Motors (Coimbatore) Limited, who placed at the disposal of the Government a sum of 1½ lakhs of rupees in Government bonds, machinery valued at about 2 lakhs of rupees and a library worth about ½ lakh of rupees, for the working of the institute. He also donated more than Rs. 10,000 for the award of scholarships and provided accommodation for the institute at the premises of the U.M.S. Workshops, Coimbatore, pending the construction of permanent buildings to house the institution. It was opened in 1945 by Sir Arthur Hope and was named after him as 'Arthur Hope Polytechnic' in token of his interest in the welfare of the youth of this State.[3] It awards diplomas and certificates in automobile engineering, auto-servicing and radio servicing and provides practical training to students in this regard by undertaking the repair of motor cars, radio sets, etc., of private owners. It may be stated here that the scheme for training demobilised and disabled military personnel has now been replaced by a scheme for imparting vocational and technical training to adult civilians in this as well as in other Polytechnics in the State.[4]

The Industrial and Commercial Museum at Coimbatore was opened in 1939 for the display and advertisement of the industrial products of

---

1 Administration Reports of the Department of Industries and Commerce from 1919.

Monthly Digest of Economics and Statistics, Madras State, January 1951, pages, 1–6.

2 Information obtained from the office of the Director of Industries and Commerce.

3 G.O. No. 1031, Development, dated 13th March 1945.

Administration Report of the Department of Industries and Commerce for 1945–46, page 51.

4 *Idem*, for 1949–50, page 17.

Idem, for 1953–54, pages 16–17.

the district, and in order to increase its usefulness it was linked up with the Central Museum established at Madras in the same year.[1] In 1947 both the central and the district museums, of which Coimbatore was one, were reorganised by the National Government. In accordance with this reorganisation the Coimbatore museum and other museums are run by the Industries Department and the direction of their affairs is entrusted to a committee consisting of the Collector of the district, two members of the Legislative Assembly and one member of the Legislative Council representing the region, three representatives of cottage and small scale industries in the region and an officer of the Industries Department.[2]

The department also gives financial aid to the following private institutions in the district;—St. Joseph's Industrial School, Coimbatore, which imparts instruction in carpentry and fitting; P.S.G. and Sons' Charities Industrial Institute, Peelamedu, which teaches mechanical engineering, electrical engineering and textile manufacture; Sri Ramakrishna Mission Vidyalaya School of Engineering, Coimbatore, which coaches pupils in general mechanics; the Women's Industrial School, Dharapuram, which gives instruction in needle work, embroidery and dress making, and the District Board Industrial School, Pollachi, which provides training in carpentry, cabinet-making and general mechanics.[3] Nor is this all. Under the scheme, for the revival of important cottage industries by the establishment of model centres started by the National Government in 1950, the department gives technical assistance and advice in the implementation of several schemes in the Lower Bhavani Community Project areas and in the several National Extension Blocks in the district.[4]

Now, let us turn our attention to trade. The chief commodities of trade are cotton, coal, coke, dyes and tans, grains and pulses, hides, skins and leather, metals, manganese, unwrought wood, provisions, spices, salt, sugar, oils and oil seeds, especially groundnuts. The inward and outward movement of marketable commodities by road cannot be ascertained, as no figures of these are available. It may, however, be stated that a good deal of commodities are transported by lorries owned by private firms and individuals and that the lorries registered in the district alone, for instance in 1956 numbered about 1,200.[5] The outward and inward movement of commodities by rail can, however, be gathered from

---

1 Administration Report of the Department of Industries and Commerce for 1939–40, pages 27–28.

2 *Idem*, for 1948–49, page 31.

3 *Idem*, for 1953–54, page 28.

4 Information obtained from the office of the Director of Industries and Commerce.

5 Report on the Administration of the Motor Vehicles Act, 1956, page 6.

the statistics of goods transported by the railways. In 1954-55, for instance, the outward movement of commodities amounted to 4,807,356 maunds of which grains and pulses accounted for 7,99,950 maunds, manufactured cotton 5,51,811 maunds, provisions 4,35,022 maunds, metals and manganese 2,60,586 maunds, raw cotton 1,92,189 maunds, oils 1,42,738 maunds, sugar 1,28,566 maunds and dyes and tans 1,01,969 maunds. The inward movement of commodities amounted to 1,73,09,115 maunds of which grains and pulses accounted for 56,84,653 maunds, oils 10,84,396 maunds, raw cotton 7,68,446 maunds, metals and manganese 691,332 maunds, salt 6,07,912 maunds, provisions 3,81,800 maunds, sugar 3,68,284 maunds, unwrought wood 3,09,614 maunds, and coal and coke 1,52,573 maunds.[1]

Since 1936 a marketing committee consisting of the representatives of the traders, growers and the Government has been constituted in Coimbatore under the Madras Commercial Crop Markets Act of 1933 in order to provide better markets for the chief commercial crops of the district. Originally (in 1936) it dealt only with cotton, confining its operation only to the area within the limits of the Tiruppur municipality. Subsequently in 1950, it extended its operation to the entire district with groundnuts added to cotton. Next year tobacco was notified as a third crop for trade regulation. It has established 4 markets so far at Tiruppur, Pollachi, Gobichettipalayam and Erode. It may be mentioned here that of these crops, cotton is the most important, occupying as it does about 3·5 lakhs of acres which is 14·6 per cent of the cultivated area of the district and 33.9 per cent of the total area grown under cotton in the State. The details about the important fairs and shandies held in the district, are as follows :—shandies are held on every Sunday in Attavanipudur, Bhavani, Jambai, Nambiyur, Polavakalipalayam and Vanipudur; on every Monday in Kugalur; on every Tuesday in Dalovaipet, Kilvani, Marudur, Satyamangalam and Siruvalur; on every Wednesday in Avanashi, Nall Road, Olagam and Vembathi; on every Thursday in Athani, Kurichi, Pollachi, Punchai Buliampatti and Vadamalaipalayam; on every Friday in Karamadai, Kondayampalayam, Perundalaiyur and Vellithiruppur; and on every Saturday in Annur, Appakudi, Mettupalayam, Modachur and Murali. Besides these weekly shandies, cattle shandies are also held on every Monday at Andhiyur, on every Tuesday in Budapudi, on every Wednesday in Kavandapadi and on every Saturday in Mylambadi.[2]

Prior to the Second World War there was no restriction on the internal movement of any commodities in the districts. But as a result of the war

---

1 Goods Revenue Statistics, Southern Railway, 1954–55, pages 5–6 and 26–27.

2 Census Handbook 1951, Coimbatore District, pages 6–7.

and the acute scarcity of several essential commodities, controls of various kinds were introduced in this State by the Government for fixing fair prices, for preventing hoarding and black-marketing and for ensuring an equitable distribution of the essential commodities. Among these measures the most important was the compulsory procurement of foodgrains, specially rice, through Government agency and its rationing through co-operative societies and other authorized dealers. Coimbatore being more or less self-sufficient in the matter of foodgrains, was left out of the scheme of compulsory procurement introduced in 1942 in the surplus districts. Rationing in urban areas was, however, introduced in Coimbatore in 1944 and procurement and informal rationing in rural areas in 1946. In December 1947 rationing (both urban and rural) was discontinued in the whole State, but in January 1949 it was again introduced in Coimbatore as well as in all other districts (except Thanjavur) on account of the extraordinary rise in prices. On 15th June 1952, however, the position having improved, both procurement and rationing were abolished in the whole State. It may be noted that almost throughout this period, restrictions were imposed on the movement and distribution of various articles like sugar, jaggery, groundnut, groundnut oil, kerosene oil and other oils, onions, chillies, etc.

It remains now to deal with the weights and measures of the district. Here 8 duddus or tolas (each weighing 180 grains) = 1 palam ; 3 palams = 1 seer; 5 seers = 1 viss; 8 viss = 1 maund (25 lb.); 50 palams = 1 tukku and 2 tukkus = 1 tulam. The weight of the maund differs widely in different places. In addition to these, special weights, such as sattai, kandagam and rattal, which vary from place to place, are also in use for weighing cotton seeds, cotton wool, etc. The goldsmiths' subdivisions of the tola are: 4 kundumanis (the small scarlet and black seeds of the Abrus precatorius) make one fanam or panavidai; 9 fanams or panavidais make one pagoda or varahanidai and 30½ fanams or panavidais make one tola or rupee. Silver is generally weighed by rupees, though in some places the palam and the viss are used.

The officially recognised table of grain measures is this: 132 tolas of rice = 1 (heaped) Madras Measure; 2 Madras Measures = 1 Vallam, 4 Vallams = 1 Marakkal; 4 Marakkals = 1 Moda and 2 Modas = 1 Salagai. Besides these, fractions of small padis are also in use. The capacity of padi and marakkal varies in some places and so is the salagai which is mostly confined to the measurement of paddy.

Liquids such as milk, curd, ghee and so on are usually sold by the ordinary grain measure and its sub-multiples. But in some places oil is measured by an ordinary earthen pot called ' kudam ' which contains 1,000 tolas. A still larger measure called ' podi ' which contains 8 kudams is used in large transactions. There are also in use fractions of the kudam up to one-sixteenth.

English acres and cents are commonly used as land measures. The old land measures of the district were; 24 feet= 1 Kol (rod); 1 square rod (576 square feet)=1 kuli or gunta; 100 kulis=1 kani (1·32 acres); 120 kulis= 1 sei (1·59 acres) and 240 kulis= 1 ma (3·17 acres). Lengths are measured by the English inch, foot and yards, but they are also measured by the popular table according to which 8 angulams (thumb's breadth)=1 jan (span); 12 angulams=1 adi (foot); 18 angulams=1 muzham (cubit, length from elbow to the tip of the middle finger); 2 muzhams=1 kajam (yard); 2 kajams= 1 mar (length from tip to tip of the fingers of the extended arms) and 16 mars=1 rope. There are no defined measures to denote distances of greater length. The term ' nazhigai vazhi ' is ordinarily used to denote the distance which can be walked in a nazhigai or 24 minutes and may be taken at about 1⅓ miles, while a ' kadam ' corresponds to ten miles. Other popular expressions are anaippu (about 100 yards), which is the favourite distance of a witness who does not care to particularize in his evidence; a kadu or a field, of which about 5 or 6 go to make one mile, etc.

Time is now reckoned on the English system of hours and minutes, but the old measures of time are also sometimes used. These are, 60 vinadis=1 nazhigai or 24 minutes; 3¾ nazhigais=1 muhurtam; 2 muhurtams= 1 jamam (watch) and 8 jamams or 60 nazhigais=1 day (24 hours). There are also in use many vague measures of time. The hour of the day at which an event occurs is sometimes indicated by phrases such as ' cock crowing time ', ' conjee time ' 'return of the cattle time', ' lamp lighting time ' and ' supper time '.[1]

---

[1] Manual of Coimbatore District, Vol. II, pages 439–442.

CHAPTER IX.

CO-OPERATION.

Co-operation has come to play an increasingly important part in the present century, alike in agriculture, in industries and in other economic and social activities. It has been claimed as the most efficient method by which planned development in various fields can be secured by providing State guidance and assistance to almost all forms of joint enterprise. It has also been hailed as a sovereign remedy both for curing the ills of capitalism and for achieving the ideals of communism, aiming as it does, at the establishment of a new economic order under which wealth, instead of being appropriated by the few, is shared and enjoyed equally by the many. As is well-known, it aims at the achievement by joint endeavour of what is difficult of achievement by individual endeavour, especially by individuals of limited means. And, nowhere is joint endeavour more necessary than in agriculture and industries which employ mostly men of very limited means. But co-operation has its uses not only for the poorer but also for the middle classes, inasmuch as it can provide them too with better facilities and greater amenities. It is the gradual realization of this that has slowly but steadily spread the co-operative movement in our country.

Agriculture has always stood in need of credit and the agriculturists have always found it necessary to borrow for meeting cultivation expenses, for maintaining their families, and, if they are indebted, as they generally are, for paying the ever increasing interest on their debts. The money-lenders are the only source from which they have been accustomed for ages to borrow and the money-lenders have not only charged them exorbitant rates of interest but very often, ultimately, deprived them of their lands and turned them into mere agricultural labourers. It was estimated in 1935 that more than 90 per cent of the credit requirements of the agriculturists were met by money-lenders.

The Government have from time to time taken several measures to afford credit facilities to the agriculturists and to free them from the clutches of the money-lenders. Of these, the formation of the agricultural co-operative credit societies is one of the most important measures.

[1] Report on Agricultural Indebtedness by W. R. S. Sathianathan, 1935, page 43.
Monograph on Rural Problems in Madras, by S. Y. Krishnaswami, 1947, pages 356–361.

But, before we deal with the co-operative societies, we may mention here something about the other measures too that have been designed to assist the agriculturists. In 1883 the Government passed the Land Improvement Loans Act (India Act XIX of 1883) under which long term loans repayable in 20 to 30 years can be granted at cheap rates of interest for making such improvements to the land as would increase its letting values, like the construction of wells, tanks, irrigation channels, etc. In 1884 they passed the Agriculturists' Loans Act (India Act XII of 1884) under which short-term and medium-term loans can be granted for the purchase of seed grain, manure, cattle, fodder, pump-sets, etc. In 1918 they acquired power under the Usurious Loans Act (India Act X of 1918) to stop recovery of usurious rates of interest. In 1935 they passed the Madras Debtors Protection Act (Madras Act VII of 1935) which fixed a reasonable maximum rate of interest and prescribed an improved system of keeping of accounts by money-lenders for the benefit of small debtors who borrow sums below Rs. 500. In the same year they amended the Agriculturists' Loans Act (Madras Act XVI of 1935) so as to permit the grant of loans to agriculturists for discharging their debts and for scaling down their debts by amicable adjustment with the creditors through Special Loans Officers. In 1936 they passed the Madras Debt Conciliation Act (Madras Act XI of 1936) which provides for voluntary and amicable settlement of debts by bringing together the agriculturist debtors and their creditors through the medium of Special Conciliation Boards. In the same year they amended the Usurious Loans Act in order to make it more effective (Madras Act VIII of 1937). Finally, in 1938, they passed the Madras Agriculturists' Relief Act (Madras Act IV of 1938) for according substantial relief to indebted agriculturists by scaling down their existing debts, by reducing the rate of interest on their future debts and by writing off their arrears of rent due to zamindars, jenmis and other landholders. Experience has, however, shown certain defects in the working of these Acts, which have, to some extent, nullified the intentions of the Government. The Takkavi loans granted under the Acts of 1883 and 1884 are stated to have failed to become popular because of the delays and irksome enquiries, because of the insufficiency of the loans granted and because of the rigour with which they are collected as arrears of land revenue. The Debtors' Protection Act of 1935 has been found to be defective, inasmuch as the creditors have been required to render accounts only if asked for by the debtors. The Agriculturists' Loans Amendment Act of 1935 and the Debt Conciliation Act of 1936 are said to have given only an infinitesimal relief to the agriculturists on account of the voluntary element involved in them. Even the Agriculturists' Relief Act of 1938 is stated to have not attained its object, as it has tended to curtail rural credit, to drive the agriculturists, as before, to the money-lenders and to drive the money-lenders to devise various ways for circumventing the Act.[1]

In industries too the conditions have been no better. Most of the cottage and small-scale industries have gradually come into the grip of capitalists, money-lenders, master weavers and master workers. Most of the workers, as a rule, have facilities neither for obtaining credit, nor for purchasing raw materials at cheap rates and marketing their finished goods at competitive prices. The State Aid to Industries Act of 1922 (Act V of 1923) under which loans are granted is said to have failed to touch even the fringe of the problem of industrial credit. Nor have the various attempts made to improve industries by opening industrial schools and museums and by rendering technical aid by demonstration removed the need to devise some machinery for procuring and distributing raw materials and arranging for the sale of finished goods.[2]

It is in this background that the value of the co-operative organisations which the Government have encouraged becomes evident. As early as 1892 they appointed Sir Frederick Nicholson as a Special Officer to enquire how far the methods of co-operation adopted in Europe could be adopted in Madras to relieve rural indebtedness. He recommended the formation of rural co-operative societies on the lines of the Raiffeisen Societies of Germany for the provision of rural credit on reasonable terms and for the encouragement of thrift among the rural population. Nothing came of this,[3] but within a few years the Government of India appointed a committee on co-operation with Sir Frederick Nicholson as one of the members and, on the recommendations of that committee, passed the Co-operative Credit Societies Act (Act X of 1904). This Act envisaged the formation of " small and simple co-operative societies for small and simple folk with simple needs and requiring small sums only " for short periods. Under this Act the Madras Central Urban Bank and two district central banks were registered with the object of financing the co-operative credit societies and several such co-operative credit societies

---

1 Monograph on Rural Problems in Madras by S. Y. Krishnaswami, 1947, pages 363–364, 369–374.

2 Idem pages 311–312.

3 Report regarding the possibility of introducing land and agricultural banks into the Madras Presidency, 1895, Vols. I and II.

G.O. No. 1576, Revenue, dated 27th April 1898.

G.O. No. 701, Revenue, dated 13th October 1899.

soon came into being. This Act was, however, replaced in 1912 by another Act (India Act II of 1912), which was more comprehensive and which made provision for the formation of central credit societies and co-operative institutions of all types and for all purposes. Under this Act, central banks were formed in one district after another as well as urban banks and societies of various types other than agricultural credit societies, such as marketing societies, the weavers' societies and the consumers' stores. Then came the First World War and close upon its heels the provincialization of the subject of co-operation under the Montague-Chelmsford Reforms, and a period of agricultural prosperity, of rapid expansion of the co-operative movement. In 1917, in order to finance the central banks and to co-ordinate their activities, the Madras Central Urban Bank was converted into the Madras Provincial (now State) Co-operative Bank. And, as these banks could not grant long-term loans to agriculturists, the formation of land mortgage banks on co-operative basis was sanctioned in 1925 for granting such loans. These banks were authorised to float debentures on the security of the lands mortgaged to them by individual borrowers. But, as each one of these banks issued its own series of debentures and caused confusion and reluctance on the part of the public to purchase them, in 1929, on the recommendation of the Townsend Committee, the Central Land Mortgage Bank was organised for the centralised issue of debentures and for financing the primary land mortgage banks. The economic depression which then began set the clock back for a time and ushered in a period more of consolidation and of reconstruction of the existing societies than of formation of new societies. This period, however, witnessed several happy auguries. It witnessed the expansion of land mortgage banks and non-credit societies. It witnessed the passing of Act VI of 1932 which remedied the defects noticed in the Act of 1912 and the passing of Act X of 1934 which regulated the working of the land mortgage banks. It also witnessed the appointment of a special committee (Vijayaraghava Achariar Committee) in 1939 which made several suggestions for the improvement of co-operative societies. Co-operation was thus put on a better footing, but its chance for an unprecedented expansion came only with the outbreak of the Second World War when, owing to the rise in prices and the scarcity of food stuffs, the introduction of controls and rationing and the need for settling ex-servicemen in profitable avocations, several new types of co-operative societies came into existence and several old types of co-operative societies began to undertake new work. And the introduction of total prohibition in this State gave also not a little fillip to co-operation since it made it necessary to absorb the ex-toddy tappers in useful industries and other avocations and provide the ex-addicts with all sorts of amenities. Meanwhile, the Government of India appointed two committees, the Agricultural Finance Sub-Committee (Gadgil Committee) and the Co-operative Planning Committee (Saraiya Committee) for suggesting post-war development of co-operation and their recommendations were considered by the conference of the Registrars of Co-operative Societies held in Madras in 1947. All these recommendations as well as the Post-War Reconstruction Schemes drawn up by the Adviser to Government in 1945 were examined, and, where necessary modified and implemented by the National Government.[1]

In accordance with the First Five-Year Plan approved by the Indian Parliament the Madras Government in 1952 provided Rs. 100 lakhs for the development of co-operation. This sum was to be spent on various schemes such as the organization of co-operative land colonization societies for the benefit of Harijans, landless labourers and ex-servicemen, the intensive cultivation of lands through village co-operatives, the construction of warehouses for the storage of agricultural produce, etc. The Government also provided a sum of Rs. 371 lakhs for several other co-operative schemes for housing, dairying and milk-supply, cottage industries, amelioration of backward classes, etc. In 1953, when the Andhra State was formed the cost of all these schemes for the residuary Madras State came to about Rs. 278·77 lakhs. About the same time, under the Indo-U.S. Technical Co-operation agreement the Indian Planning Commission allotted six Rural Community Projects to the Composite State during 1952–53. One of these projects was the Lower Bhavani Project in the Coimbatore district. Subsequently in 1953–54, two National Extension Service Blocks were set up at Tiruppur and Palladam and in 1954–55 another National Extension Service Block was set up at Kangayam. Co-operative societies were organized in the areas covered by the Project and the Blocks.

Turning to the various types of co-operative societies, the structure of co-operative credit gradually built up at different times now consists of the Madras State Co-operative Bank and the Madras Central Land Mortgage Bank at the apex for securing the needs of the whole State and the various central banks, the urban banks, the primary land mortgage banks, the agricultural credit societies, the employees' credit societies

---

1 Madras Co-operative Manual, 1952, Vol. I, pages 4–11.

Monograph on Rural Problems in Madras by S. Y. Krishnaswami, 1949, pages 364–369, 375–378.

Post-War Reconstruction and Development Schemes of Government of Madras, 1945, pages 5, 53–55, 59–75.

and other miscellaneous credit societies at the base for securing the needs of the districts. The Madras State Co-operative Bank obtains its funds from Government loans, from borrowings from the Reserve Bank of India and the State Bank of India and from deposits, and passes on these funds to the central banks which, in turn, pass them on to the primary agricultural credit societies, urban banks, etc. It normally borrows at a concessional rate of 1½ per cent interest and lends to the central banks at 2¼ per cent interest and the central banks lend to the agricultural credit and other societies affiliated to them at about 4½ per cent interest and these societies in turn lend to their members at 6¼ per cent[1]. The Central Land Mortgage Bank raises funds from the public in the shape of 20 year debentures guaranteed by the Government (up to 7 crores) at rates consistent with the prevailing market conditions, retains a margin of 1¼ per cent, and lends the funds to the district or primary land mortgage banks which, in turn, lend them to the agriculturists on the security of their lands.[2]

The agricultural credit societies form the most numerous as well as the most important of the primary societies. They obtain their funds chiefly from borrowings from the central banks. Each one of them is organized on the collective guarantee of the agriculturists of the village with unlimited liability and limited dividends. Credit is obtained on the joint security of the members who are all generally residents of one village. The societies are managed on the democratic principle of one member one vote. The general body of the society elects a panchayat which is vested with powers for executive administration and the panchayatdars elect a president and a secretary from among themselves. The bye-laws of these societies permit not only the granting of the loans but also the taking up of a wide variety of functions. Normally, however, the societies are largely confining their attention to the granting of loans, credit being the crying need of the ryots. But, during the Second World War, when rationing and controls were in force, many of these societies undertook the purchase

---

[1] *See* the pamphlet entitled the Co-operative Movement by J. C. Ryan, 1954, page 1.

Monograph on Rural Problems in Madras by S. Y. Krishnaswami, 1947, pages 368–369.

The Madras Co-operative Manual, 1952, Vol. I, pages 94–138.

Report on the Working of the Co-operative Societies, 1953, page 6.

[2] *See* the pamphlet entitled the Co-operative Movement by J. C. Ryan, 1954, pages 2–3.

Monograph on Rural Problems in Madras by S. Y. Krishnaswami, 1947, pages 375–378.

The Madras Co-operative Manual, 1952, Vol. I, pages 138–174.

Co-operation in Madras State, a pamphlet published by the Director of Information and Publicity, 1954, page 9.

and distribution of essential commodities. And since February 1949, under a scheme introduced by the National Government[1], several of them have undertaken multi-purpose activities such as the supply of agricultural, industrial and domestic requirements of the members, the marketing of their produce, the collection and sale of milk and the promotion of social and recreational activities. They have also taken part in the food production measures launched by the Government by distributing chemical manure, iron and steel, by arranging to get fallow lands on lease for cultivation and by encouraging the members to dig pits for making rural compost[2].

The non-agricultural credit societies, the urban banks, the employees' societies and the other miscellaneous credit societies are situated in the towns and cater to the credit needs of the middle class and lower middle class people such as the artisans, traders, public servants, mill hands, etc. The urban banks raise funds chiefly by obtaining deposits from the members and non-members and sometimes by borrowing from the central banks. They issue loans on personal security, on the mortgage of immovable property, on the security of non-agricultural and industrial produce, on agricultural produce where there are no marketing societies, on jewels and on insurance policies other than those coming under the Pension-*cum*-Provident Fund Scheme of the Government. Those that have a working capital exceeding one lakh of rupees and fully qualified paid secretaries have been permitted to undertake the business of discounting cheques and collection of bills of their members after adopting the necessary safeguards. The employees' societies raise funds chiefly by borrowing from central banks, collect compulsory thrift deposits from the members, issue loans to the members and recover the dues, by deduction from the pay bills, if necessary.[3]

In Coimbatore there are all these co-operative credit organizations, the central banks, the urban banks, the land mortgage banks, a rural bank, the agricultural credit societies, and the employees' and other credit societies. There is a central bank at Coimbatore. It finances all the societies in the district such as the wholesale stores, the sale

1 G.O. No. 5613, Development, dated 12th November 1948.

2 The Madras Co-operative Manual, 1952, Vol. I, pages 13–70.

Rural Problems in Madras by S. Y. Krishnaswami, 1947, pages 366–368.

Report on the Working of Co-operative Societies in the State of Madras, 1950, pages 31–34.

Pamphlet on Co-operation in Madras State, 1954, pages 6–8.

3 Report on the Working of Co-operative Societies in the Madras State, 1950, page 35.

The Madras Co-operative Manual, 1952, Vol. I, pages 71–90.

societies, the weavers' societies, the urban banks and the agricultural rural credit societies. In 1956–57, it had 1,507 members and a paid-up share capital of Rs. 8,63,106. It issued loans amounting to Rs. 91,27,240 and earned a net profit of Rs. 1,75,486. There were also in the same year 12 urban banks. They serve the middle class and the lower class people, small traders, merchants and others. They issued loans for Rs. 78,35,706. There were also ten land mortgage banks in the district situated at Sulur, Udumalpet, Pollachi, Tiruppur, Peelamedu, Bhavan, Erode, Gobichettipalayam, Kambilampatti and Perundurai. They had a membership of 19,754 and disbursed loans to the extent of Rs. 16,55,156. A rural bank was started as an experimental measure at Tudiyalur with the object of issuing medium term loans and loans on the security of jewels and produce and of affording banking facilities in rural areas. By the end of 1956–57, two more banks were started, one at Palladam and the other at Kodumudi. They had 2,904 members in 1956–57 and a paid-up share capital of Rs. 1,63,258. The deposits and borrowings amounted to Rs. 7,04,616. Jewel loans to the extent of Rs. 3,59,487 were outstanding against their members in 1957. A Senior Inspector of Co-operative Societies employed at Government expense was working as Secretary in each of the rural banks. There were also 779 agricultural credit societies with a membership of 84,828 and a share capital of Rs. 27,00,863 and they issued loans to the extent of Rs. 96,94,885. Two hundred and fifty-two of these societies were for ex-tappers, 36 were for scheduled and depressed classes, and 16 were agricultural credit societies on limited liability basis[1].

The ex-tappers societies or palm jaggery manufacturing societies, as they are called, are formed for providing alternative employment to toddy tappers who have been thrown out of work by the introduction of prohibition. In 1956–57, there were 252 such societies including one District Marketing Society in the district. They had 28,099 members and a share capital of Rs. 2,35,822 and they produced jaggery worth Rs. 27,51,963 and sold jaggery for Rs. 33,10,963[2]. For the organization and supervision of these societies, the Government have at their own cost appointed a special staff of Senior Inspectors for teaching the members of these societies the methods of manufacturing refined jaggery and for developing the industry in general. They have also appointed a State Palm Gur Organizer with headquarters at Madras. They have moreover trained a number of Palm Gur Instructors at the Government of India Palm Gur

[1] Information supplied by the Registrar of Co-operative Societies, Madras.

[2] Annual Administration Reports of the Deputy Registrars of Co-operative Societies of Coimbatore and Erode for 1954–55.

Training School established at Coimbatore and sent these instructors to the districts for giving training to the members of the societies. The manufacture of jaggery being a seasonal occupation, the members of the societies have been encouraged to take to subsidiary occupations like dairying during the off season.

The societies for Harijans receive special treatment. Their members are given loans in excess of one-eighth of their net assets which is retained as the standard borrowing power of the members of rural societies. A special staff of Co-operative Inspectors provide intensive supervision to the societies and assist them in collecting their dues and writing up their accounts. The societies are granted subsidies in deserving cases for employing clerks to maintain their accounts subject to certain conditions. As has already been stated there were 36 societies for scheduled and depressed classes of which 6 were for Harijans. They had a total membership of 1,640 with a paid-up share capital of Rs. 19,075.[1]

Turning to the non-credit organizations, there are two types of such organisations, namely, the agricultural and the non-agricultural societies. The agricultural societies of the district consist chiefly of sale societies (or marketing societies), milk supply unions and societies, cattle breeding societies, fishermen's societies, agricultural improvement societies, rural housing societies and land colonization societies.

The sale or marketing societies are intended to enable the agriculturists to market their produce profitably, holding it over if necessary until the prices rise. They generally advance loans to the members on the security of their produce, own or rent godowns for storage and deal in a wide variety of produce. They obtain their finances from the central banks not only on the security of their share capital but also on the security of their produce. During the Second World War they were utilised for distributing manure and other agricultural produce in connection with the Grow More Food Campaign. Since the year 1948–49, the National Government have given a great fillip to these societies as well as to the rural credit societies by granting subsidies to the extent of 50 per cent of the cost of godowns put up by them. In 1956–57 there were 14 such societies in the district. They had 19,457 members, their share capital amounted to Rs. 3,24,473, they advanced loans to the extent of Rs. 7,80,256 and they sold chemical manure, seeds and agricultural implements worth Rs. 8,30,481 and also the produce of members worth Rs. 24,21,066.

---

[1] Information supplied by the Registrar of Co-operative Societies, Madras.

In order to assure a better price for the sugarcane growers of Udumalpet taluk a Co-operative Sugar Mills has been registered during the year 1955–56. As on 30th June 1957, it had a membership of 450 and a paid-up share Capital of Rs. 8,86,549. The society has decided to purchase a block of 108·37 acres of lands for the location of the factory and has placed orders for purchase of Machinery. A Deputy Registrar of Co-operative Societies of the Department is working as Business Manager of this institution. If the Mills go to production, it is expected that it will be a boon to the sugarcane growers in the district.

The milk supply unions and societies are started with the object of collecting milk under sanitary conditions from the producers in the country parts and distributing it to people living in towns and cities and to public institutions like hospitals, jails, etc. The first milk supply society was formed in Madras in 1926–27. The success of this society led to the formation of similar societies in other towns and the Second World War gave them a great fillip. They have received an added impetus under the Three Year Plan inaugurated by the National Government. Under this plan the Government have given interest-free loans to the unions and societies to purchase milch animals, lorries and vans. The Government have also provided them free veterinary assistance. Nor is this all. Under the Dairy Development Scheme initiated by the Government in 1948, the milk supply unions have received technical assistance for hygienic milk production, for the feeding of animals, for the improvement of their breed and for the establishment of dry stock farms. These unions and societies have done much to provide employment to the ex-toddy tappers and counter-attractions to drink to the ex-addicts. The societies borrow the funds required by them from the unions to which they are affiliated from the central banks and from the Government. They give loans to the members for the purchase of milch animals, and maintain breeding animals for their use and buy or rent the machinery required for the preparation of by-products[1]. In Coimbatore there were one milk supply union and 34 milk supply societies in 1956–57. Seventeen of these milk supply societies were attached to the union while the rest worked as independent milk supply societies. In the same year, the milk supply union had 46 members, purchased milk worth Rs. 7,55,688

[1] Report on the Working of Co-operative Societies in the State of Madras for 1949, pages 50–56.

Idem for 1950, pages 58–61.

Idem for 1951, pages 45–50.

Idem for 1952, pages 52–56.

The Madras Co-operative Manual, 1952, Vol. I, pages 217–256.

G.O. No. 5930, Development, dated 2nd December 1948.

and sold milk and bye-products worth Rs. 9,16,269. The 34 milk supply societies had a membership of 5,672 and sold milk and bye-products worth Rs. 11,46,947.

With a view to develop the activities of the Coimbatore Co-operative Milk Supply Union a Scheme for the installation of a Pasteurisation Plant of 440 gallons capacity per hour has been formulated at a capital cost of Rs. 10,36,000, with financial assistance of 60 : 40 as subsidy and loan from Government and this is under consideration. The recurring cost under the scheme is estimated at Rs. 46,000. A scheme for the salvage of dry cows has been formulated at a capital cost of Rs. 30,000 and a recurring cost of Rs. 10,500 is pending sanction of Government.[1]

The cattle breeding societies are formed with the object of improving the breed of cows, buffaloes and sheep. They diffuse amongst their members up-to-date information on cattle breeding and arrange for the grazing of their cattle and for the joint purchase and joint sale of cattle when required. They obtain good breeding bulls under the premium scheme of the Veterinary Department and entrust them to the care of selected members. Members of the societies are bound to have their cows covered by these bulls, and also to see that their young bulls which are not required for breeding purposes are castrated. They are also bound to inform the societies whenever any of their animals fall sick and to follow the instructions of the Board of Directors for their segregation and treatment. In 1956–57 there were in the district three cattle breeding societies. One of these called the Kangayam Cattle Breeding and Marketing Society had for its object the improvement of the famous Kangayam breed of cattle. The society had 20 bulls at the beginning of the year 1954–55. It purchased 17 bulls and declared ownership of 2 bulls to the custodians after 3 years of service during the above period. It distributed the balance of 35 bulls to select custodians for their maintenance. These bulls performed 852 services during the period and produced 509 superior calves and the number of members benefited by these services was 104. Another society called the Senjeri Buffalo Improvement Society was started for distributing buffaloes for breeding purposes. It had a membership of 312 and a paid-up share capital of Rs. 1,560 and did practically no business during the year. The third one called the Appanaickenpalayam Cattle Breeding Society was started on work on 27th February 1957 with a membership of 45 and a paid-up share capital of Rs. 1,130. With a Government subsidy of Rs. 3,000, the Society purchased 5 buffaloe bulls during the period and distributed them to five custodian members. The

[1] Information supplied by the Registrar of Co-operative Societies, Madras.

Government sanctioned a subsidy of Rs. 300 towards contingencies and first aid medicines.

The fishermen's societies are intended to improve the socio-economic condition of fishermen and to promote the technical and commercial aspects of the fishing industry. Their members are mostly drawn from the fishermen community, the Harijans and other backward classes. Considering the helpless condition of these societies the Government have been giving them leases of inland fisheries at reduced rates.[1] There were four such societies in the district in 1956–57, with a membership of 476 and a working capital of Rs. 5,349. These societies are now under the control of the Fisheries Department.[2]

The agricultural improvement societies have for their object the propagation and supply of improved varieties of seeds, manure, implements, etc., and in some cases for finding a sale for the produce of the members. They encourage the members to carry on demonstrations on their own lands. There were four such societies in the district in 1956–57 with a membership of 232 and a paid-up share capital of Rs. 651. But all of them were dormant during the year.

The rural housing societies are meant for enabling villagers to build durable houses with the help of Government loans. Loans up to Rs. 5,000 are granted strictly on business lines to solvent villagers with adequate repaying capacity. The houses should have a minimum floor space of 340 square feet and should be built with durable materials which are likely to stand for 25 to 30 years. There were nine such societies in the district in 1956–57 with 630 members and a share capital of Rs. 28,483. Except the Annur Rural Housing Society no other society had commenced active work and borrowed from Government and issued loans to its members.[3]

The land colonization societies are co-operative organisations of the tenant farming type. They were originally started for encouraging the educated unemployed to take up agriculture as an occupation. But they did not prove successful. They are at present of two kinds; one exclusively for civilians, generally for the landless poor and Harijans, and the other exclusively for ex-servicemen and other demobilized personnel. They are designed not only for improving the economic condition of the agricultural labourers but

---

1 Report on the Working of Co-operative Societies for 1950, page 110, and information supplied by the Registrar of Co-operative Societies, Madras.

2 Information supplied by the Registrar of Co-operative Societies, Madras.

3 *Idem*.

also for increasing the food production by reclaiming waste lands. Government waste lands are assigned to them in compact blocks of 50 acres or more of valuable lands or of 100 acres or more of ordinary lands. The societies hold the land on ryotwari tenure and are responsible for paying the land revenue, water cess and other taxes. The members have occupancy rights in their holdings so long as they cultivate them, pay their dues and carry out the intentions of the society. If any member fails to abide by these conditions he is liable to be expelled from the society and his land is liable to be transferred to another member. A member has no right to sublet or mortgage or otherwise encumber his holding, his holding is also impartible and will, on his death, pass on undivided to his nominee or senior male heir and, failing this, to the society. Thus the ownership of the land vests permanently with the society, while the members hold the lands only as tenants. Recently, however, the Government have, on the recommendation of the Harijan Welfare Committee permitted the societies to assign lands permanently to all landless poor members (both Harijans and non-Harijans) subject to the condition that in the case of Harijans, the lands should not be alienated by them to any non-Harijan. These societies receive substantial aid from the Government such as free grants for payment of initial share capital, for the purchase of bulls, manure and seed and interest-free loans for the purchase of agricultural implements and for reclamation. They are also exempted from the payment of assessment, water-rate and cesses for three years and afforded free technical assistance by the Co-operative and Agricultural departments in the initial stages. Nor is this all. For the promotion of cottage industries and subsidiary occupations they receive free grants from the Government. There were in 1956–57, four such societies in the district with 312 members and a share capital of Rs. 22,700. So far 1,511.76 acres of land had been alienated to the societies by the Government of which 1,499.98 acres had been reclaimed and brought under cultivation. The financial assistance received by these societies from Government by way of loan amounted to Rs. 28,245. In 1956–57 a Co-operative Joint Farming Society was registered (as an experimental measure) at Nathagoundenpudur and started on work on 13th June 1957, with 24 members and a paid-up share capital of Rs. 295. The society did not commence any active business during the period. The members have pooled 105.45 acres of lands for joint cultivation. Government have sanctioned Rs. 24,000 as a loan free of interest to the society repayable in 20 years to provide irrigation facilities by digging wells and installing pump sets. Government have also guaranteed the repayment of loans that may be borrowed by the society from the Coimbatore District Co-operative Central Bank for cultivation expenses up to a maximum limit of Rs. 33,000.[1]

Coming to the non-agricultural non-credit societies, there are the urban, the semi-urban and rural co-opertaive stores, the students stores, the co-operative canteens, a printing society and several cottage industries societies like the weavers' co-operative societies, the mat weavers' societies, the house-building societies, coir workers' societies, and a motor transport society in the district.

The co-operative stores aim at eliminating the middlemen in trade by purchasing wholesale and distributing the consumers goods to their members at reasonable prices. Ordinarily they are expected to raise the funds required by them from their share capital, but they are not precluded from borrowing from central banks. They were started in this State as early as 1905, but with the single exception of the Triplicane Stores, all of them proved unsuccessful. They have, however, assumed great importance since the Second World War, when the procurement, the rationing and the controls began. During the war they purchased and sold all kinds of goods and rationed articles like mill-cloth, kerosene and sugar, not only to the members but also to the general public. Since the conclusion of the war and the abolition of controls, their activities have naturally become restricted; but still they are occupying an important place and selling goods not only to the members and the public but also to the hospitals, jails, devasthanams, hostels, etc.[2] In 1956–57 there were, in the district, 65 stores with a membership of 53,805 and a share capital of Rs. 6,57,375 . They sold goods to the value of Rs. 1,48,90,172.

As to the students' co-operative stores there were 36 of them in the same year in the district with a membership of 2,991 and a share capital of Rs. 9,764 and they supplied books and stationery to the value of Rs. 6,95,488. And as to the co-operative canteens there were two in the district, namely, the Police Hostel Co-operative Society and the Coimbatore Cotton Mills Co-operative Canteen. They had 369 members and a share capital of Rs. 1,187 and their sales amounted to Rs. 19,121.[2]

In order to assist the primary stores in obtaining their supplies at economical prices a wholesale co-operative stores has been organised at Coimbatore for catering to the needs of the whole district. Its membership includes not only the primary stores but also individuals. It makes

[1] Information supplied by the Registrar of Co-operative Societies, Madras.

[2] *The Madras Co-operative Manual*, 1952, Vol. I, pages 329–372.

See also the Reports on the working of the Co-operative Societies for 1950, 1951 and 1952.

bulk purchases from Supply or production centres at the proper time and functions as a central distributing agency for its affiliated primary stores. The latter, however, are at liberty to make their purchases from other sources, whenever it is advantageous for them to do so. The central stores obtains special allotment of coffee seeds from the Coffee Marketing Board and acts as the sole agent of the Government for stocking ammonium sulphate. In 1956–57 it had 296 members and a share capital of Rs. 2,27,750 and it purchased goods worth Rs. 76,05,469 and sold goods worth Rs. 80,89,669. The Central Stores has been selected for the export of agricultural produce like dried chillies and onions by procuring the produces from the members of primary marketing societies. During the year 1956–57 the Central Stores was given permits for the Export of 250 tons of onions and 520 tons of chillies. The quantities and the value of the produce exported during the period are as follows :—

Produce.	*Quantity.*	*Value.*
	TONS.	RS.
1. Onions	250	10,000
2. Chillies	366	8,21,530

The Stores is located in its own building and has got godown accommodation to stock about 30,000 bags. The hulling capacity of the owned rice mill situated within the store's primaries is about 3,000 bags per month. The total value of buildings, godowns, etc., is Rs. 4,09,916.[1]

The most important organisations of the cottage industries type are the weavers' co-operative societies formed principally for providing raw materials like yarn, or small cash advances to weavers, and for finding markets for their finished goods. These societies started in the earlier days were not very successful owing to the vested interests of the master weavers and other intermediaries, to the indebtedness among the weavers and to the difficulties experienced in finding a sale for their finished goods. Their chief difficulty lay, of course, in marketing, since they had to compete with cheaper mill-made cloth of all sorts. In 1935, however, they received an impetus under the Government of India subvention scheme[2] which made it possible to organise a central co-operative society for the State, called the Madras State Handloom Weavers' Co-operative Society. This State society, to which all primary weavers' societies are affiliated, purchases and distributes raw materials and appliances required by the societies, arranges for marketing their finished goods and

1 Information supplied by the Registrar of Co-operative Societies, Madras.

2 G.O. No. 368, Development, dated 8th March 1935.

gives them financial as well as technical assistance when required. The weavers' societies received a temporary fillip during the Second World War period when there was scarcity of cloth, but very soon, owing to the scarcity of yarn and loss of export markets, they suffered a set back. The societies raise funds by borrowing from the central banks, purchase yarn from the State Co-operative Society and distribute it to the weaver members specifying the varieties of cloths to be produced and receive the finished goods. The cloth is mostly sold by the societies locally, but such of it as cannot be sold by them is marketed through the State Society, through its numerous emporiums and sales depots not only in this State but also outside the State. The State Society maintains also one printing factory, some dyeing factories and one co-operative spinning mill.

In order to relieve the distress caused among the weavers by the slump in the handloom industry, the Government sanctioned in July 1952 a scheme of relief to weavers through the co-operative societies. Under this scheme, the weavers in co-operative societies were assured of a subsistence wage (maximum of 6 annas per knot) and continuous employment, and relieved of the burden of marketing their cloth, as far as possible. The weavers outside the co-operative fold were at the same time given advances of Rs. 25 per head so as to enable them to join the co-operative societies. The losses incurred under this scheme were met by the Government. This scheme was in force till 1st February 1954 when it was replaced by what is called the Cess Fund Scheme. This new scheme arose out of a cess levied by the Government of India at the rate of 3 pies per yard of cloth produced by the mills, for resuscitating the handloom industry. The proceeds of the cess were allotted to the various State to finance the schemes relating to all aspects of the handloom industry such as the granting of interest-free loans to weavers to enable them to join co-operative societies, the provision of working capital to the societies, the appointment of staff for their supervision, the opening of rural and regional depots, the running of mobile shops, the conversion of throw shuttle looms into fly-shuttle looms, the provision of standard reeds, the establishment of dyeing, warping and pattern making factories, the improvement of designs, and the subsidies to consumers on purchases of handloom cloth. Nor is this all. The Government have restricted the production of dhotis by mills to 60 per cent of what they were producing in 1951–52. All this has considerably helped the handloom industry in this State.[1] In 1956–57 there were in the district 118 weavers' societies with a membership of

---

[1] Report on the Working of Co-operative Societies in Madras for 1952, pages 75–76.

Idem for 1953, pages 80–83.

Idem for 1954, pages 78–79, 83–87.

21,721 and a share capital of Rs. 13,34,971 ; and they sold goods to the value of Rs. 1,25,08,544. So far, 17,935 looms had been brought into the co-operative field.[1]

The other co-operative cottage industries societies, though still in their infancy, hold out much scope for rural reconstruction. But co-operation in their case is greatly handicapped for want of finance. The central banks are very chary of giving loans to these societies composed generally of poor and illiterate workmen with no tangible assets.[2] Realising, however, the importance of encouraging these cottage industries societies, the Adviser Government in 1945 drew up a Five-Year Plan for their development.[3] The National Government, after much consideration, replaced this plan by a One Year Plan in 1949 and placed a lump sum grant at the disposal of the Registrar of Co-operative Societies for subsidising deserving cottage industries by giving grants for the purchase of tools and equipment and for meeting part of the establishment and contingent charges. Since then, under the Five-Year Plans, a lump sum grant has been, year after year, placed at the disposal of the Registrar for subsidising the industries. The Government have also constituted a Cottage Industries Board consisting of officials and non-officials to devise ways and means for the intensive development of the Cottage Industries. This Board aims at reviving and developing cottage industries in such a manner as to make full use of all the man power, all the traditional artistic skill and workmanship and all the raw materials available in the rural areas. It also aims at achieving the economic self-sufficiency of the villages, at raising the standard of living of the villagers, and at establishing, where possible, mechanised cottage industries based on modern technique.[4] A great deal, however, yet remains to be done. In Coimbatore, in 1956–57, there were only 21 cottage industries societies formed for purposes like mat weaving, coir making and blacksmithy. The total membership of all these societies was only 544 and their total share capital only Rs. 8,627. They purchased raw materials worth Rs. 7,491 and produced and sold finished goods worth Rs. 12,319 and Rs. 9,368 respectively.[5]

---

[1] Information supplied by the Registrar of Co-operative Societies, Madras, and Deputy Registrar of Co-operative Societies, Coimbatore.

[2] *The Madras Co-operative Manual*, 1952, Vol. I, pages 310–328.

[3] Post-War Reconstruction and Development Schemes of the Government of Madras, 1945, pages 53–54.

[4] Report on the Working of the Co-operative Societies for 1950, page 96.
Idem for 1951, pages 74–75.
Idem for 1952, pages 79–80.

[5] Annual administration reports of the Deputy Registrars of Co-operative Societies of Coimbatore and Erode for 1954–55.

The building societies, the house building societies and the house construction societies are mostly of recent growth and are generally meant for the benefit of people living in urban areas. The building societies advance long term loans to the members for the construction of houses on sites owned by the members while the house building societies generally apply to the Government for the acquisition of sites selected by the housing committee, divide the land among the members and construct houses for them as their agents. The house construction societies acquire sites, construct houses on a proprietary basis and rent them out to the members on the hire purchase system under which the tenant will become the absolute owner only after he has paid off the entire value of the site and the building. In 1956–57, there were in Coimbatore 17 building societies with a membership of 1,306 and a share capital of Rs. 1,92,055, two house building societies with 60 members and a share capital of Rs. 3,245 and three house construction societies with 329 members and a share capital of Rs. 4,19,925. These societies had built 316 houses in all. Out of three house construction societies only one society, viz., the Coimbatore Co-operative House Construction Society Limited has done some active work and the other two societies, viz., the Peelamedu Industrial Workers' Co-operative Society Limited, and the Pollachi Co-operative House Construction Society Limited, which were started on work at the fag end of the year 1955–56, have not commenced actual construction work. The Industrial Housing Scheme of the Peelamedu Industrial Workers' Co-operative House Construction Society Limited, is confined to the individual workers of the Radhakrishna Mills Limited, and Pioneer Mills Limited. It is proposed to construct 144 tenements.

The motor transport societies are formed mainly for providing employment to ex-servicemen. There was only one such society in the district in 1956–57. It had 57 actual worker-members and one sympathiser. It had a paid up share capital of Rs. 44,048. It had 14 lorries and 9 buses and earned a net profit of Rs. 60,952 [1]. A comparative statement showing the growth of the various co-operative societies in the district for the period 1921–22 to 1950–51 is appended at the end of the chapter[2].

The district has been, for administrative purposes, divided into two circles, namely, the Coimbatore Circle and the Erode Circle. Each of these circles is under a Deputy Registrar of Co-operative Societies who is assisted by a number of subordinates. In 1956–57 they had under them 10 Sub-Registrars, 97 Senior Inspectors, 42 Junior Inspectors and one

---

1 Information supplied by the Registrar of Co-operative Societies, Madras.

2 *Idem.*

Dairy Assistant[1]. In the same year there were also supervising unions in the district with a number of supervisors employed by the central banks for the inspection of societies affiliated to them. The chief function of the Deputy Registrars is that of organising new societies and auditing and guiding the existing societies and banks. They are placed under the control of the Registrar of Co-operative Societies who is the head of the department. The Registrar is assisted in his work by Joint Registrars and several Deputy Registrars on special duty and other technical officers.

1. CENTRAL BANKS.

	1941–42.	1946–47.	1950–51.
Number of banks	1	1	1
Number of members	943	1,080	1,499
Paid up share capital .. .. (Rs.)	2,80,441	3,01,297	4,64,787
Loan issued .. .. (Rs.)	19,85,682	52,76,634	98,14,487

2. LAND MORTGAGE BANKS.

	1931–32.	1936–37.	1941–42.	1946–47.	1950–51.
Number of banks.	5	10	11	11	11
Number of members.	430	4,380	8,610	10,324	13,687
Loan disbursed (Rs.)	57,500	7,85,660	4,82,546	5,61,893	11,37,378

3. AGRICULTURAL SOCIETIES.

	1921–22.	1926–27.	1931–32.	1936–37.
(1)	(2)	(3)	(4)	(5)
Number of societies ..	319	510	516	571
Number of members ..	19,333	31,789	34,200	39,500
Loan disbursed .. (Rs.)	7,68,069	13,55,205	5,07,000	16,50,600

	1941–42.	1946–47.	1950–51.
	(6)	(7)	(8)
Number of Societies ..	591	615	980
Number of members ..	47,984	53,768	97,745
Loan disbursed .. (Rs.)	..	20,45,385	51,47,629

1 Information supplied by the Registrar of Co-operative Societies, Madras.

4. SOCIETIES FOR SCHEDULED AND DEPRESSED CLASSES.

	1941–42.	1946–47.	1950–51.
Number of societies	55	51	51
Number of members	1,782	1,998	2,216
Loan disbursed .. .. .. (Rs.)	19,130	5,500	10,467
Working capital .. .. .. (Rs.)	50,290	30,299	56,589

5. SALE OR MARKETING SOCIETIES.

	1932–33.	1936–37.	1941–42.	1946–47.	1950–51.
Number of societies.	4	4	7	9	6
Number of members.	720	1,830	4,404	11,549	11,712
Loan issued. (Rs.)	3,67,700	4,93,980	13,04,097	7,14,550	7,27,278
Value of produce of members sold. (Rs.)	2,26,320	3,62,480	13,30,304	39,46,856	1,65,58,565

6. MILK SUPPLY UNIONS.

	1937–38.	1941–42.	1946–47.	1950–51.
Number of unions	1	1	1	1
Number of members ..	30	31	50	52
Value of milk purchased. (Rs.)	34,180	1,09,501	8,86,514	6,03,246
Value of milk and bye-products sold. (Rs.)	38,120	1,27,423	9,84,252	7,07,113

7. MILK SUPPLY SOCIETIES.

	1941–42.	1946–47.	1950–51.
Number of societies	6	22	31
Number of members	853	3,887	4,359
Value of milk and milk products sold (Rs.)	1,09,501	5,86,514	9,60,285

8. FISHERMEN'S SOCIETIES.

	1941–42.	1946–47.	1950–51.
Number of societies	1	1	2
Number of members	47	47	210
Working capital .. .. (Rs.)	1,093	1,093	3,666

9. AGRICULTURAL IMPROVEMENT SOCIETIES.

	1941–42.	1946–47.	1950–51.
Number of societies	2	5	5
Number of members	80	254	300
Paid up share capital .. .. .. (Rs.)	304	1,773	3,667

10. LAND COLONISATION SOCIETIES.

	1945–46.	1946–47.	1948–49.	1949–50.	1950–51.
Number of colonists.	268	268	273	254	278
Area of land assigned.	1,321	1,320	1,533·84	1,329·37	1,524·44
Total extent reclaimed and brought under cultivation.	1,321	1,274	1,476·41	1,329·37	1,473·39
Financial assistance from Government.					
	RS.	RS.	RS.	RS.	RS.
(*a*) By way of subsidy.	32,340	12,640	3,875	5,250	3,375
(*b*) By way of loan.	2,094	1,500	..	2,025	6,250

11. PRIMARY STORES.

	1936–37.	1938–39.	1940–41.	1948–49.	1950–51.
Number of societies.	2	5	28	66	68
Number of members.	650	1,290	10,130	50,929	55,738
	RS.	RS.	RS.	RS.	RS.
Value of goods purchased.	38,490	63,430	6,17,890	2,50,94,984	2,93,18,325
Value of goods sold.	45,160	71,240	6,00,860	2,66,84,670	3,32,92,047

12. WHOLESALE STORES.

	1941–42.	1946–47.	1950–51.
Number of stores	1	1	1
Number of members	77	243	263
	RS.	RS.	RS.
Value of goods purchased	4,44,940	1,52,39,821	1,53,34,790
Value of goods sold	4,24,464	1,58,74,171	1,65,83,606

13. WEAVERS SOCIETIES.

	1936–37.	1946–47.	1950–51.
Number of societies	5	36	68
Number of members	340	4,255	14,885
	RS.	RS.	RS.
Value of finished goods sold ..	13,430	24,07,432	1,07,50,036
Number of looms brought in to the field.	..	4,509	16,388

14. COTTAGE INDUSTRIAL SOCIETIES.

	1941–42.	1946–47.	1950–51.
Number of societies	1	4	3
Number of members	17	774	55
	RS.	RS.	RS.
Value of raw-materials purchased	..	..	382
Value of finished goods produced	..	31,741	382
Value of finished goods sold	..	34,963	789

CHAPTER X

WELFARE SCHEMES.

Welfare schemes are the very breath of life of modern states. And of the various welfare schemes introduced in this State none is better calculated to produce an all round improvement in rural areas than what is called the Community Development Programme, which has come in the wake of what was called the Firka Development Scheme or the Rural Welfare Scheme.

The idea of reviving the corporate life of the villages which had become almost extinct under foreign rule and of making them self-sufficient in the matter of food, clothing and other necessaries and, at the same time, of inducing the villagers to take an active and intelligent interest in all affairs affecting their welfare, is to be traced to Gandhiji. In formulating a constructive programme for the villages he said : " My idea of village swaraj is that it is a complete republic, independent of its own vital wants and yet interdependent for many others in which dependence is a necessity. Thus every village's first concern will be to grow its own food crops and cotton for its cloth. It should have a reserve for its cattle, recreation and playground for its adults and children. Then, if more land is available it will grow useful money crops, thus excluding ganja, tobacco, opium and the like. The village will maintain a village theatre, school and public hall. It will have its own waterworks ensuring clean water-supply. Education will be compulsory up to the final basic course. As far as possible every activity will be conducted on the co-operative basis. "[1] And considering that more than eighty per cent of the people in India live in villages, he remarked that, " if the village perishes, India will perish too " and with her will perish " her own mission in the world."[2] Imbued with his ideas, the National Government, as soon as they came to power in 1946, took up his programme in right earnest and formulated the Firka-Development Scheme or the Rural Welfare Scheme [3]. This scheme envisaged many reforms for the regeneration of the villages. It envisaged the construction of roads, the improvement of water-supply, sanitation

---

1 G. O. Ms. No. 65, Rural Welfare, dated 1st August 1950, page 7.

2 Community Development in Madras State, issued by the Director of Information and Publicity, 1955.

3 G.O. No. 575, Food, dated 10th September 1946.
G.O. No. 4591, Development, dated 14th December 1946.

and health, the development of agriculture, livestock and cottage industries, the introduction of electricity, the encouragement of khadi, the provision of basic education, the formation of co-operative societies and the reorganisation of the panchayats. As, however, it could not be implemented in all villages at once, the Government selected for its implementation, in the first instance, 34 firkas in the various districts, where some pioneer work had already been done by non-official agencies, where the villagers manifested enthusiasm or where the general backwardness of the villages called for urgent attention[1]. In the Coimbatore district they selected first the Palladam firka and the Vellakovil and the Avanashi centres and later on extended the scheme to the Tiruppur and the Kangayam firkas.

The Collector of each district was placed in direct charge of the scheme in the selected firkas in his district and under him were appointed for each firka, a Firka Development Officer of the rank of a Deputy Tahsildar and a few Grama Sevaks of the rank of Revenue Inspectors, each in charge of a group of five or six villages. In order to co-ordinate the work in the various firkas and to attend to the technical aspects of the scheme, a Provincial Firka Development Officer, later called the Director of Rural Welfare, of the status of a Head of a Department, was also appointed with two Regional Firka Development Officers to assist him. And, as the essence of the scheme consisted in enlisting the co-operation of the villagers, committees consisting of officials and non-officials were constituted in each firka to implement the schemes drawn up. The drawing-up of the schemes was entrusted to a State Firka Development Board formed at Madras consisting of the Heads of Departments and influential constructive workers, and this Board was assisted by a Standing Advisory Sub-Committee. Publicity and propaganda work was, at the same time, entrusted to a Central Publicity Committee set up at Madras[2].

From the very inception of the scheme the problem of finding suitable persons to work it successfully engaged the attention of the Government. For generations the villagers had lost their initiative and had become accustomed to look to the Government for even small things which they could easily and quickly do by themselves with a little co-operation. It was no easy task to change this mentality and to make them conscious of their duties and responsibilities as citizens of the State. It demanded a great deal of patience and tact and, what is more, an ability to win the confidence of the villagers. A number of persons who had already taken

[1] G.O. No. 65, Rural Welfare, dated 1st August 1950, page 8.
[2] G.O. No. 548, Firka Development, dated 19th June 1950, pages 8–11.

part in public affairs were, therefore, selected as Firka Development Officers and Grama Sevaks and given special training in the principles and practice of rural reconstruction.[1]

The Rural Welfare Scheme was in 1953 merged with the Community Development Programme. Before, however, describing this programme we may summarise the results achieved by the Rural Welfare Scheme.

One of the important measures that was initiated under the Rural Welfare Scheme was the construction of roads for linking up the villages to the main roads leading to the towns. This provided not only better facilities for communication but also greater facilities for trade. By 1952–53 in the five firkas in Coimbatore 195 miles of new roads were laid, some existing roads and cart-tracks were improved and 107 culverts, road dams and footbridges were constructed in addition to repairs made to the existing structures.

Public Health being the very foundation upon which all other activities depend, particular attention was paid to the improvement of sanitation and water-supply and the provision of medical aid. Clean drinking water is not generally available in the villages, nor are proper drains and latrines to be found in them. The digging of drinking water wells and the construction of sanitary latrines and drains was, therefore, given priority. A sanitation squad was formed in each village under the guidance of the Grama Sevaks for giving necessary advice to the villagers, for supplying cheap disinfectants, for providing sanitary latrines, dust bins, soak pits and drainage. Maternity and Child-Welfare Centres and dispensaries were also opened. By 1952–53 in the five firkas of the district 94 new wells were sunk, work on 157 new wells was taken up, 62 old wells were repaired or improved, 42 old wells were taken up for repairs and 75 latrines of the Wardha type, 47 latrines of other types and one septic tank were constructed. Besides this, 839 insanitary pits were filled up, 663 manure heaps were removed outside the dwelling places, 1,077 soak pits were dug and 57 public bath rooms were erected. In addition, 127 first-aid centres, 2 dispensaries and 5 maternity and child-welfare centres were opened.

In order to make the villages self-sufficient in the matter of food much attention was paid to agriculture and irrigation. Attempts were made to increase the productivity of lands by the supply of better seeds and manure, by the protection of crops against pests and diseases and by the use of better implements and better cattle. Agricultural implements were distributed at half the cost price to the poor cultivators and the importance

---

[1] G.O. No. 548, Firka Development, dated 19th March 1950, pages 12–12a.

of preparing and using compost manure was emphasised through the Grama Sevaks. Several Grow More Food concessions, such as the hiring out of pumpsets, the distribution of improved seeds of paddy and chemical manures at cheap rates, the supply of iron materials like cart tyres and grants of interest free loans for the purchase of seed and manure, were also extended to the cultivators. Nor was this all. Encouragement was given to the cultivation of subsidiary food crops like sweet potato, tapioca and vegetables. Model agricultural farms were started in some places, while in others, demonstration plots were laid out in private fields. Efforts were made to bring under cultivation as much waste land as possible. A village live-stock improvement scheme was devised, the object of which was to introduce improved breeds of cattle, goats and poultry. Special steps were taken to improve the minor irrigation works and the investigation of some major schemes was undertaken. The Coimbatore firkas naturally received the benefits of all these concessions and facilities granted by the Government. By 1952–53 in the five firkas of the district 4,161 manure and compost pits were dug, 11 agricultural farms and 55 agricultural demonstration plots were started, 94 stud bulls, 6 buffaloes and 12 rams were supplied to the ryots, one poultry unit was opened, poultry breeding was encouraged in several places, 15 bee-hives were set up, a centre for training in animal husbandry was started and 278 acres of waste land were brought under cultivation. Twenty-third irrigation works of all kinds were repaired and 13 ponds were also constructed.

In regard to industries, in 1946, an elaborate scheme was drawn up for the development of cottage industries in the selected firkas. The main features of this scheme were the establishment of demonstration-*cum*-training units, the reorganisation of industrial and commercial museums and the provision of financial aid to cottage industries. Under this scheme 40 training units were established in the various firkas. It was, however, soon found that the training of artisans was not so important as the production of utility article of improved quality and accordingly a revised scheme was drawn up in 1948 by which demonstration and training units were to be transferred to non-official agencies like co-operative societies and the Government were only to assist them in procuring raw materials, in obtaining technical advice and assistance and in marketing the products. The units were to be confined to 25 firkas and to 6 basic trades namely wood-work, blacksmithy, light metal casting, sheet metal work, tanning and leather goods manufacture. But, as private agencies failed to come forward to take up the demonstration-*cum*-training units, 13 out of the 40 units were by 1950, converted into production-*cum*-training centres in the 6 basic trades as well as in bamboo and rattan work. As a complement to the scheme two model centres of Village Industries were opened, one of these in the present Andhra State and the other at the Tamilnad Grama Sevak Vidyalayam, Kallupatti. The centres were placed in charge of officers who had undergone a year's training at Maganwadi, the headquarters of the All-India Village Industries Association in Wardha. By 1951, they were able to give training to selected village artisans in oil-pressing, bee-keeping, paper-making and Maganchula making.[1]

Electrification of the firkas was given priority with a view to providing power for agricultural, industrial and domestic purposes. Even where the electrification schemes were not remunerative according to the departmental standards they were pushed through with the help of subsidies from the Government and in this manner 49 villages were provided with electricity and 76 wells were given electric connection by 1953.

In order to attain self-sufficiency in cloth, the Government formulated in 1946 an intensive Khadi Scheme and in 1949 an extensive Khadi Scheme. Under the intensive Khadi Scheme which was introduced in a few centres it aimed at providing at least one charka for each family by the supply at cost price of charkas and carding and slivering equipments. In the case of the poor, payment in instalments was permitted. The spinners were encouraged to grow their own cotton and to gin, card and sliver it themselves but, where they could not grow cotton, it was supplied to them by the authorities. A subsidy was also given to the spinners to make use of the cloth spun out of their yarn. Under the extensive Khadi Scheme which was introduced into many firkas, it was aimed to supply at concessional rates, where necessary, 1,000 charkas a year in each of the firkas. Arrangements were also made under this scheme for supplying cotton and ginning and carding equipments and for giving subsidies to spinners who used cloth produced by their own yarn. The idea was that the extensive Khadi Scheme should pave the way gradually for the intensive Khadi Scheme and the entire Khadi Scheme was intended to provide an ideal subsidiary occupation to the agriculturists in the off-season. Having been included in the list of the Post-War Development Schemes, it became eligible for financial assistance from the Government of India, and for the first three years it received such financial assistance to the extent of Rs. 11·85 lakhs. The All India Spinners' Association guided the activities of the scheme till 1950, when it withdrew its men. The Government then appointed their own staff. In order to encourage

[1] Rural Welfare in Madras, 1952, pages 27–29.
Administration Reports of the Rural Welfare Department for 1949 and 1951.
G.O. No. 4591, Development, dated 14th December 1946.

Khadi, the Government ordered that it should be used for all State purposes and that all officers, except those in the Police Department of the Government, who have been allowed to use uniforms should wear Khadi uniforms[1]. In Coimbatore district the intensive Khadi scheme was introduced in two centres, namely, Avanashi and Vellakovil in 1947 and the extensive Khadi scheme was introduced in one centre, namely, Palladam, in 1949.

In the sphere of education, the old type of education which lays emphasis on learning from books was replaced by the new type of education called the basic education, which lays emphasis on learning by doing. The old types of schools that existed were, wherever possible, converted into basic schools and new basic schools were also opened. Night schools for the benefit of adults and libraries, reading rooms, cinemas and radio sets for the benefit of all were provided. The object was nothing less than the speedy liquidation of illiteracy and the quick dissemination of general knowledge. By 1952–53, in the five firkas in the district 92 elementary schools, 87 night schools, 71 adult schools and 27 basic schools were opened. 24 reading rooms, 9 central libraries and 41 branch libraries were also opened. Besides this, 52 school buildings were constructed and 5 radio sets were installed.

Co-operative societies were formed in many firkas coming under the scheme. In 1951, in the five firkas, there were 118 rural credit societies, 9 stores societies, 26 jaggery producers' societies, 6 weavers' societies, 2 Harijan societies, 3 milk supply societies. 1 building society, 1 sale society and 5 other types of societies.

In some other miscellaneous directions too the villagers of the several firkas showed considerable interest. In the same year, 1,267 charkas were purchased, 31,956 trees were planted, 135 houses for Harijans were built and 301 Grama Sanghams and 45 Valibhar Sanghams were formed.

Such were the results achieved by the Rural Welfare Scheme in the district. As has already been stated, this scheme was merged with the Community Development Programme. This programme which is subsidised by American aid was ushered in by the Indian Planning Commission in 1952, and, today, it covers wide areas in the various parts of India. Its aim is the same as the aim of the Rural Welfare Scheme, namely, that of securing an all round rural development. But it seeks to achieve this aim in a more intensive as well as a more comprehensive manner. Under it there are Community Projects located in favourable areas of

---

1 G.O. No. 135, Firka Development, dated 15th March 1948.
G.O. No. 965, Firka Development, dated 22nd October 1949.

assured rainfall or irrigation facilities. There are Community Development Blocks located in select areas and there are also National Extension Service Blocks located in less developed areas. In the Community Project areas and the Community Development Blocks a higher standard of development than that of the National Extension Service Blocks has been planned; but in all the three areas the people have been enthused to act as a body, or a community, and to do all that they can to contribute their own welfare. They are to contribute funds as well as labour and, through joint effort, backed by Government aid, financial as well as technical, provide themselves with various amenities. This programme is to be progressively expanded until it covers the entire State by the end of the Second Five-Year Plan. New National Extension Service Blocks are to be opened every year, and a certain number of the old National Extension Service Blocks are to be taken up annually for intensive development as Community Development Blocks.

The programme was launched in 1952 in four Community Projects in this State, namely, the Lower Bhavani Project comprising certain portions of the Coimbatore and Tiruchirappalli districts, the Periyar Project comprising certain parts of the Madurai district, the Malampuzha Project covering the Palghat taluk and the South Kanara Project covering certain portions of the South Kanara district. The Lower Bhavani Project comprises parts of Gobichettipalayam, Erode, Bhavani and Dharapuram taluks and three villages in the Karur taluk of the Tiruchirappalli district. These parts cover an area of 701·3 square miles and contain 187 villages with a population of 5,62,996. The result achieved under the project from 1st October 1952 up to 30th September 1956 are by no means inconsiderable.

In the sphere of agriculture, 25,468 compost pits were dug, 8,32,162 maunds of chemical fertilizers were supplied, 6,401 maunds of improved seeds were distributed, 1,001 lb. of green manure seeds were issued, 198 new agricultural implements were supplied, 522 acres were brought under fruit cultivation and 1,251 demonstration plots were cultivated. Advances to the extent of Rs. 5,13,050 were made to the cultivators for purchasing seeds, manure, etc. Vegetables were raised on 1,621 acres of land. 17,435 acres of waste land were rendered fit for cultivation and advances to the extent of Rs. 1,05,800 were made to the ryots for the purpose. Irrigation was extended to 1,67,575 acres of land. For purchasing pumpsets, loans were granted to the extent of Rs. 10,85,000. As regards animal husbandry, two artificial insemination centres were established for the improvement of cattle, besides 4 veterinary hospitals and 2 veterinary dispensaries; 3,863 bulls were castrated and 70 pedigree bulls were supplied; 66,082 cattle were inoculated and 14,842 cattle were treated; 598 pedigree fowls and 92,853 fingerlings of fish were distributed. For improving sanitation, 4,091 soakage pits were dug, 260 village latrines were built and 13 miles of drainage were constructed. 145 new wells were dug and 113 old wells were repaired with the object of providing good water-supply; 4 hospitals and 16 maternity centres were also opened.

In the field of education 25 elementary schools were converted into basic schools and 49 new schools were opened and 48 schools were provided with buildings. 54 adult schools were also opened and 1,832 persons were taught in them. Besides this 84 recreation centres were started and 81 of them were provided with radio receivers; 169 Community entertainments were organized. For improving communications 248 miles of Pucca and Kutcha Roads were constructed. As for co-operative societies, 35 weavers' Co-operative societies, 137 credit societies and 37 jaggery manufacturing societies were formed. 29 regular panchayats and 155 non-official committees were also formed. 22 youth clubs were also started. In order to improve the condition of the Harijans, building sites were allotted to them in six villages and houses were built in thirteen villages affected by the Lower Bhavani Irrigation canals. The inhabitants of the Project area contributed towards all these improvements labour worth Rs. 6,17,105 and Rs. 4,24,416 in cash and others.

A scheme for starting small scale village industries with the help of the materials available in the project area was started in November 1955 and a Community Project Officer (Industries) was appointed to execute it. Under this scheme about 6,000 people are employed in making Khadi, model smithy work, manufacture and demonstration of Wardha pattern chekkus (oil mills), and training in its use, preparation of leather goods, especially shoes, construction of bullock carts with improved materials, training in bamboo work, palm-fibre industry manufacture of soap with non-edible oil, etc.

One of the villages in the Project area, Rasiyanur, has been awarded a prize of Rs. 1,000 by the Prime Minister. This village contains a maternity centre, a community centre, a reading room, a co-operative agriculture society, a recreation centre with a radio, a higher basic elementary school and a children's playground. The village has also been provided with a good drainage and adequate roads. A Harijan Colony has been built here in the midst of the caste Hindu quarters

The people of the village have spent Rs. 20,000 towards these amenities and the Government have contributed Rs. 5,000.

With the completion of 4 years of community project activity the Lower Bhavani Project area has been converted into six National Extension Service Blocks for post intensive development with effect from 1st October 1956. This permanent organization is necessary, as improvement of rural life is a continuous process. Turning to the Community Development Blocks there are three of these in the Coimbatore district. These are the Palladam, the Tiruppur, and Kangayam blocks. The Palladam block was started in October 1953 as a National Extension Service Block and was converted into a Community Development Block from April 1953. It comprises the Palladam and Varapatti firkas and covers an area of 228·15 square miles containing 41 villages with a total population of 1,09,507. The Tiruppur Block was started as a National Extension Service Block in October 1963 and was converted into a Community Development Block from April 1956. It originally consisted of the Tiruppur and part of the Sulur firka of Palladam taluk and Avanashi and parts of the Cheyur and Annur firkas of the Avanashi taluks, covering an area of 224.79 square miles and containing 50 villages with a total population of 1,39,273. But as this block was found to be very unwieldy and as it cut across two taluks, the Avanashi, Cheyur and Annur firkas were taken away from it and these were formed into a National Extension Service Block, called the Avanashi Block. The Kangayam Block was also started in October 1954 as a National Extension Service Block and was converted into a Community Development Block from April 1956. It comprises the Kangayam and the Vellakovil and Pongalur firkas and covers an area of 307.24 square miles containing 34 villages with a population of 1,23,234.

The results achieved in these three Blocks in the various fields upto the end of March 1957 were as follows: 3,724 manure or compost pits were dug; 1,59,048 maunds of chemical fertilizers, 10,083 maunds of improved seeds and 364 new agricultural implements were distributed; 2,292 plots were cultivated as demonstration plots under improved methods of cultivation; 218 acres were planted with fruit trees; and vegetables were raised on 580 acres; 6,531 acres of waste land were rendered fit for cultivation and 7,249 acres were provided with facilities for irrigation. 4,516 bulls were castrated, 116 pedigree bulls and 1,340 pedigree fowls were supplied; 71,192 herds of cattle were inoculated; 34,236 cattle were treated for various diseases; and 19,859 fingerlings of fish were supplied to fishermen. One thousand and one soakpits and 286 latrines were constructed, 431 new wells were dug and 491 old wells were repaired.

One hundred and four new schools were opened and 24 elementary schools were converted into basic schools; 83 adult schools were also opened and 3,260 adults were taught in them; 135 recreation centres were likewise opened and 818 entertainments were organised. One hundred and two miles of pucca roads and 124 miles of katcha roads were constructed. Twenty-nine new co-operative societies were started with 4,331 members. These societies disbursed Rs. 20,68,615 as loans. For all these improvements the inhabitants of the Blocks contributed Rs. 3,88,932 by way of labour and Rs. 1,80,097 in cash and others.

Besides the three Blocks mentioned above, a new block, named the Kundadam National Extension Service Block, was formed in October 1955. It consists of the Kolumanguli and Kundadam firkas of the Dharapuram taluk and covers an area of 296.47 square miles containing 31 villages with a population of 85,504. Another National Extension Service Block which was started in October 1956 was the Avanashi Block. As has been indicated already, this was formed by partly taking away portions of the Tiruppur Community Development Block. It consists of the Avanashi firka and a part of Annur firka and Cheyur firka of the Avanashi taluk and covers an area of 133·25 square miles containing 35 villages with a population of 1,06,622. At the same time was formed the Dharapuram National Extension Service Block comprising the Dharapuram and Mulanur firkas of the Dharapuram taluk and covering an area of 271·95 square miles containing 27 villages with a population of 1,01,886.[1] After the formation of the Avanashi National Extension Service Block, the Tiruppur and the Kangayam Community Development Blocks were rearranged. Under the Tiruppur Block were brought the Tiruppur and the Pongalur firkas and part of the Sulur firka of the Palladam taluk with headquarters at Tiruppur and under the Kangayam Block were placed the Kangayam and Vellakovil firkas of the Dharapuram taluk with the headquarters at Kangayam.[2] Under the Second Five-Year Plan the entire district is to be brought under the programme of National Extension Service. The areas not covered by the project and the blocks already formed are to be formed into 26 National Extension Service Blocks.[3]

While the Community Development programme has for its object the improvement of the economic condition of the people in the villages, prohibition has for its primary object the amelioration of not only the economic but also the moral condition of the people, not only in the villages, but also in the towns. Temperance reform, the fore-runner of

[1] Based on the information furnished by the Director of Statistics.

[2] G.O. Ms. No. 3146, Public (R.D.P.), dated 19th September 1956.

[3] G.O. Ms. No. 2089, Public (R.D.P.), dated 12th June 1956.

prohibition, was hailed as a blessing by all thinking persons in India, from the very dawn of political consciousness. The Indian National Congress had it at heart from the very beginning. As early as 1889 the Congress welcomed the endeavours made by the British temperance leaders to reduce drunkenness in India, and in 1900 it appealed to the Government "to pass measures like the Marine Liquor Law of America and Sir Witham Wilfred Lawsons's Permissive Bill or the Local Option Act and impose an additional tax upon intoxicants not intended to be used as medicine "[1] From that time onwards the temperance movement gathered momentum under the impulsion of the national leaders. But it become a formidable force in Coimbatore and elsewhere only from the time of the Non-co-operation and the Khilafat Movements. In Coimbatore as we have seen, picketing of liquor shops and auction sales of toddy licenses assumed serious proportions in 1921. All this led to considerable losses of revenue to the Government.[2] In 1921–22 for instance, the excise revenue in the State fell from Rs. 546·46 lakhs to Rs. 486·23 lakhs, resulting in a loss of no less than Rs. 60·23 lakhs.[3]

The agitation entered the legislature itself where the Government were again and again urged to pass laws for the gradual introduction of prohibition. Between 1921 and 1927 one Temperance Bill and two Local Option Bills were brought forward with a view to introducing prohibition in all areas where the majority of the people were in favour of it. These attempts, however, failed chiefly because the Government were not prepared to forego the excise revenue before finding alternate sources of revenue and also because the Government held that Madras had already gone far ahead of the other States in the field of temperance by placing as many restriction as possible in the way of getting drink by reducing the spirit content in liquor and by eliminating road-side liquor shops, etc.[4] But the agitation outside the Legislature still went on. In the 1930–31 Civil Disobedience Movement large scale picketing of toddy shops was launched by the Congress in Coimbatore,[5] as in other districts. The cause of prohibition was also, at this time, not a little strengthened by the issue of

---

1 *The History of the Congress* by B. Pattabhi Sitaramayya, 1935, page 83.

2 *See* page 116 of chapter IV.

3 *Excise and Temperance in Madras by* D. N. Strathie, 1922, page 60.
G.O. No. 1103, Revenue, dated 21st July 1923.

4 G.O. No. 2040, Revenue, dated 15th November 1922.
G.O. No. 1103, Revenue, dated 21st July 1923.
G.O. No. 521, Revenue, dated 19th March 1927.
G.O. No. 587, Revenue, dated 26th March 1927.
G.O. No. 1457, Revenue, dated 28th July 1927.
G.O. No. 1029, Revenue, dated 10th May 1928.

5 *See* page 116, of Chapter IV.

two important pamphlets by Sri C. Rajagopalachari, entitled the Indian Prohibition Manual in English and *Ur Kattu Padu* in Tamil. The former dealt with all aspects of drink and its evils and stressed the need for prohibition, while the latter pointed out that the most effective way to achieve prohibition was by forming caste compacts in the villages for ostracising all those who indulged in drinking.[1]

The British Government were throughout sceptical of the sincerity of the Congress. They thought that the whole campaign was designed to cripple their revenues and to make political capital out of the financial distress of the State. They even thought that it was a grand stunt skilfully engineered for discrediting them, for encouraging lawlessness and for holding out the hope of millennim to the masses under the Congress regime.[2] But in this, they were completely mistaken. The moment Sri C. Rajagopalachari formed the first Congress Ministry in 1937, he took up prohibition with ardour and introduced it boldly by a special Act (Madras Act X of 1937) first in the Salem district and then in the Cuddapah, Chittoor and North Arcot districts.[3] Other districts would have also soon come under prohibition but for the resignation of his Ministry in 1939. There is evidence to show that the measure proved a success in all the four districts. It was reported that it was " a real boon to that large class of the population who lived on the border line of want ", that it had improved their standard of living and put an end to drunken brawls and domestic quarrels, that their women one and all, had welcomed it, and that it had on the whole led to better home life, better outlook on life and better building up of character.[4] But, as soon as the ministry resigned, popular enthusiasm for prohibition began to wane, illicit distillation began to increase and the Adviser Government suspended the Prohibition Act in all the four districts. In 1944 toddy shops were opened and in 1945 arrack shops were also opened.[5] This was, however, a passing phase.

---

1 G.O. No. 126, Public (General) (Confidential), dated 21st January 1932.

2 G.O. No. 1103, Revenue, dated 21st July 1923.
Excise and Temperance in Madras by D. N. Strathie, 1922, pages 59–62.

3 G.O. No. 197, Legal, dated 1st October 1937.
Report on the Administration of the Excise Revenue for 1937–38, pages 18–23.
Idem for 1938–39, page 19.
Idem for 1939–40, page 19.

4 Report on the Administration of Excise Revenue for 1937–38, pages 21–22.
Idem for 1938–39, page 23.
Idem for 1939–40, page 23.

5 Madras in 1942, page 46.
Madras in 1943, page 56.
Madras in 1944, page 33.
Madras in 1945, page 17.

When the National Government came to power in 1946 they introduced prohibition again not only in the four districts but also in all other districts, so that by 1948 the whole State went dry.[1]

In Coimbatore prohibition was introduced from 1st October 1946 by extending the Prohibition Act of 1937 to that district.[2] All dealings in liquor and intoxicating drugs were prohibited, except for medicinal scientific, industrial or such like purposes. Permits for possession and consumption of liquor were issued only in exceptional cases. They were issued to a few persons who were accustomed to take foreign liquor, to non-proprietary clubs for sale to such of their members as held permits and to the church authorities for sacramental wine. Licences were also prescribed for the possession and sale of denatured spirits and rectified spirits, for the possession and sale, on prescription, of brandy and medicated wines by chemists, for the possession of brandy in hospitals for medicinal purposes and for the tapping of trees for sweet toddy for making jaggery. Opium was issued on permits to opium addicts, but no permits were issued for ganja and bhang. On the recommendation of the Madras Prohibition Enquiry Committee, the quantity of opium issued to addicts was directed to be reduced annually from 1st October 1949 by 20 per cent and the issue was ordered to be completely stopped after a period of five years except on medical grounds under special circumstances. The enforcement of prohibition was entrusted to the Police Department.[3] In certain other districts, the Excise department was in charge of the enforcement of prohibition. On 3rd January 1955, the enforcement work throughout the State was transferred to the Police leaving the residuary work of dealing with the supervision and control of various licences and permits and proper realisation of revenue to the Excise department. Consequently one post of Inspector of Excise along with the necessary subordinate staff was sanctioned for the Coimbatore district. The inspector has jurisdiction over the Nilgiris district also.

A series of measures were, at the same time, taken in the district to provide counter attractions to drink and employment to ex-toddy tappers. A special staff was appointed under the Collector consisting of a Special Development Officer, an Assistant Development Officer and a Ballad Singer in every Revenue Division, and a Rural Welfare Officer and a Village

---

[1] Madras in 1946, page 12.
Madras in 1947, page 17.
Madras in 1948, page 22.

[2] Madras in 1948, pages 22–23.

[3] Excise Revenue Administration Report for 1937–38, pages 18–19.
Idem for 1949–50, page 1.

Guide in every taluk, to organise ameliorative work. A number of tea shops and refreshment stalls were opened, first by the Government and later by private persons. The Indian Tea Market Expansion Board, through their mobile canteens, distributed tea and light refreshments at concessional rates throughout the district. Taluk and Village Committees and a District Advisory Council were constituted to help the enforcement machinery in the detection of offences and to advise on measures to tighten the enforcement of prohibition. Grama Sanghams were formed to undertake various kinds of rural uplift work. All kinds of games, tournaments, ballad singing parties, bhajanas, kathaprasangams, cinema shows, dramatic performances, public readings of the Ramayana and the Mahabharatha as well as rural uplift schools and thrift schemes were organised on a wide scale. The unemployment of ex-toddy tappers in this district did not assume any serious proportions; by 1951 they were gradually absorbed without difficulty either in agriculture or in trade, or in the newly formed milk supply societies, jaggery manufacturing societies, etc.[1]

As might be expected illicit distillation and smuggling followed in the wake of prohibition. In 1949–50 there were 677 cases of illicit distillation and 1,527 other prohibition offences. These rose to 685 and 2,390 in 1950–51, 861 and 3,301 in 1951–52, 2,116 and 7,785 in 1952–53, 2,279 and 11,314 in 1953–54, 2,331 and 14,985 in 1954–55 and 2,688 and 17,055 in 1955–56.[2] Smuggling however, showed a gradual decrease during the same period owing chiefly to the steps taken by the States of Mysore and Travancore-Cochin to introduce prohibition in the areas in their States adjoining the Coimbatore district.[3] While there were 40 cases of smuggling in 1949–50, there were only 24 in 1950–51, 18 in 1951–52, and 6 in 1952–53 and 2 in 1954–55. No cases of smuggling were reported in the years 1953–54 and 1955–56. In spite of the increase of illicit distillation and other offenses, prohibition has effected a general improvement in the moral and material condition of the people of the district. The improvement in the condition of the women and children has been particularly noticeable. They are stated to be leading happy and peaceful lives.[4] The labouring classes and especially the womenfolk of the

[1] Madras Information, 15th July 1948, pages 14–21.

See, e.g., G.O. No. 1065, Development, dated 14th March 1952.

[2] Administration Reports of the Madras Excise and Prohibition department, 1949–52 and particulars furnished by the Board of Revenue (Excise), Madras.

[3] G.O. No. 342, Revenue, dated 27th February 1950.

[4] G.O. Ms. No. 180, Revenue, dated 22nd January 1947.

exaddicts have greeted it as a veritable boon. Street brawls and criminal offences resulting from drunkenness have decreased considerably.[1]

Harijan Welfare, another important social reform, had its origin in the resolution moved by the Hon'ble Sri Dadabhoy Navroji in the Imperial Legislative Council on 16th March 1916. It has since 1920 formed an important plank in the Congress programme. Of all the reforms urged by the Congress, none was more dear to Gandhiji than the removal of the social, economic and religious inequalities of the Harijans. He called the " Untouchables ", the " Depressed Classes " or the ' Scheduled Castes ' as the Harijans, ' God's Children ', a name which has since stuck to them everywhere. He made untiring efforts to remove untouchability, an evil which has been for centuries responsible for keeping down socially, morally as well as economically all the suffering millions of the Harijans. He believed with a conviction not to be shaken that "swaraj was a meaningless term " without the removal of the taint of untouchability. And, as every one knows, he undertook on behalf of the Harijans the epic fast of 1932 which for the first time impressed in a manner not to be forgotten, the importance of Harijan Uplift. As soon as the Congress Ministries came to power, they introduced various measures for securing the welfare of the Harijans.

Not that the previous Government were unconcerned about the Harijans. In Madras, Mr. Paddison was appointed as a Labour Commissioner as early as 1920,[2] as a result of the resolution of the Imperial Legislative Council of 1916 and, on his recommendation, several steps were taken to improve their condition. Steps were taken to relieve congestion in Harijan quarters by allotting to the Harijans, house-sites either by assignment or by acquisition, the cost of acquisition being advanced by the Government as a loan to be recovered in instalments. Steps were also taken to provide them with sanitary amenities such as wells, pathways and burial and burning grounds. Steps were likewise taken to open schools for them and to award scholarships to them, in order to encourage their education. But notwithstanding all this, the Harijan uplift movement never assumed the same importance as it did under the Congress and National Governments.

The credit for passing legislation for the removal of the civil and social disabilities of the Harijans belongs to the first Congress Ministry presided

[1] G.O. Ms. No. 88, Revenue, dated 10th January 1949.

[2] G.O. No. 748, Revenue, dated 29th March 1919.
G.O. No. 271, Revenue, dated 2nd February 1920.

over by Sri C. Rajagopalachari. During the period of this Ministry, two Acts called the Removal of Civil Disabilities Act (Madras Act XI of 1938) and the Temple Entry Authorization and Indemnity Act (Madras Act XII of 1939) were passed. The first enactment removed several disabilities of the Harijans, their inability to have access to public streams, rivers, wells, tanks, pathways, sanitary conveniences and means of transport, as also their disability to be appointed to public offices.[1] The second enactment indemnified and protected the officers of the Government, trustees, etc., of the Sri Meenakshi Sundareswarar Temple in Madurai as well as six other temples against legal action for having permitted the Harijans to enter those temples and offer worship and, at the same time, permitted the trustees of other temples also to throw open the temples to the Harijans, provided the worshippers were not opposed to the measure.[2]

The two Acts mentioned above were further modified and amplified by three more Acts passed by the National Government in 1947 and 1949 (Madras Act XI of 1947, Madras Act V of 1947 and Madras Act XIII of 1949). The first of these Acts prohibited all discrimination against the Harijans in secular institutions like refreshment rooms, hotels, boarding and lodging houses, laundries, hair dressing saloons, etc., and forbade all dealers from refusing to sell to the Harijans any goods kept for sale.[3] The second Act which repealed the earlier Act of 1938 conferred on the Harijans the right of entering any temple which is open to the general Hindu public and to offer worship in the same manner and to the same extent as other classes of the Hindus.[4] And the third Act enabled the Harijans even to enter and offer worship in temples meant for special communities.[5] The Constitution of India, which was soon afterwards passed, gave even greater facilities to the Harijans. It declared that the educational and economic interests of the Harijans (the Scheduled Castes and Scheduled Tribes) should be promoted with special care and that the Harijans should be protected from social injustice and all forms of exploitation. It also reserved seats for the Harijans in the Legislature for a period of ten years, gave them special preference in the matter of appointments to services and provided for the appointment of a special officer to look

---

[1] G.O. Nos. 227–229, Legal, dated 21st October 1937.
G.O. No. 43, Legal, dated 3rd February 1939.

[2] G.O. No. 224, Legal, dated 11th July 1939.
G.O. No. 293, Legal, dated 11th September 1939.

[3] G.O. No. 2896, Development, dated 4th July 1947.

[4] G.O. No. 53, Legal, dated 13th May 1947.

[5] G.O. No. 664, Firka Development, dated 20th July 1949.

after their welfare.[1] It is needless to say that the Harijans of Coimbatore enjoy all these benefits granted by these Acts and the Constitution.

Nor is this all. As soon as the National Government came to power in 1946, they set apart one crore of rupees as a special fund for ameliorative work among the Harijans (in addition to the expenditure incurred from general revenues) and appointed a State Harijan Welfare Committee for formulating a Five-Year Plan and acting as a standing advisory committee on all questions connected with Harijan Welfare Work.[2] Since then, a separate department, called the Harijan Welfare Department, under a Director of Harijan Welfare, has been organised.[3] The Collectors of the districts are primarily responsible for the work of the department in the districts and they are assisted by the District Harijan Welfare Officers. The Director of Harijan Welfare, however, co-ordinates the activities of the Collectors and formulates and controls the implementation of the various measures for Harijan Welfare[4].

These measures, in the main, consist of the provision of house-sites, the grant of special educational facilities, the provision of water-supply and sanitary amenities and the assignment of lands for cultivation. The chief difficulty of the Harijans is that they do not generally own the house or huts in which they live and, even where they own a hut, the land seldom belongs to them. They are thus liable to be evicted from their huts at any time by unscrupulous landlords. They have, therefore, been given house-sites on suitable vacant lands belonging to the Government and, where no such lands are available, private lands have been acquired under the Land Acquisition Act and distributed to them. Formerly the cost of the sites was recovered from them, but from 1949 sites have been given free of cost to them, except in cases where they can afford to pay for them. Each family is assigned 3 cents in wet areas and 5 cents in dry areas exclusive of the land required for common places like streets, lanes and pathways. There they have already built houses on Government poromboke lands, such lands, if unobjectionable, have been assigned to them and, if objectionable, alternate sites have been allotted to them. Thus, from the commencement of the Harijan Welfare operations in Coimbatore down to 1956–57, 96 house-sites were assigned to the Harijans on Government

[1] *Harijan Welfare in Madras State*, 1951, pages 32–33.

[2] *Idem* pages 26–27.
G.O. No. 2628, Development, dated 16th June 1947.
G.O. No. 199, Finance, dated 25th March 1947.

[3] *Harijan Welfare in Madras State*, 1951, pages 4, 28–29.

[4] *Idem*, pages 29–30.

lands and 44 house-sites were assigned to them on lands acquired from private persons.[1]

Education of the Harijans which had been more or less neglected has, in recent times, been fostered in various ways. The policy of the Government has been to get the Harijan pupils admitted into the existing schools and to open special schools for them only in exceptional cases. The authorities of the private schools were formerly compelled to take in the Harijan pupils on the threat of withdrawal of grants, but since the passing of the Civil Disabilities Act of 1947 the Harijan pupils have equal rights with other pupils for admission into all educational institutions. Ten per cent of the seats in all recognized Secondary and Training Schools and all Arts and Professional Colleges have also been reserved for them and a number of special schools too have been opened for them.[2] In 1956–57 there were in Coimbatore 22 schools for the Harijans and eligible communities in which were studying 893 boys and 401 girls. In these schools in Coimbatore as elsewhere mid-day meals have been supplied free to children, and in 1956–57 in Coimbatore Rs. 5,949·25 was spent over these mid-day meals.[3] As for fees, education in all elementary and secondary schools, whether special, public or private, has been imparted free to all the Harijan pupils whatever be the income of their parents. In the case of high schools, however, the full concession fee has been allowed only where the income of the parents does not exceed Rs. 1,200 per annum; and in the case of colleges only if the annual income does not exceed Rs. 1,500. This is not all. Poverty certificates for fee concessions which were formerly required to be produced from Government officials are not now insisted upon. Many scholarships, including residential scholarships have been offered to the Harijan students in elementary and secondary schools as well as in colleges.[4] In 1956–57 in Coimbatore 1,591 non-residential scholarships of the value of Rs. 28,159·50 were given to the Harijan students.[5] Full exemption from the payment of examination fees has also been granted to the Harijan students in the case of all Government examinations, and in the case of University Examinations, whenever half exemption is granted, the Government have made grants to the students

---

[1] Administration Report of the Harijan Welfare Department for 1956–57, pages 156–158.

[2] Harijan Welfare in Madras State, 1951, pages 7–9.

[3] Administration Report of the Harijan Welfare Department for 1956–57, pages 168–171.

[4] Harijan Welfare in Madras State, 1951, pages 9–13.

[5] Administration Report of the Harijan Welfare Department for 1956–57, pages 11 and 122.

to meet the other half. Several Government hostels for the Harijan students have likewise been provided and, where private hostels for such students exist, they have been subsidised by the Government.[1] In 1956–57 in Coimbatore there were 18 private hostels for the Harijans subsidised by the Government at a cost of Rs. 81,360.[2]

In regard to the provision of water-supply and sanitation to the Harijans, the Collectors of the districts have been authorised to sanction a non-recurring expenditure up to a limit of Rs. 4,500 in each case for the construction of wells, tanks, pathways, latrines, levelling of house-sites, etc., and the Director of Harijan Welfare has been empowered to sanction a similar expenditure up to a limit of Rs. 7,500. Up to 1956–57 in the Coimbatore district 22 wells were constructed and 42 wells were repaired at a cost of Rs. 1,64,816·64.[3]

A liberal policy has been pursued in the matter of assignment of lands to the Harijans for cultivation purposes. A fair proportion of waste lands in each village is reserved for them for free assignment. So also is reserved for them a good portion of the large blocks of lands such as unreserved forests, unassessed waste lands and porambokes whenever they are transferred to the head of assessed lands. Even in the case of valuable lands, like wet lands which are generally sold in public auction to the highest bidders, a concession has been shown to the Harijans. Such lands are sold to them privately at a fair market price and the price collected in easy instalments. When necessary, large blocks of lands are also assigned to land colonization co-operative societies consisting mostly of the Harijans.[4] In the Coimbatore district, during 1956–57, 138.39 acres were reserved for the Harijans and of these 18.96 acres were assigned to them.[5]

As to the special preference shown to the Harijans in the matter of appointments to public services, they are considered to possess general educational qualification even if they obtain a lesser number of marks than those prescribed for others in the Secondary School-Leaving Certificate Examination. They are exempted from paying the prescribed fees when they sit for competitive examinations conducted by the Madras Public

[1] Harijan Welfare in Madras State, 1951, pages 13–15.

[2] Administration Report of the Harijan Welfare Department for 1956–57, pages 31 and 141.

[3] Administration Report of the Harijan Welfare Department for 1956–57, page 187.

[4] Harijan Welfare in Madras State, 1951, pages 18–20.

[5] Administration Report of the Harijan Welfare Department for 1956–57, pages 78 and 188.

Service Commission, provided they have passed in the Intermediate Examination. They are also exempted from the age limits prescribed in the service rules for appointments under certain conditions. In deserving cases, they are even given special preferences in the matter of appointments by the relaxation of service rules, if necessary.[1]

Thus the dream of Gandhiji is now being made capable of realization. The Government have deliberately and systematically endeavoured to remove the social disabilities of the Harijans and to improve their economic condition. But the Government alone can by no means solve this vast and age-long problem. A change of heart among all the caste Hindus is absolutely necessary before the Harijans can take their rightful place as equal members of society. In socio-religious matters like this, legislation and executive action can only pave the way, but the goal can be reached only with the whole hearted support and co-operation of the people.

Industrial Labour Welfare, to which we now turn and which now-a-days causes not a little anxiety to all Governments owing to the increasing prevalence of strikes, has had a history of more than seventy years in India. The idea began undoubtedly as a humanitarian reform, but it gradually assumed a political complexion until today it has become one of the most crucial problems confronting all States. The Indian Factories Act (India Act XV of 1881) was passed for regulating the employment of children in big factories and providing fencing for machinery for protecting the workers against injury. It was amended in 1891 for bettering the working conditions of children as well as women and for bringing in smaller factories also under its scope. In 1911 another Act was passed which reduced the hours of work alike in the case of men, women and children and made provision for their health and safety. Then came the amending Acts of 1922, 1923, and 1926 and the comprehensive Act of 1934 (India Act XXV of 1934), which was based on the recommendations of the Royal Commission on Labour in India. The last Act divided the factories into seasonal and non-seasonal factories, brought in many more small factories under its scope, regulated the hours of work of all workers and required the big factories to provide rest sheds and creches. But even this Act was soon found to be inadequate. It was amended in 1935, 1936, 1937, 1940, 1941, 1944, 1945, 1946 and 1947 and when eventually in 1948 it was repealed and replaced by a new Act (India Act LXIII of 1948) by the National Government, based on the standards set by the International Labour Organisation. The 1948 Act which is now in force includes many progressive features. It provides for the licensing and registration of all factories, including non-power factories employing 20 or more persons

[1] Harijan Welfare in Madras State, 1951, pages 24–26.

and power factories employing 10 or more persons. It abolishes the distinction between seasonal and non-seasonal factories and shifts the entire responsibility for taking up safety precautions like fencing and guarding of machinery on the factory owners. It prescribes standards of comfortable working conditions such as adequate ventilation, lighting and prevention of over-crowding, dust, nuisance, etc., the prior approval of plans by the Chief Inspector of Factories for the purpose of enforcing the above standards in the case of construction of new factories and extension of existing factories, higher standards of safety provisions based on modern industrial practices relating to working conditions, the periodical inspection of hoists, lifts, cranes, revolving machinery and pressure plant and the grant of leave with wages at the rate of one day for every 20 days of work for adults and one day for every 15 days of work for children. It prohibits the employment of children below 14 years, reduces the hours of work of young persons to 4½ hours a day within a spread over of 5 hours, regulates the hours of work of adults to 9 hours a day and 48 hours a week, provides for the payment of over-time wages to the workers at double the ordinary rate of wages including all allowances; and insists upon the provision of sitting facilities, spittoons, latrines, good drinking water, first-aid facilities, canteens, rest sheds and creches. It provides also that young persons who have not completed 18 years of age should not be allowed to work as adults without certificates of physical fitness. Factories employing 500 workers or more are required to appoint Special Welfare Officers. All the factories in the District covered by this provision have appointed such Welfare Officers. In 1956 there were 863 factories in Coimbatore district employing 69,893 workers. Among these factories were those manufacturing food beverages and tobacco, a number of rice mills, oil mills and textile mills. There were also some printing presses, engineering works and coach building and motor-repairing works.

Besides the Factories Act, the Government have enacted several laws aiming at the social welfare and security of the workers and employees. The earliest of these laws, the Workmen's Compensation Act of 1923, assures the disabled workers and the dependants of the workers who sustained injuries and die in the course of their work, the payment of monetary compensation. Under this Act, compensation amounting to Rs. 9,389·19 was deposited by employers in Coimbatore district during 1956. The Indian Trade Unions Act (India Act XVI of 1926) provides for the registration of trade unions and lays down the rights and obligations of registered trade unions. There were 89 registered trade unions in Coimbatore district on 1st September 1957. The Payment of Wages Act of 1936 (India Act IV of 1936), ensures prompt and regular payment of wages to the workers in factories and certain other concerns whose wages and salaries average below Rs. 200 per month. It also provides for the appointment of authorities to enquire into and pass orders in cases arising out of delayed or non-payment of wages and wrongful deductions from wages, and to award compensation. The amounts awarded are recoverable as though they are fines imposed by a Magistrate. The Industrial Employment (Standing Orders) Act of 1946 (India Act XX of 1946), requires the employer of every individual establishment in which one hundred and more workmen are employed to submit to the Certifying Officer, for certification, draft standing orders proposed for adoption in his industrial establishment. It requires the draft standing orders to contain provisions on matters relating to terms of service specified in it. Such provisions shall, as far as practicable, be in conformity with the model standing orders prescribed by the State Government. The Commissioner of Labour, who is the Certifying Officer, sees whether the draft complies with the above requirements and before certifying it gives the employers and the representatives of the workers an opportunity of being heard. This Act was amended by the Industrial Disputes (Amendment and Miscellaneous Provisions) Act, 1956. The amended provisions, which came into force on 17th September 1956, empower the Certifying Officer to adjudicate on the fairness and reasonableness of the provisions of any of the standing orders and also bestow on the workmen a right to apply for the modification of Standing Orders. The State Government have extended the provisions of the Act to all registered factories engaged in the manufacture, assembly or repair of goods or articles of iron, steel, non-ferrous metals and plastics by the use of machine tools, including the foundries and forging plants which produce materials for the manufacturing, assembling and repair establishments. The provisions of the Act have also been extended to the newspaper establishments by the Working Journalists (Conditions of Service and Miscellaneous Provisions) Act, 1955.

The Industrial Disputes Act of 1947 (India Act XIV of 1947), provides for the investigation and settlement of industrial disputes and specifies the machinery for the purpose. The Conciliation Officers appointed under the Act try to settle the industrial disputes arising in their jurisdiction and where a settlement by conciliation is not possible, the Government are empowered to refer the dispute to a Board or to a Court of Enquiry for promoting a settlement or to an Industrial Tribunal for adjudication. The awards passed by the Tribunal and the settlement brought about by Conciliation Officers are binding on both the parties. The Act also imposes restrictions on strikes and lock-outs being declared during the pendency of conciliation proceedings, proceedings before a Tribunal and during the period of operation of settlements and awards, and also prohibits strikes and lock-outs in Public Utility Services without due notice. The managements of industrial establishments in which 100 or more workmen are employed, are required to constitute Works Committees consisting of representatives of the employers and workmen with a view to promoting measures for securing and preserving amity and good relations between the employers and workmen. The Act was amended in 1950, 1951, 1952, 1953, 1956 and 1957. The important amendments provide for the enforcement of awards, empower the Government to extend the period of operation of the awards and further improve the privileges given to the workmen in the matter of retaining conditions of service unchanged during pendency of proceedings and representation of parties in such proceedings. The Industrial Disputes (Amendment) Act of 1953, besides providing for payment of compensation for involuntary unemployment, requires the employers to give a months' notice, or wages in lieu thereof, and a compensation of 15 days' wages for each year of service in cases of retrenchment. The retrenched workers will also have a preferential claim over outsiders at the time of future recruitment. The benefits of lay-off compensation which apply to factories and mines employing 50 workmen and more have since been extended to workmen in Plantations. The Industrial Disputes (Amendment) Ordinance of 1957 provides for retrenchment compensation even in cases of *bona fide* closures and change of ownership of the management.

The Industrial Disputes (Appellate Tribunal) Act of 1950, which provided for an appeal against the awards of Industrial Tribunals, was repealed by the Industrial Disputes (Amendment) and Miscellaneous Provisions Act of 1956, and some of its important provisions have been incorporated in the Industrial Disputes Act itself. The important amendments introduced by this Act include the introduction of a three tier system of adjudication machinery, viz., Labour Courts, Tribunals and National Tribunals, provisions for voluntary reference of disputes to arbitration, liberalisation of the definition of the term 'workmen', provision for giving notices of proposed changes in conditions of service by employers to workmen, recognition of settlements arrived at between the parties otherwise than in the courses of conciliation proceedings, imposition of the penalty of imprisonment for breach of settlement or award and recognition of a specified number of office-bearers of unions as 'protected workmen'.

The provisions of the Industrial Disputes Act have also been extended to cover working journalists by the Working Journalists (Conditions of Service and Miscellaneous Provisions) Act of 1955, which also aims to regulate the conditions of service of the working journalists and other persons employed in Newspaper establishments.

The Minimum Wages Act of 1948 (India Act XI of 1948), requires the fixation of minimum rates of wages for specified employments in which it is considered that 'sweated labour' is most prevalent or in which there is a vast scope for exploitation of labour. Employment in agriculture, plantations, oil mills, rice mills, dhall mills, tanneries and leather manufactories are some of the more important items which at present come under the scope of this Act. The Government have fixed minimum rates of wages for all the employments covered by the Act except for employment in agriculture and employment in lac manufactories. The Government have since revised the minimum rates of wages for all the employments for which minimum rates were fixed except for the employment in mica mines. The minimum rates of wages for the employment in Beedi and Cigar Industries are not in force, as they have been held to be invalid by the High Court.

The Employees' State Insurance Act, 1948 (India Act XXIV of 1948), provides for sickness benefit, maternity benefit, dependant benefit and medical benefit to the workers. The scheme was first inaugurated in Coimbatore in January 1955. The Madras Maternity Benefit Act of 1935 (Madras Act VI of 1935), prohibits the employment of women in factories for 4 weeks after confinement and provides for the payment during the period of maternity benefit to them during the period of 3 weeks before and 4 weeks after confinement. The Employees Provident Fund Act of 1952 (India Act XIX of 1952), originally covered six major industries, viz., cement, cigarettes, electrical, mechanical or general engineering products, iron and steel, paper and textiles. The Act has subsequently been extended to 30 industries such as matches, edible oils and fats, sugar, rubber and rubber products, electricity including the generation, transmission and distribution thereof, tea, etc. Workers are required to contribute 6¼ per cent of their wages towards the Provident Fund and the Act makes it obligatory on the part of employers also to make an equal contribution.

And finally the Madras Shops and Establishments Act of 1947 (Madras Act XXXVI of 1947), which has been made applicable to all shops, hotels, theatres and commercial establishments in municipalities and first-class panchayats in the State, provides several benefits to the employees more or less similar to the benefits provided to the workers under the Factories Act. Under this Act, adults are not allowed to work for more than 8 hours a day and 48 hours a week, young persons between the ages of 14 and 18 years are not allowed to work for more than 7 hours a day or 42 hours a week and children below 14 years are prohibited from working in any establishment. It also provides for the grant of a weekly holiday with wages, grant of 12 days' annual leave, 12 days' casual leave and 12 days' sick leave with pay every year and the prompt payment of wages without deductions other than those authorised. It confers on any dismissed employee a right of appeal against his dismissal to an appellate authority.

In addition to the above measures some employers have paid attention to the welfare of their workers and have, of their own accord, provided at considerable cost, housing and other facilities to their employees. The problem of housing labourers has been engaging the attention of both the Central and State Governments. The Central Government have introduced the subsidised Industrial Housing Scheme which contemplates assistance for the construction of tenements for industrial workers who come within the scope of the Factories Act as amended from time to time and those employed in mines. The State Government Statutory Housing Boards' employers and registered Co-operative Societies of industrial workers are granted assistance for undertaking housing schemes. The financial assistance is in the shape of subsidies and loans. The State Government and Statutory Boards are granted 50 per cent of the approved ceiling cost of the building as loan and the remaining 50 per cent as subsidy. Private employers are eligible for a loan of 37½ per cent and for a subsidy of 25 per cent and Co-operative Societies for a loan of 50 per cent and a subsidy of 25 per cent. A proposal to increase the extent of financial assistance to Co-operative Societies is under consideration. The loans will be recoverable in 25 annual equated instalments from State Government and Co-operative Societies and in 15 such instalments from private employers. The scheme also prescribes the standards of accommodation, the maximum cost of construction for the purpose of calculation of financial assistance, the constitution of managing committees for the tenements constructed with the assistance under the scheme, the maximum rent that can be charged, etc. The Government also are considering proposals for taking assistance under the scheme and for constructing houses for the industrial workers in the State including those in this district.

The inspectorate which enforces the provisions of the Factory Act and the allied Acts concerning labour welfare, originally consisted of the

Deputy Commissioner of Police in Madras City and the District Magistrates in the Districts. In the year 1900, an Inspector of Factories was appointed to relieve the Deputy Commissioner of Police of the work connected with the Factories Act. In 1914, in order to assist him in inspecting the factories in the State, an Assistant Inspector of Factories was appointed. In 1920, a Labour Commissioner was appointed. He looked after not only Harijan Welfare work but also industrial labour welfare work and took upon himself the supervisory duties till then exercised by the Board of Revenue. He became also the Chief Inspector of Factories. After the introduction of the Factories Act of 1934, the Madras Maternity Act of 1934 and the Payment of Wages Act of 1936, his responsibilities increased and his department was rapidly expanded. Additional Inspectors of Factories were appointed in 1941, 1942, 1945 and 1947. A Deputy Chief Inspector of Factories was appointed in 1945 and Woman Inspectors were appointed, one in 1941 and two in 1947. With the passing of the Industrial Disputes Act of 1947, a Deputy Commissioner and an Assistant Commissioner of Labour and Labour Officers in the Districts were appointed. In 1948, after the passing of the Madras Shops and Establishments Act of 1948, the Factories Department was reorganised. At the end of March 1957, the Department consisted of the Commissioner of Labour who was also the Registrar of Trade Unions, Certifying Officer under the Industrial Employment (Standing Orders) Act and Commissioner for Workman's Compensation; an Assistant Commissioner of Labour, a Personal Assistant to the Commissioner of Labour; 10 Labour Officers and a Labour Welfare Officer on the labour side ; and a Chief Inspector of Factories, a Personal Assistant to the Chief Inspector of Factories, 5 Grade I Inspectors of Factories, 7 Grade II Inspectors of Factories, one Inspectress of Factories, 5 Inspectors of Plantations and 126 Assistant Inspectors of Labour, who were also additional Inspectors of Factories on the Factories side.

There are 2 labour officers for taking up conciliation proceedings in respect of industrial disputes arising in the District, namely one at Coimbatore with jurisdiction over Coimbatore, Avanashi, Gobichettipalayam, Palladam, Erode and Bhavani taluks and the other at Pollachi with jurisdiction over Pollachi, Udumalpet and Dharapuram taluks. There are also one Inspector of Factories, Grade I at Coimbatore and another Inspector of Factories, Grade II at Tiruppur for the administration of the Factories Act, besides 13 Assistant Inspectors of Labour for the administration of the Madras Shops and Establishments Act in the District.

With effect from 1st November 1956, the Government have taken over the administration of the Employment Exchanges and the Commissioner of Labour has been appointed as the Director of the National Employment Organisation. He is assisted by a Deputy Director, an Assistant Director and 17 District Employment Officers. There is a District Employment Office under the control of a District Employment Officer at Coimbatore.

One of the important welfare schemes undertaken by the Government is the Women's Welfare Scheme. This Scheme had its origin in the Women's Auxiliary A. R. P. Corps started in 1941 during the Second World War for instructing illiterate and ignorant women in air raid precautions. In 1945, after the cessation of the war, the corps was reconstituted to undertake general social welfare work among women and its name was changed to Indian Women's Civil Corps. It had a central organisation and centres both in the city and in the districts and it did useful work in slums by holding classes in cooking, knitting and handicrafts, by giving talks on various subjects connected with women's welfare and by organizing excursions and undertaking similar activities intended to make homes brighter. As soon as the National Government came to power, they decided to utilize this useful organisation for carrying on systematic social work among women on a wider scale. In 1948, they constituted it into a separate department called the Women's Welfare Department with a Women's Welfare Officer as its head and a number of Assistant Women's Welfare Officers and Women's Welfare Organizers in the District.[1] In 1933, the post of the Women's Welfare Officer was abolished and the Department was added to the charge of the Director of Rural Welfare, but it has been revived again in 1955 under the designation of the Director of Women's Welfare. In 1956–57, Coimbatore had one Assistant Women's Welfare Officer and 4 Women's Welfare Organizers.

The Department aims at the social, economic and cultural improvement of women at large and endeavours to achieve these aims by providing for field work, maternity welfare, service homes and industrial training. Field work consists of regular house to house visit by trained welfare organizers for advising and assisting women in matters like health, hygiene, maternity, child care, nutrition, cooking, gardening and means of earning supplementary income by poultry farming, handicrafts, etc. It also consists of inducing women to take an active part in community centres organized for the free mingling of women of all classes, for providing recreation like indoor and outdoor games for them

---

[1] *Madras in* 1949, *Part I,* pages 144–145.

Women's Welfare in Madras State, 1952, page 3.

Handbook of Information issued by the Department of Women's Welfare, 1952, pages 3–4.

G.O. No. 2921, Public, dated 19th September 1947.

G.O. No. 3376, Public, dated 13th November 1947.

and for training such of them as need training, in house crafts and cottage industries like spinning, weaving, tailoring, etc. It likewise consists of holding pre-basic classes for children aged between 3 and 7 years and of helping destitute women by securing admission for them in the Service Homes set up at Madras and Madurai and, after they are trained and discharged from these Homes, in finding useful employment for them. Each Welfare Organizer is in charge of three centres in each branch and several of these branches are located in the villages. Of the three centres in each branch, one is normally a model centre provided with a reading-room, an information bureau, a show room, a sales depot, a balavadi section, a maternity and health clinic and facilities for games and practical demonstration in handicrafts. In Coimbatore in 1956–57, there were altogether 4 branches and 8 centres situated in villages and towns. Some of these branches rendered assistance in ameliorative work connected with prohibition by arranging for various games.

Maternity welfare is sought to be provided for by appointing a trained midwife in each selected village branch. The midwives are trained in social work as well and are expected to work in co-operation with the Welfare Organizers. It is hoped to provide, in due course, one midwife for each rural branch.

As has been said already, there are two Service Homes, one of these is situated at Royapuram in Madras, and the other called Sevikasram, is situated at Gandhigram in Madurai. It is proposed to start more Homes in the Districts. The Homes are intended for helping destitute women to re-establish themselves and to lead respectable lives. They take in women with children also where necessary. Whenever the Welfare Organizers find deserving cases of destitute women, they recommend them for admission into the Home, and here they are maintained free, educated up to the middle school standard and trained as teachers, house-keepers, balasevikas and midwives. They are also trained here in handicrafts like spinning, weaving, tailoring, basketry and rattan work, printing and dyeing, paper making and soap making. After they are so trained, they are either absorbed in the field staff or are assisted to start life independently. The Sevikasram at Gandhigram was opened in 1949 with 10 inmates and in 1951 it had 40 inmates[1]. Besides the Service Homes, there is also an Industrial School for Women at Madras in which a one year course of training in cutting and tailoring, weaving of sari lace borders, ribbon and gotha (Silver laee borders) and making

1 Administration Report of the Women's Welfare Department for 1949 and 1951.

of glass beads and bangles is provided to women who, though not destitute, are poor and are anxious to learn a trade and earn an independent livelihood. The destitute and poor women of Coimbatore as of other districts have availed themselves of the facilities provided by the Homes and the Industrial School. For women who had received a limited education and who were anxious to pursue their studies further there was a Ruarl College at Tanjavur. This college which was formerly under the Education Department was, in 1950, transferred to the Women's Welfare Department. It offered a two years' course in subjects like history, geography, economics, co-operation, political science, sanitation, everyday science, food, nutrition, clothing, home craft, mother craft and care of the pre-school child. Instruction was given in Tamil through lectures delivered by lecturers from colleges, teachers from high schools and training schools, lawyers, doctors and agricultural demonstrators. The college was, however, closed in 1952 as the response from students was poor[1].

At this period, when women are claiming equal rights with men and when the Constitution of India has tacitly conceded these rights and placed them on an equal footing with men, women welfare assumes at once a special importance. If it is admitted that the women have a vital role to play in the building of New India, it should also be admitted that this can be made possible only by improving alike the social, the economic and the cultural position of women. The work being new and important, great attention is being paid to the selection of right type of welfare workers and to their training. Equal attention is also being paid to propaganda by bringing out a new journal called the Women's Welfare Journal[2].

While the Women's Welfare Scheme is of very recent origin, electrification of urban and rural areas is of some years standing. Madras City began to receive electricity through a private undertaking as early as 1908; Ootacamund received it through another private undertaking in 1924; but the Districts began to receive it in a large measure only after the Electricity Department was organized in 1927 and the Pykara, the Mettur and the Papanasam Hydro-Electric Schemes were completed in 1933, 1937 and 1941 respectively. The credit for initiating an active policy for developing the power resources of the State goes to Dr. C. P. Ramaswami Ayyar, who as a Member of the Executive Council, did much to organize

---

1 Report on Public Instruction in Madras for 1950–51, pages 41–42.
G.O. No. 1791, Public (Political), dated 6th April 1950.

2 *See* Women's Welfare in Madras State, 1952 ; and Handbook of Information issued by the Department of Women's Welfare, 1952.

the Electricity Department and to start the Pykara Scheme. And the credit for pushing through all the three schemes successfully belongs to Sir Henry Howard, the Chief Engineer, for Electricity.

In Coimbatore district electricity was first supplied by the proprietor of a cinema theatre called the Variety Hall. He was running an electric plant and generating the power required for his cinema. He obtained a permit from the Government to supply temporarily electricity to some buildings near the cinema. This was in 1923[1]. When his demand increased, he obtained permission to supply power to an extended area in 1926[2]. Three years later the firm of Stanes & Company was given similar permission to supply electricity to certain private buildings situated close to their mills[3].

Even before these two firms were permitted to supply electricity, the Government had granted in 1920 a licence to Tata & Sons, Limited, Bombay, to supply electricity to the municipalities of Ootacamund, Coonoor and Coimbatore. This licence was transferred by them in 1921 to the Nilgiri Power Syndicate, but as the Syndicate did not execute the necessary work within the stipulated period, the licence was cancelled by the Government in 1926[4]. The Syndicate was, however, given to understand at the same time that when power began to be generated at Pykara it would be permitted to distribute it in Coimbatore. This led to difficulties, for, when power was about to be generated at Pykara, the Coimbatore municipality insisted that it should be permitted to distribute it in the municipal areas[5]. It protested vehemently against the proposal to grant the licence to distribute electricity to the Nilgiri Power Syndicate. Public opinion was also very strong against the granting of the licence to anyone except the municipality. But the Syndicate would not abandon its claim. It threatened to bring legal proceedings against the Government ; and the firm of Stanes & Company which had an active voice in the management of the Syndicate and which was expected to be the biggest power consumer, refused to take power if the licence was not granted to the Syndicate. Matters were, however, compromised after a great deal of discussion and the Syndicate gave up its claims on the payment of a compensation of Rs. 75,000[6]. The Coimbatore, Tiruppur and Pollachi municipalities were granted licences to distribute

1 G.O. No. 991, Public Works, dated 4th October 1923.

2 G.O. No. 1796, Public Works, dated 25th November 1926.
G.O. No. 1633, Public Works, dated 4th July 1928.

3 G.O. No. 1904, Public Works, dated 2nd July 1929.

4 G.O. No. 27, Public Works, dated 8th January 1926.

5 G.O. No. 2585, Public Works, dated 13th September 1930.

6 G.O. No. 1114 (S-), Public Works, dated 19th May 1932.

low tension power within the municipal areas on the condition that the distribution system would be constructed and worked by the Government for three years or until the scheme was satisfactorily established. The right of distributing high tension power was retained in the hands of the Government as also the right to distribute power in the rural areas. This was in 1933[1]. Two years earlier, Erode had been supplied with electricity from the excess supply received at Mettur for the anicut project at that place from the Government of Mysore, but when the Pykara power became available the contract with Mysore Government was terminated[2]. The municipality could not be granted a licence, as the private licensees to whom a licence had subsequently been granted for Salem and Erode refused to terminate their contract. A licence was granted to the Udumalpet municipality[3] in 1935 and to the Dharapuram municipality in 1937. In 1937, the Government transferred the management of the works to the Coimbatore and Tiruppur municipalities[4] and in 1940 to Udumalpet[5].

Outside municipal areas also power began to be distributed. In 1932, Mettupalayam was supplied with electricity[6]. In 1933, supply was made to the cement factory at Podanur (Madukkarai) and to the tea estates on the Anaimalais[7]. In the same year an extension was made from Tiruppur to Avanashi and from Coimbatore to Peelamedu[8]. Sulur began to be supplied from 1934[9]. In the same year, a second circuit was established from Pollachi to Iyerpady on the Anaimalais and the Anaimalai Planters' Association was in the same year permitted to supply Valparai[10]. In 1937, supply was extended to Palladam[11]. Shortly afterwards came the second World War, when new extensions were restricted to essential purposes. These restrictions were removed after the war. At the same time the National Government passed legislation to acquire

1 G.O. No. 2615, Public Works, dated 9th December 1932.
G.O. No. 193, Public Works, dated 24th January 1933.

2 G.O. No. 238, Public Works, dated 28th January 1931.
G.O. No. 470, Public Works, dated 24th February 1933.

3 G.O. No. 1267, Public Works, dated 31st May 1935.
G.O. No. 1363, Public Works, dated 11th June 1935.

4 G.O. No. 300, Public Works, dated 12th February 1937.
G.O. No. 301, Public Works, dated 12th February 1937.

5 G.O. No. 231, Public Works, dated 1st February 1940.

6 G.O. No. 1237, Public Works, dated 8th June 1932.

7 G.O. No. 871, Public Works, dated 11th April 1933.

8 G.O. No. 2173, Public Works, dated 6th October 1933.
G.O. No. 200, Public Works, dated 23rd January 1934.

9 G.O. No. 328, Public Works, dated 8th February 1934.

10 G.O. No. 2180, Public Works, dated 2nd October 1934.
G.O. No. 2402, Public Works, dated 5th November 1934.

11 G.O. No. 2218, Public Works, dated 30th October 1937.

all private electrical undertakings under the Madras Electricity Supply Undertakings (Acquisition) Act XLIII of 1949. This was done with the object of improving and extending electricity, especially in the rural parts. Under this Act were acquired the electricity systems of Tiruppur, Dharapuram and Udumalpet with effect from 15th May 1951[1]. In 1952, no less than 448 towns and villages were supplied with power under the Pykara System and 40 towns and villages under the Mettur System. There were also 2 towns and a few villages supplied by a private licensee[2]. Madras leads all other States in rural electrification and a large number of villages have been electrified already. About 1,128 villages including hamlets and 21 towns were electrified in the District till 31st March 1957. Supply to large number of pumpsets and house-service connections were effected considerably during the last three years.

A welfare scheme which came directly in the wake of electricity was the Rural Broadcasting and community listening scheme. Early in 1934 the Government recognized the propaganda as well as the educative and entertainment value of broadcasting and engaged the services of an engineer of the British Broadcasting Corporation for formulating a broadcasting scheme for this State. He recommended the erection of two broadcasting stations, one at Madras and the other at Tiruchirappalli and the installation of 500 village receivers. But, as the Government of India desired to retain control over all transmitting stations in their own hands and installed the All-India Radio Stations at Madras and Tiruchirappalli (1938), the Madras Government, then under the First Congress Ministry, turned their attention only to the provision of facilities for rural broadcasting and community listening. It is to this Ministry that goes the credit for organising the Provincial (State) Broadcasting Department and installing the first community receiver sets. The scheme thus launched was expanded by the National Government which came to power in 1946. That Government felt that it was essential to explain to the people the logic behind all their administrative, executive and legislative activities that this could best be done by the spoken word, and that this spoken word might be made to reach as many people as possible, it was necessary to increase the broadcasting facilities. They, therefore, made representations to the Government of India to give a high priority in their development plans for the construction of more stations. This led to the starting

[1] G.O. No. 162, Public Works, dated 12th January 1951.
G.O. No. 173, Public Works, dated 12th January 1951.
G.O. No. 181, Public Works, dated 12th January 1951.
G.O. No. 3652, Public Works, dated 7th September 1951.
G.O. No. 3653, Public Works, dated 7th September 1951.
G.O. No. 3758, Public Works, dated 12th September 1951.

[2] Administration Report, Electricity Department, 1951–52.

of the All-India Radio Stations at Vijayavada and Kozhikode. Meanwhile more and more community receiving sets, public address systems and wireless broadcasting systems in various rural centres were installed by the State Government and suitable arrangements were made for their field maintenance. Wherever these facilities have been given and they have been given in many places the people can listen to the programmes broadcast by the All-India Radio, including rural programmes, on subjects like public health, sanitation, agriculture, prohibition, education, etc. The sets are worked generally for about two hours a day[1].

Nor was this all. In 1949, the Government authorised the Collectors of all districts, except Madras, to sanction from the allotment of their discretionary grant, the cost of battery operated radio sets, including the cost of installation not exceeding Rs. 500 in each case of villages in all the firkas and centres selected for intensive rural reconstruction work[2]. In 1950, they authorised the Collectors to sanction half the cost of mains operated radio sets, including cost of installation or Rs. 200 whichever is less, to villages wherever electricity was available in the firkas and centres[3]. The Government also allowed concessional rates of maintenance charges in respect of radio sets installed by the local bodies and sanctioned schemes for assembling cheap sets capable of receiving all the short and medium wave stations. The State Broadcasting Department now consists of a Radio Engineer, some Assistant Radio Engineers and a number of Radio Supervisors besides the usual supervisory staff. It has also a well equipped laboratory and workshop suitable for research and other work at Madras and many service stations in the Districts[4].

The Coimbatore district began to receive this amenity from March 1939[5]. By March 1957, the Department was maintaining in this district 188 sets in the panchayats, 19 sets in municipalities, 20 sets in the schools, one set in the propaganda van, one set belonging to a private body and six sets belonging to Government institutions. They were either main or battery sets. The district is in the charge of an Assistant Radio Engineer

---

1 G.O. No. 3081, Public Works, dated 18th July 1952—See the note at the end. Annual Administration Reports of the State Broadcasting Department from 1938 to 1953–54.

2 G.O. No. 330, Firka Development, dated 23rd March 1949.
G.O. No. 123, Rural Welfare, dated 8th February 1951.

3 G.O. No. 421, Firka Development, dated 12th May 1950.

G.O. No. 3081, Public Works, dated 18th July 1950—See the note at the end.

Administration Report of the State Broadcasting Department for 1938–1939, page 9.

who has headquarters at Tiruchirappalli. It has five service stations, viz., Coimbatore, Pollachi, Erode, Gobichettipalayam I and Gobichettipalayam II, the first two service stations having their headquarters at Coimbatore and the last three having their headquarters at Erode[1].

We may close this chapter by referring to certain important measures undertaken by the Government for the proper upkeep and maintenance of the hundreds of temples, maths and other Hindu religious institutions existing in this State. These have a history going back to a period of more than a century. As early as 1817, a Regulation (Regulation VII of 1817) was passed for enabling the Board of Revenue and, through it, the Collectors of the various districts, to exercise control over all endowments in land or money belonging to the religious institutions[2]. In 1841, however, on the instructions of the Court of Directors, the Government divested themselves of this responsibility and handed over the management to the trustees[3]. This having led to mismanagement and complaints, in 1863, they passed an amending Act (Madras Act XX of 1863) to prevent the abuses[4].

Regulation VII of 1817 divided the religious institutions into two classes, namely, those in which the nomination of trustees, managers or superintendents was vested in the Government and those in which this was not the case. For the superintendents of the institutions falling under the first description, the Act of 1863 provided for the appointment, once for all, by the Government, of local committees of three or more persons to exercise the powers of the Board of Revenue and the Collectors, the vacancies in the committees being filled up by election. But it left the institutions of the second class in the hands of the then existing trustees, free from the control of any local committees, the trustees, however, being made liable to be used by any person for breach of trust or neglect of duty[5]. This arrangement was soon found to be by no means satisfactory.

1 Administration Report of the State Broadcasting Department for 1956–1957, pages 40 and 42.

2 Madras Code, pages 68–71.
Board's Consultations, No. 56, dated 20th November 1817.

3 Revenue Consultations, Nos. 19–24, dated 15th June 1841.

4 Board's Consultations, No. 32, dated 24th March 1842.
Idem, Nos. 5–6, dated 3rd November 1842.
Idem, No. 4, dated 21st November 1842.
Idem, Nos. 9–16, dated 19th November 1846.
G.O. Nos. 1586–1587, Revenue, dated 13th September 1860.
G.O. No. 118, Judicial, dated 31st January 1872.

5 The unrepealed Acts of the Governor-General in Council (1898), Vol. I, pages 405–412.

It was found that the trustees could not be compelled to perform their duties; that the committees' powers were, to say the least, ill-defined; and that both the trustees and the committees being unpaid agencies had little inducement to discharge their responsibilities[1]. Various attempts were, therefore, made between 1870 and 1920 to bring in further legislation. First came Sri V. Ramiengar's Bill (1871)[2]. Then followed several Bills framed by various committees presided over by Sir William Robinson (1877)[3]; by Mr. Carmichael (1883); by Mr. Sullivan (1886)[4]; by Justice Muthuswami Ayyar (1893)[5]; and by Sri Chentsal Rao (1896)[6]. Some individual Bills were also brought forward by the members of the Imperial as well as the Madras Legislature. Sri Kalyanasundaram brought forward a Bill in the Madras Legislative Council in 1896[7]; Sri Ananthacharlu brought forward another in the Imperial Legislative Council in 1897[8]; Sri Srinivasa Rao brought forward a third in the Madras Legislative Council in 1902[9]; and Sri T. V. Seshagiri Ayyar and Sri L. A. Govindaraghava Ayyar, brought forward a fourth in the same Council in 1912[10]. Next came Imperial Legislation by the passing of the Religious and Charitable Trusts Act of 1920[11]. But even this Act proved a failure. It was not till 1925 that something was sought to be done to place the religious institutions on a better footing by the passing of the Madras Hindu Religious Endowments Act I of 1925; and it was not till 1927 that certain

---

1 G.O. No. 1975 (A), Judicial, dated 23rd October 1874.

2 G.O. No. 118, Judicial, dated 31st January 1872.
G.O. No. 1975 (A), Judicial, dated 23rd October 1874.

3 G.O. No. 639, Judicial, dated 4th April 1876.
G.O. Nos. 33–34, Judicial, dated 10th January 1879.
Copy of the Bill of 1879.
G.O. No. 1471, Judicial, dated 21st June 1880.
G.O. No. 1681, Judicial, dated 15th January 1880.

4 G.O. No. 58, Legislative, dated 5th February 1884.
G.O. No. 543, Public, dated 15th April 1887.
G.O. No. 364, Public, dated 4th April 1888.

5 G.O. Nos. 72–74, Legislative, dated 26th May 1894.
G.O. No. 114, Legislative, dated 30th October 1894.

6 G.O. Nos. 1065–1066, Public, dated 23rd September 1899.
G.O. No. 223, Public, dated 2nd March 1900.

7 Legislative Council Proceedings, dated 26th February 1896 and 9th April 1897.

8 G.O. Nos. 183–184, Public, dated 13th February 1899.

9 G.O. No. 14, Legislative, dated 12th March 1903.
G.O. Nos. 627–628, Public, dated 28th May 1912.

10 G.O. Nos. 627–628, Public, dated 28th May 1912.

11 G.O. No. 363, Public (Confidential), dated 10th March 1915.
G.O. No. 250, Public (Confidential), dated 11th February 1916.
G.O. No. 1982, Local and Municipal, dated 18th October 1922.

doubts regarding the validity of this Act were removed by the Madras Act II of 1927[1].

This Act set up a statutory Board consisting of a President and certain Commissioners in whom was vested, subject to the provisions of the Act, the general superintendence and control of all Hindu religious institutions in the State, with judicial and administrative powers over them[2]. The Hindu Religious Endowments Board which thus came into being sought to set right matters; it succeeded to an extent in preventing mismanagement and alienation of temple properties, but failed to exercise effective control, as the institutions continued to remain under the jurisdiction of elected committees. Complaints of mismanagement and inefficient supervision still began to pour in, until at last the first Congress Ministry under Sri C. Rajagopalachari, resolved to take over the direct administration of the endowments. Before, however, it could do so, it resigned office[3]. Some amendments were then made to the existing Act by Act V of 1944 and Act X of 1946[4]; but, the important step, that of direct administration, was taken by the National Government only in 1951 by passing the Madras Act XIX of 1951[5]. This Act consolidates the law relating to the Hindu religious and charitable institutions and endowments of the State, and specifies several controlling authorities, the Commissioner, the Deputy Commissioner, the Assistant Commissioners and the Area Committees. It empowers the Commissioner to exercise general superintendence and control over the administration of all religious endowments. It invests the Area Committees with jurisdiction over the temples and specific endowments attached to the temples with an annual income of less than Rs. 20,000. And, it required the trustees of every religious institution to keep regular accounts of all receipts and disbursements and also provides for rules being framed for the proper leasing of properties and the proper investments of funds of religious institutions. The Act also provides for the prevention of mismanagement of charitable endowments by authorising the Government to extend its provisions to

---

1 G.O. No. 1982, Local and Municipal, dated 18th October 1922.
G.O. No. 272, Law (Legislative), dated 5th December 1922.
G.O. No. 29, Law (Legislative), dated 27th January 1925.
G.O. No. 2612, Local and Municipal, dated 17th June 1926.
G.O. No. 43, Law (Legislative), dated 5th February 1927.

2 G.O. No. 45, Law (Legislative), dated 5th February 1927.

3 G.O. No. 2640, Public Health (Confidential), dated 10th June 1940.
G.O. No. 4026, Public Health, dated 1st November 1939.

4 G.O. No. 16, Legal, dated 3rd July 1944.
G.O. No. 15, Legal, dated 1st April 1946.

5 For the Bill, *See* G.O. No. 6, Legal, dated 14th January 1949.

charitable endowments. The Government have under the provisions of the Act since then arranged for the audit of accounts of the religious institutions, the annual income of which is not less than 1,000 rupees by the Local Fund Audit Department, instead of by private auditors. The cost of such audit is met from the fund collected at the rate not exceeding $1\frac{1}{2}$ per cent of the income of the religious institutions. Further, the Act enables the Commissioner to utilise the surplus funds of religious institutions for religious educational or charitable purposes.

The religious institutions of Coimbatore have naturally been affected by all these measures. In 1817 they came under the supervision of the Board of Revenue and the Collector; in 1841 they were left to be managed without any interference, by their own trustees and managers; in 1863 they came to be controlled either by the local committees or by their own trustees; in 1925 they came under the supervision of the Religious Endowment Board; and finally, in 1951, they came under the control of the Commissioner and his assistants under a separate department of State Government maintained from the fund collected at the rate not exceeding 5 per cent of the income of the religious institutions having an annual income of Rs. 200 under the slab system. There are now 834 religious institutions in the district under the jurisdiction of the Assistant Commissioner appointed under the Act[1].

---

1 Information furnished by the Commissioner, Hindu Religious and Charitable Endowments (Administration), Madras.

CHAPTER XI.

COMMUNICATIONS.

In the beginning of the last century there were hardly any roads in the district. But now the district has a network of roads traversing it in all directions. It has, in fact, a much larger mileage of roads than any other district in the State covering as they do not less than 3,840 * miles. Of these roads, 1,057 miles are under the Highways Department, 2,516 miles are under the District Board, 2 miles are under the Public Works Department and 265 miles are under the control of Municipalities. There is one National Highway and there are four State Highways in the district. These five roads and many of the major district roads are managed by the Highways Department. The rest of the major district roads and other district roads and village roads are managed by the District Board, while the Public Works Department roads are managed by that Department and the Municipal roads by the Municipalities. The Highways Department takes under its management more and more major district roads every year so that, in course of time, it might completely control all the major district roads in the district.

As to the length of the roads, the National Highway constitutes 78 miles, the State Highways 197 miles, the major district roads under the Highways Department 775 miles and under the District Board 368 miles, the other district roads, 7 miles under the Highways Department and 583 miles under the District Board, and the village roads, 1,565 miles under the District Board. The length of the roads in charge of the Public Works Department and the Municipalities has already been stated. 52 miles of the Highways Department roads and 7 miles of Municipal roads are cement concrete roads; 645 miles of the Highways Department roads, 16 miles of the District Board roads, 2 miles of the Public Works Department roads and 103 miles of Municipal roads are black top surface roads; 354 miles of the Highways Department roads, 1,169 miles of the District Board roads, and 94 miles of the Municipal roads are metalled roads; 5 miles of the Highways Department, 1,331 miles of the District Board roads, and 61 miles of the Municipal roads are unmetalled roads[1]. Large sums of money are being spent annually over the capital works and repairs

---

* The mileages was 4012 prior to the transfer of Kollegal to Mysore State.

1 Administration Report of the Highways Department, 1956–57—Annexure 5.

of all these roads. For instance, in 1956–57 the expenditure over Government roads amounted to Rs. 42,30,168[1], and over the District Board roads to Rs. 19,29,757[2].

Of the roads in the district the National Highway is, of course, the most important. It is the old Trunk Road from Madras to the West Coast. It enters the district at Bhavani on the Cauvery river and passes through the towns of Perundurai, Avanashi and Coimbatore before crossing into the Kerala State near Walayar. All the four State Highways start from Coimbatore and traverse the district in different directions. The first of these runs southward to the town of Pollachi and then turns east and after passing through the town of Udumalpet enters the district of Madurai and by way of Dindigul reaches the town of Madurai. The second Highway runs east and passing through Palladam and Kangayam enters the district of Tiruchirappalli and by way of Karur reaches the town of Tiruchirappalli. The third Highway runs north to Mettupalayam and passes thence to Ootacamund. The fourth Highway runs in a north-easterly direction to Satyamangalam and thence passes into the Mysore State. The district and other roads are too numerous to be described. A list of some of the major district roads is, however, appended at the end of this Chapter.

The soil of the district is favourable to road-making. Road metal like granite, kunkur and quartz are available in plenty almost everywhere and the formation and maintenance of roads is, therefore, not very costly. As the rainfall is scanty and the soil hard, the roads, whether metalled or gravelled, are generally in a good condition and permit easy draught almost throughout the year. The important roads are sufficiently broad[3].

As has been stated already there were in olden days no roads in the district and consequently merchandise and travellers were carried on the backs of pack-bullocks and ponies[4]. Even after the roads were formed the wear and tear could not have been much when the bullock and the pony cart were the fastest means of transport. But to-day the wear and tear is great. Merchandise is carried on heavily loaded motor trucks, 3 to 5 tons, and sometimes over 5 times in weight and people travel in buses equally heavily loaded. The number of these vehicles is also large.

---

1 Administration Report of the Highways department, 1956–57—*See* Annexure XI.

2 *Ibid.*

3 Gazetteer of the Coimbatore District, Vol. II (1933), pages 137–138—*See* also the Administration Reports of the District Board.

4 Manual of the Coimbatore District, Vol. II (1898), page 131.

In 1956 for instance there were in the district no less than 444 buses, 957 public lorries and 196 private lorries[1]. They covered more than 140 routes running in all directions of the district from important towns like Coimbatore, Dharapuram, Erode, Gobichettipalayam, Mettupalayam, Tirupur and Udumalpet. There were also town buses operating on different routes in Coimbatore and Tiruppur. Lorries carry goods in and out of the district from towns like Coimbatore, Mettupalayam, Erode, Pollachi, Tirupur and Udumalpet[2]. Besides these buses and lorries there were also in that year (1956), 724 motor cycles, 5,309 motor cars including station wagons and jeeps, 1,476 other special vehicles[3] and a few auto-rickshaws. Traffic exceeds 1,000 tons per day on several roads[4]. In addition to motor vehicles numerous carts drawn by excellent bullocks and ponies also carry passengers and goods on all the roads.

The roads in the district are not noted for their avenues. The hard soil and the poor rainfall are not favourable to the growth of trees and it is difficult and expensive to rear avenue trees. Along roads traversing wet lands, as in the Erode taluk, and the places where water is available, there are, however, avenues of coconut trees. On other roads tamarind trees are generally grown although they are not suitable avenue trees. They however, fetch a good revenue. The work of planting avenue trees is mostly in charge of the Highways Department, but the District Board also plants trees on the margins of some roads. In 1956–57 there were 55,287 trees on 1,057 miles of Government roads and 10,592 trees on 2,516 miles of District Board roads[5]. These figures show that the number of avenue trees per mile is extremely low.

Most of the rivers and streams which cross the roads have been provided with bridges or culverts or causeways. The most important bridge is that which spans the Cauvery where the National Highway enters the district. It is an old bridge and was badly damaged during the floods of 1924. The Bhavani is spanned by three bridges constructed in the last century at Mettupalayam, Satyamangalam and Bhavani town and by two other bridges constructed in 1931 at Nanjaipuliyampatti and Savandipur. The Noyyal has bridges at Coimbatore, Tiruppur, Ondiputtur,

1 Report on the Administration of the Motor Vehicles Act and Rules and the Madras Traffic Rules for 1956.

2 The Coimbatore and the Nilgiris Directory, 1957–58, pages 40–49.

3 Report on the Administration of the Motor Vehicles Act and Rules and the Madras Traffic Rules for 1956, pages 7 and 9.

4 Administration Report of the Coimbatore District Board for 1949–50.

5 Administration Report of the Highways department for 1956–57, Annexure 26.

Palayakottai and on the road to Iruttipallam. Minor rivers like the Uppar, the Aliyar and the Palar have also been bridged at important road crossings. Across streams which carry off storm water for a few days in the year and for the remaining part of the year are dry and sandy, causeways (road dams) have been constructed to render the passage of wheeled traffic easy[1].

There are a number of ferries for crossing the rivers at places where there are no bridges. They are all under the control of the District Board, though the farms are leased out by the Highways Department. They numbered 101 in 1951 and the District Board earned a net income of Rs. 59,298 from them[2].

For the benefit of travellers using the roads there are a number of travellers' bungalows, choultries, rest houses and watersheds. Many of the choultries which were built and endowed in olden days have fallen into disuse after the advent of motor cars and buses which enable people to cover long distances in a short time.

In 1956–57, the District Board maintained 18 rest houses all of which were under the control of the Highways Department, 26 choultries (there were 114 about 60 years ago) of which 16 were under the control of the Highways Department and two watersheds. Twenty-one of the choultries and the two watersheds received in the shape of money allowances from Government and income from endowments a sum of Rs. 4,541. A sum of Rs. 15,564 was spent by the Board on the maintenance of the choultries and watersheds. Besides these, the Highways Department also maintained two inspection bungalows in the district and their cost of maintenance for 1956–57 amounted to Rs. 628·25. A list showing the inspection bungalows, rest houses and choultries is appended at the end of the Chapter.

Turning to the history of roads, as has already been stated, there was none when the district passed into the hands of the British at the end of the eighteenth century. However, roads began to be constructed from about 1,800. In the early days of the East India Company, the construction and maintenance of roads were attended to by three different agencies, the Maramath department of the Board of Revenue, the Trunk Road department and the Engineering department of the Military Board. In 1858 these three departments were abolished and the Public Works

---

[1] Gazetteer of the Coimbatore District, Vol. II (1933), page 133.

[2] Administration Report of the Coimbatore District Board, 1950–51—*See* page 27 of G.O. No. 22, Local Administration, dated 4th January 1952.

Department was for the first time organized with the Chief Engineer at the head and several District Engineers under him. In the same year a road cess of 2 per cent of land revenue was imposed in ryotwari taluks for the proper maintenance of roads. In 1866 the Madras District Road Cess Act was passed, which legalised the levy of cess at half an anna in the rupee on the rent value of occupied land, so as to form a fund for the construction and maintenance of district roads.

But the chance for more rapid expansion of the roads came only with the passing of the Madras Local Funds Act of 1871. This Act repealed the District Road Cess Act of 1866, transferred the road funds raised under the latter Act to the Local Fund Boards and authorized the local bodies to levy a cess similar to the district road cess but with a maximum of one anna in the rupee and to establish tolls upon roads for their development[1]. In 1879–80 the entire execution of the maintenance and construction of roads was transferred from the Public Works Department to the Local Fund Boards which thereafter employed their own engineering staff directly responsible to them. Close on the heels of this came the Local boards Act of 1884 which created the district boards and the taluk boards. But this Act took away the salutary restriction imposed by the Act of 1871 which laid down that, besides the income from tolls, a sum of not less than two-thirds of the land cess should be spent on communications. This gave a handle to the district boards to spend less and less upon roads with the result that the Government found it necessary in 1895 to interfere and direct by an executive order that the local bodies should spend not less than half the income from their land cess upon roads. This order, however, was withdrawn in 1900 and the Government thereafter began to grant to the local bodies 25 per cent of their land cess for the improvement of roads in addition to the sums allotted from the imperial grants. From 1920 special grants were also made from time to time for the special repairs of important roads, for the maintenance of second class roads and for the construction of bridges and culverts, subject to a maximum. In 1930–31, on the introduction of the Motor Vehicles Tax, the tolls were abolished and the local bodies were given compensation for the loss of income from tolls [2].

Consequent on these changes the Coimbatore District Board began to pay more and more attention to its roads. In 1885–86, for instance, it

1 Manual of the Administration of the Madras Presidency by C. D. Maclean, Volume I, 1885, *see* the foot-notes on pages 365–367 and 379–380.

2 G.O. No. 2486, Local Administration, dated 16th November 1945, pages 5 and 9.

maintained 1,179 miles of roads. In the same year it spent a sum of Rs. 1,43,148 on the construction and maintenance of roads[1]. In 1935–36 it maintained 3,019 miles of roads. 2,103 miles of these were village roads, 702 miles were second class roads and 214 miles were trunk roads. The expenditure on these roads in the same year was Rs. 6,37,128. Out of this the Government grant amounted to Rs. 1,93,690[2].

Meanwhile the Government became more and more road conscious. In 1933 they appointed a Special Officer to draw up a comprehensive programme of road development and upon his recommendation[3] created in 1937 a separate class of roads called important marketing roads and granted subsidies for their maintenance subject to the condition that the District Boards should spend at least an amount equal to the subsidy from their own funds either on the important Marketing Roads or on second class roads. But no uniform practice of spending a fixed percentage of the road cess was adopted by any District Board. While some of the District Boards spent a good percentage of their land cess on roads, others spent very little. So far as this district was concerned, it spent only 18 per cent of the land cess on roads. Then came the Second World War and the continual heavy wear and tear of the roads caused by the military vehicles which led to their speedy deterioration. So in 1941 the Government directed that a minimum allotment should be made for the maintenance of roads by every District Board and Municipal Council [4].

All this time other measures too were being taken by the Government to have a greater control over the engineering staff employed by the local bodies. It has already been seen that from about 1880 the District Boards began to employ their own engineering establishments. The Municipalities also, from about the same time, began to employ their own engineering staffs. By the Local Boards Act of 1884 and the Municipalities Act of 1884 the appointment of District Board and Municipal Engineers was made subject to the general control of the Government. But this general control amounted in practice to no control. It was not till 1923 that the District Board Engineers' service was provincialised[5] and not till 1938 that the Assistant Engineers' service of the local

---

[1] G.O. No. 1260, Financial (Local Funds), dated 4th October 1886—*See* page 12.

[2] G.O. No. 2787, Local Administration, dated 23rd July 1937, page 41.

[3] *Scheme of Road Development for the Madras Presidency* by A. Vipan, Special Engineer, Road Development, 1935.

[4] G.O. No. 2486, Local Administration, dated 16th November 1945, pages 9–13 and 225.

[5] G.O. No. 242, Local Municipal, dated 25th January 1923.

bodies was constituted into a separate service[1]. In the meantime the Superintending Engineers of the Public Works Department were required to inspect the trunk roads and all works costing above Rs. 50,000 situated within the jurisdiction of the District Boards. In 1936 the Government appointed a Special Engineer (Road Development) as Inspecting and Superintending Officer in respect of all operations of the Engineering departments of all District Boards [2]. In 1940 they made the Chief Engineer (Buildings and Roads) the Controlling authority for the District Board Engineers' service and the Local Fund Assistant Engineers' Service and created three posts of Superintending Engineers (Communications) for the better inspection and superintendence of district roads. In 1942 they went further and created a new post of Chief Engineer (Communications),[3] and soon after created six Road Divisions and a Roads Circle [4].

But the times were fast changing, revealing new defects and demanding new remedies. The District Boards and Municipalities failed to make the minimum allotments for the maintenance of roads, while the wheels of war rolled on reducing the roads to ruin everywhere. All over India experts and laymen alike now began to clamour for more metalling, for more surface topping, more cement concreting and more mileage of roads. This led to the convening of a conference of Chief Engineers at Nagpur (1943), to the appointment of a Special Officer in Madras to review afresh the whole subject of road development[5] and to the drawing up a Five-Year Postwar Development Plan for the construction of National Highways, State Highways, major district roads and village roads and for the widening and repairing of the existing roads wherever necessary. The aim of this plan was to provide eventually access by road to all villages having a population of 500 or more and to so plan the Highways and district roads that every village would be within 2 miles of a district road or a highway in densely populated areas and within 5 miles in thinly populated areas. The Five-Year Plan drawn up for the Coimbatore district roads comprised 23 items of importance[6]. The Post War Development Plan was merged with the First Five-Year Plan formed by the Planning

[1] G.O. No. 1445, Local Administration, dated 22nd April 1938.
G.O. No. 2092, Local Administration, dated 6th June 1938.

[2] G.O. No. 1353, Local Administration, dated 31st March 1936.

[3] G.O. No. 800, Public Works, dated 16th March 1942.

[4] G.O. No. 2486, Local Administration, dated 16th November 1945, pages 16–17.

[5] For the Special Officer's Report, *see* G.O. No. 2486, Local Administration dated 16th November 1945.

[6] G.O. Ms. No. 3750, Public Works, dated 15th September 1948.
G.O. Press No. 1856, Revenue, dated 11th May 1950.

Commission of the Government of India in consultation with the Madras Government in 1951, a plan for which 5 crores of rupees were allotted to Madras under ' roads '[1]. The First Five-Year Plan has now been completed and the Second Five-Year Plan is in progress. In this Plan ample provision has been made for the extensive development of roads, especially village roads which are very necessary for the successful implementation of all social services. It is proposed to construct no less than 3,688 miles of roads. This will assure access by road to every village with a population of 500 or more. To meet the demands of increasing traffic, fast as well as slow, it is proposed to lay cement concrete pavements over a total distance of 40 miles and to increase the existing 571 miles of black top surface by another 578 miles. 195 miles of road will be up-graded by the use of hard metal surface. Roads will also be widened where the traffic is exceptionally heavy. Side by side with this, old culverts will be repaired or replaced and 12 new bridges and causeways will be built. The cost of this development is estimated to come to 374 lakhs of rupees[2].

In the meantime for the execution of the Post-war Development Plan a separate department called the Highways Department had been formed in 1946[3]. This Department took under its management all national Highways, all Provincial Highways, and in the first instance about 10,000 miles of important district roads, leaving the remaining roads as before, under the District Boards and the Municipalities[4].

This is how the Highways Department has now come to manage all the important roads in the district and to exercise a general supervision over the District Board and Municipal roads. The Department has one Chief Engineer, several Superintending Engineers, a number of Divisional Engineers, each in charge of a district or a portion of a district and a larger number of Assistant Engineers each in-charge of a subdivision. The expenditure on the Divisional Engineer and his office is shared by the Government and the District Board, while the expenditure on the Assistant Engineers and the Subordinate Staff engaged on District Board works is borne solely by the District Board concerned. In the Coimbatore District there are two Divisional Engineers (Highways), one for the Coimbatore Division with headquarters at Coimbatore and the other for the Erode Division with headquarters at Erode, with three Assistant Engineers for

[1] Administration Report of the Highways department for 1952–53, page 25.

[2] Second Five-Year Plan, Madras State, Coimbatore district (1955), page 36.

[3] G.O. No. 114, Local Administration, dated 18th January 1946.
G.O. No. 598, Local Administration, dated 28th March 1946.

[4] Madras in 1950, pages 107–112.

each Division and their work is supervised by the Superintending Engineer, Coimbatore Circle who has his headquarters at Coimbatore[1].

Coming to the railways, for a district of its size, Coimbatore is not well served by railways. Several towns and important villages are situated far from railway stations. The total mileage of railways is 202½. Of these 125¾ miles are broad-gauge and the rest metre-gauge[2]. The Chief broad Gauge Railway is the railway from Madras to West Coast. This line enters the district near Erode after crossing the Cauvery and passing through Tiruppur and Coimbatore, leaves the district through the Palghat gap. This line, which was opened in 1862, at first ran through Podanur, three miles south of Coimbatore town, and a separate line opened in 1873 ran from Podanur to Coimbatore and thence to Mettupalayam[3].

From Erode a line runs south to Kodumudi and thence to Tiruchirappalli. This line was opened in 1868. It was constructed as a broad-gauge line at first, but when it was taken over in 1879 by the South Indian Railway Company from the old Madras Railway Company, who constructed it, it was changed into the metre-gauge to be uniform with the other lines owned by the South Indian Railway Company. Fifty years later, in 1929, the line was reconverted into broad-gauge owing to the establishment of a common workshop at Tiruchirappalli for both the broad-gauge and the metre-gauge lines[4]. The importance of Podanur declined with the removal of the workshops from that place to Golden Rock in Tiruchirappalli town. At the same time the town of Coimbatore became an important industrial centre. A direct connection was, therefore, established to Coimbatore in 1939 by means of a chord line from Singanallur to Coimbatore[5]. When Coimbatore began to grow still further in importance and size this chord line was replaced in 1953 by another and longer chord line from Irugur to Coimbatore North on the Coimbatore-Mettupalayam line. The old line to Podanur has at the same time been retained for the use of trains which do not have to touch Coimbatore on their way to the West Coast.

With the exception of these two chord lines no new railway was constructed in the district till 1915 when the Coimbatore District Board

[1] G.O. No. 61, Health, Education and Local Administration, dated 10th January 1957.

[2] 1951 *Census Handbook, Coimbatore District*, page 4.

[3] *History of Indian Railways*, 1924, page 184.

[4] *Gazetteer of the Coimbatore District*, Vol. II (1933), pages 139–140.

[5] G.O. No. Ms. 2481, Public Works, dated 16th October 1939.

constructed a metre-gauge line from Podanur to Pollachi. This line was carried eastward to Dindigul via Udumalpet and Palni in 1928 by the South Indian Railway Company. Four years later, in 1932, a line running westward from Pollachi to Palghat was also opened by the Company. These new lines reduced considerably the distance from the West Coast to Dindigul, Madurai and other places in the Southern part of the State[1]. The line from Podanur to Pollachi was worked on behalf of the District Board by the South Indian Railway Company until 1945 when it was sold to the Government of India for Rs. 16,46,703 being 120 per cent of the capital outlay[2].

As has been stated already several parts of the district are unconnected by railways. No line, for instance passes through the headquarters of the taluks of Avanashi, Gobichettipalayam and Dharapuram. Several schemes have been considered from time to time for connecting the remote parts of the district by railways. A metre-gauge line from Erode to Nanjangud in Mysore State via Satyamangalam with branches from Satyamangalam to Mettupalayam and Gobichettipalayam to Palani via Dharapuram was under contemplation for a long time. The Government of Mysore was very much interested in this line, as it would connect directly Mysore with the Southern district of the Madras State. The scheme was, however, found to be unremunerative and was given up when the line from Erode to Tiruchirappalli was converted into broad-gauge and thereby through connection between Mysore and the Southern districts was rendered impossible[3]. Another scheme to connect Chamrajanagar to Mettupalayam via Satyamangalam was then taken up and investigated[4]. This scheme too has not been carried out till now. Another line which was considered was one from Pollachi to Vannanthorai; it was intended to serve the Anaimalai plantations. This line too has not been constructed[5].

The outlying parts of the district are now served by a number of out agencies for passengers and goods; Bhavani for passengers and goods is served by Erode railway station; Bhavanisagar for parcels and goods is served by Mettupalayam railway station; Dharapuram for passengers and goods is served by Tiruppur railway station and Palni railway station

---

1 *Gazetteer of the Coimbatore District*, Vol. II (1933), page 140.

2 Administration Report of the Coimbatore District Board for 1945–46, paragraph 34 (*a*).

3 *Gazetteer of the Coimbatore District*, Vol. II (1933), pages 140–141.
G.O. Ms. No. 2263, Public Works (Railways), dated 7th September 1931.

4 G.O. Ms. No. 3644, Public Works, dated 28th September 1949.

5 *Gazetteer of the Coimbatore District*, Vol. II (1933), page 141.

in the Madurai district; Palladam for passengers and goods is served by Tiruppur; and Valparai for passengers and goods is served by Pollachi[1].

Mention may be made in this place of Anaimalai ropeway which serves the plantations on the Anaimalais. It was constructed in 1928 by the joint endeavour of several planting concerns and has been of great use in transporting the produce of the plantations from the hills to the plains. The bottom station is situated near the Vannanthorai bridge at the foot of the Anaimalai ghat road and the top station is in the Iyerpady estate. The length of the ropeway is 9½ miles[2].

The town of Coimbatore is connected by air with Madras, Madurai, Trivandrum, Cochin and Bangalore and connections are available with previous arrangements at Madras and Bangalore for Calcutta, Bombay and Delhi. At present three air services which originate and terminate at Madras are touching Coimbatore[3].

The Coimbatore aerodrome is situated six miles north-east of the town on the Avanashi Road. It was originally a landing ground under the maintenance of the Coimbatore Municipal Council. In 1941, the landing ground was taken over by the Government from the Municipal Council for internal security and was subsequently developed into an aerodrome. The aerodrome was used by the Airforce authorities till 1946 when it was transferred to the Civil Aviation Department of the Government of India. Recently the aerodrome has been modernised to receive medium heavy type of aircraft and standard facilities such as passengers lounge, telephone, restaurant, etc., are available. There is also a flying club in the aerodrome to impart training in flying[4].

As to the posts and telegraphs, there were in the district in 1956–57 one head post office, one post and telegraph head office, 39 post and telegraph sub-offices, 32 non-combined sub-post offices and 577 branch post offices[5].

In regard to telephone facilities there are exchanges in the towns of Coimbatore, Mettupalayam, Pollachi and Tiruppur. In Coimbatore,

---

1 1951 *Census Handbook, Coimbatore District*, page 4.

2 G. O. Ms. No. 1282, Development, dated 27th July 1929 *Gazetteer of the Coimbatore* District, Vol. II. 1933, pages 141–142.

3 Based on the information furnished by the Controller of Aerodromes, Madras Region.

4 *Idem*

See also G. O. No. 896, Public Works (Confidential), dated 24th March 1942.

5 Information supplied by the Indian Posts and Telegraphs department, Madras.

there are 1,499 lines with 26 internal extensions, in Mettupalayam 90 lines, in Pollachi 174 lines and in Tiruppur 255 lines. From the Tiruppur Exchange, besides local connections, connections are available to Avanashi. From the Pollachi Exchange, besides local connections, connections are available to Anamalais[1].

COIMBATORE.

List of Major District Roads in the District.

	Length.		Maintained by whom.
	Mls.	Fur.	
Ambarampalayam Sothumadai Road.	10	..	Highways.
Anamalai Bridle paths	25	6	Do.
Anamalai Ghat Road	26	1	Do.
Anamalai Pulankinar Road ..	20	2	Do.
Andhiyur Ammapet Road	10	7	Do.
Andhiyur Attani Road	10	7	Do.
Arachalur Kodumudi Road ..	17	..	District Board.
Avanashi Puliampatty Road ..	11	..	Highways.
Bhavani Chellampalayam Road ..	19	2	District Board.
Chennimalai Uthukuli Road ..	11	3	Do.
Cheyur Erode Sathy Road ..	10	7	Do.
Coimbatore Pollachi to Nadupum Road.	10	7	Do.
Coimbatore Siruvani Road ..	18	5	Highways.
Coimbatore Thadagam Road ..	11	6	Do.
Dharapuram Palani Road	10	6	Do.
Dharapuram Pollachi Road ..	11	2	District Board.
Dharapuram Pollachi Road ..	21	6	Do.
Dharapuram Tiruppur Road ..	16	..	Highways.
Dharapuram Tiruppur Road ..	13	3	Do.
Erode Kangayam Road	27	4	Do.
Erode Karur Road	24	6	Do.
Erode Muthur Road	22	2	Do.
Erode Perundurai Road	10	5	Do.
Gobi Dharapuram Road	52	5	Do.
Kangayam Kodumudi Road. ..	11	..	District Board.
Karatholuvu KomaralingamRoad.	14	6	Highways.
Kattampotti To Koduvoi (via) Vavipalayam and Sonjeri Road.	22	5	District Board.
Kinathukadavu Kattampatty Road.	10	6	Do.
Kollegal Chellampalayam Road ..	25	..	Do.
Kollegal Hassanur Road	17	7	Highways.
Mettur Bhavani Road to Tiruppur.	11	2	District Board.

1 Telephone Directory, Coimbatore Division.

COIMBATORE—*cont*.

LIST OF MAJOR DISTRICT ROADS IN THE DISTRICT—*cont*.

	Length.		*Maintained by whom.*
	MLS.	FUR.	
Palladam Cochin Frontier Road ..	20	..	Highways.
Palladam Dharapuram Road ..	10	4	Do.
Porundurai Kangayam Road ..	20	..	Do.
Perundurai Kunnathur Road ..	12	2	Do.
Perundurai Maccanacombai Road	24	2	District Board.
Pollachi Munkarai Road	13	6	Highways.
Pollachi Palladam Road	30	2	Do.
Pollachi Vannanthorai Road ..	13	6	Do.
Sathy Attani Bhavani Road ..	32	..	District Board.
Sathy Mottupalayam Road ..	11	5	Highways.
Thoppur Muthur Bhavani Road ..	19	1	Do.
Tiruppur Kunnathur Road ..	11	7	Do.
Tiruppur Mottupalayam Road ..	32	7	Do.
Tiruppur Vijayamangalam Road ..	12	4	District Board.
Udumalpet Chinnadharapuram Road	34	2	Highways.
Udumalpet Chinnadharapuram Road	34	2	Do.
Udumalpet Chinnar Road	18	..	Do.
Udumalpet Komaralingam Road	11	4	District Board.
Udumalpet Senjeri Road	17	2	Do.
Udumalpet Tiruppur Road ..	38	6	Highways.

LIST OF TRAVELLERS BUNGALOWS, REST HOUSES, ETC., IN COIMBATORE DISTRICT.

Serial number and inspection bungalows, rest houses and choultries.	*Type of accommodation.*		*Location.*
	Class.	*Number of suites or rooms.*	
(1)	(2)	(3)	(4)
I. INSPECTION BUNGALOWS UNDER THE HIGHWAYS DEPARTMENT.			
1 Manupatti	II	2 suites ..	At mile 8/6 of Udumalpet Chinnar Road and 8¾ miles from Udumalpet R.S.
2 Attakatti	II	2 suites ..	At mile 7/2 of Anamalai Ghat Road and 21 miles from Pollachi R.S.

II. Rest houses owned by the District Board.

Serial number and inspection bungalows, rest houses and choultries.	*Type of accommodation.*		*Location.*
	Class.	*Number of suites or rooms.*	
(1)	(2)	(3)	(4)
1 Avanashi	I	2 sets ..	At mile 304/0 of Madras Calicut Road and 8 miles from Tiruppur R. S.
2 Annur	I	2 sets ..	At mile 20/1 of Coimbatore-Sathyamangalam Road and 12 miles from Mettupalayam R. S.
3 Karumathampatti ..	I	2 sets ..	At mile 313/0 of Madras Calicut Road and 2 miles from Somanur R. S.
4 Palladam	I	2 sets ..	At mile 103/4 of Tiruchirappalli Coimbatore Road and 12 miles from Tiruppur R. S.
5 Bhavani	I	4 suites ..	At mile 266/3, ½ a furlong away on the left side from the Salem Cochin Road and 12 miles from Erode R. S.
6 Periapatti	II	1 Set ..	At mile 12/3 of Udumalpet Pollachi Road and 13 miles from Udumalpet R.S.
7 Karamadai	II	2 suites ..	At mile 17/0 of Coimbatore-Mettupalayam Road and 2 furlongs from Karamadai R.S.
8 Kodumudi	II	3 suites ..	At mile 23/1 of Erode Karur Road and 3 furlong from Kodumudi R. S.
9 Porundurai	II	2 suites ..	At mile 279/8 of Salem Cochin Road and 3½ miles each from Porundurai R.S. and Ingur R. S.
10 Satyamangalam ..	II	2 suites ..	At mile 0/0 of Sathy Mettupalayam Road and 43/0 of Coimbatore - Sathy Road and 24 miles from Mettupalayam Railway Station.

II. Rest houses owned by the District Board—*cont.*

Serial number and inspection bungalows, rest houses and choultries.	*Type of accommodation.*		*Location.*
	Class.	*Number of suites or rooms.*	
(1)	(2)	(3)	(4)
11 Gobichettipalayam ..	II	3 suites ..	At mile 24/2 of Erode Sathy Road and 24 miles from Erode R. S.
12 Kangayam	II	3 suites ..	At mile 35/6 of Gobi–Dharapuram Road and 14 miles from Uthukuli R.S.
13 Dhimbam	II	1 suite ..	At left side of Coimbatore-Sathy - Chamarajanagar Road at mile 66/0 and 7 miles from Sathy towards Chamarajanagar. Nearest R. S. is Mettupalayam.
14 Uthukuli	II	2 sets ..	At mile 21/7 of Gobi-Dharapuram Road and within 100′ from Uthukuli R. S.
15 Vellakoil	III	3 suites ..	At mile 73/0 of Trichy-Coimbatore Road and 18½ miles from Kodumudi R.S.
16 Andhiyur	III	2 sets ..	At ½ a furlong off 12/2 Bhavani Chellampalayam Road.
17 Sirumugai	III	2 suites ..	At mile 21/0 of Sathyamangalam-Mettupalayam Road and 7 miles from Mettupalayam R.S.
18 Koduvoi	(Occupied by Elementary School).		

III. Choultries owned by the District Board.

1 Mettupalayam	III	2 rooms ..	At mile 22/6 of Coimbatore Mettupalayam Road and one mile from Mettupalayam R.S.
2 Gomangalam	III	1 set ..	At mile 35/4 of Coimbatore Dindigul Road and one mile from Gomangalam R.S.

III. CHOULTRIES OWNED BY THE DISTRICT BOARD—*cont.*

Serial number and inspection bungalows, rest houses and choultries.	*Type of accommodation.*		*Location.*
	Class.	*Number of suites or rooms.*	
(1)	(2)	(3)	(4)
3 Kinathukadavu	III	2 suites ..	At mile 13/4 of Coimbatore-Dindigul Road and 1/2 mile from Kinathukadavu R.S.
4 Punjaipuliampatty ..	III	2 sets ..	At mile 30/0 of Coimbatore Sathy - Chamarajanagar Road.
5 Sivanmalai	III	3 rooms ..	At mile 33/2 of Gobi-Dharapuram Road.
6 Udhiyur (Chatram Bungalow)	III	2 rooms ..	At mile 44/1 of Gobi-Dharapuram Road.
7 Mulanur (Chatram Bungalow)	III	2 sets ..	At mile 37/0 of Udumalpet-Chinnadharapuram Road.
8 Nambiyur	III	1 set ..	At mile 10/0 of Cheyur to Erode-Sathy Road and 34 miles from Tiruppur R. S.
9 Kundadam	III	2 rooms ..	At one furlong off mile 16/7 of Palladam-Dharapuram Road and 24 miles from Tiruppur R. S.
10 Attani	III	1 room ..	At the junction of Sathy-Attani Bhavani Road and Gobi-Savindapur Road.
11 Nerinjipet	III	1 room ..	At mile 237/2 of Thoppur-Mettur-Bhavani Road.
12 Talavady	III	1 room ..	At mile 5/4 of Kumbargundy-Talavady Road.
13 Kangayam	III	10 rooms (3 rooms occupied by elementary school)	At mile 27/4 of Erode-Kangayam Road.
14 Malayampalayam ..	III	1 set ..	At mile 14/2 of Erode-Karur Road.
15 Vijayamangalam ..	II	1 set ..	At mile 286/3 of Salem Cochin Road.

III. CHOULTRIES OWNED BY THE DISTRICT BOARD—*cont.*

Serial number and inspection bungalows, rest houses and choultries.	*Type of accommodation.*		*Location.*
	Class.	*Number of suites or rooms.*	
(1)	(2)	(3)	(4)
16 Sathyamangalam ..	III	2 rooms ..	At mile 43/1 of Coimbatore-Sathy Chamarajanagar Road.
17 Bonnari	III	2 rooms ..	At mile 51/6 of Coimbatore-Sathy Chamarajanagar Road.
18 Dhimbam	III	2 rooms ..	At mile 60/0 of Coimbatore-Sathy Chamarajanagar Road.
19 Kothamangalam ..	III	1 room ..	At mile 7/4 of Sathy-Kothamangalam Road.
20 Hassanur	III	2 rooms ..	At mile 66/1 of Coimbatore-Sathy - Chamarajanagar Road.
21 Talamalai	III	1 room ..	At mile 14/0 of Talamalai Talavady (via) Chikkalli Road.
22 Kannapuram	III	2 rooms ..	At 1 furlong off of 78/1 Trichy-Coimbatore Road and 20½ miles from Uthukuli Railway Station.
23 Avanashi	(Occupied by District Board Elementary School.)		
24 Annur	Do.		
25 Gundalore	(Occupied by Public Health Centre.)		
26 Perianaickenpalayam ..	(Abandoned.)		

CHAPTER XII.

PUBLIC HEALTH.

A hot, dry climate and a scanty rainfall are by no means conducive to good health. And the major portion of the Coimbatore District which present these characteristics cannot, therefore, be considered to be healthy. The only places where the climate is pleasant are some parts of the Coimbatore, Pollachi, Udumalpet and Dharapuram taluks which get cool currents from the west coast through the Palghat gap during the south-west monsoon[1].

Cholera has been known to exist in the District for more than a century. There are evidences to show that severe epidemics of cholera occurred in 1853–54, 1856–58, 1860–61, 1863–66, 1870, 1875–77, 1883–85, 1887, 1889-92, 1921, 1926–27, 1930–32, 1936–37, 1944 and 1950–51. In 1857 the disease carried away 12,383 persons; in 1866, 7,780; 1875, 14,220; 1876, 26,933; 1877, 12,528 and 1898, 8,397. In recent years its ravages have become less, but all the same, in some years it has suddenly flared up and done not a little havoc. Thus in 1926, it claimed 2,124 victims; in 1931, 2,100; in 1936, 2,400; in 1937, 3,310 ; in 1943, 9,649; in 1950, 3,158[2]; and in 1957, 151[3].

The frequent occurrence of cholera, in this as in some other districts, is to be traced to the spread of infection by pilgrims resorting to festivals at sacred places (although this has now been controlled to some extent), to the congregation of labourers in large numbers during harvest time in places without protected water supply, to the indiscriminate fouling of rivers, streams, channels and tanks, to the inveterate habit among the poorer classes of drinking such contaminated water and eating contaminated food and to the want of protected water supply and lack of public latrines. The disease, as is well known, is caused by germs which are given out in very large numbers in the motion and vomit of the cholera patients. These germs contaminate food through flies and drinking water through the washing of infected clothes, etc., and any person who takes such contaminated food or water immediately catches the disease.

---

1. *See* Chapter I.

2. *Manual of Coimbatore District*, Volume II, page 91.
Administration Reports of the Public Health Department from 1921 to 1951.
1951 *Census Handbook. Coimbatore District*, 1953, page 10.

3. Information furnished by the Director of Public Health, Madras.

Before the separate Health Department came into existence in 1922, no systematic efforts were made to check the ravages of cholera. Since then, however, several steps have been taken to control its outbreaks. Among the preventive measures, the most important are protected water supply, proper disposal of night soil and sanitary control over the preparation and sale of food. But these measures have been found difficult of execution owing to the lack of finance and want of public co-operation. Among the control measures, isolation and treatment of patients, disinfection of infected material, and immunization of the people by anti-cholera inoculation, have been considered the most important. These measures, however, have been enforced by the Public Health authorities to a great extent with good results[1].

Systematic anticipatory cholera inoculations of pilgrims as well as labourers moving for groundnut harvest in certain parts of the District are being carried out regularly every year and this has greatly helped in the control of the disease. An important recent achievement in the matter of control of the epidemic is the provision of mobile vans and jeeps for prompt and quick transport of staff, drugs, equipments and distribution of food supplements and for the immediate transport and isolation of patients for treatment[2].

Plague also has harassed the District in the past. The first outbreak of the disease in the District was in 1903 and it has become more or less endemic and has taken a heavy toll. In 1903 it carried away 3,045 persons; in 1904, 2,973; in 1909, 5,582; in 1917, 3,284; in 1920, 3,869; in 1921, 4,123 and in 1923, 3,888. In recent times its incidence has been very much reduced, but, all the same it has flared up in some years and taken a heavy toll. Thus in 1943 it caused 4,295 deaths; in 1944, 1,184; in 1945 nearly 1,000; in 1946, 1,798 and in 1947, 1,240. Since 1948 the disease has been occurring only in a sporadic form and thus there were 244 deaths in 1948, 7 deaths in 1949 and only one death in 1950.

The disease, as is well known, is primarily a disease of rats which can be communicated to men and a few of the lower animals by bites of rat fleas which have fed on plague infected rats. The association between human beings and rats in our country being intimate, an outbreak of plague among rats is sure to be followed by an outbreak of plague among human beings. Several steps have been taken to control the outbreak

---

1. Report of Health Survey and Development Committee, 1946, Volume I, pages 112–114.

Public Health Pamphlet No. 2—Control of Epidemics, 1949, pages, 5–7.

2. Information supplied by the Director of Public Health, Madras.

of plague. Among the preventive measures, the most important are the construction of rat-proof godowns, better housing conditions and control over the location of trades and industries which are likely to attract rats. Among the control methods, improvement of sanitation, isolation and treatment of patients, mass inoculation of the people against plague, intensive destruction of rats and fleas by the use of cyano gas, use of D.D.T. against fleas and disinfestation of grains and other articles coming from plague affected areas, have been considered as the most important.

These measures have been enforced to a great extent with good results in Coimbatore. The disease is now endemic in Coimbatore, Tirupur, Udumalpet and Pollachi towns, and in the Talavadi firka of the Gobichettipalayam taluk. Special plague staff is working in these areas throughout the year treating all the houses once a year with D.D.T. systematically and regularly. This has very greatly reduced the flea index on the rat population. Since 1951 the District is free from plague and it is expected that such sytematic and continued work with D.D.T. for a few more years will completely eradicate the disease from the district[1].

Smallpox has not been very severe in the district. Occasionally, however, it has come with virulence and taken a considerable toll. Thus in 1882 it claimed 2,075 victims; in 1892, 2,676; in 1922, 1,197; in 1951, 1,210; in 1956, 55 and in 1957, 309[2]. But normally it carries away only a few hundreds of people. The disease spreads by contact, direct or indirect through clothing, etc., and also by droplet infection through air over short distances or through dust particles. Medical science has not yet discovered a cure for the disease, but on the preventive side it has discovered a most effective remedy, namely, vaccination. Vaccination, however, does not confer permanent immunity. A person has to get himself re-vaccinated particularly during the outbreak of the epidemic. If all children are vaccinated as required by law and, if all adults get themselves periodically re-vaccinated, the disease can be completely eradicated as in most of the European countries. But this has not been found practicable here for want of public co-operation, although the public has been familiar with

---

1. *Coimbatore District Gazetteer*, Volume II, 1933, page 129.
Administration Reports of the Public Health department for the years 1921 to 1951.
1951 *Census Handbook, Coimbatore District*, 1953, page 10.
Information furnished by the Director of Public Health, Madras.
Public Health Pamphlet
No. 2—Control of Epidemics, 1949, pages 7—10.

2. *Manual of Coimbatore District*, Volume II Page, 102.
Administration Reports of the Public Health department for 1921–51.
1951 *Census Handbook, Coimbatore District*, 1953, page 10.
Information furnished by the Director of Public Health, Madras.

vaccination for over a century and a half, it having been introduced in this State as early as 1802. Besides vaccination, the other measures necessary for controlling the spread of the disease are prompt notification, isolation, disinfection and protection and surveillance of contracts. Prompt notification has seldom been done by the people, but the rest of the measures have been more or less effectually taken by the Public Health authorities in the district.[1]

The other diseases, the incidence of which may be said to be heavy in Coimbatore as compared with some of the districts in this State, are guinea-worm, inflammatory disease of eye, otitis media and mastoiditis and other diseases of the central nervous system and sense organs, influenza, broncho-pneumonia, bronchitis, digestive diseases like gastro enteritis, chronic enteritis, colitis, etc., scabies and other skin affections and rheumatism. The incidence of some other diseases like tuberculosis, syphilis, yaws, gonococcal infections, malaria, hook-worm and other diseases due to the helminths is also fairly heavy in the District. Thus in 1957 for instance, the number of indoor and outdoor patients treated in the Public Local Fund and Private Aided hospitals and dispensaries in the district for the diseases mentioned above were as follows: Guineaworm accounted for 119 patients; the inflammatory diseases 53,322; otitis media and mastoiditis 57,683; other diseases of the central nervous system and sense organs 32,581; influenza 134,844; broncho-pneumonia 7,314; bronchitis 97,651; digestive diseases like gastro enteritis, chronic enteritis and colitis, etc. 1,36,513; scabies and other skin infections 95,536; rheumatism 45,226; tuberculosis, 19,161, syphilis 11,981; gonococcal infection 7,618; hook-worm (Ankylostomiasis), 1,718; malaria 25,159 and dysentery 127,973.[2]

Special attempts have been made to control some of these diseases. We have already seen that measures have been taken for preventing cholera, plague and smallpox.

Guineaworm is endemic in the Gobichettipalayam, Dharapuram Bhavani, Pollachi and Tiruppur taluks. The prevalence of disease is due to the use of stepwell water without filtration or boiling, for drinking purposes. Cyclops breeding in the water get infected when diseased persons step into the water. It is sought to be controlled by converting the stepwells into draw-wells and by vector control measures. Super-chlorination and D.D.T. treatment of water sources are the chemical measures adopted for vector control. D.D.T. is applied to the water

1. *Public Health Pamphlet No.* 2—Control of Epidomics, 1949, pages 1–5.

2. Report on the Working of Civil Hospitals and Dispensaries for 1957.

sources as 0·5 per cent suspension of 50 per cent D.D.T. wettable powder at a dosage of 5 parts per million [1].

Yaws are endemic in the Avanashi and Palladam taluks. This disease is brought on by environmental factors, physical, social and economic. It is due to infection with a spirochaete allied to syphilis but it is not the result of man's purposeful anti-social behaviour as in the case of syphilis. It is a contact infection, transmitted non-venereally. It is predominently seen amongst Harijans. Total mass treatment of the entire population in the endemic taluks with Procaine Penicillin G in oil with aluminium monostearate has brought the incidence of the disease to a hypo-endemic level. A maintenance programme to surveil the area is being instituted [2].

Treatment of leprosy is afforded in leprosy clinics attached to all the Government Hospitals. According to the census of 1951, the incidence of the disease among the population in the District is as follows :—

Taluks.	*Males.*		*Females.*		*Total.*
	Leprosy cases.	*Doubtful cases.*	*Leprosy cases.*	*Doubtful cases.*	
(1)	(2)	(3)	(4)	(5)	(6)
Avanashi	70	25	82	24	151
Bhavani	119	41	44	26	230
Coimbatore	170	34	99	24	327
Dharapuram	162	32	57	13	264
Erode	95	47	50	51	243
Gobichettipalayam ..	60	25	18	9	112
Palladam	61	21	37	25	144
Pollachi	14	1	7	1	23
Udumalpet	91	14	42	9	156
Total ..	842	240	386	182	1,650

The incidence is very low as compared with the other districts, it being found in only 5 persons out of every 10,000 of the population.[3]

Tuberculosis, the incidence of which, as has already been seen is fairly heavy in the District, has also attracted attention. In 1933 in response to an appeal made by the Viceroy Lord Wellington for the prevention and treatment of tuberculosis, the Coimbatore District Tuberculosis Sanatorium Society was formed by a group of disinterested persons and thanks to the generous contribution from the public and local bodies and an

1. Information furnished by the Director of Public Health, Madras.

2. *Idem.*

3. 1951 *Census Handbook, Coimbatore district*, 1953, pages 77–78.
Census of India, Madras and Coorg, Part I, page 224.

allotment of Rs. 60,000 from the District collections for the Silver Jubilee Celebration, the Society constructed and started in 1939 a Tuberculosis Sanatorium at Perundurai which enjoys a salubrious climate throughout the year.[1] Another private sanatorium was opened in 1950 at Peelamedu about three miles east of Coimbatore for the treatment of the disease.[2]

A campaign of Mass B.C.G. vaccination was started in Coimbatore town and belt areas (10 miles around) in November 1954. The T.B. infection among pre-school and school children was found to be wide-spread. A third of the population was given B.C.G. vaccination. Though B.C.G. alone could not be expected to control the tuberculosis problem, it has a distinct contribution to make when combined with other measures like isolation, case finding and domiciliary chemotherapy. The incidence of the disease can be said to be in the neighbourhood of 3 to 4 per cent in the urban area of Coimbatore based on miniature X-ray surveys in urban areas of India. The number of persons tested with tuberculin and vaccinated with B.C.G. were 6,47,699 and 2,46,077 respectively.

Malaria was endemic in the hills and foot-hill villages in the taluks of Pollachi, Coimbatore, Bhavani, Avanashi, Gobichettipalayam and Udumalpet. A District Anti-malaria Scheme started functioning in 1947–1948. Control measures were instituted in the taluks of Pollachi and Bhavani to begin with and later on were gradually extended to other malarial areas in the District, year after year especially after the advent of National Malaria Control Programme in the State from 1955. The control measures adopted consisted of D.D.T. in-door—residual—spraying and intensive anti-parasite measures by free Distribution of anti-malarials. The prevalence and incidence of malaria in the operational areas were reduced to low levels as a result of sustained measures. The introduction of three new irrigation projects, namely, the Lower Bhavani Project, the Amaravathi Reservoir Project and the Mettur Right Bank Canal Irrigation, in the District in recent years has created considerable malariogenic conditions in their respective ayacut areas. Separate schemes of malaria control measures were in operation in connection with these irrigation projects during and after the construction of the engineering works. The entire ayacut areas of these new projects have been kept free from any outbreaks of malaria.

---

1. G.O. No. 1235, Public Health, dated 13th August 1936.
   G.O. No. 2721, Public Health, dated 22nd October 1937.
   G.O. No. 1516, Public Health, dated 11th April 1940.
2. G.O. No. 2665, Health, dated 28th July 1951.

A certain amount of urban and semi-urban malaria problem in towns like Erode, Tiruppur, Bhavani, Perundurai, Cithodu, Chennimalai, etc., in the District has been observed. This problem has also been taken up on hand. With the introduction of National Malaria Eradication programme for 1958 the seeds for the solution of eradication of the disease have been firmly laid.

Most of these diseases were known to be prevalent in the district even about a hundred years ago. In 1853 for instance, the most common diseases were said to be cholera, fevers, diseases of the lungs, diseases of the stomach and bowels, rheumatic affections and venereal diseases.[1] Cholera in those days was treated with what were known as "Patterson's Pills" without opium and diluted sulphuric acid combined with tincture of quassia[2] or "Patterson's Pills", compound chalk mixture with tincture catechu and Colombo arrack.[3] Smallpox was controlled, where possible, by vaccination, while the other diseases were dealt with by in-patient or out-patient treatment in the civil hospitals and dispensaries.

As regards vital statistics the average birth and death rates of the district during the period 1951–57 are 25.4 and 12.3 respectively per 1,000 of population, as against the birth rate of 27.15 and the death rate of 15.2 for the Madras State as a whole. The infant mortality rate is 94.6 per 1,000 live births, while the average rate for the State is 11.7.[3] The average maternal mortality rate is only 3.6 per 1,000 births during the period. The incidence of cholera and smallpox has steadily decreased from 1951 to 1957. In fact, only sporadic cases have been reported during the last 4 years from 1954 to 1957. The District has been entirely free from plague during the period under review, although there were some endemic centres in Coimbatore District in the past. The mortality from fevers, dysentery and diarrhoea and respiratory diseases also show a tendency to decrease during the period. The above facts indicate that the health of the people in the District has been steadily improving.

Turning now to the history of the public health administration of the District, the first steps in this direction, in this as in other districts, were taken in 1871. In that year the Madras Local Funds Act (Act IV of 1871) and the Madras Towns Improvements Act (Act III of 1871) were passed, making sanitation the responsibility of local bodies. These Acts contained provisions for the extension of vaccination in rural areas and municipal

1. Report on Civil Dispensaries for 1853, page 44.

2. *Idem* for 1870, page 29. *Idem* for 1861, page 38.

3. Report on Civil Dispensaries for 1866, page 65.

towns, for the construction and repairs of hospitals and dispensaries, for the sanitary inspection of towns and villages, for the cleaning of roads, streets, tanks, etc. and for the registration of vital statistics. The next instalment of public health legislation was embodied in the Madras Local Boards Act, 1884 (Act V of 1884) and the Madras District Municipalities Act, 1884 (Act IV of 1884) which replaced the former Acts. Under the first Act, unions were formed and the local bodies were required to undertake measures for scavenging and cleaning streets and other public places, for improving sites, for providing water-supply, for making sanitary arrangements during fairs and festivals and for constructing markets, slaughter-houses, latrines, dust Pins and drains. The third instalment of public health legislation was incorporated in the Madras Local Boards Act, 1920 (Act XIV of 1920) and the Madras District Municipalities Act, 1920 (Act V of 1920). These Acts imposed additional obligations on local bodies and marked a further advance in public health legislation. But even these Acts were found inadequate and ill-designed to secure proper Government control over public health matters. The first Congress Ministry, therefore, passed the Madras Public Health Act, 1939 (Act III of 1939) embodying all provisions essential for the advancement of public health in the State. This comprehensive Act which is now in force provides for many things. It provides for the constitution of a public Health Board in the State. It gives statutory recognition to the Director of Public Health and sufficient powers for the effective discharge of his duties. It empowers him to compel the major local bodies to employ Health Officers and to fix their scales of pay as well as the scales of pay and the conditions of service of the public health establishments. It stipulates that the local bodies should earmark a definite percentage of their income for public health expenditure. It imposes an obligation on local bodies (at the discretion of the Government) to provide a sufficient supply of drinking water by a compulsory levy of water tax if necessary. It makes effective provision for the maintenance of proper drainage and the construction of an adequate number of public latrines, for the prevention and abatement of nuisances, for the prevention and eradication of nfectious diseases, for the prevention, treatment and control of venereal diseases, for the adoption of maternity and child welfare measures, for the enforcement of mosquito control, for the reservation of areas for residential purposes, for the registration of lodging houses, for the exercise of control over the making and sale of food and finally, for the undertaking of special measures during fairs and festivals. The Act is an admirable piece of legislation, but its enforcement demands full public co-operation.

Side by side with all this legislation, steps were taken to organise an efficient Public Health Department in the State. Prior to 1922–23, the District health problems in Coimbatore as in other districts were left to the supervision of the District Medical Officer who was then called the District Medical and Sanitary Officer. It is true that, so far as the central machinery of public health was concerned, there was a Sanitary Commissioner in Madras from 1869 and that he was assisted by two or three Deputy Sanitary Commissioners. But until 1922 he had to depend mostly on the District Medical and Sanitary Officer for supervising the District health administration. The District Medical and Sanitary Officer had, in practice, very little to do with public health beyond offering advice on sanitary matters to the local bodies. Several of the District Boards and Municipalities, including those of Coimbatore, had their own staff of rural sanitary officers whose main duty then consisted of vaccination and nothing else. In order to check the work of the vaccinators, the Government maintained in the State about a hundred deputy inspectors of vaccination; and in order to check cholera they maintained eight cholera parties. In order to check plague, the Collectors of the Districts engaged a staff of plague inspectors at the expense partly of provincial and partly of local funds.[1] In 1918 the Conference of Sanitary Officers held at Delhi commented very strongly on the absence of any organization for rural sanitation in India and recommended that each district should have a complete self-contained public health staff and the Government of India urged this recommendation for adoption.[2] Shortly afterwards, under the Reforms Act of 1919, Sanitation and Public Health became a transferred subject under the control of the Provincial Minister in charge of Local Self Government and the new Government lost no time in organizing a separate Health Department and in introducing an efficient District Health Scheme. The title of the Sanitary Commissioner was changed to that of the Director of Public Health, of the Sanitary Department to that of the Public Health Department and of the Deputy Sanitary Commissioner to that of the Assistant Director of Public Health.[3] Three Assistant Directors, one in charge of vital statistics and propaganda, another in charge of vaccination and smallpox and the third in charge of fairs and festivals were appointed.[4] Health officers were constituted into a regular provincial service, individual officers being lent to local bodies when required. The qualifications of the First and Second Class Health Officers

---

1. *Public Health Code*, 1928, Part I, pages 9–11.
   Idem (Revised Edition), Volume I, pages 1–6.
2. G.O. No. 954, Local, dated 22nd July 1918, pages 1–4.
3. G.O. Nos. 367–368, Public Health, dated 8th March 1922.
4. *Public Health Code*, 1928, Part I, page 13.

were fixed;[1] District Health Committees were set up.[2] First Class Health Officers were ordered to be employed under all District Boards and in Municipalities having a population of 50,000 or more[2] and Second Class Health Officers were ordered to be appointed to the other fairly large municipalities. The services of the deputy inspectors of vaccination and of sanitary inspectors of the cholera parties were amalgamated and all were designated as sanitary or health inspectors.[3]

The District Health Scheme was introduced in Coimbatore in 1923.[4] Since then it has undergone hardly any important change. Under it, at present, there is a District Health Officer with his headquarters at Coimbatore, seven Municipal Health Officers at Coimbatore, Dharapuram, Erode, Mettupalayam, Pollachi, Tiruppur and Udumalpet, an Assistant District Health Officer and an Assistant Municipal Health Officer at Coimbatore, a Health Officer for Anti-Malarial Scheme with headquarters at Coimbatore and another Health Officer at Udumalpet in charge of Anti-Malaria General Health Measures for Amaravathi Reservoir Project, and all these Health Officers have under them a large number of Health Inspectors and vaccinators. The duties of the Health Officers are various. The District Health Officer as the Executive head of the District health staff has to tour not less than 60 days in each quarter and has to inspect all Municipalities without Health Officers at least once a year. He has to examine, verify and see the correctness of village statistics (maintained by the village officers of the Revenue Department) to make recommendations for improving sanitation and drinking water-supply of the villages, to make sanitary arrangements for the conduct of fairs and festivals, to inspect areas affected by epidemics,to concentrate, if necessary, his whole health staff to check them to supervise the work of the District health inspectors especially their vaccination work, and to perform such other duties as the Director of Public Health or the President of the District Boardmight call upon him to perform. He has to submit his reports to the President of the District Board who has to forward them to the Director of Public Health and whenever he has reason to consider that the mortality in any area is abnormal or that any local area is threatened with an epedemic, he has to bring the fact to the notice of the President of the District Board or the Chairman of the Municipal Council with his recommendations. He, as the Additional Factory Inspector, has to inspect

1. G.O. No. 533, Public Health, dated 18th May 1921.

2. G.O. No. 1354, Public Health, dated 19th October 1921.
G.O. No. 165, Public Health, dated 1st February 1922.

3. G.O. No. 817, Public Health, dated 10th June 1922.

4. Triennial Report on Civil Hospitals and Dispensaries for 1920–1922, page 9.

all factories, not less than 50 per cent every half year. Nor is this all. He has to pay special attention to conservancy, cholera, small-pox, plague and the control of all epidemics; to supervise maternity and child health centres, to conduct health propaganda in rural areas by talk, demonstration, lantern lectures, cinemas, etc.; and to attend the meetings of the District Board at which any important sanitary matter is discussed and offer his advice on all matters connected with public health.[1]

The Municipal Health Officer as the Executive head of the public health services of the municipality has to be responsible to the Commissioner of Municipal Council for its efficient working. He has to supervise sanitation and conservancy by frequent inspections, to check the work of the municipal health staff, to prevent the accumulation of rubbish and filth in private premises, to scrutinize the scheme for town improvement, to submit proposals for relief of congestion, to approve plans for the construction of new buildings, and to inspect markets, slaughter-houses, eating houses and sources of drinking water-supply. He has to check the work of the vaccinators, to ensure the accurate registration of births and deaths, to inspect all places affected by epidemics and diseases, to take preventive measures and to submit a report on them with his recommendations to the Municipal Commissioner and the Director of Public Health. He has moreover to supervise maternity and child welfare centres, to undertake health propaganda, to offer advice on public health matters at the meetings of the municipal council and to co-operate fully with the medical officer of the place.[2] He has also to attend to the issue of licenses to the dangerous and offensive trades and the enforcement of the Food Adulteration Act and to inspect factories as Additional Factory Inspector.

The Public Health Act of 1939 and the District Health Scheme of 1922 are not the only measures that have been undertaken to improve public health in the districts. The Madras Town Planning Act of 1920 (Act VII of 1920) has been passed to improve the environment in municipal areas. Under this Act the Municipal Councils have been enjoined to prepare proper plans for the development of urban areas. Since 1913, several steps have also been taken to improve rural as well as urban water-supply. In that year a number of typical designs for the improvements of rural water-supply, were prepared and issued. In 1915 the Government with the object of providing at least one well in every village of 500

1. G.O. No.1393. Public Health, dated 11th August 1926.

2. G.O. No. 1960, Public Health, dated 21st September 1926.

inhabitants began to make lump-sum grants to the local bodies. The local bodies carried out a few works in areas of acute distress, but this only touched the fringe of the problem and no substantial progress was made. The first serious attempt to tackle the problem was made only in 1937 when the Government drew up a comprehensive ten years' programme of protected water-supply for rural areas, financed from State funds. Although the scheme was interrupted on account of the Second World War it was continued by the National Government, as a post-war development scheme. It was subsequently devetailed with the First Five-Year Plan which was started in 1951–52 at an estimated cost of 40 lakhs for each year. As to urban water-supply and drainage, the National Government constituted a Water-Supply and Drainage Committee in 1947 and upon its recommendation agreed that the water supply-and drainage schemes drawn up by it with order of priority should be permitted to be taken up by the local bodies irrespective of their financial resources. They have also agreed to grant the additional loans required by the local bodies and stipulated 20 years as the maximum period within which all the urban areas in the State should be provided with water-supply and drainage facilities. The provision of water-supply has also been taken up under the Community Development and National Extension Service and Local Development Schemes, priority being given to villages prone to cholera or endemic for guineaworm.

This is not all. Every attempt has been made in this century to afford the much needed maternity relief to rural as well as urban areas. The credit for starting maternity and child welfare centres for the first time in this State belongs to the Madras Corporation. In 1917 it started two such centres in the city and since then the work had been taken up and expanded by voluntary associations alike in the city and in the Districts. Under the Madras District Municipalities Act of 1920 and the Madras Local Boards Act of 1920 provision for adequate facilities for maternity and child welfare work has been made the responsibility of the local bodies and the local bodies have been specially enjoined (1923) to attend to this work in accordance with a comprehensive plan drawn up by the Director of Public Health. This plan envisages the establishment of ante-natal and post-natal clinics and child welfare centres, the employment of lady health visitors, paid or voluntary, the provision of maternity labour wards and children's hospitals and the extension of maternity and child welfare propaganda. In order to give a practical shape to this plan the Government have also created (1931) a special section in the Public Health Department in charge of an Assistant Directress of Public Health and entrusted the supervision over the work of the maternity and child welfare centres in the Districts to the District Health Officers and the Municipal Health Officers[1].

Some of these public health measures have undoubtedly borne fruit in the Coimbatore District. The Public Health Act of 1939 has secured the necessary Government control over public health matters administered by the local bodies. Its provisions, though not always, at least on occasion, of outbreaks of epidemic have considerably strengthened the hands of the Public Health authorities and enabled them to undertake adequate measures for the control and prevention of diseases. The District Health Scheme has provided the District with a District Health Officer and several Municipal Health Officers who supervise all public health matters and exercise adequate control over the subordinate health establishments. The Town Planning Act, however, has not yet produced any substantial results. Until 1950, only the Coimbatore Municipality is stated to have made good progress in executing the sanctioned works for town-planning[2]. Nor have the schemes for protected water-supply made much headway. Protected water-supply has been provided only in the towns of Coimbatore, Erode, Mettupalayam, Pollachi and Tiruppur[3]. Nearly 1,200 wells were sunk under the Rural Water-supply Scheme, while under the First Five-Year Plan about 1,500 wells have been dug by the end of 1954–55.[4] But many people are still accustomed to take water for drinking purposes indiscriminately from unprotected sources of water-supply, as has already been stated. Drainage is even more unsatisfactory. Proper underground drainage has been provided only in Coimbatore town[5]. Conservancy is confined mostly to the municipalities and a few of the smaller towns. Several maternity and child welfare centres have indeed been opened. There were 140 such centres in the end of 1957 of which 93 were maintained by the Government and the remaining 47 by the local bodies[6]. There are also a number of midwives attached to the hospitals and dispensaries. But with all this, the arrangements for maternity and child welfare cannot be said to be adequate. On the whole much remains to be done to promote public health and to control, if not eradicate diseases.

1. *Public Health Code* (Revised Edition), pages 132–147.
Monograph on Rural Problems in Madras by S. Y. Krishnaswami, 1947, pages 424–427.

2. G.O. No. 1013, Health, dated 27th March 1952.
See also Administration Report of Town-Planning for 1950–51.

3. 1951 *Census Handbook, Coimbatore District*, 1953, page 6.

4. *Second Five-Year Plan for Coimbatore District*, 1955, page 15.

5. 1951 *Census Handbook, Coimbatore District*, 1953, page 6.

6. Information supplied by the Director of Public Health, Madras.

Coming to the curative side of public health, very little was done in that direction by the Government in this or in other districts till about 1840. There was indeed a Surgeon General in Madras from 1786, but his duties were confined to the British forces. There was also a Medical Board in Madras from the same year, but its duties were confined to the supervision of the work of the Surgeons employed in that East India Company's Settlements and to look after the welfare of the Company's servants. There were likewise Zilla Surgeons in the Districts, but their duties too were confined to the care of the European Officers at the headquarters stations and to the preservation of the health of the prisoners confined in the jails[1]. The only kind of medical aid which the Government rendered to the public in those days was by requiring the Zilla Surgeons to control the work of vaccinators in the Districts and by permitting the Collectors to afford medical relief to the people through the Indian Medical Practitioners, whenever any serious outbreaks of cholera took place[2]. In all other matters the public were entirely left to themselves and they obtained whatever medical aid they could from private indigenous institutions or practitioners of Indian Medicine.

From 1840, however, a change came to be introduced. In that year, on the recommendation of the Medical Board, the Government began to open for the first time civil hospitals or dispensaries as they are called, in large towns for the treatment of the public, especially of the poor. But it was not until after a lapse of ten years that one such dispensary was opened in Coimbatore in 1850. It was located in the Indian quarters of the town nearly opposite the Koniamman temple and occupied a triangular plot of ground formed by two converging roads with residential quarters at its base. Another dispensary was opened at Pollachi in 1858. The building for this dispensary was erected by public subscription and a further sum of Rs. 17,700 was contributed and invested as an endowment towards the upkeep of the institution[3]. There is evidence to show that the Coimbatore dispensary attracted every class of inhabitants, rich as well as poor, who came to appreciate its benefits. The Pollachi dispensary also was popular and did a great amount of good to patients who hailed from considerable distances, *viz*., Travancore, Cochin and Malabar territories[4]. It may be

1. *Madras Manual of Administration* by C. D. Maclean, Volume I, 1885, pages 507–511.

2. Judicial Consultations, dated 29th September and 13th October 1820.
Judicial Despatch to England, dated 11th March 1820.

3. *Manual of Coimbatore District*, Volume II, page 104.
Gazetteer of Coimbatore District, Volume II, page 130.

4. Report on Civil Dispensaries from 1853 to 1872.
Manual of Coimbatore District, Volume II, page 104.

stated here that the present hospital at Coimbatore has grown out of the dispensary opened in 1850. The hospital at the present site was first opened in 1909 by Sir Arthur Lawley, the then Governor of Fort St. George and was run by the Coimbatore Municipality till 1918. In that year the hospital was taken over by the Government. The bed strength of the hospital which at that time was only 81 rose to 500 by 31st March 1957. After the passing of the Local Funds Act and the Towns Improvement Act of 1871, the local bodies began to open new dispensaries at several places, so that by 1900 the District had 24 dispensaries[1].

In the meantime the medical organization of the whole State underwent some important changes. In 1857 the Medical Board was replaced by a Director General or Inspector-General of the Medical Department[2]. In 1880 his post was converted into that of the Surgeon General with the Government of Madras. The Surgeon General whose designation has now been changed to that of the Director of Medical Services was then entrusted with the control and superintendence of the civil hospitals and dispensaries and the medical establishments of the Indian Army. In 1883 the Zilla Surgeons who had by now come to be called Civil Surgeons were supplied with Assistant Surgeons in all the Districts, including Coimbatore and required to tour and inspect all the Civil hospitals and dispensaries in the District and to supervise also all sanitary work, especially vaccination. Thenceforth they came to be called the District Medical and Sanitary Officers[3]. It has already been seen how in sanitary or public health matters they came to be replaced in 1922 by the District Health Officers. Since then their designation has been changed to that of District Medical Officers.

Side by side with these changes, several changes in policy were also effected. In 1870 the Government medical institutions were by the Local Boards Act and the Towns Improvement Act, placed under the Local Boards and Municipalities and subsequently all Local Boards institutions came under the District Boards when the District Boards took the place of the Local Boards. In the early stages the Government gave only very small grants to the local bodies for the maintenance of their medical institutions. But from 1915 the Government began to adopt a more liberal attitude by granting one half of the initial and recurring cost of these institutions opened after that date. In 1917 they went a step further.

1. Report on Civil Hospitals and Dispensaries for 1900, page 16.

2. *Madras Manual of Administration* by C. D. Maclean, Volume I, 1885, page 507.

3. G.O. No. 945, Public, dated 21st June 1880.
G.O. No. 391, Public, dated 22nd February 1883.

They took over the entire management of the District and taluk headquarters hospitals with a view to making them model centres for medical aid[1]. This policy has since been vigorously pursued in all the Districts with the result that several of the important hospitals and dispensaries in the State are now run directly by the Government. In regard to the other non-Government hospitals and dispensaries, they have continued to contribute grants in some cases and have also in other cases lent their own medical officers. They have, moreover, from 1911 and more particularly from 1929, extended the system of appointing honorary medical officers in all district headquarters hospitals and Government hospitals[2]. In 1929 they introduced a scheme for the training of Dhais or indigenous midwives in all district headquarters hospitals except those in Madras. In 1943, however, it was given up, as it was not popular among the Dhais.

Nor is this all. They have introduced a scheme of subsidized rural dispensaries for providing medical relief in areas in which it is not possible to establish regular dispensaries. Under this scheme, which was started in 1924, men qualified either in the Western or the Indian system of medicines who settle permanently in specified villages and agree to treat the poor free of charge, are given subsidies partly by the Government and partly by the local bodies. The liability of the Government is restricted to the payment of subsidy to the medical practitioner and the midwife, while the cost of medicines and contingent charges are met by the local bodies. The medical practitioner is, however, at liberty, to accept fees from well-to-do patients. Besides these subsidized dispensaries, the District Boards have set up rural dispensaries of their own for rendering medical aid to the rural population[3].

In 1948–49 a departure was made from this system of rendering medical relief in rural areas. Having regard to the primary need for improving public health in rural areas as an overall measure, it was then decided to open combined Medical and Public Health Centre as otherwise called Primary Centres in areas other than self sufficiency firka areas. Unlike the existing rural dispensaries, these Primary centres are intended to render both curative and preventive services. Each centre is provided with 6 beds (4 for maternity and emergency and 2 for isolation) and is

1. G.O. No. 397, Local, dated 9th March 1915.
G.O. No. 1149, Local, dated 16th August 1915.
Madras Presidency, 1881 to 1931, by G. T. Boag, 1933, page 117.

2. *Madras Presidency*, 1881 to 1931 by G. T. Boag, 1933, page 117.

3. G.O. No. 1005, Public, dated 1st June 1937, page 1394.
Monograph on Rural Problems by S. Y. Krishnaswami, 1947, page 423.

in charge of a Medical Officer who is assisted by a staff both medical and public health[1].

Another measure that has been undertaken for expanding the scope of medical aid to rural areas is that of training as many persons as possible in the indigenous system of medicine, so that they may settle down as medical practitioners in the villages or take charge of the rural dispensaries belonging to the District Boards. A school of Indian Medicine was opened for this purpose in Madras in 1925 and since then, in order to provide higher training, a college of Indian Medicine has also been opened (1947–48). A scheme has also been recently evolved (1949) for improving the knowledge of the practitioners of the indigenous systems residing in rural areas. Under this scheme, called the Village Vaidya Scheme, selected practitioners receive training for six months in first aid, minor surgery, hygiene, preventive medicine, etc., and are afterwards examined in these subjects as well as in subjects dealing with Indian Medicine and those who pass the examination are declared village Vaidyas and made eligible for appointments by village panchayats on an honorarium. Four centres have been opened in the State for training these Vaidyas[2].

All these schemes have naturally contributed to increase the medical facilities in Coimbatore. The district has now a number of Government, Municipal and Local Fund Hospitals and dispensaries besides some aided and private medical institutions. On 31st March 1957 there were Government Hospitals belonging to Class I at Coimbatore, Dharapuram, Erode, Gobichettipalayam, Mettupalayam, Pollachi, Tiruppur and Udumalpet, 11 primary health centres belonging to Class I at Avanashi, Chennimalai, Chithode, Ganapathipalayam, Kasipalayam, Kunnathur, Muthur, Punjaikolanali, Perundurai, Sivagiri and Thukkanaickenpalayam and Government dispensaries at Bhavanisagar, Topslip and Amaravathinagar. There were also some other Government institutions belonging to classes II and III at Coimbatore and Cinchona Plantations, Anaimalai. There were 32 District Board and Municipal dispensaries belonging to class III in various towns. There were, besides, the Ramakrishna Mission dispensary at Periyanaickenpalayam, two Railway hospitals at Erode and Podanur, a Railway dispensary at Mettupalayam, two Eye Hospitals at Coimbatore and Podanur, a hospital for women at Coimbatore, a dispensary for women and children at Pollachi, a Maternity Home at Singanallur in addition to the Tuberculosis Sanatoria at Perundurai and

1. G.O. No. 3818, Public Health, dated 19th November 1947.
G.O. No. 2390, Public Health, dated 12th July 1948.
G.O. No. 3371, Public Health, dated 24th September 1949.

2. *Public Health in Madras* (*Pamphlet*), 1952, pages 24–25.

Peelamedu already mentioned while dealing with tuberculosis, and the rural dispensaries set up in several places. All these institutions treated no less than 71,174 in-patients and 1,706,142 out-patients during the calendar year 1956 [1]. There were also several rural dispensaries of indigenous medicine, State as well as private-aided and these treat every year a large number of patients[2]. It may be stated here that in 1924 the medical school at Calicut was transferred to Coimbatore where extensive buildings had been constructed for its accommodation and that the first and second year students of the L.M.P. course were trained in the school. But it was abolished subsequently in 1930 and the buildings were made over to the Government Arts College [3].

---

1. Information furnished by the Director of Medical Services, Madras.
2. *See e.g.*, G.O. No. 1729, Health, dated 17th May 1951—Report, pages 20–21.
3. *Gazetteer of the Coimbatore District*, Volume II, 1933, page 132.
   G.O. No. 1670, Public Health, dated 9th July 1930.
   G.O. No. [6-S], Public Health, dated 27th April 1931.

CHAPTER XIII

EDUCATION

In the early period of British rule, education was solely in the hands of the people, alike in Coimbatore and in other districts. It was not till 1813 that the British Parliament sanctioned a lakh of rupees for encouraging education in India; and it was not till 1822 that Sir Thomas Munro started a State-wide educational enquiry in Madras with a view to introducing reforms. This enquiry revealed that the District was by no means backward in education. For its population of 638,199, it had no less than 763 schools and 173 colleges with 8,930 pupils. While the percentage of pupils to the total population was 1·39, the percentage of male pupils to the male population was 2·79. Of the 8,930 pupils, 1,642 were Brahmins, 6,976 were non-Brahmins and 312 were Muslims. It is said that among these students there were 82 females who were mostly dancing girls belonging to the Kaikolar caste. The schools were, in fact, nothing more than pial schools and the colleges no other than Sanskrit and Tamil Veda Patasalas, both of which have existed for ages in India. The pupils in the schools, it would appear, were taught reading, writing and arithmetic, were made to read popular versions of religious books, such as the Ramayana, the Mahabaratha and the Panchatantra, and instructed to decipher up-country letters and to draw up legal documents, like deeds, which played no small part in village transactions. The pupils usually attended the schools at the age of five and studied till the age of thirteen or fourteen. They seem to have attended the schools from 6 a.m. to 10 a.m. and from 1 p.m. or 2 p.m. to 8 p. m. Besides the several festivals, they had regular holidays, 4 days in each month, on the full moon and new moon days and on the day following each. They invariably paid their fees which ranged from Rs. 3 to Rs. 14 per annum according to the circumstances of the parents. A fee was also given, whenever the pupil began a new book. Besides the fees, the school master received presents from the parents at the Dusserah and other great festivals. In the colleges or Veda Patasalas, which were usually located in Agraharam villages, instruction was gratuitously given to more advanced pupils in theology, law, astronomy and the Vedas. The pupils were all Brahmins and they usually commenced their studies at the age of fifteen and "continued to frequent the colleges until they attained a competent knowledge in the sciences or until they obtained employment". The colleges had been endowed with lands granted by the Hindu rulers for their support, but these endowments were subsequently resumed either by the Muhammadan rulers or by the British Government[1].

These schools and colleges were in no way affected by the measures undertaken as a result of Munro's enquiry. For, these measures consisted of the establishment of only a few Collectorate and Tahsildary schools, a normal school at Madras for training the teachers required for the Collectorate schools, a Board of Public Instruction in Madras for supervising all these schools and a grant to the School Book Society that had been then formed in Madras for translating good books into Indian languages. According to the plan proposed, in every Collectorate there were to be two Collectorate schools, one for the Hindus and the other for the Muslims, under one or more teachers trained in various subjects in the Normal School at Madras. In every Tahsildary there was to be a Tahsildary School under a competent school master. Candidates for the teachers' posts in the Tahsildary school were to be nominated by the respectable men of the locality, a provision which was specially designed to create local interest in education. The Tahsildary teachers were not to receive any training in Madras as the Collectorate teachers. The former were to be paid Rs. 9 and the latter Rs. 15 per mensem. Both were to be at liberty to give private tuition to any of their pupils and to receive fees in return, in addition to their salary. In the Collectorate schools, English was to be taught; but it was to be taught only as one of the languages along with the language of the district. In the Tahsildary schools, the entire teaching was to be conducted in the language of the district. It does not appear that the subjects taught in these schools were in any way different from the subjects taught in the indigenous schools. The underlying object of the scheme was to establish a few well managed, efficient schools so as to hold them out as models for imitation to the numerous indigenous schools which were reported to be in an unsatisfactory condition[2]. In accordance with this scheme, one Collectorate school and two Tahsildary schools were opened in the district; the former was presumably located at Coimbatore, while the latter were located at Coimbatore and Satyamangalam[3]. But all these schools, in this as well as in other

---

1. Board's Consultation Nos. 43–44, dated 2nd December 1822.

Manual of Coimbatore District, Volume II, pages 117–118.

Studies in Madras Administration, by B. S. Baliga, Volume II, 1949, pages 56–57.

2. *Studies in Madras Administration*, by B. S. Baliga, Volume II, 1949, pages 64–66.

3. Selection from the Records of the Madras Government No. II,—Papers relating to Public Instruction, 1855, pages Lxv–Lxvi.

districts, soon proved complete failures. The teachers of the Collectorate schools were described as "the refuse of the expectants on the Collector's list", while the teachers of the Tahsildary schools were said to be "inferior, on the whole to the common village masters"[1].

But a new era was now dawning. The Court of Directors of the East India Company advocated in 1830 the theory known as the filtration theory of education according to which the best results could be obtained by educating the higher classes in the first instance and leaving it to them to create a desire for education in the masses. They directed that the higher orders should be given instruction in English language and European literature and science and thereby trained to become fit persons for taking a larger share in the civil administration of the country. Then came the Anglo-Vernacular controversy as to whether English or Indian languages should be given prominence in the scheme of education. It reached its climax in the famous minutes of Lord Macaulay of 1835 and the equally famous Resolution of Lord William Bentinck dated 7th March 1835 which endorsed it, observing that "the great object of the British Government ought to be the promotion of European literature and science" and that all funds appropriated for the purpose of education would be best spent on English education alone. In consequence of this policy, the Collectorate and Tahsildary schools in Coimbatore as well as in other districts were abolished (1836), the Board of Instruction was superseded by a "Committee of Native Education", and the Committee was directed to organize a Normal School for training teachers for the new English schools which were to be eventually opened in the different parts of the State. No provision was, however, made for collegiate education. The "Committee of Native Education" was shortly afterwards replaced by the University Board constituted in 1840 by Lord Elphinstone for governing an institution to be styled as the Madras University. The University was to consist of a High School for the cultivation of English literature, Indian languages and elements of philosophy and science and a college for the cultivation of higher branches of literature, philosophy and science. To this University were to be tagged on by fellowships a few Provincial schools, to be established in the districts. One of the first measures of the University Board was to procure the services of Mr. E. B. Powell to organize the new institution and under his headmastership the High School was opened in April 1841. But it was not until January 1853 that the standard was considered by the Government sufficiently advanced to justify the establishment of

[1]. *Studies in Madras Administration*, by B. S. Baliga, Volume II, 1949, page 67.

a collegiate department. At the same time Provincial schools came to be opened in several places in the State.

In 1854 a series of propositions of first rate importance were propounded by the Court of Directors. The filtration theory was to be displaced by the theory of mass education. Elementary education was not to be sacrificed at the altar of higher education. Instruction in Indian languages was not to be superseded by instruction in English. Both were to be encouraged side by side and the indigenous institutions which formed the basis of elementary education were to be revived, reformed and assimilated into one comprehensive scheme of education. All this ushered in a new chapter in the history of education. The University of Lord Elphinstone was remodelled and received the name of the Presidency College. A department of education was organised (1855), the post of the Director of Public Instruction was created and under him were appointed 4 Inspectors of Schools, 20 Assistants (later called Deputy Inspectors) and 20 Sub-Assistant Inspectors or Taluk Visitors. Provision was also made for a Normal School, a few Provincial schools, some zilla schools, several Taluk schools, a depot for school books and educational presses and scholarships. Provision was likewise made for Normal Schools and Anglo-Vernacular schools in the districts and, what is more, for grants-in-aid to all private schools which came under the Government departmental inspection. The first set of rules governing grants-in-aid were issued in 1855 and this was followed by other sets which gradually tended to absorb indigenous schools into the public system. In 1857 by an Act of the Legislative Council of India the present Madras University was constituted on the model of the University of London as purely an examining body for conferring degrees in Arts, Law, Medicines and Civil Engineering[1].

But so far as the Coimbatore district is concerned, no zilla school was opened under the scheme of 1855. The need for such a school was, however, served by the Anglo-Vernacular school at Coimbatore which came under the inspection of the Government. This private school was established in August 1852 by Mr. E. B. Thomas, the then Collector, with the aid of European and native gentlemen, following his enquiries into the condition of education in the district. In the beginning it occupied an intermediate place between a taluk school and a zilla school and had five classes, " the fifth class ranking pretty nearly with the fourth class of

[1]. *Studies in Madras Administration*, by Dr. B. S. Baliga, Volume II, 1949, pages 68–73.

Standing Information regarding the official administration of the Madras Presidency, by C. D. Maclean, 1877, pages 364–383.

a Government zilla school, but being somewhat more advanced ". Its curriculam consisted of a grammatical study of English and Tamil, Arithmetic, Geography, History, Geometry, etc[1]. In 1858 a normal school and a taluk school were opened at Cheyur, which was then a taluk headquarters. The normal school was engrafted on the taluk school and the latter or a portion of it was constituted as a practising school in which students under training were instructed in the practice of their pro- ession. Provision was made in the normal school for training two classes of teachers, one consisting of village schoolmasters and the other of persons seeking to qualify for masterships in the taluk schools[2]. The teachers trained in this school were of three classes. One class consisted of those who obtained certificates of the 7th grade which required a knowledge of Vernacular, English, Arithmetic, Geometry, Algebra, Geography, History together with a practical knowledge of the art of teaching and of school management. Another class comprised those who obtained certificates of the 8th grade for which no English was demanded, while in other subjects, the requirements were somewhat lower. The third class included those who obtained certificates of the 9th grade, the examination for which was restricted to the elementary prose in Vernacular language and to the elements of Arithmetic, Geography and History[3]. In the Taluk school both English and Tamil were taught, as well as Arithmetic, Geography and Elements of History, Geometry and Algebra. It had four classes to start with, but subsequently a fifth class was added.

Subsequent years witnessed more Taluk schools, rate schools and aided schools. In April 1859 one taluk school was opened at Pollachi upon a subscription by the people of Rs. 1,050 for a school house[4]. In August of the same year, two more taluk schools were opened at Udamalcottai (Udumalpet) and Dharapuram and in 1860 three more at Anamalai, Erode and Satyamangalam[5]. But in 1861 the normal school at Cheyur had to be abolished, as the removal of the Taluk Cutcherry had greatly reduced the number of students[6]. In 1864 the taluk school at Anamala

1. *See* Report on Public Instruction for 1858–1859, pages 64–65.
Idem, 1862–1863, page 45.
Manual of Coimbatore Disrtict, Volume II, page 120.

2. Report on Public Instruction for 1857–1858, pages 39–40.

3. Idem 1859–1860, page 21.

4. Idem 1858–1859, Appendix (A), pages Ix–X.
Manual of Coimbatore District, Volume II, page 120.

5. Report on Public Instruction for 1862–1863, Appendix (E), page 76.

6. Report on Public Instruction for 1859–1860, page 21.
Manual of Coimbatore District, Volume II, page 120.

was also abolished for want of support, the attendence having fallen from 35 to 11[1]. In 1866, seven rate schools were established in the district under Act VI of 1863 which enabled the inhabitants to raise a cess or rate for the maintenance of such schools; but their number subsequently dwindled to two[2]. In 1868 the London Mission opened two Anglo-Vernacular schools, one at Coimbatore and the other at Mettupalayam[3]. In the meantime several other missionary and private schools also came to be aided, so that in 1870–71, on the eve of the introduction of the Local Fund Act and the Towns Improvement Act of 1871, the district had 6 taluks or middle schools with 353 pupils, second rate schools with 42 pupils, 6 missionary schools with 390 pupils and 205 other aided private institutions with 4,891 pupils. Besides these, there were 175 private schools with 2,898 pupils, which came under Government inspection, without receiving any grants-in-aid. Of all these private institutions, the most important was the Coimbatore Anglo-Vernacular School which had in 1867–68 become a high school and for the first time sent up candidates for the Matriculation examination[4].

In order to avoid confusion, we may, at this stage, trace the history of higher education down to the present and then turn to the history of secondary and elementary education. In 1868–69 the Anglo-Vernacular school at Coimbatore was raised to the rank of a second grade college and it sent up two students for the First Arts examination held in that year. In 1871, however, the college department was abolished probably for want of adequate number of students. But the high school continued to prosper under Mr. Flanagan, the Headmaster, and in 1874 its strength grew so large that the junior classes were removed to form a branch school. In 1875–76 the F.A. classes were re-established and the high school became once again a college of second grade. The institution was from the beginning managed by a committee of local residents and was entirely dependant upon the Government and Municipal grant.[5] In 1919 the committee found itself unable to manage the institution and upon its request the Government took it over under their management and has been maintaining it since then. From 1929 several representations were

[1]. Report on Public Instruction for 1864–1865, page 45.

[2]. *Idem* for 1866–1867, page 4.
Idem for 1869–1870, page 5.

[3]. *Idem* for 1868–1869, Appendix (A), page Cxxxii.

[4]. Report on Public Instruction for 1870–1871, pages 5 and 272.
Idem, 1867–1868, Appendix IV, page cxliv.

[5] Manual of Coimbatore District, Volume II, Maye 125–126. Report on public Instruction 1871, pages 23 and 182 for 1820. Idem for 1814–1777, page 44.

made from time to time for raising the college to the first grade. But, as the Palghat College was considerably expanded with provision for B.Sc. as well as Arts courses and for admitting a large number of students, it was considered unnecessary to reduplicate these classes in the Coimbatore College which is so close to Palghat. In 1942, the leading citizens of Coimbatore formed themselves into a committee and it offered to take over the institution under its management and develop it into an ordinary first-grade college in order to provide better educational facilities for the people in the district. But, in view of an immense amount of faction in the town of Coimbatore over its transfer, the Government refused to transfer the management to any outside agency. They, however, decided in 1945 that the development of the college to the first grade would be justified but that it should not provide for courses which were then given in the neighbouring college at Palghat[1]. Accordingly degree classes were opened in 1946–47 and the college now provides instructions for the B.A., B.O.L., and B.Com. degree courses[2]. It is worth remarking here that this is one of the colleges which have introduced the regional language as the medium of instruction in the third group subjects in the Intermediate classes[3].

Another private institution which became a college and then a high school was the Roman Catholic High School at Coimbatore. It was started as a small Anglo-Vernacular School in 1860 by the Fathers of the Foreign Mission Society, Paris, for the education of the children of the Catholic residents at Coimbatore. Though the school was intended chiefly for the Catholics, children of other religious persuasion were also admitted on the principle of non-interference. In 1886, the school became a high school; and in the next year it began to send up students for the Matriculation examination and produced fairly satisfactory results at the examination. Seeing the success of the institution, the Roman Catholic Mission desired " to place the benefits of a liberal education within the reach of the Catholic community ". To this end it applied in 1891 for the affiliation of the school to the Madras University and the school was made

---

1. *Gazetteer of the Coimbatore District*, Volume II, page 138.
G.O. No. 1370, Education, dated 13th October 1943.
G.O. No. 910, Education, dated 16th June 1945.

2. Report on Public Instruction for 1946–47, page 42.
G.O. No. 137, Education, dated 28th April 1950.
G.O. No. 1102, Education, dated 3rd May 1948.

3. G.O. No. 1986, Education, dated 16th October 1946.
G.O. No. 373, Public Health, dated 5th February 1949.

a second-grade college under the name of St. Michael's College[1]. In 1907, however, the F.A. classes were abolished and since then the institution has continued to be a high school[2].

In recent years, four private Arts colleges have come into existence in the district. They are the P.S.G. Arts College, Peelamedu, for men; The Mahajana College, Erode, for men; the Nirmala College, Coimbatore for women; and the Sri G.V.G. Visalakshi College, Udumalpet[3] for women.

The P.S.G. Arts College was opened in 1947 by the P.S.G. and Sons [1] Charities as a second-grade college. The laboratories of the P.S.G. Industrial Institute also run by the Charities were altered suitably to meet the needs of Physics and Chemistry students with the result that the college could open Science courses in the very first year of its existence. In 1953, the college started the diploma course in Social Service, but with the object of expanding the course, a separate School of Social Work was organized shortly afterwards. The college was raised to the status of a first-grade college in 1957 and now offers the Three-year B.A. and B.Sc. degree courses.

The Mahajana College, Erode, has grown out of the Mahajana High School, Erode, which was started in 1887–88 by Sri Thasappier and Sri Annaswamy Iyengar under the name of " Town High School ". In 1899, the school was taken over by a Committee called the Mahajana Schools' Committee consisting of the prominent citizens of the town and under its management the institution gradually expanded in various ways. As there was not a single college in and around Erode to provide higher education, the Mahajana School's Board decided in 1953 to start a second grade college and obtained from the Government a grant of 12 acres of land for the site of the college. The college was inaugurated by Periyar E. V. Ramaswami on 12th July 1954. In 1957, it became a first-grade college and it now coaches students for the Pre-University Course as well as for the B.A. and B.Sc. degree courses. It is open to all castes and creeds and its motto is " One Race, One God " (ஒன்றே குலம், ஒருவனே தேவன்). The college building is a magnificent one situated

---

1. *Manual of Coimbatore District*, Volume II, page 126.
Report on Public Instruction for 1889–1890, page 57.
Idem for 1891–1892, page 38.

2. *Gazetteer of the Coimbatore District*, Volume II, page 133.

3. Report on Public Instruction for 1947–1948, page 7.
Idem for 1948–49, page 29.
Idem for 1952–53, page 31.
Idem for 1953–54, pages 88–89.

on an elevated ground; it commands a panoramic view and enjoys cool fresh breeze[1].

The Nirmala College was the first college for women to be opened in the district. It was established in 1948 and is under private management. It was started as a second-grade college with 53 students. The subjects taught were English, Tamil, Malayalam, Mathematics, Natural Sciences, History, Logic and Indian Music. Subsequently Physics, Chemistry and Geography were added. In 1956, the Pre-University Course was introduced. Lately in July 1957, the college has been raised to the status of a first grade college. The college which was formerly located at R. S. Puram has also been removed to Red Fields.

The G.V.G. Visalakshi College for Women situated at Udumalpet was started in 1952 by Sri G. V. Govindaswami Naidu in memory of his daughter Srimathi Visalakshi. It now offers the Pre-University Course and the Three-year B.A. and B.Sc. degree courses.

There is a Training College for Men, called the Sri Ramakrishna Mission Vidyalaya Teachers' College, in Periyanaickenpalayam. This college was founded in July 1950 and coaches students for the B.T. course.[2] Provision is made in this college for imparting instruction in Mathematics, English, Social Studies, Basic Education, Science and Tamil and also for the teaching of two crafts, viz., wood-work and card-board modelling. The college is housed in Appar Nilayam and contains, among others, a Curriculam Laboratory, an Audio-Visual Laboratory, a Psychological Laboratory and a Research Department. There is also an Extension Department which conducts extension work in the surrounding villages and organizes week-end discourses and seminars in important towns in the district. The college is a residential one and all the teacher-trainees reside in the hostel as a self-governing community. It upholds the ideals of Sri Ramakrishna, Swami Vivekananda and Gandhiji in all its activities and provides for religious instruction and utilization of festivals for the purpose of education [3].

There is also a Government Training College for Women at Coimbatore, which was started in 1956 under the Second Five-Year Plan. It was

1. Based on the information furnished by the Principal, Mahajana College, Erode.

2. Report on Public Instruction for 1950–51, page 25.
Idem for 1953–54, page 90.

3. Based on the information furnished by the Sri Ramakrishna Mission Vidyalaya Teachers' College, Periyanaickenpalayam.

formerly inaugurated by Sri T. T. Krishnamachari, then Minister for Industries and Commerce. It now offers instructions in optional subjects, such as Mathematics, General Science, Social Studies, Tamil and English. There is a hostel attached to it, where students reside under the supervision of a Deputy Warden[1].

Like all industrial towns and cities, Coimbatore has two colleges of Technology and one Institute of Technology to serve the growing needs of the industries of the town. One of them is the Government College of Technology which was sanctioned under the post-war development scheme. The idea of founding a College of Technology in Coimbatore originated from the mill owners of Coimbatore, who in 1942 offered to contribute a substantial amount towards its maintenance. The scheme was that the college should be started by the Madras University and financed both by the mill owners and the University. It, however, fell through, as the University started its own College of Technology in Madras with the aid of substantial grants from the Government. Subsequently in 1945 Sri G.D. Naidu, a prominent industrialist, came forward with a donation of two lakhs of rupees for the starting of an Engineering College in Coimbatore and also offered to place his buildings, workshops, equipments, etc., at the disposal of the Government temporarily for a period of three years. As the town has a large and growing textile industry as well as groups of small industries and engineering workshops and as it is within the easy reach of cheap electric power from the Mettur and Pykara Projects close by, the Government considered that it would be an ideal place for establishing a College of Engineering and Technology with special reference to textile, electrical and automotive industries. They, therefore, accepted the offer of Sri G. D. Naidu and sanctioned the opening of a College of Technology in Coimbatore with effect from July 1945 under their own management. The college was named after Sir Arthur Hope who was then the Governor of Madras; and pending the construction of new buildings, it was located in the buildings of the National Electric Works belonging to Sri G. D. Naidu, but subsequently owned by the Argus Engineering Company of Bombay. In 1950, the college was shifted from the buildings of Argus Engineering Company to the new premises erected on the estates of the Agricultural and Forest Colleges; and its designation was changed to that of the Government College of Technology. Although it was decided at the time of opening the college that it should provide for the courses of study in Civil, Electrical and Automotive Engineering and

1 Higher Education in South India, Volume II, page 307.

in Textile Technology, affiliation has so far been granted only in the B.E. degree course of Civil, Electrical and Mechanical Engineering [1].

The other engineering college is the P.S.G. and Sons' Charities College of Technology, Peelamedu, founded in June 1951 by the Board of Trustees of the P.S. Govindaswami Naidu and Sons' Charities, who have dedicated themselves to the spread of technical education. The founders of the Charities started in 1926 an industrial school called the P.S.G. and Sons' Charities Industrial Institute which offered artisan courses for the careers of mechanics, electricians, weavers, dyers and printers. In 1939, the institute gained the status of a polytechnic and began offering diploma courses in Mechanical Engineering, Electrical Engineering and Printing Technology. With the growth of textile mills in and around Coimbatore, the institute opened diploma course in textile manufacture also. In 1949 the Board of Trustees felt that in spite of " the very many Colleges of Technology run by the Government and the University ", there was still a dearth of technical personnel to meet the growing needs of the industries in the State; and emboldened by the calls of National Leaders for the starting of more colleges, they ventured upon the project of upgrading the institute into a College of Technology in order to provide advanced industrial education to the public. To this end they took concerted measures to secure the affiliation of the institute to the Madras University, which was granted in 1951. Another important object of the Board of Trustees in opening this College is the promotion of research to ensure not only the efficient production of machinery, but also to train students in the methods of research. The college is now affiliated in the B.E. degree courses of Mechanical, Electrical and Civil Engineering. It also offers instruction in Pre-Professional course for Engineering [2].

The Institute of Technology is the Coimbatore Institute of Technology which is also situated at Peelamedu. This was established by Sri V. Rangasami Naidu, an industrialist of Coimbatore and the members of his family, several of whom are qualified engineers and industrialists. With the

---

[1] G.O. No. 2491, Education, dated 19th November 1947.
G.O. No. 2637, Education, dated 10th December 1947.
G.O. No. 2649, Education, dated 22nd October 1948.
G.O. No. 43, Education, dated 6th January 1950.
G.O. No. 1877, Education, dated 27th June 1950.
G.O. No. 1476, Education, dated 2nd July 1952.
Report on Public Instruction for 1953–54, page 91.

[2] Based on the information furnished by the P.S.G. and Sons' Charities College of Technology and Polytechnic, Peelamedu.
See also G.O. No. 22, Education, dated 4th January 1950.
Letter No. 2672, Education, dated 21st November 1952.
Report on Public Instruction for 1953–54, page 91.

object of providing an adequate number of educational institutions in the arts, sciences and engineering, a trust was founded in 1955. And in the following year the trust opened the Coimbatore Institute of Technology. Although the aim of the founders is to develop the Institute on the lines of the well-known Massachussets Institute of Technology and to offer facilities for post-graduate studies and research work, it now coaches students only for the B.E. Courses in Civil, Mechanical and Electrical Engineering.

Apart from these Arts and Professional colleges, the district has also an oriental college called " Tavattiru Shantalinga Adigalar Tamizh College, Perur ". This institution came into existence in 1953 as a result of the endeavours of Sri R. K. Shanmugam Chettiar, Sri C. M. Ramachandran Chettiar and other prominent citizens of the district who felt the need for improving the study of Tamil language and wanted to impart knowledge in Tamil to the young and coach up students for the Vidwan course of the Madras University. Besides the ordinary tuition in Vidwan course, the institution conducts congregational worship each Monday at the famous temple of Perur. The students also visit the Central Jail, Coimbatore and give religious talk to prisoners [1]. Besides these professional colleges, Coimbatore has also an Agricultural College and a Forest College which have already been described in the chapters on Agriculture, Irrigation and Forest.

Turning now to the later history of secondary and elementary education, a great fillip was given to these in Coimbatore as in other districts only after the formation of the local boards and the municipalities. Under the Local Fund Act No. IV of 1871, all public schools were transferred to the local boards and made a charge upon local funds, and under the Towns Improvement Act No. III of 1871, the municipalities were entrusted with the diffusion of education, with the construction and repair of school houses, with the establishment and maintenance of schools either wholly or by grants-in-aid, as well as, with the inspection of schools and the training of teachers. The Local Boards Act No. V of 1884 and the District Municipalities Act No. IV of 1884 which superseded these Acts and created new local bodies, emphasized still more the duties of these bodies in the matter of education. The Local Boards Act made it the duty of the district boards and taluk boards to diffuse education and, with this end in view, to construct and repair school houses, either wholly or by means of grants-in-aid and also to provide for the inspection of schools and the training of teachers. The District Municipalities Act

[1] Higher education in South India, Volume II, page 307.

enjoined the municipalities to make provision, where possible, for the instruction in schools of all children of school going age and, for this purpose, to maintain the schools or to give grants-in-aid or to contribute towards the cost of Government schools. They were also required to provide for the inspection of schools, for the training of teachers and for the maintenance of public libraries, reading rooms, gymnasiums, etc. All this time, the Government grants were also given to a large number of private educational institutions.

The effects of these measures soon began to be felt. The opening years of the twentieth century, for instance, revealed a marked advance in education in Coimbatore. In 1900–01 there were in the district 1,306 educational institutions imparting instruction to 39,724 scholars. There were then 2 Arts Colleges, 8 Upper Secondary Schools, 16 Lower Secondary Schools and 1,243 Primary Schools for boys and 3 Upper Secondary Schools, 8 Lower Secondary Schools and 22 Primary schools for girls, one Training School for masters, one Training School for mistresses and two Technical, Industrial and Art schools. There were also 166 Indigenous schools imparting instruction to 2,946 pupils. The percentage of total scholars to the total population of school age was 12·0 [1].

During the last fifty years Coimbatore in common with other districts, has witnessed some far reaching changes in the field of secondary education. In 1911, in lieu of the Matriculation Examination conducted by the University, the Secondary School Leaving Certificate Examination conducted by a Government Board was introduced. Thereafter the Government began to grant more and more subsidies both to the schools maintained by the local bodies and to the schools managed by private agencies. In 1923 they established an advisory board, called the District Secondary Education Board in every district (save the Nilgiris and the Agency tracts) and in 1928 they reorganised these Boards. In 1925 they gave perfect liberty to the managers of the schools to choose English or the language of the district as the medium of instruction in Forms IV, V and VI of a Secondary School [2].

But all these measures, beyond increasing the number of schools in the State, contributed little to improve the quality of instruction or to turn out good citizens. It was left to the National Government in 1948 to chalk out a sound plan of secondary education. They got the various subjects of the school curriculam drafted by specially constituted sub-

---

1 Report on Public Instruction for 1900–1901, *See* Statements.

2 *Madras Presidency* 1881–1931, by G. T. Boag, 1933, pages 108–109.

committees and subsequently finalized them after obtaining the opinion of the teaching profession, the public and the Board of Secondary Education.

The salient feature of the scheme of re-organisation thus made in Forms I to III is the building up of the curriculam in correlation with several educative school activities with a main or basic craft as the chief among the activities. Handloom weaving, woodwork, gardening and agriculture are taken up as the basic crafts for boys, and home craft as the basic craft for girls. Most of the general school activities are comprehended under citizenship training which has been introduced as a new subject in all these forms to be conducted formally up to Form IV and informally in the higher forms. Purpose and unity have been introduced in the subjects of history, geography and civics, integrating them into one subject under the head social studies. The other subjects of the curriculam, namely, languages, mathematics, general science, physical education and religious and moral instruction continue to have their due and important place in the curriculam, but their teaching is now required to be practical and based upon the life and activities of the pupils, especially of the crafts which they practice in the school and which are expected to give the necessary technical bias to the instruction. English is taught as second language from Form I. The academic course leading to the University and the diversified courses comprising the Secretarial, the Pre-technological, the Aesthetic and Domestic Science courses are the main features of the scheme in Forms IV to VI.

The underlying object of the scheme of diversified courses in the Secondary Schools is to provide a variety of courses, instead of the merely academic one, to suit the varied requirements of students of different aptitudes. Care has been taken to see that such students are not shut out from pursuing higher studies if they so choose. Instruction in all subjects is now normally given not in English as before, but in the regional languages, thereby lightening the burden of the pupils and giving a fillip to the study of the hitherto more or less neglected languages. Indeed the language scheme has been adopted with a view to enabling the students to study the regional language, the mother tongue or a classical language and Hindi, besides English. The first language is the mother tongue or the regional language, consisting of two parts of which the study of Part I is compulsory, while under Part II, students are permitted to study either the first language or a classical or any other Indian language. The second language is English and this is compulsory and the third language is Hindi, which is optional, those who do not choose Hindi being allowed to learn an additional craft or approved activity. With a view to enabling teachers to get acquainted with the general principles of the reorganised scheme of studies and making them more efficient in the discharge of their duties, more especially in such subjects like crafts, citizenship, etc., courses have been organized in Citizenship Training, Home Science, and Home Craft and Training in Museum Technique [1].

As a result of all these, the Secondary schools in Coimbatore as well as in other districts have begun to improve. In fact Coimbatore has made considerable progress in secondary education, as will be seen from the following statements:—

NUMBER OF INSTITUTIONS.

Agency.	1910–11		1930–31		1950–51	
	Males.	*Females.*	*Males.*	*Females.*	*Males.*	*Females.*
(1)	(2)	(3)	(4)	(5)	( )	(7)
Government	1	..	1	1	..	3
Municipal	1	..	5	..	11	4
Local Board	6	..	10	..	27	..
Private	12	1	9	..	27	7
Total number of institutions	21		26		79	

NUMBER OF STUDENTS.

	1910–11	1930–31	1950–51
(1)	(2)	(3)	(4)
Total number of boys	4,764	10,028	28,671
Total number of girls	181	354	7,743
Total number of Scholars	4,945	10,382	36,414

In 1956–57, it had 37 schools including a panchayat school under the District Board, 17 schools under municipalities and 36 schools under Missionary and other private agencies for boys, imparting education on the whole to 40,247 boys and 5,837 girls. Among girls' schools, it had 3 Government schools, 5 municipal schools and 9 private schools teaching on the whole 8,309 girls and 55 boys. Out of the total male population of 1,720,393 in the district, 40,302 boys attended the public secondary schools in 1957, thereby giving it a percentage of 2.34 boys to the male population; and out its total population of 1,707,654 females, 14,146 girls attended public schools in the same year, giving it a percentage of 0.82 of girls to

[1] *See* the Reports on Public Instruction 1930.

the female population. While the percentage in the case of boys was exceeded in the districts of Kanyakumari, the Nilgiris, Madras, Thanjavur and Tirunelveli, the percentage in the case of girls was higher than in other districts, save Kanyakumari, Madras and Nilgiris [1].

As regards elementary education in general till 1920, it was left in the hands of the local boards, municipal councils, missions and other private agencies. In that year was passed the Madras Elementary Education Act (Act VIII of 1920) which introduced a number of changes. It created in each district, a District Educational Council consisting of some members nominated by the Government and others elected by the local bodies, to prepare schemes for the extension of elementary education, public as well as private, for that purpose, to regulate the recognition of all elementary schools, to disburse all grants-in-aid from provincial funds to these schools and to advise the department of education generally in all matters connected with elementary education, including the provision of trained teachers. It provided for the levy, with the previous consent of the Government, of an educational tax, subject to the prescribed minimum, by the local bodies and, wherever the local bodies had levied such a tax, the contribution of an equal sum from the provincial funds in addition to the provincial subsidies usually made on behalf of elementary education. And, what is more, it provided for the introduction of compulsory education in suitable areas with the previous sanction of the Government. About the same time, the District Municipalities Act and the Local Boards Act were revised, and elementary education was completely removed from the purview of the district boards and entrusted to the taluk boards and the municipalities. In 1923, two conferences convened by the Government stressed the need for the gradual expansion of elementary education by establishing a school in every village with a population of over 500 inhabitants, by developing and improving existing indigenous schools and by requiring the local bodies to open new schools. In 1924 a special survey of elementary education was undertaken in all taluks of the State and, as a result of this, liberal subsidies were given by the Government for the opening of a large number of schools in places hitherto unprovided with schools [2].

Within a few years, however, this policy of expansion showed everywhere some serious defects. The indiscriminate growth of elementary schools led to much stagnation and wastages. In most schools the boys were rarely retained up to the fifth standard to produce any real literacy

1 Report on Public Instruction 1956–57.

2 *Madras Presidency*, 1881–1930 by G.T. Boag, 1933, pages 110–111 .

among them; in most schools they stagnated for years in the First and Second standards until their parents withdraw them from the schools altogether. In order to remedy this state of affairs, the Madras Elementary Education Act was amended and a modified form of compulsion was adopted so that every child that entered a school may have opportunities for continuous study in the school up to the school-going age. And, in order to make this compulsion effective, the chairmen of municipal councils and the presidents of the newly reconstructed district boards in the place of the taluk boards (which were abolished) were empowered to impose penalties on all parents who withdrew their children from schools, while they were of school-age, in all areas where compulsory education had been introduced. Subsequently this power was transferred to the District Educational Officers (1946). Various measures were also taken for eliminating ineffective and inefficient elementary schools and for establishing in their places, well equipped and complete schools with five standards, so that the pupils enrolled in them might go through the full primary course and become permanently literate. In the meantime the District Educational Councils were replaced by Taluk Advisory Councils in 1939 and the Taluk Advisory Councils were in turn abolished in 1941 and their duties entrusted to the Education Department. These measures have everywhere proved very successful; the percentage of pupils reading in standard V rose from 9·5 in the case of boys schools and 9.9 in the case of girls schools in 1937–38 to 42·9 and 27·9 respectively in 1950–51. This is much above the 25 per cent aimed at by the department [1].

While stagnation and wastage were considerably controlled, steps were taken to give a rural bias to elementary education which had all along remained mostly bookish and, therefore, divorced from practical life. The necessity of giving such a bias was stressed by Sir Meverel Statham, who afterwards became the Director of Public Instruction as early as 1927. Some experiments were made thereafter and finally a scheme was worked out and a proper syllabus was framed for that purpose in 1939–40. According to this scheme, which is now in force, emphasis is laid on the teaching of the mother tongue and on the teaching of handicrafts in the lower secondary standards, and at least one pre-vocational subject in the higher elementary standards. Practical subjects of daily utility such as hygiene including home craft for girls and gardening and recreational subjects like music are made compulsory for all pupils in the

---

1 *See* the Annual Reports on Public Instruction from 1933–1934 to 1950–1951.

Monograph on Rural Problems in Madras by S. Y. Krishnaswami, 1947, pages 390–395.

Madras in 1946, Part I, page 6.

lower elementary stage. Instruction is also imparted in elementary Mathematics, History and Geography, Nature Study and Physical Training. Among the handicrafts and pre-vocational subjects are included spinning and weaving, mat-making, bee-keeping, pottery, embroidery, lace-making, preserving and pickling, etc. Among the optional subjects are included English, First Aid and a second language. Special steps have been taken to train teachers in the new syllabus by organising refresher courses.[1]

Coimbatore has shared all these benefits along with the other districts; but still, it has not made much progress in elementary education as will be seen from the following statements :—

NUMBER OF INSTITUTIONS.

Agency.	1910–11.	1930–31.	1950–51
(1)	(2)	(3)	(4)
Government	8	41	17
District Board	160	923	774
Panchayats	..	..	22
Municipal	15	92	82
Private	1,209	1,084	335
Total ..	1,392	2,140	1,230

NUMBER OF PUPILS.

	1910–11.	1930–31.	1950–51.
(1)	(2)	(3)	(4)
Total number of boys	41,435	77,105	99,043
Total number of girls	7,441	22,459	47,710
Total number of pupils	48,876	99,564	1,46,753

In 1956–57 there were in the district 1,985 elementary schools with 1,37,505 boys and 72,379 girls studying in them. Of these schools, 23 were managed by the Government, 1,428 by the District Board, 79 by the Panchayat Boards, 109 by the Municipalities and 354 by aided private agencies. But its percentage of boys in classes I to V to its male population in the age group 6 to 12 worked out only to 60, a percentage which gave it only the twelfth rank among the districts. Its percentage of girls to its female population similarly worked out only to 32.6 which gave it the eleventh rank among the districts. Described in another way, it may be stated that out of 516 villages with a population of more than 2,000 persons, 507 villages in Coimbatore had one or more public schools; that out of

1 *Monograph on Rural Problems in Madras* by S. Y. Krishnaswami, 1947, pages 396–398.

Report on Public Instruction for 1939–40, pages 24–25.

222 villages with a population of 1,000 to 2,000 persons, 211 villages in it had one or more schools; that out of 117 villages with a population of 500 to 1,000 persons, 106 villages in it had one or more schools; that out of 55 villages with a population of 200 to 500 persons, 36 villages in it had one or more schools; and that out of 29 villages with a population of less than 200 persons; 11 villages had one or more schools.[1] Compulsion for boys had been introduced in the Municipality of Tiruppur and for both boys and girls in the Municipalities of Coimbatore, Mettupalayam, Gobichettipalayam and Erode. Compulsion had also been introduced in 48 centres in rural areas and in 19 centres in urban areas.[2] It may also be stated here that the distinction between boys' schools and girls' schools has now been removed and that all elementary schools have been converted into mixed schools open to boys and girls alike.[3]

A new orientation has recently been given to elementary education by the introduction of what is called the basic education. The idea underlying this system of education is that the children should learn by doing instead of merely learning about them from books, so as to develop in them initiative, enterprise and resourcefulness. Productive work is made the basis of learning. The children are taught basic crafts like spinning and weaving and are made to take pleasure in producing things of utilitarian value. Personal and environmental cleanliness are given an important place in the curriculam. They are given a great deal of freedom in these schools, the teacher acting more like a friend than as a disciplinarian. The aim of the Government is to convert, in course of time, every elementary school into a basic school and to provide at least one basic school for every village with a population of 500 or more. The chief difficulty has been that of training a sufficient number of teachers in this new method. In Coimbatore in 1956–57, there were 125 basic schools with 11,293 boys and 6,500 girls studying in them. Of these, two were Government schools, 91 were District Board schools, seven were Municipal schools and 25 were aided private schools.[4]

Another new development is adult or social education. Until about 30 years ago nothing was being done for educating the adults who had not had the benefit of school education. Some attempts were from that time

1 Report on Public Instruction for 1956–57.

2 *Idem.*

3 *Madras in* 1949, Part I, page 49.

4. Report on Public Instruction for 1956–57.

made to open night schools for adults by non-official agencies like the Y.M.C.A. with the object of producing literacy among adults. These night schools received some assistance from the Government but they failed to achieve any substantial results. It was not till the National Government came to power that something tangible was done and definite scheme of adult education was sanctioned by the Government. In accordance with this scheme, several measures have been undertaken in the State. A special Adult Education Officer has been appointed as also some special propaganda Deputy Inspectors for conducting lectures and showing educational films with the help of mobile vans fitted with projectors, generators, loud-speakers and gramaphone records. Many teachers have been trained for adult literacy work. Student volunteers have been persuaded to spend more weeks (40 days) in villages in order to disseminate general knowledge among the villagers and to instruct them through dramas, exhibitions, etc. A few rural colleges have also been opened for imparting higher education to such of the adults as had already received some education.[1] A three-year course has been drawn up for the benefit of those adults who achieve literacy with the object of making them able to read and understand the contents of a daily newspaper and a number of schools for adults have been opened. So far as the Coimbatore district is concerned, there were in 1956–57, 165 adult schools (District Board, Private Aided and Unaided) with a strength of 3,105 men and 1,019 women.[2]

It may, however, be noted here that there were in 1956–57, three Government, two District Board, three Municipal and three Aided schools under private management for Scheduled Castes imparting instruction to 1,079 boys and 483 girls, and 2 Government schools for Scheduled Tribes imparting instruction to 86 boys and 11 girls.[2] The district has also some training schools, industrial schools and commercial schools. In 1956–57 there were four ordinary training schools for men, one ordinary training school for women, six basic training schools for men, one basic training school for women, four industrial schools and 27 commercial schools.[3]

---

[1] *Monograph on Rural Problems in Madras* by S. Y. Krishnaswami, 1947, pages 403–404.

Progress of Education in Madras State (*Pamphlet*) 1954, pages 9–15.

Report on Public Instruction for 1950–51.

G.O. No. 846, Education, dated 9th January 1948.

G.O. No. 1401, Education, dated 1st May 1950.

[2] Report on Public Instruction for 1956–57.

[3] *Idem*.

In spite of all this, the overall picture of education and literacy in Coimbatore is by no means good when compared with the other districts. The following statement shows the progress of education from 1910–50.

Year.	*Population by census.*		
	Males.	*Females.*	*Total.*
(1)	(2)	(3)	(4)
1910–11 ..	1,044,429	1,072,135	2,116,564
1930–31 ..	1,106,171	1,113,677	2,219,848
1950–51 ..	1,653,494	1,639,710	3,293,204

	Scholars (public and private).			*Percentage of scholars to population.*			*Number of Institutions.*
	Males.	*Females.*	*Total.*	*Males.*	*Females.*	*Total.*	
	(5)	(6)	(7)	(8)	(9)	(10)	(11)
1910–11 ..	46,384	7,679	54,063	4·4	0·7	2·6	1,419
1930–31 ..	87,138	23,963	111,101	7·9	2·2	5·0	2,194
1950–51 .	134,518	58,005	192,523	8·1	3·5	5·5	1,431

The district had, in 1956–57, 2,451 educational institutions imparting instruction to 199,743 males and 96,005 females out of a total population of 1,720,393 males and 1,707,654 females. The percentage of scholars to population thus worked out to 11.6 in the case of males and 5.6 in the case of females and 8.6 in the case of both males and females and these percentages gave it only the twelfth rank among the districts in the matter of male education and the eleventh rank both in the matter of female education and in the matter of male and female education.[1] As to literacy it is 26.3 per cent among males and 7.6 per cent among females, which percentage is also exceeded in several districts.[2]

The district has also a number of elementary schools mainly intended for Scheduled Castes or Harijans and Backward Classes. The various educational concessions granted to the Harijans have already been described in the Chapter on Welfare Schemes.

The education of the district is under the control of the District Educational Officer who has his headquarters at Coimbatore. He looks after all schools, except the girls' schools which are under the charge of the Inspectress of Girls' Schools who has her headquarters at Salem. Coimbatore is also the headquarters of a Divisional Inspector of Schools. All these officers are under the administrative control of the Director of Public Instruction.

1 Report on Public Instruction for 1956–57.

2 *Census of India*, 1951, Madras and Coorg. Part I, pages 209–210.

CHAPTER XIV.

LOCAL ADMINISTRATION.

Local Administration in the Coimbatore district began with the passing of the Education Cess Act VI of 1863,[1] and the District Road Cess Act III of 1866.[2] Both these Acts were intended to make local education and local roads, as far as possible, a direct charge upon the people, and both these Acts created a machinery for administering the funds raised from the people. The former enabled the people of a locality to levy a rate for the upkeep of schools while the latter enabled the people of the district to impose a cess not exceeding half an anna in the rupee on the rental value of occupied land to constitute a fund for the construction and maintenance of local roads. But these were only the beginnings in local administration. Very soon the scope of that administration was expanded by the inclusion in it of sanitation and medical aid as well.[3]

This was done by the passing of the Towns Improvement Act X of 1865 and the Local Funds Act IV of 1871. The first created the municipalities and the second the local fund boards in the State which subsequent legislation has changed into the present district boards and the panchayats. Legislation altering and enlarging the nature and scope of the municipalities and the local boards has gone hand in hand almost ever since 1871, but for the sake of clarity we may first deal with the growth of the local boards and then with the development of the municipalities.

The Local Boards Act of 1871 divided the whole State into a number of circles and constituted in each of these circles a local fund board consisting of three or more non-official members nominated by the Government and an equal number (but not more) of official members appointed by the Government. The term of office of the members was to be three years. The non-official members were to be chosen from among owners or occupiers of land or persons carrying on business or residing in a circle. The Collector of the district was made ex-officio president of each board situated within his jurisdiction. The Act repealed the District Road Cess

---

1 G.O. No. 266, Education, dated 20th August 1864.

2 G.O. No. 3358, Revenue, dated 13th December 1866.

3 *Manual of Administration of the Madras Presidency*, Vol. I, 1885, by C. D. Maclean—Footnote on pages 638–640.

Standing Information regarding the Official Administration of the Madras Presidency, 1877, by C. D. Maclean, pages 207–208.

Act of 1866 and the Education Cess Act of 1863 and the existing funds and the charges appertaining to local roads and to schools were transferred to the newly constituted local funds. The Act also provided for the imposition of a cess similar to the District Road Cess but with a maximum of one anna in the rupee, for the establishment of tolls upon roads and for the levy of a house-tax. Two-thirds of the cess and the whole of the tolls were made applicable exclusively to roads and communications, and the house tax was made applicable for schools and it was to be imposed only in villages in which schools existed or were about to be established. The house-tax, however, having become very unpopular, was discontinued from 1873-1874. The local funds were made applicable for the maintenance of roads and communications; for the upkeep of schools either wholly or by grants-in-aid; for the construction and repair of hospitals, choultries, markets, tanks and wells; for the training and employment of vaccinators and sanitary inspectors; and for the cleansing of roads, streets, tanks, etc. The Act also provided for the transfer to the local fund board of public dispensaries, choultries, tanks, etc., endowed and un-endowed; for vesting the endowments in the board, for enabling the Board of Revenue which was vested with the supervision of local boards, to transfer to the local fund board the powers of control over charitable endowments conferred by Regulation VII of 1817.[1]

This Act was introduced into Coimbatore in 1871 itself. The district was divided into two circles, namely, the Northern and the Southern Circles, the former comprising the Coimbatore, Perundurai, Pollachi, Bhavani, Satyamangalam and Kollegal divisions and the latter comprising the Karur, Palladam, Dharapuram and Udumalpet divisions. In each of these circles a local fund board was constituted, consisting of official and non-official members, and presided over by the Collector or the Sub-Collector.[2] In 1872, however, both the circles were amalgamated and a single Local Fund Board was constituted consisting of 17 official and 17 non-official members or 34 members in all. The Collector acted as the president and a non-official member, as the vice-president of the Board. The receipts of the board amounted to about Rs. 2,50,000 of which the rates and taxes came to just over Rs. 2,00,000 and these were spent on roads, schools, hospitals and dispensaries, sanitation, vaccination, markets, choultries and traveller's bungalows. It is of some interest to note that

---

1 *See* the provisions of Madras Act IV of 1871 in the *Fort St. George Gazette*.

2 G.O. No. 619, Public, dated 9th May 1871.
G.O. No. 763, Finance, dated 9th December 1871.

when the Act was introduced, the non-official members were reported to have evinced little interest in local affairs.[1]

But the wheel of Juggernaut had been set in motion; and local self-Government gradually gathered momentum and made steady progress in the subsequent years. In 1884 it was felt necessary to widen its field and to increase its efficiency by increasing the powers and augmenting the strength of the non-official element of the local bodies. The Local Boards Act V of 1884 was accordingly passed for repealing Act IV of 1871 and constituting new local bodies. By this Act the control over the local boards exercised by the Board of Revenue under section 71 of Act IV of 1871 was assumed by the Government and the administration of local affairs was vested in a single district board constituted for each revenue district consisting of a president and not less than 24 members who might all be appointed by the Government or might be partly so appointed and partly elected by the members of the newly created taluk boards from among their own members or, in any part of the district where there was no taluk board, by the union boards (another set of newly created local bodies) and by the tax payers of the rural parts of the district. The members were to hold office for three years. All Revenue Divisional Officers were made ex-officio members. The proportion of the official members was reduced from one half to one-fourth of the total strength. Under the old Act the local fund board had no powers to levy taxes on its own authority but could only administer the funds raised on its behalf by the Government. Under the new Act, the local boards were empowered to levy with the approval of the Government any of the taxes authorised by the Act. Under the old Act the Collector as has been seen, was to act as the president of the local fund board. Under the new Act the president of the district board might be elected from among the members of the district board, if the Government so directed.

The taluk boards were formed for each taluk or group of taluks consisting of a president with not less than 12 members who might either *all* be appointed by the Government or partly so appointed and partly elected from among the members of the union boards or elected by the tax payers of the taluk, one-third of the members being officials. The term of office of the members was fixed at three years. The taluk board's jurisdiction then coinciding with the Revenue Divisional Officer's jurisdiction, that officer was made the ex-officio member and president of the board. The

[1] G.O. No. 1175, Finance, dated 4th September 1872; G.O. No. 1510, Finance dated 12th November 1872.

G.O. No. 1345, Finance, dated 4th October 1872; G.O. No. 626, Finance, dated 9th May 1871.

taluk board's funds consisted of one half of the proceeds of the tax levied by the district board in the taluk board's area and transferred to it by the district board and other fees collected within the area of the taluk board, such as licence fees for markets, etc. The district board might, with the approval of the Government, or should, at their direction, transfer any other sums from its funds to the taluk board.

The revenues of the district board and the taluk boards were derived from a tax not exceeding two annas in the rupee on the annual rent value of all occupied lands in certain districts and not exceeding one anna in the rupee in certain other districts; from a railway cess of three pies in the rupee on an annual rent value of lands; from tolls; and from fees for the use of cart-stands, markets, slaughter-houses, etc. The duties and responsibilities of the district board and the taluk boards were the maintenance of roads, bridges and other means of communication; the construction and maintenance of hospitals, dispensaries, etc.; the diffusion of education and for that purpose the construction and repair of school houses, the training of teachers, etc., the enforcement of measures relating to sanitation and public health; the establishment and maintenance of relief works in times of famine and scarcity; and the adoption of other acts of local public utility.

The union boards were constituted for individual villages or groups of villages called unions, the members consisting of not less than 5 persons, the headmen of the villages constituting the union, being ex-officio members. One of these headmen was to be appointed chairman. Members other than village headmen were to be either all appointed by the Government or partly so appointed and partly elected by the tax-payers. Their term of office was to be three years. The resources of the union boards were to consist of the proceeds of a house-tax levied in the union varying from 4 annas to 5 rupees according to the classification of the house and any other sums placed at the disposal of the union by the taluk board. The duties and responsibilities of the union boards were declared to be the lighting of the public roads, the cleaning of public roads, drains, wells and other public places, the establishment and maintenance of dispensaries and schools, the making and repairing of roads and drains, the constructing and repairing of tanks and wells and generally doing such things as might be necessary for the preservation of the public health.[1]

---

1 *Manual of Administration of the Madras Presidency*, 1885, by C. D. Maclean, Vol. I, pages 638–651 and footnotes on pages 641–642.

Madras Presidency, 1881–1931, by G. T. Boag, 1933, pages 11–13.

See the provisions of Madras Act V of 1834 in the *Fort St. George Gazette*.

The Act was introduced into the Coimbatore district in 1885–1887. To begin with, the maximum strength of the district board was fixed at 56 members of whom 28 were to be nominated and 28 elected from among the members of the taluk boards[1]. But within a couple of years, this strength was reduced to 32 members of whom 16 were to be nominated and 16 elected from among the members of the taluk boards[2]. Five Taluk Boards, namely, Coimbatore, Erode, Pollachi, Satyamangalam, and Kollegal were formed. The Coimbatore and Kollegal Taluk Boards covered the revenue taluks of the same name and consisted of 12 members each, while the Erode Taluk Board covered the revenue taluks of Erode, Dharapuram, Karur (subsequently transferred to Tiruchirappalli district) and Bhavani and consisted of 20 members and the Pollachi taluk board covered the revenue taluks of Pollachi, Palladam and Udumalpet and consisted of 16 members. Sixteen union boards were formed each covering one or more villages and consisting first of 5 and later of more members[3]. The district board was presided over by the Collector and the taluk boards were presided over by the Revenue Divisional Officers of the district while the union boards were presided over by the village headmen. The principal revenues of the district board were derived from a land cess of one anna in the rupee on the rent value of the lands, and tolls and market rents. Its other revenues came from school fees, income from endowments, choultry rents, traveller's bungalow fees, ferry rents, fishery rents, avenues, and contributions from the Pound Fund and State Funds for education and choultries. All these revenues were spent on roads, buildings, schools, hospitals and dispensaries, vaccination, sanitation, markets, choultries, etc. The revenues of the taluk boards were derived from a moiety of the land cess levied by the district board, school fees, choultry rents, contributions from State Funds for education and choultries and allotment from district board funds. They were expended on choultries, taluk and village roads, schools, dispensaries, sanitation and chatrams. The revenues of the union boards were derived from house-tax, miscellaneous fees and contributions from taluk boards and these were spent on roads and sanitation. The total revenues of the district board, the taluk boards and the union boards amounted for instance in 1888–1889, to Rs. 1,60,666, Rs. 2,80,830 and Rs. 18,083 respectively and their total expenditure in the same year, amounted to Rs. 1,41,353, Rs. 2,45,463 and Rs. 15,931 respectively. For some years even these new boards, save the taluk boards, seem to have failed to evoke sufficient enthusiasm among the

---

1 G.O. No. 598, Finance, dated 19th March 1885.

2 G.O. No. 1862, Local, dated 26th August 1889.

3 G.O. No. 1161, Local Fund (Finance), dated 4th December 1885.
G.O No. 856, Local, dated 5th May 1888.

people. Very few of the non-official members took any real interest in local affairs or attended the meetings regularly [1]. In 1895 the revenue taluks of Coimbatore and Satyamangalam were constituted into a single taluk board, called the Coimbatore Taluk Board [2]. In 1910, the Coimbatore Taluk Board was bifurcated into the Coimbatore and Gobichettipalayam Taluk Boards[3]. In 1918 the maximum strength of the District Board was raised from 32 to 36 members, the number of elective seats being at the same time, increased from 16 to 24[4]. The union boards were gradually increased so that by 1920 they numbered twenty-eight.

The next important milestone in local administration came with the passing of the Local Boards Act V of 1920 and the Village Panchayats Act XV of 1920, the Local Boards Amendment Act VI of 1900 having made only some minor amendments to the Act of 1884. By this time, however, much water had flowed under the bridge; political agitation had come, and people had become more and more interested in Local Self-Government. The Royal Commission on Decentralization had also suggested the enlargement of the powers of the local bodies. The Local Boards Act of 1920 which was consequently passed gave an independent status to each class of the local boards and increased not only their strength but also their proportion of elected members, their resources and their powers. The strength of the district board was raised to a maximum of 52 and a minimum of 24 members, that of the taluk board to a maximum of 24 and a minimum of 12 members and that of the union board to a maximum of 15 and a minimum of 7 members. The proportion of elected members in all these boards was fixed at not less than three fourths of the total strength, the remaining members being appointed by the Government in the case of the district boards, by the President of the District Board in the case of the taluk boards, and by the President of the Taluk Boards in the case of the union boards. The term of office of the members of the local boards was fixed as three years. The Collector ceased to be the president of the district board and the Revenue Divisional Officer ceased to be either the president or even a member of the taluk board. The president of the district board could be elected by the members of the district board or appointed by the Government; but the presidents of the taluk boards and the union boards could only be elected. The presidents of the taluk boards became ex-officio members of the district boards. The taxation powers of all the three boards were enlarged to increase their resources and each board was

---

1 G.O. No. 2401, Local, dated 17th October 1889.

2 *Coimbatore District Manual*, Volume II, by Horold A. Stuart, 1898, page 277.

3 G.O. No. 1370, Local, dated 17th October 1910.

4 G.O. No. 855, Local, dated 24th June 1918.

allowed to raise the authorised taxes separately. In addition to the obligatory land cess of one anna in the rupee of rent value of lands shared equally by the district board and the taluk boards, these boards were given the option of levying an additional land cess up to a maximum of 3 pies in the rupee. The railway cess was abolished but three new taxes, the profession tax, the companies tax and the pilgrim tax were authorised to be levied by all the three boards. The method of levying the house-tax by the union boards which was defective under the old act was modified to make the levy just and proportionate to the capital or rental value of the buildings. The local boards were moreover given a free hand in framing their budgets. Provision was made for the appointment of a District Board Engineer and a District Health Officer and for the enforcement of sanitary and public health measures. The local boards thus became more or less autonomous and the Collector and the Government were empowered to interfere only in cases of emergency and mal-administration. In order to inspect and superintend all the operations under the Local Boards Act an officer called the Inspector of Local Boards who was also the Inspector of Municipal Councils was also appointed[1].

About this time was passed the Madras Elementary Education Act VIII of 1920 which made it obligatory on the taluk boards and the municipalities to levy an education tax for the purpose of expanding elementary education, and on the Government to contribute a sum equal to that realised by the cess. When the taluk boards were abolished subsequently in 1934 the duty of levying the cess and running the schools devolved upon the district board.

Meanwhile on the introduction of the Local Boards Act into the Coimbatore district in 1921–22, the district board was reconstituted and its strength was increased from 36 to 44. The taluk boards too were reconstituted, the existing five taluk boards being increased to six by the bifurcation of the Pollachi taluk board into the Pollachi and Palladam taluk boards. As to the union boards, they were reduced from 28 to 27 consequent on the conversion of the Pollachi Union into a municipality[2]. The revenues of all the local boards increased considerably under the new Act. Thus, for instance, in 1923–24 the revenues of the District Board amounted to Rs. 7,68,930, those of the six taluk boards to Rs. 2,93,989 and those of the 27 union boards to Rs. 86,160 making the

---

1 *Madras Presidency*, 1881–1931 by G. T. Boag, page 13.

2 G.O. No. 928, Local and Municipal, dated 25th May 1922.
G.O. No. 476, Local and Municipal, dated 22nd February 1923.

total revenues of all the boards amount to Rs. 11,49,079[1]. There was now an all round improvement. The attendance of the non-official members became more regular and this showed in an unmistakable manner the greater interest evinced by the people in local administration[2].

The Government, at the same time, began to assist the local boards in various ways. They began to give grants for the maintenance of roads and schools; they began to take over the managment of headquarters hospitals; they began to provide District Engineers and District Health Officers for each district board; they began to take over the Veterinary institutions and they organised a separate audit department for auditing local fund accounts[3].

Meanwhile soon after the Local Boards Act was introduced, the Village Panchayats Act was passed. Informal village panchayats constituted on a voluntary basis had already, by 1915 come into existence in several districts for looking after village forests, village conservancy and village water-supply. These were doing useful work but were handicapped by not having any legal sanction for levying taxes or enforcing their decisions. It was now considered that the time had come to remove the handicaps of the existing panchayats, to constitute new panchayats and to place all the panchayats on a statutory basis. The Village Panchayats Act XV of 1920 which was accordingly passed, authorised the constitution of panchayats in rural areas (where there were no union boards) for the administration of village affairs by the villagers themselves. The panchayat was to be entirely an elective body consisting of not less than 7 and not more than 15 members. Its election was to be held once in three years. There was to be no property restriction in the franchise; all residents of the village who were not less than 25 years of age were to be entitled to vote and to be elected as members of the panchayat. The absence of property qualification gave opportunities to the members of the depressed classes and, in most villages, the voters elected members of their own community on the panchayats. The functions of the panchayats were defined to be the construction and maintenance of village roads, culverts and bridges; the lighting of streets and public places; the construction of drains and the disposal of drainage water and sullage; the cleaning of streets, the removal of rubbish, etc., the provision of public latrines; the maintenance of burning ghats and burial grounds; the construction and repair of wells, ponds and tanks for the supply of water

1 G.O. No. 571, Local and Municipal, dated 17th February 1925.

2 *See*, e.g., G.O. No. 571, Local and Municipal, dated 17th February 1925. G.O. No. 985, Local and Municipal, dated 12th April 1924

3 *Madras Presidency*, 1881–1931, by G. T. Boag, 1933, page 16.

for drinking, washing and bathing purposes; the control of cattle sheds, threshing floors, chatrams, village ponds, etc., the extension of village sites, the enforcement of vaccination and the registration of births and deaths. The district or taluk board within whose jurisdiction a panchayat was constituted was, in addition, authorised to empower the panchayat to exercise other functions such as the construction and control of markets, the provision of sanitation during festivals, the control of fairs and fisheries, the planting and preservation of avenue trees, the establishment and maintenance of elementary schools and the provision of medical relief. And the Government were authorised to transfer to a panchayat, village forests or village irrigation works or any other village works or institutions.

The Act placed no specific resources at the disposal of the panchayat but it enabled the panchayat with the sanction of the Government, to levy a tax on the capital value of the buildings situated in the village; a profession tax; fees for cattle stands, threshing floors, village sites, cart stands, markets and slaughter houses; fees for the occupation of choultries, chatrams and rest houses; fees for the cleaning of private latrines, fees for quarrying and excavation, and fees for the permits for grazing or the removal of fuel or other forest produce. The panchayat was also enabled to levy any other suitable taxes or fees approved by the Government. The Government reserved to themselves the right of suspension or cancellation of the proceedings of the panchayat, and of the dissolution of the panchayat itself in case it abused its powers. The Inspector of Local Boards and Municipal Councils was also appointed as the Registrar-General of Panchayats and placed in direct charge of the panchayats in the State. It may be mentioned here that State aid to panchayats was started since 1925–26 and that it took the shape of grants for panchayat libraries, grants for elementary schools and grants for the improvement of village communications and water-supply[1].

In the Coimbatore district the Act was introduced in 1921–22. Here as elsewhere the panchayats were organized mostly with the help of the presidents of taluk boards and other honorary workers. It was no easy task to overcome the apathy of the villagers in village affairs, they having for over a century come to look to the Government for everything. Nor was it an easy task to overcome the opposition of vested interests, both official and non-official[2]. However, the panchayats were gradually

---

1 *Madras Presidency*, 1881–1931, by G. T. Boag, 1933, pages 14–15.

2 G.O. No. 2645, Local and Municipal, dated 22nd June 1926.

3 G.O. No. 107, Local and Municipal, dated 10th January 1924.

organized; in 1923 they numbered only 26[1], but by 1931 they numbered 123. Of these about half the number were functioning efficiently; the rest were inactive either for want of proper guidance or for want of proper supervision. Their revenues in 1930–31 amounted to Rs. 28,510 comprising Rs. 8,114 from taxes, fees, etc., Rs, 12,557 from Government grants and Rs. 7,806 from other receipts. A few of them levied a house tax, a fewer still a profession tax and they spent their revenues mostly on roads, schools and other civic amenities of village life[1].

The position created by the Local Boards Act and the Village Panchayats Act of 1920 was modified in some respects and improved by the Local Boards Amendment Act XI of 1930. This Act repealed the Village Panchayats Act; brought the village panchayats within the scope of the local boards and, at the same time, converted the union boards into panchayats for as they are sometimes called, panchayat boards. It rearranged the taluk board areas making them normally co-terminous with the Revenue Taluks. It declared that all members of every local board, whether a district board, a taluk board or a panchayat board, were to be elected but that seats were to be reserved in these boards for certain communities and women. It laid down that the members of the district board were to be chosen by direct election. It extended the franchise of local boards to every person who was assessed to any tax payable to the local board, or to any other local authority or to the Local Government or to the Government of India. It made all offices of the presidents of the local boards elective and provided for the provincialisation of the services under the local boards. It modified the provisions relating to taxes and tolls, fixed the land cess at one and a half anna in the rupee of the rent value of the lands, and allotted one-third of the proceeds of the cess to the district boards, an other one-third to the taluk boards, onesixth to the panchayat boards, and one-sixth to the Village Development Fund. It provided for votes of no confidence in presidents and vice-presidents, for the suppression of panchayats by the local Government, and for the adjudication of disputes between local authorities by the Government themselves, or by an arbitrator, a board of arbitrators or joint committees appointed by the Government. It empowered the presidents of the district boards and taluk boards to exercise control over the affairs of the panchayats. Finally, it provided for the appointment of a District Panchayat Officer and for the formation of a Village Development Fund[2].

---

1 G.O. No. 2272, Local and Municipal, dated 14th June 1932.

2 *Madras Presidency*, 1881–1931 by G. T. Boag, 1933, pages 15–16. See the provisions of Madras Act XI of 1930 in the *Fort St. George Gazette*.

The changes subsequently made in local administration can, with a single exception be easily described. The levy of tolls and tax on motor vehicles by local boards were abolished consequent on the passing of the Madras Motor Vehicles Taxation Act III of 1931, the boards being compensated out of the proceeds of the tax levied by the Government under the Act[1]. All taluk boards were abolished in 1934, their assets, liabilities and main functions being taken over by the district boards. The Village Development Fund was also abolished and its resources were placed at the disposal of the district boards[2]. Rules were framed for the appointment of Electrical Engineers, Additional District Board Engineers, and District Panchayat Officers[3]. Relevant portions of the electoral rolls of the Legislative Assembly were ordered to be adopted as electoral rolls of the local bodies[4]. Presidents and Vice-Presidents removed by the Government were debarred from standing for election for these again for a period of six months, except when there was a general election[5]. Persons who were in arrears to local boards were disqualified from standing for election and members who were in arrears were made liable to be removed from office[6]. Powers were taken by the Government to become ultimate authorities in all disputes between local boards[7], to supersede district boards for a maximum period of three years[8], as well as to resume control over endowments transferred to the district boards[9]. Provision was made for the appointment of Executive Officers for the panchayats and the duties and powers of these officers were defined[10]. The Collector was empowered to appoint a member of the local board to exercise the duties of a president or a vice-president in cases in which the latter failed to discharge his duties[11]. Land cess was raised from one and a half anna to two annas per rupee of the annual rent value of all occupied land and the additional cess so raised was given entirely to the district board[12]. The local boards were authorised to levy a surcharge on stamp duty payable under the Indian Stamp Act of 1899 in respect of the instruments of sale, gift, mortgage with possession and transfers by way of

---

1 *Madras Presidency,* 1881–1931 by G. T. Boag, 1933, page 17.

2 Madras Administration Report for 1933–1934, page XXVI.

3 *Idem* for 1938–1939, page 5.

4 *Idem* for 1937–1938, page 6.

5 *Idem* for 1939–1940, page 4.

6 *Madras in* 1940, page 4.

7 *Madras in* 1941, page 2.

8 *Idem.*

9 *Madras in* 1943, page 4.

10 *Idem,* page 5.

11 *Madras in* 1944, page 2.

12 *Madras in* 1945, page 4

exchange and leave in perpetuity of immovable property[1]. Roads of military and other importance were transferred from the district boards to the Highways Department[2]. Some of these changes, it is clear, were designed to control the infiltration of politics into the local bodies and to tide over any local opposition that might be created during the war period. Others were intended to improve the finances and increase the usefulness of the local bodies.

The only far reaching change that has been recently introduced and that demands a fuller description is the passing of the Village Panchayats Act X of 1950. From about 1940 it became increasingly clear that the dual control exercised over the panchayats by the president of the district board and the Inspector of Municipal Councils and Local Boards was not only unsatisfactory but ineffective. The Adviser Government thought that the best way to rectify matters was to exclude the panchayats from the scope of the Madras Local Boards Act and to place them in charge of the District Collectors, and for this purpose they enacted Act XII of 1946. This Act was, however, not brought into operation and was allowed to lapse as the National Government which succeeded the Adviser Government wanted to introduce a more comprehensive legislation which would make the panchayats really autonomous. They wanted also to invest the panchayats with powers under the Village Courts Act of 1888 and the Indian Registration Act of 1908[3]. They, therefore, introduced fresh legislation and passed the Village Panchayats Act of 1950.

Under this Act a panchayat is compulsorily to be formed in every village with a population of 500 and above and where the population is less than 500 one or more villages have to be clubbed to form a panchayat. Panchayats having a population of 5,000 and above and an annual income of Rs. 10,000 are to be classified as Class I panchayats and others as Class II panchayats. Every panchayat is to have not less than 5 and not more than 15 members and all members are to be elected, but seats are to be reserved for Scheduled Castes for a period of ten years. The term of office of the members is to be three years, and franchise is to be exercised by all adults as in the case of the Legislative Assembly. No village officer or an officer under the Government or a local board can be elected as a member. The president of the panchayat is to be elected by the entire

---

1 *Idem*, page 5.
G.O. No. 144, Legal, dated 26th May 1950.
Madras in 1950, page 6.

2 *Madras in* 1946, pages 5–6.

3 G.O. No. 105, Legal, dated 7th June 1949, page 71.

electorate but the vice-president is to be elected by the members of the panchayat. Executive Officers may be appointed by the Government, where necessary, by notification. The Executive Officer is to carry out the resolutions passed by the panchayat but, where the president thinks that any resolution is in excess of the powers of the panchayat, or is likely to endanger human life or health or public safety, the Executive Officer is to refer the matter to the Government whose decision is to be final. The Government may dissolve or reconstitute a panchayat if it fails to discharge its duties while the Inspector of Municipal Councils and Local Boards may suspend or cancel a resolution or remove a president, a vice-president or a member, in case of misconduct.

It is obligatory upon every panchayat to provide, within the limits of its funds, for the construction and repair of roads, bridges, culverts, drains, etc., for the lighting of public places, for the cleaning of streets, the removal of rubbish, etc., for the construction of public latrines and the maintenance of burning ghats and burial grounds; for the sinking or repairing of wells or tanks for drinking, washing and bathing purposes; and for the carrying out of preventive and remedial measures connected with epidemics or malaria. A panchayat may also make provision for the planting of avenues, for the opening of public markets and slaughter-houses; for the control of fairs and festivals; for the extension of village sites and regulation of buildings; for the improvement of agriculture and agricultural stock; for the promotion of cottage industries; for the opening and maintenance of elementary schools, reading rooms and libraries; for the establishment of wireless receiving sets, play-grounds, sports clubs and centres of physical culture; for the running of dispensaries and maternity and child welfare centres for the rendering of veterinary aid and for the undertaking of any other measures of public utility.

Every panchayat is required to levy a house-tax, a profession tax, a vehicle tax and a duty on certain transfers of property. It may also, with the permission of the Inspector of Municipal Councils and Local Boards, levy a land cess at the rate of 3 pies in the rupee on the rent value of all occupied lands, a tax on agricultural land and fees on commercial crops bought and sold in the village. In addition to these sources of revenue the panchayats receive pilgrim tax, tolls and ferries and fishery rents, market fees, and contributions from the district board for elementary education.

The panchayats are vested with control over all unreserved forests in the villages, all village roads, all irrigation works not under the Public

Works Department and all water courses, springs, tanks and communal property in the villages. They may also be vested with control over charitable endowments and empowered to execute kudimaramath works by levying fees for that purpose. Nor is this all. All panchayats enjoy the powers of the panchayat courts under the Village Courts Act of 1888, their pecuniary jurisdiction being increased from Rs. 50 to Rs. 100, and such of them as do not possess sub-registrars' offices may be authorised to exercise also certain functions performed by the sub-registrars under the Indian Registration Act of 1908. The district boards are to have no longer any control over the panchayats, nor are the Collectors to have any, except in cases of emergency. The working of the panchayats is to be supervised by the Inspector of Municipal Councils and Local Boards and the officers under him[1].

This Act which enlarged alike the powers, the resources and the responsibilities of the panchayats was brought into operation in this State on 1st April 1951[2]. Turning to the other local boards, we have already seen the position created by the Local Boards Act of 1920 in Coimbatore until the passing of the amending Act of 1930. It remains now to review the position in the district created by the legislation passed since 1930. The taluk boards in Coimbatore were abolished in 1934 and their assets, liabilities and main functions were transferred to the district board. But, as the Government considered that the district board was unable to cope with the increased work, they bifurcated the board in 1936 into two district boards, one called the Coimbatore District Board with headquarters at Coimbatore and the other called the Erode District Board with headquarters at Erode[3]. The bifurcation, however, was short lived. As soon as the Congress Ministry came to power, they amalgamated the two boards and restored the original position (1938)[4]. Then came the Second World War when no district board elections were held, the term of the district board being extended from year to year. In November 1946 on the accession of the National Government, the district board was dissolved and the Collector was appointed as the Special Officer pending fresh elections[5]. It was only in 1949[6] that the district board elections were held and a fresh district board was constituted.

---

1 G.O. No. 223, Legal, dated 29th July 1950.
Madras in 1950 (*Pamphlet*), pages 91–96.

Madras Information, April 1954, page 30.

G.O. No. 4948, Local Self-Government, dated 12th November 1936.

G.O. No. 4214, Local Administration, dated 21st October 1938.

G.O. No. 1723, Local Administration, dated 22nd October 1946.

Madras in 1949, page 47.

An idea of the District Board administration in general in Coimbatore can best be obtained by looking into some of the details of the working of the District Board in 1956–57. At the beginning of the year it consisted of 52 members of whom 45 occupied non-reserved seats and 7 occupied reserved seats. The reserved seats were occupied by 2 women and 5 persons belonging to the scheduled castes. But with the transfer of Kollegal taluk from November 1956, the strength of the district board was reduced to 49 of which 43 were non-reserved seats and 6 were reserved seats, 2 for women and 4 for the scheduled castes. Its revenues amounted to Rs. 87,43,006. One main source was the education cess and it was levied at first at 3 annas in the rupee of land revenue for augmenting the Elementary Education Fund. This brought in Rs. 9,10,907. Another source was the land cess and it was levied at the rate of 2 annas in the rupee of land revenue. The cess collected in the panchayat areas was shared by the district board and the panchayat boards, the former receiving one and a half annas in the rupee and the latter half anna in the rupee. The District Boards' income from the land cess amounted to Rs. 5,42,954. The third main source was the surcharge on land revenue which fetched Rs. 5,02,221. Besides these, the contribution of Government under Motor Vehicles Taxation Act brought to the district board Rs. 4,09,098, market fees Rs. 13,39,583, license fees on motor vehicles Rs. 1,71,538, school fees Rs. 2,96,289, education grant Rs. 5,37,844, license fees Rs. 49,544 and sale of tree produce Rs. 4,934.

The District Board spent its revenues mostly on roads, education and medical aid. Its total expenditure in 1956-57 amounted to Rs. 87,52,156. It maintained 368 (398) miles of major district roads, 582 (650) miles of other district roads and 1,565 (1,596) miles of village roads at a cost of Rs. 12,10,513 and spent Rs. 1,57,900 on the construction of bridges, culverts, etc. It maintained 79 (92) ferries and derived from them an income of Rs. 40,992. It maintained 1,692 miles of avenues and derived from them an income of Rs. 6,845. It maintained 18 (21) rest houses and 26 (28) choultries at a cost of Rs. 27,699 and derived from them an income of Rs. 9,959. It maintained 1,514 (1,604) elementary schools including 649 (668) schools opened under the scheme for the relief of the educated unemployed and 71 schools under the Second Five-Year Plan with 157,955 (166,531) pupils of which 371 had buildings of their own, 321 occupied rented buildings and the rest occupied rent-free buildings. Its receipts under elementary education came from the education cess, Government grants, endowments, and contributions from general funds and amounted to Rs. 25,38,435 and its expenditure amounted to Rs. 28,83,655. It maintained 36 (39) secondary schools with a strength of 16,901 (18,158 consisting of 15,203 boys and 2,955 girls) in the secondary department, of whom 1,546 appeared for the S.S.L.C. examination. Thirty-two schools had buildings of their own and 4 occupied rented buildings. Its receipts under secondary education came from fees, Government grants, etc., and amounted to Rs. 6,91,467 and its expenditure on secondary education amounted to Rs. 11,31,435. It maintained 3 hospitals, 11 (14) regular dispensaries of modern medicine, 12 (13) rural dispensaries and 7 (11) part-time dispensaries under the western system of medicine which treated 1,644 in-patients, and 4,28,086 out-patients, as well as 6 (7) regular ayurvedic dispensaries, 17 (19) rural ayurvedic dispensaries, 1 regular siddha dispensary and 5 rural siddha dispensaries which treated 2,91,606 out-patients. It maintained a maternity home and 17 maternity and child welfare centres. And, finally it maintained 135 (143) markets and derived from them an income of Rs. 11,62,037[1].

The District Board exercised control over the panchayats till 1951 when, under the new Act, a District Panchayat Officer and several Deputy Panchayat Officers were appointed and placed in charge of the panchayats. All these officers were placed under the control of the Inspector of Municipal Councils and Local Boards. In 1956–57 the district had 30 class I and 407 class II Panchayats. Their receipts amounted to Rs. 20,28,615 and Rs. 13,53,906 and their expenditure to Rs. 18,88,051 and Rs. 10,77,798 respectively. Their revenues were derived from land cess, the library cess, the house tax, profession tax, licence fees levied on dangerous and offensive trades and fees from markets, cart stands and slaughter houses. The revenues were generally spent on sanitation, lighting, roads, libraries, parks and water supply.

We now come to municipal administration. Leaving out of consideration the Madras City, municipal activities in the districts originated from the passing of India Act XXVI of 1850. This Act authorised the Government to introduce it in any town in which the inhabitants were desirous of making better provision for "constructing, repairing, cleaning, lighting or watching any public streets, roads, drains or tanks or for the prevention of nuisances or for improving the town in any manner". The Act might be introduced even for a few of these purposes if the inhabitants

1 G.O. No. 308, Local Administration, dated 20th February 1958. The figures within brackets represent figures as at the beginning of the year and are inclusiv eof Kollegal taluk which was transferred to the Mysore State on 1st vemb r 1956.

so wished.The councillors, or the commissioners as they were then called, consisted of the magistrate and such of the inhabitants as the Government might appoint and they were removable at pleasure. The raising of the necessary ways and means, the definition and prohibition of nuisances and the fixing of penalties as well as all matters connected with the establishment needed for carrying out the purposes of the Act were left to be provided for by the bye-laws to be framed by the councillors and approved by the Government. Under this Act which was merely an enabling Act, a voluntary association was formed in Coimbatore town which derived a precarious income from a tax on houses. It was, however, only after the passing of the next Act, called the Madras Towns Improvement Act X of 1865, that a regular municipality was established there.

This Act primarily originated in the intention of the Government to make the inhabitants bear as much as possible, the charges of maintaining police in towns. But it was eventually resolved that the funds compulsorily raised under it should be made applicable not only to the expenses of the police but also to "the construction, repairing and cleaning of drains; the making and repairing of roads, the keeping of roads, streets and tanks clean; and doing such things as may be necessary for the preservation of the public health". The amount to be raised for these purposes was to be fixed by the Government, who were also to indicate the means of taxation and one-fourth of the sum so fixed was to be paid by the Government as a grant-in-aid. Besides the sums compulsorily fixed by the Government the councillors were, with the sanction of the Government, empowered to raise further sums for other municipal purposes such as lighting, prevention of fire, water supply, etc. The independence of the councillors was restricted in more than one direction. They were bound to raise the amount fixed by the Government and, if they failed to do so, the District Magistrate was empowered to raise the sums himself. Three ex-officio councillors, namely, the District Magistrate, the local magistrate and the range officer of the Public Works Department sat on the council itself. The District Magistrate who acted as the president, appointed the vice-presidents of all municipalities within the district. He was invested with the power of appointing such establishment as the councillors might sanction for the purposes of the Act and, in case of emergency, he could exercise all the powers of the councillors. The councillors were to consist of not less than 5 inhabitants of the town appointed by the Government and their term of office was limited to one year, subject to re-appointment. The nature, amount and the method of collection of the various rates, taxes, tolls and fees were defined and several conservancy clauses were enacted in the place of the optional rules and the bye-laws which the councillors were empowered to make under the old law[1].

It was under this Act that the Coimbatore Municipality came into existence in 1866. It had the District Magistrate as the president and the range officer of the Public Works Department as one of their councillors. Excluding these officers there were 11 councillors of whom 6 were officials and 5 were non-officials. These six officers were the Head Assistant Magistrate, the Superintendent of Police, the Zillah Surgeon, the Tahsildar, the District Munsif and the Sheristadar[2]. The municipality derived its income from a tax on houses and buildings, tolls, a tax on carriages and animals, fees for registration of carts, fees for licensing slaughter houses, cart stands and offensive trades, fines and contributions from Government. It spent a major portion of this income on the police and the rest on roads, buildings, wells, and sanitation. To give an idea of its income, it had an income of Rs. 29,000 in 1868 and Rs. 32,000 in 1869. The municipality seems to have done much to improve conservancy[3].

The Act of 1865 had hardly been brought into operation in the State, when the necessity of extending its scope and revising its provisions began to be felt. It was found that beyond collecting the taxes fixed compulsorily by the Government, the inhabitants had shown hardly any enthusiasm for providing for lighting, water supply, etc. It was also found that the voluntary Education Cess Act IV of 1863 had practically remained a dead letter. In order to set right these matters, a new Act known as the Towns Improvement Act III of 1871 was passed which included the above mentioned objects among those to which the funds raised under the Act should ordinarily be applicable. At the same time the Government withdrew the grant-in-aid of 25 per cent of the compulsory expenditure which under the Act of 1865 they were bound to contribute. This was done partly for financial reasons and partly for consistency, as there was no justification for giving such a grant to the municipalities when it was denied to the local boards which were being then formed under the Local Funds Act IV of 1871. By this change the municipalities gained in the direction of having no longer to contribute the police charges;

1 *Manual of Madras Administration* by C.D. Maclean, Vol. I, 1885—Footnote on pages 225–226.

Standing Information regarding the Official Administration of the Madras Presidency by C. D. Maclean, 1877, pages 207–209.

2 G.O. No. 1187, Public, dated 20th November 1866.
G.O. No. 1044, Public, dated 26th August 1868.
G.O. No. 886, Public, dated 20th June 1869.

3 G.O. No. 1044, Public, dated 26th August 1868.
G.O. No. 866, Public, dated 30th June 1869.

they lost, however, in having had thrown on them four new charges, namely, those for hospitals and dispensaries, those for schools, those for birth and death registration and those for vaccination. It was at the same time provided that the Government might appoint any person whatever as a councillor even though he might not be an inhabitant of the town, subject only to the limitation as to the number of officials on each council. This provision was made to enable the Government to appoint an European Officer as a working member of the municipality. The qualification for the members was made more elastic. Their term of office was increased from one year to three years. The number of ex-officio members was reduced from 3 to 2, the Collector of the district being substituted for the District Magistrate as president and the local revenue officer taking the place of the local magistrate and the range officer of the Public Works Department. The appointment of the vice-president was taken out of the president's hands and vested in the Government. Provision was made for the election of the councillors by the rate-payers under rules that might be framed by the Government and a similar provision was also made for the election of the vice-president. The Government's contribution of 25 per cent of the sanctioned expenditure having been withdrawn, and there being no police charges to provide for, there was no longer the same necessity for giving the Government the power to fix the amount of taxation and to levy it through the president if the councillors failed to do so. Consequently the old provisions made in this regard were not re-enacted. The general right, however, to fix the amount of taxation was still maintained by the Government by providing that the Government might pass such orders as they deemed fit on the annual budgets of the municipalities. Provision was likewise made for the appointment by the Government of inspecting officers to superintend the working of the Act. The result of the Act of 1871 was to place the councillors in a more responsible position and to diminish the Government interference in matters of detail, while the provisions rendering permissive election of councillors and of vice-presidents furnished the machinery for granting a larger measure of independence than before[1].

This Act was introduced not only in Coimbatore but also in Erode which was then growing into importance. The Coimbatore Municipality now came to consist of 23 councillors of whom 1 was an ex-officio councillor and 22 were nominated councillors; and of these 10 were officials and the rest were non-officials. The Erode Municipality was

1 *Manual of Administration of the Madras Presidency* by C.D. Maclean, Vol. I, 1885—*See* footnote on page 226.

For the provisions of Act III of 1871—See *Fort St. George Gazette.*

constituted consisting of 16 councillors of whom 2 were ex-officio and 14 nominated councillors and of these 8 were officials and the rest were non-officials[1]. The income of both these municipalities was derived from a tax on houses, a tax on vehicles, a tax on carts, tolls, fees, fines, endowments and a contribution from the Local Fund Board. To convey an idea of their receipts and expenditure, in 1874–75, for instance, the Coimbatore Municipality collected and spent Rs. 37,200 while the Erode Municipality collected and spent Rs. 8,916. The municipal funds were no longer spent on police; they were spent on roads, conservancy, sanitation, lighting, education, hospitals and dispensaries, vaccination and registration of births and deaths. It was reported that the working of both the municipalities was quite satisfactory[2].

About this time an interesting discussion took place on the introduction of the elective system in the municipalities. Lord Hobart, the Governor, stood for the system of election and stressed the need for giving immediate effect to the permissive provisions of the Act. But his colleagues were opposed to the measure, as the people were evincing but little interest and still less in taxing themselves for the common good. It was eventually agreed to try the experiment as regards half the councillors in ten selected towns. This experiment, however, was not tried in any of the Municipalities in Coimbatore. Meanwhile the financial pressure having become great, largely owing to the famines of 1876-1878, the Government once more went back to the policy of 1865 of taxing the people for the maintenance of the town police. Act VII of 1878 was accordingly passed, making the municipalities liable to 75 per cent of the police charges. This state of things, however, lasted only for 3 years. In 1881 the Government of India gave it as their opinion that the municipalities might be relieved of the charges for police on the ground that it was a department " over which they had no control and in the efficient and economical expenditures of which they had but little direct interest and no immediate responsibility ". At the same time they considered that an equivalent burden on education, medical aid and public works of local interests might be transferred to the municipalities together with such control over the details of expenditure as might be deemed necessary. In 1882 a committee was appointed by the local Government to go into the whole question of local administration and on its

1 Report of the Committee on Local Self Government, 1882, pages 128–129.

2 G.O. No. 1100, Financial, dated 20th May 1875.
G.O. No. 1081, Financial, dated 18th May 1875.

recommendation, a new Act, entitled the Madras District Municipalities Act, IV of 1884 was passed[1].

This Act superseded the Towns Improvement Act of 1871 and for the first time introduced the term " municipality " into the title, the former Acts being styled only as Towns Improvement Acts. It also adopted the new terms, so well known today, ' Council ' and ' Councillors ' in lieu of the old terms ' Commission ' and ' Commissioners ' employed in the earlier Acts. Under the provisions made in this Act the Government could withdraw the Act from municipalities which had become reduced in population and importance by famine, pestilence, floods or other calamities and thus subject them to lighter taxation and less onerous duties of unions under the local boards. The municipal council was to consist of not less than 12 persons. Their term of office was to be three years. The revenue officer in charge of the division of the district in which any municipality was situated, was to be an ex-officio councillor. All the other councillors might be appointed by the Government, or with the permission of the Government; any portion not exceeding three-fourths of them might be elected by the tax payers but more than one-fourth of the whole number of the councillors might be salaried officers of the Government, unless they had been elected as councillors by the tax payers. Each council was to have a chairman who might be either appointed by the Government, or, with the permission of the Government, elected, by the councillors from among their own number. He was to be the executive officer of the council answering to the former vice-president and was to be responsible for carrying out all the purposes of the Act. The Government were to have the power to remove a chairman or municipal councillor at any time. The Collector was to have emergency powers over the municipality. The position of the Government servants lent to the municipalities was defined and the position of the municipal servants was improved. The only new tax authorised by this Act was the water tax to be levied at the rate of 4 per cent on the annual rent value of houses and lands and applicable only to the purposes of water-supply by means of works of more or less permanent character.

The main sources of revenue of the municipalities at this time consisted of a tax on professions; a tax on lands and buildings not exceeding 7½ per cent on their annual value; a water tax as mentioned already not exceeding 4 per cent on their annual value; a tax on vehicles, tolls on vehicles and animals entering the municipal limits and licenses to carry on offensive or dangerous trades. Other sources consisted of fees or rents for the use

1 *Manual of Administration of the Madras Presidency* by C.D. Maclean, 1885—*See* footnotes on pages 226–228.

of municipal gardens, choultries, markets, slaughter houses, cart stands, etc., fines and forfeitures, payments for municipal services, and grants-in-aid from State funds. The revenues so raised were applicable to the construction and repair of streets, bridges, etc., the construction and maintenance of hospitals, dispensaries, choultries, markets, tanks, wells, drains, sewers, etc., the training and employment of medical practitioners, vaccinators and sanitary inspectors; the registration of births and deaths, the lighting and cleaning of streets; the diffusion of education and, with this in view, the construction, repair and maintenance of schools either wholly or by means of grants-in-aid and the inspection of schools and the training of teachers [1].

This Act came into force in Coimbatore in 1885 [2]. Under it the position of the two municipalities in the district became as follows; Coimbatore came to have 20 councillors of whom 15 were elected and 5 were nominated and Erode came to have 12 councillors of whom 4 were elected and 8 were nominated. Their income was derived from taxes on property, professions, vehicles and animals, from tolls, travellers' bungalows, avenues, markets and fisheries and license fees and fines and proceeds from the sale of street refuse. Their revenues and expenditure showed a marked increase; the Coimbatore municipality collected and spent Rs. 57,316, while the Erode municipality collected and spent Rs. 22,501[3].

For some years the district saw no new municipalities. In 1915–20, however, four new municipalities were constituted, that of Dharapuram in 1916, that of Tiruppur in 1917, that of Udumalpet in 1917, and that of Pollachi in 1920. The strength of the first three municipalities was fixed at 12 nominated councillors while the strength of the fourth was fixed at 16 nominated councillors [4].

Meanwhile an important change in municipal administration was made in the State. As a result of the recommendations of the Royal

1. *Manual of Administration of the Madras Presidency* by C. D. Maclean, 1885—Footnotes on pages 229–230 and pages 228–243.

For the provisions of Madras Act IV of 1884—*See* the *Fort St. George Gazette*.

2 G.O. No. 597, Finance, dated 19th March 1885.

3 G.O. No. 1069, Municipal, dated 26th July 1901.
G.O. No. 1093, Municipal, dated 30th July 1901.

4 G.O. No. 673, Municipal, dated 3rd May 1915.
G.O. No. 1647, Municipal, dated 18th October 1915.
G.O. No. 1850, Municipal, dated 27th October 1916.
G.O. No. 2062, Municipal, dated 4th December 1916.
G.O. No. 1401, Municipal, dated 18th August 1917.
G.O. No. 1527, Municipal, dated 7th September 1917.
G.O. No. 2037, Local and Municipal, dated 27th November 1917.
G.O. No. 1332, Municipal, dated 24th September 1920.

Commission on Decentralisation, the Madras District Municipalities Act V of 1920 was passed for repealing the Act of 1884 and for increasing the elected proportion of the members of the municipal councils as well as the resources and powers of the municipalities. In that year also an Inspector of Municipal Council was appointed to supervise the working of the municipalities. The Act of 1920 provided that the Government might, by notification, declare any town or village as a municipality or abolish any municipality. The municipal council was to consist of 16 members in municipalities with a population not exceeding 20,000; 20 in those between 20,000 and 30,000; 24 in those between 30,000 and 40,000; 28 in those between 40,000 and 50,000; 32 in those between 50,000 and 1,00,000; and 36 in those exceeding 1,00,000. The elected portion of the councillors was not to be less than three fourths of the total number; the rest were to be appointed by the Government having regard to the representation of Muslims and other minority communities. The term of the councillors was to be three years. They were to elect the chairman and vice-chairman; the former might, however, be also appointed by the Government. The council might appoint standing committees or special committees for carrying out the purposes of the Act. The Collector of the District might exercise control over the council in cases of default or emergency; and the Government might suspend the execution of any resolutions of the council, appoint officers of their own to superintend the municipalities or remove a chairman or dissolve or supersede a council in cases of misconduct. The council might and, if directed by the Government should appoint a health officer and a municipal engineer. The Government might also lend their own officers to the council.

Every municipal council might levy a property tax, a tax on companies, a profession tax, a vehicle tax and tolls on vehicles and animals entering the municipality. The rates of taxes were not fixed, latitude being given in this matter to the council. It might also with the previous sanction of the Government levy a surcharge on income tax in lieu of the tax on companies and of the profession tax as well as a pilgrim tax. The Government were to appoint auditors to audit the municipal funds. All streets, public water courses, wells, tanks, etc., were to vest in the council and the Board of Revenue might transfer to it also the control of endowments. The council might, with the sanction of the Government, construct and maintain water works. It should provide for lighting public streets, drainage, latrines, scavenging, removal of rubbish, etc. It should maintain and repair the streets, regulate the construction of buildings, take precautions against outbreaks of fire and issue licenses for various purposes, like the keeping of animals, the starting of industries and factories and the running of markets and slaughter houses. It should maintain a register of vital statistics and arrange for the prevention of diseases and for compulsory vaccination [1]. Nor is this all. Besides these duties imposed by the District Municipalities Act it was made to provide for the expansion of elementary education by the levy of an education tax under the Elementary Education Act VIII of 1920 [2].

The District Municipalities Act and the Elementary Education Act of 1920 were introduced in all the six municipalities of the district in 1921. The position of the six municipalities now became as follows; in Coimbatore 32 councillors, in Erode 20 councillors, in Dharapuram, Tiruppur, Udumalpet and Pollachi, 16 councillors each. Three-fourths of all these councillors were elected by the rate-payers and one-fourth were nominated by the Government. The municipalities levied the taxes permitted by the Acts and spent them as usual, but in a larger measure, on public works, sanitation, lighting, public health, medical aid, vital statistics and education. Both their revenues and expenditure now considerably increased. They amounted in Coimbatore to Rs. 1,81,523 and Rs. 1,79,984; in Erode to Rs. 91,023 and Rs. 1,05,015; in Dharapuram to Rs. 50,249 and Rs. 50,249; in Tiruppur to Rs. 54,245 and Rs. 54,071; in Udumalpet to Rs. 54,657 and Rs. 54,657 and in Pollachi to Rs. 44,853 and Rs. 34,009 [3].

The District Municipalities Act of 1920 was modified in some important respects by the Act X of 1930. This Act did away with nomination and laid down that every municipal councillor should be elected. It, however, provided for the reservation of seats for minority communities, Muslims, Indian Christians, Harijans, Europeans, Anglo-Indians and Women. It also removed the disqualification of women to stand for election and extended the franchise to every person assessed to any tax to the Government of India, or the Local Government or any other local authority. It made the office of the chairman and vice-chairman elective and provided for the provincialisation of any class of municipal officers. It likewise provided for the passing of votes of no-confidence in the chairman and vice-chairman and for the adjudication of disputes between local bodies [4].

---

1 G.O. No. 64, Legislative, dated 21st June 1920.

2 For Act VIII of 1920—See *Fort St. George Gazette.*

3 G.O. No. 1254, Local and Municipal, dated 27th July 1922.
G.O. No. 1867, Local and Municipal, dated 10th October 1922.
G.O. No. 2051, Local and Municipal, dated 25th October 1922.
G.O. No. 2089, Local and Municipal, dated 30th October 1922.
G.O. No. 2355, Local and Municipal, dated 29th November 1922.
G.O. No. 2573, Local and Municipal, dated 20th December 1922.
G.O. No. 65, Local and Municipal, dated 10th January 1923.

4 For Act X of 1930—*See* the *Fort St. George Gazette.*

Subsequent municipal legislation ran on lines similar to those chalked out in the case of local boards, which we have already seen. The Motor Vehicles Taxation Act abolished the levy of tolls and tax on motor vehicles in municipalities, and compensated the municipalities out of the proceeds of the tax on motor vehicles collected by the Government (1931). The Government were empowered to appoint commissioners to the municipalities (1933) [1]. The relevant portions of the electoral rolls of the Legislative Assembly were prescribed as the electoral rolls for the municipal elections also (1938) [2]. The Government were authorised to secure ultimate control over electrical undertakings managed by municipal councils and to appoint Municipal Electrical Engineers (1938) [3]. Municipal chairman and vice-chairman removed from office by the Government were debarred from standing for election again for either of the offices for a period of six months except when ordinary elections took place (1939) [4]. The municipal elections were postponed and the term of office of the existing councillors was extended (1940). Persons who were in arrears to the municipalities were debarred from standing for elections [5]. The Collectors were empowered to nominate any municipal councillors to discharge the functions of the chairman or vice-chairman who failed to discharge their duties (1944)[6]. The Government were empowered to direct the municipal councils which were levying a low rate of property tax, to increase the tax (1944)[7]. The municipal councils were authorised to levy a surcharge on stamp duty payable under the Indian Stamp Act, in respect of the instrument of sale, gift and mortgage with possession (1945)[8] and transfers by way of exchange and lease in perpetuity (1950)[9]. All important and military roads in the municipalities were transferred to the Highways Department (1946)[10]. And finally, the provisions contained in the Act of 1930 relating to the reservation of seats for Muslims, Indian Christians and Europeans were deleted, those relating to the Anglo-Indians, Harijans and women, however, being left intact (1950)[11].

The elections to the municipalities which were postponed from time to time during the war period were held in 1947. In the meantime two new

---

1 Madras Administration Report for 1932–33, page 22.
2 *Idem* for 1937–38, page 6.
3 *Idem* for 1938–39, page 5.
4 Madras Administration Report for 1939–40, page 4.
5 *Madras in* 1940, pages 3 and 4.
6 *Madras in* 1944, page 2.
7 *Madras in* 1944, page 3.
8 *Madras in* 1945, page 5.
9 *Madras in* 1950, page 6.
10 *Madras in* 1945, pages 5–6.
11 *Madras in* 1950, pages 9–10.

municipalities were constituted in the district, namely, the Mettupalayam Municipality in 1948 and the Gobichettipalayam Municipality in 1949, the former with a strength of 16 councillors and the latter with a strength of 20 councillors [1]. The revision of the wards and the reallocation of the seats were, about this time made in the several existing municipalities. In 1956, the eight municipalities in the district presented the following picture.

The Coimbatore Municipality had 36 councillors, of whom six occupied the reserved seats. It levied a property tax, a profession tax, a tax on vehicles and animals and a tax on carts and derived also an income from surcharge on stamp duty, entertainments tax, motor vehicles tax and Government grants under several heads. Its receipts amounted to Rs. 1,31,07,647 and its expenditure to Rs. 1,30,30,878. It maintained 83½ miles of roads lit partly by electricity and partly by kerosene. It maintained thirty-two elementary schools with an average strength of 15,777 pupils as well as five high schools, four middle schools, one deaf and dumb school, one hostel, one library and twenty-four reading rooms. It ran five maternity and child welfare centres, one infectious diseases hospital, nine dispensaries and these dispensaries treated 5,27,522 out-patients. It had a First-class Health Officer, one Assistant Health Officer, two selection grade Sanitary Inspectors and twenty Sanitary Inspectors. It had five daily markets, two cart-stands and two slaughter-houses. It had also eleven town planning schemes, namely, (1) the Red Fields Scheme, (2) the Ramanathapuram Scheme, (3) the Pappanaickenpalayam Scheme, (4) the Rathnasabapathypuram (R. S. Puram) Scheme, (5) the Power House Scheme, (6) the Service Reservoir or the Goshen Park Scheme, (7) the West of Thadagam Road Scheme, (8) the Race Course Scheme, (9) the South of Kempatty Colony Scheme, (10) the Raja Vaikal area Scheme and (11) the Distillery area Scheme. Of these, the first six schemes were under execution, while the other schemes were under consideration [2].

The Erode Municipality had thirty-two councillors of whom five occupied reserved seats. It too levied a property tax, a profession tax and a tax on vehicles and animals and derived an income from surcharge on stamp duty, entertainment tax, motor vehicles tax and Government grants under various heads. Its receipts were Rs. 16,69,099 and its expenditure was Rs. 13,48,149. It maintained 34 miles of roads lit by electricity, seventeen elementary schools (of which two were exclusively intended for Muslim girls) with an average strength of 4,705 pupils, one

1 G.O. No. 1662, Local Administration, dated 4th September 1948.
G.O. No. 1698, Local Administration, dated 12th August 1949.

2 G.O. No. 241, Local Administration, dated 11th February 1958.

high school and one library and five reading rooms. It had two ayurvedic dispensaries of which one was a general one and the other exclusively for women and children. They all treated 41,703 out-patients. It had a second-class Health Officer, six Sanitary Inspectors and four Health Assistants. It had one maternity home, two maternity and child welfare centres, two daily markets and one weekly market, two cart-stands, one bus-stand and two slaughter-houses. It had six town-planning schemes under consideration [1].

The Dharapuram Municipality had 20 councillors, of whom two were occupying reserved seats. It levied a property tax, a profession tax, a tax on vehicles and animals and a cart tax and derived an income from surcharge on stamp duty, the entertainment tax, the motor vehicles tax and Government grants under various heads. Its receipts were Rs. 3,75,427 and its expenditure was Rs. 3,27,199. It maintained 16½ miles of roads lit by electricity, six elementary schools (of which one was for Muslim girls) with a total strength of 1,593 and one high school with a strength of 285 pupils. It had a Second-Class Health Officer, two Sanitary Inspectors and one child welfare centre and one ayurvedic dispensary which treated 90,152 out-patients. It had two daily markets, one weekly market, one bus-stand and one slaughter-house [2].

The Tiruppur Municipality had thirty-two councillors of whom four occupied reserved seats. It levied like the other Municipalities, a property tax, a profession tax, a tax on vehicles and animals and a cart tax, and derived also an income from surcharge on stamp duty, entertainment tax, the motor vehicles tax and Government grants under various heads. Its receipts amounted to Rs. 94,31,107 and its expenditure to Rs. 92,63,899. It maintained 40 miles of roads mostly lit by electricity, nineteen elementary schools with 6,380 pupils, four high schools (of which two were for girls), with 3,145 pupils, one middle school, one hostel, one public library and six reading rooms. It had a dispensary which treated 11,840 out-patients and two maternity and child welfare centres. It had a Second class Health Officer and five Sanitary Inspectors. It maintained one daily market, two weekly markets, two cart-stands and one slaughter house. And it had five town-planning schemes under consideration [3].

The Udumalpet Municipality had twenty councillors of whom two occupied the reserved seats. Its receipts were Rs. 4,74,696 and its expenditure was Rs. 4,05,181. It maintained 14 miles of roads lit by electricity.

---

1 G. O. No. 427, Local Administration, dated 10th March 1958.
The names of the town-planning schemes are not available.

2 G.O. No. 100, Loal Administration, dated 22nd January 1958.

3 G.O. No. 149, Local Administration, datod 30th January 1958.
The names of the town-planning schemes are not available.

It maintained 8 elementary schools with a strength of 2,708 pupils, one middle school with a strength of 264 pupils and two reading rooms. It had a Health Officer, two Sanitary Inspectors and two Health Assistants. It had one weekly market and one slaughter-house [1].

The Pollachi Municipality had twenty-eight councillors, six of whom were occupying reserved seats. Its receipts were Rs. 15,98,236 and its expenditure was Rs. 16,73,613. It maintained twenty miles of roads lit by electricity. It maintained fifteen elementary schools with a strength of 5,463 pupils, three high schools (of which one was for girls) with a strength of 2,725 pupils, three libraries and three reading rooms. It ran three dispensaries one for women and children, one Allopathic and one Siddha, which treated 1,66,283 out-patients. It ran also three maternity and child welfare centres. It had a Health Officer, four Sanitary Inspectors and three Health Assistants. It maintained one daily market, one weekly market, one cart-stand and one slaughter-house. It had three town-planning schemes under consideration, namely (1) the market by-pass scheme, (2) the Palladam Road Extension Scheme and (3) the Kottur Road Extension Scheme. Besides these there was also a detailed town-planning scheme under consideration [2].

In the Mettupalayam Municipality there were twenty councillors, four of whom occupied reserved seats. Its receipts amounted to Rs. 5,53,275 and its expenditure to Rs. 5,82,342. It had under its control twenty-two miles of roads, part of which were lit by electricity. It ran five elementary schools with a strength of 953 pupils, one girls' high school with a strength of 188 pupils and four reading rooms. It also ran one Indian medicine dispensary which treated 29,257 out-patients. It had one Health Officer and two Sanitary Inspectors. It maintained one daily market and two slaughter houses. It had four town-planning schemes under consideration [3].

In Gobichettipalayam, the Municipal council consisted of 20 councillors, of whom four occupied reserved seats. Its receipts amounted o Rs. 10,82,370 and its expenditure to Rs. 10,23,995. It had under its control, 32 miles of roads partly lit by electricity. It ran seven elementary schools with 1,527 pupils, one high school with 281 pupils, one adult literary school and four reading rooms. It had two Sanitary Inspectors and one Health Assistant. It had two town-planning schemes under consideration, namely the Gobichettipalayam North Scheme and the Gobichettipalayam West Scheme [4].

---

1 G.O. No. 1823, Local Administration, dated 16th December 1957.

2 G.O. No. 1792, Local Administration, dated 12th December 1957.

3 G.O. No. 138, Local Administration, dated 29th January 1958. The names of the town-planning schemes are not available.

4 G.O. No. 50, Local Administration, dated 6th January 1958.

CHAPTER XV.

LAW AND ORDER.

The seeds of the present system of law and order, of civil and criminal justice as well as the magistracy and the police were first sown in Coimbatore, as in other districts, by what is known as the Cornwallis System. This system was originally established in Bengal in 1793 and subsequently extended to Madras in 1802. Under this system, a series of Regulations were passed in this State for establishing a hierarchy of civil and criminal courts and for defining their powers. First among these Company's Courts at the top there was the Sadr and Foujdari Adalat having jurisdiction over all the districts, below it there were the four Provincial and Circuit Courts, each having jurisdiction over a group of districts, and below these Courts, the Zillah Courts. The higher courts had both civil and criminal jurisdiction. The Sadr Adalat was so called when it sat as a civil court, but when it sat as a criminal court it was called the Foujdari Adalat. Similarly, the Provincial Court was so called when it sat as a civil court, but when it sat as a criminal or sessions court it was called the Court of Circuit. The Zillah Court was both a civil and a magisterial court and the Zillah Judge was both a civil judge and a magistrate. The magisterial powers till then exercised by the Collector were transferred to him. So also were transferred to him from the Collector the powers of control over the police. The police was, at the same time, reorganised in several districts by replacing the village watchmen by Darogas and Thanadars. This system was, however, not applicable to the Madras City where there were a Crown Court called the Supreme Court (1801), some Justices of the Peace, a Poligar and his police peons and later a Superintendent of Police and his Daffadars, Harkaras and Peons. [1]

The Cornwallis System underwent some important changes first in 1816 when, on the recommendations of Sir Thomas Munro and the Court of Directors, the magisterial powers and the control of the police were transferred from the Zillah Judge again to the Collector and Indian agency was more and more employed in judicial administration, and next, in 1843 when the Provincial and Circuit Courts were abolished and their powers were vested in a new Zillah Judge called the Civil and Sessions Judge.

---

1 Report on the Madras Records by H. Dodwell, 1916, pages 60 and 62 to 74.

But for these changes, it continued to retain its old lineaments till 1862 when the Sadr and Foujdari Adalat as well as the Supreme Court were abolished and their powers transferred to the High Court. About this time came also the several codes, which substantively changed the character of judicial administration, civil as well as criminal. We may, for convenience, first trace the history of the civil and criminal justice in the district separately till about 1862 and thereafter describe the changes subsequently introduced. We may also, for convenience, trace the history of the police separately after dealing with the civil and criminal justice.

It was not till 1799 that the Coimbatore district came into the hands of the company; and it was not till 1806 that the District received the blessings of a regular system of justice. From 1799 to 1806 the Collector of Coimbatore administered civil as well as criminal justice and controlled the police assisted by his revenue subordinates. In 1806, however, the Cornwallis Code having been introduced in the District, these duties were transferred from him to the Zillah Judge whose court was established at Dharapuram.[1] The jurisdiction of the Zillah Court extended not only over the entire district of Coimbatore, but also over the Dindigul palayams of Ayakkudi, Idaiyakottai, Mambarai, Palni, Reddiambadi and Virupakshi and the taluk of Karur which was then included in the Coimbatore district [2]. The Zillah Judge came under the control of the Provincial and Circuit Court of the Southern Division which then had its headquarters at Tiruchirappalli.

In administering civil justice the Zillah Judge was assisted by a Kazi and a Mufti as well as a Pandit. He followed the Muslim and Hindu Law as expounded by these Law Officers in all suits regarding succession, inheritance, marriage and caste and all religious usages and institutions. Where however neither legal opinions, nor the Regulations, nor the works on Hindu and Muslim Law prescribed the law, he proceeded according to justice, equity and good conscience. This meant that at a time when there was no law of contract, no law of succession, no law of administration of deceased estates, etc., he had a very wide field within which to exercise his discretion. [3] The procedure that he followed in his court as well as the procedure that his subordinate judicial officers followed in their courts

---

1 Judicial Consultations, dated 13th and 14th May 1806, pages 1007, 1054–1055.

Idem, dated 29th July 1806, pages 2264–2265.

2 Judicial Consultations, dated 14th May 1806, pages 1054–1055. Regulation XI of 1808.

3 *Manual of Administration of the Madras Presidency* by C. D. Maclean, Vol. I. 1885, page 270—*See* foot-note.

was prescribed by the Regulations.[1] And he was given the benefit of a Government Pleader,[2] while the parties were given the benefit of employing licensed pleaders or vakils to argue their suits.

The Zillah Judge, to begin with, had a Register's (Registrar's) Court and some Native (Commissioners') Courts under him. The Commissioners were chosen from among respectable Indians belonging to certain classes like land-owners, jagirdars, tradesmen, Kazis etc. They were appointed by commissions issued under the seal and signature of the Zillah Judge with the previous approval of the Sadr Adalat; and the number of Commissioners to be appointed for each Zillah was left to be determined by the Zillah Judge. They acted in three capacities. They acted as Referees in suits for money or other personal property not exceeding Rs. 80 in value, referred to them by the Zillah Judge. They also acted as Arbitrators in any suit referred to them by the parties, without the intervention of the court under a written arbitration bond. They acted likewise as Munsiffs in suits against under-renters and ryots in jagirs.[3] The Registrar had powers to try for money or other personal property not exceeding Rs. 200 in value, suits for revenue-paying land the annual produce of which did not exceed Rs. 200, and suits for revenue-free land the annual produce of which did not exceed Rs. 20. His decisions were final in suits not exceeding Rs. 25 in value subject to the discretionary power of revision of the Zillah Judge on the ground of obvious error or injustice. In suits above that value, a second appeal lay to the Provincial Court.[4] The Zillah Judge had powers to try all other suits, but his decisions were final only in suits for money or other personal property not exceeding Rs. 1,000, in suits for revenue-free land the annual produce of which did not exceed Rs. 20 and in suits for zamindari or other revenue-paying land the annual produce of which did not exceed Rs. 200. In 1809, however, all decrees of the Zillah Judge in original trials were made appealable to the Provincial Court.[5]

The Provincial Court, which consisted of three judges and sat at Tiruchirappalli, tried appeals from the Zillah Courts under it as well as original suits referred to it by the Sadr Adalat. Its decisions were final

---

1 *Idem*, page 271—*See* foot-note.
Also Regulations III, XIII, XIV and XV of 1802.

2 Regulation II of 1802, Section 15 and Regulation X of 1802, Sections 22 and 24.

3 Regulation XVI of 1802.

4 Regulation XII of 1802, sections 6, 9 and 10.

5 Regulation II of 1802, section 21.
Regulation VII of 1809, section 24.

when the amount did not exceed Rs. 100 in suits for revenue-paying lands or zamindari lands the annual produce of which exceeded Rs. 1,000 and in suits for money or other personal property above Rs. 5,000 in value.[1]

The Sadr Adalat as constituted in 1802 consisted of the Governor and Council.[2] In 1806 its constitution was altered, the Governor functioning as the Chief Judge and the other two judges being selected from among the covenanted civil servants of the Company other than the members of the Council.[3] In 1807 some changes were again made. The Governor ceased to be the Chief Judge and the latter came to be appointed by the Governor first from among the members of the covenanted civil service outside his Council and then from among the members of his own Council. The Commander-in-Chief also came to be appointed as one of the Judges, and three other puisne judges came to be appointed from among the covenanted civil servants.[4] The Sadr Adalat had powers to decide finally all suits up to Rs. 45,000 and above that sum an appeal lay to the Governor-General in Council.[5]

In 1809 the jurisdiction of the Registrar of the Zillah Judge was extended to suits for money or other personal property not exceeding Rs. 500 in value, to suits for revenue-paying lands the annual produce of which did not exceed Rs. 500 to suits for revenue-free lands the annual produce of which did not exceed Rs. 150 and to suits for other property the value of which did not exceed Rs. 500. But his powers of hearing appeals were reduced, it being laid down that no appeals from 'Native Commissioners' were to be referred to him.[6] His powers of final decision were also abolished,[7] but in suits in which the Zillah Judge reversed his decree or disallowed a sum not exceeding Rs. 100, an appeal was made to lie to the Provincial Court.[8] In the same year, the Hindu and Muslim Law Officers of the Zillah Court came to be appointed as Sadr Amins or Head Referees,[9] with powers to try suits referred to them by the Zillah Judge for personal

1 Regulation IV of 1802, sections 6, 7 and 12.
Regulation V of 1802, section 10.

2 Regulation V of 1802, section 2.
Regulation VIII of 1802, section 3.

3 Regulation IV of 1806, section 3.

4 Regulation I of 1807, section 2.
Regulation III of 1807, section 3.

5 Regulation V. of 1802, sections 31–36.

6 Regulation VII of 1809.

7 Regulation VII of 1806, section 6.

8 Regulation VII of 1809, section 8.

9 Regulation X of 1809, section 2.

property for Rs. 100, for revenue-paying lands the annual produce of which was Rs. 100 and for revenue-free lands the annual produce of which did not exceed Rs. 10.[1] The Zillah Judge's decision now became final in all appeals from the decisions passed by the 'Native Commissioners' but an appeal was made to lie from his decision in suits tried by him in the first instance to the Provincial Court.[2] The Provincial Court was also authorized to admit special appeals in all cases from his decision where a regular appeal might not lie to it from his decrees, if such decrees appeared erroneous or unjust, or if the case was considered important.[3] Similar powers of admitting special appeals were also granted to the Sadr Adalat.[4] At the same time the Provincial Court was given original jurisdiction in suits above Rs. 5,000 and in suits for revenue-free land the annual produce of which exceeded Rs. 500.[5]

In 1811 the Zillah Court was transferred from Dharapuram to Coimbatore.[6] In 1813, when the District was on the eve of some important changes, the state of civil justice was as follows. The Zillah Judge tried in that year 9 original suits and 4 appeals from the Native Commissioners, the Registrar tried 56 original suits and the 'Native Commissioners' tried 2,107 original suits. Of these suits, 17 suits were adjusted by *razinamah* by the Registrar and 1,752 suits by the 'Native Commissioners'. The value of the property decreed in all these suits amounted to 5,854 pagodas. As to the arrears of suits, on 1st January 1814 there were 28 appeals and 15 original suits pending in the Zillah Court, 106 original suits in the Registrar's Court and 135 original suits in the Courts of the 'Native Commissioners'. The property in litigation in all these courts was valued at 11,235 pagodas.[7]

Then followed a period of changes, of the introduction of new courts and the enlargement of the powers of the existing courts. The credit for all this goes in a large measure to Colonel (later Sir) Thomas Munro who saw with unerring foresight the imperative need for increasing Indian agency in administration and entrusting it with wider powers. He believed that in a populous country like India justice could be well dispensed only with the aid of Indians themselves. He observed that it

1 Regulation VII of 1809, section 9 (1).

2 Regulation VII of 1809, sections 23–24.

3 Regulation VII of 1809, sections 25–26.

4 Regulation VII of 1809, sections 28–29.

5 Regulation XII of 1809, sections 2–3.

6 Judicial Consultations, dated 26th July 1811, pages 3516–3517.

7 Selection of Papers from the Records of the East India House, Vol.II, Part I, 1820, pages 284 and 286.

was absurd to suppose that the Indians were so corrupt as to be altogether unfit to be entrusted with the discharge of important duties and that their place could ever be supplied by a few foreigners imperfectly acquainted with their customs and languages. He urged, therefore, that as much as possible of the administration of justice should be entrusted to the Indians, and that the European Judges should only watch over their proceedings and see that they executed their duty properly. He pointed out that it was because the existing system ignored these fundamentals, that vast arrears of suits had accumulated in the Zillah Courts. He had to contend with an immense amount of opposition from his superiors. But the Court of Directors supported his views, appointed him as the head of a Judicial Commission to reorganize the existing system and, upon his recommendations, ordered a number of important changes in civil as well as criminal justice and police. [1]

As a result of all this, in the field of civil justice, from 1816-1817onwards District Munsifs and Village Munsifs came to be appointed in this as in other districts. In 1816 five District Munsif's Courts were ordered to be established in the District.[2] They appear to have been set up at Cheyur, Coimbatore, Dalavaypatti, Karur and Udumalpet. [3] The jurisdiction of the District Munsifs included one or more taluks. The Village Munsifs, who were also the heads of villages, had powers to try and finally determine all suits for money or other personal property not exceeding Rs. 10 in value. The Karnams assisted the Village Munsifs by conducting and recording the court proceedings and by acting as assessors, although the responsibility for the decision naturally lay solely on the Village Munsifs. [4] The Village Munsifs could also assemble Village Panchayats for the adjudication of civil suits of any amount (except suits for damages for personal injuries) within their village jurisdiction; and the decisions of such panchayats were generally made final. [5] The Village Munsifs could moreover act as arbitrators to determine suits where the value of money or personal property did not exceed Rs. 100 whenever both the parties voluntarily agreed to such arbitration. [6] The District Munsif was empowered to try suits for land and personal property (except for revenue-free lands wherein their powers were restricted to lands the annual produce

---

1 For full details, *See* selections from Papers from the Records at East India House, Vol. II, Part I, 1820, page 105 *et seq.*

2 Judicial Consultations, dated 15th July 1816, pages 2635 to 2645.

3 *Manual of Coimbatore District*, Vol. II, page 236.
Judicial Consultations, dated 20th March 1827, pages 827-31.

4 Regulation VI of 1816, sections 2, 3, 5 and 10.

5 Regulation V of 1816, sections 2-12.

6 Regulation IV of 1816, section 27.

of which did not exceed Rs. 20) upto Rs. 200 and his decisions were made final in such suits upto Rs. 20 and in suits for revenue-free lands the annual produce of which did not exceed Rs. 2.[1] Above these sums an appeal lay from his decisions to the Zillah Court whose decision was regarded as final.[2] The District Munsif could also try any suits for damages referred to him but not suits filed *in forma pauperis*. He could likewise assemble District Panchayats on lines similar to those of the Village Panchayats.[3] These District Panchayats could try suits without limitation as to value, except suits for damages for personal injuries, if the parties agreed in writing to abide by their decisions. Such decisions were not open to appeal but were liable to be set aside and annulled, if partiality or corruption was proved to the satisfaction of the Provincial Court. The parties in such cases had the option of having recourse to another District Panchayat or any other competent court. The District Munsif had moreover powers to act as an arbitrator in suits voluntarily referred to him for real or personal property of the same amount as his primary jurisdiction, his arbitration in such cases being final except on proof of corruption or partiality.[4]

The jurisdiction of the Sadr Amins (the Hindu and Muslim Law Officers of the Zillah Court and the Hindu Law Officers of the Provincial Court) was at the same time raised to Rs. 300, except in suits for revenue-free lands where the limit was fixed as annual produce not exceeding Rs. 30 in value. An appeal was made to lie from their decision to the Zillah Judge and the Zillah Judge was also empowered to refer to them appeals from the District Munsif, for final disposal.[5] The Sadr Adalat was later empowered to call up from the Provincial Courts and try in the first instance suits for Rs. 45,000 and upwards, the then appealable amount to the Governor-General in Council. The Provincial Court was then debarred from admitting regular appeals from the decisions passed by the Zillah Judge on appeals from his Registrar, but it was empowered to admit special appeals from his decisions in regular appeals from the original judgments of the Registrar, the Sadr Amins and the District Munsifs.[6] Finally all original suits tried by the Provincial Court were made appealable to the Sadr Adalat.[7] Provision was also made for

1 Regulation VI of 1816, section 11.

2 Regulation IV of 1816, section 43.

3 Regulation VII of 1816, sections 2–11.

4 Regulation VI of 1816, sections 57, 58.

5 Regulation VIII of 1816, section 16.

6 Regulation XV of 1816, sections 2 and 3.

7 Regulation XV of 1816, section 6.

reviewing the judgments of the Zillah and Provincial Courts in cases where no regular appeals lay.[1]

In 1818 the Governor-General ceased to hear appeals from the Sadr Adalat and the Privy Council became the ultimate appellate authority.[2] In 1820 the Zillah Judge was empowered to try suits brought by Indians against British subjects, residing in the districts and an appeal was made to lie in such suits to the Supreme Court or the Sadr Adalat.[3] In 1821 the jurisdiction of the Registrar, the Sadr Amin and the District Munsif was extended to Rs. 1,000, Rs. 750 and Rs. 500 respectively except in the case of rent-free lands where the limits were fixed at Rs. 100, Rs. 75 and Rs. 50 of annual produce respectively.[4] In 1825 all decisions of the District Munsifs in suits for property in land were made open to an appeal in the Zillah Court.[5]

Meanwhile, in 1816, the jurisdiction of the Zillah Court of Coimbatore was made co-extensive with that of the Collector, by transferring the Dindigul palayams of Ayakkudi, Idaiyakkottai, Mambarai, Palni, Reddiambadi and Virupakshi to the jurisdiction of the Zillah Court of Madurai.[6] In 1821 the Zillah Court of Coimbatore was abolished and the District was placed under the jurisdiction of the Zillah Court of Salem.[7] In 1827 an Auxiliary Zillah Court with increased powers came to be established at Coimbatore under an Assistant Judge.[8] It had territorial jurisdiction over the district with the exception of that part of it composing the jurisdiction of the District Munsifs of Karur and Dalavaypatti[9] and exclusive cognizance of suits not exceeding Rs. 5,000 in value. The Assistant Judge exercised appellate jurisdiction over the District Munsifs stationed within his territorial limits. A special appeal or second appeal lay to the Zillah Judge of Salem from the decision of the Assistant Judge in appeal, if the decision was contrary to judical precedent or usage having the force of law or involved an important question of law not covered by judicial authority. In suits not exceeding Rs. 1,000 tried by him, an appeal

1 Regulation XV of 1816, Section 6.

2 Regulation VIII of 1818.

3 53rd George III C-55, Regulation II of 1820.

4 Regulation II of 1821, sections 2–4.

5 Regulation V of 1825.

6 Judicial Consultations, dated 9th December 1816, pages 5187–5190.

7 *Idem,* dated 30th November 1821, pages 3477–3478 and 3481–3482.

8 *Idem,* dated 30th January 1827, pages 225–229 and 253, dated 20th March 1827, pages 827–831.

9 *Idem,* dated 20th March 1927, pages 829, 831.

lay to the Zillah Judge of Salem and, above that sum, to the Provincial Court at Tiruchirappalli. A Sadr Amin (other than the Law Officer appointed as such under Regulation III of 1816) was appointed by the Auxiliary Court and an appeal from his decision was made to lie to the Assistant Judge. A second appeal was also open to the Assistant Judge from the decisions of the Sadr Amin in appeals referred to him from the District Munsifs. [1]

In the matter of second appeals an appeal lay to the Zillah Judge from the decrees of the Assistant Judge in appeals from the Sadr Amin of the Auxiliary Court. Similarly an appeal lay to the Provincial Court from the decrees of the Zillah Judge in appeals from the Assistant Judge. An appeal likewise lay to the Sadr Adalat from the decrees of the Provincial Court in appeals from the Assistant Judge. [2]

In 1833 the jurisdiction of the Registrar, the Sadr Amin and the District Munsif was raised to Rs. 3,000, 2,500 and 1,000 respectively, except in suits for revenue-free land where the annual produce did not exceed Rs. 300, 250 and 100 respectively. [3] In 1836 the special appeals which the British subjects enjoyed from the decisions of the Zillah Court to the Supreme Court were abolished, and it was enacted that no person by reason of birth or descent should be exempted from the jurisdiction of the Company's Courts[4] or be incapable of being appointed as a Principal Sadr Amin or a Sadr Amin or a District Munsif. [5] In 1843 (by Act III of 1843) special appeals were made to lie to the Sadr Adalat from all decisions passed on regular appeals in all subordinate civil courts when such decisions were inconsistent with law or usage or the practice of the courts or involved doubtful questions of law, usage or practice. [6]

In 1840, a Munsif's Court had been established at Ootacamund, the civil administration of which was till then conducted by a Military 'Court of Requests ', although the Nilgiris were then part of the Coimbatore district. [7] In 1843 another important change was introduced in the

---

1 Regulation I of 1827, sections 2–7.

2 Regulation XI of 1827.

3 Regulation III of 1833, sections 3–5.
Judicial Consultations, dated 3rd May 1833, page 1875.
Idem, dated 31st May 1833, pages 2018–2025.

4 Act XI of 1836.

5 Act XXIV of 1836, sections 1–5.

6 Act III of 1843, section 1.

7 *Manual of Coimbatore District*, Vol. II, page 237.
See also Judicial Consultations, dated 18th August 1840, pages 5097–5099.

administration of justice. Both the Provincial Court and the Zillah Court were abolished and a new Zillah Court was established at Coimbatore, presided over by a Judge styled as the Civil and Sessions Judge.[1] In the same year Bhavani and Karur, which till then had been subject to the Zillah Court of Salem, were transferred to the jurisdiction of the new Zillah Court of Coimbatore with a Munsif's Court at each station.[2] The original jurisdiction vested in the Provincial Court for amounts of less than Rs. 10,000 was now transferred to the Subordinate Judge that might be appointed (The Assistant Judge came to be so designated except in the case of officers appointed under Section 32 of Act VII of 1843) and the Principal Sadr Amin[3] and both were given jurisdiction over Europeans and Americans also.[4] The new Zillah Judge as Civil Judge was empowered to hear appeals from the decrees of the Subordinate Judge, the Sadr Amins and District Munsifs. He could also refer appeals from the decisions of the District Munsifs to the Subordinate Judge or call up to his own court appeals received from those courts.[5] Appeals from his court lay to the Sadr Adalat.[6] The new scheme, however, deprived him of the assistance of the Registrar's Court, that court having been abolished. Summary appeals lay to his court from the decisions of the subordinate Judge,[7] and from his court to the Sadr Adalat.[8] In Coimbatore, however, no Subordinate Judge was appointed. In 1844 all suits within the competency of the Sadr Amins to decide came to be ordinarily instituted in their courts but they were made liable to be withdrawn by the Zillah Judge to be tried by him.[9] And in 1853, Act III of 1843 was repealed and another Act was passed specifying the grounds on which appeals were to lie to the Sadr Adalat.[10] After this, however, practically no change occurred until the introduction of the codes and the establishment of the High Court. At this stage, therefore, we may survey the state of civil justice in the District.

---

1 Act VII of 1843, section 1.
Judicial Consultations, dated 20th June 1843, pages 1665-1675.

2 *Manual of Coimbatore District*, Vol. II, page 237.

3 Act VII of 1843, section 4.

4 Act VII of 1843, section 5.

5 Act VII of 1843, section 7.

6 Act VII of 1843, section 9.

7 Act VII of 1843, section 8.

8 Act VII of 1843, section 9.

9 Act IX of 1844, sections 1, 2 and 4.

10 Act XVI of 1853.
See also *Manual of Administration of the Madras Presidency* by C. D. Maclean, Vol. I, 1885—Footnotes on pages 271-272.

In 1855, for instance, there were in the District one civil or Zillah Judge, one Principal Sadr Amin, one Sadr Amin with headquarters at Coimbatore and six District Munsifs with headquarters at Coimbatore, Udumalpet, Cheyur, Bhavani, Ootacamund and Karur. Coimbatore was regarded as one of the more or less litigious districts, and in 1855 the total number of original suits filed in all the courts in that year in the District came to 4,896 involving an amount of Rs. 1,98,957. In the number of suits filed, the District stood ninth in the whole State. The bulk of the litigation was in the lower courts; there were thus 1,617 suits pending and instituted in the Village Munsif's Courts, of which 259 were decreed on merits, 435 were disposed of by *razinamah* and 514 were dismissed. The gross value of the suits disposed of by these courts amounted to Rs. 6,177. There were also 4,824 suits pending, instituted and referred to in the District Munsif's Courts, of which 1,475 were decreed on merits, 900 were disposed by razinamah and 1,443 were dismissed. The gross value of the suits disposed of amounted to Rs. 1,32,697 and pending amounted to Rs. 69,015.[1]

Turning to criminal justice, by the Cornwallis System introduced in the District in 1806, the Zillah Judge became the Zillah Magistrate and was empowered to dispose of all petty criminal cases,[2] in accordance with the Muslim law which was declared to be the criminal law of the State. He was assisted by a Kazi and a Mufti who as Law Officers expounded the Muslim law in his court.[3] He disposed of all petty offences, such as abusive language, calumny, inconsiderable assaults and affrays, by imprisonment for a term not exceeding 15 days or by a fine not exceeding Rs. 50 except in the case of Zamindars and other landed proprietors in which case he was authorized to impose a fine up to Rs. 200.[4] He disposed of also all petty thefts by the infliction of corporal punishment not exceeding 30 rattans or by imprisonment for a period not exceeding one month.[5] All other cases he had to commit for trial before the Southern Court of Circuit.[6]

The Court of Circuit sent one of its Judges on Circuit with a Kazi and a Mufti periodically to the Coimbatore and other districts within its jurisdiction for the trial of sessions cases. This court could finally dispose of all cases committed for trial except those involving sentence of death

1 Report of the Sadr Adalat on Civil Justice for 1855, pages 3, 8, 10, 12, 35 and 36.

2 Regulation VI of 1802.

3 Regulation VII of 1802, section 15.

4 Regulation VI of 1802, section 8.

5 Regulation VI of 1802, sections 9–10.

6 Regulation VII of 1802.

or imprisonment for life wherein it dissented from the fatwa of the Muslim Law Officers. Sentences of death or imprisonment for life, it had to refer for final sentence to the Foujdari Adalat.[1] It had to be guided in its decisions entirely by the rules of Muslim Law as expounded by the fatwas of the Kazi and the Mufti.[2] But it was authorized to commute certain harsh penalties prescribed by the Muslim law to imprisonment. It could commute Deyut, or the price of blood, in cases of homicide to imprisonment for a term of years[3]; and it could commute Hud, or amputation, to imprisonment for 14 years in the case of a prisoner adjudged to lose two limbs and for seven years in the case of a prisoner adjudged to lose one limb by the fatwas of the Law Officers.[4] In fact punishment by mutilation was entirely forbidden. It had also powers to visit the crime of perjury with the punishment of Tasheer or public exposure or corporal punishment or imprisonment.[5] The Foujdari Adalat had powers to dispose of all cases referred to it for final sentence and to punish the crime of murder with death.[6] In other cases it had to be guided by the fatwas of their Law Officers, the Kazi and the Mufti. Whenever, however, it considered the penalties awarded in those fatwas too severe or unwarranted by the evidence, it could represent the case to the Government with a view to mitigating or entirely remitting the punishment adjudged.[7] In cases in which a sentence of imprisonment for life or for a limited period of not less than seven years was adjudged, it could order the prisoner to be transferred beyond the sea.[8] It could also, after obtaining the sanction of the Government, offer conditional pardon to accessories in the commission of crimes with a view to apprehending or convicting the principal.[9] In cases of robbery by open violence in which discretionary punishment was awarded in the fatwas of the Muslim Law officers, the Judge of Circuit and the Foujdari Adalat could inflict whatever punishment they thought proper. However, the Judge of Circuit could inflict only up to a maximum number of 39 stripes and imprisonment with hard labour in irons for seven years. Where a severe punishment was called for he

---

1 Regulation VII of 1802.
Regulation VI of 1808.

2 Regulation VII of 1802, section 15.

3 *Idem.*

4 Regulation VII of 1802, section 21.

5 Regulations VII of 1802, sections 36 and 40.
Judicial Consultations, dated 9th April 1811, page 157
Idem, dated 23rd April 1811, page 1590.

6 Regulation VIII of 1802, section 10.

7 Regulation VIII of 1802, section 11.

8 *Idem*, section 18.

9 *Idem*, section 20.

had to refer the case to the Foujdari Adalat or, where a strong suspicion was attached to the accused he had powers to demand security for his good conduct and appearance when required.[1] From 1811 the Zillah Judge and Magistrate began to exercise more powers; he was empowered to inflict punishment on persons convicted by him by imprisonment not exceeding one year, by corporal punishment not exceeding 30 rattans or by fine not exceeding Rs. 200.[2]

A much more important change came in 1816; in that year the Cornwallis system was replaced by the Munro System. Munro who had been appointed in 1814 at the head of the Judicial Commission to suggest measures for the reform of the judiciary held that the Zillah Judge, confined as he was to his headquarters had hardly any opportunity to acquire an intimate knowledge of the people; that such knowledge could be had only by the Collector who, in the performance of his revenue duties, frequently toured the District, and that, as this knowledge was essential for discharging the functions of the magistrate and for controlling the police effectually, the magisterial powers and the control of police should be transferred from the Zillah Judge to the Collector. This, he also remarked, was the Indian System in which the revenue, magisterial and police duties were combined in the revenue officer[3]; and his recommendation having been strongly supported by the Court of Directors, the change was introduced in 1816;[4] The office of the Zillah Magistrate of Coimbatore was now transferred from the Zillah Judge to the Collector and at the same time a Criminal Court was established at Coimbatore presided over by the Zillah Judge to which the Magistrate was required to commit all cases not adjudicable by him, instead of, as before, committing such cases for trial

---

[1] Regulation XV of 1803, sections 2 and 11.

See also Select Reports and cases of the Court of Foujdari Adalat 1826–1850, pages III to VIII.

[2] Regulation IV of 1811, section 12.

[3] Judicial Consultations, dated 24th December 1814, page 858.
Judicial Consultations, dated 1st March 1815, page 872.
Judicial Consultations, dated 28th March 1815, page 1849.
Judicial Consultations, dated 13th May 1815, page 1888.
Judicial Consultations, dated 15th July 1815, page 2856.
Judicial Consultations, dated 19th August 1815, page 3070.

For a full discussion on the subject *see* Selections of papers from the Records at East India House, Vol. II, 1820, Parts I and II.

See also Judicial Consultations, dated 25th June 1816, page 2461 and dated 8th July 1816, page 2612.

[4] Regulation IX of 1816.

Regulation X of 1816; *see* also Judicial Consultations, dated 18th November 1816, page 4760, dated 25th November 1816, page 4832.

to the Court of Circuit.[1] The magistrate was empowered to apprehend offenders and in certain cases to pass sentence.[2] He was authorized to punish persons guilty of petty thefts and other minor offences by stripes not exceeding 18 rattans, by imprisonment not exceeding 15 days or by fines not exceeding Rs. 50[3]; in other cases he had to send the offenders for trial to the Criminal Judge of the Zillah [4]. The Zillah Judge could punish offenders in some cases with stripes not exceeding 30 rattans; and in cases of thefts, in addition, with imprisonment not exceeding six months, and in other cases with a fine not exceeding Rs. 200.[5] Persons charged with more serious offences had to be committed by him for trial before the Court of Circuit[6].

The years that followed witnessed the gradual enlargement of the powers of all judicial officers of the District. In 1818 the Zillah Magistrate was empowered to delegate the whole or any part of his authority to his assistant.[7] In 1820 he was given jurisdiction over British subjects residing in the interior for assaults and trespasses against Indians; their convictions, however, in such cases were made removable by *certiorari* to the Supreme Court. [8] In 1822 the Criminal Judge was authorized to take cognizance of burglary and, if not attended with violence, to punish the offenders with 30 stripes and imprisonment with hard labour for two years, but, if accompanied with violence, to commit them to the Court of Circuit. The Court of Circuit was authorized to punish such offenders by 39 stripes and imprisonment by banishment for fourteen years, if the burglary was not attended with attempt to murder or wounding, but, if otherwise, on conviction, to refer the trial to the Foujdari Adalat.[9] The Criminal Judge was likewise authorized to punish thefts not exceeding Rs. 50 and not attended with attempt to murder or with wounding by imprisonment with hard labour for two years and 30 rattans; but otherwise to refer the trial to the Circuit Judge.[10] The Criminal Judge was also empowered in certain cases to try and punish offenders for receiving or purchasing stolen goods [11] and convicts for escaping from jail.[12] In 1825 he was required to

---

1 Regulation X of 1816.
2 Regulation IX of 1816, section 18.
3 Regulation IX of 1816, sections 32, 33 and 35.
4 Regulation IX, 1816, section 34.
5 Regulation X, 1816, sections 2, and 7.
6 Regulation X, 1816, section 9.
7 Regulation IX, 1818.
8 Regulation II, 1820.
9 Regulation VI, 1822, section 2.
10 Regulation VI, 1822, section 3.
11 Regulation VI, 1822, section 4.
12 *Idem*, section 5.

commit for trial before the Circuit Court all offenders involved in thefts exceeding Rs. 300.[1] Meanwhile, as has already been seen, the Zillah Court of Coimbatore having been abolished (1821) and that District having been placed under the jurisdiction of the Zillah Court of Salem, the Zillah Judge of Salem became the Criminal Judge of Coimbatore; and in 1827 he came to be assisted by an Assistant Judge who also acted as a Joint Criminal Judge at the Auxiliary Court set up at Coimbatore.

Then came the trial by jury and some humanitarian reforms. In 1827 a regulation was passed for the gradual introduction of the trial by jury into the Criminal Judicature and it was declared to be unnecessary for either the Judge of Circuit or the Foujdari Adalat to require a fatwa from their Law Officers as to the guilt of the prisoner, that being established by the verdict of the jury.[2] It is interesting to note that only Hindus and Muslims were eligible to serve as jurors and that every juror received one rupee a day for his expenses. In 1828 the use of the rattan was abolished and the cat-of-nine tails was substituted.[3] In 1830 the 'Korah' was also substituted by the cat-of-nine tails.[4] In 1832 the Magistrate, the Criminal and the Joint Criminal Judges of the District were empowered to adjudge solitary imprisonment in all cases cognizable by them.[5] In 1833 females were exempted from the punishment of flogging.[6]

These were succeeded by changes of a general nature. In 1833, Criminal and Joint Criminal Judges were authorized to employ the Sadr Amins in the investigation and decision of criminal cases, except in cases committable for trial before the Court of Circuit. These judges had powers to overrule the decisions of the Sadr Amins who were moreover declared not to have jurisdiction over Europeans or Americans.[7] In

---

1 Regulation I, 1825, section 90.

2 Regulation X, 1827, section 33.
Judicial Consultations, dated 28th December 1827, pages 3970–3974.
Judicial Consultations, dated 3rd July 1827, page 2046.
Judicial Consultations, dated 11th September 1827, page 2893.

3 Regulation VIII, 1828.
Judicial Consultations, dated 15th April 1828, page 1091.
Judicial Consultations, dated 29th April 1828, page 1611.
Judicial Consultations, dated 20th June 1828, page 2158.

4 Regulation II, 1830.
Judicial Consultations, dated 28th May 1830; dated 23rd February 1830, page 769.

5 Regulation XIII, 1832, section 4.

6 Regulation II, 1833.
Judicial Consultations, dated 12th April 1833, page 1495, dated 26th April 1833, pages 1807–1808.

7 Regulation III of 1833.

1840 the Foujdari Adalat was empowered to dispense altogether with the fatwa but not with the Muslim law.[1] Until 1841, treason, rebellion or other crimes against the State had been tried by the Judges of Circuit or by special courts appointed by the Government and consisting of three judges.[2] In 1841 the Government were empowered to issue a Commission to one or more judges with or without law officers for the trial of treason, rebellion or any other crime against the State. The Commission had to report its sentences, whether of acquittal or of punishment, to the Foujdari Adalat; and the latter in turn had to report its sentence to the Government and await orders for three months before executing the same.[3] In 1843 sentences passed by the Justices of the Peace in the Mofussil (the Magistrate) on the British subjects residing in the District for assaults and trespasses against the Indians were made appealable in the regular course in the same manner as ordinary sentences passed in ordinary exercise of a Magistrate's jurisdiction and, when so passed, were declared no more to be liable to revision by *certiorari* by the Supreme Court[4].

As has already been stated, in 1843 the District saw the abolition of the Court of Circuit and the establishment of the new Zillah Court under the new Zillah Judge, called the Civil and Sessions Judge, invested with enlarged powers.[5] The Judge of the new Zillah Court was empowered to exercise all the powers of the Judges of the Old Court of Circuit,[6] which now disappeared. He was directed to hold permanent sessions for the trial of all persons accused of crimes formerly cognizable by the Court of Circuit.[7] He could avail himself of the aid of respectable Indians or other persons either by constituting them as assessors or members of the court with a view to benefiting by their observations particularly in the examination of witnesses, by or employing them more nearly as a jury, to attend during the trial, to suggest points of enquiry and, after consultation, to deliver in their verdict. He was, however, authorized to pass decision according to his opinion whether agreeing with the assessors or jury or not; but if his decision was in opposition to their opinions, it was to be referred to the Foujdari Adalat.[8] He had also the power of overruling the

---

1 Act I of 1840.
Judicial Consultations, dated 12th November 1839, pages 8684–8687, dated 13th August 1839, page 6300.

2 Regulation XX of 1802.

3 Act V of 1841, sections 1–5.

4 Act IV of 1843.

5 Judicial Consultations, dated 1st August 1843, page 2720.
Judicial Consultations, dated 15th August 1843, pages 2844.

6 Act VII of 1843, section 26.

7 Act VII of 1843, section 27.

8 Act VII of 1843, section 32.

criminal sentences passed by the Sadr Amins.[1] The powers of the Magistrate were also extended, but an appeal was made to lie over from his decision to the Sessions Judge.[2] The District Munsifs were also, in 1854, given criminal jurisdiction in petty offences and petty thefts.[3] In 1855 the Sessions Judge was invested with the duty of holding sessions from time to time at Ootacamund, for the trial of offences committed in the Nilgiris.[4] No material changes having taken place till the passing of the codes and the establishment of the High Court. We may pause now to cast a glance at the state of criminal justice in the district.

In 1855, for instance, the same year for which we have given civil statistics, the district had 1 Sessions Judge, 1 Principal Sadr Amin, 1 Sadr Amin, 1 District Magistrate, 2 Joint Magistrates, 1 Head Assistant Magistrate, 1 Assistant Magistrate, and 1 Special Assistant Magistrate. The total number of crimes committed against persons and property like murder, highway robbery, gang robbery, house-breaking, arson, embezzlement, fraud and forgery were 1,622 in which 5,922 persons were involved. Besides these, there were a very large number of petty offences like assault, theft and cattle stealing. Among the major crimes, murder, gang robbery, house-breaking and thefts were the most prevalent.[5]

Shortly afterwards, in 1863, the Nilgiris were removed from the jurisdiction of the Coimbatore District Court and placed under a separate Civil and Sessions Court set up at Ootacamund.[6] In 1868 they were constituted into a separate district and placed under a Judicial Commissioner.[7] But subsequently in 1881 they were again included in the jurisdiction of the District and Sessions Judge of Coimbatore for purposes of civil and criminal justice. Under this arrangement the District Judge was empowered to hold sessions, when necessary, at Ootacamund and to hear appellate suits and dispose of emergent miscellaneous civil work. The District Magistrate Court of the Nilgiris was constituted into an

---

1. *Idem*, section 36.

2. *Idem*, sections 54, 55.

3. Act XII of 1854.
See also Manual of Administration of the Madras Presidency by C.D. Maclean, Vol. I, 1885, Footnotes on pages 272–273.

4. Act XXV of 1855.

5. Report of the Foujdari Adalat on the Administration of Criminal Justice for 1855, pages 26–27.

6. G.O. No. 761–762, Judicial, dated 19th May 1863.
G.O. No. 1610, Judicial, dated 6th October 1863.
G.O. No. 1658, Judicial, dated 19th October 1863.

7. *Manual of Coimbatore District* Vol. II, pages 237-238.

Additional Sessions Judge Court with powers to try all offences not punishable with death or transportation for life. A Subordinate Judge's Court was at the same time established at Ootacamund with jurisdiction over the Nilgiris district and with powers to try small causes up to Rs. 500. [1]

In the meanwhile a series of important changes were made not only in the structure of the judiciary but also in the law to be administered and the procedure to be followed in the courts. In 1859 the Civil Procedure Code was enacted and this was followed by the Penal Code in 1860 and the Criminal Procedure Code in 1861. These Codes replaced the Regulations and Acts hitherto governing judicial administration. The Sadr and Foujdari Adalat and the Supreme Court were, at the same time, replaced by the High Court established by Letters Patent under charters issued in 1862 and 1865 and the High Court was invested with civil and criminal jurisdiction over all the courts in the State.[2] Since then the three Codes have been amended on several occasions and a large number of Acts have been passed defining the law governing specific subjects. It is neither possible nor necessary to enter here into this vast field of legal enactments. But it must be stated that, after the codification of the law, the Kazis, the Muftis and the Pandits disappeared from the courts and that, about the same time, the constitution and jurisdiction of the courts themselves underwent some important changes. The present set up of the civil courts came into existence in 1873 by the passing of the Madras Civil Courts Act of 1873; [3] and the present set up of the criminal courts came into existence in 1872 by the passing of the Criminal Procedure Code of 1872.[4] Under the Civil Courts Act of 1873 the civil judiciary in the district came to consist of the District Court, the Subordinate Judge's Court and the District Munsif's Courts ; the Courts of the Assistant Judge and the Sadr Amins now ceased to exist. Under the Criminal Procedure Code of 1872,

---

1. G.O. No. 250, Judicial, dated 7th February 1880.
G.O. No. 2051, Judicial, dated 21st August 1880.
Manual of Coimbatore District Vol. II, pages 237, 238.

2. *Manual of Administration of the Madras Presidency* by C. D. Maclean, Vol. I, 1885, *see* footnote on page 274.
G.O. No. 37–40, Judicial, dated 10th June 1859.
G.O. No. 26–31A, Judicial, dated 5th August 1862.
G.O. No. 180, Judicial, dated 15th August 1862.
G.O. No. 99–100, Judicial, dated 11th August 1862.
G.O. No. 18–19, Judicial, dated 3rd December 1862.
G.O. No. 39–40, Judicial, dated 12th January 1863.
G.O. No. 83–84, Judicial, dated 12th March 1866.
G.O. No. 341–342, Judicial, dated 25th October 1866.

3. The Civil Court Manual (Madras Acts), 1949, Vol. I, pages 266–277.

4. *Manual of Madras Administration* by C. D. Maclean, Vol. I, 1885, page 274 *see* footnote.

the criminal judiciary in the district came to consist of the Sessions Court and the Courts of the First, Second and the Third Class Magistrates. The Village Munsif's Courts and the Panchayat Courts, however, continued to function under Regulations IV and V of 1816 as amended by Madras Act IV of 1883 and Act I of 1889.

The administration of civil justice is now under the exclusive superintendence of the High Court. The High Court originally consisted of a Chief Justice and a few Puisne Judges. The Chief Justice and one of the Puisne Judges were barristers of the United Kingdom, while the other Judges were experienced members of the civil Service. All these were appointed by the Crown.[1] Subsequently the Judges were increased and their appointments came to be made on the principle that one third of them should be barristers from the United Kingdom, one third should be members of the Indian Civil Service and the remaining one third should be Advocates of some years standing in the High Court.[2] Under the new constitution (1950) it now consists of a Chief Justice and nine other judges appointed by the President under his hand and seal. No person is eligible for appointment as a Judge of the High Court unless he is a citizen of India and has for at least ten years held a judicial office in India or has for at least ten years been an Advocate of a High Court in India.[3]

The High Court has all along exercised ordinary original jurisdiction over all suits the cause of action in which has arisen within the limits of the City of Madras and appellate jurisdiction over all civil courts established throughout the State. It has also all along decided original cases by a single judge from whose decision an appeal has laid to a division bench consisting of two judges. It has, in the same manner, heard and determined appeals from district courts by a division bench of two judges and when the judges have differed in opinion, they have stated the question of law on which they differed and referred the matter to a third judge. When important questions of law have arisen, it has had then decided by full Benches consisting of three or more judges. It has heard and decided all second appeals, i.e., decrees passed in appeal by the subordinate courts wherein the decision has been contrary to law or usage, or has failed to determine some material issue of law or usage or had made a substantial error in procedure. It has exercised powers of extraordinary original jurisdiction by which it can call up and determine any suit or appeal from any court, subject to its superintendence. It has

1. *Manual of Madras Administration* by C. D. Maclean, Vol. I, 1885, pages 209–210.

2. Report of the Indian Statutory Commission, 1930, Vol. I, page 294.

3. *The Constitution of India*, 1950, Madras Edition, page 73.

had powers to hold sittings for the relief of insolvent debtors and it has exercised testamentary and matrimonial jurisdiction.[1] And recently, under the new constitution, it has come to exercise original jurisdiction in respect of any matter concerning revenue and its collection.[2]

Except for the transfer of the District Munsif's Court of Karur to the jurisdiction of the Sessions Judge of Tiruchirappalli in 1910,[3] the jurisdiction of the several other courts in the Coimbatore district has practically remained unchanged from 1873. Ever since that time whenever Additional Subordinate Judges and Additional District Munsifs have been appointed to one and the same Subordinate Judge's Court or District Munsif's Court, one of the Subordinate Judges and District Munsifs has been called the Principal Subordinate Judge and the Principal District Munsif respectively.[4] The District Judge and the Subordinate Judge have throughout exercised jurisdiction in all original suits and proceedings of a civil nature.[5] The District Munsifs exercised jurisdiction over such suits and proceedings till 1916 where the amount did not exceed Rs. 2,500 but in that year this limit was raised to Rs. 3,000.[6] Regular appeals against the decrees and orders of the District Court go to the High Court; and appeals against the decrees and orders of the Subordinate Judges' Courts and District Munsifs' Courts go to the District Courts, except where the amount or value of the subject matter of the suit has exceeded Rs. 5,000 in which case an appeal has to be placed before the High Court.[7] In certain cases the Subordinate Judges have exercised the powers of disposing of appeals from the District Munsifs within their jurisdiction and the District Judge has, in such cases, exercised the powers of moving those suits to his own court, and, with the permission of the High Court, of referring any appeals from the decrees and orders of the District Munsifs preferred to his court to any Subordinate Judge under him.[8] And finally all the courts have all along administered the Hindu or Muslim Law in all matters regarding succession, inheritance, marriage or caste or any religious usage or institution, according as the parties involved have been Hindus or Muslims. Where, however, these have not existed, they have followed

1. *Manual of Administration of the Madras Presidency* by C. D. Maclean, Vol. I, 1885, pages 209–210.

2. *The Constitution of India*, 1950, *Madras Edition*, page 75.

3. G.O. No. 74, Judicial, dated 12th January 1910.

4. Madras Civil Courts Act of 1873, sections 4 and 4-A.

5. *Idem*, section 12.

6. *Idem*, section 12 and Madras Civil Courts Amendment Act, 1916, section 2.

7. Madras Civil Courts Act of 1873, section 13.

8. Madras Civil Courts Act of 1873, section 13.

any custom having the force of law unless such custom has been by legislative enactment altered; and, where no specific rule as existed, they have acted according to justice, equity and good conscience.[1]

The Village Munsifs and the Village Panchayats have all along continued to exercise petty civil powers. We have already seen that the Village Munsifs, since 1816, exercised civil judicial powers in simple disputes. In 1883 under Madras Act IV of 1883, their powers were extended to suits for personal property up to Rs. 20, their decision not being open to appeal. They were also empowered, in case the parties consented, to try and determine similar suits up to Rs. 100 as arbitrators. They were likewise empowered, when the parties agreed, to summon panchayats as before to decide suits for personal property of any value.[2] By the Village Courts Act of 1889 (Madras Act I of 1889) the Village Munsifs' Courts as well as the new Panchayat Courts that could be constituted for one or more villages, were invested with powers to try civil suits up to Rs. 50 and, where the parties gave their consent in writing up to Rs. 200.[3]

It may be stated here that there have also been revenue courts in the district from 1822. The Collectors, Sub-Collectors and Assistant and Deputy Collectors in charge of divisions have been authorised to sit as revenue courts and exercise judicial powers under the Madras Regulations XII of 1816 on claims to lands or crops, under Madras Regulation IX of 1822, III of 1823 and III of 1832 on charges against revenue subordinates for corruption, exaction, embezzlement, etc.,[4] under Madras Regulation VI of 1831 repealed by the Madras Hereditary Village Officers Act III of 1895 on claims to hereditary village officers; [5] and under Madras Act VIII of 1865 repealed by the Madras Estate Land Act I of 1908 on disputes between the landlord and tenant in which no title is involved.[6] The revenue courts have also under the Acts of 1865 and 1908 exercised powers to enforce terms of tenancy, to compel the exchange of pattas and muchilikas, to settle rates of assessment or rent, to order sales under distraint, etc.

---

1. Madras Civil Courts Act of 1873, section 16.

2. *Manual of Administration of the Madras Presidency* by C. D. Maclean Vol. I, 1885, pages 212–213.

3. *The Civil Courts Manual* (*Madras Acts*), Fifth Edition, 1940, pages 1854–1858.

4. Regulations of the Government of Fort St. George by Richard Clarke, 1848, pages 434–441, 517–518.

5. Idem pages 507–509.
The Civil Courts Manual (Madras Acts), 1940, pages 1007–1025.

6. *The Madras Code*, 1888, pages 230–231.
The Madras Code, 1915, Vol. II, pages 1107–1182.

Since the establishment of the High Court and the passing of the several Acts connected with civil justice, the judicial officers have been invested with certain special powers. Under the Madras Civil Courts Act of 1873 the Subordinate Judges and District Munsifs were invested with the powers of a Small Cause Court up to Rs. 500 and Rs. 50 respectively. In 1914 the powers of the District Munsifs were raised to Rs. 100 generally and Rs. 200 in the case of a few District Munsifs recommended by the High Court. In 1926 the powers of the Subordinate Judges were raised to Rs. 1,000 and in 1942 the powers of the District Munsifs were raised to Rs. 300. It may also be mentioned here that the District Judge exercises special jurisdiction under enactments like the Guardians and Wards Act, the Indian Divorce Act, the Native Converts Marriage Dissolution Act and the Administrator-Generals Act. The Subordinate Judges also exercise jurisdiction under special enactments like the Provincial Insolvency Act, the Guardians and Wards Act, the Indian Succession Act, the Madras Hindu Prevention of Bigamy and Divorce Act and the Land Acquisition Act. The District Munsifs likewise exercise certain jurisdiction under the Provincial Insolvency Act and the Indian Succession Act. Mention may also be made here of Official Receiver appointed under the Provincial Insolvency Act for the administration of insolvents' estates. Originally the Official Receiver was a part time officer appointed for a term of five years and remunerated on a Commission basis. In 1939 he was made a full time officer of the Government and remunerated by salary. In the same year he was also appointed ex-officio Official Liquidator under the Indian Companies Act to carry on proceedings in the liquidation of companies ordered to be wound up by the High Court.

The following statement will give an idea of the State of litigation in the district during the last 50 years:—

Year.	*Suits.*			*Appeals.*		*Total of suits and appeals instituted.*
	Before Village Courts.	*Before Panchayat Courts.*	*Before Civil Courts.*	*To District and Subordinate Judges Courts.*	*To High Court.*	
1900	8,840	..	10,567	229	48	19,684
1910	6,946	..	13,622	326	93	20,987
1920	6,741	..	19,993	318	91	27,143
1930	1,294	15,611	17,228	399	119	34,651
1940	762	16,365	11,460	364	152	29,103
1950	99	1,447	12,973	491	189	15,199

The percentage of total number of suits and appeals in the district to the State total was 5·56 in 1900, but it fell to 4·81 in 1910. It then rose to 5·47 in 1920, 6·35 in 1930 and 6·72 in 1940, but again fell to 5·43 in 1950.

In 1956-57 the state of the civil justice in the district was as follows : There were in the district one District Judge's Court presided over by two permanent District Judges, one Subordinate Judge's Court at Coimbatore presided over by four Subordinate Judges (two permanent and two temporary), one District Munsif's Court presided over by two permanent District Munsifs all at Coimbatore,—one Subordinate Judge's Court at Ootacamund (permanent), one at Erode (temporary) and six District Munsifs' Courts at Dharapuram, Erode, Gobichettipalayam, Gudalur, Tiruppur and Udumalpet respectively. The post of the temporary II Additional Subordinate Judge at Coimbatore was sanctioned in 1951 and the sanction is being continued right through, the period being extended each year. The temporary III Additional Subordinate Judge started functioning from 1952 but this post was abolished with effect from 5th June 1956. The same has been renewed with effect from 24th June 1957 and is still continuing. A temporary Subordinate Judge's Court was established at Erode with effect from 5th June 1956 with territorial jurisdiction over the revenue taluks of Erode, Bhavani, Gobichettipalayam, Satyamangalam and Dharapuram. That Court was originally sanctioned for a period of one year and has been extended for another year. The Subordinate Judges of Coimbatore and Erode do not exercise Small Cause jurisdiction. A part time Official Receiver is functioning in the district from 1st January 1955. There were also in the district 234 Village Panchayat Courts and 91 Village Munsif's Courts which tried cases. There were as many as 19,861 suits and appeals before these various Courts. The Village Munsif's Courts disposed of 4 suits ; the Village Panchayat Courts disposed of 3,840 suits ; the District Munsif's Courts disposed of 6,794 Ordinary and 8,901 Small Causes suits, the Subordinate Judge's Courts disposed of 609 ordinary suits and 1,459 Small Causes suits and 286 appeals ; and the District Judges Court disposed of 11 Ordinary suits and 310 appeals. Powers of a Sessions Judge were exercised by the Sessions Judge and the Additional Sessions Judge and powers of an Assistant Sessions Judge were exercised by the Subordinate Judges of Coimbatore, Erode and Ootacamund. All the Sessions Judges and Assistant Sessions Judge together disposed of 290 Sessions cases and the two Sessions Judges disposed of 409 Criminal Appeals and 26 Criminal Revision Cases and among all the courts in the State, this District appears to have the maximum number of Civil and Sessions Cases[1]. The proportion of suits filed was one to every 182 persons in 1956 and one to every 255 persons in 1957; and the percentage of total number of suits and appeals to that of the State total was 13·79 in 1956 and 11·61 in 1957.

1. Information furnished by the District Judge, Coimbatore.

The District ranked first in the whole State in the matter of litigation in 1956 and second in the year 1957.

A subject connected with civil justice is the registration of assurances. As early as 1802 a Regulation was passed (Regulation XVII of 1802) with the object of giving security to the titles and rights of persons purchasing or receiving in gift, or advancing money on mortgage or taking on lease or other limited assignment of real property. The Regulation also aimed at preventing individuals from being defrauded by entering into transactions in respect of any property that might have been previously dealt with, at obviating litigation regarding wills and any written authority to adopt and at providing against injury to rights or title by the loss or destruction of deeds relating to transactions of the above nature. The Regulation came into force only in 1805 and the registry was placed in charge of the Registrar of the Zillah Court. The documents registerable consisted of sales and gifts, mortgages and certificates of discharges of mortgages, leases and other limited assignments or temporary transfers of property, wills and written authorities to adopt. The registration was, however, optional[1]. In 1831, Officiating or Deputy Registrars as well as Zillah Assistants and Indian Judges were permitted to perform the duties of the Registrar where specially appointed for the purpose. In 1834 the Court of Directors suggested the enactment of a law for making registration of deeds relating to immovable property compulsory. But the suggestion bore fruit only in 1864 by the passing of India Act XVI of 1864. This Act was amended in 1877, 1879, 1886 and 1889 and was consolidated in 1908 by India Act XVI of 1908[2]. The chief object of registration is to obviate the difficulties arising from the purchase of a title to immovable property the validity of which cannot be checked. The Act provides the machinery for registration, and lays down what documents should be compulsorily registered in order to obtain validity in a court of law and what documents may or may not be registered at the option of the parties. Ever since the passing of the Act of 1864 the work of registration has been placed in charge of a separate department under an Inspector-General of Registration assisted by a number of Registrars and Sub-Registrars. Coimbatore has been under a Registrar since the passing of the Act of 1864. As for the Sub-Registrar's Offices there were 33 of them in 1955–56, located in towns and important villages. In the same year these offices effected 57,306 registrations, compulsory and optional, relating to immovable property

---

1. Regulation XVII of 1802, *see* also Act I of 1943.

2. *Madras Presidency*, 1881 *to* 1931 by G. T. Boag, 1933, page 59.
Manual of Administration of the Madras Presidency by C. D. Maclean, Vol. I, page 214.

worth Rs. 8,12,14,134 and collected thereby fees amounting to Rs. 4,14,272. They also registered 1,147 documents relating to movable property worth Rs. 16,73,662 and realised thereby fees amounting to Rs. 10,363. They likewise registered 1,065 wills and realised thereby Rs. 11,841 towards fees[1]. There are now two District Registrars, one at Erode and the other at Coimbatore. The latter is also in charge of the Nilgiris.

Another subject connected with civil justice is that of court fees. In order to discourage frivolous litigation and the filing of superfluous exhibits and the summoning of unnecessary witnesses, a Regulation was passed as early as 1808 (Regulation IV of 1808) prescribing the levy of stamp duty on every petition, answer, reply, rejoinder or supplemental pleadings in suits on appeals to the Zillah, Provincial or Sadr Court on all miscellaneous petitions and applications which were treated as pleadings, on sanads of appointment granted to Kazis or authorized pleaders and on all copies of judicial papers granted to parties on application. The scale of stamp duty ranged from 4 annas to Rs. 2[2]. In suits and appeals the scale was revised in the same year[3]. Complaints to Magistrates or Police Darogahs were charged a stamp duty of annas 8. Provision was at the same time made for the institution of suits *in forma pauperis*. In the same year by another Regulation (Regulation V of 1803) a scale of court fees was prescribed on all suits. The fees collected by the Registrars, the District Munsifs, the Sadr Amins and the 'Native Commissioners' were appropriated by them towards their remuneration ; but the fees collected by the Zillah Judges, the Provincial Courts and the Sadr Adalat were credited to the Government.[4] No fee was, however, collected in the case of suits filed before the Village Courts which came into existence in 1816[5]. In 1817 the stamp duty was made payable also on documents like promissory notes, bills of exchange, letters of credit, receipts, deeds of gift, sale, devise, lease, mortgage, etc., and the court fees leviable on institution of suits and appeals was also revised. The court fees varied from Re. 1 for suits and appeals not exceeding Rs. 16 in value, for Rs. 2,000 for suits and appeals exceeding Rs. 1,00,000 in value[6]. The Registrars, the District Munsifs, etc., continued to appropriate the fees collected by them. From 1834, however, the District Munsifs ceased to be remunerated with the fees

1 G.O. No. 4637, Revenue, dated 22nd December 1956.

2 Regulation IV of 1808, sections 2, 3.

3 Regulation V of 1808, section 3.

4 Regulation V of 1808.

5 Regulation IV of 1816, section 32, Regulation V of 1816, section 13 Regulation VII of 1816.

Regulation XIII of 1816, section 13,

and in lieu thereof were paid monthly allowances for themselves.[1] The next change in the court fees on judicial stamps was made in 1860 when a comprehensive Act containing several new provisions taken from the English statutes was passed and made applicable to the whole of India.[2] Some minor amendments were made to this Act in 1862.[3] In 1867 stamp duties on judicial proceedings were increased.[4] In 1870 another comprehensive Act was passed reducing the stamp duties and making various changes in detail in the judicial part of the stamp law.[5] This Act was amended in 1922 mainly for raising the stamp duties and thereby meeting the increased cost of administration.[6] A minor amendment to this Act was made in 1945[7].

Coming to criminal justice, the High Court has all along exercised original and appellate jurisdiction, the former in the case of the City of Madras and the latter in the case of the districts. It has tried all ordinary cases before a common jury and all important cases, in which the State is interested, before a special jury.[8] Appeals have been, usually heard by one judge unless they related to death sentences, in which case two judges have sat and decided appeals. Appeals posted before one Judge have sometimes been referred by him to a Bench of two Judges and appeals posted before a Bench of two Judges have sometimes been referred by them to a Full Bench consisting of three or more Judges. The High Court has exercised the powers of revision over all the Criminal Courts in the State, such as those of revising their calendars and sentences, calling for their records and annulling, suspending or altering their sentences.[9]

The Sessions Court in the Coimbatore District has all along been the highest court within the limits of its jurisdiction which includes the Nilgiris also. It has not generally taken cognizance of any offences as a court of original jurisdiction; it has taken cognizance of cases only when committed by competent magistrates. It has held trials with the aid of assessors or jury.[10] It has possessed powers to pass the maximum

1 Regulation II of 1834, Act V of 1835.

2 India Act XXXVI of 1860.

3 India Act X of 1862.

4 India Act XXVI of 1867.

5 India Act of VII of 1870.

6 Madras Act V of 1922.

7 Madras Act XVII of 1945.

8 G.O. No. 11–12, Judicial, dated 2nd December 1865.

9 *Manual of Madras Administration* by C. D. Maclean, Vol. I, 1885, pages 198–199, *Code of Criminal Procedure*, 1898, section 31 (1).

10 *Code of Criminal Procedure*, 1898, section 268,

punishment prescribed for each offence by the Penal Code; and, except in the case of death sentence its sentences have been effectual without further reference, subject only to appeals to the High Court. All capital punishments passed by it, however, have had to be confirmed by the High Court[1]. It has also possessed appellate jurisdiction and heard and determined all appeals from the decisions of the District Magistrates and First Class Magistrates. Whenever the work of the Sessions Court has been heavy, an additional Sessions Judge or an Assistant Sessions Judge has been appointed. The Additional Sessions Judge has exercised the same powers as the Sessions Judge; and the Assistant Sessions Judge has exercised all the powers of the Sessions Judge except those of passing sentences of death or of transportation or of imprisonment for more than seven years.[2]

Below the Sessions Court there have been all along three grades of Criminal Courts in the district presided over by the Magistrates of the First, Second and Third Class. The Collector has exercised First Class Magisterial powers under the designation of the District Magistrates and, as the head of the district, he has had jurisdiction and control over the other magistrates. The Sub-divisional Magistrates, whether Sub-Collectors or Deputy Collectors, have also exercised First Class Magisterial powers. The Tahsildars have been vested with Second Class Magisterial powers, but they have rarely exercised these powers for the trial of cases. The Deputy Tahsildars as Sub-Magistrates have been vested with Third Class Magisterial powers to start with and after six months have been invariably vested with Second Class powers;[3] and such of the Sub-Magistrates doing exclusively magisterial work have been designated as the Stationary Sub-Magistrates. As to the magisterial powers the magistrates of the First Class have throughout possessed powers of passing sentences of imprisonment not exceeding two years, of imposing fines to the extent of Rs. 1,000 and of whipping[4]. Magistrates of the Second Class have similarly possessed powers of passing sentences of imprisonment not exceeding six months and of imposing fines not exceeding Rs. 200[5]. Magistrates of the Third Class have possessed powers of passing sentences of imprisonment not exceeding one month and of imposing fines not exceeding Rs. 50[6]. The First- class Magistrates,

---

1 *Code of Criminal Procedure*, 1898, section 31 (2).

2 *Idem*, section 31 (3).
Manual of Madras Administration by C.D. Maclean, Vol. I, 1885, pages 198–199.

3 Board's Standing Orders, No. 139.

4 *Code of Criminal Procedure*, 1898, section 32 (1).

5 *Idem*.

6 *Idem*.

when empowered by the Government, have also heard appeals from the decisions of the Second-class and Third-class Magistrates.

Besides these magistrates there have been other magistrates too in the district. There have been from a long time, from about 1861, benches of Honorary Magistrates and Honorary Special Magistrates, mostly in towns,[1] who have exercised generally the Third or Second Class powers or sometimes even First Class powers.[2] There have been also the Village Munsifs who have exercised magisterial powers in petty cases of minor assault, affrays, abusive language, etc., under Regulation XI of 1816 as amended by Act II of 1920; they have had powers to imprison offenders in the village choultry for a period not exceeding twelve hours.[3] There have moreover been the Panchayat Courts which have exercised powers of imposing fines in petty offences under the Village Courts Act I of 1889.[4]

Recently in 1951, an important change has been introduced in the district, namely, the separation of the Judiciary from the Executive.[5] The separation has a history of its own dating from almost the very inception of the Indian National Congress. We have dealt with it fully elsewhere,[6] but here we must note that the agitation for the change was made mainly on the principle that the prosecuting agency should not also be the trying agency, inasmuch as such a combination of powers violates the first principles of justice and equity. In spite of the various attempts made from 1886, however, the separation began to be actually effected in the State only from 1949, after the advent of the National Government. Under the Scheme of separation then introduced, the Collector and his subordinates ceased to have powers to try criminal cases, but their powers for preserving public peace and for maintaining law and order were retained in them. A separate class of Sub-Magistrates, Sub-divisional Magistrates and District Magistrates possessing legal qualification have been brought into existence purely for trying cases. This

---

1 *Manual of Madras Administration by* C. D. Maclean, Vol. I, 1885 p. 200.
G.O. Nos. 172–173, Judicial, dated 29th May 1861.
G.O. No. 154, Judicial, dated 21st July 1874.
G.O. No. 156, Judicial, dated 16th February 1875.

2 G.O. No. 1729, Judicial, dated 14th August 1914.
G.O. No. 1537, Law (General), dated 20th June 1922.

3 *Criminal Courts Manual Madras Acts*, 1949, *page* 509.

4 *Idem*, page 815.

5 G.O. No. 51, Public (Separation), dated 5th January 1951.
G.O. No. 1545, Home, dated 20th April 1951.
G.O. Nos. 1627–1634, Home, dated 26th April 1951.
G.O. No. 2107, Home, dated 28th May 1951.

6 *Studies in Madras Administration* by B. S. Baliga, Vol. I, 1949, pages 184–240.

system, however, does not involve any change in the law relating to the administration of criminal justice.[1]

Such is the history of criminal justice. Before leaving it, however, we may have a glance at the statistics relating to it in the district. The following statement will show the work turned out by the several criminal courts in the district during the last 50 years :—

	1900	1910	1920	1930	1940	1950
Cases—						
Village Magistrates Courts	266	142	95	6	2	700
Panchayat Courts.. ..	..	..	..	2,462	2,083	..
Regular Courts—						
1. Bench Magistrates ..	1,612	2,214	3,443	7,797	16,977	21,461
2. Special, Stipendiary, Deputy, Assistant, Joint and District Magistrates..	8,117	7,385	11,179	7,580	14,333	30,117
3. Sessions	122	129	133	159	236	189
Appeals—						
Magistrates Courts ..	511	448	308	223	253	309
Sessions Court	100	106	78	105	154	185
High Court	74	64	38	102	129	62
Total ..	10,802	10,488	15,274	18,434	34,167	53,023

The percentage of total number of criminal cases and appeals in the district to the State total was 4·29 in 1900 and it gradually rose to 4.35 in 1910, 5·31 in 1920, 6·46 in 1930, 6·52 in 1940 and 7·11 in 1950.

In 1956–57 the position of criminal justice in the district was as follows: There were in the district one Sessions Judge and one Additional Sessions Judge, both of whom exercised jurisdiction over the Nilgiris. The post of the Additional Sessions Judge was created in 1924 on a temporary basis in view of the large number of crimes committed to the sessions in the district. It was continued year after year until it was made permanent in 1937.[2] Besides these, there were in the district one District Magistrate common with the Nilgiris, one City First-class Magistrate, two Additional First-class Magistrates, two Subdivisional

[1] *Madras in* 1950, pages 40–43.
G.O. No. 78, Public, dated 10th January 1947.
G.O. No. 3105, Public, dated 9th September 1949.

[2] G.O. No. 58, Judicial (Magisterial), dated 9th February 1924.
G.O. No. 252, Judicial (Magisterial), dated 15th June 1924.
G.O. No. 722, Law (General), dated 4th March 1927.
G.O. No. 5054, Home, dated 11th December 1937.

Magistrates and thirteen Sub-Magistrates (12 in Coimbatore Division and one in the Nilgiris, all exercising second class powers). There were also several Panchayat Courts and Courts of Village Magistrates, but none of them tried any criminal cases. There were four Honorary Special First-class Magistrates in Coimbatore Division, two in Erode and two in Tiruppur Division. One Court of Second-class Bench Magistrate was functioning at Coimbatore Town. The Sub-Registrar at Sulur was appointed as Special Magistrate invested with third-class powers and was trying S.P.C.A. cases arising within his jurisdiction. In the Gudalur area of the Nilgiris district wherein separation has not been introduced, there was one Executive Revenue First-class Magistrate called Taluk First-class Magistrate functioning at Gudalur. There was also a Sheristadar Second-class Magistrate functioning at Gudalur to try second-class cases arising within the area. The Honorary Bench and Special Magistrates disposed of 11,586 cases, while the regular courts disposed of 79,975 cases. The number of appeals in the District Magistrates' Courts was 750 and in the Subdivisional Magistrates' Courts was 150, and all of them were disposed of. The fines realised by the courts (including the Nilgiris) amounted to Rs. 9,14,109. The percentage of total number of cases and appeals in the district to the State total was 12·44 in 1956 and 14·44 in 1957 and the district ranked 3rd in 1956 and second in 1957, in its contribution to the State total.[1]

Turning to police, on the decay of the Vijayanagar empire, the district was divided among a number of self-created petty poligars who, taking advantage of the troubled times, became independent of the Kings of Madurai who were then ruling the country. These predatory chieftains assumed judicial powers and maintained under them a number of head kavalkars and village kavalkars who acted either as police or as plunderers, according as occasion or their masters' command might serve. When the district came under the rule of the Mysore Kings, they established an efficient military police not only to overawe the poligars and to maintain internal peace, but also to defend the country from foreign invasion. This force is estimated to have been in the taluks north of Noyil, between 10,000 and 15,000 men called 'kandacharada peons'. They were supported by endowments of land and were employed partly in garrisoning the forts under Killedars and partly in police stations under Hoblidars at various centres. This police system was considered little better than " a military despotism under which a subject's property might have been secured from common robbery, but not from the licentiousness of those

1 Information furnished by the District Magistrate, Coimbatore and Registrar of High Court, Madras.

who held the sword ". Under Hyder this system became one of terrorism; and while he did not prevent plunder which eventually supplied his own coffers, his vigilance against crime or offences was unremitting and his punishment was heavy and summary. He added a postal system to this police system, using its officials as officers of an intelligence department to penetrate the secrets of the wealthy and to transmit the information direct to him. The system continued unaltered till 1790 when Tipu Sultan ordered the forts to be evacuated and their garrison to be disbanded, so that they might not furnish the British then in the country with additional means of carrying on the warfare against him. He did not, however, take any measures subsequently to re-establish these forts or to substitute a police. In fact the Coimbatore country was very much neglected by him during his last war with the British which terminated in his downfall. This relaxation of authority gave rise to the greatest excesses by the revenue servants and their oppression afforded an opportunity to rebels and robbers to overrun the country and to commit plunder and other offences with perfect impunity.[1]

When the district came under the British authority in 1799, the duties of the police devolved entirely on revenue officers and the village sibbandy. But, " as their situation and pay depended on the performance of their revenue duties which would occupy almost the whole of their time and attention ", the police work was considered as of a secondary nature and, being unremunerative, was naturally neglected.[2] In view of this inefficient means for the detection and prevention of offences, people in many villages maintained at their own expense, private kavalkars of Koravars and Valiars, who preserved the villages from depreciation and, in case of robbery, either detected the chief and recovered the property or made good the loss. As regards towns, they were divided into wards or sections according to the number of houses and the members of the wards jointly maintained three or four totis under the orders of a Kotwal or other principal officer. The duty of these totis was to patrol the streets by day and night, to apprehend suspicious persons, to keep the streets clean of dirt and to preserve the avenues of trees planted in them.[3]

In 1806 on the establishment of the Zillah Court at Dharapuram the old village police system was abolished and the tana or station system was introduced. Under this system the whole Zillah was divided into

---

1 Coimbatore Collectorate, Vol. I, No. 617, pages 125–139.
Manual of Coimbatore District, Vol. II, pages 246–247.

2 Judicial Sundries Vol. No. 4 (B), pages 279–280.

3 Coimbatore Collectorate, Vol. No. 617, pages 125–139.

Superintendencies in charge of Darogahs. Each Superintendency was divided into Hoblies in charge of Hoblidars or Duffadars; and each Hobly was divided into Tanahs or police stations in charge of Tanahdars who were responsible for the vigilance of the peons in the station in the discharge of their duties. Besides these police establishments maintained by the Government, there was another system called the Native Co-operation and Preventive Police introduced in 1807. The object of this system was " to inspire the people with a spirit of self-defence against gangs of robbers and thieves of every kind when attacked, to unite them on such occasions in defence of each other, of each other's property and the property and persons of the community to which they belonged and by this means to divert them of the fear on which those who attacked them entirely depended for success in their lawlessness ". Under this system the people in the villages, with the exception of certain castes, were divided into one or more sections and the inhabitants of each section were distributed into separate bodies corresponding in number with the month of the year. The section for the particular month to which it belonged and the people forming it were to remain on duty till the end of the month when the section for the ensuing month would enter on their duty and so on in regular rotation throughout the year. In case of emergency the people of the other sections who were not on duty were liable to be called out to resist an actual attack or to act in co-operation with the public police in the pursuit and apprehension of gang robbers and other offenders.[1]

In 1808 a further change was introduced in accordance with the Cornwallis Code; the police were transferred from the Collector to the Zillah Judge. The Zillah Judge who, now became responsible for the maintenance of public peace, had under him in that year three Daroghas, nine Rozsum, 90 Duffadars and 726 peons. The total expenses of the establishment amounted to 9,648 pagodas per annum.[2] This change however, by no means, improved matters. Crimes continued to increase. Between 1806 and 1812, for instance, there were 82 murders, 80 gang robberies, 107 gang burgalaries, 274 thefts, 53 cases of poisoning and killing cattle, eighteen cases of receiving stolen property, fifteen cases of arson, ten cases of wounding, seven cases of conspiracy to commit murder and liberate convicts, four cases of rape and one case of riot.[3] Moreover, the police as introduced by the Cornwallis Code had no means of knowing the State of the country, because neither the Darogah nor the peons

1 Judicial Sundries, Vol. No. 4 (B), pages 249–255.

2 Judicial Sundries, Vol. No. 5 (A), page 507.

3 *Idem*, Vol. No. 4 (B), pages 268–269.

serving under him had any natural authority or influence in it. The Darogah did not know where crimes were likely to be committed; nor could he remove any of the causes which frequently gave rise to crimes and disorders. In fact " he had no respect in the country, and he usually sought to keep up his consequence by terror, and to increase his income by fomenting disputes in families, by alarming them with threats of making disclosures against their women, by exacting money for concealment and by every kind of vexation."[1]

The police reforms introduced in all the districts in 1816 as a result of the recommendations of a Special Police Committee abolished the Kaval system altogether, resumed all the Kaval fees and maniums, reorganised the police under the heads of villages, the Tahsildars, the Zamindars, the Amins of police and the Kotwals and retransferred the magistracy and the control of the police from the Zillah Judge to the Collector. The heads of villages were assisted in their duties by the Talaiyaris and other village watchers and the Tahsildars were assisted by the Peshkars, the Gumsthas and the peons. The Zamindars were appointed as heads of police within their Zamindaris and the Amins of police were appointed as Tahsildars chiefly for furnishing supplies for travellers, and the Collector-Magistrate, who was placed in control over the entire police of the district, was held responsible for the maintenance of public peace.[2]

But even these changes were soon felt to be inadequate. The Collector-Magistrate, because of his more frequent tours and more intimate connection with the people, was undoubtedly found to be more capable of exercising a better control over the police than the Judge-Magistrate. But, saddled as he was by his growing revenue duties, he and his subordinates found little time to attend to police duties. The Talayaris who were the backbone of the police system were never properly paid; in the original settlement, allowances were granted for revenue servants, but not for the police duties of the Talaiyaris whose manium lands had been resumed by Tipu. They were consequently unwilling to work, although they were liable to punishment, if they failed to detect crimes which occurred in their respective villages. Several attempts were made by District Magistrates to get their position bettered, but with no avail. In 1844 waste lands were assigned as inams for their support; but since the lands were of poor quality, they required for their development. So, being almost without pay, the Talayaris neglected their police duties with

---

1 Selection of Papers from the Records of, at East India, Home, Vol. I, pages 70–71.

2 Regulation XI of 1816.

See also G.O. No. 672, Judicial, dated 30th May 1960.

the result that crime became more rife and detection less successful (1846).[1] The crimes went on incressing, as we have already seen while dealing with criminal justice.

Affairs were not better in other districts. In 1859, therefore, the police of the whole State was reorganized and made into a separate department. It was considered that the Collector-Magistrates, through their Assistants and revenue subordinates, were not in a position to exercise adequate supervision over the police establishments, that the control exercised by the Sessions Judges over the Collector-Magistrates, ever since the abolition of the Courts of Circuits, was illusory, since the Sessions Judges were occupying the same status as that of the Collectors, and that the police establishments themselves demanded a thorough revision. For all these reasons an Inspector-General of Police was appointed as the Head of the Department and under him were appointed a few Deputy Inspectors-General in charge of groups of districts and District Superintendents of Police each in charge of a district. The District Superintendents of Police, except in matters affecting discipline, etc., were placed under the District Magistrates. In matters affecting discipline, service, etc., they were placed under the Inspector-General of Police. And, finally each District Superintendent of Police was provided with a separate police staff of Inspectors, Constables and Village police.[2]

This system was introduced into the Coimbatore District in 1860. The district, including the Nilgiris, was now provided with one District Superintendent of Police, 24 Inspectors, 1,074 Constables, 275 Village Inspectors, 1,947 Village Talaiyaris. This establishment was distributed into 11 taluks then existing, and in each taluk were posted one or more Inspectors and a number of parties of constables attached to police stations and out-posts. There were thus 18 Inspectors with 53 police parties; 48 out-posts and 804 constables under them. At the same time separate police establishments were stationed in the towns of Coimbatore, Ootacamund and Wellington. Separate police establishments were also appointed for jails, treasuries and courts and some parties were kept as Reserve Police.[3]

The changes made in 1860 have remained the same in essentials to this days. The only important additional changes that have since been made are the formation of the Criminal Intelligence Department branch and the

---

1 *Manual of Coimbatore District*, Vol. II, page 248.

2 Judicial Consultations, dated 4th January 1859, papers connected with the reorganization of the Police, 1859.

3 G.O. No. 672, Judicial, dated 30th May 1860.

Railway Police. In about 1880 it was felt that, in order to prevent refined crimes such as forgery, false evidence, poisoning, cheating and conspiracy, it was essential to have a separate staff of police for criminal intelligence work and that, in order to prevent thefts on railways and at railway stations, it was equally essential to have a separate Railway Police.[1] Subsequently both the Criminal Intelligence Staff[2] and the Railway Police[3] were reorganized. It may be mentioned here that in 1910 the Nilgiris were removed from the Coimbatore district and placed under a separate District Superintendent of Police.[4]

Coimbatore is a heavy district in crime. Thus it stood fifth in grave crimes committed in 1954 and 1955.[5] But in 1956 the position became somewhat better and the district occupied the seventh place in the State. In that year 133 cases of murder, 15 cases of decoity, 22 cases of robbery, 612 cases of housebreaking, 209 cases of cattle theft and 1,365 cases of ordinary theft were committed in the district. The district, however, accounted for the highest number of murders and decoities followed in the case of the former, by Salem, Tirunelveli, Madurai (North) and Tanjore and, in the case of the latter, by Madurai (North), Tanjore, Ramanathapuram and Salem.[6]

Most of the crimes are attributable to certain criminal tribes in the district. Of those, the Valayars and the Salem Melnad Kuravars have been the most notorious from a long time. The Valayars are found over the greater part of the district, but more especially in the Avanashi, Coimbatore, Palladam and Satyamangalam taluks. Their name is said to have been derived from their being constantly employed in netting games in the jungles. Although many of them are frequently employed as talaiyaris and village menials, they live chiefly by committing crimes. They do not work in permanently organized gangs, but frequently they join together to commit a single crime or perhaps even several crimes at a time. Their favourite crime is theft of sheep or goat which they kill and dispose of, before the police even hear of the crime.[7]

---

1 Madras Police Report for 1881.

2 G.O. No. 1152, Judicial, dated 10th July 1906.

3 G.O. No. 1463, Judicial, dated 8th October 1897.

4 G.O. No.1045A–1046, Judicial, dated 4th July 1905.
G.O. No. 1616, Judicial, dated 7th October 1905.
G.O. No. 712, Judicial, dated 1st June 1909.
G.O. No. 712, Judicial, dated 11th May 1910.
Gazetteer of the Coimbatore District, Vol. II, 1933, page 196.

5 Report of the Administration of Police for 1955, page 2.

6 *Idem*, for 1956, pages 2, 3 and 5.

7 Papers relating to the Criminality of Tribes notified under the Criminal Tribes Act, pages 109–111.

The Salem Melnad Kuravars reside chiefly in the Bhavani and Erode taluks. Although village watching is stated to be their means of livelihood, they really live upon crime. They constitute themselves as village Kavalkars and extort kaval fees from villagers who have no other means of protection against their depredations. In return for the kaval fees, the Koravars are supposed to protect the villagers against crime and make good the losses they may incur. But in practice they do neither; and the villagers dare not dismiss them or withhold their fees, as they know that either course will entail the loss of their property at the hands of the kavalkars. The only people who are benefited by the existence of these kavalkars are the rich landlords who employ the Koravars as servants or in their capacity as criminals for the purpose of committing decoities on their enemies. To these landlords the Koravars remain obsequious and submissive and thereby gain a license to pray upon the less fortunate and unprotected villagers. Their kaval duties which are by no means lawful provide them with a means of evading the watch of the police and of facilitating their participation in crime.

These Koravars are criminals by tradition and training. Their aim and object in life is to be successful in the commission of offence. When a Korava marries, his wife, it is said, takes an oath that she will not reveal her husband's complicity in crime; nor does she admit that his absence from home is due to his participation in a criminal raid. The children of the tribe are brought upon the same line, and they further undergo an apprenticeship in crime. The mother conceals some articles with the child's knowledge and warns him not to tell his father. The latter endeavours to get the child to reveal the hiding place, using promises, threats and force in turn. As soon as the child is sufficiently hardened by these means, he is sent out to commit petty thefts and, on reaching the age of fifteen, participates in the crimes of the adults.[1]

The other criminal class of the district is Thottiya Nayaks who are believed to be an off-shoot of the Donga Dasari tribe so well-known in the Ceded Districts and Northern Circars of the Andhra Pradesh. The Thottiya Nayaks are purely nomadic in their habits and their chief crimes are theft and housebreaking. They move about in small parties with a 'Pattayam' or brass plate bearing an inscription which authorizes them to collect money from artizans, particularly blacksmiths. Under cover of one of these 'Pattayams', the nucleus of a gang travels through the district begging and doing a little work. While it is so occupied, the members engaged in committing crime remain out of sight and travel parallel to

1. Papers relating to the Criminality of the Tribes notified under the Criminal Tribes Act, pages 61–64.

them, keeping in secret touch with them for the purpose of obtaining information and disposing of stolen property.[1]

All these criminal classes were declared as criminal tribes under the Criminal Tribes Act of 1911 (India Act III of 1911),[2] and restrictions were imposed upon their movements. This Act was re-enacted in 1924, but was repealed in 1947 (Madras Act X of 1947) by the National Government which considered that, in the new set-up, it was altogether unjust to brand whole communities as criminals.[3] The individuals of the criminal tribes who are habitual offenders are, however, now dealt with under the Madras Restriction of Habitual Offenders Act (Madras Act XX of 1943) which places restriction on all habitual offenders, irrespective of the tribe or community to which they belong.[4]

Being the most important industrial district in South India it consists of a large number of labourers who are controlled by several unions, sponsored by the various political parties. Due to jealousy and rivalry among these divergent groups and common labour problems, the city and its surroundings are often beset with disturbance of peace. Of the riots and disturbances witnessed by the district, those which took place in connection with political agitation have already been described in the Chapter on Nationalism and Independence. Among others, the most serious in recent years were those which took place at Kothavadi, Coimbatore and Erode. The first flared up in August 1934 when a police party, proceeding from Kinathakadavu to Kothavadi to help a court amin in executing an order of the court for the delivery of certain lands sold in court auction, was way-laid and stoned by a crowd of 250 obstructors armed with sticks and other weapons. The police opened fire in order to save themselves from being over-whelmed by the obstructors and, as a result, two persons were killed and seven were injured.[5] The second riot which occurred in November 1946 originated from the lock-out of the Coimbatore Spinning and Weaving Mills, Coimbatore, on account of certain demands of the Communist Labour Union. When the mills reopened, a large mob of communists collected and attacked the property of the mills as well as the police who arrived on the scene. The mob, however, was dispersed by the police and curfew was imposed in the

1. G.O. No. 2968, Judicial, dated 12th December 1916.

2. Papers relating to the Criminality of the Tribes notified under the Criminal Tribes Act.

3. G.O. No. 2427, Home, dated 20th June 1947.

4. G.O. No. 231, Home, dated 26th January 1944.
G.O. No. 73, Home, dated 10th January 1945.

5. G.O. No. 273, Public, dated 14th February 1935.

disturbed area.[1] The third riot took place in January 1948 in consequence of a rumour which spread in Erode, shortly after the broadcast of the news of the assassination of Gandhiji. The rumour was to the effect that a Muslim boy in the guise of a Hindu assaulted two or three Hindu boys. Thereupon a large mob gathered in the town, committed looting and arson on the properties of the Muslims and attacked the police with sticks and stones. The rioters, however, dispersed on the arrival of the armed reserve.[2]

The police force in the district is under the charge of a District Superintendent of Police and Additional District Superintendent of Police who have their headquarters at Coimbatore. The latter was appointed in 1955 when the enforcement of prohibition was taken over by the Police Department. They have now under their control 6 Deputy Superintendents of Police in charge of Sub-Divisions, 19 Inspectors, 108 Sub-Inspectors 216 head-constables, 1,502 Constables of Taluk Police and one Sergeant Major, eight Sergeants, seven Jamedars, 42 Head Constables, 37 Naiks, 35 Lance Naiks and 424 Constables of Armed Reserve. There is also a District Intelligence Bureau functioning at the headquarters under the supervision of the District Superintendent of Police with one Inspector and seven Head Constables. Its primary duty is to collect and disseminate information regarding property, incidence of crimes and the *modus operandi* and sphere of operation of criminals. This, in short, is an 'Information Bureau' for the district regarding crimes and criminals. It also directs and co-ordinates the detection work in respect of organized crimes or any special type of crimes. It publishes weekly sheets and a monthly review relating to the district, which greatly facilitate both detection and prevention of crimes. It likewise publishes prohibition reviews and important notifications and circulars. The registration of foreigners and the issue of passports are also dealt with by this Bureau. The most important work of the Bureau is that of the Head Constables who are trained in developing finger prints and taking cast prints of the feet and toes for the scientific investigation of crimes. On the occurrence of crime, in which the possibility of such investigation exists, the investigating agency wires for the experts from the Bureau and their services are utilised for developing and lifting the latent finger prints.[3]

The District Special Branch, with one Inspector, five Sub-Inspectors, 20 Head Constables and one Police Constable is working directly under the District Superintendent of Police to deal with the political, labour

[1] G.O. No. 2701, Public, dated 14th December 1946.

[2] G.O. No. 1118, Public, dated 25th April 1949.

[3] *South Arcot District Gazetteer*, page 384.

and other matters as also security work in connection with the visits important persons. The Sub-Inspectors and the Head Constables arespr;, all over the district for getting quickly information about the situations in their respective spheres. Of late, this staff is being utilized also for gathering information about concentrations in illicit distillation of arrack and other offences under the Prohibition Act for incessent raids in the district.

There are two mobile raid parties consisting of one Sub-Inspector, one Head-Constable and ten Police Constables each and a van for its transport. They are under the direct control and supervision of the District Superintendent of Police and raid black spots (both *suo moto* and under instructions from the District Superintendent of Police) which are either neglected by or inaccessible to the regular Police. This apart, special mobile prohibition parties were formed in each Sub-division, in accordance with the decision arrived at during the last District Superintendents' Conference at Ootacamund to deal with only Prohibition Crimes within the sub-division. The strength of one Sub-Inspector and ten per cent of the Police Constables in the Sub-Division required for each party is drawn from the existing strength in turns and the transports are supplied from the existing Armed Reserve strength.

One Sub-Inspector and two Head-Constables form the Motor Vehicle Taxation staff at Coimbatore, working directly under the District Superintendent of Police exclusively for general and surprise checks of motor vehicles for detecting violations of the Motor Vehicle Taxation Acts all over the district by planned tours. This staff also works in co-ordination with the Regional Transport Officer, Coimbatore.

Besides this, there is also a Central Recruits' School at Coimbatore for the training of constables. This school was originally sanctioned in 1907 on the recommendation of the Police Commission of 1902.[1] It was, however, closed in 1923 when the vacancy reserve of 15 per cent of the total strength of Head Constables and constables was abolished. But subsequently in 1926 it was again re-opened.[2] and has been in existence continuously from that time. It can accommodate up to 600 recruits at a time. It trains the recruits for the districts of Coimbatore, Salem, the Nilgiris, Tiruchirappalli, Madurai Urban, Madurai North, Tirunelveli and Kanyakumari. It is in charge of a Deputy Superintendent of Police who is designated as Principal. There is a Chief Law Instructor of the rank of Inspector who is assisted by a number of Assistant Law Instructors of the

---

1. G.O. No. 1487, Judicial, dated 22nd August 1907.
   G.O. No. 712, Judicial, dated 1st Juno 1909.

2. G.O. No. 210, Judicial, dated 7th April 1926.

rank of Sub-Inspectors according to the number of recruits under training at the time. Similarly instruction in drill is imparted by a Chief Drill Instructor of the rank of Sergeant Major assisted by an Assistant Drill Instructor usually of the rank of Head Constable. [1] Recruits are admitted in the school every month in batches of not less than 20 to 30 according to the requirements of the districts served by the school.[2] The course of training extends over six months and includes instruction in drill, discipline, elementary law and procedure and manner in which police officers should conduct themselves towards the public. [3] The district comes under the jurisdiction of the Deputy Inspector-General of Police, Western Range, who has his headquarters at Coimbatore. The Deputy Inspector-General of Police is under the control of the Inspector-General of Police, Madras.

Coming to the jails, before the introduction of the Cornwallis system, there were no regular jails in the district. The few offenders who had to be confined were kept by the Collector in the town or village choultries. After the introduction of the Cornwallis system a jail was constructed at Dharapuram in 1807 for the accommodation of the prisoners. This jail was subsequently shifted to Coimbatore in 1811 when Coimbatore became the seat of the Zillah Court. The Zillah Judge who exercised supervision over the jail was assisted by a jailor and a number of prison guards, and medical aid was provided to the prisoners through the Zillah Surgeon. The Judges of Circuit were required to inspect the jail during their circuit and to submit a report to the Foujdari Adalat. Rules were at the same time drawn up and prescribed for the separate accommodation of different classes of prisoners, for the segregation of men and women, for the supply of proper food and clothing to them, for the ensuring of cleanliness and sanitation among them and for the regulation of their labour. But these rules were not always enforced. Prison discipline was then lax and prison escapes were not uncommon. [4]

In 1861, the Government sanctioned the construction of a new Central Jail which was completed in 1868 at a total cost of Rs. 3,42,690. The work was carried out by convicts under the supervision of Mr. Grimes, the first Superintendent of the jail. The jail was constructed in the north-eastern part of the Coimbatore town, covering about 44 acres and with an extent of 160 acres of land attached to it. It is not built on the standard plan,

---

1. Information furnished by the Deputy Inspector-General of Police, Western Range, Coimbatore.

2. G.O. No. 2813, Home, dated 20th June 1950.

3. G.O. No. 1487, Judicial, dated 22nd August 1907.

4. *Studies in Madras Administration* by B. S. Baliga, Vol. II, 1949, pages 169–173.

but contains twelve compartments of yards radiating from a central tower, the hospital wards being in a separate enclosure on the north-west side. The inner prison and factory are contained in separate enclosures on the south-west side, while the quarantine ward, female prison and civil prison are outside the main wall. Immediately after the completion of the prison a pise wall was constructed round the whole of the jail lands and completed in 1871. Considerable additions have been made to it in recent years. To day, it is one of the Central jails in the State. It had got accommodation for 1,166 prisoners in separate cells and for 762 in association wards. The prisoners are employed chiefly in the manufacture of textiles required for police uniforms, hospital bedding and clothing, convict bedding and clothing and many smaller items. They are also employed in dyeing, tailoring, tent-making, carpentry and blacksmithy. There is a well equipped elementary school within the jail to impart education to those convicts who are likely to be benefited by it. Besides this Central jail, there are sub-jails at the several taluk headquarters except at Coimbatore[1].

As has already been stated, the Zillah Judge and the District Judge were in charge of the Zillah Jail for a long time. In 1855 all the Jails in the State, including that coimbatore, were placed in charge of an Inspector of Prisons. In 1858 the designation of the post was changed to that of the Inspector-General of the Jails and in 1894 it was again changed to that of the Inspector-General of Prisons. From 1864 medical men came to be appointed as Superintendents of Jails in the place of District Judges.[2] This has since been replaced by the present system of appointing non-medical men, i.e., by officers belonging to the Madras Jail Service. There is now a Superintendent of Jails in charge of the Coimbatore Central Jail and he has under him one Deputy Superintendent of Jails, one Jailor, some subordinate officers and a number of warders.

Besides of Central Jail and Sub-Jails, Coimbatore has a Reception Home, a Vigilance Rescue Shelter, a branch of the Discharged Prisoners' Aid Society and three Probation Officers under the Probation Department. The Reception Home which is managed by the Discharged Prisoners' Aid Society was started in 1949 under the Madras Children Act, 1920 ; and the Rules framed thereunder for the reception and custody of under trial juvenile delinquents, destitutes and uncontrollable under the provisions of the Act. This Home is intended for both boys and girls of ages below 14. The children are looked after in the Home till

---

1 *Gazetteer of the Coimbatore District*, Vol. II, pages 187–199.
See also the Report of the Administration of Jails for 1956.

2 *Manual of Madras Administration* by C. D. Maclean, Vol, I page 177.

their cases are disposed of after necessray enquiries, by committal to a Certified School or otherwise disposed of by the Court as laid down in the Madras Children Act, 1920. The Vigilance Rescue Shelter started in 1950 is a short stay home established under the Madras Suppression of Immoral Traffic Act, 1930 for the reception and intermediate custody of rescued minor girls from brothels and young women below 30 years of age committed for street solieitation under the provisions of the Act. The inmates are afforded shelter and protection in the Home till their cases are disposed of after necessary enquiries by committal to a Rescue Home or Vigilance Home has the case may be, or otherwise disposed of by the courts as laid down in the Act. This Home is run under the direct control of the Tahsildar, Coimbatore. Both the above institutions are under the administrative control of the Chief Inspector of Certified Schools and Vigilance Service, Madras. The Discharged Prisoners' Aid Society assists generally the prisoners discharged from jails and the persons discharged from Borstal and Certified Schools in securing employment and in becoming useful members of the society. It maintains also a Discharged Prisoners' Home for affording shelter to homeless discharged prisoners. The Probation Officers came to be appointed for the first time in this State in 1937 under the Probation of Offenders Act of 1936 (Madras Act III of 1937). They discharge several useful functions under various Acts. Under the Probation of Offenders Act they make preliminary investigations in cases referred to them by the courts and also exercise supervision over the offenders placed under them. Under the Madras Children Act of 1920 (Madras Act IV of 1920), the Borstal School Act of 1926 (Madras Act V of 1926) and the Suppression of Immoral Traffic Act V of 1930), they perform the After-care work of persons discharged from certified schools, Borstal Schools and the Shri Sadana and the Vigilance Home and assist in the rehabilitation of persons discharged from these institutions. They also do the After-care work of Parole prisoners, i.e., prisoners, released conditionally and prematurely under the Advisory Board Scheme. And finally, under Chapter XXXVI of the Criminal Procedure Code, they try to effect reconciliation between entranged husbands and wives. In 1955, for instance, the three Probation Officers of the district made 1254, preliminary enquires, supervised 678 persons, paid 2,697 visits and submitted 2,434 periodical reports about their progress.

CHAPTER XVI.

REVENUE ADMINISTRATION.

In Coimbatore, as in other districts, land revenue administration has had the longest history. This is not surprising seeing that, until recently, land revenue constituted the main source of Provincial Revenue and seeing also that it has always affected the welfare of millions engaged in the cultivation of land. We shall do well, therefore, to deal first with land revenue and then with the other sources of revenue.

Land revenue administration in Coimbatore under the British began with the acquisition of that district from Tipu by the East India Company in 1799. In that year, the tracts north of the Noyyil, now known as Erode, Bhavani, Gobichettipalayam, Coimbatore, the Nilgiri hills, Avanashi, part of Palladam and Kollegal were placed under Mr. Macleod, while the rest of Palladam, Karur, Dharapuram, Udumalpet and Pollachi were placed under Mr. Hurdis.[1] Of these tracts, the Nilgiris were separated in 1868, Karur was transferred to the Tiruchirappalli district in 1910 and Kollegal was added to the Mysore State in 1956.

Both the Collectors, Mr. Macleod and Mr. Hurdis (who was also the Collector of Dindigul) having served previously under Mr. Read, the well known Collector of Salem and the father of the Ryotwari System, it was only natural that they should have thought of introducing the same system in Coimbatore. They were also disposed to adopt that system, because it was the system in vogue under Hyder and Tipu. Omitting all details, what they did can be described in a few words. In both the divisions surveys were conducted; the lands of each village were divided into a limited number of classes according to their productive powers; the villages themselves were divided into groups with reference to the general quality of their lands and to their proximity to markets and towns; the second rate of the first and the most favourably situated groups of villages was applied to the best lands of the second group, the third group villages were assigned as their highest rates the second rate of the second group villages and so on; and the grain values of each class of field were determined with reference to the opinions of the Karnams and the ryots and

---

[1] Proposals for a New Settlement of the Land Revenue, etc., of Coimbatore by Mr. H. F. Clogstoun, dated 1st September 1875, printed, page 3.

Manual of the Coimbatore District by F. A. Nicholson, 1887, page 96.

commuted into money at the average price prevailing in the previous favourable seasons.

Thus far, the course pursued by Mr. Macleod and Mr. Hurdis in the two divisions was the same in all essentials. But, in determining the total assessment to be levied and thus in obtaining a guide as to what portion of the produce should be exacted as assessment, the two officers seem to have gone different ways. Mr. Macleod, in the Northern Division sought to equalise the assessment without rendering the total revenues of the country too high or too low in comparison with the collections of former years. Finding, therefore, after his classification was completed, that the tentative rates which he had at first fixed upon as being fair and equitable would result in an excessive increase of revenue, he, at once, cut them down by nearly one-third; having, however, satisfied himself that the rates thus arrived at, which showed an increase of about 12 per cent over the revenue of Fasli 1209 (1799)—the first year of British rule—would represent fairly what the country could bear. These rates, he judged, would be rather below than above the rates which could be afforded by the ryots. The assessment, he added, took less than two-fifths of the gross produce of dry lands and below half the gross produce of wet and garden lands. Mr. Hurdis, in the Southern Division, on the other hand, sought to fix the revenue at that proportion of the produce to which the Government was generally entitled, regardless of all considerations, as to the amount of revenue which the division had previously borne. The proportion of produce leviable, he decided, should be half of the net produce in the case of wet lands and two-fifths of the gross produce in the case of dry and garden lands; and these proportions of the produce commuted into money, the ryots were compelled to pay. The rates thus determined by different ways were introduced into the Northern Division in the first half of Faslies 1211 and 1212 (1801 and 1802) and into the Southern Division in the latter half of the same Faslis. They resulted in the Northern Division in an increase of 8 per cent and in the Southern Division in an increase of 17 per cent over the revenues collected by Tipu, the assessment in the Southern Division averaging on the whole, about 35 per cent above those of the Northern Division. [1]

There is evidence to show that during Faslis 1212–17 (1802–07), the Southern Division suffered much from continued bad seasons. There

1. Proposals for a New Settlement of the Land Revenue, etc., of Coimbatore, etc., by H. F. Clogstoun, dated 1st September 1875, pages 7–9.

For details, see *Manual of the Coimbatore district* by F. A. Nicholson, 1887, pages 96–102.

Board's Consultations, dated 5th January 1818.

is evidence to show that it was thrown into not a little confusion during the same period by the rebellion of one of the Palayakars. There is also evidence to show that, during the same period, it was subjected to a most malignant type of fever. These factors might have been partly the cause for a considerable fall in the collection of revenue in the Southern Division. But, the main cause was undoubtedly the high pitch of assessment in this Division. That is what the Board of Revenue and the Government thought when they ordered an immediate reduction to the standard rates prevailing in the Northern Division. This reduction was carried out in 1807 by Mr. Garrow who had been appointed as the Collector of both the divisions in 1805.

The reduction, however, did not, by any means, bring relief to the ryots. The work was "badly and imperfectly done ". Instead of assimilating the assessment of the two divisions, a reduction of 37 per cent was made in the punja (dry) assessment only, while the garden assessments were left at their original high standard, and, to compensate further for the loss of revenue which the reduction would have caused, the ryots were compelled to pay full rents for their waste grass lands, instead of the usual rate of one-fourth of the assessment. The settlement of Fasli 1217 (1807) thus made increased the revenue of the whole district from Rs. 19,63,657 to Rs. 21,31,986. It was upon the basis of the average collections of these high assessments that the village leases were concluded.[1]

This new system, called the village settlement, obtained recognition in Madras in 1807. It was first recommended by what is called the Tanjore Commission and was at once unhesitatingly approved by the Government as being the system least liable to objection and better calculated for an ultimate measure of permanency which they were then contemplating than the ryotwari or zamindari or muttadari settlements. It was given a further fillip by Mr. Hodgson, a Member of the Board of Revenue, and of the Tanjore Commission. Having toured through the districts of Coimbatore and Tirunelveli, he submitted two reports to the Government towards the end of 1807. These reports urging the necessity for the adoption of village settlements were referred by the Government to the Board of Revenue for remarks, with a direction to state its opinion on the expediency of substituting the village for the ryotwari settlement in the whole State. The Board lost no time in reporting strongly in favour of the village system. That system, it said, was formerly prevailing in most

1. Proposals for a New Settlement of the Land Revenue, etc., of Coimbatore by H. F. Clogstoun, dated 1st September 1875, page 9.
Manual of the Coimbatore district by F. A. Nicholson, 1887, pages 104–105.

parts of the State. Under it, the whole country was divided into villages with generally fixed boundaries, including large tracts of land, both arable and waste. Under it the Government share was usually received from the nanja lands (wet lands) in kind at rates varying from 40 to 60 per cent of the gross produce after deducting a certain portion distributed before the threshing season, and from punja lands (dry lands) in cash at so much for a fixed measure of land, or so much for the same measure of land, varying with the produce. Of the two other systems recommended for permanency, the Board felt that the zamindari or the muttadari system must be ruled out as being unsuitable in the southern districts and that the ryotwari system propounded by Munro must also be ruled out, as it had several drawbacks. According to Munro's plan, the existing assessment under the ryotwari system was to be lowered by 25 per cent with a still greater remission on land watered by picotahs, etc. This remission was to provide for all contingencies and nothing further was to be allowed for bad crops, except in extraordinarily bad seasons. Further, the waste lands were to be regarded as Government lands and taxed when brought under cultivation ; the repairs of large tanks alone were to be carried out by the Government, and advances for cultivation were to be gradually discontinued. This plan, the Board said, Munro had advocated, instead of a permanent zamindari settlement, believing that, while it permanently settled the minimum income of the Government, it provided for the future augmentation of that income with the extension of cultivation and increase of population. It was, however, the Board remarked, impracticable for the Government to make so large a sacrifice as one-fourth of the existing revenue. The ryotwari system also involved the employment of a large number of subordinate revenue officials, upon whose conduct no proper checks could be easily imposed. The danger of delegating authority to corrupt Tahsildars, the general inability of the ryots to pay in all seasons the assessments fixed on their holdings, the constant change of field occupants and the resulting deterioration of cultivation, all these, seemed to the Board insuperable objections to the ryotwari system. The village system was, on the other hand, the Board observed, as old as the age of Manu. It was familiar to the people. It would facilitate and reduce the charges of collection and it did not demand much attention from the Collectors. On grounds such as these, the Board recommended the village lease for a period of three or five years and the Government agreed with it and ordered the conclusion of triennial leases in Coimbatore as well as in all other districts not permanently settled. The Government also directed the Board to prepare materials for effecting a permanent settlement of the villages at the expiration of the triennial leases in districts which might admit of that measure. Accordingly a triennial lease was introduced in 1808 in Coimbatore and several other districts. [1]

Under this system the assessment on each village was fixed for a period of three years with reference to the accounts of cultivation and the assessment and actual collections of past years. The rents fixed were declared to be payable under all circumstances, extraordinary calamities excepted. In villages suffering under adverse seasons or other drawbacks, a progressive rent was fixed or the lease was deferred for a term of one year with the principal ryots of the villages. Ordinary repairs were ordered to be done by the ryots but repairs of magnitude or new works, it was declared would be undertaken by the Government on the condition of a proportionate increase of assessment. The ryots were held jointly and severally responsible for the assessment and pattas were ordered to be issued by them to the cultivating tenants for their mutual security against loss on the one hand and oppression on the other. [2]

But this triennial lease introduced into the district proved a complete failure. Based as it was on the high assessments and collections of past years, it led to a system of rack rents which left the district in a state of utter exhaustion. The revenues also fell from Rs. 21,14,960 to Rs. 18,59,342 and again to Rs. 16,92,283. [3]

And yet, the Board of Revenue and the Government refused to lose faith in the village system and did their best to make it permanent not only in Coimbatore but also in other districts. In 1811 when the, triennial leases in the various districts were about to expire, the Board again took up the subject into consideration. The village leases, it said, had failed because of unfavourable seasons, the low price of grain, the short period of the lease and the freedom from compulsion which the cultivators enjoyed

1. Board's Consultations Nos. 9–10, dated 7th May 1807.

General Report of the Board of Revenue, Vol. V, pages 51–52.

Revenue Consultations No. 258, dated 4th December 1807 and No. 244, dated 27th November 1807.

General Report of the Board of Revenue, Vol. V, dated 5th October 1808, pages 170–178.

Board's Consultations No. 11, dated 25th April 1808.

Board's Consultations Nos. 17–18, dated 4th February 1808.

Board's Consultations Nos. 21–23, dated 11th July 1808.

Revenue Despatch to England, dated 24th October 1808, paragraphs 59–76.

Board's Consultations No. 2, dated 1st August 1808.

2. General Report of the Board of Revenue, Vol. V, dated 5th October 1808, pages 178–181.

Board's Consultations Nos. 21–23, dated 11th July 1808.

3. Proposals for a New Settlement of the Land Revenue of Coimbatore, etc., by H. F. Clogstoun, dated 1st September 1875, page 10.

under the new system of judicature. And the village system, it went on to observe, first made on a long lease, say of 7 or 10 years and then permanently *fixed* at a standard rent or *shist*, was the system best calculated to give the ryots " a permanent interest in the improvement of the land, if not a proprietary right in the soil, without involving the necessity of considerable remissions and without introducing strangers or shocking and fettering the people with novel and arbitrary regulations ". Such a *shist* might be determined on " a calculation of the average collections of former years and the general capabilities and permanent resources of the village ". In villages where the principal inhabitants might agree to pay the *shist*, they should receive a cowle investing them with all the rights of the Government in all the waste lands of the village and assuring them that, so long as they continued to pay the *shist*, they would remain in possession of their lands without any additional assessment. In those villages where the poverty of the inhabitants, the low state of cultivation, or the large extent of waste lands might preclude an immediate settlement on adequate terms, a temporary settlement might be formed on a moderate, progressive rent and the inhabitants informed that on their agreeing to pay the *shist* they would be placed on the footing of permanent lessees. The Board was sanguine that under this system "private property would be established and land would become saleable property and the occasional remissions and the expenses of taccavi and tank repairs . . . would diminish by degrees in proportion to the gradual improvement of the country ". It, however, said that the settlements should be formed with the principal ryots or head inhabitants of the village to be made permanent, subject to the approval of the Court of Directors.[1]

The Government sanctioned these proposals, ordered the village settlements to be made decennial in the first instance subject to permanency on the approval of the Directors, and strongly recommended the measure to the Home Authorities dwelling at length on its merits. They also ordered the Board to incorporate all rules relating to the settlement in a Regulation so that the rights of the Government, the principal ryots as well as the cultivating tenants might be clearly defined and each party maintained in its just rights by the civil courts. It was believed that the immediate advantages of the settlement would be the simplification of the revenue system, the avoidance of all labour involved in temporary settlements, the decrease in the charges of collection, the reduction in taluk establishments and the consequent savings to the public treasury,

1 General Report of the Board of Revenue, dated 30th January 1812, pages 127–135.

Board's Consultations No. 12, dated 9th May 1811 and No. 14, dated 1st July 1811.

the release of ample time for the Collectors to devote adequate attention to their other duties, and, hence, an all round improvement in the administration of the districts.[1]

It was under these circumstances that, on the expiration of the triennial lease, a decennial lease was introduced into Coimbatore. But, by the time that this lease was extended to two-thirds of the district,[2] the Court of Directors condemned the village system in no uncertain terms and ordered its discontinuance and reversion to the ryotwari system. In 1812, they wrote an important despatch to Madras. They were, they said, surprised at the general establishment of the village system as a measure of permanency conditional on their sanction, when they had not been apprised of the result of the triennial leases attempted in the several districts. They had ample evidence from Bengal that great errors had been committed in concluding the permanent settlement in that Province. A similar settlement formed in Madras, they stated, had not been found successful. They could see little difference between the muttadari settlement which had already failed in the Baramahal and other places in Madras and the permanent village system which had been urged for general adoption. "The difference between the two systems appears to be in degree, not in principle, both having a tendency to affect the interests, feelings and rights of the small landed proprietors." The Patta Regulation which was intended to protect the rights of the ryots in the Zamindaris "had almost become a dead-letter" both in Bengal and Madras. The Zamindars had habitually disregarded this Regulation and the principal ryots under the village system might likewise do the same. The chief objection raised against the ryotwari system was its detail, but Munro, alike in the Baramahal, Kanara, and the Ceded Districts, had not found his administration impeded by the ryotwari system. The detail must be carried out by somebody, and the question was whether it had better be carried out under the Collectors or under the Zamindars. Moreover, the details were involved chiefly in the jamabandi and, once the jamabandi was over, the collection went on by itself. Arguing thus in favour of the ryotwari system, the Directors quoted the authority of several of the Company's servants, including the views of Lord William Bentinck, in support of that system. Nor is this all. They pointed out that the ryotwari system had two great advantages. One was that it secured effectually to the State, better than

1 General Report of the Board of Revenue, Vol. 6, dated 30th January 1812, pages 141–152.

Revenue Despatch to England, dated 29th February 1812, paragraphs 195–256.

2 Proposals for a New Settlement of the Land Revenue in Coimbatore, etc., by H. F. Clogstoun, dated 1st September 1875, page 10.

any other system, an adequate revenue from waste lands as they were brought under cultivation. The other was that it was quite in consonance with the Hindu Law of inheritance which divided and subdivided properties and brought them " to a state similar to that they would be under the ryotwari management ". For these reasons they ordered that in all unsettled districts the ryotwari system should be adopted, and that, where the village rents had been already established, the leases should be declared terminable at the expiration of the period for which they had been granted. They warned the Government of the responsibility that would attach to them for any detriment to the Company's interests from disobedience to their orders.[1]

These orders were obeyed, though with not a little reluctance, by the Government. In Coimbatore as well as in other districts, the ryotwari system was again ordered to be introduced on the expiry of the decennial leases.[2] In Coimbatore it was introduced in 1815. In that year, a special commission consisting of Mr. Munro and Mr. Sullivan exposed a series of abuses committed in the district by the subordinate revenue officers in collusion with the renters, and as a result, as soon as Mr. Sullivan took charge of the district from Mr. Garrow, he cancelled all the village leases on the ground of universal fraud and re-introduced the ryotwari system.[3]

From that date till to-day the ryotwari system has continued in the district not without, however, many modifications. From 1815 to 1878, the year in which the modern ryotwari system was introduced, the old system underwent several changes, and these changes can be conveniently classified under the following heads ; (1) the patkat system which refused the ryot complete freedom of relinquishment, (2) the reductions of assessment, (3) remissions and cowles, (4) gross rents and payments for waste, (5) the garden assessments, (6) second crop assessment, (7) takavi and (8) the dittam, the jamabandi and the patta.

The patkat system was introduced by Mr. Thackeray in 1818. It was a departure from the field system to which the ryots were immemorially accustomed and which was the starting point of Mr. Macleod and

---

1 Revenue Despatch from England, dated 16th December 1812, paragraphs 3–47.

2 Revenue Despatch to England, dated 5th March 1813, paragraphs 123–136.
Idem, dated 25th August 1813, paragraphs 1–20.
Idem, dated 12th August 1814, paragraphs 1–30.
Revenue Despatch from England, dated 12th April 1815, paragraphs 57–80 and 113–125.

3 *Manual of the Coimbatore District* by F. A. Nicholson, 1887, pages 106–107.

Mr. Hurdis. Mr. Thackeray found or assumed that, whatever be the intention of the ryotwari settlement, there was, in practice, a variety of inequalities and errors and this led to many fields being assessed too high, and many too low. He also assumed that, in the fifteen years which had elapsed since the settlement, these errors had to a great extent been rectified by the action of the ryots and of the officials, chiefly in the matter of gross and garden rents, so that the possession of lands favourably assessed was balanced by that of heavily assessed lands and vice versa. He moreover considered that the continual struggle for favours, the evasion of rules, and the opportunities for fraud were debasing the ryots and revenue officers, while the absence of permanency in the demand were discouraging the ryots who felt that any improvement, such as the digging of a well or the conversion of a so-called grass land into arable land, was followed by a great increase in the Government demand. He further noticed that the demand varied both with the purpose to which the field might be appropriated, e.g., grass or dry cultivation or garden culture, and with the circumstances of the ryot, and he broadly stated that it was " the ryotwari settlement only in name " and that " it taxed the ryot and not the land ". Believing, therefore, that the then existing demand of about 21 lakhs of rupees was as much as the district could pay, he proposed to limit the demand to that sum, to regard existing holdings or farms, or " estates " as he called them, with their existing assessments as the revenue unit, instead of the settlement field, and to the ryots upon their holdings for a considerable term of years during which, without further increase of payments, they might dig wells and grow garden crops, convert grass lands into arable lands and so forth. In case of division of the holdings by inheritance, the apportionment of the demand upon the divisions, he stated, should be made by panchayats, so that gradually, without any revision of field assessment, each little holding or estate would eventually be equitably assessed according to its productive power as gauged by the owners themselves or their predecessors in holding.

Nor is this all. He supposed that the existing inequalities could be set right by the denial of freedom in relinquishment. Assuming that the holding of bad lands was necessary to compensate a supposed advantage in good lands, he argued the justice of the rule that forbade the ryot to give up bad land without a due proportion of good land; just as a tenant in England would not be allowed to rent only the good fields in a farm, so a ryot ought not to be allowed to pick and choose his holding. He also stated that, if the ryots were given freedom of relinquishment, they would throw up bad lands assessed at about 2 lakhs of rupees, and concentrating their attention and stock on the smallest extent of the best and lowest assessed land, would crop the fields to exhaustion and eventually throw up those fields as well.[1]

This system, with some modifications, having been approved by the Board of Revenue and the Government, was introduced into the district from 1818 onwards. In 1832, Mr. Drury, the then Collector of the district described it thus: " a ryot whose means were known to be affluent could not throw up any part of his farm unless another ryot engaged to take it, or he himself agreed to occupy other land paying equal rent ", while a poor ryot was allowed to throw up land, provided he gave up good and bad together, remissions being granted for waste land and " distressed circumstances ". On a similar report submitted by him in 1835, the Board of Revenue promptly ordered him to put all ryots, rich and poor alike, under the same rule, viz., freedom of relinquishment of good and bad together, and this did away with a great hardship to ryots of actual or reported affluence. It must be stated that this restriction on freedom of relinquishment was, as time went on, gradually evaded and relaxed, so that, in 1853, the Collector reported that the system no longer existed.

Reductions in assessment were periodically effected in nanja, punja as well as garden lands. So that the Collector, Mr. Thomas, could report in 1855-56 as follows: " The Coimbatore Settlement is now to all intents and purposes a permanent settlement under real ryotwar, and I cannot honestly see what more could be desired for the ryot. He is certainly content . . . his assessment is light, fixed, unvarying, on the soil, not on the crop; he grows what he pleases without injury. His lease is permanent, it runs for as many years as he chooses unchanged, but he can reduce or enlarge his farm *ad libitum* by simply making known his wish; any labour and capital he sinks in improvement is entirely untaxed; he reaps the whole benefit " [2].

Remissions covered a multitude of difficulties. There were the remissions of assessment on grass lands, and second-crop cultivation, and other remissions necessitated by the patkat and compulsory holding system, by the want of freedom in the matter of land relinquishment. There were also the remissions caused by the dittam system under which the ryot agreed to take more land than either the season subsequently permitted or he himself had stock and capital to cultivate.

---

[1] Coimbatore Collectorate, Vol. No. 611, pages 25–57.
Idem, Vol. No. 588, pages 51–123.
Manual of the Coimbatore District by F. A. Nicholson, 1887, pages 109–110.

[2] *Idem*, pages 110–112.

In fact the weight of assessment at the prevailing prices was considerable and its incidence were unequal, so that various expedients had to be resorted to in order to retain the full area in cultivation; and of these expedients none was considered so efficacious as the remissions. Under Mr. Sullivan, under the patkat system then in vogue, remissions became the rule. He granted cowles of remission, temporary as well as permanent by alleging the pitiable condition of the ryots and survey inequalities and the Board of Revenue and the Government fulminated in vain. It was pointed out that they amounted to tampering with the principle of a fixed survey assessment, that they could be regarded as nothing but temporary expedients " unsound and fictitious ", that they led to a " premature extension of cultivation " of bad soils for the mere show of extension of cultivation and that they converted the annual settlement into "a scramble for remissions " and led to corruption and venality. In 1832, the then Collector, Mr. Thomas, clearly saw that they were necessitated by the patkat system of restriction of freedom and recommended a return to the free ryotwari system proper, arguing that the ryots were the best judges of what they could occupy, and stated that the permanent cowles and other remissions could be got rid of. But though the Board and the Government admitted the inadvisability of indiscriminate cowles and remissions and ordered their revocation and abandonment, they adhered to the restriction of the patkat system. They laid down that, except on particular occasions, the only cowles should be for the reclamation of waste and conversion of dry into garden lands but retained the objectionable restrictive rules. The result was the remission system continued at least in part. It was not till 1841 that permanent remissions were ordered to be discontinued and not till 1856 that temporary remissions became extinct. Seasonal remission have, however, been continued to this day [1].

In regard to grass rents, there were two such rents, one called ayan pilluvari or pancham hissa, and the other called pilluvari. The former was not an assessment, but a remission of three-fourths of the regular survey assessment of 1801 on one-fifth of the patta holding, while the latter was the rental of the unoccupied waste lands, which were not held by any ryot but which were let out for grazing purposes only. The pancham hissa system arose as follows. Under former Governments, all lands, if left waste, paid a small tax of about 1 to 4 annas per acre. At the settlement of 1801, Mr. Macleod fixed one-third of the survey assessment as the payment for occupied waste in the Northern Division, while Mr. Hurdis retained the old rate of the Southern Division, which, however, was raised to one-fourth of the assessment in 1805. The remission

1 *Manual of the Coimbatore District* by F. A. Nicholson, 1887, pages 112–116.

amounted in 1818 to Rs, 3,22,536, rose to Rs. 4,22,961 in 1835–36 and fell to Rs. 2,73,852 in 1836–37, probably because the Board ordered in 1835 that the remission on all land held on grass tax in addition to the regular one-fifth should be discontinued and full rates charged. From that time onwards it steadily decreased till, in 1873, it was only Rs. 21,252 and was finally abolished at the original settlement in 1880–83. The second form of grass revenue, called parava pillu was a true tax, also amounting to one-fourth of the assessment. The unoccupied land was let out to whatever ryot would take it and in any quantity, and was held for a year or longer period, if no one wanted it for cultivation. It amounted occasionally to about a lakh of rupees, but rapidly fell after 1863, when waste lands were taken up for cultivation, so that, in 1872, it amounted to only Rs. 151. It was found that the richer ryots sometimes only one or two, intentionally kept lands out of cultivation for this purpose and retained them for grazing "to the exclusion of poorer ryots who were willing to cultivate, but afraid to come forward". This was noticed by several Collectors, and in the Dharapuram taluk it was early found necessary to assess at full rates ayan pillu lands occupied by rich ryots beyond the customary one-fifth, since they kept poor ryots from getting the land. [1]

As to payments, for waste, it may be stated briefly that the rule under the former Governments varied and that Tipu appears to have ordered that all occupied land should pay full rates, the grass rent for unoccupied being retained. Tipu's practice was changed by the British by allowing grass remission on occupied waste up to one-fifth of the holding, the remaining fallow being, after 1835, fully charged. The practice of fallowing, it may be stated, is of immemorial antiquity. And, as has already been seen, the grass remission on occupied land gradually decreased and was abolished at the original settlement [2].

The next item, the garden assessments, were the subject of a great deal of correspondence. Originally based upon a share of the crop, they formed an undue burden on the ryot, since he shared with the Government the profit on his own capital, in spite of the extra labour involved in well-irrigation. The assessment averaged about four times that on dry lands, but was higher in the south than in the north. It was usual to grant favourable terms for the first year or two, gradually increasing it to the full rate in the fifth year. There were different modes of classifying the lands; in some taluks whole fields were classed as garden, irrespective of the

[1] *Manual of the Coimbatore District* by F. A. Nicholson, 1887, pages 116–118.

Proposals for a New Settlement of Land Revenue in Coimbatore, etc., by H. F. Clegstoun, dated 1st September 1875, pages 50–53.

[2] *Manual of the Coimbatore District* by F. A. Nicholson, 1887, page 118.

irrigable area; in others only the area actually irrigable. The former rule was soon found to be unworkable, as it was often equivalent to doubling the rates and various expedients therefore, such as charging half-rates or dry rates on the non-irrigable area, were resorted to and the irrigable area was sometimes determined by the quantity of water in the well and sometimes by the area originally irrigated. The circumstances of the ryot were also another factor in the change so that there was little certainty for the cultivator. To add to all this, there was incessant change, and one Collector treated gardens in one way only to have his expedients criticised and altered by his successor. The problem was to show the largest possible increase of revenue, and the temptation to charge full rates for garden lands was checked only by the certainty of discouraging an increase in well-digging and the abandonment of many wells. In practice however, many remissions and reductions were granted, and consequently the wells steadily increased, the Collectors being fully aware that " nothing but cultivation from wells can secure the people of this district against heavy loss and very often ruin, consequent upon successive seasons of severe drought ". It may be stated here that all gardens were, from the beginning, saleable and were the subject of the peculiar form of property known as " adhinam ", by which a ryot who had given up a garden could reclaim it, even if it had passed into other hands, upon paying the value of any improvements as decided by a panchayat. Neither time nor absence affected his ownership, which was that of absolute private property, and this right was always recognized by the former Governments and continued under the British.

Gradually, however, the impolicy of taxing improvements, especially wells which, in a dry district like this, act as a famine insurance came to be realized. As early as 1818, the Board of Revenue proposed to declare that in future all dry land converted into garden at the sole expense of the ryot should not be liable on that account to any additional charge, but this liberal suggestion was not carried out. The patkat theory and the idea of "once a garden always a garden" seem to have at first stood in the way of equitable rules; a dry field, if made into a garden, was promptly charged garden rates, but if a garden failed, even by reason of the springs drying up, the ryot got into difficulties. In 1833, Mr. Drury, the then Collector, proposed to settle the demand at the highest dry rate of the village upon gardens no longer cultivable as such and to treat only " the area within the range of the well " as garden land and to charge it garden rates, the rest being charged as dry. This was approved of with the alteration that the dry rate appropriate to the land should be charged, but as the rules left everything to the discretion of the authorities, nothing tangible resulted.

It was not till Mr. Thomas, when he was Collector, took up the subject in earnest, that more liberal views prevailed. Owing chiefly to his advocacy, a rule was passed in 1852 and was carried into effect in 1854, whereby all lands watered from new wells were charged only the ordinary dry rates or, in other words, not interfered with, all extra assessment on garden lands with ruined wells was struck off, and, even if a well was repaired no further charge was made. At the same time, 12 per cent in the northern taluks and 15 per cent in the southern taluks were remitted on all garden lands. In 1864, the matter was again brought up and the Collector pressed for the concession of 25 per cent upon the old gardens as recommended by Mr. Thomas; but the Government being not convinced, directed that assessments should only be reduced in all cases to the highest dry rate of the village. [1]

Another matter was second crop cultivation. It may be noted that the principal sources of irrigation in the district are the Bhavani, the Noyyil and the Amaravathi rivers and the rain-fed tanks. A consolidated assessment was at the settlement of 1801 imposed on the greater part of the irrigated area under the rivers. But, about the year 1832, the levy of a second-crop assessment, in cases where no second-crop was raised, was discontinued, save under the Kalingarayan channel. A portion generally two-thirds of the consolidated assessment was taken as representing the assessment on a first crop, and, with the exception of the Kalingarayan lands, the additional assessment was only levied in the event of a second crop being grown. The concession was even greater in some cases; thus, for lands under the Noyyil, the charge for the second crop was only imposed when the second crop was either arecanut, or coconut or betel-vine, or sugar-cane or turmeric or plantains, a second crop rice being allowed free of charge, while in lands irrigated by the Kodiveri anicut no charge whatever was made, except for lands under coconut or arecanut. The limitation of the charge for second crop to certain special products other than rice had nothing to recommend it, but this limitation survived until the introduction of the original settlement [2].

As to takavi, or the system of annual advances to aid current cultivation, it was never much in vogue in the district. And as to dittam and jamabandi, which were annual settlements, the former was abolished in 1858, while the latter still continues, The dittam calls for some

1 B.P. No. 2502, dated 10th September 1878.

Manual of the Coimbatore District by F. A. Nicholson, 1887, pages 118–122.

2 *Proposals for a New Settlement of the Land Revenue of Coimbatore, etc.*, by H. F. Clogstoun, dated 1st September 1875, pages 48–49.

Manual of the Coimbatore District by F. A. Nicholson, 1887, pages 122–123.

explanation. It was an arrangement or a settlement "in theory an account taken by the revenue subordinates at the commencement of the cultivating season, of the land that the ryots intended to cultivate and what of the previous holdings they intended to give up. In practice, however, it was accompanied by inducements and injunctions to take up larger extents of land than the ryots had the means of cultivating, in order to make a great show on paper, and the ryots used to consider themselves obliged to cultivate what was then saddled upon them"[1]. The dittam was thus merely the cultivation proposals or engagements of the ryots made in April or May for the coming season, and, as this was very uncertain, it became customary at the jamabandi to make all kinds of abatements which, though nominally for reasons arising out of the season or for "unavoidable causes", really included other reasons, such as the reported insolvency or poverty of the ryot and so on. These abatements were made at the jamabandi, which was at the close of the cultivating season, and the jamabandi, therefore, became a scramble for remissions as stated by more than one Collector. But, when on the one hand the ryot obtained greater freedom from all restrictions and on the other was refused remissions, the dittam became useless and was consequently done away with, as has been already stated, in 1858. The jamabandi, or settlement proper determined the revenue, after all deductions had been made, and was properly preceded, then as now, by elaborate village to village enquiries by the tahsildars, who were subsequently aided by peshkars and revenue inspectors. On the report of these officers at the jamabandi, the accounts were made up and closed, and pattas issued, which were thus mere bills for the amount due by each ryot and not title deeds for lands. As permanency and fixity increased, especially after the abolition of the dittam, and the importance of the jamabandi as a scramble for remissions diminished, the money entries in the pattas became of less, and of land entries, of greater relative importance, so that the patta came to be regarded as a title deed than as a bill[2].

Such was the old ryotwari system followed in the district until the introduction of the new or the modern ryotwari system, in 1874–1881. The new system based upon a detailed survey and classification of soils had, as early as 1855, become the only recognized system of settlement in the State. It had been, since then, introduced into district after district. Its lineaments were as follows : A revenue survey showing all the physical features, such as hills, jungles, roads, channels, tanks, topes, houses and cultivable lands, was to be conducted. In the case of the cultivable lands,

1 B.P. No. 2353, dated 9th July 1858.

2 *Manual of the Coimbatore District* by F. A. Nicholson, 1887, pages 123–124.

the sizes of the fields were to be accurately shown. Permanent boundary marks were to be established and field, village, and taluk maps were to be prepared. As to the settlement operations, the soils were to be divided into a few series based on differences of composition, like the alluvial and exceptional, the regar or regada, (the black cotton soil), the red ferruginous, the calcareous and the arenaceous. The alluvial and exceptional were to be further classified into the alluvial and the permanently improved while the others were to be classified as clayey, loamy or sandy. Thus there would be fourteen classes of soils, namely : (1) alluvial, (2) permanently improved, (3) regar clay, (4) regar loam, (5) regar sand, (6) red ferruginous clay, (7) red ferruginous loam, (8) red ferruginous sand, (9) calcareous clay, (10) calcareous loam, (11) calcareous sand, (12) arenaceous clay, (13) arenaceous loam and (14) arenaceous sand. All the lands were to be further divided into five sorts, namely: (1) the best, (2) the good, (3) the ordinary, (4) the inferior and (5) the worst. The grain outturn for each class and sort of soil was to be then carefully determined by actual experiments with reference to the standard grains grown, i.e., paddy for irrigated lands, and cumbu, cholam or some other grain, for unirrigated lands. These grain outturns had to be commuted into money at the average of the selling prices for a series of years, generally 20 non-famine years, preceding the settlement. From the amount arrived at by such commutation a deduction of 15 per cent was to be made for marketing charges and a deduction of one-sixteenth to one-fourth for vicissitudes of the season and for uncropped areas like irrigation channels. Against the average value of the produce thus determined was to be set off the cost of cultivation, the estimation of which was to be done with every care. The items of cost to be usually included in the cultivation expenses, were ploughing cattle, agricultural implements, seed, manure, and labour required for ploughing, manuring, etc. The method of calculation of these was to vary according to the crops grown and the method of culture, as well as the mode in which these items were usually paid, whether in grain or money, or in both grain and money. Payments in grain were to be commuted into money at the commutation price adopted for the settlement. The cost of the bullocks and the implements of husbandry was to be distributed over the number of years during which they were estimated to be serviceable and other items were to be calculated for each year. The calculations were to be first made for the area which could be cultivated with one plough and one pair of bullocks and the required calculations for an acre were to be deduced from them. The expenses of cultivation were to be taken to be the same as had been already determined in neighbouring settled districts. The cultivation expenses thus arrived at being deducted from the gross assets, i.e., the value of the total outturn, the result would be the approximate net produce of the land under examination and half this, or rather less than half, was to be taken as the Government demand. The straw was to be usually taken as a set off against the item "feed of bullocks".

Nor was this all. For purposes of simplicity and for avoiding multiplication of rates, the classes and sorts of soil which were alike were to be arranged in grades called "tarams". The values of half the net produce of the different classes and sort of soil falling in the same taram being very nearly equal, only one rate of assessment was to be fixed for each taram and the rates so fixed were to be so adjusted that their descent from the highest to the lowest might be by a uniform amount in each taram. Again, the productive powers of the soils different in lands irrigated and dry, two scales of tarams were to be adopted, one for wet lands and another for dry lands. And, as all villages would not have the same advantages in respect of proximity to markets, facility of communication, means of irrigation, etc., villages were to be arranged in groups, generally two or three for a district, according to circumstances. The irrigation sources were also to be arranged in classes according to the nature of water-supply. All these factors were to be taken into consideration in correcting the assessments on the fields. The final accounts of the settlement thus arrived at were to be entered in a Settlement Register which was to be the foundation of the whole revenue administration, containing as it did, information regarding every holding, large or small. From this register, a ledger was to be prepared for giving the personal account of each ryot and this was to form his patta. The settlement so made was to last for thirty years. During this period, neither the grain outturn, nor the commutation rates, were to be altered, but each ryot was to be free to hold or relinquish whatever fields he liked or to take up other available fields. There was, therefore, to be an annual settlement of accounts with the ryots and this was to be called the annual jamabandi [1].

It was broadly upon these lines that the survey and settlement of the district were conducted. The survey was begun by a small party attached to the settlement department in 1860 and was continued by the survey department from 1867. The settlement scheme was submitted by the Settlement Officer, Mr. Clogstoun, in 1875. It was somewhat modified by the Director of Settlements, Mr. Puckle, and the Board of Revenue and sanctioned by the Government in 1878. The scheme, it may be noted, was prepared for the five northern taluks, Erode, Satyamangalam,

---

[1] *Memorandum upon Current Land Revenue Settlements by* E. Stack, 1880, pages 333–352.

Administration Report, Madras, for 1901–1902, pages 68–76.

Palladam, Coimbatore and Bhavani, (exclusive of Kollegal), and as these taluks were considered as fair samples, it was proposed and sanctioned for the whole district. The settlement operations were completed for the entire district by 1881.

As regards classification, the system adopted by Mr. Clogstoun for drawing up the preliminary scheme was that of field classification as distinguished from the block system. It attempted to give a strictly accurate valuation of each field, regardless of the fact whether the result was an increase or decrease of assessment. Under it a classifier visited a village and, with a map in his hand, inspected every field accompanied by the Karnam and by the field owners and, on the spot, made a complete registry of the field in a form which gave particulars of the member, class, irrigation, crops, area, assessment, etc., in the columns entered for the purpose. He then classified the field according to the nature and quality of the soil under the following classes, black or red clay, black or red loam, or black or red sand, each of these classes being divided into three sorts called good, middling or bad. His classification was then marked with symbols on the map which to a practised eye thus became a picture of the soils of the village. Various precautions were adopted in the way of supervision by head classifiers, supervisors and Deputy Directors, to ensure evenness and correctness of classification. This system, Mr. Clogstoun claimed, ensured great accuracy without unnecessary minuteness in detail.

In reviewing the scheme, however, Mr. Puckle, the Director of Settlement, observed that it was impossible to ignore existing facts, that the ryots would not, under the system followed by Mr. Clogstoun, understand the great variations upon adjoining fields introduced to satisfy theoretical nicety, and that the classifiers would find it difficult to rate individual fields, unless regard were had to surrounding circumstances and existing assessments. In other words, Mr. Puckle favoured the block system, which, although based upon a field survey and classification, took no account of individual fields in assessing a village, but having fixed upon an appropriate rate for each class of soil, blocked out a village into areas of fairly homogenous character and applied to each area the appropriate rate. These blocks with appropriate symbols were entered at first on village sketches and then were transferred to small maps embracing a series of villages, so that the Settlement Officer could see at a glance that a sketch of say " red gravelly upland running through several villages is treated uniformly throughout, or that all the lands under a channel are classed systematically with reference to soil, situation, and level, though they may be in several villages ". In making the settlement

Mr. Clogstoun's plan was to equalize the incidence of assessment on each field by raising or lowering each field to an assumed standard, and he thought that a settlement which did not make a vast difference condemned itself. Mr. Puckle' s plan was to avoid making any great difference and to endeavour to levy similar assessments, over large tracts, such assessments approximating, as far as possible, to existing relations, so far as consistent with the general principles of revision. The Board of Revenue and the Government accepted Mr. Puckle's plan and ordered it to be carried out. It was upon this plan that the settlement of the whole district was made.

Of the fourteen classes of soils mentioned above (see page 536), only five classes of soils were found in the district, namely, black clay (class 3), black loam (class 4), black sand (class 5), red loam (class 7) and red sand (class 8). Each class was divided into five sorts, namely, best (1st), good (2nd), ordinary (3rd), inferior (4th) and worst (5th), instead of three as originally proposed. Beyond this classification, no grouping of dry villages was done, since it was thought that such grouping was not necessary in the district which had so many weekly markets and excellent roads. Grouping in regard to wet lands was done with reference to the nature and quality of the source of irrigation. Three wet groups were made. Lands irrigated, for instance, by the Bhavani, with the exception of those under the Kaniepalayam Anicut and those under the Kodiveri Anicut which were only allowed a sufficient supply of water for the growth of a crop of kar paddy, were placed in the first group. Lands under the Noyyil and also lands under the Kodiveri Anicut which were only allowed a sufficient supply of water for the growth of a crop of kar paddy were placed in the second group. And all lands irrigated by tanks not supplied by either of the above rivers, as well as all lands irrigated by jungle streams and those under the Kaniepalayam anicut were placed in the third group.

The determination of the grain values of the different soils, based upon the outturn, was done with every care. One thousand five hundred and forty experiments were made in the dry staples (kambu, cholam and ragi) and 1,572 in paddy. The seasons of these experiments were those of 1872–73 and 1873–74 for dry grains and the same two seasons and that of 1874–75 for paddy.

On the basis of these experiments, the different soils of wet lands were divided into nine tarams and those of dry lands into eight tarams according to their productivity. The outturns of these tarams of lands were estimated as follows :—

Wet.		*Dry.*	
Number of taram.	*Outturn in Madras measures.*	*Number of taram.*	*Outturn in Madras measures.*
(1)	(2)	(3)	(4)
1	1,200	1	250
2	1,000	2	225
3	900	3	200
4	700	4	175
5	580	5	150
6	480	6	125
7	400	7	100
8	350	8	100
9	300		

Cultivation expenses were also calculated with equal care. The lower rates of soil were granted smaller allowances since they were not so highly cultivated as the better sorts. In most dry lands the allowance was above half the gross produce in all but the first rate, after allowing one-fifth for vicissitudes, while in the case of other dry lands it was much less than half the produce. It was assumed that a pair of bullocks would last six years cost Rs. 50 and would suffice for 10 acres and the cost of the cattle was accordingly calculated at 13 annas 4 pies per acre. This did not allow for interest on the cost, as the ryot had other uses for his cattle, which, again, did not cost more than Rs. 30 to 40, and usually lasted longer than six years. Taking one field with another, the allowance for implements, seed, and manure was liberal and also that for labour, which, on the better classes nearly represented per acre the labour of one man for 25 days or one man and two women for 10 days. The price of labour was calculated at the ordinary wages in grain, which was turned into money at the settlement commutation rate. For wet land, the assumption was that three acres could be ploughed with one pair of oxen of the same cost and duration as in dry land. The cost of ploughing was, however, variously estimated at Rs. 3 to Rs. 1—4—0 per acre, the latter rate being obviously too low as the assumed rate of three acres and a life of only six years. The rates for tools and seed were high, while those for manure and labour were low. It was common to put on the better lands four cart-loads of green manure per acre per crop and it was seldom that this cost less than one rupee per load. The labour in such fields was very considerable, for treading the green manure, transplanting, weeding, reaping and threshing. The rates for garden crop cultivation were not separately entered ; the cost was, of course, much above that of dry cultivation. No allowance was made for feeding charges of cattle, it being assumed that the straw, which *per contra*, was not credited to the outturn, was a sufficient equivalent.

The next important matter was commutation rate. According to the general scheme laid down, the average prices in the ryots selling months during a series of 20 years (1845-64) were taken and the rate was based upon their average. Prices having greatly risen from 1860 to 1870, the ryots were much favoured by the selection of an earlier series of years. The month and the average so obtained were as follows :—

—	*Selling month.*	*Average price per garce over 20 years.*		
(1)	(2)	(3)		
		RS.	A.	P.
For first-sort paddy	February	144	0	0
,, second-sort paddy	May	133	0	0
,, Kambu	December	115	0	0
,, Cholam	November	154	0	0
,, Ragi	Do.	128	0	0

These were town prices and from them a 10 per cent deduction was made as the dealer's profit, the result being the supposed price obtained by the ryot.

The next difficulty was to obtain a simple rate that should apply for all dry crops. The first thing was to class all dry crops, other than the standard kambu, cholam, or ragi, under one of those crops either at an equal or other proportion. For example cotton was considered equal to cholam; horsegram or kambu ; gingelly, castor, etc., were rated at three-sevenths of cholam and four-sevenths of kambu, and so on. Waste, which occupied 13 per cent was charged similarly to gingelly. The average area occupied by each crop during the previous four years was then ascertained and, when found, was re-distributed in terms of the standard crops according to the scale laid down, with the result that 51 per cent was treated as kambu, 40 per cent as cholam and 9 per cent as ragi. To this area was then applied the commutation rate for each standard crop, the added result being taken as the general commutation rate. The commutation rate for paddy was obtained by averaging the prices of first and second sort of paddy. The commutation rates thus arrived at were Rs. 119 per garce for dry grain and Rs. 126 per garce for paddy.

From the grain valuation as found by experiment, it was decided to deduct 20 per cent for unprofitable seasons and inequalities of crops, inclusion of unprofitable waste, such as rocks, surface water-courses, paths, etc.

The grain valuation, cultivation charges and commutation rate having been thus determined, and the above 20 per cent deduction having been made, it became possible to settle the assessment rates. The rates so finally settled were as follows :—

Dry.

Class and sort. (1)		*Taram.* (2)	*First group.* (3)			*Taram.* (4)	*Second group.* (5)		
			RS.	A.	P.		RS.	A.	P.
3	1	1	2	0	0	2	1	8	0
4	1								
3	2								
4	2	2	1	8	0	3	1	4	0
7	1								
3	3								
4	3								
5	1	3	1	4	0	4	1	0	0
7	2								
8	1								
3	4								
4	4								
5	2	4	1	0	0	5	0	12	0
7	3								
8	2								
3	5								
4	5								
5	3	5	0	12	0	6	0	8	0
7	4								
8	3								
5	4								
7	5	6	0	8	0	7	0	6	0
8	4								
5	5	7	0	6	0	8	0	4	0
8	5								

Wet.							
Class and sort.		*Taram,*	*First group.*	*Taram.*	*Second group.*	*Taram. group.*	*Third group.*
(6)		(7)	(8)	(9)	(10)	(11)	(12)
			RS. A. P.		RS. A. P.		RS. A. P.
4	1	1	12 0 0	2	10 0 0	3	8 0 0
3 4 7	1 2 1	2	10 0 0	3	8 0 0	4	6 0 0
3 4 5 7 8	2 3 1 2 1	3	8 0 0	4	6 0 0	5	5 0 0
3 4 5 7 8	3 4 2 3 2	4	6 0 0	5	5 0 0	6	4 0 0
3 4 5 7 8	4 5 3 4 3	5	5 0 0	6	4 0 0	7	3 8 0
3 5 7 8	5 4 5 4	6	4 0 0	7	3 8 0	8	3 0 0
5 8	5 5	7	3 8 0	8	3 0 0	9	2 8 0

It will thus be seen that there were nine rates varying from Rs. 12 to Rs. 2—8—0 in wet lands and eight rates varying from Rs. 2 to annas 4 in dry lands.

The assessment proposed for wet lands was that for a single crop, and Mr. Clogstoun went on to propose the mode of fixing the second-crop assessment. Hitherto the practice had been peculiar. For instance, in Dharapuram, if land was cultivated with a second crop, no extra charge was made ; if only with one crop, a certain amount was remitted. There was, however, no uniform practice. This practice was done away with. The lands under the Kalingarayan were now charged at a consolidated rate of half the additional assessment to the single crop assessment and the ryots under other works were allowed to the option of compounding at one-third or one-fourth the additional rate, no exception being made in the case of rain-fed tanks. It was also ordered that half the single crop rate should be levied on second crops whenever grown on land assessed only as single crop, but, in 1880, the ryots were permitted to effect composition at any time in respect of single survey numbers or letters on the same scale as that adopted for similar lands in the same village.

This was how the survey and settlement was carried out throughout the district. It resulted in increasing the area by 6⅛ per cent and in increasing the assessment by 8 per cent or a little over 2 lakhs of rupees (Rs. 2,10,223). The total outlay for survey and settlement came to Rs. 19,65,870. " The benefits of the settlement ", it was remarked " do not consist in enhanced revenue but in the certainty and accuracy of areas, equality of existing assessments, and the permanent recording in printed registers and accurate maps on a large scale, of the area and assessment of every field."[1]

On the expiry of the thirty years period of the Original Settlement, in 1909–12, a resettlement was carried out in all the taluks of the district. It was based on the proposals of Mr. Lancashire, the Special Settlement Officer. Two scheme reports were submitted by him, one on the resettlement of the Bhavani, Palladam, Coimbatore, Satyamangalam, Dharapuram, Erode and Karur (transferred to Tiruchirappalli district in 1910) taluks in 1909,[2] and the other on the resettlement of the Pollachi, Udumalpet and Kollegal (transferred to the Mysore State in 1956) taluks in 1911.[3] The resettlement of the former taluks was ordered in 1910 and that of the latter taluks in 1912. Opportunity was also then taken to settle for the first time certain villages (93 villages) in the Bhavani, Satyamangalam and Coimbatore taluks and 50 villages of the Kollegal taluk which had been left out at the original settlement.

[1] B.P. No. 1760, dated 26th June 1879.
G.O. No. 1964, Revenue, dated 6th December 1878.
G.O. No. 2123, Revenue, dated 30th October 1879.
G.O. No. 49, Revenue, dated 12th January 1880.
G.O. No. 979, Revenue, dated 19th August 1880.
G.O. No. 649, Revenue, dated 16th April 1881.
B.P. No. 1229, dated 4th May 1882.
G.O. No. 124, Revenue, dated 15th February 1894.
G.O. No. 1017, Revenue, dated 23rd September 1882.
Manual of the Coimbatore District by F.A. Nicholson, 1887, pages 131–152.

[2] G.O. No. 102, Revenue, dated 10th January 1910.

[3] G.O. No. 1972, Revenue, dated 3rd July 1912.

Taking first the resettlement of the Bhavani, Palladam, Coimbatore, Satyamangalam, Dharapuram, Erode and Karur taluks, it was based mainly on the rise in the prices of the staple foodgrains since the last settlement, and it involved no general reclassification of the soils. The changes which it effected can be summarised as follows. In regard to wet lands, no change was made in the classification of the irrigation sources adopted at the original settlement except in a few cases. These few cases related to the Odathurai tank in the Bhavani taluk which was transferred to the third class, to the Kanniyampalayam anicut in the Satyamangalam taluk which was removed from the list of irrigation sources, its registered ayacut being classified as dry, and to the Chadivayalpallam channel, which irrigated the wet lands in the village of Madavarayapuram in the Coimbatore taluk, was registered as second-crop source. It was at the same time declared that, if at any time the defect on account of which an irrigation source had been placed in a lower class was remedied by the Government, or if any new sources were constructed by the Government, they were at liberty to revise the existing classification or to impose wet rates of assessment or water rates on the lands commanded by them with reference to the revised classification. The existing classification of soils into two main series, i.e, " regar " and " red ferruginous " and the sub-division of each of these series into three classes, clayey, loamy and sandy, was retained. The gradation of each of these sub-divisions into five sorts, i.e., best, good, ordinary, inferior, and worst and the existing block system was retained. Reclassification was resorted to only in exceptional instances of transfers of land from dry to wet made by the Revenue Department where the soil classification adopted did not properly represent the productive capacity of the land. Paddy was taken as the standard crop and the out-turn fixed at the original settlement for the several tarams was retained. The allowance of one-fifth deducted from those gross out-turns on account of vicissitudes of season was also retained. After allowing a deduction of 10 per cent for merchant's profit and cartage, a commutation rate of Rs. 126 a garce was adopted at the Original Settlement. The commutation rate calculated in a similar manner on the average price of paddy during the 20 years of normal prices preceding the year 1907–1908 came to Rs. 167 per garce. There was thus an increase in prices of 32½ per cent since the last settlement. The allowances made at the last settlement on account of cultivation expenses were now increased by 50 per cent although the prices had risen only by 32½ per cent.

The rates of assessment in wet lands worked out on these lines exceeded the previous rates by 8 to 36 per cent, but actually the rates were increased only by 15 per cent. The new rates were as follows :—

Taram.	*Rates.* RS.	AS.	PS.
1	13	12	0
2	11	8	0
3	9	4	0
4	6	14	0
5	5	12	0
6	4	10	0
7	4	0	0
8	3	8	0
9	2	14	0

Lands under the first class source which received an assured supply for two wet crops were registered as "double crop" with an assessment of 1½ times the single crop charge. It was declared that these lands would be entitled to remission of the difference between double and single crop charge, if the irrigation supply were to be insufficient for two crops in any year. The charge for second crop on lands registered as single crop was fixed at one half of the single crop assessment in respect of wet lands under the Cauvery—Korambu channels which had hitherto been subject to a second crop charge of only one-third of the single crop assessment, while in the case of wet lands under the Upper Amaravati channels and the Noyyil river anicut channels and tanks, the rate of composition for second crop charge was continued at one-fourth of the single crop assessment. All lands under rain-fed tanks and jungle streams were registered as single-crop and the ryots were given the option of compounding the charge for second-crop at one-fourth of the single-crop assessment. It was also declared that the lands on which the charge for second-crop had been compounded were not entitled to separate remission of second-crop charge, but that the full compounded rate would be collected even if only one wet crop were raised.

Fields registered as dry which had been regularly cultivated with wet crops for five years and which, in the opinion of the Settlement Officer, could be transferred to wet without prejudice to the existing wet ayacut, and fields registered as dry from which, in the opinion of the Settlement Officer, it was impossible to exclude water, were ordered to be transferred to wet. Fields registered as wet which had not been cultivated with wet crops for five years or which, in the opinion of the Settlement Officer, it was not advisable to retain a registered wet lands, were ordered to be transferred to dry. When lands were transferred from dry to wet or from wet to dry or from one registered source to another, a soil classification suitable to their new registration was assigned to them. When water from a Government source was supplied for the registration of dry lands, water-cess was charged in accordance with the following rules—Rule I (*a*) for a single wet crop, the difference between the dry and wet rates was assessed; (*b*) for a second or third wet crop one-half of the charge shown against (*a*) plus half the dry assessment; (*c*) for a first, second and third dry crop, one-third of the charge shown against (*a*); (*d*) for sugarcane, betel, plantains and other wet crops which ordinarily remain on the ground for more than six months, the sum of the charges specified against (*a*) and (*b*); (*e*) for dry crops which ordinarily remain on the ground for more than six months one and a half times the charge shown against (*c*). Rule II—When water used for irrigation could not be obtained without raising it by baling or by some other mechanical contrivance, the water-rate charged would be three-fourth of the rates specified in Rule I. Besides this, the Government reserved to themselves the power to alter at any time during the term of resettlement the water rate on lands not registered as wet. The remission of one rupee an acre usually allowed in the case of lands irrigated by baling was continued. And the irrigation cess then paid by the ryots in respect of certain channels continued to be collected, the Government reserving to themselves the right to enhance the wet assessment on the lands commanded by the channels, should the cess be abolished at any future date.

In regard to dry lands the original grouping was adhered to in most cases. No change was made in the classification of soils except in the following cases : (*a*) lands left unclassified or registered as poramboke at the original settlement and since granted on patta and assessed by the Revenue Department, and (*b*) the blocks of land in certain villages which were sub-divided during the survey made in 1903. Compact blocks of assessed waste lands which had remained unoccupied even under sivoijama cultivation for three years continuously were not re-classified but their existing classification was reduced by one taram. In carrying out the classification of these lands, the classification adopted for dry lands at the original settlement was followed. The resettlement was based mainly on the rise in the prices of staple grains since the previous settlement. The staple grains adopted at the previous settlement were, as has been seen, cumbu, cholam and ragi and the prices showed an increase of 55 to 70 per cent above the old commutation rates. In calculating the average prices of the last 20 non-famine years, the famine years, faslis 1300, 1301 and 1302 were excluded. The deduction of 10 per cent for cartage and merchant's profits and the deduction of 20 per cent for vicissitudes of season and unprofitable areas allowed at the previous settlement were continued unaltered, while the allowance for cultivation expenses was increased by 70 per cent. The new rates worked out on these lines justified an enhancement of the existing dry rates by 17 to 54 per cent; but the Government increased the existing dry rates by only 12½ per cent or two annas in the rupee. The new rates worked out as follows :—

Taram.	*New Rates.*		
	RS.	AS.	P.
1	2	4	0
2	1	11	0
3	1	6	0
4	1	2	0
5	0	13	0
6	0	9	0
7	0	7	0
8	0	5	0
9	0	4	0

In the Coimbatore taluk, however, the existing rates for sixth and seventh tarams were continued unaltered. Assessment on special rate lands was, at the same time, everywhere enhanced from the existing rates of Rs. 2 and Rs. 2—8—0 to Rs. 2—4—0 and Rs. 2—12—0. The Special concession to hold lands at one-fourth the taram assessment, which had been granted to certain jungle tribes in the Coimbatore taluk in 1873 and 1877, was continued.

When the resettlement resulted in a 25 per cent increase in the assessment payable on any individual patta, the increased assessment was imposed gradually, i.e., by increase spread over a series of years. This temporary abatement of the full resettlement assessment was called " increment remission ". In estimating the increase which gave a claim to increment remission, enhancements due to increase in area by resurvey, increase due to transfer of old land from dry to wet and increase due to transfer from single crop to double crop was not taken into account. Increases due to re-classification of soil or sources of irrigation or to revision of grouping were, however, taken into account, but in all these cases, minor increase in area was not deducted, the increment remission being calculated on the total enhancements of the new assessments on the holding over the old assessment. If the increase of assessment in individual cases exceeded 25 per cent of the old assessment, an amount equal to the old assessment plus 25 per cent thereof was levied at once and the remainder by annual increments equal to 12½ per cent of the old assessment. Increment remission was not granted when the total increase did not exceed Rs. 3. If the whole or a portion of the land held by a pattadar at the resettlement was relinquished or transferred, the full assessment was charged for the lands remaining in his patta and for those which had passed into other hands. This was, however, not done in cases in which the change in the holdings was due to causes beyond the ryot's control, i.e., when a portion of his land was washed away by a river or he was obliged to relinquish it, or when a piece of land was taken up for public purposes. In the latter class of cases, the excess assessment on what remained of the holding was levied in the same number of instalments as those fixed for the entire holding. Similarly, when one of the joint holders of a patta transferred his interest therein either to a co-pattadar or to a stranger, increment remission was granted. Pattas were issued at the resettlement in accordance with the registry in the re-settlement registers prepared on the basis of adangals corrected upto date and embodying the results of the supplemental survey due to revision of adangals and rectification of errors and discrepancies in field maps.

The initial settlement of the 93 villages of the Bhavani, Coimbatore and Satyamangalam taluks, already referred to, was also made in accordance with the foregoing rules subject however to the following modifications. In the first place, the whole of the surveyed area was classified and an appropriate soil classification was assigned to the ands. In the second place, the wet lands in a few villages which were included in the ayacut of the Kaniyampalayam anicut were transferred to dry. And, in the third place, such newly surveyed areas as had been included in the reserved forests were formed into a third dry group for which new money rates were fixed.[1]

The re-settlement and the initial settlement so made were declared to remain in force for the usual period of thirty years. The cost of the survey and settlement of the seven taluks came to Rs. 7,40,348; the survey cost Rs. 3,44,469, the adangal revision Rs. 1,61,702 and the settlement Rs. 2,34,117. The financial result of the application of revised rates to wet and dry in all the seven taluks was an addition to the existing revenue of Rs. 2,40,613 or 12·77 per cent, including transfers from dry to wet, single crop to double crop and vice versa, or of Rs. 2,27,634 or 12 per cent excluding these transfers. The total revenue demand, it may be stated, rose from Rs. 2,80,516 to Rs. 3,21,077.[2]

---

[1] G.O. No. 909, Revenue, dated 23rd March 1910.

[2] G.O. No. 297, Revenue, dated 30 March 1913.

The re-settlement of the Udumalpet, Pollachi and Kollegal taluks of the district was carried on in the following manner. As in the case of other taluks, it was based mainly on the rise in prices of the staple food grains since the last settlement. No general re-classification of the soils was made. Taking the wet lands first, no change was made in the classification of the irrigation sources adopted at the original settlement, except in the following cases. The Aliyar river and its channels in the Pollachi taluk were registered as first class sources of irrigation in regard to such of the wet lands irrigated by them as might fairly be expected to receive a steady supply of water in all normal years for second crop. As to the remaining portions of their ayacuts, the Aliyar and its channels were continued to be treated as second class sources. The Kumaralingam channel of the Amaravathi river in the Udumalpet taluk was placed in the first class in respect of those wet lands irrigated by it for which an unfailing supply of water for two crops could be assured in all normal years. The remaining portion of the ayacut of the channel was continued to be treated as a second class source. For purposes of baling, the Aliyar and the Amaravathi were regarded as first-class sources. Power was also taken by the Government to revise the existing classification or to impose wet rates of assessment or to levy water rates wherever any new irrigation sources might be constructed by the Government. The existing classification of soils into two main series, the regar and the red ferruginous, and the sub-division of each of these series into three classes, clayey, loamy and sandy, was retained. The gradation of each of these subdivisions into five sorts and the existing block system was also retained. Re-classification was resorted to only in exceptional instances of transfers of land from dry to wet made by the Revenue Department where the soil classification adopted did not properly represent the productive capacity of the land. Paddy was taken as the standard crop and the out-turn fixed at the original settlement for the several tarams was retained. The allowance of one-fifth deducted from these gross out-turns on account of vicissitudes of season and unprofitable areas was also retained. The commutation rates and cultivation expenses were fixed on the same lines as those followed in the other seven taluks, which have already been described. The rates of assessment worked out were the same as those of the seven taluks, which also have already been stated.

As to second crop charge, lands under a first-class source which received an assured supply were registered as double crop with an assessment of one and a half times the single wet crop charge; and these lands were given a remission of the difference between double and single crop charges, if the irrigation supply was insufficient for two crops in any year. In accordance with these rules--which, as has been seen, were followed also in the seven taluks,—the wet lands under the Amaravathi channels in five villages, namely, Karattolur, Kadattur, Kanniyur, Sholamadevi and Sircar Kannadiputtur, of the Udumalpet taluk which had hitherto been permitted to compound for the second crop charge at one-third of the single crop assessment, were now registered as permanent double crop lands, with the exception of 70 acres of single crop land at the tail end of the Kanniyur channel and a similar extent of single crop land at the tail end of the Karattolur channel. In the case of the wet lands, in regard to which the channels under the Aliyar river and the Komaralingam channel of the Amaravati river were registered as first-class sources at resettlement, as there was a large enhancement of the existing rates of assessment the Government as a matter of grace, restricted the enhancement on these lands to about 35 per cent by allowing them to be compounded for the second crop charge at special consolidated double crop assessments. The rate of composition for second crop in the case of wet lands under the Kallapuram channel of the Amaravati which was a second crop source of irrigation was raised to the normal rate of one-third of the first crop charge. The same rate was also applied in the case of all other second class wet lands under the Amaravati and of similar lands under the Aliyar, in lieu of the favourable rate of one-fourth of the first crop charge hitherto allowed. For all other sources of irrigation the rate of composition was the same as at the original settlement, i.e., one-fourth of the first crop charge.

In Pollachi taluk there were certain dry lands which regularly grew paddy or a dufassal wet crop by the aid of irrigation from natural rivers, streams or springs without the aid of any Government irrigation works. These were registered as wet as far as that could be done with due regard to the interests of holders of wet lands under the same or other sources of irrigation. Under some other sources which had been constructed or improved by private enterprise, a remission of 4 per cent on the capital outlay had hitherto been deducted from the water rate leviable year by year in consideration of the expenses incurred by the ryots on the works executed. This remission was taken away and the lands were registered as wet at resettlement, their soil classification being reduced by one sort. In regard to transfer of lands from dry to wet, and wet to dry the same rules as were followed in the seven taluks mentioned already, were followed in these taluks also.

Coming to dry lands, no change was made grouping of dry lands and, except in the following cases, the classification of the soils adopted at the original settlement was unaltered. The exceptions were lands transferred from wet to dry by the Revenue Department, lands left unclassified or registered as "poramboke" at the original settlement; and the blocks of lands in 28 villages of the Kollegal taluk which were subdivided during the survey of 1903. The resettlement was based mainly on the rise in prices of staple food grains since the previous settlement, and the same rules as were followed in the seven taluks were followed in these taluks also for fixing commutation rates, allowance for cultivation expenses, etc. The same dry rates as were applied in the seven taluks were applied in these taluks also, and the same rules governing increment remission, registration of holdings, etc., as were followed in the seven taluks, were followed in these taluks also. It may be also mentioned here that the resettlement in the three taluks was declared to be in force for 30 years as in the case of the seven taluks and that the rights of the hill tribes in respect of 1,712 acres of land in Mavadap and Pundi villages which they held free of all payment of land revenue or cesses, were left undisturbed.[1]

The resettlement of the three taluks resulted in an increase of Rs. 47,041 or 11 per cent on dry lands and of Rs. 25,187 or 22 per cent on wet lands, or total increase of Rs. 72,228. The net increase by resettlement came to Rs. 72,228 or 13 per cent of the total revenue of Rs. 5,60,480 for the year preceding the resettlement after allowing for transfers from dry to wet and composition for second crop charge. The cost of resurvey and resettlement operations in the three taluks amounted to Rs. 15,419.

Taking the district as a whole the resettlement resulted in a total net increase of Rs. 3,51,319 or a little over Rs. 3½ lakhs on a total revenue of Rs. 28,70,968 or 12 per cent after making allowance for transfers from dry to wet and single to double crop. And the cost of survey and resettlement operations came to Rs. 9,50,106.[2]

Excluding the Karur and Kollegal taluks which no longer form part of this district, the extent of dry and wet lands under each taram in each of the remaining nine taluks and the assessment fixed on these lands under the resettlement are given in the following statements.[3]

---

1. G.O. No. 2990, Revenue, dated 5th October 1912.

2. G.O. No. 1334, Revenue, dated 9th May 1914.

3. G.O. No. 297, Revenue, dated 30th January 1913.
G.O. No. 3364, Revenue, dated 19th November 1913.
G.O. No. 1334, Revenue, dated 9th May 1914.

STATEMENT SHOWING THE EXTENT AND ASSESSMENT OF DRY LANDS IN EACH TALUK UNDER EACH TARAM.

Taluk.	Taram 1. Extent in acres.	Taram 1. Assessment in rupees. RS.	A.	P.	Taram 2. Extent in acres.	Taram 2. Assessment in rupees. RS.	A.	P.	Taram 3. Extent in acres.	Taram 3. Assessment in rupees. RS.	A.	P.
Avanashi	52·86	118	15	0	14,180·23	23,945	14	0	45,690·57	63,140	14	0
Bhavani	24·26	54	9	0	3,115·12	5,250	10	0	31,074·50	42,762	6	0
Coimbatore	6,002·30	13,509	9	0	27,291·98	46,084	4	0	39,470·67	54,322	11	0
Dharapuram	4·64	10	8	0	7,012·74	11,841	4	0	23,640·40	32,522	3	0
Erode	79·50	178	15	0	45,493·70	76,805	15	0	79,386·74	1,09,222	7	0
Gobichettipalayam	13·38	30	2	0	17,923·83	30,265	9	0	71,986·78	99,027	7	0
Palladam	16·65	37	8	0	63,501·57	1,07,204	13	0	43,734·08	60,125	13	0
Pollachi	5,680·77	12,785	1	0	20,689·54	34,929	2	0	33,471·16	46,039	14	0
Udumalpet	4,220·95	9,499	6	0	25,979·02	42,165	1	0	19,055·54	26,211	4	0

Taluk.	Taram 4. Extent in acres.	Taram 4. Assessment in rupees. RS.	A.	P.	Taram 5. Extent in acres.	Taram 5. Assessment in rupees. RS.	A.	P.	Taram 6. Extent in acres.	Taram 6. Assessment in rupees. RS.	A.	P.
Avanashi	58,149·64	65,470	5	0	46,050·91	37,444	15	0	25,419·76	12,896	9	0
Bhavani	40,259·51	45,328	7	0	34,834·30	28,334	12	0	31,444·80	17,701	3	0
Coimbatore	28,512·41	32,103	0	0	50,323·18	40,919	7	0	25,753·03	12,890	5	0
Dharapuram	61,232·68	68,916	14	0	1,58,697·86	1,28,990	15	0	155,761·84	87,680	3	0
Erode	1,09,232·81	1,22,957	5	0	53,478·56	43,481	5	0	10,086·47	5,686	4	0
Gobichettipalayam	61,781·22	69,557	8	0	30,756·67	25,009	5	0	12,275·81	6,911	8	0
Palladam	59,975·47	67,555	6	0	92,814·70	75,466	3	0	46,771·55	26,332	15	0
ollachi	60,309·90	67,877	13	0	57,341·35	46,615	5	0	11,561·10	6,509	10	0
Udumalpet	26,985·10	30,373	6	0	41,350·99	33,617	4	0	38,713·86	21,791	8	0

STATEMENT SHOWING THE EXTENT AND ASSESSMENT OF DRY LANDS IN EACH TALUK UNDER EACH TARAM—*cont.*

Taluk.	Taram 7.		Taram 8.		Taram 9.	
	Extent in acres.	*Assessment in rupees.*	*Extent in acres.*	*Assessment in rupees.*	*Extent in acres.*	*Assessment in rupees.*
		RS. A. P.		RS. A. P.		RS. A. P.
Avanashi	11,223·11	4,226 5 0	632·48	197 10 0	17·21	4 6 0
Bhavani	19,656·34	8,605 9 0	2,892·68	904 2 0	5,176·30	1,294 2 0
Coimbatore	1,075·60	404 5 0	..	..	..	..
Dharapuram	4,725·57	2,080 13 0	..	..	..	..
Erode	1,145·83	502 4 0	..	..	..	..
Gobichettipalayam	4,707·35	2,064 12 0	431·59	135 1 0	4·25	1 2 0
Palladam	104·16	45 13 0	..	..	..	..
Pollachi	56·59	24 13 0	..	..	..	..
Udumalpet	4,069·21	1,781 3 0	..	..	..	..

STATEMENT SHOWING THE EXTENT AND ASSESSMENT OF WET LANDS IN EACH TALUK UNDER EACH TARAM.

Taluk.	Taram 1.		Taram 2.		Taram 3.	
	Extent in acres.	*Assessment in rupees.*	*Extent in acres.*	*Assessment in rupees.*	*Extent in acres.*	*Assessment in rupees.*
		RS. A. P.		RS. A. P.		RS. A. P.
Avanashi	..	..	..	..	1·25	14 7 0
Bhavani	..	..	..	..	50·31	506 4 0
Coimbatore	..	..	458·19	6,199 4 0	4,821·97	48,555 13 0
Dharapuram	1,165·11	19,235 11 0	1,313·55	17,304 12 0	1,657·82	16,861 9 0
Erode	898·07	18,524 13 0	2,434·72	41,990 12 0	2,481·61	33,889 12 0
Gobichettipalayam	3,464·71	47,637 8 0	4,072·58	46,858 15 0	5,381·51	49,784 14 0
Palladam	..	..	..	..	1,148·52	13,164 12 0
Pollachi	..	..	..	..	54·21	501 8 0
Udumalpet		..	317·53	5,477 11 0	1,167·39	16,165 4 0

STATEMENT SHOWING THE EXTENT AND ASSESSMENT OF WET LANDS IN EACH TALUK UNDER EACH TARAM—*cont.*

Taluk.	Taram 4.				Taram 5.				Taram 6.			
	Extent in acres.	*Assessment in rupees.*			*Extent in acres.*	*Assessment in rupees.*			*Extent in acres.*	*Assessment in rupees.*		
		RS.	A.	P.		RS.	A.	P.		RS.	A.	P.
Avanashi	820·42	6,637	6	0	1,053·79	7,023	14	0	480·04	2,445	2	0
Bhavani	350·12	2,511	4	0	577·60	3,637	9	0	3,01[illegible]·14	1,457	0	0
Coimbatore	3,047·55	22,882	1	0	1,646·94	10,066	0	0	889·97	4,123	9	0
Dharapuram	1,958·58	14,767	15	0	910·35	5,768	0	0	315·83	1,616	6	0
Erode	2,216·70	21,833	7	0	787·66	6,072	1	0	293·27	1,[illegible]73	5	0
Gobichettipalayam	4,277·58	29,413	3	0	535·07	3,172	7	0	84·05	388	12	0
Palladam	1,244·34	10,511	14	0	412·04	2,790	8	0	46·32	264	2	0
Pollachi	1,965·80	17,158	5	0	2,637·49	17,904	14	0	2,265·08	11,785	9	0
Udumalpet	934·82	8,887	7	0	1,785·31	13,722	0	0	1,533·82	9,203	7	0

Taluk.	Taram 7.				Taram 8.				Taram 9.			
	Extent in acres.	*Assessment in rupees.*			*Extent in acres.*	*Assessment in rupees.*			*Extent in acres.*	*Assessment in rupees.*		
		RS.	A.	P.		RS.	A.	P.		RS.	A.	P.
Avanashi	1,097·87	4,931	2	0	..	..			..	..		
Bhavani	152·69	620	6	0	5·36	18	11	0	..	..		
Coimbatore	119·86	485	1	0	..	..			..	..		
Dharapuram	..	..			..	..			..	..		
Erode	..	..			70·16	307	2	0	..	..		
Gobichettipalayam	18·75	75	1	0	16·02	56	1	0	..	..		
Palladam	..	..			55·34	242	4	0	..	..		
Pollachi	1,317·48	5,837	1	0	881·76	3,262	6	0	21·71	69	9	0
Udumalpet	1,599·20	8,309	2	0	872·35	3,868	4	0	417·21	1,367	4	0

In the period that followed, the policy of resettlement underwent complete change. From 1930 onwards prices having fallen on account of the general economic depression, special remissions were granted in all districts and in 1937 it was decided to hold in abeyance all resettlement operations and the system of periodical resettlement itself was abandoned as a matter of state policy.[1]

The original settlement and the resettlement were applicable only to the Government lands. They were not applicable to the inam and zamindari or palayam lands. These were settled at different times under different principles. As to the inams of the district they were first surveyed in 1801-1802. A special enquiry into the titles of inams was also held between 1801 and 1805, and during this enquiry, 1,16,000 out of the 2,96,000 cawnies of inam lands which were then in existence were resumed and the remainder which were considered to be held on good titles were confirmed subject, however, to a jodi varying from one-sixteenth to six-sixteenth of their value. The next inam enquiry and the inam settlement in the district was made only after the appointment of the Inam Commissioner for the whole State in 1858. In 1862, Mr. Blair, the acting Inam Commissioner, reported to the Government that the early inam enquiries made in the district in 1801-1805 had greatly simplified matters, and that the inams which then remained were of unquestionable validity, either having originated under former Governments upwardes fifty years ago on being new grants made under the authority of the British Government. He found that all the necessary information in regard to the locality, extent, assessment, age and title of the inams was contained in the registers prepared at the time of the survey and special enquiry in 1801-1805. He only wanted an enquiry to be made to ascertain whether the assessment fixed originally on the inams had been reduced or not on subsequent occasions and to fix the assessment on them upon the same principles and at the same rate as was then actually paid on Government lands. He also stated that in the northern division of the district the inam land bore one consolidated assessment while in the southern division they were distinguished as that of one and two crops. These distinctions, he proposed to maintain, as also the practice of levying fasaljasti prevailing in the whole district. He said that there were in the district 2,599 religious inams, 435 charitable inams, 3,223 personal inams, 5,818 service inams and 10 shrotrium and jagir inams, i.e., altogether 12,085 inams. He proposed to continue the religious and charitable

[1]. G.O. No. 3412, Revenue (Confidential), dated 20th December 1939.
G.O. No. 804, Public, dated 26th April 1937.
G.O. No. 1067, Revenue, dated 21st May 1937.
Rural Problems in Madras by S. Y. Krishnaswami, pages 57—58.

inams on their existing tenure and to enfranchise the personal inams, as well as service inams (subsequenty after enquiry). As to the shrotrium and jagir inams, which comprised ten entire inam villages, he said, nine of these villages comprised two grants made by the British Government to certain public servants for three lives. And he went on to observe that under paragraph XV of the Inam Rules, these grants were allowed to be enfranchised and rendered permanent at the option of the holders, but that, as the grants expressly conveyed only the right to the Government share of the revenue, it might be desirable to consult the wishes of the cultivating ryots before extending the period of the grants. The one jagir inam, he said, was a permanent one conferred on T. Ramaswami Mudaliyar, his heirs and successors for the construction of two bridges across the Cauvery as well as for their future preservation. In addition to the above, there were, he continued, a number of Ardhabagam, Trashbagam and Chaturbagam villages in the northern division of the district which were assumed by the Government in 1804. The Agraharamdars were once assigned half, one-third and one-fourth of the cultivated lands. He proposed to treat them as personal inams.[1]

The Government generally approved all these proposals, save the one which related to the entire inam villages. They thought that there was no valid reason to treat these inams differently from similar grants given elsewhere or to consult the wishes of the ryots. They, therefore, ordered that these inams might be dealt with under Section XV of the Inam Rules as usual.[2] It was under these proposals and orders that the inams in the district were settled.[3]

There were originally 13 palayams in the district namely, Uttukuli, Samattur, Kattampatti, Negamam, Avalappampatti, Poravipalayam and Ramapatnam in the Pollachi taluk, Metrathi, Thungavi, Jothampatti, Vedapatti and Maivadi in the Udumalpet taluk and Andipatty in the Karur taluk. They paid an annual peshkash of Rs. 28,019, fixed in 1808;[4] and this peshkash represented 70 per cent of the assets of the estates.[5] They were all permanently settled on the existing peshkash and given istimarar sanads only in 1865-1871.[6]

---

1 Collection of papers relating to the Inam Settlement in Madras, 1948, pages 270–273.

2 Collection of papers relating to the Inam Settlement in Madras, 1948, pages 273–274.

3 Inam—Selection No. 45—Coimbatore.

4 B.P. No. 375, dated 15th January 1862.

5 G.O. No. 2730, Revenue, dated 10th November 1865, page 57.

6 B.P. No. 4828, dated 9th June 1868.
B.P. No. 2721, dated 5th July 1871.
B.P. No. 210, dated 14th January 1873.

Both the palayams and the whole inam villages of this as well as other districts have been vitally affected by the general legislation governing estates passed in the State in recent years. The Rent Recovery Act of 1865 (Madras Act VIII of 1865), the Madras Estates Land Act of 1908 (Madras Act I of 1908) and the Madras Estates (Abolition and Conversion into Ryotwari) Act of 1948 (Madras Act XXVI of 1948) have all alike treated them as estates. The Rent Recovery Act of 1865 was passed to define the rights of the tenants in estates and to 'consolidate and improve the laws which defined the process to be taken in the recovery of rent'. The Act however failed to improve the lot of the tenants and the landholder was given the veiled right to enhance the rent on grounds similar to those upon which the Government could enhance the revenue in ryotwari areas. This led not only to exactions but to confusion in the minds of jurists as to the exact rights of the tenants. It was thought that their tenancy was from year to year and that they could be evicted at the end of the year. The position was not fully clarified till 1908 when the comprehensive Estates Land Act of that year was passed. This Act defined for the first time the substantive and relative rights and obligations of landholder and their tenants or ryots. It secured a permanent right of occupancy to every ryot who at its commencement was in possession of ryoti land or who subsequently was admitted to possesssion of such land. This right was made heritable and transferable by sale, gift or otherwise. Nor was this all. He could use the land without materially impairing its value or rendering it unfit for agricultural purposes. He could enjoy and cut down all trees planted by him after the passing of the Act, or those which grew upon his holding. He could make improvements to his land except when the land holders wanted it in order to benefit other ryots as well. He could not be subjected to any enhanced rent on the ground of the improvements effected by the landholder, unless it had been registered in accordance with the provisions of the Act. He had a right to have evidence of improvements effected by him recorded; and had a right to the sole benefits accruing from such improvements. He was protected against all unlawful exactions and given the right to a reduction of rent in certain circumstances. He could also insist upon a patta from the landholder. The Act at the same time conferred certain rights on the landholder. He required a first charge for rent and interest thereon not only upon the ryot's holding but also upon its produce. He could reserve mining rights, receive a premium when first admitting any person to possession of ryoti land, enhance the rent under certain conditions, and recover arrears of rent by a suit before the Collector by distraint and sale of movable property, crops, etc. The

Act also provided for a survey and a record of rights to be made by the Collector in certain cases.[1]

Now, this Act brought under the definition of estate " any village of which the land revenue had been granted in inam to a person not owning the kudivaram right thereof provided that the grant has been made, confirmed or recognised by the British Government or any separated part of such villages ". This definition was made to set right certain doubts that had arisen consequent on the Inam Settlement. The inam title deeds issued under that settlement were so drawn up that they conveyed an impression as if the land belonged to the inamdars irrespective of the fact whether they possessed the kudivaram right in it or not. As a result of this some of the inamdars claimed the right in the soil to the injury of the actual kudivaram holders. An Act was, therefore, passed declaring that nothing contained in any title deed issued to any inamdar should be deemed to define, limit, infringe or destroy the rights of any description of holders or occupiers of the land from which any inam was derived or drawn. When this Act was passed the Government held the view that an inam on the face of it carried only the melvaram right and that if any inamdar set up a claim to the kudivaram right also, it was for him to establish that right. This view which practically amounted to saying that kudivaram right should be considered to belong to the cultivators unless the contrary was proved was upheld for a long time and the validity of this view was recognised by the courts in several cases and was presumed when the whole inam villages were included in the above mentioned definition of estate in the 1908 Act. But this view was completely upset by the Privy Council in 1918. In that year, in a well-known decision, the Privy Council held that there was no presumption in law that an inam conveyed the melvaram right alone, and ruled that whoever claimed the kudivaram right must prove it in a court of law. This decision as well as some other decisions to more or less the same effect practically threw on the cultivators the onus of proving that they possessed the kudivaram right in each and every case. The hardship to the ryots involved in it was removed by the Government by amending the definition of estate by Madras Act VIII of 1934. The definition was changed by this Act into " any village of which the land revenue without the kudivaram has been granted in inam to a person not owning the kudivaram thereof, provided that the grant has been made, confirmed or recognised by the British Government ". The alteration so made virtually amounted to laying down that, if the inamdar of a whole inam village wanted to escape the

1 *Monagraph on Rural Problems in Madras* by S. Y. Krishnaswami, 1947 page 41.

provisions of the Estates Land Act, he had to prove in a court of law that he possessed the kudivaram right in that village. The onus of proving the kudivaram right in the case of whole inam villages was thus again shifted back from the cultivators to the inamdars and the cultivators were for all practical purposes, considered to possess the kudivaram right. By Madras Act XVII of 1936 the definition of 'estate' was further extended so as to include within its scope any inam village of which the grant had been made, confirmed or recognised by the British Government. The effect of the amendment was to bring all inam villages within the scope of the Madras Estates Land Act. In the case however of inam villages which became estates by virtue of this amending Act, the inamdars were given an opportunity to prove that they possessed the kudivaram right in lands in such villages by lodging applications before a special tribunal.[1]

Meanwhile the zamindari system in all its aspects came to be criticised, discredited and condemned with more and more vehemence. In 1937, in consequence of the agitation in the Legislature, the Congress Ministry appointed a Committee presided over by Sri T. Prakasam, the Revenue Minister, to enquire into the whole question. On the basis of its recommendations the Estates Land Reforms Bill of 1938 was drafted. Both this Bill and a revised Bill prepared in 1939, however, could achieve nothing, as the Congress Ministry soon afterwards resigned office.[2] In 1940 the Adviser Government, which succeeded the Congress Ministry drew up a scheme for the conversion of zamindari tenure into ryotwari by buying out zamindars and paying them compensation on the basis of net income.[3] In 1945 the Working Committee of the Congress issued a manifesto urging comprehensive land reforms, including the abolition of the zamindari system, and the acquisition of estates by the payment of equitable compensation. Early in 1947 after the National Government came to power the legislature passed a Resolution accepting the general principle of the abolition of the zamindari system.[4] In pursuance of this resolution the Government as a first step, passed an Act called the Madras Estates Land (Reduction of Rent) Act XXX of 1947, for reducing the high rents which prevailed in the estates. It provided for the reduction of rents payable by the ryots in estates approximately

---

1 *Studies in Madras Administration* by B. S. Baliga, Volume I, 1949, pages 93–94.

Extracts from Papers relating to Tenency Right in Inams, Vol. I—III.

2 *Monograph on Rural Problems in Madras* by S. Y. Krishnaswami, 1947, pages 43–44.

3 *Madras in* 1950, pages 58–60.

4 G.O. No. 114, Legal, dated 13th September 1947. *See* the Statement of Objects and Reasons.

to the level of the assessments imposed on ryotwari lands in the neighbourhood.[1] The Government also brought forward a Bill in the same year for abolishing all estates. The zamindari system, they stated, had perpetuated an assessment which was not only high but also had no relation to the productive capacity of the land. It had led to loss of contact between the Government and the actual cultivators. It had acted as a brake on agricultural improvements. It had allowed most of the irrigation works to fall into disrepair. It had, because of its complexities, brought in an immense amount of litigation in which the illiterate ryots had been placed at the mercy of the unscrupulous agents of the zamindars. It had rarely, if ever, resulted in administration as efficient as that of the Government areas, and consequently it had led to a great deal of discontent and agitation among the ryots. Indeed the system, having outlived its usefulness, had nothing to recommend its continuance.[2]

The Bill was passed into the Madras (Estates Abolition and Conversion into Ryotwari) Act XXVI of 1948. It applies to all zamindaris, all unsettled palayams, and all whole inam villages except those which became estates by virtue of Act XVIII of 1936. When an estate is notified under the Act all the earlier enactments relating to estates, except the Rent Reduction Act of 1947, cease to be applicable to it; and the entire estate, including all communal lands and porambokes, waste lands, pasture lands, lanka lands, forests, mines and minerals, quarries, rivers and streams, tanks and irrigation works, fisheries and ferries stand transferred to the Government and vest in them free of all encumbrances. The estate is then to be surveyed and settled on ryotwari principles by Settlement Officers appointed under a Director of Settlements who works under the Board of Revenue. The Settlement Officer is to enquire and determine whether any inam village in his jurisdiction is an inam estate or not in order to find out whether it can be notified and acquired. His decision is to be appealable to a Special Tribunal constituted under the Act. He is also to decide on application whether an under-tenure estate was created before or after the principal estate was permanently settled so as to determine whether the compensation is to be paid entirely to the under tenure holder or partly also to the holder of the principal estate. The ryots are to be given ryotwari pattas for their holdings with effect from the notified date and the landholders, zamindars, inamdars and under-tenure holders are also to be given ryotwari pattas in respect of their private lands and certain other lands which had been in their continuous occupation from certain

[1] G.O. No. 3, Legal, dated 7th January 1948.

[2] G.O. No. 114, Legal, dated 13th September 1947. *See* the Statement of Objects and Reasons.

specified dates. Appeals from the decisions of the Settlement Officers in these cases also are to lie to the Special Tribunal.

Compensation is to be paid to the landholders only after the estates are surveyed and settled. Meanwhile the landholder is to be entitled to an interim payment representing roughly the estimated basic annual sum. This interim payment is not to be counted against the final compensation. As to the method of calculating the basic annual sum in the case of the zamindari estates, the gross annual ryotwari demand in respect of all lands for which persons other than the zamindar are entitled to ryotwari pattas under the Act and the average net annual miscellaneous revenue from all other sources in the lands have to be computed; and one-third of this figure has to be taken to be the zamindar's share. This one-third portion is, however, to be made subject to two deductions, a deduction of five per cent of the gross annual ryotwari demand on account of establishment charges and another deduction of three and one-third per cent on account of the maintenance of irrigation works which is the zamindars' responsibility. In calculating the basic annual sum for inam estates the annual gross ryotwari demand and not any fraction of it is to be taken as the starting point. From this figure three and one-third per cent is to be deducted on account of maintenance of irrigation works in the estate which the landholder is obliged to maintain. Then the quit-rent or the jodi, etc., payable annually to the Government by the landholder is also to be deducted. The balance represents the basic annual sum for the inam estate. The compensation is to be the basic annual sum multiplied by a figure which varies between 12 and 30. Where the basic annual sum does not exceed Rs. 1,000 the multiplier is 30; over one lakh of rupees the multiplier is 12½. There are to be four intermediate stages 15, 17½, 20 and 25 depending on the annual basic sum. Payments are not to be made direct to the landholders but are to be deposited with the two tribunals constituted under the Act. Provision is also made for the appointment of more tribunals when necessary.[1]

These are, in the main, the provisions of the Estates Abolition and Conversion into Ryotwari Act. This Act was amended by Act I of 1950, to provide for the payment of a portion of the compensation without waiting for the completion of the survey and settlement operations. Under the latter Act advance compensation is to be adjusted towards the compensation as finally determined. The Act also ensures the payment of a minimum of 12½ crores of rupees as compensation for the zamindari

1 G.O. No. 75, Legal, dated 18th April 1949.
Madras in 1950, pages 60–64.

estates in the State of Madras as it was before the creation of the Andhra State.[1] In Coimbatore the estates have been taken over by the Government.

The present land revenue of the district including the additional surcharge amounts to Rs. 81,70,144–0–10, as detailed below* :—

Taluk.	*Land revenue.*			*Additional surcharge on the land revenue.*		
	RS.	A.	P.	RS.	A.	P.
Avanashi	3,71,842	7	6	33,063,	12	0
Bhavani	7,23,649	2	1	50,659	6	4
Coimbatore	5,19,491	15	6	51,047	13	0
Dharapuram	8,20,952	14	3	70,875	12	0
Erode	20,90,149	0	3	1,63,953	10	3
Gobichettipalayam	14,99,452	3	2	1,13,688	7	0
Palladam	5,05,534	10	1	50,783	11	9
Pollachi	6,50,315	3	0	61,461	3	11
Udumalpet	3,59,031	10	9	34,191	2	0
Total	75,40,419	2	7	6,29,724	14	3

* These are the figures for 1956–57, furnished by the Collector of Coimbatore district.

As for the machinery employed for collecting it and administering all other revenue and general matters, the district as we have already seen, has had first two Collectors and thereafter one from the early days. The Collector was, from the beginning, assisted by Sub-Collectors. From 1859 he came to be assisted by Deputy Collectors as well.[2] As for the taluks there were originally ten taluks, namely, Coimbatore, Udumalpet, Pollachi, Palladam, Bhavani, Erode, Karur, Kollegal, Dharapuram and Satyamangalam. In 1910 Karur was transferred to the Tiruchirappalli district, Satyamangalam was formed into the Gobichettipalayam taluk and parts of Palladam and Coimbatore taluks were constituted into a new taluk called the Avanashi taluk. Kollegal was transferred to the Mysore State in 1956. So that, at present, there are nine taluks in the district, namely, Coimbatore, Pollachi, Udumalpet, Palladam, Dharapuram, Erode, Gobichettipalayam, Avanashi and Bhavani. As for the Revenue Divisions they have naturally changed from time to time. At present these consist of Pollachi, Erode and Gobichettipalayam. The Pollachi Division comprises the taluks of Coimbatore, Pollachi and Udumalpet ; the Erode Division comprises the taluks of Palladam,

1 G.O. No. 26, Legal, dated 25th January 1950.

2 G.O. No. 379, Revenue, dated 22nd March 1859.

Dharapuram and Erode; and the Gobichettipalayam Division comprises the taluks of Gobichettipalayam, Avanashi and Bhavani. The Revenue Divisions have been invariably under the charge of Sub-Collectors or Deputy Collectors and the taluks under the charge of Tahsildars. The Tahsildars have been having under them the usual revenue subordinates, the Deputy Tahsildars and Revenue Inspectors. The Village establishments have always consisted of the village headmen (the Nattamaikarans), the Karnams, etc.

As to land tenures, both the fixed rent and the varam tenures are prevalent in the district. The former is a system by which lands are leased out by the landlords for fixed rents to the tenants, while the latter is a system by which the lands are leased out by the landholders to the tenants for a share of the produce. There are also some other systems in vogue in the district. There is thus the system known as the 'kootu' tenancy where the landholder also works with the tenant and takes one-fourth more yield in addition to the usual half varam. There is the system called the 'Kattuveli bogium' under which a piece of land is mortgaged to a creditor for a stipulated number of years, the creditor cultivating the land, taking all the yield, having complete possession and paying all the taxes upon the land. After, however, the loan is discharged from the yield of the land in the mortgaged period, the land is returned to the landholder, no interest being payable on the loan. There is yet another system, the usufructuary mortgage on the land, under which the mortgager advances a loan on a piece of land but allows the mortgager to cultivate the same on the execution of a lease bond for a rental equivalent to the interest on the loan.[1]

The leases for fixed and varam rents run from 1 to 10 years or more, but the most common are the one-year, three-year and five-year leases.[2] In most cases, as has been stated already the lessee pays half the produce as varam rent, but in some, half the produce and straw, and even two-thirds of the produce and one-third straw or three-fourths of the produce. The high rents prevail especially under the big project areas, like the Bhavani and the Amaravati project areas.[3] In the case of second crop the lessee pays from one-third to one-sixth of the first crop rental.[4] In most cases the lessee is required to pay the rent whether the land is cultivated or not;

---

[1] Report of the Special Officer on Land Tenures in the Ryotwari Areas of the Madras Province, 1947, pages 38, 163.

[2] *Idem*, page 68.

[3] *Idem*, pages 62, 84.
G.O. No. 1357, Revenue (Confidential), dated 8th April 1918. *See* page 90.

[4] *Idem*, *see* Moir's Report, page 90.

but in some cases he is allowed remission if the crops fail. The instalments in which the rents are paid are generally two, but more instalments are allowed in the case of garden crops, cocoanut topes, etc.[1] Compensation is sometimes paid for the improvements made by the tenants.[2] Advances to tenants are sometimes given.[3] As to cultivation, the lessee is most commonly required to deliver up the land free from prickly pear, weeds, etc., and to manure the crops properly and deepen the well.[4] Restriction on cultivation of particular crops is fairly common; mulberry, cotton groundnut, hemp and gingelly are usually prohibited.[5] A rotation of crops is sometimes prescribed, or the crop to be last grown is specified.[6] Sub-letting is prohibited in some cases.[7] Suits for ejectment of tenants is fairly high;[8] and the percentage of absentee landlords is 10.[9]

Since the accession of the National Government tenancy and other land reforms have been actively considered. In 1946 the Government appointed a Special Officer and in 1950 a Special Committee presided over by Sri M. V. Subramanian, I.C.S., a Member of the Board of Revenue to consider and report on various tenancy as well as other land revenue matters.[10] Their reports are still being considered and in the meanwhile, upon their recommendation, two important Acts affecting tenancy matters have been passed. The first Act, the Madras Cultivating Tenants Protection Act XXV of 1955, extends to all areas in the State, excepting the Gudalur taluk of the Nilgiris district and in the areas in which the provisions of the Tanjore Tenants and Pannaiyals Protection Act XIV of 1952, is in force. It prevents the owners of land, in anticipation of land reforms legislation, from evicting cultivating tenants, with a view to bringing the lands under their personal cultivation. It, however, withholds protection

---

1 *Idem*, page 9.0

2 Report of the Special Officer on Land Tenures in the Ryotwari Areas of the Madras Province, 1947, page 70.

3 Report of the Special Officer on Land Tenures in the Ryotwari Areas of the Madras Province, 1947, page 70.

4 G.O. No. 1357, Revenue (Confidential), dated 8th April 1918—*See* Moir's Report, page 90.

5 *Idem*, page 90.

6 Report of the Special Officer on Land Tenures in the Ryotwari Areas in the Madras Presidency, 1947, page 69.

7 *Idem*, page 69.

8 *Idem*, page 199.

9 *Idem*, page 182.

10 *See* the Reports of the Special Officer on Land Tenures in Ryotwari Areas (1947) and on the Investigation of Land Tenures (1949)—*See* also the First and Second Reports of the Land Revenue Reforms Committee (1951).

from tenants who are in arrears of rent or have done any act which is destructive of or injurious to the land or any crop thereon, or have ceased to cultivate the land or have used it for any purpose other than that for which it was let.[1] The second Act, the Madras Cultivating Tenants (Payment of Fair Rent) Act XXIV of 1956, extends to the whole State. It fixes the fair rent payable by the cultivating tenant to the land owner. This rent is, in the case of wet land at 40 per cent of the gross produce or its value in money ; in the case of wet land, where the irrigation is supplemented by lifting water, at 35 per cent, and in the case of any other class of land, at 33 1-3rd per cent. It calls upon the tenant to bear all the cultivation expenses, allows him a reduction in cases of baling water, provides for the payment of fair rent by him either partly or wholly, in cash or in kind, and constitutes Rent Courts and Rent Tribunals to decide disputes arising under the Act between him and the land-owner.[2]

The Madras Plantations Agricultural Income Tax Act V of 1955, levies a tax on agricultural income from coffee, tea, rubber, cinchona and cardamom plantations. This tax is levied over and above the land revenue assessment on every person whose total agricultural income is not less than Rs. 3,000 and in the case of joint families, not less than Rs. 6,000. Its rates are these. On the first Rs. 1,500 of total agricultural income, nil, on the next Rs. 3,500 at 9 pies in the rupee; on the next Rs. 5,000 at one anna and 6 pies in the rupee; on the next Rs. 5,000 at 2 annas and 6 pies in the rupee; on the next Rs. 5,000 at 3 annas and 6 pies in the rupee; on the next Rs. 5,000 at 4 annas in the rupee; on the balance at 5 annas and 6 pies in the rupee.[3]

So much about land revenue administration. The history of the other revenues is soon told. We can deal here only with such of them as were formerly or are now administered by the Madras Government. Taking those that have been throughout under the Madras Government first, excise was till lately, until prohibition was introduced, the most important source of revenue. But today, with the introduction of prohibition, it has dwindled into a very small sum. In 1945–46, for instance, when prohibition had been suspended by the Advisor Government, it amounted to about Rs. 15·89 crores in the State. But, in 1955–57, the whole State having gone dry for some years, the

[1] *See* the *Fort St. George Gazette* for the Act.

[2] *Idem.*

[3] *Idem.*

total (gross) revenue, excluding refunds, was only Rs. 20,86,086 in the State and Rs. 53,298 in the district.[1]

This revenue was in pre-prohibition days derived from the manufacture and sale of arrack, and toddy, and from the sale of foreign liquors, opium, ganja and bhang. It is now derived chiefly from foreign liquor. Its history is now merely of antiquarian interest, but none the less it has to be recounted in as much as it affected the administration of the district for more than a century.

From the early days of British rule till 1875 the arrack and toddy farms were leased out conjointly, usually by taluks, for triennial periods. From 1859–60 to 1869–70, however, the whole district was leased out in one farm to induce large capitalists to take up the business, but, as the plan did not answer the purpose, the taluk farms were reverted to at the end of that period. Until 1850 the selection of renters was made on a consideration of tenders received and subsequently of bids made at open auctions. The renter paid a fixed rent and could sell any quantity of liquor or further the sale of one kind of liquor at the expense of another, i.e., arrack at the expense of toddy. The only restriction imposed on him was that he could not sell below certain minimum rates fixed by the Board of Revenue, but even this was practically inoperative, as the minimum rates were fixed without any reference to the strengths of liquor sold. The privilege of sub-renting almost every shop was availed of by the renters, and practically every shopkeeper had a still. Under this system the Government had no means of gauging the consumption of liquors, of regulating taxation, and controlling the traffic so as to secure the object of maximum of revenue with the minimum of consumption. The farming system had accordingly in 1875–76 to give way to what was called "the improved excise system". Under this system the exclusive privilege of manufacture and sale of country spirits for the whole district was assigned to a contractor selected by tender after public notification. Distillation was permitted only at the headquarters of the district, at which sufficient guard and gauging establishments were maintained at the contractor's expense. The revenue was taken in the shape of an excise duty on each gallon issued at rates defined with references to strength, and to guard against the contractor giving his attention only to the easily managed portions of his farm, neglecting the outlaying parts, it was stipulated that he should guarantee a minimum revenue. In addition to the duty leviable at the distillery, a surcharge of duty was made on liquor sold in shops within the limits of certain towns, where the

1 Report on the Administration of the Madras Excise and Prohibition Department for 1955–56, 1957, Page 23.

consumption of liquor was high and the drinking classes could afford to pay a higher duty than the rural population. The contractors were bound to keep accounts of receipts and disbursements and of manufacture and issue of liquors, to see that a sufficient number of hydrometers were supplied to the shops for testing the strength sold so as to check dilution, to sell liquor only at the prescribed strengths, and at prices between certain maximum and minimum limits, to use proper measures and to allow inspection of premises by Officers of the Government. The excise duty was at first fixed at Rs. 1—12—0 and subsequently raised to Rs. 2. The contractor was expected to maintain the necessary establishment for the detection and suppression of illicit traffic in liquor. The toddy farms were now separated from those of arrack, as it was found that the tendency was for contractors to extend the sale of arrack at the expense of toddy which was considered the more wholesome beverage.

It was however soon found that this system was responsible for a serious growth of illegal practices. As all the shops were in the hands of the manufacturer and he had to pay the duty only on the quantity issued to the vendors, it mattered little to him, if the shops sold illicit liquor. Further, the renter failed to maintain the preventive staff required to put down the illicit practices. The Government, therefore, appointed a Committee in 1884 to suggest improvements and, upon its recommendation, passed Act I of 1886. The 'improved excise system' was now in the case of arrack replaced by the free supply system which was one of free competition among the licensed distillers in respect of manufacture and supply. This led to unhealthy competition and finally to the danger of a monopoly. The system was accordingly abandoned in 1900 and replaced by the contract distillery system. Under this system the privilege to manufacture and to vend were entirely separated; the manufacturer was given the privilege of supplying a fixed area at a definite rate per gallon, the Government supervising the process and ensuring the purity of liquor. The liquor was issued from a central source of supply and the right of retail sale was disposed of by auction. By this arrangement the prevention of illicit practices was left in the hands of the Government.

In the case of toddy, a tree tax system was introduced in the district from 1897. Under this system tapping for fermented toddy was allowed for licensed shops after the trees were marked for tapping on payment of the prescribed tree tax by the renter. Licences and permits were issued for tapping and transport respectively. The rate of tree tax was fixed from time to time and was usually greater for the coconut than for the palmyra or the date tree. Coconut and palmyra were most commonly tapped in the district. The renters of toddy shops used to lease trees from the owners for annual payments. Sweet juice industry was carried on, on a fairly large scale and the juice was chiefly converted into jaggery. As to foreign liquor, town licences were granted for consumption on the premises, the fees being determined by auction. But wholesale licences and retail licences for consumption off the premises, for refreshment rooms, bars, etc., were granted on payment of fixed fees. The sale of opium was administered under Act I of 1878 and that of Ganja under Act I of 1886 and the right of retail vend to the public was sold by auction[1].

Such was the position till 1946 when prohibition was introduced into the district. We have already seen in the chapter on welfare Schemes how prohibition was introduced and with what results.

The loss of revenue caused by prohibition has been more than made up by the levy of new taxes called commercial taxes. The credit for devising and introducing these new taxes belongs to the first Congress Ministry presided over by Sri C. Rajagopalachari. In 1939 the Madras General Sales Tax Act (Act IX of 1939), the Madras Entertainments Tax Act (Act X of 1939), the Madras Sales of Motor Spirit Taxation Act (Act VI of 1939) and the Madras Tobacco (Taxation of Sales and Licensing) Act (Act VIII of 1939) were passed; and there began a new era in taxation.

The Madras Tobacco (Taxation of Sales and Licensing) Act was suspended in 1944 on account of the levy of central excise duty by the Government of India and a lump sum compensation was given by that Government thereafter to the Madras Government for the loss of State Revenue. In 1953, this Act was repealed and the State enacted the Madras Tobacco (Taxation of Sales and Registration) Act of 1953 (Act IV of 1953). This Act came into force from 20th April 1953. It enabled a single point tax on the first sales to be levied on all varieties of cigarettes sold at the retail point at more than 3 pies per cigarette on a graduated scale ranging from 10 per cent, of the turnover to 30 per cent of the turnover according to the rate of the retail price of the cigarette, and at 30 per cent of the turnover on cigars and cheroots sold at not less than two annas per cigar or cheroot and on pipe tobacco or cigarette tobacco. In 1955, the tax was extended to cigarettes of which the price at retail point was not more than three pies per cigarette or at the rate of 3 1/8th per cent of the turnover. The tax realised for the year 1955-56 for the whole State was Rs. 30,10,191, Coimbatore contributing Rs. 3,056[2].

---

1 *Manual of Coimbatore District*, edited by Harold A. Stuart, Vol. II, 1898 pages 220–225.

Gazetteer of the Coimbatore District, Vol. II, 1933, pages 186–188.

The Madras Presidency 1881–1931, by G. T. Boag, 1933, pages 55–58.

2 G.O. No. 3363, Revenue, dated 6th September 1956.

It may be of some interest to state here that in olden days there was a tobacco monopoly in the district. It was introduced by Tipu, abolished in 1799, and was revived in 1807. In Malabar, tobacco has immemoriably been considered a necessity of life by ryots working throughout the day for months together on swampy wet land, it being found in practice to be a preventive of fever and chills. But the climate not being suitable to the growth of tobacco, a large import trade of the leaf was carried on with Coimbatore where it was grown with ease and in abundance. Until 1807 there were no restrictions on the trade. In that year the sale in Malabar was made a Government monopoly and in 1811 the monopoly was extended to Coimbatore, both as regards cultivation and sale, the whole crop being taken up by the Collector at certain rates. The required quantity was then despatched to Malabar and the balance was sold by Government agents to retailers for local consumption. This system led to frightful abuses, and the growth and sale of tobacco were freed from control in 1816, from which date till 1826, one or other Collector entered into contracts with merchants and others to supply a determined quantity of Coimbatore tobacco to the Government depots in Malabar at fixed rates. This system, in turn, worked ill and, in 1827, a new system came into force under which the cultivation in Coimbatore of tobacco suited for Malabar market was prohibited except under permission of the Government Officers, who, having settled the quantity required for Malabar, made advances to select cultivators. The tobacco thus grown was brought to depots at Coimbatore, where it was paid at rates varying according to its quality, the quality being determined by the Government Officers with reference to a panchayat in cases of dispute. The possible frauds practised upon the ryots and the Government by the subordinates might easily be imagined. Apart from this the evils inherent in the monopoly system itself soon began to be felt. The price at which tobacco was sold in Malabar to the licensed vendors by the Tahsildars, was Rs. 202 per candy of 500 lb. or Rs. 2⅛ per lb.; but as excellent tobacco could be sold at a profit at one anna or so per lb., the monopoly price came to 700 per cent advance upon its actual value. As the frontiers of the two districts adjoined, and as a head load was worth Rs. 20 at the monopoly price, the temptation to smuggle became irresistible. The result was a rapid approach to general demoralization. Tobacco smugglers, chiefly Moplahs, went about in armed gangs, even attacking and plundering the Government depots when not engaged in secret contraband traffic. On the other hand, the frauds and oppressions practised by the preventive force when they were not conniving at the contraband trade, their frequent domiciliary visitations with their attendant exactions, led to many collusions between themselves and the people, the result being in the highest degree injurious to peace and good order. The Government were at last obliged to put down the violence of the smugglers by military force and permanently to locate an additional force in Malabar, and in 1845 they finally called on the Collectors, to report, through the Board of Revenue, on the practicability of a beneficial modification of the monopoly, or in default, to suggest some substitute for this source of revenue, such as a tax upon the mercantile classes who had just (1844) been releived of the inland custom duties (sayer). The Board reported that no modification would be of any use in freeing the monopoly from the evils attendant upon it and stated that between its entire ‘surrender and the retention of the present system with all its evils, there is no practicable middle course’. The Government finally adopted the Board's view and abolished the monopoly in 1852[1].

To go back to the commercial taxes, the General Sales Tax came into force on 1st October 1939[2]. It was levied on all business the turnover of which exceeded Rs. 10,000, thereby exempting all small traders dealing in food, clothing, etc. To facilitate its levy and to avoid detailed investigations into the exact turnovers in the case of smaller businesses, the amount of the tax was fixed at Rs. 5 per month when the turnover was between Rs. 10,000 and Rs. 20,000. A tax at half a per cent was levied when the turnover exceeded Rs. 20,000. Safeguards were provided in the Act to avoid the taxation of both the seller and the buyer in respect of one and the same transaction and also on both the purchases and sales of the same goods of the same dealer. Exemptions were made in the case of certain articles like bullion and species, cotton, cotton yarn and cloth woven on handlooms and sold by persons exclusively dealing in such cloth. In the case of hides and skins provision was also made to levy the tax at the single point in a series of sales by successive dealers. In the case of certain finished articles of industrial manufacture a rebate of one half of the tax levied on sales of such articles for delivery outside the State was allowed. The sale of electrical energy, motor spirit and manufactured tobacco was exempted from the tax[3]. In 1940–41 the rates of tax were reduced to Rs. 4 per month on turnovers between Rs. 10,000 and Rs. 20,000 and to one-fourth per cent on turnovers exceeding Rs. 20,000[4]. In 1944 the rates of taxation were raised to Rs. 8

[1] *Manual of the Coimbatore District* by F. A. Nicholson, 1887, pages 175–176.
For a detailed account of the Tobacco Monopoly, *See Studies in Madras Administration* by B. S. Baliga, Vol. I, 1949, pages 174–213.

[2] G.O. No. 338, Revenue, dated 12th February 1941.

[3] *See* the Act in the *Fort St. George Gazette*.

[4] G.O. No. 2528, Revenue, dated 5th November 1941.

per mensem on turnovers between Rs. 15,000 and Rs. 20,000 and to one per cent on turnovers exceeding Rs. 20,000[1]. In 1948 the slab system of taxation was abolished, except in the case of fruit and vegetable dealers and a tax at 3 pies per rupee was levied in all cases in which the turnover was Rs. 10,000 or more. In respect of certain luxury goods an additional tax at the rate of 3 to 6 pies for every rupee was also levied at the stage of sale by the first dealer[2]. In 1949 the slab rate system was made inapplicable to dealers in coconuts, canned, preserved, dried or dehydrated vegetables and fruits. In the same year a tax on food and drink sold in hotels, boarding houses and restaurants was raised to 4½ pies in the rupee when the turnover was Rs. 25,000 or more; and the sale of cotton which had been exempted from tax prior to 1st August 1949 now became liable to a tax at a single point at the rate of half a per cent on the turnover[3]. From 1950, by virtue of Article 286 (1) of the Constitution of India, sales in the course of export outside the territory of India were exempted from tax, while the taxes on other sales, including sales in the course of export to the other States in India, continued to be levied under the special permission of the President till 1955[4]. From 1954 the levy of additional tax was extended to certain varieties of mill cloth, fine or superfine cotton cloth other than handloom cloth, hosiery goods other than those made wholly of cotton and medium cotton mill cloth, at the rate of one anna three pies and precious stones at the rate of six pies. From 1956 the sale of sugar was also subjected to the additional tax at the rate of one anna in the rupee. A single point tax of six pies was also levied on the sale of raw tobacco and certain varieties of manufactured tobacco which were not subjected to tax under the Madras Tobacco (Taxation of Sales and Registration) Act, 1953. From 1st April 1954, exemptions were granted to certain articles like handloom cloth, eggs, meat, fish, flowers, vegetables and fruits and from 1st April 1955 to onions, potatoes, betel leaves and plantain leaves, and to co-operative societies effecting sales of palm gur and to sales effected by cottage industrial co-operative societies. The net result of all this brought in Rs. 9,94,17,279 to the State, in 1955–56, Coimbatore contributing Rs. 1,28,35,400[5].

The entertainment tax came into force on 1st August 1939[6]. This Act repealed a previous Act of 1926 (Act V of 1927) by which local bodies

---

1 G.O. No. 769, Revenue, dated 28th March 1947.

2 G.O. No. 429, Revenue, dated 23rd February 1949.

3 G.O. No. 2601, Revenue, dated 27th September 1950.

5 *Madras in* 1949, page 25.

5 G.O. No. 4207, Revenue, dated 17th November 1956.

6 G.O. No. 3075, Revenue, dated 10th December 1940.

could levy a tax on entertainments and provided compensation for such bodies. It authorised the levy of a tax on a graduated scale according to the value of the payment made for admission to any entertainment. When the payment was not more than 2 annas, the tax was levied at 3 pies; when it was more than 2 annas but less than 6 annas, it was levied at 6 pies. In the case of higher payments it rose gradually from one anna in the case of payments between 6 annas and 12 annas to Rs. 2 in the case of payments between Rs. 9½ and Rs. 10. When the payment was Rs. 10 or more it was Rs. 2 for the first 10 rupees and Rs. 2 for every 10 rupees or portion thereof in excess of the first 10 rupees. Provision was made in the Act for compounding the tax for a fixed sum as well as payment of a fixed percentage of the gross proceeds, when the proprietors applied for such lump sum payments. Provision was also made for exempting entertainments, the proceeds of which were devoted to philanthropic, religious or charitable purposes, and entertainments which were of an educational, cultural and scientific character[1]. In 1945, the rates of tax on payments for admission above 2 annas was increased by fifty per cent. From 1947, the tax was levied at the following rates. Where the payment, inclusive of the amount of the tax, is not more than 5 annas at one-fifth rate, where it is more than 5 annas but is not more than Rs. 1—8—0 at one-fourth rate; and where it is more than Rs. 1—8—0, at one-third the rate. A concession was also given to cinematograph exhibitions for which the tax was calculated at the above rates, after excluding from such payments, the amount of the tax. In addition to the above tax, a show tax calculated at different rates for Madras City, big municipalities, etc., has been levied since 1949. The rate of tax prescribed for dramatic and music performances, Indian dances, exhibitions of works of arts, manufactures, etc., is as follows:—Where the payment inclusive of the tax is not more than 3 rupees, the rate of tax is one-eighth; where it is more than 3 rupees but not more than 5 rupees, it is one-fifth; and where it is more than 5 rupees, it is one-third. All dramatic performances, other than dance-dramas and all music and dance performances and variety entertainments by approved registered sabhas and similar associations have been exempted from entertainment tax. In 1955–56 the tax yielded Rs. 93,37,492 in the State, Coimbatore contributing Rs. 11,74,585[2].

The Sales of Motor Spirit Taxation Act came into force on 1st April 1939[3]. It provided for a levy of a tax of one anna and six pies per gallon on all retail sales of petrol and six pies per gallon on the sale of motor

---

1 *See* the Act in the *Fort St. George Gazette.*

2 G.O. No. 3864, Revenue; dated 19th October 1956.

3 G.O. No. 265, Revenue, dated 16th March 1943.

spirit other than petrol. The tax was payable only once and the dealers were required to register themselves and maintain proper accounts[1]. In 1947 the rates of tax were raised to 4 annas in the case of petrol and 1½ annas in the case of motor spirit other than petrol[2], and in 1952 the rate of tax on petrol was enhanced to 6 annas per gallon[3]. This tax amounted to Rs. 1,11,33,680 in the State for 1955-56, Coimbatore contributing Rs. 16,17,671[4].

The revenue realised from these new taxes being very considerable, a new department, called the Commercial Tax Department, was organized to administer them. The General Sales Tax was, from the beginning, administered by this department[5]. A notable feature in the administration of this Act was the constitution of the Sales Tax Appellate Tribunal from 1951 to hear appeals against the appellate orders of the Commercial Tax Officers and the *suo motu* orders of the Deputy Commissioner of Commercial Taxes. The Sales of Motor Spirit Taxation Act was administered by the Collectors and the Entertainments Tax Act was administered by the municipalities in municipal areas and Commercial Tax Department in non-municipal areas till 1943. In that year the working of these two Acts was also placed entirely under the Commercial Tax Department[6]. This Department is under a Commissioner of Commercial Taxes, who is a member of the Board of Revenue and there are three Deputy Commissioners, a number of Commercial Tax Officers, Deputy Commercial Tax Officers and Assistant Commercial Tax Officers under him. There are two Commercial Tax Officers in the district, one at Erode (Coimbatore South) and another at Coimbatore (Coimbatore North and the Nilgiris).

The other revenues administered by the State Government are registration fees and stamp revenue. The history of registration fees and revenue from judicial stamps has already been indicated in the chapter on Law and Order. The revenue from registration fees amounted to Rs. 49,48,085 in the State and Rs. 4,36,476 in the district in 1955-56[7]. In the same year, the revenue from judicial stamps amounted to Rs. 1,51,24,423 in the State and Rs. 16,65,264 in the district. The law

1 G.O. No. 111, Legal, dated 21st March 1939.

2 G.O. No. 2990, Revenue, dated 6th September 1947.

3 G.O. No. 2228, Revenue, dated 4th August 1952.

4 G.O. No. 2833, Revenue, dated 6th July 1956.

5 G.O. No. 338, Revenue, dated 12th February 1941.

6 G.O. No. 265, Revenue, dated 16th March 1943.
G.O. No. 20, Revenue, dated 6th January 1947.

7 G.O. No. 4637, Revenue, dated 22nd December 1956.

relating to non-judicial stamps is contained in India Act II of 1899 (Stamp Act) as amended by the Madras Acts VI of 1922, VI of 1923, XIII of 1924, VI of 1950, XXV of 1950 and XIV of 1951. The Stamp Act imposes duties on all commercial transactions recorded in writing, such as conveyances, bonds, cheques, bills of exchange and the like. The revenue from non-judicial stamps amounted to Rs. 2,43,77,772 in the State and Rs. 37,67,978 in the district in 1955–56[1]. The administration of the stamp revenue is vested in the Board of Revenue. The management of the stamp revenue in the district is vested in the Collector of the district.

Salt and Income Tax are administered by the Government of India. As the district is not a maritime district, it has no sea salt manufacture. It draws its supply of salt from the factories on the East Coast, principally from the Tuticorin group of Salt Factories though it is free to get supply of its quota from any other sources within Madras Zone. Based on the population of 1951 and per capita consumption, the District requires about 8 lakhs maunds of salt per year. " Salt earth " has been declared contraband in the district; though the saline areas are not sufficiently rich to prove dangerous to the salt revenue. During salt duty days Coimbatore was the headquarters of a Salt Preventive Party, who controlled the private manufacture of salt in the district. After the abolition of duty on salt from 1st April 1947, the manufacture of Saltpetre, which was previously licensed, is no longer controlled[2].

Income Tax was first imposed in India in 1860 in order to meet the financial dislocation caused by the Mutiny. It was levied at the rate of 4 per cent on all incomes of Rs. 500 and upwards. Since then many changes have been made in the system from time to time. According to the present schedule in force on 31st March 1957, the first Rs. 4,200 are exempted. In the case of incomes exceeding this amount the tax is levied as follows:—On the first Rs. 1,000 in the case of an unmarried person and Rs. 2,000 in the case of a married person, nil; on the next Rs. 3,000 at 9 pies in the rupee; on the next Rs. 2,500 at one anna and 9 pies in the rupee; on the next Rs. 2,500 at 2 annas and 3 pies in the rupee ; on the next Rs. 5,000 at 3 annas and 3 pies in the rupee; and on the balance at 4 annas in the rupee. A surcharge of 1/20 of the basic tax is also levied. On high incomes, i.e., over Rs. 20,000, a super tax ranging from 1 anna to 9½ annas in the rupee with a surcharge of 1/20 of the super tax is also levied as shown thus. On the first Rs. 20,000 nil ; next Rs. 5,000 at one

[1] G.O. No. 1666, Revenue, dated 7th April 1957.

[2] Information furnished by the Deputy Commissioner of Salt, Government of India, Madras.

anna in the rupee; next 15,000 at 3 annas in the rupee ; next Rs. 10,000 at 5 annas in the rupee; next Rs. 10,000 at 6 annas in the rupee; next Rs. 20,000 at 7 annas in the rupee; next Rs. 20,000 at 8 annas in the rupee; next Rs. 50,000 at 9 annas in the rupee; and on the balance at 9 annas 6 pies in the rupee.

Originally the administration of the Income Tax Department was vested in the State Government and was carried on by the Board of Revenue and the Collectors of the districts, assisted first by the ordinary revenue staff, and later by Special Deputy Collectors, Tahsildars, Assistant Tahsildars and Inspectors[1]. In 1922 a Chief Commissioner, who was a Member of the Board of Revenue, four Assistant Commissioners and many Assessors and investigating officers, called Surveyors, came to be appointed. Subsequently, as a result of the 1919 Reforms, the administration of the Department was taken over by the Government of India and their officers.

The district is now divided into two income tax circles, the Coimbatore circle and the Erode circle. The Coimbatore circle comprises the revenue taluks of Coimbatore, Palladam, Pollachi, Avanashi and Udumalpet; the Erode Circle comprises the revenue taluks of Erode, Dharapuram, Bhavani and Gobichettipalayam. Each circle is in charge of an Income Tax Officer. The number of assesses in the district in 1956–57 was 6,079 as against 60,861 for the whole State, and the amount of demand was about Rs. 2·7 crores in the district as against the demand of 17·97 crores for the whole State. Important industries, trades, etc., which contribute the tax in the Coimbatore circle are textile mills, ginning factories and groundnut oil mills, and these are mostly confined to the taluks of Coimbatore, Pollachi and Udumalpet. The main businesses which contribute tax in the Erode circle are those of gingelly oil, turmeric, groundnut oil, tobacco and tannery. There is no foreign trade worth mentioning in the district.

Since 1953 the Estate Duty has been introduced into the district. It is levied in accordance with the Estates Duty Act of 1953 (India Act XXXIV of 1953) on the capital value of all property real or personal, settled or not settled, which passes or is deemed to pass, on the death of any person. In the case of property which consists of an interest in the joint family property of a Hindu family, it is levied as follows. On the first Rs. 50,000 nil; on the next Rs. 50,000 at 5 per cent; on the next Rs. 50,000 at 7½ per cent; on the next Rs. 50,000 at 10 per cent; on the

[1] G.O. No. 275–276, Finance (Separate Revenue), dated 18th November 1921.

next Rs. 1,00,000 at 12½ per cent; on the next Rs. 2,00,000 at 15 per cent; on the next Rs. 5,00,000 at 20 per cent; on the next Rs. 10,00,000 at 25 per cent; on the next Rs. 10,00,000 at 30 per cent; on the next Rs. 20,00,000 at 35 per cent; and, on the balance of the principal value of the estate at 40 per cent; In the case of property of any other kind, it is levied as follows. On the first Rs. 1,00,000 of the principal value of the estate, nil; on the next Rs. 50,000 at 7½ per cent; on the next Rs. 50,000 at 10 per cent; on the next Rs. 1,00,000 at 12½ per cent; on the next Rs. 2,00,000 at 15 per cent; on the next Rs. 5,00,000 at 20 per cent; on the next Rs. 10,00,000 at 30 per cent; on the next Rs. 20,00,000 at 35 per cent; and on the *balance* of the principal value of the estate at 40 per cent. In the case of shares held by a deceased member, however, it is levied thus; if the principal value of the estate held does not exceed Rs. 5,000 nil, and, if the principal value exceeds Rs. 5,000 at 7½ per cent. The amount of the demand under the Estate Duty for 1956–57 for the district was Rs. 6·71 lakhs as against Rs. 46·07 lakhs for the whole State.

CHAPTER XVII

GAZETTEER

Avanasi Taluk

This taluk was formed in 1910 out of the northern portions of the old Palladam and Coimbatore taluks. Its area is 493 square miles and its population 2,72,536. Its greatest length is 40 miles east to west and 15 miles from north to south. It is a huge open plateau with the Nilgiris and their spurs forming prominent features of the landscape to the north and west. Isolated hillocks are found here and there towards the east, the chief of which are Kuruntamalai and Thogamalai in the Mettupalayam firka and Othimalai in Sinnakallippatti village. Each of these has a temple on it. The places of historical or antiquarian interest in the taluk are described below :—

Annur.—(Population 8,305), twenty miles north-north-east of Coimbatore on the road to Satyamangalam, contains an ancient Siva temple supposed to have been built by Kongu Cholas. The place was once fortified, but the traces of the old fort no longer exist. There is also a tradition that it was an opulent town and that the temple is built on the site of an 'aswamedha' or horse sacrifice. The old name of the place is Vanniyur.

On the western part of the village is a temple dedicated to Mannarswamy with some large earthenware horses and stone effigies near it.

Avanashi.—(Population 7,986), the headquarters of the taluk, is called in ancient Tamil works as Pokkoliyur or Tiruppukoliyur. It contains an old Siva temple dedicated to Avanashisvara which is one of the seven Kongu Sivalayams. The Nandi of the temple is of colossal size. In the outer porch of the temple are two stone alligators, each vomiting forth a child in memory of the story of the child who, through the intercession of Sundaramurthi Nayanar, was disgorged uninjured after having been swallowed by an alligator. A shrine to this saint exists not only within the temple but also stands on the bund of the tank called the Tamaraikulam (pond of lotuses). The walls of the temple contain inscriptions of Veera Pandya and Sundara Pandya of the Kongu Pandya dynasty. On the passing of the district into the hands of the Mysore

Rajas in the middle of the eighteenth century the temple received considerable attention from them. Krishna Deva Udayar completely renovated it in 1756 and the towers, walls, mantapams and the tank used for the floating festival were all repaired. Sankarayya, the agent of the Mysore Dalavoy Devarajayya, supervised the repairs and had a lingam, called Sankareswara, installed within the temple to mark his connection with the renovation.

Inscriptions on the walls of the shrines of the goddess refer to the Vikrama Cholar Teruveedi or the street of Vikrama Chola. There is, however, no street of this name now. Several of the inscriptions relate to Kongu Cholas, especially to Veera Rajendra (1207–52). A village named Papparapundi renamed Veera Rajendranallur is stated to have been granted rent free to the temple. Another village named Vanavasi or Veeracholanallur is stated to have been similarly granted on the occasion of the king's coronation. The former village is now known as Kanampundi and the latter as Sembiyanallur. During the time of the Hoysalas Madappa Danda Nayaka, son of Perumal, the founder of Danayakkankottai, granted to the temple a village called Tenpalli Nattam or Sitakaragandanallur. This village has not been identified.

Avanashi is known as Dakshina Kasi (Benaras of the South) in the inscriptions of certain Ummattur Chiefs of the fifteenth century and pilgrims still believe that a visit to the temple confers upon them as much merit as a visit to Benaras.

The big tower over the entrance to the temple had its five upper storeys pulled down about 1860 as it had become dilapidated to a dangerous extent. Only the bottom floor is now in existence.

A number of dolmens have formerly been found in the neighbourhood of the town as well as a subterranean vault built of large slabs of stone. These have, however, now disappeared. The bridge over the river is built in the old Hindu style as seen at Vijayanagar, on stone pillars sunk in the bed of the river with slabs resting on them.

There is a tradition that in ancient days there was a large City near the present town with palaces and temples and in 1860 a handsome bronze jug supposed to have been brought by Greek and Phoenician sailors was dug up from what is supposed to have been the site of the city.

Karamadai.—(Population 2,756), a railway station, 17 miles north of Coimbatore, is noted for its Vishnu temple dedicated to Ranganathaswami the car festival of which is largely attended. It is said that the processional car which was in use until some years ago was provided by the famous Tirumala Nayaka of Madurai.

Karavalur.—(Population 2,751), about 5 miles north west of Palladam, contains two old temples one dedicated to Vishnu and the other to Siva. An inscription on the wall of the former records a grant of land to the temple by a king called Konerimaikondan who has not been identified. There is also a famous temple of Mariamman in the village the annual festival of which is largely attended. There is a belief among the devotees that worship for eight weeks continuously at the temple would cure blindness caused by small-pox.

Mondipalayam.—(Population 275), a hamlet of Pongalur about 12 miles north-west of Avanashi, contains a famous Vishnu temple dedicated to Venkataramanaswami. Large numbers of people visit it especially on the Saturdays in the Tamil month of Purattasi. People who cannot go to Tirupati to fulfil their vows perform their vows like the shaving the head, at this temple.

Sevur (Cheyur)—(Population 3,974).—about 5 miles north of Avanashi, contains two old temples one dedicated to Venkataramanaswami and the other to Kapaleswara or Valiswara. The inscriptions in the former show that it was repaired by Sundara Pandya (1251–70), that Veera Ballala III bestowed lands upon it, that during the reign of Veera Pandya (1253-74) a village called Karugampadu was granted to it and to certain Vaishnavite Brahmins and that in those days Manavala Muni's birthday was regularly celebrated at the temple. The Saivite temple was patronised by the Kongu Cholas and the Ummattur Chiefs. One of the inscriptions records the grant of a village called Kuladipanallur to the temple by Konerimaikondan.

The village contains the tomb of a holy person named Muthukumara Devar at which Senguntha Mudaliars offer worship once in two years. This person is believed to have lived several centuries ago and to have cut up his limbs and offered them to birds of the air before he died. It is said that when his tomb was opened for repairs some years ago the body was found to be fresh and that this circumstance added to his sanctity.

The water of one of the tanks in the village called Sembiyankulam is considered to have a curative value. There is a tradition that this water used to be taken daily on the back of elephants to Mysore for the use of one of its rulers and that it cured him of his illness.

Thirumurugampundi.—(Population 4,492), four and a half miles north-north-west of Tiruppur railway station, contains a very old temple dedicated to Muruga or Subrahmanya and included among the seven Kongu Sivalayams. Sundaramurthi Nayanar is said to have visited it on his way to Cranganore in Malabar and that, on his praying to the God, his belongings which had been robbed from him were restored to him. There are several inscriptions in the temple relating to the period of the Kongu Cholas and the Ummattur Chiefs recording mostly gifts of land made to the temple. There is a belief that lunatics are cured by bathing in the temple tank and worshipping the God for a number of days. Consequently a number of lunatics are always found there.

BHAVANI TALUK.

This taluk is situated on the north-east corner of the district and is extremely hilly. It was formerly through this taluk that one of the routes from Mysore passed, but this route has now been almost abandoned in favour of the route, via., Satyamangalam and Hassanur. The area of the taluk is 572 square miles and its population 2,35,170. The places of historical or antiquarian interest in the taluk are described below :—

Andiyur.—(Population 15,750), twelve miles north-west of Bhavani, contains an old Siva temple with fine sculptures and some inscriptions. There is also an old fort.

Appakudal.—(Population 4,019), seven and a half miles north-west of Bhavani, contains an old Siva temple with good sculptures and some inscriptions. It was sold by Hyder Ali to a banker named Valman Das, who gave sixty thousand pagodas on condition of holding it as a jaghir. It was invaded by the British about the close of the eighteenth century. A famine followed the invasion and destroyed most of the inhabitants.

Bhavani.—(Population 12,133), the headquarters of the taluk is situated at the confluence of the Cauvery and the Bhavani. Bathing at this place is regarded as sacred and large number of pilgrims, especially from Palghat, visit the place. There is a temple dedicated to Sangameswara which is situated at the end of the tongue of land at the actual confluence, the bathing ghats occupying the extreme point of the rock. According to the local legend four Asuras tried to steal a pot of nectar presented by Vishnu to a Rishi (Parasara Muni) and when the Rishi prayed to Vishnu for protection the latter sent some Kalis who slew the Asuras and guarded the nectar. At the end of his devotions the Rishi found that the nectar had become solid. He then worshipped it as Amrita Lingam. Several

Rishis attained salvation by bathing at this place. The temple is well-sculptured and there are a few inscriptions on its walls which show that it was built by Getti Mudali a Palayakkar under the Nayakas and another person and that Krishna Raya Udayar of Mysore added some mantapams round the main shrine in the eighteenth century. There was a fort near the temple in olden days. The remains of this fort were said to have been in existence even as late as the closing years of the last century. These are, however, no longer to be found. During the extraordinary floods of 1924 a small temple was exposed in the bed of the Cauvery just above its confluence with the Bhavani. According to a local tradition this temple was dedicated to Gayatrilingeswara and was buried under ground for several centuries. It has been covered up again now by sand.

Several stories are told about Mr. Garrow, one of the earliest Collectors of the district. He made Bhavani his headquarters and his charge included part of the Salem district also. He is stated to have occupied a bungalow near the entrance to the temple and presented to the temple a number of jewels, vahanams, and vessels, some of which are said to be still in existence. The most valuable of these is an ivory cot. People believed that he was a devotee of the Goddess, that he was directed by the Goddess in his dream to leave his house and that soon after he left it, it crumbled down. Certain holes in the wall of the temple are stated to be those through which Mr. Garrow used to look at the deity.

Gettisamudram.—(Population 4,298), 14 miles north-west of Bhavani, contains an old Siva temple dedicated to Gurunathaswami with inscriptions. A car festival is held at the temple every year in the month of August.

Coimbatore Taluk.

This taluk is situated in the north-west part of the district. It is a arge open plateau of considerable elevation, sloping away from the foot of the Nilgiris to the south-east. The Nilgiris and their spurs are notable eatures in the landscape to the north and west, the higher ranges to the north being partly concealed by a nearer spur, the sharp pinnacle of Lambton Peak being within 5 or 6 miles of the town. To the west the Velliyangiri hills, within 15 miles of the town, form a rampart against the south-west monsoon. Further to the south-west is the Palghat Gap. On the other side of the gap rise abruptly the spurs of the Anaimalais known as the Kuchmalai range while the splendid peaks of the Anaimalais themselves bound the landscape on the south at a distance of some 35 or 40 miles. The area of the taluk is 528 square miles and its population

5,62,522. The places of historical or antiquarian interest in the ta are described below :—

Coimbatore.—(Population 1,97,755), the headquarters of the taluk and the district, is a town of importance and antiquity. From its position which commands the approach to Palghat on the west and to the Gazzalhatti pass on the north, it was formerly of great strategical importance. It originally formed part of the Chera Kingdom, but was captured by the Nayakas of Madurai and was considered as one of their strongholds. Later, it fell into the hands of the rulers of Mysore. During the wars of the British with Hyder Ali and Tipu Sultan it changed hands many times. In 1768 the British took it and lost it. In 1783 it was again taken and lost. In 1790 it was occupied a third time, but Tipu, after a siege of five months, compelled the British to surrender it. In 1792 provisionally, and in 1799 finally, it was ceded to the British and from that time it ceased to be a military station. Hyder and Tipu frequently stayed here occupying a palace situated in the street now known as Madaraja Mahal street. This Madaraja or Madayya is said to have been a local chief under the Mysore king, Chikka Deva Raya. Sir Thomas Munro owned a garden with a tank in this street, situated at the western end of the same street. He presented it to one of his subordinates named Govinda Rao. Near the tank is a Hanumar temple evidently constructed by Govinda Rao. There was once a fort in Coimbatore, but it was dismantled during the wars. Its site continues to be known as Kottamedu. A mosque which stands near the temple of Koni Amman is believed to have been built at the time of Tipu.

Maileripalayam.—(Population 2,886), situated at about 10 miles south-south-east from Coimbatore is the chief village of a Jaghir of seven villages which was given to Govinda Rao by the East India Company in 1829 in recognition of his valuable services to the Company in the Revenue Department. The garden and tank in Coimbatore town presented to him by Sir Thomas Munro have already been referred to under Coimbatore. The following is an extract from the letter of Munro granting the garden :—

" The garden which I have relinquished to you at Coimbatore is a very good one. I advise you particularly to take care of the trees of oranges and pumple mosses and if you get some grape vine and attend to those that are there you will find them succeed very well. There are also two or three trees of Arabian dates which produce fine fruit when they come to maturity and some plants of Cadda Pannu which you might have seen in the Malayalam country used for Chutturs when the leaf is full grown. I sincerely wish you the happiness of an easy old age free from trouble or sickness. I know that you have for a long time been a very useful servant of the Company.

Your friend,

T. MUNRO."

Marudamalai.—(Population 101), eleven miles north-west of Coimbatore, contains a small hill with a temple on its top. The temple is visible from Coimbatore and is largely visited by the people of Coimbatore for worship. Below the temple is a spring of excellent water.

Perur.—(Population 2,955), four miles west of Coimbatore, is also known as Mel Chidambaram and is one of the seven Kongu Sivalayams and its temple is of great sanctity. It is one of the few temples that Tipu Sultan respected. The inner shrine is of great antiquity, but the outer buildings are supposed to have been erected by Alakadri Naidu, brother-in-law of Tirumala Nayaka of Madurai (1623–59). The temple has been completely renovated by the Nattukottai Chettiyars and a new Kalyana Mantapam has been erected. The festival of Arudra Darsanam conducted in the Tamil month of Margazhi (December-January) attracts large crowds of people from all parts of the district and from Malabar. A car festival is also celebrated on the Panguni Uttaram day in March-April.

Another curious festival called the Nattu Nadavu Utsavam (the festival of transplanting seedlings) takes place in the month of Ani (June-July) when the god and goddess are taken in procession to a neighbouring field and some transplanting of seedlings is done. The story connected with this festival is as follows. When Sundaramurthi Nayanar came to Perur the god was unwilling to see him and therefore left the temple and proceeded to an adjacent field with the goddess, disguised as a Paria man and woman. Before doing so, however, the god warned Nandi not to divulge his whereabouts to Sundaramurthi Nayanar. The latter being unable to find the god and goddess in the temple turned to Nandi who kept silent according to his master's orders. When, however, the saint threatened to curse him, he turned his head in the direction of the field. For this he was punished by his master with the loss of a portion of his lower jaw. The stone image of Nandi in front of the dwaja stambha illustrates this incident.

The country round about Perur was in ancient times called Perur Nadu and Coimbatore was a small village within it. It was a flourishing country under the Kongu Cholas and the Pandyas whose inscriptions are found on the walls of the temple. The earliest inscriptions is dated in the tenth century and refers to the Chola King Parantaka I. A temple to Vishnu was built in the village in the eighth century by an early Pandyan King. No trace of it is, however, now found, as it was pulled down by a later Saivite chief and the materials were used by Madayya, son of Sankarayya of Terkanambi, in the fifteenth century for the construction of the stone revetted tank in front of the temple. Karikala Chola is said to have dug a lotus pond here and one of the bathing ghats on the river Noyyal is called after him. Large numbers of people bathe in the river during the month of Aippasi (October-November) . People from Kerala are in the habit of immersing the bones of their deceased ancestors into the river which is here known as the Kanchimahakanadi. The village was the residence of a Tamilian saint named Santhalingaswami whose name is perpetuated by a mutt in which his disciples reside and celebrate with great pomp every year the anniversary of his death.

Singanallur.—(Population 19,852), four miles east of Coimbatore, was once a large fortified town, but its fort was destroyed by the Marathas. The village was granted as an inam to Brahmins by Singammal, the queen of a Kongu Chola King. Some of the Brahmins in the village wear the *namam* of the Vaishnavites even though they are Saivites. The reason for this is said to be that, after a visit by the Vaishnava teacher, Ramanuja, to their village, they agreed to adopt his mode of dress and worship.

Tudiyalur.—(Population 3,076), six miles north of Coimbatore, contains an old Siva temple dedicated to Virundiswaraswami (the god who gave the feast). According to the legend the god of this place gave a feast to the god of another place who was proceeding to a distant place.

Vellalur.—(Population 11,695), four and a half miles east-south-east of Coimbatore, was known as Annadana Sivapuri in ancient days, according to the inscriptions found in the old Siva temple of this place. Two of these inscriptions show that the place was in the ninth century under the Chera Kings. There is also a Vaishnavites temple with an inscription of the Hoysala King, Veera Ballala III. In 1842 an earthen pot was dug up at this place which contained 522 Roman silver denari, chiefly of Tiberius and Augustus with a few of Caligula and Claudius. In 1931 also several coins dating from Augustus to Constantine were unearthed here. All this indicates that the place was a centre of trade with the Roman Empire. Pre-historic burial places called Pandavakulis containing well made earthen vessels have been found near the village.

DHARAPURAM TALUK.

This taluk lies in the southern part of the district. It is an undulating plain mostly sloping gently eastward towards the Cauvery. Its area is 854 square miles and its population 3,23,307. Its places of historical or antiquarian importance are dealt with below :—

Dharapuram.—(Population 24,163), the headquarters of the taluk, is stated by tradition to have been the place where the Pandavas spent their year of exile *incognito*. An uncommon use of such names as Arjuna, Bhima and Draupadi and the existence of a fine breed of cattle for which king Virata's country was famous are pointed out as evidences to prove the truth of the tradition. Kiranur, ten miles from Dharapuram, is believed to have been the place where Keechaka was killed by Bhima, Kongu Cholas appear to have had their capital either here or at Karur, both on the Amaravathi and both situated on the Karavazhi or high road to the Chera country. The town came to be called Parantakapuram after it came under the Cholas. In 1667 it was taken from Madurai by the Mysoreans. In the wars of the British with Hyder Ali and Tipu Sultan it was a point of some strategical importance, being captured by the British in 1768, retaken by Hyder in the same year, again occupied by the British in 1783, given up by the treaty of Mangalore and finally resumed in 1790. In 1792 the fort was dismantled. The town also nearly disappeared, but was rebuilt after 1799 upon plans drawn up by Mr. Hurdis who made it the headquarters of the Southern Division. The zillah court was also located here from 1800 to 1828. In the village of Korinjivadi close to Dharapuram is an old Siva temple with inscriptions of the Pandya and the Vijayanagar rulers.

Kangayam.—(Population 12,920), twenty one miles north of Dharapuram, gave the name to one of the twenty four divisions into which the country was divided in ancient days, namely, Kangaya Nadu. Kangayam is said to be a corrupt form of Gangeya (Subrahmanya) the God of the temple on Sivamalai hill. This part of Kongu Nadu seems to have been a prosperous and populous tract in the time of the Kongu Cholas and Pandyas. No other taluk contains such a variety of temples and epigraphical materials relating to these two dynasties. There is an old Siva temple in Kangayam with some inscriptions.

Muttur—(Population 4, 887), twelve miles north-east of Kangayam, contains a Siva temple which is at least 800 years old. It is said to have been built by Kulottunga Chola and the deity is called Kulottunga Choleswara-Udaiyar. Inscriptions in the temple show that a local chief called Paparaja was ordered by the Kongu Chola King to provide for the offerings in the temple out of the tax due to him from the chief; that the temple treasury lent out money and that offerings were made to the temple by all classes of the inhabitants.

Padiyur.—(Population 1,576), six and a half miles north-west of Kangayam, was formerly celebrated for the aquamarine or beryl which used to be mined here. These gems were in great demand among the ancient Romans. Pliny says that the best beryls have a peculiar sea green tint and come mostly from India, being seldom found elsewhere. Even in India no other place is known to produce the gem. The mines, however, have been completely worked out long ago and do not yield any more gems.

Paranchervazhi.—(Population 5,000), six miles north by east of Kangayam, contains two temples, one a Saivite temple dedicated to Madhyapuriswara or Natturamarndar, and the other, a Vaishnavite temple dedicated to Veera Narayana Perumal. Inscriptions in these two temples show that they received endowments in the days of Vikrama Choladeva (1120–1135).

Pazhayakottai.—(Population 3,413), about 10 miles east by north of Kangayam, is the seat of the well known Pattagar who raises the famous Kangayam breed of cattle. About a mile from the residence of the Pattagar is a village called Nattakadayur with an ancient Siva temple with an inscription of King Rama of Vijayanagar, dated 1622. On its wall there is an inscription which says that Nallathambi Gounder Viswanatha Chakkarai Mandradiyar of Karaiyur gave certain lands to the temple. The Viceroy of Madurai at this time was Muthu Veerappa Nayaka. The Pattagar is the religious and social head of a section of the Kongu Vellalars who claim to be immigrants from the Chola country along with a princess who married a prince of the Kongu Mandalam. A Pattagar, called Sarkara, was a general under Jatavarman Sundara Pandya (in the thirteeth century) under whom the people of Kongu Nadu took refuge, being oppressed by their own king, an Uttama Chola. The Pattagar distinguished himself in this battle and was given the title Uttama Kaminda Nalla Senapathi and the religious and social head-ship of the Kongu Vellalars.

Sankarandamapalayam.—(Population 6,608), eight miles north-east of Dharapuram, is the residence of a Pattagar similar to the Pazhayakottai Pattagar. He also exerts some influence over another section of the Kongu Vellalars. It is stated that an ancestor of this Pattagar, called Venadan, was a general under a Karikala Chola and that he defeated a

Pandyan King. Another ancestor, also called Venadan, who was living at Sivayam in the Kulitalai taluk of the Tiruchirappalli district, was ordered by a Chola King to capture Kaviripoompattinam. It is said he did this and was allowed to rule over it. Subsequently at the behest of a Chola King, whose daughter married a Chera King, the Vellalars of Chola mandalam with a Venadan at their head were ordered to go and settle in Kongu Nadu which was then under Chera rule. The family of the Venadan settled at Sangarandampalayam then called Korrainagar.

Sivanmalai.—(Population 5,489), three miles north of Kangayam, contains five temples of which two dedicated to Siva and Vishnu are very old.

Vellakovil.—(Population 10,537), twelve miles east of Kangayam, contains an old Siva temple dedicated to Parakrama Choleswara. The inscriptions on its walls are stated to be indistinct.

Velliyarachal.—(Population 3,509), eight miles east of Kangayam was in ancient days known as Raja Kesaripuram. It contains an ancient Siva temple dedicated to Mandiswara with some inscriptions in Vattezhuthu (archaic Tamil) characters.

Erode Taluk.

This taluk is situated in the north-east part of the district. It consists of a gently undulating plain sloping east and south-east towards the Cauvery, except for a slight ridge the peaks of which are Sennimalai, Arachalur and Ezhumattur. There are also several small isolated hills. Its area is 599 square miles and its population 4,39,641. Its places of historical or antiquarian interest are described below :—

Chennimalai.—(Population 2,804), eight miles south of Perundurai, is a considerable hill surmounted by a temple reached by a long flight of steps and dedicated to Subrahmanya. This temple, which is an ancient one, is visited by a large number of people, especially Vellalars.

Erode.—(Population 57,576), on the north-east border of the district close to the Cauvery, is the headquarters of the taluk. In Hyder's time it was in a very flourishing condition with 3,000 houses and a population of 15,000. But owing to the successive waves of the Maratha, Mysore and British invasion, it became almost utterly deserted and ruined. As soon, however, as peace was restored by the British, the people returned and settled in a more advantageous and fertile place and within a year it began to grow with 400 houses and a population of over 2,000. The garrison was withdrawn in 1807 and the ruined fort levelled as a relief work during the famine of 1877, the place enclosed within the ramparts having long before been occupied by houses. It is now a municipal town of considerable importance. About a mile and a half east of the town, there is an old bridge which spans the Cauvery. The well at Pechiparai situated in the municipal park was once celebrated for its milky and wholesome water. But it is no longer used as a source for the supply of drinking water, the municipality having built a reservoir on the Pechiparai rock. There are two old temples here one dedicated to Siva and the other to Vishnu.

The name of the town, which in Tamil means " wet skull " is apparently derived from the skull of Brahma found in one of the hands of Ardra Kapaleswarar, the presiding deity of the Siva temple. According to the legend narrated in this regard, Daksha-Prajapati, who had given his daughter, Dakshayani, in marriage to Siva, performed a yagam or sacrifice to which he invited all the gods except Siva. Dakshayani, however, after taking the permission of Siva, went to her father's mansion to witness the sacrifice. But neither he, nor her mother nor any of the attendants welcomed her. She was sorely vexed and throwing herself in the flames of the yaga-kundam, burnt herself to ashes. On hearing this Siva got highly enraged, proceeded to the sacrificial spot and punished every one who was present. Among them was Brahma who had come there to receive the usual Havir bhagam. Siva in his rage tore off one of his five heads and returned with the skull.

The Siva and Vishnu temples contain numerous inscriptions, the earliest of which is that of the Chola King, Madurai Konda Parakesarivarman (905–947) and the Kongu Chola King,Vira Rajendra (1207–1249). One of the inscriptions refers to Rajakesari Varman Vira Pandya (1255–1281), which is a unique instance of a Pandyan King bearing a Chola title. The other inscription relates to the Hoysala King, Ballala III (1340) and the Parvata Rahutta(1510) who is believed to have been the Viceroy under Krishna Deva Raya of Vijayanagar in the territory newly acquired by the latter. They also refer to Kantirava Narasaraja (1638–1659) and his Dalavoy Hampayya who defeated and overthrew Tirumala Nayak of Madurai. The inscriptions show that Erode was situated in Kanchittundum, a Sub-Division of Melkarai-Nadu, that the adjoining country was called Perundurai-Nadu and that its people made gifts of lands and villages to these temples.

Ezhumattur.—(Population 4,320), eleven and a half miles south-south-east of Erode, contains two temples on a rock, one of which is dedicated to Siva and the other to Vishnu.

Kanakapuram.—(Population 1,597), seven miles south-south-west of Erode, contains three Siva temples. There is a beautiful cave in a rock adjoining the village.

Kanjikkovil.—(Population 1,862), nine miles north-north-west of Erode, once contained five temples dedicated to Siva, but only one Siva temple is now found in the village. The annual festival of the temple is well attended. Corundum is said to have occurred in a field in the village.

Kodumudi.—(Population 8,098), on the banks of the Cauvery twenty-one miles south-south-east of Erode, contains an ancient Siva temple which is one of the seven Sivalayams in Kongu Nadu. Extensive repairs have been made to this temple by Nattukkottai Chettiars. Opposite to it is the Subrahmanya temple built in 1923 by an Andi by raising subscriptions from local people. It is said that this Andi who was originally an illiterate labourer was able to cure diseases by his touch. It is also said that he built a matam with a cellar and desired that his body should be deposited in the cellar after his death, but that he went away subsequently leaving the temple and the matam in charge of trustees.

Mudavandi Satyamangalam.—(Population 2,914), this was originally an inam village granted by the Hindu Kings and subsequently confirmed by Tipu Sultan, for the support of 32 mudavandis (cripples) of the Vellala or agricultural caste in Erode and the adjacent taluks. But, when the district came into the possession of the British, the village was resumed and the endowment was commuted for a grant of land, the proceeds to be enjoyed in shares by the 32 mudavandis (cripples) and 42 kaladis (or able-bodied men) who were in attendance on them. Subsequently the proceeds of the inam lands came to be utilized for the maintenance of a langar-khana, or alms-house at Coimbatore to give relief to lame persons. In 1887 the inam lands were resumed and an annual grant of Rs. 1,000 was ordered to be paid to the municipality for the maintenance of the alms-house.

Nallampatti.—(Population 2,299), is six miles north-north-west of Perundurai. A great group of dolmens and stone circles have been found close to this village.

Perundurai.—(Population 14,037), eleven miles south-west of Erode, was once the headquarters of the taluk. It is now the headquarters of a Deputy Tahsildar and contains an old Siva temple.

Sarkar Periyapalaiyam.—(Population 1,457), half a mile from Kulipalaiyam railway station, is a village of historical interest. It is called

Suralur and Sundara Pandyanallur in the several inscriptions found on the walls of the Sugriveswara temple in this place. There is a reference in them to an irrigation tank called Nanjarayan tank which was named after an Ummattur Chief, Nanjaraya, who had repaired the tank. He established himself firmly in this part of the country in the 15th century, but subsequently became a vassal of Krishna Deva Raya of Vijayanagar. The village was called after Sundara Pandya who had granted the village to the temple. An inscription of his reign shows that the irrigation tank existed in his time and that rules were framed for its maintenance and supervision. The village was also called Mukundanur in the inscriptions.

Thingalur.—(Population 2,364), contains ancient Hindu and Jain temples with inscriptions of the 11th, 12th and 13th centuries relating to Hoysala, Kongu Chola and Kongu Pandya kings. The Jain basthi is dedicated to Pushpanada.

Unjalur.—(Population 2,407), seventeen and a half miles south-east of Erode, contains an old Siva temple with numerous inscriptions.

Vijayamangalam or *Voyppadi.*—(Population 1,791), a railway station, contains small Jain Basthis with small land endowments for the use of the priest.

The Jain Basthi has been described as follows :— " The plan of the Jain Basthi at Vijayamangalam is similar in some respects to that of the Hindus. A column rises through the roof, and a choultry faces the principal gateway, which is surmounted by the usual propylon or tower of several storeys. In the middle of the court-yard, encompassed by four walls, stands the body of the pagoda consisting of an oblong stone building with a flat roof. The entablatures of the exterior are ornamented with figures of Adi Iswara, the very image of Budha, and seated like him cross-legged, in some places holding a bell in one hand, and in others seated under the shade of an umbrella. There are also figures of the god canopied by the elevated trunks of two elephants, one on each side of him, men on elephants, miniature pagodas, men playing on various musical instruments, men riding on lions, and other animals, figures with a horse-tail punkah fanning a cross-legged image of Adi Iswara and figures in gothic niches. Inside the pagoda there are effigies of Krishna treading on the snake, Ganesa, the five Pandavas, Hanuman and other mythological beings; these occur chiefly on a cornice running round the top of the wall. Outside the pagoda is a deep well traditionally reputed to be the work of Bhima, one of the Pandavas, who, wanting water, struck the ground with his club and formed the well. "

There are numerous inscriptions on the walls of the Siva and Vishnu temples and Jain basthis in this village. An inscription in one of the Jain basthies refers to the Nisidika of Pullappa, younger sister of Chamundaraja who, it is surmised, was the same as the minister of the two Ganga Kings, Narasimha II and Rachimalla II who built the Jain Colossus at Sravana Belgola. The village once contained a big tank called Virapandyaneri in the 13th century, in memory of a Kongu Pandya king who repaired it. This tank irrigated the lands granted to the Nageswaraswami temple free of rent. There is only a small tank in the village now called Rajankulam (king's tank) with the Nageswaraswami temple on its bank. Apparently this tank is the same as the one dug by the Kongu Pandya King. Jainism appears to have been fairly widespread in this part of the country, as there are still several Jain families living in this and in a few neighbouring villages.

GOBICHETTIPALAYAM TALUK.

This taluk which was formerly called Satyamangalam taluk is the northernmost of the taluks below the ghats. On the north, north-east, north-west and west, it is surrounded by mountain ranges, the Nilgiris lying to the west and the ghat south of the Mysore plateau to the north-west and north. Through these latter run the Talamalai, Hasanur and Gazzalhatti passes by which Hyder and Tipu launched their armies into the plains during the Mysore wars. The area of the taluk is 1,129 square miles and its population 3,94,267. The places of historical or antiquarian interest in the taluk are described below :—

Danayakkankottai.—(Population 57), twenty-six miles west by south of Gobichettipalayam, was formerly the headquarters of a taluk of the same name, but it became subsequently almost deserted. When the Bhavanisagar dam was constructed in 1949–1955, the village was submerged in the waterspread area. Three miles away from the village, there was an old ruined fort which stood on the north side of the Bhavani, a little above the junction of the Moyar. Inside the fort, there were two temples, one dedicated to Siva and the other to Vishnu. These temples contained many inscriptions, the oldest of which related to the reign of the Hoysala King, Vira Ballala III. Another inscription referred to Singayya Danayaka, the Governor of the fort, which was then called Nilgiri—Sadaran—Kottai or the fort of the subedar of the Nilgiris. It appears that the idols in the Siva and Vishnu temples were removed to Satyamangalam on two occasions. The circumstances in which they were removed to Satyamangalam and the period during which they were kept there on the first occasion are not precisely known. The removal on the second occasion was caused by the construction of the Bhavanisagar dam which, as mentioned above, submerged Danayakkan Kottai. On this occasion the idols were retained at Satyamangalam until a new temple was specially constructed for them near the dam. The idols are now kept and worshipped in the new temple. It appears that the place was named after Perumal Dandanayaka, a general under Narasimha III, who conquered the Kongu country from the Pandyas. An inscription at Perur near Coimbatore records that Virachikka Ketaya, son of Vira Madhava-Dandanayaka, built the Madhava Perumal temple in this village and endowed it with the revenues of thirteen villages. The village was also called Thuravalur in the inscriptions. The place was considered as an important strategical point by the Hoysalas and the Nayakas. Between this place and the Davalagiri hill, Col. Floyd fought a severe battle with Tipu in the third Mysore war.

At Kallampalla in the neighbourhood of Danayakkankottai, there is a Siva temple containing the image of 'Mariamma' to which the hill tribes used to make offerings of goats and cocks.

Gazzalhatti (the elephant track), was formerly the principal pass from Coimbatore to Mysore, one track leading from Satyamangalam and another from Coimbatore town via. Danayakkankottai to the foot of the ghat where an old fashioned bridge is still standing. The head of the pass, which is 2,800 feet above sea level, is seventeen miles from the Mysore frontier. A mud fort said to have been built by the son-in-law of Tirumala Nayaka of Madurai commanded the forts at the foot of this pass. Being of considerable strategic importance, it changed hands several times during the wars with Mysore. It was taken over by Mysore in 1657, was captured by Colonel Wood in 1768 and recaptured by Hyder in 1769. In 1790 Col. Floyd occupied the place and fought a severe battle with Tipu between this fort and Danayakkankottai. Traces of this old fort no longer exist.

Guttiyalathur or Kuttalathur.—(Population 6,860), twenty-two miles north-west of Gobichettipalayam, contains an old fort with a temple in ruins.

Kugalur (Population 10,504), six miles east-north-east of Gobichettipalayam, contains two old temples, one dedicated to Siva and the other to Vishnu, which are said to have been built by a Chera king. The inscriptions in the Siva temple record the endowments made to it by Kulottunga, the Kongu Chola king, and Sundara Pandya Deva, the

Kongu Pandya king, as well as the valuable grants given by a native of this village, called Sokkan, during the time of the Hoysala king, Vira Ballala III. But the stones bearing the old inscriptions are no longer found in the temple, having been displaced during its renovation some years ago.

Nambiyur.—(Population 8,517), twelve and a half miles south-east of Gobichettipalayam, was originally called Nambiperur. The Siva temple in this village which is dedicated to Tantoniswaram-Udaiyar was specially favoured by Vira Pandya Deva. There is a trident-marked stone in the market place here, which records that the profits of the market should go to the temple.

Periyur.—(Population 4,558), contains an old Siva temple which was patronized by Kongu Cholas and Hoysalas. One of the inscriptions found in the temple describes the twenty nadus into which the North Kongu was divided in ancient days. A tank called Araiyar-kulam is said to have been assigned to the villagers by a Kongu king on a permanent tenure, the tenants (Stanattars) agreeing to pay a third of the profit to the temple to celebrate its chief festival established in the name of the king. But this tank-bed has been converted into wet land and is now owned by certain Vellalars of Pudupalaiyam who conduct the temple festivals. There is also a Pidari temple in the village, in front of which a fire-walking ceremony takes place every year in February-March. The place was perhaps named after the ancient chieftain, "Pari" who was the friend and patron of the celebrated poet 'Kapilar' of the Sangam age. He was very famous for his munificence and is praised in the Sangam literature for having donated his golden chariot to a jasmine creeper which was without any support, during one of his excursions.

Perundalaiyur.—(Population 2,885), thirteen miles east of Gobichettipalayam, is the end of the rice producing tract with the tank known as Anantasagaram. The old Siva temple in the village contains many inscriptions, one of which relates to the reign of Sundara Pandya Deva. There is a Kannada copper-plate grant in the temple recording gifts of lands by Krishna Raja Udaiyar of Mysore.

Satyamangalam.—(Population 14,018), lies thirteen miles west-north-west of Gobichettipalayam, on the Bhavani river, which is here more than 100 yards broad. It was once the headquarters of the taluk of the same name. From here the Gazzalhatti and Hasanur ghat roads lead to the uplands, the latter having been the most frequented route into Mysore. The Vishnu temple here has a large richly carved ratha or car. As stated under Danayakkankottai the idols of the Siva and Vishnu temples of Danayakkankottai were kept and maintained with regular worship in this temple for some time as Danayakkankottai was submerged under the water-spread area of the Bhavanisagar dam. The idols are now kept and worshipped in a new temple built near the Bhavanisagar dam. There is also an ancient Siva temple here dedicated to Minakshi Sundareswarar, which contains the inscriptions of Kulottunga and Virarajendra, both Kongu Chola kings. A copper plate grant in another Siva temple records a grant of Krishna Raja Udaiyar of Mysore. Copper plate grants issued by the Udaiyar kings of Mysore have also been found in the possession of certain private individuals in the town. The Devalagiri hill at the confluence of the Bhavani and the Chintamani rivers contains a temple on its top dedicated to Kumaraswami. The place was known as Durvasakshetra, perhaps called after the ancient Hindu rishi, Durvasa, who was notorious for his short temper. The temple was built by the Mysore king, Chikka Deva Raya, who also endowed it with the revenues of the village of Bestrapalaiyam or Kumarapalaiyam situated at the foot of the hill. The inscription in this temple dated Saka 1598 (1675–76 A.D.) reveals that the country around Satyamangalam was called Oduvanga Nadu.

Siruvalur.—(Population 5,947), eight miles south of Gobichettipalayam on the road to Perundurai railway station, contains an old Vishnu temple with an inscription mentioning repairs to the temple. There is also another temple in the village dedicated to Siva.

Talamalai.—(Population 1,814), forty-six miles west by north f Gobichettipalayam, contains an old ruined fort and another at Hanumamalai, five miles north of Talamalai.

Palladam Taluk.

This taluk lies in the centre of the district. It is somewhat a flat dreary plain, having neither hills nor forests. Its area is 585 square miles and its population 351,734. The places of historical or antiquarian interest in the taluk are described below :—

Alagumalai.—(Population 2,787), thirteen miles south-east of Tiruppur, contains a temple dedicated to Subrahmanya on the top of a hill bearing the same name.

Avanashipalaiyam.—(Population 5,052), about twelve miles south-east of Tiruppur, contains an old Siva temple in the hamlet of Koduvoy, with inscriptions of the 18th century. One of the inscriptions found in the Vishnu temple of the same place relates to the 15th century and records an arrangement made amongst the villagers for the performance of temple service. In the hamlet of Pudupalaiyam, there is another old Siva temple with several inscriptions.

Irugur.—(Population 10,154), twenty-four miles west of Tiruppur, contains several pandavarkulis in which were found pieces of pottery and weapons and implements and some human bones.

Karumathampatti.—sixteen miles east of Coimbatore and fourteen miles west of Tiruppur on the trunk road to Madras and two miles away from the Somanur railway station, was an ancient Roman Catholic settlement. It was the centre for nearby villages where christianity was introduced in the middle of the seventeenth century by the Jesuit foreign missionaries, prominent among them being Robert de Nobili. In 1660 a small church was built at this place for the use of the Christian converts and in 1684 two priests were appointed to be in charge of this centre. It was about this time that St. John De Britto visited this place on three occasions. It continued to be the residence of the Jesuit missionaries till 1759 when they were removed from there by the orders of the Portuguese Government and the Christians in this centre were left without their pastors. During the wars with Tipu Sultan, they were dispersed and their church was destroyed. After the defeat of Tipu Sultan by the British, Rev.Father Dubois of the French Society visited Karumathampatti in 1803 and built a new church on the site of the old church with the help of an Indian priest called Gnanapragasam. The place again became a Catholic centre with French Missionaries residing in it. In 1846 it was made the headquarters of a new Bishop appointed for the diocese of Coimbatore. But when the Bishop transferred his headquarters to Coimbatore in 1850, leaving the neighbouring out-stations in charge of residential priests, Karumathampatti became in course of time a deserted village except for the gathering of 5,000 pilgrims for the annual feast of the church held on the first Sunday in October. Recently owing to the efforts of the present Bishop (Francis Savari Muthu), it got life again and has become an educational centre spreading culture all round.

Palladam.—(Population 9,238), ten miles south-south-west of Tiruppur, was the old headquarters of the taluk. The place was once fortified, but traces of the fort no longer exist.

Savadipalaiyam.—(Population 732), a hamlet of Kettanur sixteen miles south-south-west of Tiruppur, contained ancient tombs known as pandavarkulis in one of which was discovered a large hoard of punch-mark coins. A dolmen and a stone circle have also been found near this place.

Tiruppur (Population 52,479), a railway station about twenty-six miles from Coimbatore, is the headquarters of the taluk. The car festival celebrated here in honour of the local deity in the month of Vaikasi (May-June) attracts a large crowd from the adjoining villages.

Pollachi Taluk.

This taluk is one of the most interesting in the district by reason of its fertility, climate and scenery. It lies on the extreme south-west of the district under the shadow of the Anamalais and their spurs on the south and the west. The whole surface is diversified by gentle undulations which pleasantly break the monotony of a plain. Its area is 709 square miles and its population 3,84,677. The places for historical or antiquarian interest are described below :—

Anaimalai (Population 10,348), seven and a half miles south-west of Pollachi on the river Aliyar and 8 miles from the lower spurs of the Anaimalai range, was an important town in the middle of the eighteenth century. The forests adjoining the place abounded in destructive and formidable elephants which killed many people who ventured into the forest tracts, but they have now become scarce in the neighbourhood. It contains the ruins of an old Siva temple which is said to have been destroyed by Tipu. It owes its origin, according to tradition, to the Chola kings, but it was repaired several times by the kings of Mysore. It is elaborately sculptured and contains many inscriptions. A copper plate records the grant of lands of Madayya, agent of the Mysore Rajahs at Coimbatore. A little to the west of the village there are a Vishnu temple and a fort called Chakragiridurgam on the summit of a small hill named Jain-Kal-durgam, or ' hill of the Jain stone '. This fort was constructed by the Rajahs of Mysore, using the materials of an old ruined fort near the river, said to have been built by the Rajahs of Madurai. Tipu repaired it with the materials of the temple he had demolished. South of the village there was another ruined Vishnu temple, but this has now disappeared.

Avalappampatti (Population 1,169), situated about nine miles north-east of Pollachi and three miles south of Negamam was the chief village of a palaiyam of the same name. It remained an unsettled palayam till 1871 when it was granted a permanent sanad. In 1891 it was attached for debts due by the Poligar and sold in two lots known as Avalappampatti division and Nugur Division.

Garudan Kottai.—There is at present no village or hamlet bearing the name of Garudan Kottai in Pollachi taluk. However tradition ascribes the south-western portion of Somandurai village in Pollachi taluk as the site where the fort existed. There is at present only a small mound at this place, in the midst of wet fields. A few stone-pillars are found near the mound but they are neither carved nor inscribed. According to the local traditions, there was a temple here which was destroyed during a Muslim invasion and later on the stones were used up in the construction of the Vadakalur anicut on the Aliyar nearby. About twelve years ago, a beautiful bronze idol of Somaskandha was un-earthed from a wet field near the mound. This is now housed in a small brick shrine built at the place of the discovery. The idol is a late Chola bronze and may have been the utsava-vigraha of the Someswara Temple, an ancient temple at Anamalai, a mile to the west of the mound. In the court-yard of the modern brick shrine there lies a granite stone slab containing a fragmentary inscription in the Tamil characters of about the 13th Century, which seems to record a taxfree grant of lands to the temple by an agreement made by the villagers.

Kottur (Population 14,435), eight miles south-south-west of Pollachi at the fort of a pass in the Anamalais, contains a large ruined temple with good sculpture and some inscriptions. Three copper images found here, were kept in the temple at Anamalai.

Marchchinayakkanpalaiyam. (Population 11,163), three and a half miles west of Pollachi, contains a ruined fort.

Nattukkalpalaiyam. (Population 980), lies three and a half miles south-east of Pollachi. There was in former days a large group of megalithic monuments amongst the cultivated fields of this village. Mr. Walhouse, the Collector, described them as "large cairns close to one another, each surrounded by a circle of unusual height and uniformity, the stones tall and painted, often exceeding 6 feet in height." *

Negamam. (Population 6,470), lies three miles to the north of Avalappampatti palayam. This was the head village of a small Palaiyam consisting of two villages. It remained an unsettled palaiyam till 1871 when it was granted a permanent sanad. It has been assigned to the Srirangam temple, of which the poligar has constituted himself as the agent.

Pollachi (Population 41,744), the headquarters of the taluk, has from ancient days been a place of trade on account of its position on

* The Journal of the Royal Asiatic Society, New Series VII for 1875, pages 19 and 20.

the highway from the west to the east coast. Alexandrian merchants used to frequent this place as they did at Karur and other parts of India. A number of Roman silver coins of Emperors Augustus and Tiberius were discovered here in 1800. A number of dolmens or rude stone circles called 'Mandavarkuli' or 'Pandavarkuli' have been found in the neighbourhood of the town. They all formed circles of various sizes, ranging from 10 to 45 feet in diameter and contained fragments of human skulls and bones broken pieces of earthenware and a few implements and ornaments at a depth of five to seven feet below the surface. Among the other articles found in these cairns were three blocks of images containing the figure of a male and female both seated. They proved to be an offering made to fulfil a vow for progeny.

Several suggestions have been made for the derivation of the name, 'Pollachi'. One suggestion is that it was derived from Pollachi, the second wife of a Vellalar who came to the place which was then covered with forest and cleared it for cultivation. Another suggestion is that it is made up of two words, viz., Porul acchi, meaning possession of wealth. It has also been suggested that the name is a corruption of Pullacchi, which means possession of birds, the town being so called on account of its extensive woods, which form a favourite home for birds.

Poravaippalaiyam (population 5,755), seven miles to the north-east of Pollachi was the chief village of an old palayam consisting of three small villages. This palayam remained an unsettled palayam till 1871 when it was granted a permanent sanad.

Ramapattanam (population 5,693), eight miles to the north-east of Pollachi was the chief village of an old palayam consisting of three villages. It remained an unsettled palayam till 1871 when it was granted a permanent sanad.

Samattur and Kottampatti (population 3,184 and 1,436), lying three miles to the south of Pollachi, are the chief villages of an old palayam. This palayam remained an unsettled palayam till 1871 when it was granted a permanent sanad.

Uthukkuli (population 5,315), a little to the west of Pollachi, is the chief village of a palayam of the same name, consisting of 10 villages. The palayakars of this palayam trace their origin to the Chola times when Kalingan, one of their ancestors, was appointed chief of Perundurai-nadu with Vellodu as capital, in the Kongu country, soon after it came under the Chola rule. He opened the great irrigation channel of the

Erode taluk called the Kalingarayan Channel and his statue is said to be found close to the anicut across the Bhavani from which the channel draws its water. But subsequently, owing to the jealousy of the neighbouring chiefs, he removed his family to Uthukuli in Kavalikkanadu about 80 miles west of Vellodu. The place was rebuilt and the country around brought under cultivation during the time of Deva Raya of Vijayanagar who recognized the rights of the Kalingan family to its chieftaincy and conferred on it the title of Raya. When Viswanatha Nayaka was Viceroy at Madurai, the then Kalingarayar of Uthukkuli was made a palayakar and placed in charge of one of the bastions of the Madurai fort. The 23rd palayakar is stated to have subdued Coorg for the Udaiyar Raja of Mysore who rewarded his services with a golden palanquin. The palayakar then commanded an army of 5,000 foot and 5,000 horse and owned a number of war elephants. He regularly supplied several elephants to the Mysore army and guarded the pass leading to Malabar. Later, a palayakar was defeated by the Zamorin of Calicut at Edapalli at the close of the 18th century, while one of his successors, Kumaraswami Kalingarayar, the 29th palayakar was harassed by Tipu's armies on their marches to and from Palghat. He, however, remained loyal to the English and the East India Company recognized his rights to the palaiyam. The palaiyam remained unsettled till 1871, when it was granted a permanent sanad. There is an old fort in the place.

Udumalpet Taluk.

The taluk, which lies in the Southern part of the district, was formerly known as Chakragiri. But no proper explanation is offered as to why it was called so. A Tamil poetical work dealing with Sankaramanallur refers to the gift by Siva and Vishnu of a Chakragiri fortress on the hill of Andigoundanur to a king named Kondramalai. Whether the hill had a fortress on its top or not, it is impossible to stay. But the hill to the west of Anamalai village, in Pollachi taluk, with a fort on its top is still called Chakragiridurg. It is possible that the old Chakragiri taluk included Udumalpet and derived its name from this hill fortress. The country is an open, gently undulating plain, flat in the black-cotton tract on the west and north, but less so in the south and east. Its area is 555 square miles and its population 190,442. The places of historical or antiquarian interest in the taluk are described below.

Cholamadevi (population 2,348), eleven miles north north-east of Udumalpet, contains three old temples dedicated to Siva, Vishnu and a village goddess. The Siva temple is in ruins and bears many inscriptions recording gifts from Kongu Cholas as well as from private individuals. It is recorded in one of the inscriptions that the properties of one of the residents of the village was made over to the temple for treason against the king. This was perhaps the usual way in which treason in villages was punished in those days. There were matams to the east and west of the Siva temple. The country around the village was called Karaivalinadu.

Dali or Dhali (population 2,788), seven miles south-west of Udumalpet and about 4 miles from Tirumurti hills, was the chief village of a former palayakar, but the estate was resumed after his rebellion in 1800. Two miles to the south of the village, there is a ruined temple of Subrahmanya with good sculptures. This temple is stated to have been destroyed by Tipu. There is no worship in it now; nor has any attempt been made to renovate it.

Gudimangalam (population 2,374), eight miles north-north-east of Udumalpet, contains an old ruined Siva temple bearing some inscriptions, one of which is dated S.S. 1450 (158 A.D.).

Jothampatti (population 1,394), seven miles to the east of Udumalpet was a small palayam consisting of a single village. It remained an unsettled palayam till 1871 when it was granted a permanent sanad.

Kadattur (population 2,701), eleven miles east of Udumalpet, contains an old Siva temple with some inscriptions. The temple is stated to have been built by one of the Chola kings.

Kaniyur (population 5,170), nine miles east of Udumalpet, contains a small ruined fort which is stated to have belonged to a king named 'Kumaran' whose exploits are celebrated in country ballads. There is also a small ruined temple here with several inscriptions, one of which mentions the repairs made to the temple in S.S. 1265 (1343 A.D.).

The inscriptions in this temple as well as those found in the villages of Kadattur, Kannadiputtur, Kolumam, Kumaralingam and Sankarama-nallur date from the time of the Chola king, Parantaka I, the great ancestor of Rajaraja, the Great. According to the 'Kongudesa Rajakkal', the Kongu country was conquered by Aditya I, a Chola king who reigned from 871 to 907 A.D. This is confirmed by the inscriptions of Parantaka I, the son and successor of Aditya I, one of whose generals was a native of Kongunadu.

Five miles west of Kaniyur are the remains of some ruined Muslim buildings.

Kannadipputtur (*Sirkar Kannadiputtur*) (population 5,566), eight miles south-south-east of Udumalpet, contains an old Siva temple which is stated to have been built by a Chola king. The inscriptions on the walls of this and other temples in the village record gifts of land and money by the Cholas. The village was also called Virapandya-Chaturvedi-Mangalam. It was situated in Karaivalinadu.

Kolumum (*Kozhumum*) (population 1,221), eleven miles south-east of Udumalpet, contains an old ruined mud fort. There is also an old Siva temple here bearing inscriptions. The village is mentioned in a copper plate grant of Chokkanatha Nayaka of Madurai during the reign of Sri Ranga Raya of Vijayanagar.

Kumaralingam (population 5,966), ten miles south-east of Udumalpet contains an ancient Siva temple dedicated to Kasiviswanatha, which was largely patronized by Veera Rajendra Chola who ruled the Kongu country. There is another temple dedicated to Vishnu containing many inscriptions, one of which refers to Adiraja Voikal of Kolumum in Karaivali Nadu and also to a matam in which three ascetics, followers of Sundaramurthi, the Tamil saint, lived. The channel mentioned in the inscriptions is apparently the Kumaralingam Rajavoikal. Ramasamudram included in this village is said to have been granted as an inam to a Brahmin by Chokkanatha Nayaka of Madurai. It was also called Kumarangabhima-chaturvedi-mangalam and a Paradarasahodara-Chaturvedi-mangalam evidently after the Danayakkankottai chiefs who bore the title (biruda) *Paradarasahodara*.

Maivadi (population 2,512), five miles east of Udumalpet was a small palayam consisting of one village. It remained an unsettled palayam till 1871 when it was granted a permanent sanad.

Metratti (population 3,759), nine miles to the north-east of Udumalpet was a small palayam, of one village. It remained an unsettled palayam till 1871 when it was granted a permanent sanad.

Pundi (population 212), fourteen miles south-west of Udumalpet, is a village of the hill tribe called Malaiyarasar (Malasar) or 'hill kings'. It lies on the slopes of the Anamalai mountains between 2,000 to 3,000 feet above the sea. Some interesting dolmens and built cairns have been discovered four or five miles from this village. Mr. Walhouse the Collector described them thus : " The Kistvaens are surrounded by a low wall of squared stones built together, not heaped like cairns. The nearest approach is the extraordinary and characteristics tombs on the Nilgiris, consisting of circular walls of rough stones, but these are circular and never enclose a dolmen or kistvaen. Moreover, the Pundi sample, being built upon a surface of rock, must always have been free-standing, but kistvaens on the plains were, originally at least, always subterranean. Their existence may seem strange in these difficult fever haunted mountain tracts when their builders possessed the fertile plains beneath, which are so thickly sprinkled with their tombs, unless it be supposed that they were the last raised after the primitive race had been given to the hill fastnesses by alien invaders."

Sankararamanallur (population 7,642), ten miles east of Udumalpet contains an old Siva temple called the Choleswara temple which was founded during the reign of a certain Konerimaikondar. It is said that this king built this temple on the occasion of a solar eclipse which occurred under the star of his nativity and that the temple architect was granted rent-free lands and other privileges on the opening of the temple. The latter contains many inscriptions referring to the various gifts made by successive rulers including Tirumala Nayaka of Madurai. One of the inscriptions reveals that several temples in that locality were destroyed by an army of invasion and that the general who led the army repented for this and gave the village of Rattiyambadi in Vaigavinadu to meet the expenses of the renovation of the temple. There is an inscription on the tower of the temple which records a request to the soldiers to spare the tower, the temple and its premises from destruction.

Somavarapatti (population 2,260), lies six miles north-west of Udumalpet. A car festival used to take place here in honour of a goddess called Kandiamman in Masi (February-March) which attracted a large crowd of Chucklers and Kammavars. But, owing to the superstition that the person who leads the celebration dies soon afterwards, the festival has not been celebrated for many years now.

Trimurtikovil or (*Kurumalai*) (population 170), eleven miles south-west of Udumalpet and two and a half miles east-south-east of Pundi, is another hill village on the slopes of the Anamalai hills 2,000 or 3,000 feet above the sea. It is difficult of access and is inhabited by Malaiyarasars (Malasars). At the bottom of the valley there is a sculpture on an immense boulder about 40 feet high which was described by Mr. Walhouse, the Collector, as follows :—" At two-thirds of its height, there was indistinctly engraved the outline of a personage sitting with hands and feet folded in front and wearing a tall mitre; each side of it was another figure, very indistinct and smaller than the central; but the whole group was not in a perpendicular, but a horizontal position, with heads to the east; the outlines were all much worn and seemed very old, and being so high up, could only with difficulty be discerned. Beneath, at the bottom of the boulder, there was a step and over it an emblem engraved on the rock and copiously smeared with oil. A canopy covered with flowers, gilt and filigree was raised over the step and emblem. None but a Brahmin might approach it closely. A ceremony is held there every Sunday and the rocky ground in front is covered with the graven prints and outlines of feet ". There is a choultry close by and near this there are eight stone images surrounding a stone pillar. This place is called the Trimurtikovil, but the group is suspected to be Buddhist or possibly Jain. Pilgrims largely resort to the hill on Sundays in Avani (August-September) and on Saturdays in Purattasi (September-October).

Tungavi (population 3,468), lying six miles east-north-east of Udumalpet, was an old palayam of one village. It remained an unsettled palayam till 1871 when it was granted a permanent sanad.

Vedappatti (population 982), lying eight miles east of Udumalpet was an old palayam of one village. It remained an unsettled palayam till 1871 when it was granted a permanent sanad.

BIBLIOGRAPHY

ENGLISH BOOKS.

Arokiaswami, M. .. .. *The Kongu Country*, 1956.

Baliga, B. S. .. .. .. *Studies in Madras Administration, Volume I*, 1949.

Bamford, P. C... .. .. *Histories of the Non-co-operation and Khilafat Movements*, 1925.

Beveridge, H. .. .. .. *A Comprehensive History of India, Volume II*, 1867.

Boag, G. T. .. .. .. *Madras Presidency*, (1881–1931), 1933.

Bowring, L. B. .. .. *Haidar Ali and Tipu Sultan*, 1893.

Clarke, Richard .. .. *Regulations of the Government of* Fort St. George, 1848.

Clogstoun, H. F. .. .. *Proposals for a new settlement of the land revenue, etc., of Coimbatore*, 1875.

Dodwell, H. .. .. .. *Report on the Madras Records*, 1916.

Dodwell, H. (Ed.) .. .. *The Cambridge Shorter History of India*, 1934.

Francis, W. .. .. .. *Gazetteer of the Madura District, Volume, I*, 1906.

Hayavadana Rao, C. .. .. *History of Mysore, Volume III*, 1946.

Jouveau-Dubreuil, G... .. *Ancient History of the Deccan*, 1920.

Krishnan, M. S. .. .. *Mineral Resources of Madras*, 1951.

Krishna Rao, K. .. .. *The Gangas of Talkad*, 1936.

Krishnaswami, S. Y. .. .. *Rural Problems in Madras, Monograph*, 1947.

Krishnaswami Aiyangar, S. .. *Hindu Administrative Institutions in South India*, 1931.

Do. .. *South India and her Muhammadan invaders*, 1921.

Krishnaswami Aiyar, K. N. (Ed.) *Gazetteer of the Coimbatore District, Volume II*, 1933.

Le Fanu, H. .. .. .. *Manual of the Salem District, Volume I*, 1883.

Maclean, C. D. .. .. .. *Manual of the Administration of the Madras Presidency*, Volume I, 1885.

Do. .. .. .. *Standing Information regarding the officials' Administration of the Madras Presidency*, 1877.

Malcom, J. .. .. *History of India*, Volume II.

Martin, M. (Ed.) .. .. *Marquis of Wellesley's Despatches*, Volume I, 1837.

Mill, J. .. .. *History of India*, Volume VI.

Nambiar, P. K. .. .. *Second Five-Year Plan, Coimbatore District*, 1955.

Nelson, J. H. .. .. .. *Madura District Manual*, Part III, 1868.

Nicholson, F. A. .. .. *Manual of the Coimbatore District*, 1887.

Nilakanta Sastri, K. A. .. *Studies in Cola History and Administration*, 1932.

Do. .. *The Colas*, Volumes I and II, 1935.

Do. .. *The Pandyan Kingdom*, 1929.

Do. .. *A History of South India*, 1955.

Do. .. *History of India*, 1950.

Owen, J. (Ed.) .. .. .. *A Selection from the Despatches, etc., of the Marquis of Wellesley*, 1877.

Pattabhi Sitaramayya .. *The History of the Congress*, 1935.

Do. .. *The History of the Indian National Congress*, 1947.

Pearse, R. (Ed.) .. .. *Memoirs of the Marquis of Wellesley*, Volume I, 1846.

ENGLISH BOOKS—*cont.*

Ramachandra Dikshitar, V. R.	*Pre-Historic South India*, 1951.
Rice, B. L.	*Mysore*, Volume I, 1897.
Roberts, P. E.	*India under Wellesley*, 1929.
Ryan, J. C.	*The Co-operative Movement*, 1954.
Sathyanatha Aiyar, R. ..	*The History of the Nayaks of Madura*, 1924.
Sesha Aiyar, K. G.	*Chera Kings of the Sangam period*, 1937.
Sewell, R.	*List of Antiquities, Madras*, Volume II, 1884.
Sinha, N. K.	*Haidar Ali*, 1949.
Stack, E.	*Memorandum upon Current Land Revenue Settlement*, 1880.
Strathio, D. N.	*Excise and Temperance in Madras*, 1922.
Stuart Harold, A.	*Manual of the Coimbatore District*, Volume II, 1898.
Thurston, Edgar	*Castes and Tribes of Southern India*, Volumes I, II, III, IV, V, VI, VII, 1909.
Venkataramanayya, N. ..	*Eastern Chalukyas*, 1951.
Do. ..	*Studies in the History of the Third Dynasty of Vijayanagar*, 1935.
Do. ..	*Early Muslim Expansion in South India*, 1942.
Vipan, A.	*Scheme of Road Development for the Madras Presidency*, 1935.
Vriddhagirisan, V.	*The Nayakas of Tanjore*, 1949.
Wilks, Mark	*History of Mysore*, Volume I, 1869.

ADMINISTRATION REPORTS.

Agricultural Department, 1951–52 to 1954–55.

Animal Husbandry Department, 1949–50 to 1954–55.

Department of Industries and Commerce from 1919 *to* 1956.

Deputy Registrars of Co-operative Societies of Coimbatore and Erode, 1954–55.

Electricity Department, 1951–52.

Harijan Welfare Department, 1956–57.

Highways Department, 1952–53,—1956–57.

Jail Department, 1956.

Madras Excise and Prohibition Department, 1949–52.

Motor Vehicles Act, 1956.

Public Health Department, 1921–51.

Public Works (Irrigation) Department for 1955–56.

Rural Welfare Department, 1949–56.

State Broadcasting Department, 1938 *to* 1954.

Women's Welfare Department, 1949 *and* 1951.

OTHER REPORTS.

Agricultural Indebtedness By W. R. S. Sathianathan, 1935.

Archaelogical Survey of India—Annual for 1902–1903.

Board of Revenue—General Reports.

Civil Dispensaries, 1853–1872.

Civil Hospitals and Dispensaries, Triennial 1920–22.

OTHER REPORTS—*cont.*

Court of Foujdari Adalat, 1826–1850—Select reports and cases.

Fortnightly Reports (Confidential), 1946–1957.

Health Survey and Development Committee, Volume I, 1946.

High Ranges of the Anaimalai Mountains, by Lt. Col. Douglas Hamilton, 1886.

Indian Statutory Commission, 1930.

Land Revenue Reforms Committee, First and Second Reports, 1951.

Land Tenures in the Ryotwari Areas of the Madras Province (1947) *and on the Investigation of Land Tenures* (1949).

Madras Forest College, Coimbatore, 1948–49 *and* 1951–52.

Public Instruction in Madras, 1857–58 to 1956–57.

Report regarding the possibility of introducing Land and Agricultural Banks into the Madras Presidency, Volumes I and II, 1895.

Sadr Adalat on Civil Justice for 1855.

Season and Crop Reports for 1953–54 *to* 1956–57.

Working of Civil Hospitals and Dispensaries, 1900–1955.

Working of Co-operative Societies in the State of Madras for 1949, 1950, 1951, 1952.

MISCELLANEOUS.

Amaravathi Reservoir Project, 1953.

Census Handbook, 1951, *Coimbatore district*, 1953.

Census of India, 1901, Volume XV, Part I.

Census of India, 1951, *Madras and Coorg*, Part I.

Civil Courts Manual (Madras Acts), 1949.

Code of Criminal Procedure, 1898.

Coimbatore and the Nilgiris Directory, 1957–58.

Coimbatore Collectorate Volumes.

Community Development in Madras State, 1955.

Constitution of India, 1950.

Co-operation in Madras State, 1954.

Goods Revenue Statistics, Southern Railway, 1954–55.

Grow More Food Campaign Pamphlets, 1942–47.

Handbook of Information issued by the Department of Women's Welfare, 1952.

Handbook of Rules and Regulations relating to the Agricultural College, Coimbatore, 1954.

Harijan Welfare in Madras State, 1951.

Higher Education in South India, published by the University of Madras, Volume II.

History of Indian Railways, 1924.

Judicial Sundries.

Madras Civil Courts Act of 1873.

Madras Code, 1888 *and* 1915.

Madras Co-operative Manual, 1952.

Madras Information, 1948.

Memoirs of the Department of Agriculture, Madras, No. 36, 1954.

Memoirs of the Geological Survey of India, Volume 33.

Monthly Digest of Economics and Statistics, Madras State, January 1951.

Notes on Irrigation by V. N. Kudva, 1953.

Papers relating to the Criminality of tribes notified under the Criminal Tribes Act.

MISCELLANEOUS—*cont.*

Papers relating to Public Instruction, 1855.

Papers relating to Tenancy Right in Inams, Volume I—III.

Popular Account of the progress of the work of the Madras Agricultural Department, 1922–1935.

Post-war Reconstruction and Development Schemes of the Government of Madras, 1945.

Public Health Code, Part I, 1928.

Public Health Pamphlet—No. 2 Control of Epidemics, 1949.

Rural Welfare in Madras, 1952.

Second Five-Year Plan—a symposium, 1956.

Selection of papers from the Records of the East India House, Volume II, Part I, 1820.

Short Note on Mettur-Canal Scheme, 1956.

Southern Forest Rangers' College Magazine, October 1955.

Statistical Atlas (1940-41), 1949.

Unrepealed Acts of the Governor-General in Council, Volume I (1898).

Women's Welfare in Madras State, 1952.

Working Plan for the Coimbatore South Forest Division from 1954–55 to 1968–69 by Sri K. A. Bhoja Shetty.

Working Plan for the Forests of the Walayar, Bolampatty and Thadagam Valleys, Palghat Forest Division, 1937–46 by T. V. Venkateswara Aiyar (Revised).

Working Plan for the Kollegal Forest Division, 1942–43 to 1957–58 by V. S. Krishnaswami.

Working Plan for the North Coimbatore Forest Division, 1932–1942 by C. R. Ranganathan.

Working Plan for the North Coimbatore Forest Division, 1934.

GLOSSARY

Ahanikams	Daily religious observances of Brahmin.
Adigārigal	Officers of trust in the army and in the Administrative Departments of Government.
Alungānam	Ruling group of a village.
Amāni	Collection of revenue direct from the cultivators by the officers of Government.
Ānaiyātkal	Elephant corps.
Andalagattalār	Fort garrisons.
Ankurārpana	Seed sowing ceremony in marriage.
Annaprāsanam	Food giving ceremony for the child.
Āraiyan	Title conferred on officers occupying very high civil positions.
Ārathi	Waving of lights, and water mixed with turmeric and chunam to ward off the evil eye.
Arumaikkaran and Arumaikkaris.	Priest and Priestess of Kongu Vellālārs.
Aswamedha	Horse sacrifice.
Ātman	Infinite spirit.
Ayan Pilluvari	Remission of assessment on grass lands.
Balchitāngadu	Game of catching while holding breath.
Bhajana	A congregation where devotional songs are sung.
Bhattavrithi	An assignment of revenue or lands to Brahmins.
Bhōga	Land held by service tenure holders.
Bondhu	Strings of unbleached cotton.
Bottu	Sacred ornament tied around the neck of the bride.
Brahmādayam	Any grant or perquisite appropriated to Brahmins.
Brahmāyagyna	Daily Worship of fire.
Choulam	Tonsure ceremony.
Dārōgha	The head of a police, custom or excise station.
Dēvadāna	Lands or allowances for the support of a temple.
Dēvapuja	Daily worship of God at home.
Dhāra	Pouring water.
Dharadattam	Giving away the bride.
Dhonige	Cloth roller.
Drāvida	South.
Ellaiamman	Goddess of the boundary.
Enādi	Distinguished title of Civil Officers.
Fatwā	Written opinion of the Muslim Law Officer of a Court.
Foujdāri Ādālat	Company's Supreme Court of appeal (Criminal)
Garbhādānam	Impregnation ceremony.
Garuda	Brāhminy kite (bird).

Gōdhānam	Presentation of cows.
Gōtra	A tribe, primitive spiritual head.
Gramadevatas	Village deities.
Grāmani	Headman.
Harkārās	Messengers.
Homam	Sacrificial fire.
Jāghir	A tenure by which the revenues of a tract of land were made over to a servant of the State.
Jaghirinam	Lands conferred by Government for some permanent service rendered to the public.
Jātakaranam	Naming ceremony.
Jiva	Soul of man.
Jivita	Land held by service tenure.
Kadāgams	Cantonments.
Kāltācchār	Stone mason.
Kankanam	Wrist threads.
Kannār	Brass-smith.
Kannikādhānam	Giving a girl in marriage without demanding a bride price.
Karavazhi	High Road.
Karumār or Kollar	Blacksmith.
Kattam	A kind of chess game.
Kavalgārs	Village watchmen.
Kazhagam	Association.
Kāzi	Muslim law officer.
Kodachimani	Hooked jewel; necklace of gold beads presented to a girl by her maternal uncle.
Kodikkāl	Field in which betel vine is grown.
Kolattam	Play.
Kottukāran	Village chief.
Kuda vilakku	Pot light.
Kudiraiccēvagar	Cavalry.
Kurram	Big size villages.
Malaiyadi	Foot of the hill.
Mandalam	Province.
Māngalyadhāranam	Tying the tāli or bottu.
Manjanīr pillai	Adopted son.
Mārāyan	Military title indicating distinction won on the field of battle.
Mufti	Muslim law officer
Mulapāl Kuli	Bride's price or the price of suckling.
Muthugunīrkuththal	Pouring water on the back.
Nādū	Unit of administration.
Nagaram	Primary assembly of merchants of important towns.
Nāmakaranam	Naming ceremony.
Nattām	Village site.
Nāttāmāikkārar	Headman.
Nattukavundan or Poriyatanakkaran	Chief of a nadu or province.

Nazzur	Presents.
Nischayathartham	Betrothal.
Otti	Tossing and catching tamarind seeds.
Pachaikudirai	Game ; a kind of leap frog.
Padaitalais	Leaders of armies.
Padinettāmperukku	A festival falling on the 18th day of the Tamil month of Adi (July-August).
Pālayagārs	A petty chieftain.
Pāligai Vilakku	Seedling light.
Pancham hissa	Remission of assessment on grass lands.
Pānigrahanam	Bridegroom taking over the hand of the bride.
Pānsupāri	Betel and arecanut.
Paradōsapravōsam	Mock pilgrimage to Benaras, which is a part of the Hindu marriage ceremony.
Parava pillu	Grass revenue.
Parisappanam	Bride's price.
Pariyam	Bride's price.
Pāshāna sthāpanam	Stone fixing in funeral ceremonies.
Pavalankatti	Wearers of Coral.
Pērāriyan	Titles conferred on officers occupying very high civil positions.
Pilluvari	Rental of the unoccupied waste land.
Pothurājā	King of buffaloes.
Prajā	People.
Pujari	Priest.
Pumsavanam	Ceremony performed seventh or ninth month of the first pregnancy.
Rāzināmah	Settlement between parties.
Sabhā	An assemblage of persons of rank or respectability.
Sadr Ādālat	Company's supreme court of appeal (civil).
Sadr Amins	A class of native civil judges.
Samskārās	Hindu religious rites.
Sapthapathi	Taking of the seven steps by the married couple.
Senāpathis	Military Commanders under Gangas.
Sendalais	Red-headed man.
Sīmantham	Ceremony performed during seventh or ninth month of first pregnancy.
Srādhā	Memorial rites.
Taniyūr	A town apart.
Tarapadi maniams	Rent free grants of land.
Tarpana	Oblations of water.
Thāmbulam	Presenting of betel leaves, arecanut and chunam.
Thānādār	A petty police officer subordinate to a Dārogha.
Ṭilakam	Mark on the forehead.

Tirumandira Ōlai	An officer who writes the verbal orders of the king.
Tirva	Money assessment of revenue on land.
Udan Kūttan	Heads of various departments in Chola Administration.
Upanayanam	Ceremony of initiation ; first wearing of the sacred thread.
Vapitta	Head of a village.
Vēērakal	Stone of valour or victory.
Vellan vagai	Peasant proprietors.
Vellikkai	Hands made of silver.
Vivāham	Marriage ceremony.
Vritti	Land held by service tenure holders.
Zimmi	Vassal.

INDEX

A

A—*cont.*

A—*cont.*

A—*cont.*

A—*cont.*

A—*cont.*

B

B—*cont.*

C

C—*cont.*

C—cont.

C—*cont.*

C—*cont.*

C—*cont.*

D

D—*cont.*

D—*cont.*

E—*cont.*

F

F—*cont.*

G—*cont.*

H—*cont.*

I

I—*cont*.

I—*cont.*

J

J—*cont.*

K

K—*cont.*

K—*cont.*

L

L—*cont.*

M—*cont.*

M—*cont.*

M—*cont.*

M—*cont.*

N

N—*cont.*

O

P

P—*cont.*

P—*cont.*

P—*cont.*

R

R—*cont.*

R—*cont.*

PAGE

R—*cont.*

PAGE

S—*cont.*

S—*cont.*

PAGE

S—*cont.*

PAGE

S—*cont.*

T

PAGE

T—*cont.*

T— *cont.*

PAGE

T—*cont.*

PAGE

U—*cont.*

V

PAGE

V—*cont.*

PAGE

V—*cont.*

W

PAGE

W—*cont.*

Y

Z

1. Sculpture of Bikshandavamoorthi on a pillar in Natana Sabha Mandapa, Siva Temple, Perur.

2. Sculpture of Kali on a pillar in Natana Sabha Mandapa, Siva Temple, Perur.

4. Jain Temple, Mettupudur.

3. Closer view of Sugriveswara Temple, Sircar Periapalayam.

6. Agricultural College, Coimbatore.

5. A general view of the Siva Temple at Perur.

8. Forest College, Coimbatore.

7. (*a*) Kangeyam Bull.

7. (*b*) Burgur Bull.

10. Nachimuthu Polytechnic, Coimbatore.

9. Rural College, Perianaickenpalayam.

12. Lower Bhavani Dam, Bhavanisagar.

11. Amaravathy Dam, Amaravathy Nagar.

13. (*a*) A Cotton Mill at Coimbatore.

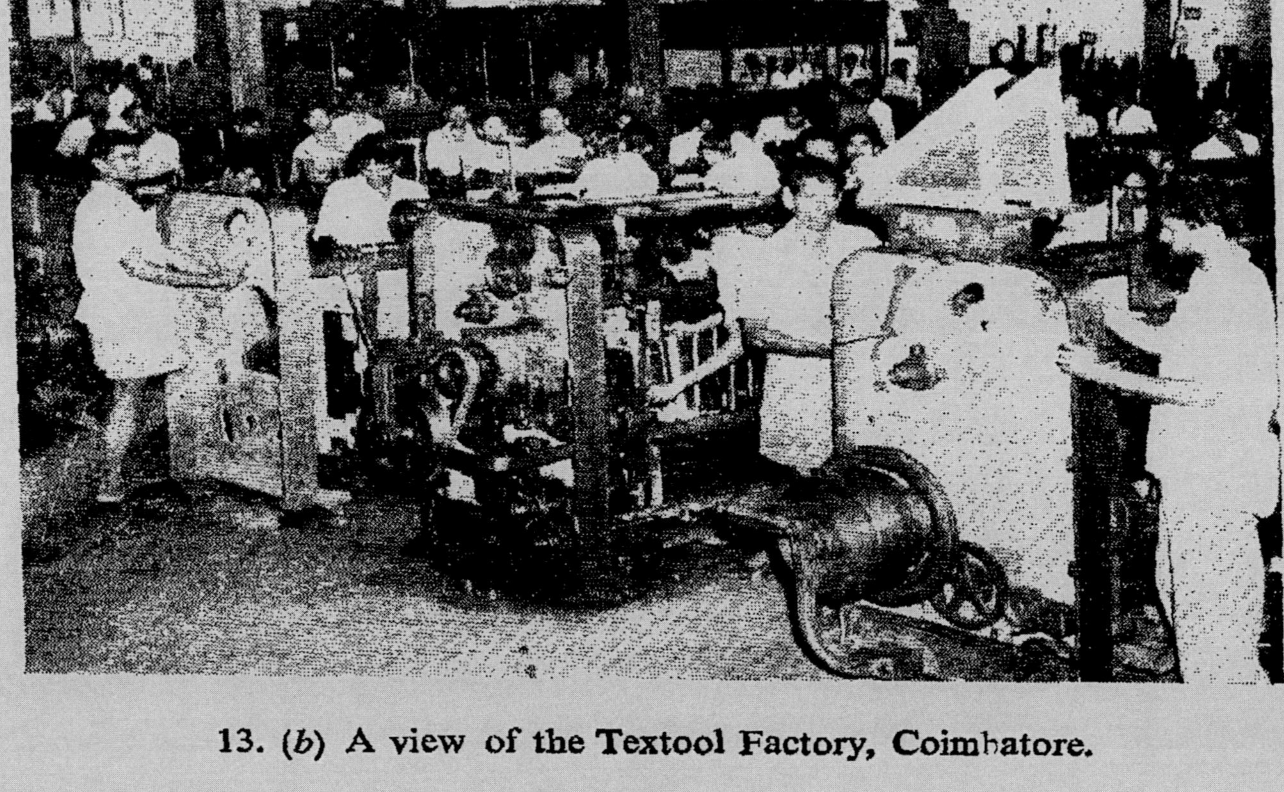

13. (*b*) A view of the Textool Factory, Coimbatore.